P9-EEO-339

Clyde Bedell's

CONCORDEX
OF THE
URANTIA BOOK

Clyde Bedell's

CONCORDEX

OF THE

URANTIA BOOK

CLYDE BEDELL SANTA BARBARA CALIFORNIA

THE MISSION OF THE URANTIA BOOK

THE time is ripe to witness the figurative resurrection of the human Jesus from his burial tomb amidst the theological traditions and the religious dogmas of nineteen centuries. Jesus of Nazareth must not be longer sacrificed to even the splendid concept of the glorified Christ.

What a transcendent service if, through this revelation, the Son of Man should be recovered from the tomb of traditional theology and be presented as the living Jesus to the church that bears his name, and to all other religions!

Surely the Christian fellowship of believers will not hesitate to make such adjustments of faith and of practices of living as will enable it to "follow after" the Master in the demonstration of his real life of religious devotion to the doing of his Father's will and of consecration to the unselfish service of man.

Do professed Christians fear the exposure of a self-sufficient and unconsecrated fellowship of social respectability and selfish economic maladjustment?

Does institutional Christianity fear the possible jeopardy, or even the overthrow, of traditional ecclesiastical authority if the Jesus of Galilee is reinstated in the minds and souls of mortal men as the ideal of personal religious living?

Indeed, the social readjustments, the economic transformations, the moral rejuvenations, and the religious revisions of Christian civilization would be drastic and revolutionary if the living religion of Jesus should suddenly supplant the theologic religion about Jesus. *

URANTIA BOOK, p. 2090

* by permission of the Urantia Foundation

v

"I readily believe that there are more invisible beings in the universe than visible. But who shall explain to us the nature, the rank and kinship, the distinguished marks and graces of each? What do they do? Where do they dwell? The human mind has circled round this knowledge, but never attained to it. Yet there is profit, I do not doubt, in sometimes contemplating in the mind, as in a picture, the image of a greater and better world; lest the intellect, habituated to the petty details of daily life, should be contracted within too narrow limits and settle down wholly on trifles."

E. Bernbaum's translation.

T. Burnet, ARCHAEOLOGICA PHILOSOPHICA, A.D. 1692

"The worlds teem with angels and men and other highly personal beings..." *

URANTIA BOOK, p. 260

"This narrative cannot be more than a brief outline of the nature and work of the manifold personalities who throng the universes of space administering these creations as enormous training schools, schools wherein the pilgrims of time advance from life to life and world to world until they are lovingly dispatched from the borders of the universe of their origin to the higher educational regime of the superuniverse and thence on to the spirit-training worlds of Havone and eventually to Paradise and the high destiny of the finaliters--the eternal assignment on missions not yet revealed to the universes of time and space." *

URANTIA BOOK, p. 417

* by permission of the Urantia Foundation

ABOUT THE URANTIA BOOK

THE THREE Most Vital Questions being asked by the most people on earth today are these: "Who am I? What am I doing here? Where am I going?"

It should be obvious that only an intelligence above man's, with cosmic wisdom and perspective, can provide the answers. Yet men seek human answers, asking these questions over and over of intellectuals, philosophers, politicians, educators, and ecclesiastics! Most of these in turn ask the same questions of one another, while they grope through a secularistic tunnel, wondering why the unresponsive darkness doesn't answer.

THE URANTIA BOOK provides the answers, in depth and with the highest authority. It is the first epochal revelation to this planet since Jesus of Nazareth who, in his person, was the fourth epochal revelation since the planet's birth.

URANTIA is the true name of this planet in the universe and on the records of creation. It is one of the youngest and least advanced among 619 inhabited worlds in our system.

The first two-thirds of the BOOK set up the immeasurable panoply of the cosmos, within which our vast local universe is a tiny peripheral unit of only 10 million inhabited planets among a total of 7 trillion.

And yet, among the celestial hierarchy, our backward and presently quarantined little URANTIA is the distinguished sentimental favorite among the 10 million! For Michael of Nebadon, a Paradise Creator Son of God, creator of this universe, in self-bestowal was born on URANTIA as a normal mortal babe. And here he lived a man-God life as Jesus---the Christ---of Nazareth.

The last third of the 2100 pages of the URANTIA BOOK is the detailed narrative of the entire life of Jesus, year by year, almost day by day, without embroidery or omission, and <u>with</u> all his supernal instruction.

Jesus, our local universe creator and Father was---of course---the wisest, most compassionate, most perfect, most practical, and most realistic being ever to walk this earth. Although one would hardly know it from much of the pallid gospel teachings of today.

The most important thing any men may learn anywhere in this entire universe ---if human civilization is not to destroy itself---is what this all-wise Creator knew and taught (and can teach) men to enable any society, primitive or advanced, to thrive and progress. The URANTIA BOOK is complete and magnificent in the full presentation of these teachings.

THE URANTIA BOOK AND THE BIBLE

With the BIBLE on earth, why do we need a URANTIA BOOK? Jesus, in his life on earth, quoted from the best of the religious writings in the Scriptures, which he knew thoroughly. But he made clear that the Biblical writings were human and fallible, not all inspired. He rejected much of the Scriptures which were the legend heritage of primitive Bedouin peoples, and of the Babylonian writers of secular---not sacred---history. He also rejected, as unacceptable, Biblical writings which were clearly misrepresentative of the loving God---his Universal Father.

With the URANTIA BOOK you may love and honor much of the BIBLE. And embrace too the magnificent revelations of science and the unfolding evidences of God's majesty and awesome invention in the material creation. You will know from the URANTIA BOOK that the God of personality and spirit is inevitably also the God of all matter and energy.

THE URANTIA BOOK WILL CHANGE YOU

If you develop a deep interest in the URANTIA BOOK, as you likely will if you permit yourself to become really acquainted with it, your life will change.

Part of the Universal Father's progressive plan of evolution includes serial bestowals of Creator Sons, who in winning full sovereignty of their universes, intimately live lives as, and among, their lowliest creatures.

On this lowly planet we mortals are intelligent enough in this age to film and record important events and lives. No doubt our unseen celestial friends have for millions of years been recording—with invisible techniques—every vital minute of every Creator Son's bestowals of whatever kind throughout creation.

These records are available for revelation to mortals whenever a major up-stepping of spiritual comprehension is necessary to save or to improve a civilization.

Jesus' life on this planet was a revelation of God to man, and also a revelation to God of the perfection to which mortal man can attain. That life was lived here, not for the edification of URANTIA mortals alone, but for the creatures of millions of worlds in our universe more advanced than our own, who could follow on "space reports" (perfected interplanetary audio-visual) how a Creator God of a far flung universe submitted himself to the machinations of human mortals and of mortal life.

It is doubtful if anyone could read and ponder this life, and not be somehow changed. The URANTIA BOOK, if you are susceptible to learning, will change you.

AN EXCITING AND REWARDING CHALLENGE

IF YOU develop a deep interest in the URANTIA BOOK you will likely wind up with a profound over-riding conviction that you are the son (or daughter) of a benevolent, loving Father, and that—inescapably—all men are your brothers.

Even the slightest acknowledgement of this truth can provide any man of any age a challenge so overwhelming as to make his life continually active and exciting—and rewarding.

In this century many individuals have rejected the claims religion would seem to impose upon them. Traditional religion promised loss of many earthly and earthy satisfactions, and a dreary sort of existence apart from the mainstreams of life.

Many churches reacted by going over to worldly things. They substituted social "activism" and permissiveness-in-conduct for conventional religion. They became good fellows instead of trying to make fellows good. They have told men what to do instead of what to be.

This has not spiritualized adherents to the substitutions, and it has lost those with spiritual insight who know the "way has been lost".

The URANTIA BOOK will show you clearly that religion is not social action. It will make equally clear that true religion inevitably leads to social action. The difference here is crucial to the human heart, to those in need, and to the world.

The religion of the URANTIA BOOK is easy to accept for it is genuine and of the very nature of the Gods themselves. It doesn't dull life---it sharpens life. It doesn't attempt to set you apart as a saint in an unsaintly world.

DON'T BE AFRAID OF THE RELIGION OF CHRIST

DO NOT be afraid to embrace the URANTIA BOOK because of what it will do to you. Live in this BOOK as a companion to Jesus of Nazareth, and find Him the most understanding, compassionate, wise, and practical of men. His optimism would be contagious. Religionists do thus live in companionship with Christ.

The BOOK should, if you like it, make you want to be a Christian in the sense of the Gospel as Jesus himself taught it. That original Gospel, set forth so fully, beautifully, and practically in the URANTIA BOOK is infinitely more help-ful and satisfying than the garbled and diluted Gospel of much of the so-called Christian community today. The URANTIA BOOK gives you the religion OF Jesus. Usual Christian instruction presents a religion ABOUT Jesus. This is the difference between a vast power generator and a flashbulb.

Do not be afraid to embrace the URANTIA BOOK because you feel you are not ready to be as good as some day you may want to be. Or because you believe its religion will make too great demands upon you. Do not think you will be led to unhappy sacrifice and unacceptable asceticism. Christ's genuine brand of Christianity will provide you the most joyous life possible. The URANTIA BOOK will make of you a better man or woman, a better companion, a more faithful better friend, husband, wife, parent, son or daughter. Oh yes, it will!

God must achieve whatever good He would on earth through men. He accepts help where He can get it from whom He can get it. If He can get cooperation from you He will take it from you as you are now. He knows you will change. He doesn't demand perfection from the mortal who discovers his own awesome sonship. He demands only trend and effort. Perfection is man's goal and destiny. It is not his condition.

Even as little good as any of us may do his fellow man is appreciated on high. God's incalculable computerized spiritual bookkeeping credits men generously. Even the smallest good that pours from the most imperfect human vessel is not overlooked.

C. S. Lewis, English atheist who became a great Christian leader, wrote that the happiness God provides His higher creatures is an ecstacy of love and delight compared with which the most rapturous love on earth is mere milk and water. Don't bet against its being true. Man in partnership with God is man new and enlarged and invincibly confident and happy. You can find this out for yourself through the URANTIA BOOK.

Do not delay the soul-stretching satisfaction to be had from the URANTIA BOOK. You will find yourself still human and perhaps for the first time, free, exultant.

THE URANTIA BOOK PROVIDES ANSWERS

THE URANTIA BOOK is the answer for all sorts of religious and anti-religious problems and confusions. In Jesus' religion there is no sorry introspection, no depreciating self-examination, no pawing through the forgotten files of the ugly basement of the subconscious. The URANTIA BOOK restores to Christianity

Jesus' bright and shining "instant psychiatry" of the "new birth through faith".
It is efficacious and priceless.

The URANTIA BOOK gives us education for the service of men—not education
for imposing upon men—and society. This is a restoration of self-reliant, responsible man, as the maker of civilization. The difference between this and the
permissive education which has contributed to our enormous dilemma is profound.

The URANTIA BOOK gives us politics of ideals, not ideas; of self-control
instead of people control; of fairness and justice, hence liberation.

THERE are no gross and upsetting blank spots in the URANTIA BOOK'S stupendous cosmology. None in the celestial architecture of the physical creations.
None in the hierarchy of Deity and personality and spiritual wholeness. You will
find the answers. You will find them to be revealing beyond the greatest
stretches of imagination. And they are unequivocal.

No writing on earth has so reconciled science and religion. Why not? Celestial revelators composed these papers. The URANTIA BOOK comes from where
the creations were planned, and where all salvable mortal and spiritual experience is recorded.

ENTHRALLING READJUSTMENT AHEAD

THE URANTIA BOOK calls for changes and improvements in our SOCIAL and
ECONOMIC institutions. It will tell you that we are on the brink of one of our
earth's "most amazing and enthralling epochs of social readjustment, moral
quickening, and spiritual enlightenment". You know of the gravity of our problems in this desperate century. From the URANTIA BOOK will come understanding, recognition of the part you will want to play in these crucial years, and
optimism for mankind's and for your own immortal destiny.

In the forthright teachings of Jesus for seven-days-a-week living for all men
are the answers our minds and spirits tell us are the cures for all our ills.
There are no other answers. They come from transcendent intelligence.

They are the answers for us all, regardless of age, race, beliefs, or our
conditions of life. Answers for already convinced believers, answers for conservative religionsts who love Christ but yearn too, for intellectual respectability and integrity. Answers for those who have loved God outside the church,
because they find magic ritual of blood and flesh repellent. Answers for those
who find it impossible to accept a wrathful God who demands for his forgiveness,
a faultless son be crucified as price.

Answers for those who doubt that an incomprehensibly great God can at the
same time live as a differentiated always unique Spirit in every one of his mortal
sons and daughters. Answers for the agnostic who demands intellectual plaus-
ibility to balance the mysteries which some Deified beings themselves may never
understand. Answers for atheists who can learn that a viable civilization without God is an illusion, who must conclude that it is easier to accept the truth of
a transcendent original Intelligence than the absurdity of an accidental ordered
creation.

You will find in the URANTIA BOOK the simple formulas which can give all
good men of earth spiritual freedom and unity, without requirement for spiritual
uniformity. This was Christ's way.

A NEW CHURCH?

READERS of the URANTIA BOOK will not want to establish a new church. They will want no one-day-in-the-week recognitions. They may want to belong to a seven-day-a-week brotherhood or society of believers for whom Christ's formulas shape a way of life. They will know their brotherhood will be world-wide --cutting across nations, races, religions, and all conditions of men.

There are unnumbered millions of people over the earth who can fully accept the wholly revealed Christ of the URANTIA BOOK. Whereas they look at so-called Christian nations today--and flee from Christianity.

Modern man beholds the technology of the past few decades with its astonishing lightninglike progressions. He knows this technology will be manipulated by men either to destroy the earth or--possibly--to make of it a sphere of peaceful and enlightened peoples.

It will be what men believe in their hearts and with what convictions they hold those beliefs that will determine the alternative. Today's decent man wants this earth's salvation, not its destruction. He must be ready to see that man's intelligence cannot save the world, unless it is augmented by a Higher Intelligence.

He knows earth's salvation will not be through the churches that summons him with trumpet blasts of the Middle Ages. He knows it will not be through those whose liberal contemporary trumpets emit thin and watery notes of social, not spiritual, change. He knows it will not be through conservative churches that demand acceptance of the validity of Christ, while at the same time they deny the equal validity of science.

The searching spirit-conscious man, together with those ecclesiastics who never abandoned the living God or the robust living Christ, will find the URANTIA BOOK a sustaining soul feast. It emphasizes Christ's life, not his death--a Christ who lived a bold and perfect life, and taught truth, was shamefully put to death, then rose to resume His universe responsibilities, as though he had never submitted himself to the capricious wills of men.

Members of a URANTIA brotherhood will have their work cut out for them--to the extent they embrace the BOOK'S truth. They will become persistently busy in the tough, absorbing job of world-remaking and soul-building.

WILL OUR WORLD BE RE-MADE, OUR CIVILIZATION SAVED?

OF COURSE, the URANTIA BOOK illuminates such questions. It is as boundless in its cosmic erudition as it is intimately personal in its instruction for the individual.

URANTIANS believe the BOOK was given this planet because it is desperately needed--to save our civilization. And if enough of mankind puts the BOOK'S ineffable wisdom to work, we will see a trend reversal and an era of improvement and progress for human society.

I believe the URANTIA BOOK is mankind's only prescription for saving civilization. It is most compassionate but it is equally realistic in its specifics against the coddling and multiplying of the baser orders of humanity.

It does not confuse compassion with the false sentiment that retards civilization by sacrificing true progress on the altars of formalized, specious pity.

The URANTIA BOOK says that on enlightened evolutionary worlds the profit motive gradually becomes augmented and superseded by the service motive. It wastes no time on the wicked and selfish who are either over- or under-privileged. A progressive society is doomed that will not defend itself against those who would either exploit or destroy it--whether they be unwise do-gooders, animal men, criminal defectives, weak and lazy drones, or the wealthy power-ful.

But--to the question. Grave as are civilization's problems today, the URANTIA BOOK should fill you with optimism for the long term. One of the most encouraging and inspiring sentences in the BOOK is in a paper on "GOVERNMENT ON A NEIGHBORING PLANET."

Moral instruction in the dominant nation on that planet is in the schools. (Our schools used to be strong in teaching morality.) Most religious training is in the home--not in churches. There are none there. Religious training is public only in temples of philosophy. In their philosophy, religion is the striving to know God and to manifest love for one's fellows through service to them. Spiritual advisers and examiners (for education without religious train-ing is a contradiction in terms) are under a Foundation of Spiritual Progress.

This nation has learned to deal with criminals and defectives. The homicide rate is 1% of that among the sphere's backward nations, which are on other continents. The visitation of justice there is swift and sure. And now for that encouraging and inspiring sentence I referred to: "...in the average state (of this nation) the police force is now only one-tenth as large as it was fifty years ago."

This fills me with hope and inspiration. If it has been done elsewhere it can be done here. If...if through religious understanding people can become moral! And if also--we can select men and policies to govern us in the interests of the normal and superior constitutives of a good society, instead of --as often now seems the case--in the interests of the subnormal, deviate, and inferior constitutives of society.

There is, I say, no end to the stimulating and provocative wisdom in the URANTIA BOOK. So, come to know this blessed revelation and attain to a level of perception and a universe perspective no other way possible on earth.

IF I have sounded over-enthusiastic, test for yourself fully and honestly the wisdom, the spiritual fragrance, the social significance, the awesome uplift, the brilliant illumination, the sheer wonder and beauty and utility of the URANTIA BOOK. In my own heart, I know I have failed miserably to do it jus-tice here, and in this CONCORDEX. (The URANTIA BOOK is a divine revela-tion. This CONCORDEX is a purely human, and imperfect work.)

On this earth, I know I can do no greater favor to a hungering, eager, questioning heart, than to lead it to useful possession of the URANTIA BOOK and the most important thing of earth to know--what Jesus of Nazareth believed and taught, which is the essence of this "most recent revelation of truth to the mortals of this planet."

WHY THIS KIND OF VOLUME
--THE CONCORDEX?

READING and STUDYING the URANTIA BOOK is something like travelling over a vast and strange, yet mysteriously familiar country on a limitless network of great highways and beautiful feeder roads. Within the 2100 pages are answers to endless questions. There are complete projections of our future careers in the universes, and outlines of celestial wonders beyond imagination.

But--this kind of travel without a road map can be frustrating and provoking. How--in the vast complex of highways and byways can one find again some idyllic spot, or awesome vista, or comforting pastoral valley, it seems urgently important to return to? And quickly!

The word CONCORDEX is not in the dictionary. In attempting to provide myself and you with an "index" of some sort that would helpfully direct us to all pertinent references on all topics touched in the URANTIA BOOK, I found I had undertaken an impossible job.

A conventional index or concordance wasn't the answer. Either would refer you to a thousand appearances, or hundreds at least, of words like "mortal", "man", "mind", "personality", "Thought Adjuster", and so on.

A straight TOPICAL INDEX was not the answer either. I finally found that I was preparing references that would simply, in my opinion, be as helpful to readers as I could make it. It turned out to be something like and unlike an index or concordance or topical index. Hence the name CONCORDEX.

Through the long, yet fleeting years I have worked through the URANTIA BOOK in this task, the need for more references and cross-references, and more categorical groupings of ideas, has seemed ever greater the more I include.

This CONCORDEX is not a complete mapping of the limitless intellectual and spiritual travel the URANTIA BOOK affords. Some time in the future a professional staff may do the job as it should be done.

Until then, I hope that it will be more helpful than I dare expect (knowing its limitations) it will be. I know that if I worked another year or so and my perhaps 80,000 references grew to 300,000--it would still be incomplete, for every new avenue of approach opens onto many more.

This then is my humble apology for the shortcomings, the omissions, the inconsistencies, the errors, which may annoy you. I pray each user of the CONCORDEX will, for each disappointment, be partially compensated by finding something else rewarding and new to him.

It was the thought of you, the URANTIA BOOK READER, running a finger down a page, and rediscovering a precious lost reference, that held me to my task many and many an hour.

Lest that last sentence give you the wrong impression, I hastily add that I have been the most privileged of men, having opportunity to prepare this CONCORDEX. Years ago I said: "If I had to give up either my library (some thousands of books) or the URANTIA BOOK, I would not hesitate. I would keep the URANTIA BOOK and part with all others." That is still true.

I am grateful indeed to the URANTIA FOUNDATION and to many URANTIA BROTHERHOOD MEMBERS for their warm encouragement and eagerness to have the CONCORDEX completed. Their enthusiasm has made my privileged task refreshing rather than fatiguing.

While the Urantia Foundation has given this effort its approval, the CON-CORDEX is a private and personal labor of love. It is not an official Foundation publication. I alone am responsible for whatever shortcomings, errors, and judgments, make the CONCORDEX unworthy of the BOOK to which it is companion.

I extend my thanks to a number of individuals who have here and there given me deeply appreciated help--with early typing, spot-checking for errors, "testing the listings", opinions, and production.

Clyde Bedell, 120 Camino Alto, Santa Barbara, California 93103

ORGANIZATION OF THE URANTIA BOOK

PART III. THE HISTORY OF URANTIA

xix

HOW TO GET THE MOST
FROM YOUR URANTIA BOOK

WHY YOU SHOULD READ AND STUDY THE URANTIA BOOK TWO WAYS

The URANTIA BOOK is the last BOOK in the world for anyone to read from front to back and then put aside with the feeling--"mission accomplished". It is a BOOK to live with and by--a Manual of Instruction and Action which no mortal on earth can quickly absorb, master, and profit from fully with one reading.

Surely, like any other book it should be read from the beginning, but there is a catch here. The most difficult part of the BOOK to understand and profit from is at the front. The easiest part to read, the "Life and Teachings of Jesus", is at the end.

I know many readers who have started to read this as an ordinary BOOK, have soon put it down. They say, in effect: "What am I doing, trying to understand Deity, the Nature of God, Energy and Pattern, the Absolutes, and so on? What have these to do with me?" And if such readers have little spiritual curiosity, concern, and foundation, it's a good question.

The average spiritually conscious man or woman who can have a wonderful religious experience through the Jesus papers, may not make immediate headway with a scholarly front-of-the-BOOK approach.

Nevertheless, the front-of-the-BOOK should not be ignored. On page 215 of the BOOK itself you can read why our celestial friends begin this revelation with the highest cosmic reality and proceed from it to lower reality--even to the reality of lowly evolving will creatures--you and me.

Read the reasons for their approach. It is only through learning of the vast and complex cosmos and the hierarchy of spirit personalities that control energies and work through myriad other personalities in cosmic affairs that we can achieve cosmic wisdom.

You can learn from the Jesus Papers of God's love for you. But you cannot through them alone understand WHO YOU REALLY ARE--of your standing in and planned ascendant (really inward) course through, an almost infinitely great cosmos. Or of your personal importance to God in his plan of progressive evolution. You need the BOOK'S vast overall picture for that.

The next question vital to you is WHAT YOU ARE DOING HERE. You can learn the purpose of living through the Jesus Papers. But only in the rest of the BOOK will you come to a proper perspective of your present situation on the threshold of eternities, spending an almost "momentary life" here in preparation for eternal life. This perspective gained, you next want to know "whither"-- WHERE YOU ARE GOING. Again, the Jesus Papers will no doubt convince you that you have an immortal soul to "create", and an eternal career. But it takes the rest of the BOOK for you clearly to see how you will progress from this "first life" to the mansion worlds. Then how your volitional course goes on with choices among alternates, until you become a finaliter on Paradise--where you will ultimately face and see God. And still more--where you will be prepared for assignment for a still more fabulous and endless career in celestial service.

HOW CAN you then accept the advice--difficult to follow--of those to whom we are indebted for this revelation, and still be buoyed up by gripping interest while you work your way through the higher essentials?

My personal suggestion is that you start at the beginning, after getting a bird's eye view of the BOOK'S construction by briefly studying the "ORGANIZATION OF THE URANTIA BOOK", p. xv, this CONCORDEX. Then begin with the URANTIA BOOK'S FOREWORD and read thoughtfully, slowly, through at least section "1", ending on p. 3. If you need to, re-read. Then if the going has been heavy, turn to some paper you select because of its engaging title, further on in the BOOK. Read it.

Each time you want to read an "easy", grippingly interesting Paper, read first, in obedience to the revelators, another section at the front.

In this way, master slowly, at least the essence of the plan of the stupendous Cosmic Arena and its Managers, for this is your home forever--and "eye hath not seen, nor ear heard" the glories it holds forth for us as we progress.

So you should read and study in two ways. From the beginning of the BOOK to stretch your mind and increase your wisdom, slowly--laboriously if need be. And then at will in the rest of the BOOK for the same purpose, but more easily.

Surely, when you start the Jesus Papers you will want to read straight through them, as time allows. But keep turning back to work your way from the front.

THIS CONCORDEX WILL HAVE 5 MAJOR USES

1. It will help you to return to, and find again, things you know you have read in the URANTIA BOOK, and want to promptly find again.

2. It will help you find related and associated references on most any subject in which you are interested.

3. It will help you find choice new interesting areas of reading.

4. It can be used to help you interest others in the BOOK.

5. It can be very helpful in study groups or "course" reading.

We will briefly discuss these ways of using the CONCORDEX.

1. OVER and over I have heard lovers of the URANTIA BOOK utter the plaintive comment: "I can't find that wonderful reference about so-and-so. I have completely lost track of it."

Since there are at least a thousand references I know I want to return to now and again, I feel for them all.

Many such "lost" quotes you will be able to find with the CONCORDEX.

2. YOU can also find through the CONCORDEX related or associated references to one that has interested you. And it is well to read as fully as you can on any subject that interests you, for a reference without associated references may delude you.

I know a young couple who became vegetarians when they read that Adam and Eve ate no flesh. When they have the CONCORDEX they will no doubt look up "vegetarian", "carnivorous", and "diet". Under any of these references they will be directed to p. 901, where we are told that it was a "great forward step" for the health and vigor of ancient humans when they added "flesh of the herds" to their diets.

A friend of mine, who through much metaphysical reading had come to believe in reincarnation, came to love the Urantia Book. He hoped the Urantia Book would confirm this belief. It doesn't. But I could refer him to 15 or 20 "reincarnation" and related references. He learned that we have many, what he may call "reincarnations" as we "ascend" through the mansion worlds, and on inward to Paradise (although none on this earth)--each one in more spiritual form than the last. And he was satisfied.

No BOOK on earth can give you such understanding and appreciation of prayer, as the URANTIA BOOK. Imagine being told everything about prayer that could be told us in a couple hundred references by such authority. There are sections that fully treat prayer, and there are references too, scattered through the BOOK from p. 65 to 2089.

If you wish to know what these transcendent ones can tell us about reality, personality, education, forgiveness, worship, mind, faith, education, the references are numerous indeed. Study any subject in the BOOK that is important spiritually or to our evolutionary progress, and you will likely be well informed.

3.   BROWSING through the CONCORDEX will put you in touch with new areas of interest. You'll find fascinating information as well as illuminating, on minor, as well as major subjects. A woman who believes animals have souls asked what the URANTIA BOOK has to say on the matter. She was able to look up a great many references about animals and animal-man differences.

Her information on the subject is now, of course--if not replete--at least authoritative.

A minister who asked for references on the "atonement" was given no end of references. How much more rational can be his understanding now, than to believe God demanded the "ransom-death" of his God-man Son in payment for his mercy to us!

Browse a little yourself. Seek answers to questions in your own mind.

Perhaps you would like to be stimulated by a few paragraphs that are direct or indirect challenges to those of us fortunate enough to possess this BOOK. Look under "CHALLENGES."

Do you want to have at least some idea, quickly, of the scale of the plan of God of which you are a part? Refer to "numbers, some". Here are a few (only about 80 of a possible two hundred or so) references that will stretch your imagination and your concepts at once.

There are over 300 references under "Personality" in the CONCORDEX. This provides an astonishing compendium of earth's most reliable information on this fascinating subject.

By browsing through the CONCORDEX you will find other things that will grip your interest.

4.   INTEREST others in the BOOK with help from the CONCORDEX.

There is a listing of 803 significant excerpts ranging from front to back of the BOOK. See that listing (p.xxvii) and you may find it of value in interesting friends whose hobbies or special fields you can identify.

Ask a friend you want to read the BOOK if there are answers he wants to any puzzling religious questions. Find references that will touch upon his subject, if you can, and give them to him.

On p. xv begins a brief outline of the plan of the URANTIA BOOK. Read, in its connection, on p.xxvii how you may use it in helping spark the attention of friends.

But, remember, Jesus admonished his apostles not to take anything "out of the hearts of those who seek salvation...labor only to put something into these hungry souls." The URANTIA BOOK should not be used to upset or destroy faith that is now serving men well.

5.   IF YOU are in a study group, use the CONCORDEX in planning and programming. It can help the leader or someone who is putting on a program come up with wide ranging information from throughout the BOOK.

Here again, the 803 excerpts might be helpful.

HOW TO FIND WHAT YOU WANT

I believe that any form of INDEX or CONCORDANCE for the URANTIA BOOK, were it complete, would be as big as the BOOK itself, with easily 2100 pages.

The CONCORDEX is not complete. It is not consistent. The further I went in its creation the more convinced I was that the larger it got, the larger it would still become. Another year of work and another complete typing and revision could have reduced inconsistencies and increased references. But-- there had to be a stopping place, and I stopped with the present listing.

You may look for a reference you should be able to find--and not find it at once. Although it may be in the CONCORDEX even in more than one place. You may look and find a reference listed one way, when your judgment tells you it should have been listed another way, in another location.

I should at least partially explain.

Under "JESUS, QUOTES", there are over 800 entries. Through thorough cross-indexing these could have become over 3000. The book would thus become unwieldy, very expensive, and more difficult (I believe) to use, with such enlargement.

I chose therefore, to list most quotes in their original word sequence, and perhaps not always starting with the word you would. Be willing to look several places.

When Searching For A Reference, Don't Quit Too Easily

For instance, Jesus said: "peacemaking is the cure of distrust and suspicion." In a true and complete concordance, one might find that quote by looking under any of the four key words. However, he might not recognize it without checking clear through to their pages several irrelevant references. Because nowhere in the concordance would the entire quote appear.

I have chosen to list it as it appears above, under "p".

He also said: "acquire the spiritual attitude of a sincere child." There are five words under which one might seek to find such a quotation depending upon the facet of the idea that recalled the quote to mind. It is listed only under "acquire".

Most of the 800 are listed in that way. Only a few are cross-indexed.

WITH some references, cross-indexing becomes very important. On p. 579 you may read in the URANTIA BOOK:

> "All through the Paradise career, reward follows effort as the result
> of causes. Such rewards set off the individual from the average,
> provide a differential of creature experience, and contribute to the
> versatility of ultimate performances in the collective body of finaliters."

That passage is important. Here is evidence that in the vast central universes which are the ultimate in perfection, it is recognized that evolving beings are unequal individuals, and since each is unique his creature experiences further differentiate him. The versatility of performance of individuals, which this leads to, is desireable.

When someone reads that quote and later wishes to find it again, where would he look for it? This is one type of problem I have been anxious to solve for readers of the Urantia Book.

Therefore, anyone who has a fair concept of the idea expressed should be able to find it, for there are references to it in 8 different places. Key words beginning the phrases that would lead to it are: "reward follows effort...", "average, rewards set off individual from", "differential of creature experience", "versatility of...performance", "Men--differentials among...", "differences desired among...", "equality, uniformity, not desired...", "ascendant career, differential of experience..." Of course, not many sentences or thoughts are so fully indexed.

When you first look for an idea, or for one you wish to relocate, don't give up if it isn't where you first look. It may be recovered by you with a little persistence and ingenuity. Ask yourself where else, or under what other word, or words, you might find it.

THERE are both advantages and disadvantages to an abridged reference list which is based on subjective decisions in many instances. I trust the advantages outweigh, as I have assumed they will, the opposite. Any believer in the URANTIA BOOK, such as this writer, must resolve every question on behalf of what he believes is most consistent with the URANTIA BOOK'S mission and intent, hence is most helpful to the CONCORDEX user. And hope he will be, in most instances, right.

Thoughts or sentences you may wish to locate, and then perhaps refer to again in the future, are sometimes very elusive within the page referred to. If you wish to familiarize yourself with the BOOK and be adept, fast, at finding references, get into the habit of marking up your BOOK. There is a practical suggestion for this on p.xxvi.

MARK UP YOUR URANTIA BOOK

I have friends who read books and never make a mark in them. I have other friends who, like me, mark up all their books as they read. Ask a non-marker reader to find some excerpt or precious passage in a beloved book, and his often fruitless effort makes you wonder why he read or possessed the book.

A book that people read has no value of its own. Its value is only in the residual sediment it leaves in the reader's mind or reclaimable possession. Take the URANTIA BOOK for example. It can leave a vast delta of tillable sediment in your possession to enrich you through its cultivation.

If, as you read through a year or so, or many years, you do not mark the BOOK so you may quickly relocate whatever you wish, the residual sediment it leaves you is small. Instead it washes out to sea, to limbo.

Therefore, if you love the BOOK, mark it. Be able through the CONCORDEX and your own markings to find quickly whatever you wish to return to.

There are approximately 650 words per page in the URANTIA BOOK. It is not always easy to find a reference you seek even after you have the right page number. A key word or two may elude the eye. I have sometimes scanned an unmarked page four times before pinpointing a reference I know is on the page.

However, once found, and the key word circled with an easy-writing ball point pen, I can next time find that reference within a second or so on the otherwise baffling page. Note the illustration. This is one way to mark your BOOK.

6. MATERIALISM

Scientists have unintentionally precipitated mankind into a materialistic panic, they have started an unthinking run on the moral bank of the ages, but this bank of human experience has vast spiritual resources; it can stand the demands being made upon it. Only unthinking men become panicky about the spiritual assets of the human race. When the materialistic-secular panic is over, the religion of Jesus will not be found bankrupt. The spiritual bank of the kingdom of heaven will be paying out faith, hope, and moral security to all who draw upon it "in His name."

No matter what the apparent conflict between materialism and the teachings of Jesus may be, you can rest assured that, in the ages to come, the teachings of the Master will fully triumph. In reality, true religion cannot become involved in any controversy with science; it is in no way concerned with material things. Religion is simply indifferent to, but sympathetic with, science, while it supremely concerns itself with the scientist.

Owning a BOOK that is a veritable treasure trove, and not being able to locate its treasures promptly, easily--is like owning a high-powered car you can't drive.

Test this idea a few times. Circle 8 or 10 key words to references on a single page of the URANTIA BOOK. Then give that marked page to one person. To another, give the same page, unmarked. Ask them both to locate those key words as you call them, in random sequence. You will be astonished at the difficulties one person has, and the easy achievement of the other.

803 BRIEF, VARIED, PROVOCATIVE, URANTIA BOOK EXCERPTS

THE VALUE OF THESE EXCERPTS AND HOW TO USE THEM

There are several ways, at least, to use the excerpts on the following pages. ONE: Start anywhere among the 800 excerpts identified on the following pages. Work forward or backward and read! Mark excerpts you particularly like by underlining or circling the excerpt number. Suggest this sampling method to a friend to whom you give or loan a book. TWO: Devoted Urantians may prefer to enter these excerpt numbers alongside the marked excerpts themselves throughout their books. The illustration shows how simply it may be done using a pen. If you otherwise mark your book, use a different colored ink for these excerpts.

NATURE OF GOD   37

natural laws and righteous spiritual mandates! "Be not deceived; God is not mocked, for whatsoever a man sows that shall he also reap." True, even in the justice of reaping the harvest of wrongdoing, this divine justice is always tempered with mercy. Infinite wisdom is the eternal arbiter which determines the proportions of justice and mercy which shall be meted out in any given circumstance. The greatest punishment (in reality an inevitable consequence) for wrongdoing and deliberate rebellion against the government of God is loss of existence as an individual subject of that government. The final result of wholehearted sin is annihilation. In the last analysis, such sin-identified individuals have destroyed themselves by becoming wholly unreal through their embrace of iniquity. The factual disappearance of such a creature is, however, always delayed until the ordained order of justice current in that universe has been fully complied with.

⑧
30
40

Cessation of existence is usually decreed at the dispensational or epochal n of the realm or real   world such as Urantia it com

---

The circled "8" means this is excerpt 8 of the 803. The numeral 30 means that the preceding excerpt (7) is on p. 30. The succeeding excerpt (9) is on p. 40.

If you enter all these excerpt identifications in your book itself, you (or anyone) may start reading at any marked excerpt and proceed backwards or forwards and find stimulating, inspiring, provocative, or at the very least, interesting, "samples".

THREE: Prior to starting a formal study group which might wish to go through the BOOK from beginning to end, several informal "orientation" meetings may be held. Have each person present read at random from this following tabulation one or two or three excerpts.

When an excerpt prompts spontaneous discussion, it might be assigned as a springboard for a subsequent meeting, with the reader (or another) designated to lead the discussion by referring to all possible references (dug out of CONCORDEX) pertaining to that subject. Some subjects would lead to an entire series of meetings: Faith, Reality, Mind, Personality--for instance.

FOUR: If you lend a BOOK and CONCORDEX to a friend, he may browse for himself with this tabulation's guidance. But you may find it more helpful to him to hand him with the CONCORDEX a pencilled list of excerpt numbers you recommend as "starters".

FIVE: When you have the CONCORDEX and you wish to introduce the URANTIA BOOK to a friend whose interests you know, science, geology, anthropology, government, or whatever, turn to the table of ORGANIZATION OF THE URANTIA BOOK in front of the CONCORDEX. Choose papers touching your friend's particular area of INTEREST: Scientist, perhaps papers 32, 41-44, 65, 81; to illustrate. The table of ORGANIZATION gives you page numbers of all these papers, and you could circle those excerpt numbers falling within the pages of those papers.

A geologist might be particularly interested in checking excerpts on pages within papers 57 through 62, excerpts 176 to 184. An anthropologist, excerpts within pages 711-771, papers 63 to 68. Someone interested in government, excerpts falling within papers 68 to 72, pages 763-819. A minister or religionist, excerpts in papers 85 through 103. And so on. These excerpts, if your friend is ready for the URANTIA BOOK, should enthrall and convince him, and lead to further papers which are equally pertinent to his specialty.

HOW to read the EXCERPTS TABULATION
(next 5 pages)

Col.	1	2	3	4
	4	27	1-2	...The God
	6	29	L	
	46	129	7	The Grand
	72	210	F	
	146	554	L+	
	407	1216	L2+2	
	683	1898	5	When a
	749	2044	3-5	...You shall

Col. 1   The figure in column 1 is the chronological number of the reference, as 4th, 6th, 749th.

Col. 2   The figure in column 2 refers to page number in the URANTIA BOOK.

Col. 3   Designations in column 3 locate the paragraphs on the given page number. "1-2" above means paragraphs "1 thro 2". "3-5" means paragraphs "3 thro 5". In counting paragraphs, always count a partial paragraph at top of page as paragraph "1". See reference "683" (col. 1) above. The 5th paragraph begins with the words "When a".

An "L" in column 3 means "Last" paragraph. An "L+" means the last paragraph plus runover onto the next page.

An "F" refers to first paragraph. "F3" would mean first 3 paragraphs.

Col. 4   On most--but not all--pp. the paragraphs indicated in "col. 3" can be counted only one way. To avoid counting confusions, where the count may be in doubt, column 4 provides guide words as to where reference starts. Reference 46 p. 129 (see above) begins with the words "The Grand".

Dots preceding the "guide words" mean that the excerpt begins WITHIN the paragraph named, (as in excerpt 4 above "...the God"). Reference 749, p. 2044 begins within paragraph 3, at the words "You shall".

NOTE: The guide words are not provided as a clue to what the excerpt is about. They are simply to LOCATE the beginning of the excerpt.

No.	Page	Par's.	Begin with	No.	Page	Par's.	Begin with	No.	Page	Par's.	Begin with
384	1178	2	As the	447	1317	2		510	1460	L2	...his relig...
385	1182	7	We know	448	1318	2		511	1462	F	
386	1183	3	Thought	449	1326	3	...From the	512	1463	2	...When in
387	1186	L+		450	1329	2		513	1464	2-3	
388	1187	4	...There are	451	1330	F5		514	1464	4	"6. If you...
389	1192	F2	...The pres...	452	1336	6	Through	515	1466	3	"Ganid
390	1193	F	...The	453	1338	3	Into	516	1467	L	
391	1193	3-4	The Adjuster	454	1338	5	...The early	517	1468	3	...Although
392	1194	All		455	1339	6	As many	518	1474	3	The miller
393	1199	5	But your	456	1339	7	By the	519	1475	4	To the travel...
394	1203	F2		457	1340	3-5		520	1475	L+	
395	1204	F		458	1341	4	...The Gos...	521	1475	L+1	
396	1204	3	The Adjuster	459	1342	6	...This is	522	1478	5-6	"The soul...
397	1204	5	When	460	1343	2		523	1479	7	My son
398	1206	3	I	461	1347	3	Gabriel's	524	1480	5	The human
399	1206	4-5	..Ignorance	462	1347	5	In all	525	1486	L3	
400	1207	5-6	There	463	1354	L2		526	1487	3	The Kingdom
401	1208	L+		464	1361	6	...But this	527	1488	7	The diff..
402	1209	5	When	465	1363	2		528	1488	L-	
403	1211	5	There is	466	1367	5	This winter	529	1489	2-4	
404	1213	2	...So few	467	1372	2	...Increasing.	530	1490	2	
405	1213	5	While	468	1373	F		531	1490	4	...If one
406	1215	F		469	1373	4	It was	532	1490	7	Another
407	1216	L2+2		470	1373	L		533	1490	L+2	
408	1217	4	But man	471	1375	L+		534	1491	3-8	Urantia
409	1217	5	Mind	472	1376	2		535	1494	3	On an
410	1219	5	The	473	1378	2		356	1494	L+	
411	1221	3-8	The doing	474	1378	L+		537	1502	3	...Only
412	122	3	The problem	475	1383	F		538	1509	F	
413	1222	5	When man	476	1383	3	After	539	1511	3	...This cerem..
414	1222	6-7	Science	477	1384	6	In silence	540	1513	3	...I bring
415	1222	8+	It is	478	1384	L+		541	1514	L4	Jesus
416	1223	4	May I	479	1386	3	As he	542	1515	5	...It had
417	1226	3	Personality	480	1388	L		543	1516	4+	
418	1227	3-5	Life	481	1389	6	During	544	1517	2	...No miracle
419	1227	7	But the	482	1393	F2		545	1521	F	
420	1228	2-5	The Uni---	483	1393	6	As he	546	1522	5	Rome
421	1228	6-7	As mind	484	1394	F		547	1523	2	
422	1232	3-4	Selfhood	475	1395	3-4	Having	548	1530	L	
423	1233	7	When the	486	1398	1		549	1532	2	
424	1234	2		487	1398	5	This year	550	1553	4	Jesus
425	1235	4	The thought	488	1404	5	..."But	551	1535	5-6	All of
426	1236	2	...In the	489	1405	5	Jesus	552	1541	2-3	
427	1245	4-5	Seraphim	490	1410	4		553	1541	5	That after...
428	1245	7	The min...	491	1412	3	Mary	554	1543	3-4	In these
429	1258	5	(The Cosmic	492	1412	6-7	Presently	555	1545	4	Jesus
430	1260	F		493	1413	2-3		556	1545	L2+	...Jesus knew
431	1260	2		494	1416	4	This year	557	1557	F2	The master
432	1261	3	The entire	495	1421	2		558	1565	7	...He must
433	1263	2	It is in	496	1422	5	...Although	559	1566	5	...That
434	1263	4	...Whatso...	497	1423	L+		560	1567	4	
435	1268	2		498	1434	4	A one-eyed	561	1569	2-3	
436	1274	3-5	The time	499	1434	6		562	1576	L+	
437	1283	5	Through...	500	1435	L+2		563	1576	L+	
438	1289	3-4	Men all	501	1440	L+		564	1581	4	...Jesus
439	1293	L		502	1447	2		565	1585	3	...While eat...
440	1299	2-3	In the	503	1447	3	...Love of	566	1591	5-6	...When Jesus
441	1300	3-5	In the	504	1445	F		567	1592	5	When Simon
442	1301	8	Mortal	505	1456	F		568	1592	L+2	
443	1303	F		506	1456	2	...we who	569	1592	5	the Master
444	1304	L+		507	1457	6	My brother	570	1592	L2+	"The only
445	1305	5-7	Some of	508	1459	L3+	But truth	571	1596	L2	
446	1307	L		509	1460	2-4		572	1601	4	The sup...

ABBREVIATIONS YOU WILL FIND IN THE CONCORDEX

A	Absolute	GrU	Grand Universe	OT	Old Testament
AE	Adam & Eve	ga	guardian angel	O	Orvonton
ams	adjustant mind spirits				
Alex	Alexandria	H	Havona	P	Paradise
AD	Ancients of Days	HS	Holy Spirit	PF	Paradise Father
Ap	Apostle(s)			PI	Paradise Isle
		I	Infinite	PTA	Personalized TA
B	Bible	IS	Infinite Spirit	PT	Paradise Trinity
br	brotherhood	IP	Isle of Paradise	p	personality
				PP	Planetary Prince
C	Caligastia	Jer	Jerusalem		
CU	Central Universe	J	Jesus	r	religion
GM	Christ Michael	Jw	Jews, Jewish	rev	revelation
Chr	Christian, Christianity				
ci	civilization	k	kingdom	San	Sanhedrin
CA	Conjoint Actor	koh	kingdom of heaven	Sc	Scripture
CC	Conjoint Creator			SM	Solitary Messenger
CS	Creator Son	LC	Life Carriers	S	Son
		lal	light and life	ST	Spirit of Truth
d	death	lu	local universe	su	superuniverse
Ds	Deities	Lur	Lucifer rebellion	SB	Supreme, Supreme Being
D	Deity				
DA	Deity Absolute	mw	mansion world(s)	TSC	Third Source and Center
		MS	Master Spirit(s)	TA	Thought Adjuster(s)
ES	Eternal Son	MU	Master Universe	T	Trinity, Paradise Trinity
		MatS	Material Son	TTS	Trinity Teacher Sons
f	faith	Mel	Melchizedek	tbg	truth, beauty, goodness
F(GF)	Father, God the	M	Michael		
FSC	First Source & Center	MiMe	Mighty Messenger(s)	UA	Universal Absolute
		MC	Morontia Companions	UF	Universal Father
Gab	Gabriel	MH	Most Highs	u	universe
G	God	MoS	Mother Spirit	uu	universe of universes
GA	God the Absolute	MM	Mystery Monitors	UqA	Unqualified Absolute
				U	Urantia
GS	God the Supreme	nP	nether Paradise	UB	Urantia Book
GU	God the Ultimate	NT	New Testament		
Gos	Gospel			V	Verondadek

Ignore articles, "a, an, the," and read references as though they were omitted

A

AARON, MAN WITH WITHERED HAND, 1664,-66
abandonters, 452
  creations of Ancients of Days and...416
  artistic skill, social adaptability, cleverness, 493
  teaching language of superuniverse, 631
Abbadon, chief of staff of Caligastia, 602
Abel, needed more age, 848
Abila (Nathaniel's work place), 1767
ability, always has an ancestral foundation, 507
  enhanced for edification of realm, 508
  implies gift of foresight...vision, 1779
  is inherited, skill is acquired, 1779
  is measure of opportunities, 1876
  special human a., 3 possible sources of, 507-8
  to learn, marks beginning of a.m.s., 739
  will gain recognition as you ascend, 508
ability and intelligence,
  some of most valuable strains lost to world, 714
Abimelech, Abraham, Joseph, J knew traditions of,
  1387
  appropriated wife of Abraham, 1022
Abirim and Segub, buried in walls of Jericho, 981
ABNER, of Hebron, Bethlehem, Philadelphia,
  head of Engedi colony, church in south and east,
    1627,-48,1772,1801,-25,-33
  and Andrew, difficulty in upholding courage of...
    1644
  and J at Engedi, 1605
  at variance with all leaders of church, 1831
  chief of John (Baptist's) supporters, 1624
  chief of the 70, 1817
  choice (his) of Urmia teachers unfortunate, 1491
  David was financial overseer for A, kingdom, 1869
  died at 89, (November 21 A.D.74), 1832
  efforts consolidated favorable kingdom sentiment,
    1789
  faithful to the end, 1832
  head of the 70 teachers, 1626
  headquarters at Hebron, 1678
  heard of plot to kill J, 1933
  help from A sought by Cymboyton's son, 1491
  J sent "death" message to A, 1966
  J spent time with A and associates, 1788,-98
  John (Baptist) fond of A, 1497
  last time A saw J in flesh, 1870
  Lazarus felt safe with A, 1849
  made head of gospel teachers, preachers, 1800
  "manifest loving devotion to A in the East", 1959
  moved headquarters to Bethlehem, 1771
  Nathaniel visited A for year after crossing Peter,
    2058
  Philadelphia center for large interests of kingdom,
    1869
  resisted Paul's attempts to change J teachings, 1831
  synagogues surreptitiously opened to A, 1741
  teaching 3 times a day, Philadelphia, 1831
  uncompromising attitude, 2072
  women's work placed under A, 1808
Abnerian kingdom of heaven, 1869
aborigines, 728
  abortion, child killing, cannibalism, 770
  Australian, African, miserable remnants, 764
  Australian a., focus religion upon the clan, 1132
  Australian, never developed tribal form of govt., 788
  Australian, prayers antedated belief in spirits, 994
  Eskimos, sole survivors of original Urantia a., 700
  Pygmies have no religious reactions as a class, 1010
  six colored races, mutated from the a., 701
abortion and infanticide, virtually exterminated some
  tribes, 770

ABRAHAM, 918, 1340, 1598, 1732, 1796
  a chosen individual, 1018
  ancestry partly Hittite, tongue Andonite, 896
  and Isaac, 981
  became terrified with fear of murder, 1022
  "before A was, I am", 1750,-86,-97
  by faith justified and made aware of salvation, 1682
  conversion of young A, 1672
  forewent Egyptian honors for spiritual work, 1019
  genealogy confused, months and years, 857
  Hebrew priests invented Noah's flood for genealogy,
    874
  introduced tithing system, 1016
  Isaac, Jacob, "I am God of", 1900,-06
  Jacob, Abimilech, 1387
  married his half-sister, 918
  Melchizedek's covenant with A propaganda pattern,
    1027
  name changed from Abram, 1021
  not racial father of all the Hebrews, 1055
  offspring formed nucleus of Jewish people, 1055
  others as prepared as A for Salem doctrine, 1018
  resorted to barbarous practice, 1018
  seed of A will sit down with gentiles, 1829
  THE SELECTION OF A, 1018
  words of Moses, Scriptures, not in existence before
    A, 1767
  victory over Chedorlaomar, 1018
  waged war for Egyptian King, relative, 1019
ABRAHAM (young Sanhedrin member) baptised, 1655,-66
  conversion of young A upset Jewish leaders, 1672
Absalom, demagogue, 1073
absolute, 1226
  level of a., one dimension of personality, 1226
  only a. is existential, unqualifiedly eternal, 1260
  personality to function to borders of a., 1226
Absolute
  only an A can be existential and experiential, 1174
absolute actuals (3), 1151, 1262
absolute and subabsolute, 7
absolute attitudes, 113
ABSOLUTE BASIS FOR SUPREMACY, 1261
absolute cosmos, conceptually without limit, 1261
Absolute, God the, 13
  level of unifying Deity expression, expansion, 4
absolute level, involves postulate of three phases, 1262
ABSOLUTE MIND, THE, 102
ABSOLUTE OR SIXTH PHASE INTEGRATION, 1167
Absolute, qualified and unqualified, unified in
  Universal Absolute, 5, 15
absolute reality
  of infinity, 1260
  three persons of D, P, 3 Absolutes, 1153-54
Absolute Trinity, unification of second experiential
  Trinity, 13
Absolute, Unqualified
  and Paradise, 126
  outer regions pervaded by space potency of U A,
    124,-34
  repository of...universes of eternal future, 45
ABSOLUTE, UNQUALIFIED, DOMAINS OF THE, 130
absolute vs. absonites and finites 7, 1260
Absolutes
  actual and potential, 1151
  all things change except A, 1434
  are manifestations of the I AM, 1157
  equal total infinite reality, 4-5, 1146-47, 1156-57,
    1261
  Father, Universal, is the a. of the A, 1148
  First Source and Center potential in 3A, 1279
  in the triunities and triodities, 1147-51
  level connoting presence of...1163

Absolutes (cont'd)
  of potentiality, 55, 1262
  presences not fully revealed, 55
  seven coordinate A of actuality, 1262
  total infinite reality is existential in 7 A, 4-5
  the two--qualified and unqualified, 5, 15
  Universal Father is the cause of the A, 1148
  Unq. A, D A, Uni. A, 1262
ABSOLUTES OF INFINITY, THE SEVEN, 1155
Absolutes of infinity (7), 5, 1150, -54-57, 1172-3
  of potentiality operative on eternal levels, 1151,
    1262
ABSOLUTES, the THREE, 13, 1279
Absolutes, will of God potentialized in 3 A, 1278
absolutum, 1149
  organization of space potency, unique, 120
absonite, 636, 643, 1264, -67, -83
  among realities...transcendental level, 1160
  attitude of Trinity toward, 113
  existence more than finite, less than absolute, 113
  Havona, training universe for a. beings, 163
  level of reality, time and space transcending, 2
  level of reality, without beginnings or endings, 2
  phases of eternal career, 1287, -92
  quest for Father on new and higher levels, 1293
  seven groups of master Architects in a. levels, 351
  superconscious of Father, ultimacy of God, 69
  three dimensions of personality on a. level, 1226
  through Supreme, finite may attain a., 12
  Ultimate Deity signifies a. unification, 12
  Ultimate is...Trinity...comprehended by a., 12
absonite grandeur, after material wisdom exhausted,
  631
absonite ministers, 7th stage of light and life, 627
absonites,
  and finites vs. absolute, 7, 1260
  realities relative with respect to time and eternity, 7
absonitized being, how could a. b. be explained to us,
  334
absonity equivalated to value of Absolute, 352

ac

accident, fifty-thousand facts incompatible with a., 665
  God is not a cosmic a., 34
  J as child, fell downstairs, 1361
  universe not an a., 52
accidents, and angels, 1830
  and inconsistencies of chance, due to finite "Gods",
    1268
  J' teaching about, 1830
  no blind a. unforeseen in cosmos, 47
  no interference usually, 1361
  part of finite drama, 56
  of living, not remedied by legislation, philanthropy,
    957
  of time, believers not immune from, 1767
  "of time, innocent victims of", 1830
acclimatize, ascenders must, 554
accounting, living trial balance, 314
  your a. with the universe, 314-5
achieved vs. unachieved space, 159
achievement, lower circles of mortal a., 1247
  main potential for, 1438   main test, Havona, 291
  prerequisite to status, 1260
  one must do something, not only be, 1260
ACKNOWLEDGEMENT by Divine Counselor, 16
acknowledgement (U Book) of midwayer once attached
  to Andrew, helped J papers, 1343
ACME OF MATERIAL DEVELOPMENT, THE, 629
ACME OF RELIGIOUS LIVING, THE, 1101

acme of virtues, rugged self-control, 927
act is ours, consequences God's, 556, 1286
act of unreserved consecration, intelligent, 2065
action, creator thought always precedes creative a., 42
ACTION, THE GOD OF, 90
Actium, battle of, 1471
active personality, no real religion without, 1120
activities, all a. not in service of self are religious, 67
  executive worlds, most varied in universe, 151
  nonreligious, all are in service of self, 67
  on Jerusem, 526
activity necessary to spirit growth, 1120
actors (1,000,000) scenes (1,000), 501
  reenact an age, 501
acts, amazing a. of loyal devotion, 757
"acts of God", inexplicable things of life, 944
acts of today are the destiny of tomorrow, 557
actuality vs. potentiality, 1262-3

ad

Adam, 901
  age of A, third planetary epoch, opens, 830
  animals in Garden, 1000's familiar to A, 831
  arrival 35,000 years ago, 702
  beginning of dispensation, 702
  confronted with well nigh hopeless task, 846
  counsellor, one of 24 for Urantia, 514
  default 35,000 years B.C., 838-9, 868, 1327
  despite default upstepped Urantians, 868
  father of the realm, 587
  foretold J, 852
  had no liking for war, 844
  impregnated 1684 women, 851
  instruction for A on earth, 827
  J the second A, Paul's doctrine, 1582
  lived 530 years, 852
  Paul called J the second A, 1025
  pure line descendants to upstep red men, 884
  Son of God, 702, 1732
  Trinity idea ever since, 1598
  (town named) John preached, 1503
Adam and Eve (Material Son and Daughter of local
  system, biologic uplifters), 821
Adam and Eve, 584, 593, 626, 627, 632, 828, 843-5, 905, 1317
ADAM AND EVE, 828 (see "Eve" also)
ADAM AND EVE, ARRIVAL OF, 829
Adam and Eve,
  biologic uplifters, descending Sons, 444
  bodies gave forth shimmer of light, 580, 834
  both are Material Sons, biologic uplifters, 580, 821
  can petition to begin Paradise ascent, 628-9
  children left Urantia, 37,000 years ago, 632
  come to a planet to augment...evolution, 437
  communicated over about 50 miles, thought
    oscillations, 834-5
  contributed much despite downfall, 846, 868
ADAM AND EVE, DEATH OF, 851
ADAM AND EVE, DEFAULT OF, 839
ADAM AND EVE, DEGRADATION OF, 845
Adam and Eve,
  desired faster progress, 839
  destined to accompany earth fellows, 1025
  energized by food and light, 834, 851
  first ever, man-woman working together, 940
  first night on earth--and it was so lonely, 830
  forgiven, 514
  found world groping in spiritual darkness, 839
ADAM AND EVE, HOME LIFE OF, 834
ADAM AND EVE LEARN ABOUT THE PLANET, 830
ADAM AND EVE LEAVE THE GARDEN, 844

Adam and Eve (cont'd)
    left potent progeny on Urantia, 869
    made a mighty contribution, 854
    Material Sons, tall, bodies glow radiantly, 580
    may elect to humanize, start for Paradise, 629
    Michael chose Urantia after default of A & E, 1316
    music, would have given us A & E in reality, 500
    normally visible heads of planet, 584
    often receive T A while on a world, 629
ADAM AND EVE ON JERUSEM, 828
Adam and Eve
    origin of A & E of each local system, 415
    perhaps return to Urantia?, 1025
    plan is not for them to mate with mortals, 593
    release from planetary duties, 628-29
    rib legend, 742, 837
    rode fandors (giant birds) to travel, 831
    ruled Eden 117 years, 838
    scope of problems, 839
    second presentation of Trinity on U, 1143
    seraphim associate told...1317
    seraphim of A & E, called "voices of the Garden",
        437
    sorry plight of Urantia, seemed hopeless to, 840
ADAM AND EVE, SURVIVAL OF, 853
Adam and Eve
    Tabamantia recommended sending Material Sons, 821
    turned from ordained way, disaster, 838
    Urantia profited immeasurably from, 580
    vegetarians, 850
    violated the covenant, 845   trapped, 583
    "where are you?", 843
Adamic departure, 629
ADAMIC MISSIONS, THE, 582
Adamic period, control of natural forces achieved, 593
ADAMIC TRAINING OF ASCENDERS, 515
Adamites, 905, 940, 979
    and Adamsonites--violet race, 868, 904
    and Nodites blended, 859
    Andite descendants sagacious militarists, 872
    augmented religion of Nile valley, 1044
    beginning of warfare, A and Nodites, 844
    cultural level deteriorated, 870
    custom: honored seventh day, 1042
    early expansions of , 860
ADAMITES ENTER EUROPES, THE, 889
Adamites, excelled surrounding peoples, 850
    had sense of humor, appreciation of music, 835
    had to wrest living from unprepared soil, 847-48
    improved family life, 940
    in Mediterranean basin, with blue men, 869
ADAMITES IN THE SECOND GARDEN, THE, 869
Adamites, long-headed, like Nodites, 904
    lost culture in passing over Eurasia, 871
    many generations throughout Turkestan, 891
    migrations halted by geologic changes, 900
    not cannibalistic, 979
    were Pacific, Nodites no, 892
    women given increased recognition, 937
ADAM'S ADMINISTRATION, 833
Adam's rib, confused condensation, 837
Adams and Eves
    appear in biological level: why, 437
    origins, 415
ADAMS, THE PLANETARY, 580
Adamson, 876, 901, 990, 1021
    and brothers, sisters, non-flesh eaters, 850
    descendants were progenitors of Greeks, 895
    founded violet race center N of 2nd Eden, 849, 861
    grandfather of secondary midwayers, 862
    halo, from portrayal of A descendants, 834

Adamson (cont'd)
    lived for 396 years, 862
    majestic, met, married Ratta, 3 months, 861
    midwayer grandchildren, 70 days to create, 862
    midwayers kept him informed, 862
    new world center for truth, righteousness, 862
    north to start new life at 120 years of age, 861
    traditions of A still fostered pre-Hellenic Greece,
        1077
ADAMSON AND RATTA, 861
Adamsonites, 868, 896
    center of high civilization, Kopet Dagh, 862
    forerunners of Greeks, 895
    maintained high culture 7,000 years, 862
    second civilization of the, 895
addiction to snake venom, 946
addressed all inhabitants of sphere (Michael), 1315
adjudication, each individual's right to eternal life, 314
    first a. when Planetary Prince arrives, 567
    highest function of government, 247
    of mortal's life based on records, 1231
ADJUSTER, THOUGHT (See "Thought Adjusters",
    separate listing)
Adjuster-fused ascendant mortals, 244, 340
    finaliters, 249
Adjuster-fusion, 538
    Urantia mortals since Christ Michael, 410
ADJUSTER-FUSION SERIES, 565, 568 (See numerous
    "ADJUSTER" listings under "Thought Adjusters")
Adjusterlikeness is Godlikeness, 1216
ADJUSTER MINDEDNESS, 1181
ADJUSTER'S MISSION, THE, 1191
ADJUSTERS AS PURE SPIRITS, 1182
adjustment, human, physical, social, econimics vs.
    moral, spiritual, 911
adjustment sleep, 7 times, mansonia career, 540
ADJUSTMENT TO PLANETARY ENVIRONMENT, 565
adjustments (readjustments), task of modern man, 1013
adjutant mind circuits, death everlastingly divorces man
    from--, 1286
ADJUTANT MIND SPIRITS, 205, (mind bestowal of
    Mother Spirit, 205, mind ministers, 738)
adjutant mind spirits, 631, 710,-34, 950, 1244,-87
ADJUTANT MIND SPIRITS, THE SEVEN, 401
adjutant mind spirits, (see also "circles"),
    activate teachable types of minds, 730
    aided by ministry from above, 739
    animals served by, 709
    beginning function, potential ability to learn, 739
    bestowal in accord with innate brain capacity, 670
    come to mortals from capitals of Creator Son, 639
    concerned with pre-spiritual mind, 457
    cosmic mind plus a.m.s. evolve physical
        tabernacle, 483
    do not contact mechanical orders of...response, 739
    function exclusively through 5 phases, 739
    function from lowest...739
    impulse of worship largely originates in, 1245
    intellect resides in pulsations of, 1286
    intuition result of, 709
    labor long before arrival mind attains human levels,
        739
    like circuits, not beings, 403
    mind is endowment of a.m.s. on, 399
    ministry aids evolutionary religion, 1003, 1110
    mind bestowal of Mother Spirit, 205
    mind ministers, 738
    mind improves under ministry of a.m.s., 737
    mortal leaves native planet, leaves a.m.s., 1237
    mother love is inherent endowment of, 932

adjutant mind spirits (cont'd)
   named, 378, 401-2
   no influences in...career comparable to, 1236
   prepare mind for T A, 118
   science, philosophy, founded on a.m.s., 1141
   source and pattern for "intuitive", 739
   sponsor, censor all of man's religious reactions,1129
   task of weaning mortal mind from...1211
   when 7 have functioned, T A comes, 1187
ADJUTANT-SPIRIT MINDS, 481
ADJUTANTS OF WORSHIP AND WISDOM, 948
administration, moral growth not had by improved
   a., 1097
ADMINISTRATION OF THE ETERNAL SON, 83
ADMINISTRATION OF THE LOCAL UNIVERSE, 366
administration, 70 divisions constellation affairs, 486
ADMINISTRATION, THE LOCAL SYSTEM, 509
administrative-advisory chain helps govern, 213
ADMINISTRATIVE ASSISTANTS, 434
administrative coordination, 209,-69
ADMINISTRATIVE READJUSTMENTS, 626
administrative uniformity on creative diversity
   (Master Spirits), 209
administrative unit, vast complex of, 456
ADMINISTRATOR SERAPHIM, 434
admirers, J had many, 1400,-03
ADOLESCENT YEARS, THE, 1395
adolescents, J a refuge for a., all ages and worlds, 1395
ADOPTED SERAPHIM, 348
adoption into clan, 787
adoption of superior captives, 779
adornment, universal physical a. of the eternal God, 125
adultery, J on, 1576
   "this woman was taken in a. in the very act",1792,-93
advance from life to life and world to world, 417
advance-tuned, on morontia worlds, 544
advanced races of earth, pre-Adam, 822
advanced semispiritual level, 730
advanced state, wars no more, governments disappear,
   630
advanced states, honors of, 804
advances, gains, not all due to secular revolt, 2082
ADVANCING GHOST CULT, THE, 962
adventure, and excitement needed, social activities, 769
   call to, 1303, 1749, 2076,-84
   career endless of a. and discovery, 2076
   cheap and sordid, avoid, 2076
   desire for, don't try satisfy in lifetime, 2076
   enthralling, partner of, 1430   magnificent, 614
   lure of time, 159
   man's great universe, 263, 364-5, 1303
   man's greatest, 2097
   man's universe a., statics to spirit dynamics, 1303
   most satisfying and thrilling, 1732
   of exploration, 1484
   Paradise a., uncertainty with security, 1223
   purely useless, 149
   stimulus of curiosity and a. through Havona, 159
   supernal a. should be our supreme study, 449
   supreme, 1608, 1732-3
   supreme, of all men all worlds, 22
   too much for one life, 2076, 2096
   tremendous a. and growth in future, 263
ADVENTURE, THE ULTIMATE, 352
ADVENTURE, THE URANTIA, 734
adventure, useless a. not for high personalities, 149
adventures in cultural adjustment, 911
   in growth, forever forthcoming, 1294
adversity, apostles, 1726
   "go with you", 1767
   viewed as God's displeasure, 1830

advertisement, first literature was a., 775
"advertising" (too many desires), 765
advice, give none voluntarily, 556, 1420
   never offered unless asked for (J), 371
   not proffered, 1420
ADVISERS, TECHNICAL, 279, 414
advisory-administrative chain helps govern, 213
advisory council to Urantia, 513

af

affectation, 557
affection, augmented by devotion, 1419
   fervent, J, 1837
   "for spiritual pursuits", 1821
   "give expression to", 1745
   shortsighted, that would pamper and spoil, 1304
affectionate "bus" (passenger) birds, 590
affectionate heavenly Father, 41
affections, man entitled to satisfactions of a., 1096
afflicted, causes of being, 1649,-64
affliction, greatest a. is, 556
   "is not the frown of God", 1831
afflictions, Father does not send, 1661
   five theories of a., 989
   greatest of a. may be unearned leisure, 1305
   "I will be with you in a.", 1662
   "in all your a. I am afflicted" (the Father), 53
   J had 3 kinds to meet, 1591
   J healed mental, people thot physical, 1836
   purpose of, 1661
   reasons why there are a. (4), 1649,-64
   study of Job's a. helped John, 1661
   undeserved a. are transient, 619
   unearned leisure, undeserved wealth, may be
      great a., 1305
afraid, J was not a. to understand, 1736
   men a. to comprehend J, 1736
   nothing on Edentia to make anyone a., 492
AFRAID, THE YOUNG MAN WHO WAS, 1437
Africa, 764, 768, 905
   and Europe rose out of Pacific depths, 662
   Baganda tribes, mana level of prayer, 994
   Bushmen, individual names don't exist, 972
   Bushmen, self-interest and group-interest, 1132
   cannibalism recently, as a war measure, 979
   fetish stones, 945
   moved slightly south (Mediterranean basin), 668
   pygmies, and religious reactions as a class, 1010
   rainbow thought to be a celestial smoke, 947
   Sicilian land bridge to A, 826
   types of primitive government now in, 789
   umbilical cord highly prized fetish, 968
African traditions, missionaries breakdown authority
   of, 750
Africans still buy wives, 923
AFTER THE CRUCIFIXION, 2011
AFTER MEETING, THE, 1712
AFTER THE NOONTIME MEAL, 1932
AFTER PENTECOST, 2069
AFTERNOON AT THE SYNAGOGUE, 1629

ag

Agaman, 1679
age, next a. of man, 1863
AGE OF ADVANCED MAMMALS, 694
age of Biologic Tribulation, 684
   of Birds, 691
   of despair and hopelessness (India), 1029
AGE OF EARLY MAMMALS, 693

AGE OF EARTHQUAKES, THE, 660
AGE OF THE ELEPHANT AND HORSE, 696
age of expanding horizons and enlarging concepts, 1146
  of Fishes, The, 679
  of Frogs, The, 682
  of J at baptism, 1512
  of mortals (longevity), normal post-bestowal, over
    300 years, 597
  of mortals, normal post-teacher Son, 500 years, 599
  of spiritual striving, 577
  plan of a new a., 1595
  the security a., 576
aged, death better than infirmity, 953
  preferred being killed to infirmity, 953
  responsibility for, 1712
agents of the Creator (miracle?), 1530
agents on earth (J'), 1570
ages, bronze, iron, not distinct, 903
  early a., courage, bravery, heroism, 729
  required to recoup loss of strain of heredity, 560
aggregations vs. systems, 1227
aggressive, be in preaching gospel, 1931
  J was, 1366, -96
aggressiveness needs balance of sagacity, 1958
agnostics, automaton conceive philosophy of auto-
    matism?, 2080
agondonters, believe without seeing, 579
agree, two or three, it shall be done, 1763
agreement, great Urantian, divinity and humanity, 1020
agricultural stage, The, 769
agricultural-industrial pop. vs. land, 770
agriculture, brought slavery and private land
    ownership, 902
  ennobling influence, 769
  man not consigned to toil to "sweat", 751
  menial to till soil in early ages, 900
  quadrupled land-man ratio, 769
  weakness of a. and industrialism, 769

ah

Ahab, King, 1074
  and Jezebel, 1374
  murdered Naboths, 1065
Ahura-Mazda, head of galaxy of 7 gods, 1049

AIDS, THE UNIVERSE, 406
aims of constitutional tribunals, 798
air breathers, water scorpions suddenly appeared, 678
air transport, and water, Edentia, 486
"airport" for celestial beings, Urantia, 326, 438

al

Alabama, coal beds 35 layers deep, 681
alabaster cruse of spikenard, 1879
alarming picture, few who can function with...1207
  spiritual decline, 1207
Alaska, 670, -89, 728
alchemy, turned into chemistry by science, 901
Alexander, armies of A aided Samaritans against
    Jews, 1612
Alexandria, believers believed in resurrection, 2029
  center of Jewish learning and culture, 1351
  Damascus center planned to outshine A, 1412
  group of Jews from A met with J, 1413
ALEXANDRIA, J AND FRIENDS AT, 1432
Alexandria, J family believed he was in A, 1483

Alexandria (cont'd)
  J visited A with Ganid and Gonod, 1427, -32
  Philo, wealthy, educated Jew of A (see "Philo")
  Joseph, Mary, J, 2 years in A, 1354
ALEXANDRIAN APPEARANCE, THE, 2044
Alexandrian proposal to J, 1413
all bona fide personalities have Holy Spirit, 1003
"all power in heaven and earth", 605
all things, for God-knowing, 1306
  work together for good, 548
all things are possible, in liaison with God, 291
  no limitation, a.t.a.p., partnership with God, 1299
  to him who really believes, 1757
Allah, 1051
allegory, rich man and beggar, 1854
  vs. parable, 1672, 1690, 1691
ALLOCATION OF CIVIL AUTHORITY, 797
ALMIGHTY AND GOD THE SEVENFOLD, THE, 1269
ALMIGHTY AND PARADISE DEITY, THE, 1270
ALMIGHTY AND THE SEVENFOLD CONTROLLERS,
    THE, 1273
ALMIGHTY AND THE SUPREME CREATORS, THE,
    1271
ALMIGHTY SUPREME, THE, 1268 (See also "God,
    the Supreme", and "Supreme Being")
Almighty Supreme, physical universes, symbolic of...
    reality of A S, 1276
alms, J refused a., 1414
  when you give a., 1577, -83
alms seekers, professional, 1580
alone, few duties to be done a., 312
  go apart to seek wisdom, strength, guidance, 1747
ALONE IN GETHSEMANE, 1968
alone, John Mark, a., with God (J), 1920
  man languishes in isolation, 1776
  no thing or being exists or lives in isolation, 647
  not good for man to be a., 283, 1775, 2055
  sorrow (etc.) worse when borne a., 1776
  tends to exhaust energy charge of soul, 1776
alphabet, basic on Uversa, 70 symbols, 503
  concept symbols of Uversa, over 1 billion, 503
  Dravidians imported a. from Sumeria, 881
  first, 500,000 years ago, 746
  first on Urantia, Fad, 25 characters, 746
  second on Urantia, Van, Edenic, 829
  third on Urantia, Adamites, Mesopotamia, 850
  Van and Amadon, new a. 24 letters (Eden), 829
Alps, dislocated plants, animals, 702
alternate routes to Havona, 538
altruism, derived from, 1133
  desirable?, 51, 52
  fire, first opportunity for a., 777
  not a. to give sympathy to inferior, abnormal, 592
altruistic drive may overdevelop if no personality
    unification, 1132

am

Amadon, modified human associate of Van, 757
  outstanding human hero of rebellion, 757
AMADONITES AND NODITES, 821
Amadonites, derived from 144 Andonites, 759
Amatha, Peter's mother-in-law, 1631
Amathus, 1409, 1827
  J and apostles 3 weeks at, 1589
AMATHUS, LAST WEEK AT, 1592
AMATHUS, THE SOJOURN AT, 1589
Amaziah, King, 1074
amazing conclusion, 95% of Paradise gravity grasp
    unused by present organized universes, 132

ambassadors, from Paradise, 371
  origin of, 371, -83, 834
AMBASSADORS, THE TRINITIZED, 248
ambition, and initiative, impaired by magic, charms,
  972
    and invention better ferment than war, 786
    and leisure combined, good, 907
    dangerous, 557, 1926
Amdon, Chaldean herder, 1015
ameba, but little modified, 732
  typical survivors of initial animal life, 673
Amenhotep, 111
  and Ka, 1215
Amenemope, 1009, -43
  Book of Wisdom, 1046-47
  colored thot of Hebrews and Greeks, 1046
  philosophy of Proverbs from A, 1046
AMENOMOPE, TEACHINGS OF, 1046
Amenomope, very great, advanced teacher, 1046
America "discovered", 729, 934
American Congress (approved), 1489
American Federal Union and peace, 1489
American government, fore-runner of, 789
American industrialism, amazing creativity due to
  secularistic revolt, 2081
American life-implantation, produced humans'
  ancestors, 703
Americans, favorable opportunity for development, 907
  result of north-south "cracking", 663
Amerinds (see "red man", "red men")
Amida Buddha, 1040
  God of the Paradise in the West, 1041
amity displaces enmity slowly, 785
ammonites, beautiful
  developed from best cephalopods, 686-87
  fossil remains found all over world, 686
AMONG THE GENTILES, 1334
Amorites, confederation, 1020, 1054
AMOS AND HOSEA, 1065
AMOS, brother of J, born,1373, died, 1400
AMOS, lunatic of Kheresa, 1695-97, 1765
AMOS, prophet, 1502, 1597, 1731, 1065
  threatened God would abandon Israel, 1071
  was a discoverer of new concepts of Deity, 1065
AMOS, young friend of John Mark, 1922
Amosad, leader of Sethite priests, 872, 1009
amphitheater, Caeserea, could seat 20,000, 1429
    Jerusem, 5 billion seats, 522
    J proposed a. for Nazareth, 1371
    Urmia, dedicated to "spirit of religion", 1485
amulets are futile, 1681
amusement madness, Rome, 2074

an

analogy, natural and spirit worlds, 1692
analysis of H$_2$O, couldn't predict put out fire, 141
analysis, technical, can't tell human capacity, 141
anarchy, augmented misery, law and order slowly
  emerge, 783
Anaxagoras, 1079
ancestor of all materialization, force-charge of
  space, 169
ancestor veneration, weakness of, 888
ANCESTOR WORSHIP, 960
ancestor worship, 767, -91, 1012, -33
ancestors, common a. of mankind (on normal planet), 587
  man's a. almost extinguished, 705, -8
  no leisure for reflection, social thinking, 901
ANCESTORS OF UNIVERSES, THE--NEBULAE, 169

ancestors (cont'd)
  our, devotion bordered on grandeur, 729
  pre-human a., narrow escapes, 705-6
  unfit, inferior, disqualify offspring for survival, 1198
ancestors of man, seaweed, slime and ooze of ocean
  bed, 731
ancestral energy, sevenfold constitution of, 481
ancestral stamp of Seven Paradise Spirits, 190
ancestral tendencies, adjust to demands of spiritual
  urges (problem), 1199
ancestry, data on a., plus projected patterns of life for
  T A, 1185-86
ancient, that which was a., supposedly sacred, 1004
Ancients of Days (21 preside over destinies of the 7
  superuniverses, 209; in connection with this U Book,
  32; reserve power of decision on a mortal's extinction, 210, 367, 372, 396)
Ancients of Days, 269, 270
ANCIENTS OF DAYS, THE, 209
Ancients of Days
  act for the 7 Master Spirits in 7 superuniverses, 197
  adjudicated rebellion in system, 11
  aided by 1 billion Perfectors of Wisdom, 178, 1311
  and 3 billion Divine Counsellors, 178
  and Universal Censors, 3 billion, 178
  assign circuit supervisors to local u, 265
  assured Michael safety of realm on bestowals, 1325
  attacked by Lucifer as "foreign potentates", 603
  beginning of personality records, 209
  can see, hear, all things, 308
  circuit supervisor assigned by, 265
  confirmed Edentia Most Highs in Authority, 489
  courts of A D are high review tribunals, 180
  decree extinction of life, establish it, 396
  each super-universe ruled by 3, 178
  hear, see,from Paradise to ends of worlds, 308
  indicated Michael's experience... finished, 1513
  J accepted as sovereign ruler of Nebadon after
    Urantia, 1317
  know mind of Spirit through Voice of Conjoint Actor,
    308
  mandate, no spiritual jeopardy during bestowal, 1326
  mete out just judgment of... fairness, 115
  midway between Paradise and evolving worlds, 1272
  most divinely endowed rulers aside from... 210
  most powerful of direct rulers, 210
  narrator of paper, attached to, 270
  only A D sit in judgment issues of eternal life and
    death, 180
  preside over destinies of the 7 superuniverses, 208
  primary seconaphim keep A D informed, 307
  Reflective Spirits, have "voices" to A D, 201
  represent beginnings of personality, 209
  reserve power of decision on extinction, 210, 367,
    372, 396
  rulers of our superuniverse (connection with U Book),
    32
  rulers of 7 superuniverses rightly called A D, 164
  see progress through universe reflectivity, 1284
  Solitary Messengers lead to A D in local u., 259
  Supreme Trinity Personalities, 207
  three preside over each superuniverse, 209, 396, 259,
    1272
  three rule, why?, 309
  three supervise each superuniverse, 178
  to be superseded by Supreme, 210
  tribunal of A D, 1214
  triune rulers of superuniverses, 1309
  uniform, superperfect offspring of Trinity, 21
    basically identical, 209

6

Ancients of Days (cont'd)
  use Image Aids in communication, 202
  when A D function, Trinity functions, 217
ancients sacrificed mother for child, 940
ANDITE CONQUEST OF INDIA, THE, 879
ANDITE CONQUEST OF NORTHERN EUROPE, 893
ANDITE DISPERSIONS, THE LAST, 873
ANDITE EXPANSION IN THE OCCIDENT, 889
ANDITE EXPANSION IN THE ORIENT, 878
ANDITE INVASIONS OF EUROPE, THE, 892
ANDITE MIGRATIONS, THE, 872
Andites (the mighty race), 937, 1077
ANDITES, THE, 871
Andites, Adamic peoples mixed with Nodites, Sangiks, 868, 892
ANDITES ALONG THE NILE, 894
Andites, ancestors of Nordics (Scandinavians, Germans, Anglo-Saxons), 893
  attracted Sangiks for mating, 919
  augmented religion (culture) in Egypt, 1044
  beginnings of the mighty A, 851
  believed ghosts returned to homelands, 953
  blend of Nodite, Adamic, Caucasoid, 905
  can't be traced by stages of pottery, 903
  children of Nodite women (mostly) and Adam, 851
  cultural ferments and biologic reserves, 900
  dispossessed of homelands, 879
  Dravidian A conquered India, 881
  Egypt, culture and religion chiefly from, 1045
ANDITES ENTER CHINA, THE, 886
Andites, families as ready for Salem doctrines as Abraham, 1018
  family-council practices of A good today, 941
  first important domesticaters of horse, 902
  greater percentage of Adamic blood than moderns, 871
  India under domination of A Aryans, 1027
  Indian heritage of monotheism from A, 881
  Iran, Turkestan, SinKiang, aridity, 907
  mixed A (Nodites and Adamites), 859
  not Aryan, but pre-Aryan, 872
  not cannibalistic until admixed, 979
ANDITES OF THE MEDITERRANEAN ISLES, 895
ANDITES OF TURKESTAN, THE, 878
  132 A to S A, established ancestry of Incas, 873
  pure-line violet plus Nodites, Sangiks, 871
  race born on periphery of 2nd garden, 871
  so-called Dravidians and Aryans who conquered India, 873
  stage set for A era of civilization, 871
  submerged by peoples of So. in India, 881
  traces of A blood reached Peru, 884
  turned westward from Turkestan to Europe, 878
Andon, ancestor of Neanderthal and blue men, 727
  discoverer of fire, 777
  invented ax, 715
ANDON AND FONTA (first human beings), 711
  about 100 best families of descendants survived, 722
  actual parents of all mankind, 711
  family held together 19 generations, 713
  greetings to Urantia not approved, 717
  loss of A F would have delayed evolution, 734
ANDON AND FONTA, THE SURVIVAL OF, 717
ANDONIC ABORIGINES, THE, 718
ANDONIC CLANS, THE, 713
Andonic germ plasm, changes in, mutant traits, 857
Andonic peoples, mated with inferior tribes, deteriorated, 719
Andonites (first human beings, 713; 100 best used to modify 100 Jerusem citizens to flesh and blood partaking of life circuits of system, 742)

Andonites (cont'd) 857-58, -62, -69, -74, 904
  access to tree of life, 756
  Amadonites descended from loyal A, 821
  among students trained in Mesopotamia, 751
  best, preserved of, nw of India, 870
  broad-headed, 904
  considerable A in white races, 889
  "discovered" stone-headed club, 768
ANDONITES, DISPERSION OF THE, 715
Andonites, distribution of, 30,000-10,000 B.C., 870-71
  early A, about 75 of them, 713
  early A evinced clannish spirit, 713
  early, not cannibalistic, 979
  early taught the Golden Rule, 783
  evolved in advance of color races, 723
  fearless, successful hunters, 715
  first creatures to use animal skins for warmth, 713
  first people to live in England, 719
  first primitive men, black eyes, swarthy, 713
  included Amadonites, noble band, 759
  Mek did much to advance culture of A, 748
  northern islands of Pacific held by, 884
  now separate two branches of white race, Europe, 896
  of Iceland, 1021
  100 modified to give material bodies to...742, 745
  purest A lived in north...728
  regarded twins as good luck, 770
  round-headed, 894
  Siberian A, profited from mixing red race, 884
  used animal skins, against cold, 713
ANDON'S FAMILY, 713
Andovontia, greetings to Urantia, 413
ANDREW, THE FIRST CHOSEN (APOSTLE), 1548, (See also under "APOSTLES")
Andromeda, collapse about fifty years ago, 464
  light we see left A 1 million years ago, 170
  outside inhabited superuniverse, 170
ANDRONOVER NEBULA, THE, 651
Andronover, 168, 651
  birth to 1,013,628 suns, 654
Ang, of Caligastia, 100, 745
Angamon, Stoic leader friend of Paul, taught by J, 1456
angel, an a. has spoken to him, 1904
  Melchizedek, a. of the Lord, 1023
  mighty a. spoke to, strengthened him, 1968
"angel of the Lord" (Brilliant Evening Star), 407
angelic army, 12 hosts, over 71 million, a unit, 421
angelic corps, are ministers, 418
  each universe has its own native a.c., 414
  what constitutes, 418
angelic hosts, 285, 314
ANGELIC HOSTS, THE VOICE OF, 309
angelic ministers, mother of all a.m. is Infinite Spirit, 205
ANGELIC NATURES, 419
ANGELIC WORLD, THE, 510
angels (see also "guardian angels", "seraphim"), 306, -19, 348, 408, 418, -20, -26, 1840, 2020
  act in emergencies and on instruction, 1246
  attenuations of Infinite Spirit, 95
  childrens', 1761
  circuits of arch-, 1254
  concepts on Urantia, come from, 438
  contact mortals for spiritual personalities, 421
  created a little lower than the a., 445
  dedicated to service of companionship, 283
ANGELS, EPOCHAL, 1255
angels, feminine, 419
  fifth order, planetary helpers, 583
  follow you through many an age, 1246
  guardian (see "guardian angels")

angels (cont'd)
  intrude into human drama (when), 1246
  keep worlds in touch with one another, 1841
  lead you in trouble as loving discipline, 1931
  love human beings, 419
  men do not become a., 1841
  mother of local universe a. is a Creative Spirit, 205
  never die, 1841, 1900
  not directly concerned with prayers, 1246
ANGELS OF THE CHURCHES, 1255
ANGELS OF DIVERSION, 1256
ANGELS OF ENLIGHTENMENT, 1256
ANGELS OF THE FUTURE, 1255
angels, "of God, ascending and descending", 1841
ANGELS OF HEALTH, 1256
ANGELS OF INDUSTRY, 1256
angels, of the Lord opened prison doors, freed
  Christians, 865
ANGELS OF NATION LIFE, 1255
ANGELS OF PROGRESS, 1255
ANGELS OF THE RACES, 1255
ANGELS OF SUPERHUMAN MINISTRY, 1256
angels, personally guard and guide you, 445
  petty frictions among, 311
  recording, 1243
  reflective, can discern motives, 313-4
  Sadducees, entangling question about a., 1901
  saving men, many engaged in, 1841
  seek to bring together working groups, 432
  share man's nonsensuous emotions, 419
  social architects, 432
  strengthened Him, 1904, -68   super, 407
  "tempt not the a. of your supervision", 1931
  twelve groups of a. in planetary supervision, 1255
  unfaithful and disobedient a. in custody, 1249
ANGELS, UNREVEALED, 420
angels, "weep because of your... intolerance", 1246
  wings, concept of, 438; no, 1246
  world intercommunication, 1841
  worlds teem with, 260
anger, and fear weaken character, 1573
  depletes the health, debases the mind, 1673
  foreign to nature of God, 57
  handicaps spirit teacher of soul, 1673
  hardly worthy to be called human, 57
  inconsistent with divine sonship, 1673
  J on a., 1673
  is a failure, 1673
  like stone hurled in hornet's nest, 557
  Moses tells us God (is of) fierce a., 1597
  not part of the kingdom, 1725
angiosperms, 695
  suddenly, 689
Anglo-Saxon forefathers, 893
Angona system, 655
angry, he who is a. in danger of condemnation, 1576
  J not even a. when, 2000
  Joseph, father of J angered by son, 1371
  Psalmist "kiss the son lest he be a.", 1725
anguish, J endured great, 1969
animal(s), Adam understood 1000's of a. shown him, 831
  advisers regarding the conquest of predatory a., 746
  all are bellicose, 784
  became fetish if ate human flesh, 967
  counted in rise of primitive society, 777
  develop from patterns of vegetable kingdom, 560, 669
  disease believed due to conspiracy, spirits and a., 991
  dog-eating greatly reduced man-eating, 980
  domesticated twice before Andite age, 902
  domestication of, 746, 778, 901
  during vogue of a., would be drawn on walls, 716

animal(s) (cont'd)   Egyptians believed in survival, 1049
  enormous profits to temple in a., 1888
  entire world of a. was man's enemy, early, 778
  form of a. worship veneration, among Andonites, 716
  great variance planet to planet, 561
  have fears but no illusions, hence no religion, 944
  husbandry reduced women to depths of slavery, 768
  in Europe from Africa, 721
  man functions as a. when fails to discriminate, 193
  man's slothful a. mind rebels at effort, 1097
  mere a. cannot possess time self-consciousness, 1479
  midwayers have definite powers over "beasts", 865
  no spiritual nature or time consciousness (J), 1431, -79
  no survival with identity, 404
  primitive men thought ancestors were a., 837
  revered by early man for power and cunning, 946
  sacrifice of a. meant much to primitive man, 978
  sacrificial a. rejected by temple inspectors, 1888
  served by adjutant mind-spirits before man evolved, 709
  sort of cross between cat and seal, 695
  speeded civilization in Asia, 902
  those who cannot know God are reckoned among a., 1468
  to angel, to spirit, to God, 558
  trait of a. in man leads to assault the superior, 1984
  Urantia races highly like a., 1207
ANIMALS, THE UTILIZATION OF, 778
animal(s), vestigial traits of a., eradicated by morontia
    career, 551
  when becomes self-conscious is primitive man, 1479
  worship of a. due to misinterpretation of G R, 946
  zoological garden within Garden of Eden, 824
animal and spirit in man, hardly be reconciled in short
    life, 381
animal forms of life, origin, 731
animal man, deliverance from shackles of animalism, 231
animal mutations (see "mutations, animal")
animal vs. man, 231, 706, 1984
  a., blind and instinctive urge, m transcends urge, 1773
  a. can't communicate ideas, can't have personality, 1775
  a. does not visualize survival after death, 766
  a. does not sense time as m does, 1439
  a. has mind, can know master, cannot know God, 1431
  a. labors instinctive, m labors by design, 773
  a. lives in present only, m visualizes future, 135
  a., motion has meaning for, m has value for, 1297
  a. never worries, never commits suicide, 1773
  a., no inquiry into purpose of life, m yes, 1773
  a. responds to urge of life, m attains art of living, 1773
  both early m and a. discarded young early, 940
  fire building, 777
  m can transcend self, a. can't, 1223
  m, early, had to compete with a. for food, 773
  m makes moral choice, a. cannot, 1131
  m, moral, religious natures distinguish from a., 193
  m only in degree possesses mind above a. level, 1435
  m transcends a., appreciates art, humor, religion, 772
  soul elevates man above level of a., 1478
animal way to live vs. human way, 1775
animalism, shackles of, 231
animalistic retrogression, slothfulness of, 1285
animism, 952, 995
annals of salvation, touching chapter in, 1313
ANNAS, VISIT TO, 1596
ANNAS (high priest emeritus, 1975, -77; father-in-law of
    high priest Caiaphas, 1978; most powerful man in
    all Jewry, 1978; distant relative of Salome, mother
    of apostles John and James Zebedee, 1420, 1596,
    1978)
  and Caiaphas, consultation on "risen J", 2033
  argued for 3 charges against J, 1983
  detained J to "kill time" for Sanhedrin, 1978

ANNAS (cont'd)
enmity aroused due to threatened revenues, 1979
enriched by temple revenues, 1978
former friend of J but turned, 1596
guided indictment of J, sought death, 1985
J to A, "Fear is man's chief enslaver and pride his
great weakness", 1596
letter from Salome about J, 1422
looked upon J as great man, 1422
most influential of Sadducees, 1420
palace outside Jerusalem, Mt. Olivet, 1981
Peter's denial of J in A courtyard, 1980
relative of Salome Zebedee, mother of apostles,
1420, 1596, 1978
reproached by J, 1979
"you are disturbing peace and order", 1979
annihilation (see also "cessation of existence",
"extinction", and "personality extinction")
after decree, fair adjudication again, 615
Gabriel, plea for a. of rebels, 609-11
rebels, instant a., perhaps if...616
repentant rebels, no extinction, 610
announcement, tremendous, J, 1589
announcements to towns, J to arrive, 1827
anonymity, why J contrived a., 1413
ANOTHER DISAPPOINTMENT, 1543
another and Greater John the Baptist, 1865
Anova, oldest world in Satania, 559
ANSWER TO PETER'S QUESTION, 1824
ANSWER TO PRAYER, THE, 1848
answer to prayer depends on...1639
antagonism(s), God never victim of attitudinal a., 38
in all successful human institution, 938
incapable of solution, 1134
irritations, frictions, among angelic hosts, 311
J a. to tradition, 1655
natural, 782, 938
positive (J), 1655
antagonistic, desires of people, natural occurrences
seem a., 1306
antagonistic cooperation, marriage highest kind of, 938-9
Antarctica, 662, -68
Antares, 60 million times volume of our sun, 458
anthems of glory (presence embellishers), 506
anthropology, 719
"missing link", fossils nearest to, India, 720
anthropomorphic God. What a mistake!, 297
anthropomorphism, highest man can conceive, 67
anti-semitism, 1339, 1788, 1909
antidote for so-called accidental ills, 957
antigravity, affects weight of evolving energy, 175
amazing power of Infinite Spirit, 82, 101
and heat disrupt matter, dissipates energy, 176
behavior of ultimatonic energies, 473
beings possessed with endowments of a., 264
employed in...functions, activities of...156
gyroscope illustrates effect, but not cause of, 101
how annuls gravity, 101
influence acts as brake, 125
neutralizes gravity action in space, 482
possessed of a. in excess of all others...326
Universe Spirit possesses full endowment of, 375
antigravity behavior, ultimatons, velocity to points of
partial a., 476
Antioch, and Philadelphia, 1869
followers of J first called "Christians", 1333
gave Christianity its name, 2068
head of church, N and W, 1831, 2029
hdqtrs, Pauline Christianity, 1869
J spent over 2 months in, 1492
largest Syrian city, 1480

Antioch believers, collections for Jerusalem
believers, 2067
Antipatris, 1404   anti-semitism, 1399, 1708, 1909
antisocial conditions, social mechanism insurance
against, 906
antisocial, defective, degenerate, unfit--disfellowship,
585
antisocially minded individuals, hindrance to progress,
910
antithesis(es), J used, 1771
(series of), 51, 52
Antonia, praetorium at A, J trial, 1987
Roman castle of A (Jerusalem) grim, 1794
anvil of justice and hammer of suffering, 100
anvils of necessity, 258, 747
anxieties, discount a. of present for certainties of
future, 548
anxiety, and dread, thoughtless panic of, 1243
can do nothing to supply material needs, 1823
man's dual situation results in a., 1221-2
must be abandoned, 557
natural state of the savage mind, 951
no! forethought, yes, 1579
vs. will of the Father, 1525

ap

Aphrodite, ritual of Ishtar, A in Greece, 1043
apocalyptic, Selta wrote an a. about Messiah, 1915
apocalyptists (teachers) arose in Palestine 100 B.C.,
1500
apostate planet, evolution dangerous, 580

apostles

APOSTLES
"about" the apostles, appraisals of (first p. no.)
admonitions, final personal, and warnings (2nd p. no.)
Alpheus twins, 1563, 1959
Andrew, 1548, 1959
James Zebedee, 1552, 1958
John Zebedee, 1553, 1955
Judas Iscariot, 1565
Matthew, 1559, 1957
Nathaniel, 1558, 1960
Philip, 1556, 1960
Simon Peter, 1550, 1962
Simon the Zealot, 1564, 1956
Thomas Didymus, 1561, 1961
adversity, baptism of a. for apostles (Chorazin), 1726
afflictions, 3 forms to meet, how, 1591
aggression, acquired spirit of positive a., 1609
Alpheus twins (see "James and Judas Alpheus" below)
AMATHUS, LAST WEEK AT, 1592
AMATHUS, SOJOURN AT, 1589
ambassadors of the kingdom, 1568, -70-71
ANDREW, ablest man of 12, 1549
"are you speaking to us in parables?", 1759
called "chief", 1549
final admonition (J), 1958
ANDREW, THE FIRST CHOSEN, 1548
ANDREW, "his" midwayer, 1332, 1547
lost record of A, 1341
Luke, edited copy A notes (purported), 1342
record of J' sayings by A, 1549
"repeat for our benefit" (J on wealth), 1823
revelators had access to lost record of A, 1341
sermon topic, The New Way, 1629
"strive for self-denial or self-control?", 1609
"whom do you seek?", 1756
"why...leave us alone with multitude?", 1635

A

archaeology, (cont'd)
  early Andon settlements are on English coast, 719
  foothills, Turkestan, vestiges of Adamsonites, 862
  fossils of Siwalik hills, near transition types, 720
  later vases, implements, often inferior to earlier, 903
  primitive communities rose on dirt and trash, 903
  stones with laws, off Mesopotamia, Persia, 751
  submerged Garden of Eden, 823, -26-27, -75
  Sumerian clay tablets tell of earthly paradise, 860
  transition fossils, man and pre-man, Siwalik Hills, 720
  vestiges of Adamsonites, near Kopet Dagh, 862
  when Sumerian clay tablets dug up, lists of kings, 857
ARCHANGELS, THE, 406-08
archangels, and their ever-ready circuit, 1254
  angels of the resurrection, 2022
  circuit of a. located on Urantia, 1250, -3, -4, -9
  circuit opened on U at resurrection roll call, 2024
  circuit used in planetary emergencies, 1254
  council of a. while J in tomb, 2020
  divisional headquarters on U, 1253
  have a technique of body dissolution, 2023
  headquarters on U. Why?, 1259
  preserve record of personality constitution, 1234
  sought body of J for dissolution, 2022-3
ARCHANGELS, THE WORLDS OF THE, 409
Archelais and Phasaelis, few believers in, 1611
ARCHELAIS, PREACHING AT, 1607
Archelaus (brother of Herod), 1356, -74, 1875
Archeozoic, last earthwide flood, 672, 875
architect, Babel, 858
  Eden, 830, -50
Architects of Being (see also "Life Carriers"),
Architects of Being, life formulated to plans of, 396
Architects, Master, of creation, 480
architects, master, universe, 329, -33
ARCHITECTS OF THE MASTER UNIVERSE, 262, 351, 354
Architects of Master Universe, Personalized T A's are their all-wise executives, 1201
  what is of survival value held for services of, 1201
ARCHITECTS, SOCIAL, 432
ARCHITECTURAL SPHERES, THE, 174
architectural worlds (spheres), 91
  accommodate physical and spiritual personalities, 358
  built for special purposes, 172, -4
  constellation government in cluster, 771 a. spheres, 485
  five billion, if...175
  foretaste of paradisiacal glory, 521
  independent of suns of space, 456
  mass organized by direct action, 170
  not luminous in space, not visible, 520
  one of 5 classifications of spheres, 172
  Salvington, capital of Nebadon, 358
  system government, cluster of 57 a. spheres, 509
  ten standard divisions of physical life, 521
  two hundred elements (including 100 morontia material), 541
arctic species, plants and animals, 702
Ardnon, Chaldean priest, 1317
  seraphim (of Adam and Eve) told A of J coming birth, 1317
AREA AND BUILDING CUSTODIANS, 546
arena, all spiritual activities in material a., 139
  home is natural social a. for ethics grasp, 941
  intellectual a. of human thought, expansion of, 1146
  living the Father's will leads to supremacy in personality a., 1175
  material mind the a. in which personalities live, 1216

ARENA, MIND A OF CHOICE, 1216
arena
  of choice, finite personality self-determines destiny in, 1301
  of society and commerce, religious life in, 1121
  our little world, a. where Michael completed...1318
  produced by encircuitment within...ministry, 1286
arguments, J, no egoistic desire in a., 1383
  overpowering, do not use (J), 1765
  verbal, substituted for blows, 797
aridity, drove Andites to rivers and sea shores, 878
  forced Andites to invent, 907
arise and shine, for your light has come, 1066
aristocracy, first century A.D., 1335
  of benign leadership, lost, 856
Aristotelian philosophy, 1338
Aristotle, 1079
arithmetic, ten men shear a sheep, 1476
  ten persons like 100, pooling moral values, 1476
Arius vanquished by Athanasius (Nicea), 2070
ark: Jewish; relics, the law, shrine, 969
Ark, Noah's, story invented by Hebrew priests, 875
  story of Ararat flood woven into Jewish story of Noah, 860
Armageddon, headquarters of orange race, 724
armaments and war, 1491
"armies of heaven, near at hand", 1934
arms, underneath are the everlasting a., 1057, 1662
army, Saul 3000, priests changed to 330,000, 1072
aroma of friendliness, 1874
Arrangements for the Last Supper, 1934
art, an a. in defeat, noble souls acquire, 1779
  appreciation of a, accords recognition to artist, 2080
  ascending mortals satiated, artistic longing, 508
  attempt to escape...lack of beauty, 2096
  beauty sponsors a, music, rhythms, 647
  color workers, one of 7 heavenly groups, 501
  dangerous when blind to spirit, 2080
  descriptive words don't equal seeing, 2083
  gesture toward morontia level, 2096
  great value of beauty in urge to worship, 1840
  handicap to advancement of a., 963
  height of finite a. is, 646
  high mission of any a., 557
  humanizes science in high culture, 2080
  improvement in Egypt through burial statues, 1044
  is only religious when spiritual motivation, 1115
  is spiritualized by true religion, 2080
  is to foreshadow higher reality, 557
  Jesus and a. at Flavius' home, 1600
  less a. from Adamics than humor, 549
  new every generation, 1772
  new every 10 generations, 1772
  new gospel, and, 1778
  no caste in ranks of spirit artisans, 508
ART OF LIVING, THE, 1775
art, of living, based on more than material stimuli, 956
    higher levels of, 1775   live on high plane, 1773
  only the inner life that is truly creative, 1220
  picturization techniques, fast learning, 503
  proves man is not mechanistic, 2079
  religion never ceases spiritual evaluation of a., 2080
  represents evaluation of reality, 67, 2080
  results from man's attempt to escape...2096
  retarded by Moses' proscription, 969
  Rodan on, 1775
  science, and a., planetary council on, 748
  science, religion, philosophy, 1775, 2096
  soul of expression absent unless...507
  spiritualized by true religion, 2080

art (cont'd)
    the artist, not a. demonstrates...2080
    true a. humanizes science, 2080
    true a. is ennobling manipulation of material
        things, 2080
    unification of contrasts, largely, 646
    vs. technique of existence, 1772, -75, -78
Artemis, temple to A of the Ephesians, 1477
arthropods, 680
artificial, means, folly of, 1521
    situations, J used no, 1521 structures doomed, 870
artificiality in human relations, n g, 432
artisans, celestial, 497
    glorify architectural spheres, 508
    we may become c. a for 1000 years, 497
artist, not art, demonstrates...2080
    sees God as ideal of beauty, aesthetics, 68
artistic triumphs of truth are...555
artists, help gifted individuals, 507
    of odor, 506
arts derived from accidental occurrences, 902
ARYAN INVASION OF INDIA, THE, 882
Aryan, invasion nearly destroyed Salem influence, 1077
    mother tongue from Turkestan, 872
    polytheism, degeneration from monotheism, 1027
    pre-Aryan, Andites were, pre-white, 872
    Sethite priests with A invasion of India, 881

as

"AS JESUS PASSED BY", 1874
ascend from humanity to divinity, 2092
ascendant, children, feast of, 291
    plan, scheme of enslavement (Lucifer), 604
ascendant career, can be with associate of earthly
    career, 283
    differential of experience, not levelling, 579
ASCENDANT DESTINIES, 452
Ascendant Evening Stars, 407
ascendants, as a. we have memory of past, 550
ascended, countless individuals have, 127, 2024
Ascender-trinitized Sons, 251
Ascender's arrival in Havona, 290
ascenders, eventually to Paradise and high destiny, 417
    from system capital with Planetary Prince, 574
    individual, three groups of, 569
    living, translated (2nd roll call), 853
    lovingly dispatched from universes of origin, 417
    mortal when admitted to finaliter corps of Paradise,
        1292
    never forget first day on sphere "Melchizedek", 387
    not destined for Paradise, some remain local u,
        410-11
    recognize spirits through extended light reactions, 436
    retain appreciation of former levels, 174
    seven mortal types, 340
    system capitals endeared to a., 436
    three groups, where they start on mansion worlds, 569
    transient assignments on lower planets, 625
ascending levels of wisdom, 806
ASCENDING MATERIAL SONS, 444
ASCENDING MORTALS, THE, 340
    seven stages universe career, 340
ASCENDING PILGRIMS, THE, 340
ascending son, nature is woven out of reality of Supreme
    by T A, 1284
ascending sons, mortals after fusion, 447, -49
ASCENDING SONS OF GOD, 443
Ascendington, 1237, -39
ASCENDINGTON "bosom of Father, Son, and Spirit", 147
Ascendington, "home address" (our), 148

Ascendington, Paradise home of ascendant souls, 147
ASCENSION CANDIDATES, 423
ascension, career, tremendous transformation of, 1205
    in spiritual flames, 623
ASCENSION, THE MASTER'S, 2057
ascension, orders of survival and a., 568-70
    scheme of the universe, 826
ascent, dead of an age entered upon a., 2053
    immediate, soon, or delayed, 1233
    in individual right, or with many end of age, 1231
    some mortals to mansion worlds at once, 1231
ascent to Paradise, no power can prevent indwelt man's,
    63
    "stupendous undertaking", 509
ascetic, J no, 1512
ascetics, do not become colorless a., 1931
ashamed, "be not a. of my teaching", 1682, 1760
    terrible feeling of being, 1984
Ashtaroth, strange preacher at A, 1764
Ashtoreth, cult of Ishtar in Palestine, 1043
Ashur, Assyrians' "God", 1067
Ashurbanipal, 1612
Asia, domesticated animals speeded civilization, 902
    homeland of human race, 878
    criminals were eaten, 979
    eastern coast line, hovers over precipice, 669
    in southwest A 25,000 years ago, potential great, 869
    looks for return of Ghengis Khan, 1008
    Minor, 1021
    neglected, 1432
    recent ages, most stable land mass, 675
Asia Minor, goddess Artemis, 1478
Asiatic people, one A p taught "God is a great fear", 1004
ask, and receive, law of universe, 1838
    "for the heavenly", 1823
    "in my name", 1639
    "what my spirit wills", 1945
Asmodean palace, 1379, 1411
asocial associations, hindrance to progress, 910
Asoka, 1037
ass, why J rode an a., 1881; assault of living faith, 1829
assemblies, advisory and research, 373
    courts, very different from primitive a. here, 373
    deliberative, for super-governments, 317, -91
ASSEMBLY, THE DELIBERATIVE, 179
assembly, membership, 100 years on Uversa, 180
    system legislative, 632
asset is liability, 1673
assets spiritual, of human race, 2076
Assigned Sentinel presides over system legislative
    assembly, 632
ASSIGNED SENTINELS, THE, 268, 413, 1251-2
ASSIGNMENT HIGHER SPIRIT ORDERS OF, 413
assignment, Solitary Messengers, million years, 259
assignments, of defeated candidates, work in realms of
    space, 295
    of eternal service, after worship, 304
ASSIGNMENTS OF SOLITARY MESSENGERS, 257
assimilation, racial, disastrous now, 726
ASSISTANT TEACHERS, 430
ASSISTANTS, ADMINISTRATIVE, (Seraphim), 434
ASSISTANTS, MOST HIGH, 409
ASSISTANTS, SUPERVISING, 432
Associate Inspector and Assigned Sentinels, local
    universe, 413
ASSOCIATE INSPECTORS, THE, 268
associate persons of Deity, (Spirit and Son), 140
ASSOCIATE POWER DIRECTORS, 324, -25
ASSOCIATE REGISTRARS, 544
associates, 2 mortals close a., 1 fails, 284
association with animals, vs. with plants, 769

ASSOCIATORS, PRIMARY, 328
assumptions, a priori, science, 191
   of reason, wisdom, faith, 1141
   of science and religion, 1139,-41
assurance of truth, the, 1642
ASSURANCES OF FAITH, 1118
Assyrians, 1067,-74,-84,1612
Astarte, cult of Ishtar called A, northern tribes, 1043
asteroids of Jupiter, 658
astrology, Caesars banished a. again and again, 988
   conjunction Jupiter, Saturn...1352
   courses of stars, nothing to do with human life, 1680
   early marriages employed "even" a., 924
   ghost cults used a., 963
   helped priesthood deteriorate, 1043
   intelligent beings still believe in a., 973
   primitive a. was world-wide belief, 988
   superstitious belief, 990,1337
   turned into astronomy by science, 901,-72
astronomers, celestial, 260,339
   confusion of a. on Urantia, produced by, 168,461
   of nearby universes, 652
   superuniverse,165
   time-space distortions because, 134
   when U a. behold amazing evolution...130
   will sometime see 10 grand divisions of...459
astronomic fact, three conjunctions Jupiter, Saturn, in
   Pisces, 1352
astronomic velocities, unreliable as regards other
   space, 134
astronomy, Antares, 450x diameter of our sun, 458
   confusion due to 7 multiple revolutionary movements,
     168
   conjunction, Jupiter, Saturn, 5/29, 9/29, 12/5, 7 B.C.,
     1352
   density of sun 1-1/2x that of water, but gaseous, 459
   disastrous electrical storms, some worlds, 563
   explosion, double star, seen Urantia, 458,1572
   "extragalactic" to our a., traveling with us, 131
   is astrology advanced by search for truth, science,
     901
   Milky Way, watchlike grouping, 1/7 of...167
   our sun mass slightly greater than estimated, 459
   relative space for enormous suns, 458
   Sagittarius, rotational center our minor sector, 168
   space respiration, 123, 134-5
   spectroscopic estimations outer space unreliable,134
   stars, old, some 6000 pounds per cubic inch, 458
   stars, ours, part of ten trillion blazing suns, 172
   telescopes, new, will reveal 375 million new galax-
     ies, 130
   thousand plus states and stages of stars, 172
   when angle propitious, we gaze toward center...167

at

Athanasius vanquished Arius (Nicea), 2070
atheism, materialistic, demonstrates spirit synthesis in
   mind, 1228
atheist, godless religion devoid of survival value, 1126
   good a. is a grafted branch, fed by roots, 1126
Athens, 1427,-76
   keen minds, 1477
   offspring of inferior slaves, 1477
Atlantic coast, first white man chanced to land on,
   (circa 934 A.D.), 729
atman (Hindu) approximates appreciation of nature of
   T A, 1215
atmosphere, determines life differences, 561
   four hundred miles high, 1/2 of it in lowest 3 miles,
     666   makes life at night possible, 666

atmosphere (cont'd)
   passage through a., people, 561
   of Urantia, 665
     shades into space matter at 3000 miles, 473
ATMOSPHERIC TYPES, THE, 561
atomic, "system" held by several factors, 478
   unpredictability (like person's), 478
ATOMIC COHESION, 478
atomic cohesive integrity, secret of is energy
   undiscovered on U, 479
ATOMIC MATTER, 477
atomic-molecular relationships, 459
atomic system, never over 100 orbital electrons in
   atom, 478
atomic types, 100 observable, 477
atom(s), almost no whole a. interior of suns, 463
   described, 478
   electronic and other ancestral components, 463
   nuclear stability due to a., 479
   similar to persons unpredictability, 478
   sizes, etc., 463,-77
   space pervaded by unknown energy, 478
   25,000 times second, alternate "jerks", 462
Aton faith (Ikhnaton took generalized doctrines), 548,1047
atonement, abandon primitive notions of a., 2017
   advanced epochs, a. supplanted by attunement, 437
   affection precludes all disposition to bargain, 1585
   animal sacrifice, then Moses, then Paul's, 716
   at-onement authorization is result of fusion, 1237
   barbarous idea of appeasing...God, 60
   bestowal not to influence Father, 227
   by shedding of blood, Semitic tribesmen, 1021
   by way of Paul, Moses, animal a., not J'idea, 716
   concepts of God are crude, grotesque, 75
   cross not symbol of sacrifice of innocent, 2019
   day of days in Jewish ritual, 1494
   day of (feast of the new year), 1360
   death of J no connection sacrificial system, 2002
   death of J not a ransom, or to atone, 229,2016,-19
   doctrine, from erroneous supposition, 41,2016
   evolutionary planets, a. idea needs supplanting, 437
   fact of cross not central truth from J, 1615
   Father had nothing to do with J' death, 1972,2019
   God not a relentless, offended sovereign, 2017,-19
   grounded in selfishness, 2017
   hatred, cruelty, of a., look of evil men, 1972
   idea, incompatible with God, 2017
     philosophic assault on...God, 41
   idea of a. supplanted by "divine attunement", 437
   innocent sufferer for guilty offender, childish, 2017
   Jesus abrogated, swept away, ceremonials of, a.,1133
   Jesus' death in relation to Passover, 2002
   Jesus' life became gospel of ransom, 2061
   Jesus not going to atone for mortals, 2003
   Jewish, not Christian, 1670
   "message not changed by my resurrection", 2052
   mistake: teaching J was sacrificed Son, 1670
   Mithraic, (partly) origin, 1339
   modified Master's concept, J as Redeemer, 1864
   no--but grim determination to kill J, 1932
   no--but "to drink cup" of mortals, 229
   no--creature experience of mortal death, 1969,-72
   no--crucifixion was price of human bigotry,1872
   no--God loved man as much before J, 2002
   no--natural events took their course, 1969,-72,-99,
     2002
   not a., J' was man-made death, 1972,-99,2002,-16
   original with Paul, some phases, 1339
   Paul "God was in Christ, reconciling", 1083
   Paul's cult blended, (Mithraic atonement), 1340
   Paul's theologic compromise, 984

atonement (cont'd)
    Philo vs. Paul on a., Philo right idea, 1339
    primitive man sacrificed to make, 1133
    religious ideas including atonement, from ghost
        fear, 1005
    resurrection, changed religion of J, 2051
    seraphim help supplant a. with attunement, 437
    services at temple, J and John Zebedee, 1494
ATONEMENT, SIN, AND SACRIFICE, 974
atonement, temple a., to J a travesty, 1494
atrocities, slaughter in name of God, 784
attacks, make, none on old ways, religion (J), 1932
ATTAINMENT OF IMMORTALITY, 1212
attainment, striving for a. distasteful, painful
    (Gautama), 1037
attainments, highest human a. -- reason, wisdom,
    faith, 1141
attempt to communicate with T A, 1475
attention, intellectual, J taught how to arrest and
    focus, 1705
attitude, assertions of a. are philosophy, 1457
    finite, absonite, and absolute, 113
    of the Jewish leaders, 1741
Attitude of the People, 1670
attitude of soul, vs. behavior, 1584
attitudes of spiritual non-progression, 2095
attribute that exclusively characterizes Deity, 1434
attributes, never lost, 499
ATTRIBUTES OF THE ETERNAL SON, 76
ATTRIBUTES OF GOD, 44
ATTRIBUTES OF THE THIRD SOURCE AND CENTER,
    98
attunement, philosophy of survival, 437
    supplants atonement idea, 437

au

audience to hear J or Peter, (4000), 1817
augments tribulation, error or evil, 138, 761
Augustus, proclaimed self Supreme God, 1081
auroral displays, why, 666
auroral phenomena, related to sun spots, 666
Australia, 674-75, 808
    almost covered by ice blanket, 699
    ancestors of kangaroo 45 million years ago, 694
    Andon's descendants to Tasmania, 719
    began to rise 800 million years ago, 662
    drifted far after breaking away, 668
    limestone layers, 685
    no large dinosaur fossils, 687
    red sandstone stratum, Devonian, 679
    sank almost 370 million years ago, 674
Australian, 979-80
Australians, Pygmies, Bushmen, 764, -68, -70, -88,
    934, -79, -94, 1010, 1132
authoritarian state direct offspring of, 2081
authoritative pronouncements, new, 1749
authoritative religions cannot unify, 1732
authoritative wisdom, from focalized experience, 453
authority, behind J' papers, 1341-43
    "by what a. do you do these things?", 1891
    "he speaks like one having a.", 1819
    must be in group, 1764
    "of facts, truth, faith", 2043
    of truth is...1768
    vs. spirit, religions of a., 1732
    watchword of Jewry, 1891
autocracy and democracy, 179
autocracy of perfection, 179
automatic self-rejuvenators, Creators are, 548
automatic, spirit gravity, 84

"automation", 909, 1186
autorevelation is from T A, 1109

av

Avalon, Brilliant Evening Star, 760
    seraphim of Nebadon taught by seraphim of A, 421
    surgeons of A, 742, 857
avenue of Creature approach to Father, 89
average, rewards (Paradise) set off individual from a.,
    579
avoid dishonesty and unfairness, 1740
Avonal sons, 407, 567
    return after bestowal "in glory with seraphic hosts",
    596
Avonals, and Michaels, bestowals of the Eternal Son,
    1308
    bestowal sons are born of woman, 225
    Paradise, 427, 587, -94, -96
awakening, epoch of great religious a., 595, 888
    ethical a. on Urantia, 597
    if men took J firsthand, not secondhand, 2083
awareness, out of material a. grows reason, 1138
    out of spiritual a. grows faith, 1138
awesome force of false fear, 957
awful human moments, one of (for J), 1969-70
ax, Andon invented, 715
Azariah, 16 year old king (called Uzziah by Isaiah), 1074

B

ba and ka, Egyptian (2 aspects of being), 1215
BAAL AND YAHWEH, 1064
Baal, followers vs. Yahweh believers, socioeconomic
    clash, 1064
    highplace of B, J visited, 1387
    the word B means "owner", 1064
    Yahweh, struggle ended, 1075
Baal-Perazim, 80% of David's soldiers were Baalites,
    1073
Baal sites, Samuel could overthrow, 1062
Baal worship, economic and social system, and soil
    fertility, 1075
    was...1074
Baalites, 80% of David's soldiers were B, 1073
Babel, Tower of, 858, -76
babies, Adjusterless b... still attached to parents, 570
    children of pre-Adjuster ages, in families of five, 532
    deceased on U, probation nursery Satania, 516
    deformed, immature, strangled by savages, 932
    infant-receiving schools of Satania, 531
    many die before choosing Paradise career, 569
    Moses, Sargon, Cyrus, Romulus, that survived being
    "abandoned", 982
    repersonalized on finaliter world, 570
Bablot, a descendant of Nod (Babel), 858
    proposed tower of Babel, 858
baby, born without education, man's opportunity, 909
    Jesus, conceived, born, as all other b, 1317
Babylon, end of Judah, people taken to Babylon, 1075
    en masse editing of Old Testament records, 1023
    Yahweh-Baal struggle ended in the captivity, 1075
Babylonian captivity, 838
    following sudden end of Judah, 1075
    Hebrew narratives altered, 1023
    return from c, enmity for Samaritans, 1612
    shocked remnant of Israel into monotheism, 1075
Babylonian priests, magical conglomerations of the, 1043
Babylonian teachers, saved Jewish theology from oblivion,
    1339
Babylonian triad of deities, 1042

Babylonians, had never outgrown forms of sex worship, 1042
Babylonians, 837
BACK IN BETHSAIDA, 1703
BACK IN CANA, 1644
BACK IN CAPERNAUM, 1531, 1655
BACK IN NAZARETH, 1356
"back to nature", not so good, 764
backward blacks, spiritual equality, 725
backward peoples, compelled to work by slavery, 779
bacteria, 679, 732, 736
badge of harlotry, 1652
Badonan people, believed in 2 souls, breath and shadow, 955
    founded center of culture, lasted over 1/2 million years, 878
    held onto some traditions of Andon, 719
    racial struggle India, about 100 families survived, 722
BADONAN TRIBES, THE, 720
Baganda tribes, Africa, 994
BALANCE OF MATURITY, THE, 1778
balance wheel, mind-spirit b w of universe, 150
balances (religion with humor, etc.), 1616
bank, account, spiritual, 556
  "draw on s b in his name", 2076
banker, early, was valorous man, 775
bankrupt, religion of J not, 2076
banner of Michael, 606
banquet, enormous, for creators of Eden, 831
    public b for J, all Bethany, Bethpage, 1878
    sometimes bid the poor, maimed, blind, 1834
baptised, in name of J, 2067
    multitude, (over 2000), 2060
    the 70 converted, 1817
    when b with the Spirit of Truth... 2043
    with the Spirit, be, 1593
baptism, 1545, 1817
    administered to believers by apostles, 1668
    admission to social organization by b, 1865
    AND THE FORTY DAYS, 1509
    became a religious ceremonial in Babylon, 947
    date of J' reconciled, 1512
    ended purely human life of J, 1512
    feature of later water ritual, 964
    for Abner's believers, not instructed by J, 1817
    in Jordan, beginning of J' public career, 1408
    Jesus' b not in repentance, 1511-12
    J said "I come (for your) b", 1504
    John, atremble with emotion at J' b, 1504
    John, b for "remission of sins", 1502
    Mithraism, Christianity, both baptized, 1083
    not a new ceremony among Jews, 1502
BAPTISM OF JESUS, 1408, 1504, 1510, 1511-12
baptism "of the spirit", 2061   of 3 spies, 1667
    serious problem, apostles of J and John, 1625
    three days of preaching, teaching b, 1654
    with holy spirit (not water), 1536, -93, 2061
Barabbas, 1993, -96, 2009
barbarian horsemen, Mesopotamia, 1042
barbaric men, appreciated wisdom and experience, 788
barbaric, we are, 591
barbarism, days of b dangerous to know much, 972
    improvement over savagery, 792
    so long as one sex tyrannizes another, 564
barbarous arbitrament of war, 598
Barnabas, Stephen, converted by Greeks, 2068
barren extremes of philosophy, 1779
barren time of this age, 2082
barrenness of formalized religion, 2083
barriers, for evolutionary balance, 1302

barriers, restraining, evolutionary, must be overcome by mind, 1302
Bartimeus, blind beggar, 1873
basalt, 668, -85
BASIC HUMAN INSTITUTIONS, 772
basic energies of space, divine rest essential to utilize, 506
basis of modern industrial society, capital, 777
basket, and John Mark, 1920
    boy, and all, 1923
    weaving, origin, 902
Basques, Berbers, survivals of blue men, 898
bastion, one inner b is unassailable, 1096
Batanea, 1724-25
bathes all creation (Son), 78
bathing, advanced as part of worship, 748
    clean, to be c, recent, 964
    primitive b was religious ceremony, 964
Bathsheba, David took 9 wives and B, 1072
    Solomon was son of B, 1073
bats, mammals, 562
batteries, recharging b of the soul, 1621
battle, issues of b are clearly drawn, 1742
    not to the strong, 951
Bautan (Salem believer), 1035
bays, social ship steamed out of sheltered, 1086

be

"be born again" (see "born again, be")
"be", J taught what to be, not do, 1584
be, not do, 1584
"be you perfect" (see also under "Jesus, Quotes")
    astounding invitation, command to finite children, 290
    command of the Universal Father, 295
    eternal urge to b p, 1583
    every mortal craves to b p, 1573
    finite creature, ascend to Paradise, through, 637
    High Commissioners have obeyed, 411
    Jesus called mankind to b p, 1091
    Jesus expected followers to strive to b p, 1573
    mandate, entrusted to Eternal Son, 86
    mortal finaliters have fully complied, 348
    mortals in local u, Corps of Perfection, 411
    the Paradise command, 297
    Rodan influenced by, 1784
    supreme mandate from the Universal Father, 21, 449, 1030
    true meaning of b y p for mortals, 21-22
    when Father is attained, injunction is obeyed, 295
    why God demands, 449
beads, 1681   once collection of sacred stones, 967
beast, mark of, eradicated, 538 (378)
"beasts", (of John), unparalleled beauty, 378
beatitudes, 1570, -73, -75
"beatniks", anti-socially minded, 910
beauty, 1912, -69
    architectural Edentia, 486, 523-4
    as an influence to worship, 1840
    galleries of, 1779, 1969
    is largely matter of verification of contrasts, 646
    Jesus' appreciation of b, Flavius home, 1600
    Jesus on appreciation of, 1600
    of Jerusem, we can't imagine, 523
    region of wondrous b (Caesarea-Philippi), 1745
    rhythm, harmony are spiritually akin, 507
    sponsors art, music, and... 647
    triumphant when, 1739
    ultimate b is eternal truth, 43
    universal b is recognition of... 647
    Urantia devoid of b in marine life era, 673, -78

bestowal (cont'd)
just such a strange, unexpected event, 1863
BESTOWAL LIMITATIONS, 1327
bestowal, Michael's 6th b, extraordinary and
amazing, 1315
necessary to precede T A, 227
normally Michael would have been received by... 584
not to influence the stern Father, 227, -29
"of divine spirit, first moral decision", 1478
BESTOWAL OF PARADISE SONS OF GOD, 227
bestowal, of personality results in self-determination,
etc., 1301
BESTOWAL OF THE SPIRIT OF TRUTH, 2059
bestowal, plan, 85
planet, U, announced 4000 years ago, 486
plans for b formulated by Michael, 1327
pre-bestowal charge by Immanuel, 1325
price Creator Sons pay for sovereignty, 1323
prime mission of, 1417, -23
pursue to natural end, 229, 1755
second, System Sovereign, 1311
seventh, as infant mortal, 1316
should unfold as ordained by Father, 1413
sixth morontia mortal, 1316
son, must live and die as mortal, 229
supreme spiritual purpose of Christ Michael's, 1331
technique is a mystery, 87, 228, 1315
third, Material Son, 1312
time of J' b most favorable in history, 1332
truths of b in danger, 2070
Urantia chosen, then Palestine, then J' parents, 1344
why Paradise Son b is necessary, 227
work, technically finished, 1513
bestowal groups, there are seven b g of Creator Sons, 239
bestowal Son, lives, dies, for spiritual uplift of races,
596
bestowal Sons, Creator or Magisterial, 229
7-fold, 234
bestowals, Avonal Sons' vs. Creator Sons', 229
career of b supreme goal of Creator Sons, 227
last steps in education for ruling universes, 1308
BESTOWALS, THE MICHAEL, 239
(Michael, the universe name of J, or Christ Michael),
all 7 a Nebadon revelation of the Supreme, 1318
each of 7 revealed nature of one of 7 Master Spirits,
1318, -24
from Melchizedek down to mortals of flesh and
blood, 1315
"instructions to Michael on", 1327, -30
intervals between, 1309
method of, even Gabriel doesn't comprehend, 1315
sequence of the Michael b, as
human being, 1316, 1323
Lanonandek Son, 1310
Material Son, 1312
Melchizedek, 1310
morontia mortal, 1315
seraphim, 1313
spirit mortal, 1314
bestowals, necessary to understanding varied,
imperfect creatures, 1308
not essential to universe management, 1308
BESTOWALS OF CHRIST MICHAEL, THE, 1308
bestowals, of the Eternal Son, 87
of non-Creator sons (Avonals), 427
of the original Michael, 87
one in 7 b, Son born of woman, 239
Paradise Sons' b, never beget offspring, 229
purpose of creature incarnations, 1308
611, 121 bestowals of Creator Sons, 1309
through b J learned safe-trust (in F) he required,
1325-26

Bethabara (Bethany ford of the Jordan), 1502, -93, 1869
Bethany, 1416, 1788, -98, 1875, -83, -95
boy J meets Mary, Martha, Lazarus, 1375
chief priests heard of dinner at B, 1880
David assisted M and M sell real estate, 1869, 2031
David had J' family come to B, 1976, -97
David married Ruth in B at end, 2031
family at B, believed this was last visit of J, 1878
first Passover of devout Jews, no paschal lamb, 1404
had accepted J, other cities rejected, 1880
Jesus and apostolic party, hdqtrs. as usual, 1648
Jesus and Jude meet Lazarus of B, trouble, 1415
Jesus dropped remarks that disturbed John Z, 1495
Jesus persuaded parents have Passover at, 1379
Jesus spent Wednesday resting at B, 1603
Jesus, Thomas, Nathaniel to Martha's for breakfast,
1811
Jesus took James to B, Passover supper, 1399
Jesus took John Z to B, Lazarus' family, 1494
Jesus took Joseph to B, Passover supper, 1409
Martha and Mary depart B for good, 2031
spent Sabbath week-ends at B, 1606
urgent message to J from B, "Lazarus sick", 1836
visit with M and M, 1797
Bethany and Bethpage, all B & B celebrated arrival of J,
1878
Bethany ford, 1502, -93, 1869
Bethel, 1374, -99, 1607
BETHESDA, AT THE POOL OF, 1649
Bethlehem, 1349-50, -54, 1788
Abner, hdqtrs. to, 1771
David's messengers hdqtrs., 1771
Jesus at, with Abner, 1798
Jesus' family fled--night before massacre, 1354
Jesus' family stayed more than year in, 1352
returned to A. D. 25, saw birthplace, 1492
returned to, 4 B. C., stayed month, 1356
thrilling announcement babe of B born on Urantia, 1316
BETHLEHEM WITH ABNER, AT, 1798
BETHSAIDA, BACK IN, 1703
Bethsaida, Capernaum's fishing harbor, 1548
BETHSAIDA HOSPITAL, THE, 1658
BETHSAIDA, RETURNING TO, 1677
Bethsaida, "woe upon light-rejecting inhabitants of", 1807
Zebedee's home near B, 1420
BETHSAIDA-JULIAS, AT, 1744, 1807
BETRAYAL AND ARREST OF JESUS, 1971
betrayal of J, not required, 1940
betterment of estate on earth, Father's will, 1661

bi

BIBLE (see also "Scriptures", "Jesus, Quotes",
"Gospels", "O. Testament", "N. Testament")
alterations, intentional and unintentional (see also
"confused, distorted" under "Bible"), 1023
altogether human, 1767   "arise and shine", 1629
beginning of B, secret writing to defeat speech
suppression, 1074
Book of Hebrew Psalms, written by Egyptian, 1045
Book of Revelation, greatly distorted, 1555
borrowed from Amenemope's Book of Wisdom, 1046-7
Christ had a religion, became a religion, 2092
confused, distorted, slurred, not factual, not inspired,
784, -95, 837, -57-58, -60, -74-75, 981, 1023-24, -43,
1068, -71, -73, 1348, 1552, -55, -99, 1660, 1725, -36,
1767-69
creation story written 1000 years after Moses, then
credited to him, 838
Deity in Job, product of 300 years' teaching, 1060
diversions from facts, 1023, 1043
Elihu, prophet of Ur, not Hebrew, 1061
erroneous writings to bolster Jewish courage, 1068

B

black (indigo) race (cont'd)
 moved to forests of Central Africa, 890
 orange, green, indigo, 3 secondary races, 564
 red man far above, 584
 Saharans b r plus green, orange, 889
 wiped out green men by force of numbers, 728
black men, least progressive, spiritually equal, 725
blame, man should not b God for afflictions...1661
blameless, "be found without spot and b", 600
blanket of hot gases (millions degrees hot), 463
"blaspheme against God" no "forgiveness", 1714, 1820
blasphemer, J called b by Caiaphas, 1983
blasphemous humor, 547
blasphemy, against God, deliberately, no forgiveness,
 1714, 1820
 charge of b, no weight with Pilate, 1985
 J provided testimony for own conviction of b, 1999
 Sanhedrin, J must be charged blasphemy, 1713
 "you charge (me) with b", 1816
 you have all heard this man's b, 1983
blendings of human and divine throughout universe, 297
"blessed is the womb that bore you", 1723
blessed, "more b to give than to receive", 1581
 objects, 969
 "who hears Word of God", 1722
BLESSING THE LITTLE CHILDREN, 1839
blessing, man's paramount b is labor, 773
blessings, appropriated, 1621
 may be appropriated up to capacity, 1621
 of secular revolt
 tolerance, social service, democratic government,
 civil liberties, 2081-2
blind, in spirit, 1458
 lead the blind, 1571, 1771, 1907
BLIND MAN AT JERICHO, 1873
blind, man, spittle, Josiah (et seq.), 1811
 universe b, disproved by, 2077
 "you are all fools and", 1907
blinded by prejudice, 1672, 1714, -26, -45
bliss, heavenly b on Edentia for us, 495
blood, and sacrifice, 984 briny deep in our b, 664
 atonement by shedding of b, 1021
 barbarous idea of appeasing God, 60
 "be on me and our children", 1996
 drinking, 748, -87, 980, 1082
 "God has made of one b all the nations", 593
 "his be on us and ours", 1996
 "I did not teach you that my b is water", 1712
 no remission of sin without b, 60
 not water of life, 1712
 "of the everlasting covenant", 984
 on house doorposts to protect first-born, 982
 "shedding of b", Paul preserved idea, 716
 shedding of b, Philo taught against atonement by, 1339
 stream, 15,000,000 chemical reactions, 737
bloodless Passover, 1648
bloodletting, 991
 individual, international, 786
bloodshed for remission of sin, 60
bloody Hebrew ritual, overthrown but for priests, 1067
"bloody way by night, dangerous", (David), 1967
blue eyes, Adamites, 850
blue man, the, 564, 725, -27-28, 748, -51
 came to an end quickly, 893
blue people, preferred by Adamics, 725, 887
blunder, exalting reaction of mind to sphere of divine
 dignity, 1208
blunders, hurt U, didn't deprive persons, 761, -64
 no matter what b, gospel will rule, 1608
 serious, in world's early administration, 578

board of animal domestication, the, 746
boat designer, J, 1420
boatbuilder of Capernaum (J), 1419, -24, -2
bodies, are "temples of God", 26
 constructed to receive Andonic life plasm, 742
 Nebadon alone, 570 successive morontia b (see
 "morontia changes"), 542
 temples of T A, 26
 temporary, occupied, 574
bodies of Material Sons, are surcharged with divine
 energy, 581
 glow, 580
body, can be killed--but not soul, 1682
 different on mansion worlds, 532
 discarded outer covering, is, 2021
 dwelling place of God, 1779
 earthly tabernacle of marvelous gift from God, 1204
 electro-chemical mechanism, animal, 8
 has spirit? No. Spirit has body, 483
 is product of supermortal design, 1303
 Jesus' b dematerialized by accelerated time, 2022
 Jesus' b "evaporated", 2037
 Jesus' b sought by archangels, 2022
 life mechanism of mortal personality, 1303
 likened to Grand Universe, 1276
 minus volitional mind is no longer human, 1230
 more enduring than b is morontia soul, 1229
 morontia b rekeyed on 70 worlds, 494
 not bread, 1712, 1942
 outer covering, an, 2021
 physical tabernacle, 532
 from liaison, cosmic mind, adjutant mind spirits,
 483
 Thought Adjuster, and mind, 1216
 unimportance of, 2021
 vehicle, a transient, 404
boldness of J at Jerusalem, 1789-90
Bon, of Caligastia 100, 746
bondage, of abstraction, (slavery, blindness) science, 141
 of ceremonialism, 1942
 of superstition and slavery of fear, 141
 to religious traditions, 1582
bones of heroes and saints preserved, 1080
Book of the Dead, 1044
Book of Wisdom, Amenomope's, 1046-47
Book, organization of U, 215 (see also "Urantia Book")
"book, stone" biogeologic record, 671-2
bookkeeper, God is not, 1590
books, living b of real knowledge on Paradise, 301
 sacred, fetishism, 969
born, anew, way to be, 1602
 readjusted to life, 1438
 "as children of eternal life", 2052
born again, be, 1438, 1576, -92, 1630, 1853
 allow faith to accomplish through...transformation,1119
 "are we willing to be b a (Rodan), 1782
 be endowed with power of perfect will of God, 1609
 change of mind by faith--the new birth, 1545
 don't enter kingdom unless you are b a, 1130
 endowed with power of perfect will of God, 1609
 "first be b a, to possess gift of eternal life", 2053
 "forever delivered from bondage...of self-denial",1610
 from above, 1602
 "he who is born of God keeps himself", 610
 "I declare that you must be reborn", 1576
 "if Sons of God, you have been born of the spirit", 1601
 "I have called you to be b a", 1731
 "in Father's kingdom, you...become new creatures",
 1609
 is spiritual birth, 1130

born again, be (cont'd)
  key to being b a, 1602
  kingdom is brotherhood of citizens, 1568
  old things pass away... become new, 1609
  price of admission to kingdom, 1545
  "regenerated, converted" Rodan, 1775
  religion, there is a "birth day", 1130
  requisite to enter kingdom, change of mind, 1861
  righteousness is natural fruit of being, 1683
  spiritual birth, in anguish or gradually, 1130
  "this day... you are to be reborn", 1438
  "those b a discern the word of God", 1732
  "those who are b a show forth fruits", 2054
  through change of mind by faith, 1545
  to become partaker of divine nature, 1609
  to transfer goal from time to eternity, be, 1775
  "unless you are b a you cannot enter kingdom", 1829
  "who has been b a can overcome all doubt", 1601
  "you would begin to bear fruits of spirit"(J), 1602
born of the spirit, evidence to world is you love one
    another, 1601
  Father's children b o s always masters of self, 1610
  "have men b o s first, then instruction in advanced
    ways of spirit", 1592-3
  how to be b o s, 1602, 2052
  must be b o s to yield fruits of the spirit, 1738, 2053
  reduce conflict with mortal natures, 383
  shall discern word of God regardless of source, 1732
  show the fruits of the spirit, 2054
  those b o s go to Eternal with spiritual forces, 380
  those who have received and recognized T A, 381
  who have recognized indwelling of God, 381
  why is it necessary to be b o s, 1660
"bosom of the Father", 64, 2015
botanic expression, Garden was a paradise of, 823
botanical beauty of... Edentia, 493
bow and arrow, 723
boy, babies under 2, all killed, 1354
  possessed by the evil spirit, 1713
  runaway, 1475
  shepherd, 1437
Brachiopod Age, The, 677
brachiopods almost unchanged, 674, -76
Brahman, description, development, weakness of, 1028
  indefinite and illusive self, 1029
  ravished and destroyed mortal desire and ambition,
    1029
Brahman-Narayana, 1030
BRAHMANIC PHILOSOPHY, 1030
BRAHMANISM, 1028
Brahmans, 1027, -31
  origin, 882, 1009
  priests exalted selves above their gods, 1028
  Vedic priesthood sank in pessimism, 1029
brain, capacity, mind is dependent on, 670
  energies cease vital pulsations, 1230
brained, -one, -two, -three, 446-7, 565-6, 1197-8
brain-power, helped by Adam, 905
BRAIN-TYPE SERIES, 566
brains, and agility replaced armor and size (animals), 695
  animals with small b, 686
  henceforth, evolution will follow growth of b, 688
  large, 697, 704-5
  too small for body size, 688, -91, -95
  two ounces in animals 35 ft. long, 688
brake on cultural evolutionary progress, material
  inertia, 1302
BRANCHES, THE VINE AND THE, 1945
"brass, sounding b and a tinkling cymbal", 84
brave, adults never shun difficulty, danger, 1575
  honest person faces mind's logic, 1773

"bravely go forth", 1726
bravery, mind, physical, spiritual, 1608
  required to face what logical mind discovers, 1773
  spiritual b is highest, 1608
bread, communion symbol, 1710, -12, 1942
  fill the belly with b of ease, 1710
  "for which you had not labored", 1710
  "I am this living b", 1711
  "I did not teach you that my flesh is the b", 1712
  man cannot live by b alone, 1777
  "my life is a bestowal of the b of heaven", 1712
  of life, 1822, -29, 1942
  of life and water thereof, 1337, 2054
  of remembrance, last supper, 1942
  true b of life, 1711 -12
  wanted without toil, 1704, -10
breakdown, prevention of transitional b as factor in
  Urantia civilization, 911
BREAKFAST WITH THE PHARISEES, 1833
breath of life, 953, -55
"breath of life" necessary to be imparted to lifeless
  forms, 404
breeding, uncontrolled, must be superseded, 734
brethren, all men are (Cynicism), 1443
  "one of the least of these", 1727
bribery of spirits, 963-4
bribes to men, called sacrifices in religion, 978
brick, early building material, 743
brick buildings, over 5000 in Garden of Eden, 824
"bridge... this world is only a", 1735
bridle your passions, 2076
"Brigand", on thieves' signs, 2005
Bright and Morning Star, 376, 423
  creation of Creator Son-Creative Spirit, 273
  first-born of a local universe, 306-7
  local U chief executive, 237
  may delegate authority, as to Melchizedek, 386
  only one created in each universe, 369
  Universe Aids, Gabriel of Salvington, 406
Brilliant Evening Stars, 406, 524-25, 1247
BRILLIANT EVENING STARS, 407
Brilliant Evening Stars, assisted locally by Paradise-
  origin beings, 409
  attended J throughout mortal bestowal, 1251
  examine Jerusemites for spirit insight,
  liaison between Michael and U, 1251
  local universe personalities, 232
  remained loyal to Christ Michael, 607
  serve as teachers, 517
  unique twofold order, 407
  Urantia Book written on U ("where you leave off down
    here"), 533
brink of, enthralling epoch, 2082
  moral quickening, 2080, -82
  social readjustment, 2082
  spiritual enlightenment, 2080, -82
"briny deep" our origin, and in our blood, 664
British Isles, missionaries to, 1021
Brittany, 899
broadcast directors, the, 504
BROADCAST RECEIVERS, 309
broadcast service of universe of universes, 270
Broadcasters, 431
BROADCASTERS, THE, 288
Broadcasters, The, Havona, operate on all basic
  circuits, 288
broadcasts, 371
BROADCASTS, THE JERUSEM, 522
broadcasts, of infinite spirit, tuning in to, 1621
  translated for local universes, 504
  universal b of love, from Father, T A translates, 1213

bronze invented by an Adamsonite, 904
brothel, woman from b, anointed J'feet, 1651
brother, great, of all creatures, the Supreme, 1285
    is more than neighbor, love as yourself, 2053-54
"brother" and "sister", Christians, 2067
brother and sister marriages, 835, 918

BROTHERHOOD
    acceptance of sonship with God and b, 1781
    affects all, 138
    and service, cornerstones of gospel, 1930
    and temporal duty, simultaneously, 1957
    and unity only through spirit within, 1672
    associated truth of Fatherhood, 2053
    astounding political, economic repercussions, 1088
    based on Fatherhood of God, 1808
    beginning of spiritual b when... 1302
    Brotherhood of Men, The, (Urmia lectures), 1485
    changed by Paul, 2092
    Christian church not a dynamic b, 2083
    church as social, displaced J' spiritual b, 1865
    civilization encompassed by love, b, 1098
    comes from Fatherhood, 196
    concealed truths of b will emerge, 2061
    discloses qualities of the whole, 138
    divine, human direction, 1570
    ecclesiasticism incompatible with b, 2084-5
    economic interdependence and social fraternity, 1093
    energies of living... unselfish service to, 2083
    epoch of philosophy and b, 577
    eventuates from practice of presence of God, 1133
    exploitation of weak, incompatible with b, 1803
    factors in world-wide realization of b, 598
    "Father is all-wise ruler of this spiritual b", 1702
    "fellowship of living association" with all believers,
        1750
    formal church was substituted for spiritual b, 1864
    forthcoming world-wide b, 1764
    fourth phase of kingdom, new social order, 1863
    gospel is fact of Fatherhood, and sonship, 2059
    greatest truths, Fatherhood and b, 2086
    Herod informed J advanced only a spiritual b, 1717
    highest concept of b is service, 2017
    "I came to establish... spiritual b", 1710
    immediate realization no, because, 763
    impossible without Fatherhood of God, 2082
    individual emerges into joy of b of faith sons, 1942
    in J'brotherhood before church, 2067
    "I will fellowship you in the b", 2034
    Jesus' b, no church, 2067
    Jesus'b vs. Paul's, 2092
    Jesus, called his b kingdom of heaven, 1717
        preferred b term to "kingdom", 1861
        regretted necessity for calling b a kingdom, 1856
        taught religion of... serving the b, 2092
        was a profound demonstration of b, 2091
    joy and satisfaction in J' b, 2095
    kingdom is exclusively spiritual b, 1088
    lack of spiritual b inexcusable, reprehensible, 1865-6
    loving materialization of the b, 1608
    made imperative, 1769
    man may acceptably fulfill temporal duties and b, 1957
    men ordained to preach gospel... and b, 2066
    more than neighbor, 2053
    must reason ourselves into, 196
    "my kingdom is b of men", 1991
    no place for assertions of infallibility, 2085
    no place for sectarian rivalry in this b, 2085
    normally begins to materialize when, 594

BROTHERHOOD (cont'd)
    not easy, even on normal worlds, 597
    not while denying God, 2082
    of culture, science vainly strives to create the, 1122
    of God's reign in the hearts of men, 1862
    of intelligent beings, 1676
    of love, the reborn citizens of... kingdom, 1568
    of man, 1608
    of man, mighty ideal of b, 966
    of men who have become the sons of God, 1991
    of sons of God, 1819
    only through ministry of seraphic spirits, 437
    on U remarkable in view of Adamic default, 437
    possible, only when, 1487
    "proclaim a spiritual b of sons of God", 1805
    quickest way to realize b on U, 598
    races don't take kindly to, 437
    recognition of, leads to better knowledge of G R, 1651
    relationship between all, 138
    religion enables man to live together, complex age,1139
    religion is... Fatherhood of God and b of man, 1603
    religious b of mankind, 1708
    (religious peace) only when b, 1487
    remarkable is as much b on U as is, 437
    "remember the moral claims of human b", 1580
    revelation necessary to b on U, 597
    secret of a better civilization bound up in b, 2064
    seldom do varied races take kindly to b, 437
    servants of the b of man, 1853
    service to others to enhance b, 1862
    Simon, hard to reconcile b with patriotism, 1611
    social b, how, 597
    social, transformations required, 597
    source of, 1093, 1133, 1863
BROTHERHOOD, THE SPIRITS OF, 437
brotherhood, spiritual b has astounding... repercussions,
    1088
    spiritual b essential, 1866
    spiritual b succeeded by "Redeemer" idea, 1864
    spiritual b superseded by church, 1864
    spiritual vs. social, 597
    supermortal b, superhuman kingdom, 1863
    "teach spiritual b", 1804
    transcendant civilizers for b, 598
    "trust me... will help you be kind to the b", 2048
    two realities, Fatherhood, and b, 2017
    ultimate goal of society can't transcend J' b, 2093
    universal, only after U Father and universal sonship,
        1299
    welfare of b, determine issues of conduct, 1763
    will be loving organism, 2085
    wisdom of b should prevail, 1764

brotherly affection, how manifested, 1603
brotherly love, 1959
brothers, all men are (J on), 1431, 1656
    get along, 1549
    Jesus'walk with two, 2034
    "terrifies me that all men my b", 1454
brown men, 727, 871
brutality vented upon the superior people, 1984

bu

Buddha, 1466
    Amida (see "Buddhism, Amida"), 1040
    became a reflective devotee of leisure, 773
    changed, like Christianity, 1034
    devotee of leisure, idleness, 773

Buddha (cont'd)
    failure, to show path to Paradise, 1035
    in Asia, his return is expected, 1008
    knew God in spirit but...1467
    one of 7 outstanding teachers, 1339
    philosophy, 1034,-37
    revered in Asia by millions, 1009
    valiant fight against transmigration of souls'
      concept, 1035
BUDDHISM, 1446
Buddhism, adaptability, 1011
    best godless philosophy, 773, 1035,-37, 1141
    despite 1000 years success, couldn't compete, 1029-30
    devotee of leisure, 773, 1144
    devotees of B, physical humiliation, 976
    Gautama fought belief in transmigration, 1035
    Gautama's theories grew into philosophy of, 1035
BUDDHISM, THE GOD CONCEPT OF, 1040
Buddhism, great strength, 1041
    grotesque perversion in later centuries, 1036
    Islam, and Hinduism, synthesized into Sikhism, 1010
    Jesus on B, 1466
    led to changes in Hinduism, 1031
    like Christianity, perversion of original, 1036
    modern B not what Buddha taught, 1036
    permits freedom of choice from all religions, 1041
    promises salvation from suffering, peace, 67
BUDDHISM, THE SPREAD OF, 1037
Buddhism, taught freedom from danger of incarnation,
    1037
    undergoing 20th century renaissance, 1041
    will it respond to new concepts?, 1041
BUDDHIST FAITH, THE, 1036
BUDDHIST PHILOSOPHY, 1038
    great advance, relativity of truth, 1039
BUILDERS, THE DIVINE, 501
builders, divine, 7 groups (morontia worlds), 502
bullocks, seventy were sacrificed, 1794
burden, of J' message, always, 1460
    "of truth is light", 1766
burial, first day, 1837
BURIAL OF JESUS, THE, 2012
Burma, 884
burned out suns, 171
Bushmen, 768,-87, 971, 1132
    Pygmies, Aborigines, backward, suspicious, anti-
      social, 764
business groups, Mediterranean society, 1st century
    A.D., 1335   hold society together, largely, 787
business methods, early b m not improved upon, 100s of
    1000s of years, 746-7
business on earth, our real, 1466
busy, man thinks he is too, 2077
"but are we willing to pay the price?", 1782
butterfly, like Christian kingdom, 1866
    metamorphosis, 480
    morontia minus material self, like b, 1235
burying property advance over burning, 781
"by faith are you saved" (see under "Jesus, Quotes" and
    "faith")

C

cabinet, advisory, 390
cadeuceus, origin of, 946
Caesar, is it lawful to give tribute to C, 1899
    render to, 1580, 1740, 1899, 1929,-57
    taxes paid by J and apostles, 1991
Caesar Augustus decrees census, 1350
Caesarea, 1411,-13,-27,-29,-92
    capital of Palestine, 1429

Caesarea (cont'd)
    harbor of C built by Herod, helped Palestine, 1334
    water system, 1429
Caesarea Philippi, 1492, 1723
CAESAREA-PHILIPPI, AT, 1727
CAESAREA-PHILIPPI, AT, 1743
Caesarea Philippi, after C P, J was same plus divine,
    1749
    before C P, J was master teacher of gospel, 1749
    much new for apostles at C P (J' changed plans), 1750
    region of wondrous beauty, 1745
Caiaphas, high priest of Jews, 1847, 1925,-81,-97
    avenging finger in Pilate's face, 1996
    "better one man die than...", 1847
    called meeting to deal with resurrection, 2033
    heart set on self-glory and self-exaltation, 1926
    Judas met J' enemies at home of C, 1924
    meeting at C', fears of resurrection, 2014
    meeting at C' house to formulate charges, 1911
    more prosecutor than unbiased judge, 1982
    orders, take J before C, 1977
    perjured testimony before C, 1999
    personally demanded death of J, 1995
    real trial of J at home of C, 1980
    Sanhedrin court decreed J' death unjustly, 1986
    servant of C gave Judas the silver, 1998
    smote J in face, 1983
CAIN AND ABEL, 848
Cain, born to Eve enroute to second garden, 847
    descendants of C glorified Eve, "mother cult", 895
    grim reminder of folly to Adam & Eve, 849
    "if C was avenged seven times", 1764
    "went to Nod, and got self a wife", 1660
    wife not edited out of O T by "editors", 837
calamity, savages feared much good luck as harbinger of,
    950
calcium, longevity, individuality, excelling other matter,
    462
    tosses electron back and forth 25,000 times per
      second, 462
CALCIUM--THE WANDERER OF SPACE, 461
calcium electron in 1 millionth second orbit, 1 million
    revolutions, 462
Caleb and Joshua lived to enter promised land, 1828
Calebites, 1072
calendar, 858
California, ancient C sea rich in marine life, 682, 686
    arctic inland sea, outlet to Pacific through C, 678
    four mile vertical fault 25 million years old, 696
    great volcanic actions, coast range, 689
    Onamonalonton, hdqtrs. among redwoods, 723
    red race culture vanished by 35,000 years B.C., 884
    rich fossil beds along coast of C, 679
Caligastia (see also "Planetary Prince"), 741, 2016
    and Lucifer, fallen children of light, 1327
    and Lucifer rebellion, 1049
    by-passed time governor of human evolution, 1302
    comparatively impotent since cross, 610
    contested Moses immediate resurrection, 596
    destroyed barriers minds had not overcome, 1302
    is "devil", 602, 753
    Jesus met and defeated C, 1512
    Jesus--no use for C' revolutionary techniques, 1522
CALIGASTIA, MISFORTUNES OF, 752

Caligastia, 100, each from a different planet, 742
    100, proclaimed...individual initiative, 749
    pleased by Judas' betrayal, 1938
CALIGASTIA, PRINCE, 741
Caligastia, prince of darkness, 1938
    "Prince of Urantia" now cast down, 610

C

ceremony (cont'd)
    one only associated with J' life mission, 1942
    to induce action, 1813
certain of God, we have right to be, 1127
certainty, about kingdom, how, 1641
    consists in, 2094
    experience, matter of personal, 1641
    fears not analysis, 1641
    from faith, 1124
    matter of faith, 1641
    more religion you have, the more c, 1119
    physical, moral, spiritual, consists of, 2094
certainty of religionist should not be disturbed by
    doubting materialist, 1140
CERTAINTY OF RELIGIOUS FAITH, THE, 1124
CERTITUDE OF THE DIVINE, THE, 1126
cessation of existence (see also "annihilation" and
    extinction")
    at end of dispensation, 37
    formal recognition of, 1247
    obliteration, "wages of sin is death", 529, 612
    withdrawal from God, man nears c e, 1285
Ceylon, 890

ch

chain of human evolution, links saved, 1246
Chaldean priests, Ardnon leader, 1317
    before Herod, 1353
Chaldeans, 1054
    among first to use animal instead of human
        sacrifice as, 980
    looked upon stars as cause of suffering, 990
    Melchizedek spoke Chaldean, 1015
    star cultists, 947
    wife could impose promise, no second wife, 927
CHALK PERIOD, THE END OF THE, 691

CHALLENGE (These are not listings of references
using the word "challenge, " but a casual (obviously
incomplete) selection of excerpts which are a challenge
to the reader.)
    all the courageous manhood you can muster, 1608
    amazing, enthralling epoch ahead, 2082
    call to the adventure of building new society...2084
    carry the pack a second mile, will c, 1770
    Christianity languishes for lack of new vision, 2082
    Christianity threatened by slow death, 2083
    CHRISTIANITY'S PROBLEM, 2082
    cooperation with T A, loving service, 1206
    do not fear the dangers, 383
    do you fully appreciate...?, 449
    each episode of existence, declaration--"if I
        cannot do...", 59
    endless unfolding of almost infinite panorama, 1194
    energies...unselfish service of brotherhood, 2083
    exchange your mind for mind of Jesus of Nazareth,
        553
    expanding and progressing cosmic citizenship, 1093
    the facts of science, beliefs of philosophy, 1127
    for leaders, society must turn to...786
    God and man need each other, 2084
    great c given to mortal man, 1284
    great c to modern man is to...2097
    the great hope of U lies in...2086
    heed the distant echo of Adjuster's call, 1223
    hour is striking for a rediscovery, 2083
    if Christian church would only dare, 2085
    independent of material environment, 381

CHALLENGE (cont'd)
    industry without morality, 2086
    in next world you will give an account, 1918
    inspires man to live courageously, religion, 1093
    Jesus' religion calling to the best in man, 43, 2083
    Jesus' religion, unsullied transcendant summons,
        2083
    knowledge without character, 2086
    leaders, religion does need new, 2082
    live up to full measure of responsibilities, 1770
    living J is the only hope, 2085
    living J should be presented, 2090
    of God the Ultimate, 305
    Paradise ascent the supreme adventure, 1608
    partial (religious) approaches must be harmonized,
        1090
    plan of God, infinite treasures yours for the
        striving, 365
    pleasure without restraint, 2086
    politics without principles, 2086
    power without conscience, 2086
    predicament of unfinished growth, 1090
    purpose of all education, 2086
    religion does need new leaders, 43, 2082
    religion needs new slogans, 2077
    religionist, dogmatic c to dogmatic unbeliever, 1127
    religious c of this age, 43
    science without idealism, 2086
    secret of survival is wrapped up in...1206
    secularistic society is slowly disintegrating, 2082
    settle down, never as in past ages, 1086
    sons of God enlisted in fighting the battle of reality...
        1117
    supreme adventure--trying to do divine will, 1732
    there must come a revival, 1866
    thousands as never before need religion, 1090
    time is ripe for figurative resurrection...2090
    to all children of light, 1918
    to gaze upon the universe from within, 1117
    "to your authority can never recur" (Immanuel to J),
        1327
    transcendant spiritual summons, 2083
    trumpet blasts of middle ages, mistake, 2077
    Urantia on brink of amazing social readjustment, 2082
    Urantia waiting for...ennobling message of Michael,
        1041
    wealth without work, 2086
    we anticipate...tremendous adventure, 263
    what an awakening world could experience, 2083
    whosoever wishes to be my disciple, 1770
    why do you not aid the Adjuster?, 1223
    worst is over, understanding...dawn, 2076

CHALLENGING THE MASTER'S AUTHORITY, 1891
chance, determines aggressive or retiring companions,
    546
CHANCE: GOOD LUCK AND BAD LUCK, 950
chance is a word signifying...951
chance, accident, 50,000 facts incompatible with laws
    of, 665
chance (opportunity) another for Jews (J), 1809-10, 1883,
    1906, -08 (see detail under "JESUS")
change,
    eternal, universe is non-static, 222
    great, suddenly, bad, 911
    in hearts, kingdom comes in, 1533
    mores yes, instinct never, 938
    new proclamation of gospel, 2057
    of mind, (rebirth), 1861

CHERUBIM, MORONTIA, 423
cherubim, much to do with details of government, 1250
  on U about same number as seraphim, 1250
  pair is a cherubim and a sanobim, 1243-4
  serve in pairs usually, 1243
  teachers, like most instructors, under Melchizedeks, 413, 550
  Urantia about 501 million pairs of c, 1250
CHERUBIM AND SANOBIM, 422
CHERUBIM AND SANOBIM, EVOLUTION OF, 423
cherubim and sanophim,
  are aids of seraphic ministers, 422
  become seraphim, 423
  three great classes of, 423
  25% are quasi-material, 422
Chicago, 1243
chief dismissed harem, was killed, 927
CHIEF EXECUTIVE, GABRIEL, 369

chief priests (rulers of the Jews)
    (see also "priests, rabbis, money")
  afraid to call J, called Josiah, 1813
  agents of c p raised a tumult, 1797
  Annas examined J, 1978-9
  answer to J' last appeal, 1909
  astounded at boldness of the apostles, 2060
  clamoring for pardon of murderer and the blood of J, 1993
  "crucify him, crucify him", 1994
  death plan for J', origin with, 1971
  death to J at any and all costs, 1909
  decision: put a stop to J' teaching, 1654
  denunciation of--in J' farewell address, 1905
  dispatched officer to arrest J in temple, 1791
  dumfounded at J' cleansing the temple, 1890
  effrontery of c p, asking Pilate for J' death, no trial, 1989-90
  fear had come over c p, result of division in own ranks, 1789
  feeding the 5000 stirred up fears of c p, 1704
  14 members resigned upon death decree, no trial, 1847
  from this day plotted for J' destruction, 1673
  greatest danger to J lay in Jer. leaders, 1647
  had officers on way to Bethsaida to arrest J, 1723
  Herod listened to all charges of the c p, 1992
  in conference with Herod Antipas, sought arrest of J, 1719
  Jesus and Sanhedrinist court to Pilate, 1987
  Jesus before the Sanhedrinist court, 1982
  Jesus favorably received by people, c p increasingly antagonistic, 1672
  Jesus must be speedily destroyed, 1891
  led crowd in shouting "Barabbas", 1993
  "make the sepulchre secure", 2014   malice, 1907
  mandate to close synagogues of all Jewry to J, 1741
  many occasions decreed death of J, 1909
  many went to Golgotha but...2007
  met Judas at Caiaphas' home, 1924
  minded to have J put to death, 1993
  mob acting under direct leadership of, 1994
  new problems with Christ risen, 2034
  objections to J' teachings listed, 1850
  offered bribes to traitorous Judas, 2023
  open warfare on J and disciples, 1708
  overawed by J' daring challenge, 1789
  paid tomb guards to lie about resurrection, 2023
  Pilate reported: "I find no fault in him", 1991, -95
  Pilate saw c p's malice, hatred, prejudice, and envy, 1993

chief priests, rulers of the Jews (cont'd)
  planned to throw J' body into open pits, 2012
  prepared to arrest J, on return to Jerusalem, 1606
  presumed to dictate to Pilate, why, 1989
  protested Pilate's sign "King of the Jews", 2005
  questions to entrap J, 1899
  "reject the gift of God and all men will reject you", 1882
  "Son of Peace, whom the c p have rejected", 1882
  spies, appointed 6 to follow J, 1654
  Stephen...in conflict with c p, 2068
  steward of Annas struck J, 1979
  struck J, spit in his face, 1983
  threatened to report Pilate to Caesar, 1996
  three quit, refused charges without witnesses, 1985-6
  to Jer. despite c p death declaration, 1871
  told crowd J brought to him by c p, 1993
  "told you how c p would put (me) to death", 2052
  trial of J, session ended in confusion, 1984
  trial proceeded along unfair, unjust lines, 1815
  we come for confirmation of death decree, 1989
  were very antagonistic, 1617
  "what shall we do with J?", 1847
  what should be done with risen Lazarus, 1880

CHIEF RECORDERS, 288
CHIEFS OF ASSIGNMENT, 300
CHIEFS OF RECORDS, 281
child, altruistic drive, overdeveloped, 1132
  become as a little c, 1960
  become as little children as the price, 1585
  "believe as, don't act as", 2048
  commend the spiritual simplicity of a, 1733
  develops love for father through...1676
  essential to come as a little c, 1861
  evaluates experience (in terms) of pleasure, 1094
  every c should early learn to sacrifice, 1575
  "except you become more like this c", 1761
  faith and trust of a c, 1536, 1861
  fear or love dominance with parents, 1013
  first conflict in mind, egoism, altruism, 1131
  first few years affect life, 1922
  first moral impulses, 1131, -86
  first promptings of c's moral nature, 1131
  introduction to worship, 1840
  Jesus' faith like unsuspecting trust of, 2089
  Judas poor loser as a c, 2056
  "little c"--why used as illustration, 1676
  moves positively, moral impulses are positive, 1131
  Nicodemus couldn't become as a little c, 1602-3
  "not mental immaturity of a c J' command", 1733
  of the worlds, isolated, 43
  raising, mansion world, 531
  religious experience of c dependent on fear or love, 1013
  spacing, 625
  Thought Adjuster's arrival signified by emergence of, 1131
  to keep free from conflicts, crises, 1131
  training, J' methods of, 1401
  "who receives not kingdom as a little", 1840
  why J so often referred to little c, 1676
child of God, approach Father as a, 1629
  each of you is a, 1629
child of promise, John Baptist, "c o p", 1497
  Mary rarely thought about J being "c o p", 1412
  Mary steadied herself, recalling "c o p", 1391, 1402
  no one told about J being "c o p", 1355

child rearing (see also "child training")
    increasingly difficult now because, 941
    Judas' life too easy as a child, 2056
    wise fathers do not punish in anger, 2017
    youth, teach how to plan, build character, 2086
child training, 1604 (see also "child rearing")
    beauty aids the urge to worship, 1840
    child evaluates as to contents of pleasure, 1094
    child learns early "it is more blessed", 1131
    commanded good, exalted it (J), 1401
    decree of older children, punishment (J), 1401
    determines subsequent life, 1922
    discipline, guidance, correction, restraint, 1604
    discussion, family welfare (J), 1401
    father supremely interested in child's welfare, 1604
    fathers not like judges, enemies, creditors, 1604
    give chance to grow own religious experience, 1094
    ideals of children, do not dislodge, 555
    introduce to worship outdoors, 1840
    John Mark's early life, 1921-2
    mind of normal child moves positively, 1131
    positive injunctions (J), 1401
    prepare young for greater responsibilities, 1604
    spirit of justice, elasticity (J), 1401
    tolerance, patience, forgiveness, 1604
    wise discipline (J), 1401
childbirth, cleansing of woman after c b, 935
    not painful to Fonta and...714
    painless for Eve, 850
    relatively easy among unmixed tribes, 935
childhood in gospel, be not content with, 1736
CHILDHOOD, JESUS' EARLY, 1355
childish scheme, substituting innocent sufferer for
    guilty offender, 2017
childlike faith, faith and trusting dependence of child,
    1536
children, Adamson and Ratta, 67 c, 861
    become as little, 1585, 1621
    best not spaced too far apart, 625
    best when contribute to mutual training, 625
    Caligastia and Lucifer, fallen c of light, 1327
    can't understand chastisement, 1597
    conform to types, but no 2 exactly alike, 1220
    custom of adopting originated because, 960
    dangerous period, transition to manhood, 1394
    deceased before spirit identity, reconstructed, 516,
      569
    delinquency due to parents, 1653
    docile, tractable, Eskimo, also red, yellow, 941
    education, improper, makes divorce, 929
    even twins never exactly alike, 1220
    Eve's weaned at 1 year, 834
    exposed to death, unwanted, ended, 2073
    factors of rearing in family, 1604
    fattened for slaughter (women too), 979
    heroes, help c choose, 1574
    impressed only by loyalties, 1094
    invisible (often) born to Adamson and Ratta, 861
    Jericho mothers brought c for J' blessing, 1839
    Jesus at 9 resented slow-acting minds, 1368
    Jesus began wise discipline, brothers, sisters, 1401
    Jesus missed c, 1421
    Jesus reared in ordinary manner of c of that race,
      age, 1317
    Jesus resented elders blaming his father, 1366
    joyous with J, 1416
    lead to highest joys in homes, 1839
    learn to love, 1675
    liberty not restrained by love, etc., 1923
    modern c need intelligent discipline of wisdom, 1923
    monogamy, best for c, 927

children (cont'd)
    "my (little)" (J), 1543, 1605, -75, 1871, 1908, -45, -59
    need fathers as well as mothers, 531
    of God, men are, 2053
    of light, 1919, 2042
    of the Supreme, 1239 -40, -44
    older, served families well, 891
    peacemakers, c as, 1575
    rearing, difficult because, 941
    religion and beauty, 1840
    respond to challenge, 1575
    shortsighted affection, pamper and spoil c, 1304
    supreme human responsibility, 941
    teach those younger, 812
    teaching, 1401, 1574, 1840, -98, 1921 (see also "child
      rearing", and "child training")
    timed close together, best, 625
    trustful, naturally, 1574
    unifier of family life, 1089
    unique, of sex and nonsex liaison, 862
    we see departed c again on high, 516, -31, -69-70
    who die before choosing Paradise career, 570
    who die before receiving T A, 570
    whosoever causes one of these...to stumble, 1761
    wise parent of, takes no sides, 1589
    wonderful c of the womb of space, 304
    young, reaction to chastisement, 1597
China, emancipation from priests, 1033
    Jesus learned about, 1427
    once head of human society due to... religion, 1035
    spiritual dark ages, 1035
CHINA, STRUGGLE FOR TRUTH IN, 1032
China, why met defeat, 833, 1033, -5
China and India needed a Paul, ready, 1430
China, India, 874, 946, 1011-12, 1215, 1430
    Andites migrated to C I, 873
    culture of Mesopotamia spread to C I, 873
Chinese, assimilated red stock, were benefitted, 884
    believed disease work of evil demons, 990
    buried in wall workers who died building it, 981
CHINESE CIVILIZATION, DAWN OF, 884
CHINESE CIVILIZATION, THE LATER, 887
Chinese, cultural stability in strength of family groups,
    939
    dragon worship survival of snake cult, 946
    early C treated women better than...937
    early turned to agriculture, 887, 901
    first to learn that in union there is strength, 883
    loyalty, ethics, morality, 888
    merchant Chang, friend of J, 1475
    once believed soul and body stay together, 953
    records, 857
    35, 000 B. C. in control central Asia, 869
    threw live maiden into metal for bell, 981
    tribute to, 888
    used magic, protection against demons, 988
choice (see also "decision")
    each reflective moral c divine invasion of soul, 2095
    every man opportunity for final, 1233
    highest moral c is c of highest value, 435
    makes sin potential in all realms, 613
    makes spiritual evolution, 1460
    not invalidated by correlation or forecast, 1300
    personal decisions of c because, 1457
    power of, ends perfection, 277
    priceless powers of c, 1219
    uncontrolled by mechanism, is unstable, 1301
    unidentified with spirit, is dangerous, 1301
    universe reality, a, 615
    when men have c no divine perfection, 277, 613
    within universe frame only, 1300

choice, free
 eventually approaches divine freedom, 1301
 increasingly liberated as universes are ascended, 1301
 limited through lower levels, for safety, 1301
 means possible self-confusion, self-disruption, self-destruction, 1301
choice stimulus, potential of value levels provide us a c s, 52
choices, connote insight (between) good and evil, human and divine, spiritual and material, time and eternity, truth and error, 2095
 three, of human mind, 2094
choosing, ability from moral nature, 193
 Father's will...spiritual attainment, 25
CHOOSING THE FIRST FOUR APOSTLES, 1524
choosing, free will c opens portals of eternity, 71
 God's will constitutes real worship, 22
 (good or evil) influenced by c, 193
 manner of c, decides spiritual presence, 150
 of mind, determines survival, 69
CHOOSING PHILIP AND NATHANIEL, 1526
CHOOSING THE SIX, 1539
Chorazin, converts few at, 1807
CHORAZIN, THE EVANGELISTS IN, 1726
Chorazin, rejected the J message, 1644
 sojourn at C very depressing, 1644
"chosen people", Amos, Lord wouldn't countenance sin among c p, 1065
 certain Semite tribes called c p, 1055
 delusion, 1005
 doctrine of c p factor in advance, but...803
 for special service of carrying truth, 1075
 individual--yes, 1018
 no such thing, 1488
 origin, 1023, -75
 priests, inventions to support idea of c p, 1068
 Samuel believed Lord concerned with c p, 1063
 why Jews thought selves, 1334
 with special mission on earth, doom sealed, 1969
CHRIST (earth name for Creator Son, Michael, sovereign of local universe, 601, 1084). (See "Jesus" and "Michael" headings.)
 add to old leaders, don't supplant, 1092
 the man, should be venerated, 1013
 Stoics better prepared Rome to receive, 2073
 supreme ideal of spiritual leadership, 1091
"Christ and Him Crucified", Paul, 2071
CHRIST MICHAEL, BESTOWALS OF, 1308
Christ Michael (see also "Jesus" sections and "Michael" headings)
 domain is universe of Nebadon, 10,000 systems of inhabited worlds, 600
 ruled as viceregent before earning sovereignty, 605
 Son of Man and Son of God, 8
 vested with "all power in heaven and earth", 605
Christendom can't win world divided, 2085
Christian, practically all great minds had become, 2074
Christian believers, pitiful subdivision of, 1866
 sect within Jewish faith ended, 2068
Christian Church, became social, instead of spiritual, 1865
CHRISTIAN CHURCH, BEGINNINGS OF THE, 2066
Christian Church, brotherhood, spiritual, early concept, 1864
 claimed powers not its own, 1866
 cocoon in which kingdom now slumbers, 1866
 crystallizing rapidly after Jerusalem destroyed, 1861
 early, largely slaves and lower classes, 1335
 early, tolerant of modified slavery because...1335
 embarrassment great, because, 1866

Christian Church (cont'd)
 father-son idea lost sight of, 1865
 first called, 1333
 membership in C C not fellowship in kingdom, 1866
 Peter real founder of, 2069, -91
 rapidly growing (50 years after), 1861
 result of apostles' failure, 1865
 so-called, is cocoon (Gospel slumber), 1866
 socialized human shadow of, 1865
 substituted for Master's ideal of kingdom, 1865
 supplanted J' concept of kingdom, 1864
 taught kingdom in future, not now, 1865
 will change ultimately to J' views, 1865
Christian concept, three separate teachings, plus experience 3 men, 67-8
Christian concept of God, 67
Christian cult, most effective ever, 965
 Paul's, 1337-8
 vital influence turned it west, 1338
Christian era, 33 years more people killed than in all history, 2082
Christian missionary mistakes, 750
Christian movement, from J, to exaltation of risen Christ, 2092
Christian New Testament, not Jesusonian, 2091
CHRISTIAN RELIGION, THE, 1083 (see also "religion")
Christian religion, about death instead of life of J, 1614
 arose through following teachings, 1084
 bitter persecution of, by Jerusalem, 1616
 compounded of following (7 things), 1084
 compromised, diluted, 1637
 early, about J, not of J, 1670
  fell back from its recognition of women, 1679
  two great mistakes, 1670
 is...1011
 is Judaism, Zoroastrianism, Greek philosophy, and Peter, Paul, Philo, 1011
 vs. Mithraism, 1083
Christian teachers, early were intolerant, 1491
 first to teach equal salvation for poor, 780
Christian theology, great difficulty in attaining consistency, 68
Christian worship, early, taken from synagogue, paganism, Mithraic ritual, 2074

Christianity

CHRISTIANITY (see also "religion")
 about death, not life of J, 1614-15
 Abnerian, Pauline, 1869
 almost exclusively Paul's experience, 2091
 and the J gospel, 1864
 AND MITHRAISM, 1083
 and poverty, unfortunate, 976
 Antioch cult, 1084, 2070
 arose through the following (7 things), 1084
 ascendency gained in that...2070
 Athanasius at Nicea, 2070
 attitude on rituals, magic, art, 2069
 bargain with pagans, shrewd, 2070
 based on, 1340
 believers were sect within Judaism, 2060
  no longer, 2068
 busies self with wrong problems, 2082
 captured best minds of Roman Empire, 2070
 cease to sponsor social, industrial policies, 2086
 challenged traditions of Western civilization, 2069
 changed by apostles, 1825
 comatose for over 1000 years, 2086
 comes from, 1011, -84, 1340, 2071
 communal, 2067

CHRISTIANITY (cont'd)

communishm, no, 1335
compromise, a, 2069
confronted with doom, 2085
Constantine won to C, 2070
could have won world, 1670
cream of Hebrew theology, 2070
described in paragraph, 2070
difficult to accept because, 1670
don't despise, 2085
drains many a pagan swamp, barbarian morass,2083
early C, free from civil, social commitments, 1088
eastern version, how lost, 2072
economic in no sense, 1335
error, built around death of J, 1614
error, marriage no sacrament, 927,-29
exhibits, presents, history of...2075
extemporized religion, 2086
faces worst struggle for existence, 2075
first religion for poor, 780
founders confused the concepts of J, 1859
FUTURE, THE, 2084
Golden Rule positive, not negative (see "Golden Rule")
great mistakes (2), 1670
greatest religion, even as changed, 2067
Greco-Roman, best classes became members, 2069
GREEK INFLUENCE, 2071
Greek, not Jesusonian, 2074
Greeks forced Romans to accept C, 2071
Greeks, C owes very much to, 2070
half-hearted attempts made, 1720
has largely forgotten Master's gospel, 1085
"hellenized" and paganized, 2070-73
hibernating in spiritual sense, dark ages, 2074
higher classes responded, 2069
history (in one paragraph), 2075
hope of, 2075
hope of modern C, 2086
how capture best minds of Roman Empire, 2070
hurt by human philosophy, 1040
ideal religion because, 1775
ideals of J compromised, ideas saved, 2070
in a paragraph, 1011
in Tibet, 1038
inelasticity, no growth possible with unity, 1010
is not J' gospel, 2059
Jesus' gospel, then Peter's, then Paul's, 2091
Jesus' ideals partially embraced in, 2072
Jesus transcended teachings of his forebears, 1671
Jesusonian C unique, no introspection, 1583
Jews and Greeks and C, 2071
kingdom, dual concept of, 1859
lower classes members at first, 2069
lowered its ideals, 2083
mighty religion because, 2086
minute summary, 2086,-91
miseries, not to ameliorate, 1335
Mithraism, won half of, 2070
moral, not religious culture of Rome, 2072
moves minds, mighty emotions, 2085
must go low gear, 2086
name from Antioch, 2068
neglecting its spiritual mission, 2082
never seriously tried on earth, 1720
new and great ideal, 2070
new and less exacting version (N. Z.), 1005
new order of human society, 2069
new problems for, 2075
not brotherhood it's supposed to be, 2083
not J' religion, 1583,1670
not teachings of J, 1036,-41,1670,2069,-91

CHRISTIANITY (cont'd)

obstacle to our own advancement, 2084
Occidental dogmas made C a white man's religion, 1032
occidentalized, 1011
ominous struggle, 2075
Orient and divided, 2084
origins, organization of, 1864
owes much to Greeks, 2070
paganization of, 2070,-73
paganized, needs teachings of J, 2082
Paul won fringe in synagogues to C, 1333
Pauline, not Jesusonian, 2091
Pauline version of life and teachings of, 2070
Paul's cult of C blended with (3) following teachings, 1340
Paul's Hellenized C, 2073
personal religion, 1629
Philo, Peter, Paul (definition), 1011
power from service and faith, 2073
pretensions of C caused clash, 2069
proselytes to Judaism, early backbone of, 2074
rapid spread, why, 1456
recent rehabilitation of, 2075
rehabilitation, relative, 2075
religion about J, not religion of J, 1670,1859
ROMAN INFLUENCE, 2072
Roman world, C conquered, 2086
Romans fought C, Greeks embraced C, 2071
Rome, 30 pivotal leaders taught by J, 1456
seemed to sponsor a "bad" society, 2086
self-examination, no, 1583
setting stage for rapid spread of early, 1456
simple spiritual appeal of J, C is not, 2069
so-called, 1637,1720
so-called C is social, cultural movement, 2083
social vs. spiritual problems, 2082
socialized, needs J' teachings, 2082
society and religion, a, 2069
spiritual regeneration of men should work on, 2082
spread, 3 factors, 1456
strength from Hebrew, Greek, 1079
struggle, C faces more ominous, 2075
suffers under great handicap, 2086
technique for conservation of moral and social values, 1083
threatened by slow death, 2083
three factors of paramount value in spread of, 1456
too passive, 1607
transplanted from Jewish to gentile soil, 1859
triumph approaching completion, 2074
triumph due to, 2069-71
truths slumber in paganized, 2070
two mistakes of early, 1670
ultrapacific, Mithraism militaristic, 1083
unique, 1769
unlike J' new religion, 2069
vs. Mithraism, 1083
walk by faith--not by sight, 1897
well adapted to social, economic mores of white races, 1084
what it withstood, accomplished, 2086
why, 1083
world waiting for unencumbered, 1041
wrong base, 1614
Zoroastrianism, Greek philosophy, Jewish theology, 1011

35

Christianity's, error, struck attitudes on law, govt.,
etc., 2069
experiences (1 paragraph), 2075
CHRISTIANITY'S PROBLEM, 2082
Christianity's, struggle ahead, 2075
superiorities over mysteries, 1337
Christianized version of J' message, 2069
Christians, Alexandrian C, disciples of Philo's
teachings, 1339   and troubles, 1767
shrewd bargain with pagans, 2070
unwitting secularists, most are, 2081
Christmas, our C date, annual festival of Mithras, 1082
Christmas gifts, 777
Christ's sacrifice, Christian travesty, 60
chromosomes, 857; units of pattern control 48 (Urantia
scientists say units of p c are only 46), 397-8
CHRONOLDEKS, THE (living mechanisms, beyond
computers), 328, 519
church (see also "Christian Church")
aloof from secular, 1092
attitude, only proper, teaching nonviolence, 1088
betrayal of Master, 2085
built on foundations of sonship, 1747
commerce, politics, no excuse to be in, 2085
dictation of c, eclipsed person, 2074
Eastern; more Jesusonian, 1430
errors, struck attitudes on government, etc., 2069
evil of, 1864   false, sentiment, too much, 1088
failure of kingdom concept, result of, 1865
founded by Peter, 2068-9
function, contrast Palestine, Greece, 1079
great hope for non-creedal, 1135
(group) member should enjoy religious liberty, 1135
head of, James, 1831
how started, Peter, 2091
how started wrong, 2059
in commerce, politics, betrayal of Master, 2085
is larval stage of thwarted kingdom, 1866
Jesus didn't found, 2069, -85
(medieval Christian) mother of modern secularism,
2081
membership is not fellowship in kingdom, 1866
must be non-secular, 1089, -92, 2069
no, just brotherhood of J, 2067
not dynamic brotherhood of J, 2083
not Jesusonian, 1825
obstacle to gospel advancement, 2085
of social action, displaced spiritual, 1864
on ideals and purposes, 1091
organized due to Stephen's stoning, 2068
outward c taken place of kingdom, an, 1866
overshadowing authority, tradition, dictation of, 2074
persecuted truth bearers, 2085
Peter first leader, 2068
politics, no excuse to be in, 2085
powerful institutionalized c dared...2085
proper attitude, only, 1088
(religion) could not save Roman Empire, 2074
saints, spiritual menace, 2074
separate from state, peace move, 784
should unite on divine oneness of J' life, 1866
smothered newborn faith, 2085
social brotherhood substituted for spiritual, 1865
social, displaced J' spiritual concept, 1864
spiritual barrenness, Rome, 2074
started teaching "kingdom" at second coming, 1865
substitute for Master's ideal, 1865
successor to spiritual brotherhood, 1864
totalitarianism, 2081
true c characterized by unity, 2085
unity, 2085

church (cont'd)
vs. kingdom, 1866
visible handicaps, invisible, 2085
church's dilemma, great embarrassment, 1087, 1866
church and state, divorce, 1930
hand in hand, 1074
church, the early
Antioch, Philadelphia, 1831
built on wrong ideas, 1825
largely slaves and lower classes, 1335
church membership, not same as kingdom fellowship,
1866
churches, appealing simplicity, c should be of, 1840
(kingdom) to be built on concept of, 1748
living J, should be presented, the, 2090
obstacles to advance of real gospel, 2084-5
ornateness does not promote spiritual, 1840
over-decorated, 1840
religious unity only with God's sovereignty, 1487
should stand aloof from secular, 1092
unconscious obstacles to gospel advance, 2085

ci

circle attainment, augments potential of human success,
1211
circle-making decisions, seraphim promote, 1245
circle of eternal purpose meshes with material cycles,
364
circle of eternity, 1776
circles, journey inward in task of self-understanding,
self-conquest, self-mastery, 1242
CIRCLES OF THE ANGELS, 525
CIRCLES OF THE ASCENDING MORTALS, 526
CIRCLES OF THE COURTESY COLONIES, 526
CIRCLES OF THE FINALITERS, 527
CIRCLES OF THE MASTER PHYSICAL CONTROLLERS,
526
circles, of progress, derived from central U, 158
CIRCLES OF THE SONS OF GOD, 524
circles, of spirituality, angels, 1242
CIRCLES OF THE UNIVERSE AIDS, 525
circles, 7 on this planet, 1233 (see "adjutant m. spirits")
7 psychic, 569, 1209-10, 1233, -37
squares, rectangles, triangles, 522
CIRCLES, THE JERUSEM, 523
circles, third, if attained before death, 1231
three concentric, Melchizedek, 606, 1015-16, 1143
circuit, emanating from the Infinite Spirit, 257
force and energy return...ordained, 468
Harmony Supervisors originate on first, 288
of enormous masses, U in, 458
outer planetary, 290
planetary-establishment, archangel of, 710
circuit, archangels', 1250
ever-ready, U, 1254
in emergency, available on U, 1254
operated for first time from U, 2024
circuit, mind
identity means man has, 1232
placed in subordination to man's will, 1232
circuit, mind gravity, preserved Adam & Eve
immortal status, 845
circuit number two, disappointed ascenders certified, 295
circuit of communication, automatically established, U,
710
circuit of energy, direct, 322
circuit of love, the great, Father to sons to brothers,
to the Supreme, 1289
circuit of the Sons, 4th Havona circuit, 293
most intriguing of Havona sojourn, 293

circuit of universes, countless times, 63
circuit, Paradise, sustenance of (S. M.), 257
circuit, personality, 9, 25, 64, 71, 196, 363, 445, -50
circuit, personality, through p c Father knows
    thoughts, acts, of all beings, 363
    thus does Father draw near to us, 445, 450
CIRCUIT REGULATORS, 543
circuit, sevenfold c of universe power, 321
circuit, spirit c of Eternal Son, 84
circuit, spirit gravity, like neural circuits in body, 84
    pulls soul of man Paradiseward, 84
    spiritual value in prayer, seized by, 84
circuit, spirit, universal, 84
Circuit Spirits, like Thought Adjusters, 203
circuit supervisors, 607
CIRCUIT SUPERVISORS, THE UNIVERSE, 265, 377
circuit universe personality, Father has encircuited
    persons in grasp of, 196
circuits, absolute-gravity, 131
    adjutant mind c, upon death, 1286
    adjutant mind spirits like c, not beings, 403
    and revolutions of electrons, 473
    energy c will ultimately be in balance, 1292
    essential to seconaphim not on U, 318
    established c of grand universe, 261
    four absolute-gravity c, Father acts over all, 131
    four, of Father, Son, Spirit, material gravity, 9
    instantaneous...gravity c of Paradise Isle, 1182
    life c of the system, for Jerusemites, 742
circuits, concentric, of worlds, 152
    35, 000, 000 to 245, 000, 000 per circuit, 152
circuits, constellation, "automatically thrown out of
    c c", 606
circuits, energy,
    basic to all...phenomena, 456
    directionized by dark island way stations, 458
    help bind space bodies into integrated unit, 456
    midwayers can traverse, 866
    Life Carriers instigate e c of living matter, 560
    of space, 319
circuits, gravity, limit Michael's power, 367
circuits, higher c of the universe, both seraphim (if
    pair) required only for, 1243
circuits, intelligence,
    of Infinite Spirit, 307
    of universes, like body's neural sensation paths, 1276
circuits, life, lost contact with life c through rebellion,
    745
circuits, life-maintenance, of Satania, 857
CIRCUITS, THE LOCAL UNIVERSE, 377
    intelligence--penetrate Gr. U, 1276
    isolation of U, not a planetary orphanage, 1258
    mind and spirit--man uses, 1287
    of cosmic mind, 1278
    three names, 177
circuits, master c of universe energy, 323
circuits, master energy c of grand universe, 321
circuits, master, of grand universe, 377
circuits, Messengers of the Havona c, 258
    of interplanetary communication, not at Eden, 830
    of space and currents of time, 257
    of universe communication, 309
    planetary c of central universe, 289
    planets in main c assured survival, 621
    puzzling Mystery Monitors and material c, 1182
    remain to be traversed, after attainment of Father, 294
    seven outer planetary c of central universe, 289-97
circuits, mind c of human will action, 1230
circuits, mind, of Infinite Spirit, mind-energy
    manipulators, students of, 505
circuits, morontia, 543

circuits of, the central universe, 441
    energy, mind, spirit, never permanent possessions
        of ascenders, 1286
    the Father, supernaphim in pairs to use, 286
    power, electronic organization of universe power,
        321
    power, segregated, not common to superuniverses,
        324
    space, directors of space reports operate on all
        basic, 288
    spiritual ministry, 1286
    the system, 591
circuits, Paradise, all open to Unions of Days, 212
circuits, presence, of Eternal Son, Infinite Spirit, Isle
    of Paradise, 45
    of gravity, of the Trinity, 176-7
circuits, seven power c from s u hdqtrs. , 322
Circuits, Seven Spirits of the, 287
circuits, spiritual,
    man never possesses s c as own, 1286
    normal worlds, post-bestowal are in s c, 598
    Urantia is presently outside s c, 439
circuits, superuniverse, 7 named, 177
circuits, system, sustain life, complement of s c for
    100 Andonites, 745
circuits, three distinct spirit circuits, Nebadon, 377
    ultimatons not in c within electrons, 476
    Urantia sometime restoration to spirit c, 413
    vital c disrupted past critical point, 1230
circuits, universal of Paradise, pervade the 7 s u, 176
circuits, universe, energy currents of u c, 438

circumcision, 102, 988, 1003, -21
    purely sacrificial (not hygiene), 982-3
circumstanced (?), apparently cruel hand, father of J
    died, 1388
    sinking (timing) of Garden of Eden, 827
circumstanced, angels seek to bring "right" people
    together, 432
    "by apparent chance", J met travelers, 1422
    by seraphic guidance, T A coordinated direction, 742
    medley of phenomena, 56
    unusual co-ordination of spiritual agencies, 1033
circumstances, all c of existence perhaps
    meaningful, 115
citadel of the spirit, absolutely unassailable, 1096
cities, dominate the country, struggle, 1074
    income sources, 815
CITIES, MANUFACTURE, AND COMMERCE, 903
cities, multiply good or evil, 770
    whose builder is God, 501, 1935
citizen exists for state is moral myth, 800
CITIZENS OF URANTIA, THE PERMANENT, 865
citizens, believers should be better c, 1930
    of U, the midwayers, 415
CITIZENSHIP, THE CORPS OF PERMANENT, 337
citizenship, cosmic, through religion, 1093
CITIZENSHIP, INTERPRETERS OF COSMIC, 434
CITIZENSHIP, JERUSEM, 539
CITIZENSHIP ON EDENTIA, 495
citizenship, on high, here now, experienced by God-
    knowing, 1985
    realization of divine destiny of perfection, 1985
    world, better, 1930
"city, greater than he who captures a", 1609
city of this (U Book) contact visitation, 1243
"city set upon a hill", 157, 172
"city whose builder and maker is God", 542
civil government, is founded on justice, 1462
civil laws, J obeyed all, 1580
civil liberties came from secular revolt, 2082

civil rights (human), everyone associated with a social
    duty, 906
    regression, 794
civil servants, 1931
civil, social, realms, J ignored, 1580

civilization

CIVILIZATION
    Aegean, perished due to slaves' descendants, 895
    advanced c 500,000 years ago, an, 745,-48
    always few suffer for majority to advance, 927
    Anora in advanced stage of progressive c, 559
    art of living more difficult as c complex, 1772
    artificial and vulnerable, unless evolved,870
    at a standstill, 909
    basic institution of c is home, 1256
    being modified by invention and knowledge, 1086
    better, c would be, on J' teachings, 1720
    better, from superconscious minds and...1220
    better, secret of, 2064
    can't long survive loss of...religion, 1727
    can't succeed if not evolved,870
    constituted by cosmic gifts, 196
    constitutive endowments of man must contribute, 196
    cosmic gifts (3) socialized, constitute c, 196
    CRADLE OF, 900
    crash of c, science, morality, religion, survive, 196
    cultural c, can't have without leisure, 769,902
    cultural leisure, with ambition for good c, 907
    cultural velocity of c determined by, 909
    DAWN OF, THE, 763
    degree of, told by public opinion's control through
        non-violence, 802
    delayed when social change lags, 911
    depends chiefly on evolution of mores, 767
    depends on family, 888
    depends on genius, resources, leisure,870
    depends on leisure, 769,902
    depends on religion, 883
    depends on tools, 901,-09
    DEVELOPMENT OF MODERN, 900
    differs on all planets, 576
    Egypt's c deteriorated by Saharans, 889
    enduring strain of a most dangerous phase, 765
    eternal foundation, guiding star, true religion, 1013
    European c culminated from, 894   epochs (7) of, 576
    European, unifying influence of Jews, 1332
    evidences striving, not stagnation, 764
    expanding c embraces 12 part program, 804
    extinguished by breeding with inferiors, 719
    family, everything of lasting value roots in f, 765
    first four great advances, 777,901
    flexible, shifting classes essential to, 793
    flourish, not without antecedent racial progression,
        905
    for advancing c and augmenting...evolution, 820
    four steps in forward march of, 768
    from S.W. Asia, 878
    great, missed occurring in No. America, 723
    groans under overload of luxury, 765
    guiding star of, 1013
    hammer, great forward step in c, 768
    has arrived, when profits from experience, 577
    held together by thread of c, 767
    high, born of, 910-11,1220
    high demands, 1088   high, 35,000 B.C., 884
    highest type of human c, 2063
    how it works, wisdom and restraints, 1302
    hypothesize world center of c in the Levant, 587
    is made by people, not vice versa, 854

CIVILIZATION (cont'd)
    is never really jeopardized until, 911
    jeopardized without able leadership, 911
    jeopardy if better Urantians mate with lower races,
        586
    jeopardy when 3/4 of youths materialistic, 1220
    Jesus' truths will emerge to transform c, 2061
    judge by purity and nobility of religion, 1127
    lifted from chaos by mighty lever, religion, 793
    made by people, not people by c, 854
    MAINTENANCE OF, THE, 906
    man can modify evolutionary course, 909
    marks of high c are, 556
    measure of advance determined by, 802
    menaced by materialism, 1457
    modern, on J' teachings, 1720
    most tenuous factors of c (justice, brotherhood),1302
    must seek realities of heaven, 2075
    needs swift augmentation of experiential wisdom,1302
    no system or regime contributes advances minus
        God, 2084
    not without leisure to think, 902
    now evolving embodying ideals of trust, 438
    of mortal maturity, 1777
    only hope of survival is the home, family, 943
    only safe method to accelerate, 802
    on U grew out of 15 factors, 906
    potential for great c 23,000 B.C., Asia, 869
    predicated on 15 factors, U, 906
    premature levels of attainment, c will recede from,
        1302
    present crisis of, 1087
    progress of c hardly alike any 2 planets, 576
    PROGRESSIVE, 576,804
    progressive, seven epochs of, 576
    progressive (12 features), 804
    qualities of superior c not inherited, 763
    realities of heaven, c requires the, 2075
    really (has) arrived when, 577
    red and yellow, high c apart from Andites, 884
    religion lifts c out of chaos, 793
    requires, moral values, 1458
        spiritual goals, 1457
    result of cosmic gifts, socialized, 196
    retarded (by churches), 88
    retrogression when "material" outruns worship-
        wisdom, 1302; retrogressions, many, U c, 768
    returns to more simplified living, 595
    Roman, harm through sudden reform adoption, 801
    ruinous maladjustment, too rapidly advancing, 767
    Saharans dispersed, 889
    scientific c increasing liberty for man, 902
    second Eden cradle of c 30,000 years, 868
    secret of a better, 2064
    secular Christianity obstacle to advancement, 2084
    security of c rests in, 941
    specialization, c enormously advanced by, 910
    specialization, c may be destroyed by, 910
    spiritual idealism, the energy that uplifts culture, 910
    status determined by, 797,1462
    status portrayed by...803
    steps to, 576
    struggle for existence drove man to c, 783
    survive, can't in loss of best in its religion, 1727
    sustenance and leisure required to build c, 769
    test of c, sex regulated by society, 914
    to accelerate, bullets give way to ballots, 802
    TOOLS OF, THE, 901
    true religion must be eternal foundation and guiding
        star of all enduring c, 1013
    unprecedented material progress of Western, 2081

CIVILIZATION (cont'd)
    Urantia c evolving through 15 factors, 906
    Vedic-Aryan c paid greatest price for rejecting
        Salem, 1029
    war an indispenable scaffolding in, 786
    weak elements incline toward excesses, brutality,577
    Western c, long night of, 2075
    wisdom, c comes from cumulative, 1775
    youth places c in jeopardy when 75%, 1220
civilizations, come and go, but science, morality,
    religion survive, 196
    mortal, normal progressive epochs (7), 576
    that would astound Urantians, 566
    unstable because they are not cosmic, 196

cl

clans, common interests among members, 788
CLANS AND TRIBES, 788
clash between new and old religions, 1893
clashes, intelligence and tolerance to avoid, 278
classes and caste in evolving civilization, 793
classes in society, 792-3, 1534
classification for cosmic force, emergent energy,
    universe power, 469
CLASSIFICATION OF ADJUSTERS, 1178
CLASSIFICATION OF MATTER, 471
classifications of instruction, Havona, 291
classless society, only lowest and highest, 792
    possible only when...793
Claudia (Pilate's wife), appeal on behalf of J, 1994
    "innocent and just man..."(J), 1994
    spread gospel, 1989-90
Claudus became preacher, (J had taught), 1440
clay and spittle, J taught material means healing be
    used, 1813
clay origin of man, how, why, 837
clean hearts vs. hands, transcended Jewish teaching,
    1671
cleanse yourselves, exalted privilege to c while seek
    perfection, 1610
CLEANSING THE TEMPLE, 1888
climate, philosophic, of Europe, America, decidedly
    secular, 2081
CLIMATIC AND GEOLOGIC CHANGES, 890
climatic, destruction, Turkestan grazing grounds, 903
    factors, 2 new appeared, 683
    fluctuations, chief factors of, 662,-96
CLIMATIC TRANSITION STAGE, THE, 682
clinic for creations, 388
clock, radium, 659
clockwise, counterclockwise flow of the galaxies, 125
clockwise, counterclockwise of space bodies, 168
closing of the synagogues, 1718
cloudbursts, violent and periodic, 685
clouds, when c gather overhead...1194
CLUBS AND SECRET SOCIETIES, PRIMITIVE, 790

co

COABSOLUTE OR FIFTH-PHASE ASSOCIATION, 1167
coabsolutes, 1162-3
coal age, life features of c a, ferns and frogs, 682
coal-bearing strata, 18, 000 feet thick, 681
coal layers indicate times land fell and rose, 681
coat, "give second", meaning, 1770
cock crow, 1962,-81
cockroaches, 1000 species, 680
cocoa, raw, early medicine, 991
cocoon, church is c, 1866
code, precursor of 10 commandments, 751

coeducation, Dalamatia, 751
COERCION AND EXORCISM, 963
coercion, no, 1765
coeternal, Son and Spirit both c with Father, 111
coherence, eternal quest is for divine c, 42
coin, search for c lost in house, 1851
coins struck in honor of Augustus, 1512
cold and hunger stimulate man, 718
COLLECTION STAGE, THE, 768
collective drives necessary, 786
College of High Ethics, 388
College of Revealed Religion, The, 747
colleges, Melchizedek, 388, 517
collision, electron gives up light, energy, 475
collisional spheres, 171
colonization, origin of, 982
color, "Son has made of one c all the nations", 593
    symphonies, 499
    tones...peal forth messages, 506
    workers, the, 501
colored races (see also "Sangiks"), 714,-18
    and Planetary Prince, same time, 701
    color castes result, 793
COLORED RACES, DISPERSION OF THE, 726
colored races, EVOLUTIONARY RACES OF COLOR, 718
    from one family, 723,-35
    multicolored races, a handicap to U, 626
    only a little inferior, 920
    only 2 of original 6 remain today, 919
COLORED RACES, ORIGIN OF THE, 722
colored races, reasons for, 715,-26,-92
    six basic evolutionary races, 564
    the six, suddenly in 1 generation from aboriginal
        stock, 701
combat, J, no, 1368-9, 1469
combat, physical, ill repute on normal worlds, 614
COMBINED CONTROLLERS, 544
combustion bodies, no transit in space, 431
come again, J will, 1603 (see also "J return")
"come all who labor...", 1590, 1627, 1808
"come, whosoever will may", 1567
"come, where I go you cannot", 1792,-95
comely creature, Nalda, 1612
comet tail, 173
comets, 967
COMFORT, LAST WORDS OF, 1953
Comforter, spirit, from 7-fold Creator Son, 230
coming, second c of J, 1876, 1915,-18 (see also "J'
    return")
command, "failed to exercise the faith at your c", 1758
commandment, greatest, 1901
    man's whole duty summed up in this one c, 1805
    new, 1939,-44,-49,-55
    new and higher, 1676
    one in place of the Pharisees 613 rules, 1805
    one (man's whole duty), 1805
commandments, five of Buddha's moral preachments,
    1036
    Gautama's secondary 7 moral preachments, 1036
    greatest, 1901
    seven of Dalamatia and Eden, 975, 1017
    seven, Prince's staff, 751
    seven promulgated by Melchizedek, 1017
    ten, 975, 1057
        early, later, 1599
    "twice recorded in Scriptures", 1599
commerce and adventure, led to exploration, 775
commerce, great civilizer
    always g c through promoting cross-fertilization of
        culture, 775, 903

commerce, great civilizer (cont'd)
  on U, peace promoted more by trade than by
    sophistry of visionary peace planning, 787
  social brotherhood through travel, commerce... 597
  through manufacture, industry, augmenting
    pleasure of life, 905
  trader, explorer, more to advance civilization than
    all else, 904
"commingle good and evil, you shall die", 842
COMMISSIONERS, HIGH, 410
commissioners, race, 411
commissions, 18 trillion in Orvonton, 278
  sent to enlarge revelation of truth, 260
common goals and motives, all the apostles, 1592
common, morals, ethics, J' and Jewish faiths, 1338
common people will respond again, 2090
common sense, religion not safeguarded by, 1768
commons, represent survival of earlier collective
  ownership, 782
commonwealth, in a real c government by experts, 803
communal, Bethsaida camp was not, 1657
  control of land failed, 782
  life, no pronouncements on, J, 1581
  living, penalties of, 2067
  supper, 1091
  vision of truth, all mankind, 1782
communicate, celestial beings--throughout universe, 371
  Thought Adjusters' unlimited ability to c with each
    other, 1181
  with T A, make every attempt, 1475
communicated, 100,000 years of knowledge can be c
  in hour, ideograph recorders, 503
communication(s), Adam and Eve, over 50 mi., 834
  after death, none from departed, 1230, 1646, 1680
  between planets is normal, 372
  between Solitary Messengers, 261
  chance meeting on high, more c than 1000 years U
    language, 503
  competition must be regulated, 805
  compossibility and omnipotence, 1299
  comprehension of infinity, impossible, 1261
  error, Van's ruling, 760
  experts of, 505
  guardians, their wards, 1248
  instant, Urantia to Uversa, 222
  intercommunication, higher forms greatly helped
    by T A, 1198
  interplanetary is normal, 529
  Jesus and spirits, 1659
  of intelligence, use currents of space, 504
  100,000 or more light years away, instant c, 308
  oral, cover U lifetime in a half hour, 503
  perfect with Master Sons and worlds, 241
  personal, all entrusted to Brilliant Evening Stars, 431
  planetary pole of space, 710
  possibility of direct, unlimited c, Father and
    creature, 1184
  symbolic, 1775
  system breakdown, Van, 760
  thirty minutes, equal to U lifetime, 503
  this, thanks to unconcerned human, 1208
  Thought Adjuster (except virgin) unlimited ability for
    intercommunication, 1181
  throughout the Universe, 371
  took 1000 years to spread news, 743
  two way--of universes, reflectivity, 201
  with the dead, none, 1230, 1646, 1680
  with spirit world only through man's spirit gift, 1681
communion (see "remembrance supper")
  interruption of spiritual c, sense of guilt, 1133
  Jesus, seasons of personal c with Father, 1618

communion (cont'd)
  Jesus' worship, understanding c with Father, 1620
  Judas in place of sincere c, 1751
  through prayer and worship, 2066
  truce in conflict--between ego and T A, 1133
  unbroken with Maker, 2066
  with spiritual forces of the universe, 1751
communism, as religion?, 1100
  Christianity, not, 1335, 1581
  cooperation more productive than c, 910
  coordination, regulation better than primitive
    methods of c, 910
  counter to 4 human proclivities, 780
  destroyed by refusal to be victimized by idlers, 780-1
  early c did not level men down, 780
  early c was not a social doctrine, 780
  early c was a practical adjustment, 780
  finally destroyed by progressive individuals, 780
  Godless c can make no contribution, 2084
  handles children like primitives, 787
  indispensable early scaffolding, 780
  no system or regime which denies God can... advance
    civilization, 2084
  well-meant experiment disastrous, sorrow-
    breeding, 2067
  what we have better than any method ancestors had,
    782
  why it can't prevail
    Adjusters limit periods of spiritual non-
      progression, 2095
    each new generation has effective spiritual
      solvent, 2060
    no social system denying God can make lasting
      contribution, 2084
    religion of J most powerful unifying influence
      world has known, 2065
    runs counter to four human proclivities, 780
    spiritual forward urge most powerful force, 2063
    suicidal weakness, worker slave to idler, 780
    "where spirit of the Lord is, there is liberty"
      (all men have spirits, demand liberty), 2065
community of religious teachers, 1486
community property, natural resources, sphere of
  light and life, 625
COMPANIONS, MORONTIA, 70 billion in Nebadon, 414, 534
companionship, provision for c, even on Paradise, 283
companionship with seraphim, superb, 419
compass, affected by sun, 666
compasses, living c of local u, John called "beasts", 378
compassion, discreet, 1369
  "Father moved by loving c", 1852
  is the essential, 1951
  Jesus taught, 1580, 1874
  mature beings tender, tolerant, with all others, 1773
  new capacity for experiencing, 1583
  of J (by Rodan) moved alike by... 1785-6
  "our God is full of c, gracious...", 38
  the poise of, 1958
  tolerance, taught by Spirit of Truth and... in J, 1958
  worship can't atone for lack of, 1951
compassionate character, heart of J' religion, 1582
"compassionate, the Lord is", 1662
compensation, an all-wise c in adjustment of...
  creation, 360
competition, better than abrogation of individual
  liberties, 805
  essential to social progress, early ages, 805
COMPETITION, EVOLUTION OF, 805
competition, gravity pulls man down, 773
  keen c produced by dense population, caste, 770
  rivalry, keen and laudatory among men, 575

competition (cont'd)
    rivalry, promoted even among seraphic hosts, 313
    slowly displacing war, 805
    struggle to qualify for Garden admission, 586
    survival of a society, new ideas, and c, 767-8
    to get into schools, keen, 575
    vs. cooperation, 805
    world-wide for garden breeding, 586
COMPLEMENTS OF REST, 296
complex of lines, circuits, etc. for Universe, 456
complex society requires spiritual energies, 1777
compliments, depreciating c, origin of, 963
components of society, 10 classes, 792
COMPOSITE RELIGIONS, THE, 1010
COMPOSSIBILITY AND OMNIPOTENCE, 1299
compound manipulators, 505
comprehend, ability to c, key to Havona, 290
comprehension, mortal, infinity is beyond, 1153
compromise, but hold to spiritual allegiance, 1199
    continuous human, temporal c necessary, 1199
    didn't ordain Greeks, was a J' c, 1924
    every Urantian serves 2 masters, must be adept
        in c, 1199
    new religion of revelation pays price of c, 1626
    out of conflict, the gospel, 2069
    rendered Christianity more acceptable, 1637
compromises of Christianity, 1637, 2069
"computers", 504
    concept recorders, permanent recording unknown on
        material realms, 503
    Custodians of Knowledge, 301
    500,000 words minute, 503
    Frandalanks, living machines, 328
    ideograph recorders, 1000-fold more than "concept
        recorders", 503
    "if any man lack wisdom, let him ask" Voice of
        Wisdom, 310-11   living genealogies, 314
    promoters of oratory, 30" cover U lifetime, 503
    Secondary Seconaphim 310
    Spirit voice-flash, Michael voice-flash, 309
    stream of wisdom of divinity, flood of wisdom of
        practicality, 311
    tertiary Seconaphim, 313
    thought preservers, chance meeting more under-
        standing than in 1000 U years, 503
    Voice of the Angelic Hosts, 309
    Voice of the Creator Sons, 308-9
conceit outruns reason, eludes logic, 2079
conceived, J c as all other babies before and since
    except...1317
concentrate energies, why, 1725
concentric circles, 606
concentric contraction rings, 170
concept (Father), expression (Son), life realization
    (spirit), 405
CONCEPT, THE NEW, 1748
CONCEPT OF GOD, THE, 28,1598
concept of the I AM, 6
CONCEPT OF SIN, THE, 975
concept of the Supreme essential to...1297
concept recorders, 503
conception "within you is ordained by heaven", 1346
concepts, beyond capacity, 145
    dead c are potential evil, 1436
    most difficult (I am and U A), 1153, 1261
CONCEPTS OF THE EXPECTED MESSIAH, 1509
CONCEPTS OF THE KINGDOM OF HEAVEN, 1858
CONCEPTS OF SUPREME VALUE, 1096
concepts, religion of J transcends former c, 1781
    static, retard all, 1436
concerned, be not c for words, 1820

concerns, science, causes; religion, personality;
    philosophy, unity, 1122
conciliating commissions, 18 trillion, Orvonton, 275,
    278
    probably 100 million in local universe, 414
conciliation, 1555
conciliators, 275
CONCILIATORS, THE FAR-REACHING SERVICE OF,
    276
conciliators, problems of temporal existence, 276
    universal, 414
CONCILIATORS, THE UNIVERSAL, 275
conciliators, Universe, 275
conclaves, great c take place on Paradise satellites, 199
    Salvington, as many as 1000 in session at once, 407
conclusions, abrupt, sometimes work of T A, but...
    1207
concubinage, 926
condensation, electronic, 6000 lbs. cu. in., 458
    ultimatonic, explosion, 459
CONDITIONS OF EFFECTIVE PRAYER, 1002
CONDUCT, DIRECTORS OF, 301
conduct, improved ethical and moral c is kingdom, 1860
    irreligious c of religionists may lead men to suspend
        efforts to find God, 2095
    what determines, 1090
CONDUCTORS OF WORSHIP, 303
confederation of divine powers for your deliverance, 381
confederation, superuniverse c of local universes, 177
conference, important to J, 1531
CONFERENCE WITH JOHN'S APOSTLES, 1624
confession, appeared early in primitive religion, 976
    doesn't mitigate consequences of sin, 984
    egoistic prayers involve c, 998
    essential to religious growth, spiritual progress, 984
    meaningless ceremony, 976, -84
    new feature of Peter's, 1748
    of J' divinity, first, 1746; second, 1747
"confide in one another", 2055
confide in others, Judas failed to, 2056
confidence in universe, in God, 2088
confidence, J had unshakable c in man, 1102
configuration, cosmic
    always pattern of the Second Triunity, 1148
    ultimaton, star, or nebula, c c prevails, 1148
conflict(s)
    Adjuster will participate in c involving real right,
        wrong, 1192
    all c is evil in that it inhibits, 1221
    avoid wasteful c between animal, spiritual natures,
        1738
    between militarism, industrialism, 786
    between self-seeking and altruistic impulses, 1131
    deadly religious, 1730
    eliminating, 1087
    emotional c lessened by religionist's motivation, 1100
    freedom from, 383, 1131
    fringe of, flesh and spirit, 1766
    internecine over Babel, 859
    is a species of civil war in the personality, 1221
    Jesus, no emphasis on c between soul and body, 1749
    mind c may lead to mind disruption, 1480
    moral c usually accompanies moral choosing, 1131
    never between true knowledge and truth, 1459
    no c among laws of the Infinite, 137
    no growth without psychic c, 1097
    none if all was material, 1766
    none if all was spiritual, 1766
    psychic, necessary to growth, 1097
    result of misguided conscience, overdeveloped
        altruism, 1132

41

conflict(s) (cont'd)
    (self) wasteful, weakening, 1738
    transition area between flesh and spirit, 1766
    unresolved c, mind disruption, 1480
    Urantia mortals' acute, why, 382
    value of, 1097
conflicting contentions of mortal natures, 413
conform versus consent, 1384, 1404
conformity of results to causes (nature's justice), 794
CONFUCIANISM, 1452
Confucianists, had a religion of ethics, 67
CONFUCIUS AND LAO-TSE, 1033
CONFUCIUS (KING FU-TZE), 1009, -34
confused by doctrines of Greeks and errors of Persians,
    1660
confused medley works out, 56
confusing misconstruction, discourse on "second
    coming", 1915
confusion, about God due to, 60, 87
    about second coming, 1915, -18
    and turmoil, why, 1460
    before growth, 1092
    due to limitations of comprehension, 6
    faith in midst, of, 1460
    of scientists, due to, 1439
    on U, ignorance of multiple Sons, 87
    on U, regarding universe rulers, 488
    quantum behavior, 474
    spiritual, 1766
confusions, amidst c man needs cosmic perspective, 1092
    disastrous, theologic, time of J, 1338
CONGREGATION AT PHILADELPHIA, 1831
congregation, brotherhood, 1763
Conjoint Actor (see also "Third Source and Center" and
    "Infinite Spirit"), 91-105, 135, 189
    Father & Son function... in C A, 135
    Father collaborates with C A, 1282
    Havona universe affords proof of C A, 161
    Infinite Spirit as (is) C A, 4, 96, 205
    is functioning entity of Spirit, 112
    is source of intelligence, reason, universal mind, 8
    mind presence of God, correlated with... mind of, 45
    one of God the sevenfold, 1270
    possesses an amazing power--antigravity, 101
    respondents to C A, we call mind, 9
    sees that mechanism of Paradise correlates, 1303
    to realms of mind, like Son to spiritual universe, 140
    "we think" initiates motion in space, 133
Conjoint Creator (Infinite Spirit)
    acts personally for the Father and the Son, 101
    is the manipulator of energy, is action, 101
Connecticut fault, 686
connection, the prayer c can be destroyed, 1638
"conquer yourself in own heart", 1870
conscience, 1005, -95
    admonishes, do right, T A tells what is right, 1208
    Egypt, first to proclaim...1046
    human and psychic reaction, 1208
    misguided, responsible for much unhappiness, 1132-4
    not directly related to T A, 1207
    not spirit-leading, 1104
    not voice of God to the soul, 1208
    responds to emotional appeal, 1722
    vs. Adjuster, 1208
    vs. "true light that lights... man", 1107
consciences and souls, J spoke to, 1632
conscious of pre-existence, 1395
consciousizing of human after death, 1247
consciousness, can't be explained by mechanistic
    materialism, 1228
    creator c vs. mortal c, 1299

consciousness (cont'd)
   during translation, 544
   Israelitish c origin, 1071
CONSCIOUSNESS OF GOD, 68
consciousness of presence of God, attained by
   intelligent prayer, sincere worship, 2089
consciousness, of sub or superconscious, never, 1216
consciousness, rests upon electro-chemical mechanism
   below, 1216
   sublime, 63
   touches spirit-morontia energy system above, 1216
CONSECRATION OF CHOICE, THE, 1221
consecration rituals perfunctory at temple, 1377
consent vs. conform, 1384, 1404
consequences, the act is ours, the c God's, 1285
conservation of social inheritance essential to
   civilization, 763
conservatism of Chinese contributed to by tradition, 887
consistency, demands Creator, 1125
   Jesus on, 1673
   savages no pretense at, 979
consolation, don't offer... who lie down before
   troubles, 1766
consort of Creator Son, (impersonal) becomes a
   person, 204
consorts of Creator Sons, 203, 236, 358 (see also
   "Mother Spirits")
conspiracies (fortuitous) of energies, intellects,
   spirits, 55
conspiracy of spiritual forces, truly exists within you,
   381
constancy of spirits, reconciled with good and bad
   fortune, 961
constellation, the, 166
Constellation Father, 487-9, 2016
CONSTELLATION FATHERS, THE, <u>390</u>, 605
CONSTELLATION GOVERNMENT, THE, 487
CONSTELLATION HEADQUARTERS, THE, 485
constellation, legislative program of, 487
   legislature, 517
   100 systems, 166
   year equals 5 U years, 488
constellation training worlds, achieve socialization of...
   personality, 494
CONSTELLATIONS, THE, 485
constellations have legislative assemblies, 373
CONSTITUTION OF HAVONA, THE, 154
constitutive factors of man, 196
consuls of constellations, representatives, 371
Consummator of Universe Destiny, 1169
contact, city of this c visitation, 1243
   Father-man, 3-fold, 34
   the human subject c of these papers, 1243
   one world with another, 1317
contact, divine, develops from accepted guidance, 381
contact (God with man), many ways, 35
contact personalities, less than a score conscious of
   preparation for crises, 1257-8
   midwayers involved, 865
contagion of contact for advancement, 193
contentment, 438, 1674
   is the greatest wealth, 1447
CONTENTMENT, LESSON REGARDING, 1674
contest, archer people vs. red race, 887
   elemental, interior of planet and crust, 659
   first c between science and religion, 774
   personality of higher level triumphs, 37
   200,000 years for Asia, red vs. yellow man, 883
continence cult, and Paul, 977
continent, one great c, 950 million years ago, 660
Continental courts authoritative, world court moral, 807

CONTINENTAL DRIFT, THE, 668
CONTINENTAL-ELEVATION STAGE, THE RECENT, 698
continental land drift continued, 663
CONTINENTAL NATION, THE, 808
continents, all tend to creep into oceans, 669
    drifted west, 663
    float upon cushioning sea of molten basalt, 668
    westward drift of Americas (cleavage), 663, -68
continuum, nonending eternal, fragments of, called
    time, 1296
contractural stars, solar catastrophes, 171
contrast, John and J, 1509
CONTROL AND OVERCONTROL, 1301
control, man increases c through knowledge of "a, b, c", 1306
    perfect c of body only after Adjuster fusion, 1303
control creatures of Salvington (four), 378
    called "beasts" in Revelation (are exquisite), 378
control of personality expression requires T A, 1303
Controller, the Great (Hinduism), 1449
    "makes no mistakes", 34
CONTROLLERS, COMBINED, 544
controllers, Master Physical, 541
CONTROLLERS, MASTER PHYSICAL, 324
Controllers, Master Physical, possess antigravity in
    excess of all other beings, 326
CONTROLLERS, MECHANICAL, 325
controllers, power, appear with Almighty, 1269
CONTROLLERS, THE SATANIA PHYSICAL, 456
controversy, conciliated, no matter how trivial
    (constellations), 277
    "defend vigorously, when attacked, truth that has
        saved you", 1932
    "only when truth despisers force it upon you", 1932
    religion has none with science, 2076
    socioeconomic, Baalites and Hebrews, 1064-5
"conventions", every millenium divine sons, 87
CONVERSION AND MYSTICISM, 1098
conversion, emotion alone is a false c, 1099
    spiritual "births", 1130-1
conversions, and mysticism, 1098
    psychologic, 1099
    slow, difficult, 1130, 1637
    two kinds, 1099, 1130
"Converter, can this be the C?", 1614
Converter, John preached about the, 1614
"conviction of truth (Spirit of Truth is the)", 1949
cooking saved early man's digestion energies, 778
COOPERATE, THE WILLINGNESS TO, 910
cooperation, Adjuster and seraphim (not accidental),1245
    as factor in U civilization, 910
    between planets, 177
    consecrated, "you are so devoid of cc" with T A, 1207
    marriage, highest...of antagonistic c, 938
    mature man wins c, 1778
    not a natural trait of man, 764
    reluctant among humans, 763
    vs. competition, 805
COOPERATION WITH THE ADJUSTER, 1205
Co-ordinate Creator Sons, 162
Co-ordinate Ministering Daughters, 162
CO-ORDINATE TRINITY-ORIGIN BEINGS, THE, 214
co-ordination and co-operation essential, 910
CO-ORDINATION OF SPECIALISTS NECESSARY, 910
CO-ORDINATORS AND LIAISON DIRECTORS, 546
CO-ORDINATORS, THE INTELLIGENCE, 289
CO-ORDINATORS, SPIRIT, 430
copper, 671
Coral Period, The, 676
cords, knotted, and beads, J denounced belief in, 1681

core, earth's, 12 times dense as H_2O, 668
    of earth, rigid as steel, 668
    of earth, temperature, 668
    25,000 tons pressure psi, 668
CORINTH, AT, 1471
Corinth, boat traveled 10 miles overland at, 1476
    Jesus, Ganid heard learned rabbi, 1471
    Jesus, Ganid 2 months in, 1476
    leader of church, former rabbi,embraced
        Christianity, 1472
    most cosmopolitan city after Rome, Alexandria, 1472
CORINTH, PERSONAL WORK IN, 1474
cornerstone, "keepsakes" origin, 981
    of J' religion, 1769
cornerstones of gospel, brotherhood and service, 1930
"corporeal ascent", not possible (combustible bodies),431
    not possible (semi-material bodies), 582
Corps of Completion, Nebadon, 453
corps of destiny, reserve (see "reserve corps of
    destiny")
CORPS OF THE FINALITY, (present known destination
    of ascending...mortals of time), 345
    about 1/10 of 1% of area for C, 156
    Adamic midwayers all routed for, 444
    after Paradise and admission to C, 148
    after satisfactions of worship on Paradise, the, 305
    ages of ascent to Paradise, trained to limits, 348
    aided by Graduate Guides, 269
    all ascendant members of C, mortal except...629
    arrivals to live on Paradise, mustered in, 343
    career of ascending pilgrims, 340
    common clay of ascending mortals (mostly), 762
    constantly in service now on U, 345
    destined to service in...outer space?, 354
    destiny guardians mustered into, 1249
    destiny of C directed by Supreme?, 1292
    destiny of surviving mortals is C, 1238-9
    exalted beings, residences on Paradise, 156
    exquisite mortals, 631
    finaliters serve in all 7 superuniverses after
        Paradise, 345
    functional grouping, agondonters, 579
    glorified mortal residents of Paradise admitted to,300
    God the Supreme evolving as unifier of, 1292
    has a Supreme Council, 199
    high and exalted destiny, Paradise C F, 451
    illumination of wisdom of Father, an, 762
    includes Trinitized Sons, 244
    is an eternity assignment, 348
    less subject to material gravity, 84
    "maleness", "femaleness" continue to, 939
    members sent back to work in local universes, 347
    mortal mind, eventually mustered into C, 84
    mortals who have attained perfection, 116
    much work on spheres, light and life, 232
    mustered in, allied in new way with...1286
    mysterious servants of the future, 762
    mystery of ultimate destiny of, 348
    new type of creation preparing for, 131
    990 in company of 1000 are mortals, 347
    no other group such a messenger corps, 347
    oath of Trinity, musters into C F, 305
    one more unknown stage for these 6th stagers, 347-8
    only Father-fused beings become, 343
    Paradise, (7 groups), 337
    revelation portrays eternal brotherhood, the C, 1122
    seven corps constitute Paradise C, 337
    seven finaliters from the 7 C, complete Trinity
        relationship, 191
    to Paradise residence and admission to C, 159
    training wise and necessary for future members, 342

CORPS OF THE FINALITY (cont'd)
   undisclosed destiny in uncreated universes, 2015
   volunteer C, come back to planets to help, 626
corps of 50 women, 1808
Corps of Mortal Finality, 444
Corps of Perfection, ascenders who remain in local u,
   411
CORPS OF PERMANENT CITIZENSHIP, 334, -37
CORPS OF SERAPHIC COMPLETION, THE, 441
correlated ministries, seraphim, Adjuster, Holy
   Spirit, Spirit of Truth, 1245
correlation of energies, motions, thoughts, ideals
   (providence), 1305
cosmic
   attitudes, approximation of, 217
   citizenship, dignity of, ours, 195
   citizenship (joyful acceptance of), 1206, 1301
   citizenship, sincere religionist is conscious of c c
      in u, 1100, -17
   compass, infallible, the T A, 1177
   configuration, whence, 1148
   consciousness, expands, sees interrelatedness, 1146
   consciousness, real birth, M World #5, 537
   dimensions, 7, 1439
   discrimination, 3 kinds, forms, 192
   disharmony (from misadaptation of life), 1434
   events, God may interpose hand in stream of, 1305
   evolution, never ending drama of c e, 1298
   gifts, socialized, constitute civilization, 196
   growth, each age is antechamber of more, 1294
   growth, through 7 circles preceding Adjuster-fusion,
      1209
   insight, 806, 1572
      constantly augmented by seraphim, 1245
   knowledge in common causation, 1477
   leasehold for Creator Son, 237
   loyalty, 1089
   meanings become discernible when, 740
   orientation, comprehension of Deity helpful to man's,
      1295
   perspective, man needs, 1092
   position, in good system all factors are in c p, 1227
   potentials, 1303
   providence, 137
   quality (a), "the evolution of dominance", 1229
   wisdom, essential to cosmic understanding, 620
cosmic circle, is universal, eternal, absolute,
   infinite, 1122
cosmic circle, third reached by more, hence more
   seraphic guardians, 626
cosmic circles, human progress measured by mastery
   of 7 c c, 569
   mastery of is related to comprehension of supreme
      meanings, 1211
   of personality growth must be attained, 1233 (see
      also "CIRCLES, SEVEN PSYCHIC")
   T A is partner in attainment of, 1209
cosmic cocoon, human life experience is the c c in
   which, 1289
cosmic configuration, ultimaton to nebula, c c of
   Second Triunity prevails, 1148
cosmic energy and divine spirit, wide gulf between, 1276
cosmic fog is star dust, 130
cosmic force, all energies from UqA, but unresponsive
   to Paradise gravity, 9, (102)
   can't understand fully, 471
   ultimatons have mutual resistance to, 476
cosmic force and energy, follow curved space path, 125
cosmic intellectuality, two extremes of, 1217
cosmic intuitions develop unfailingly, 192
cosmic levels (7), 1211

COSMIC MIND, THE, 191
cosmic mind, 1218
   and intelligence, 1949
   endows all will creatures, 192
   injects spontaneity into material worlds, 2078
   is differently functioning in the 7 s u, 1269
   is it strange that c m... be aware?, 196
   quality of "reality response", a, 191
   responds on 3 levels of reality, 191-2, -5
cosmic mind endowment, 193
   moral discrimination, 193
   spiritual insight, 193
cosmic morality, is sensitivity to and acceptance of
   duty, 1284
   relation of man to Supreme, foundation for, 1284
cosmic path, 165
cosmic poise, 1101
cosmic reality, 1275
   distinct realms of, three, 739
   physical, mental, spiritual gravity, distinct, 739
   seven relative levels of, 140
cosmic responsibility, of self-conscious personalities,
   1284
cosmic self-realization, from, 1039
cosmic stage, drama of personality performance,
   energy metamorphosis, 1160
cosmic suicide, 1283
cosmic thinking, few exercise, 192
cosmic truth, goodness attained through pursuit of, 1306
cosmic tyranny, if God decided everything for us in
   advance, 1304
cosmic unity, or animals (species) vanish, 670
   why men find it hard to believe in, 961
cosmic window is T A, 1129
cosmologic levels of thought, three, 646
cosmologies, revelation mixed up with transient c, 1119
cosmology (of U Book), destined to be outgrown swiftly,
   1109
cosmos, can never contain all of infinity of God, 45
   Creator Sons factualize c in time and space, 1283
   finite, Father originates concept of, 1283
   foreordained trend of the c, the, 1300
COSMOS INFINITE, THE, 1168
cosmos, living c is the Supreme person, 1287
   material, facts against chance origin, 665
   Supreme culminates the total finite, 1164
   Trinity functions on all levels of c, 112
   vast creation of the vibrant c, 1276
   virtue is conformity with c, 193
cost of remaining in kingdom, 1583
council of the archangels, 2020
councils of men, J not directed by, 1412
councils of supreme sanction, 373
Councils of the Trinity, executive branch of supergovernment, 178
councils, ten, early at Dalamatia, 745
COUNSEL, THE HEART OF, 312
COUNSEL, THE SPIRIT OF, 402
COUNSEL, A WEEK OF, 1717
COUNSELING THE RICH MAN, 1462
COUNSELORS AND ADVISERS, THE, 295
COUNSELORS, THE DIVINE, 216
COUNSELORS, THE FOUR AND TWENTY, 513
counselors, four and twenty
   advisory control body of U, 854
   Jerusem headquarters, 513
   membership, 513-4
counselors, system, all Urantians, 573, 854
COUNSELORS, THE TEACHING, 428
COUNTING THE COST, ON, 1869
"counting out", as in game, once serious, 988

courage, altruism, hope, faith, loyalty, etc., 51
  and sincerity to solve problems, 1773
  bravery, heroism, in early ages, 729
  enables one to face problems, 1774,-77
  greatest is to give life for truth, 1608
  heart of J' teachings, 1582
  interchange of c for fear, 1777
  is the confidence of thoroughgoing honesty, 1641
  is c desirable?, 51
  needs discretion, 1958
  physical vs. mental, 1608
COURAGE, THE SPIRIT OF, 402
courage, strength of character, desirable?, 51,152
COURT ADVISERS, 428

court of the synagogue, 1822
court of the women, and assemblies, different on high,

court, supreme planetary, advisory, 807
court (temple), of the women, 1794
  of the gentiles, 1794
  of Israel, 1794
courtesans, addressed by J, 1472
courtesy colonies, 416
courtesy, origin, 963
courts, endurance of nation depends on fairness, 1462
  equity of c is index to civilization, 797
  first, were fistic encounters, 797
  two c systems, neighboring planet, 810
courts, continental, authoritative,807
courts of major sector like those of A D, 181
COURTS OF NEBADON, THE, 372
courts of superuniverse, high review tribunals for
  spiritual adjudication, 180
courts, traveling, local universe, Universal
  Conciliators are t c, 100,000,000, 414
courts, traveling, of the worlds, velocity 558,000 mps,
  276
courts, universe, under supervision of Gabriel, 372
COURTSHIP AND BETROTHAL, 923
courtship,now passing through c of T A, 1204
cousin marriages, meaningless prohibitions of some
  types of, 933
  once obligatory, 918
covenant, beginning of religious c, 983
  between divinity and humanity, 1020
  of Melchizedek with Abraham, 1020
  Samuel preached: "...everlasting c", 1063
covenant divine, abrogated, 1910
  God does all, man only believes, 1020
COVENANTS AND REDEMPTION, 982
covering, body is an outer, 2021
"covetous, the Lord abhors the c", 1822
cow improved by careful breeding (500,000 years ago),
  746
cowardly, Abraham, 1023
  Judas, so ascribed same to J, 1927
  souls,give small pity to, 1766
cowards
  undertaking, no mission for c (Peter), 1805
cowards, moral
  halfheartedly stand up to life, 1766
  no courage to invade new levels...1114
  teachers of traditionalism who know better, 1769

cr

cradle, hand that rocks the c fraternizes with destiny,
  938
CRADLE OF CIVILIZATION, THE, 900
craftworkers of color, the, 506

crash of civilization, science, morality, religion,
  always survive, 196
craves, what every mortal, 1573
"create in me a clean heart", 1640, 1769
"create, let us c the sight of this blind", 1812
created good, evil, error, no, 1429
creation, accidental? 150,000 facts say "no", 665
  Babylonians taught man's c incompatible with day,837
  evolving, dual-energy system, 154
  greater c of the future is in formation, a, 131
  Havona so perfect, no intellectual system of
    government required, 155
  immensity of material c, 166
  in 6 days,an afterthought, 837
    false, 838
  is a creation of mind, and a mechanism of law, 481
  is a living mechanism, 1303
  Jews, spurious c story, said it was Moses', 838
CREATION, LEGEND OF, 836
creation, mechanical, moves on inexorably, 1285
  "not rest, but progressive growth", 1953
  of eternity, of time, of ultimacy, 130
  Old Testament account a distorted story, 837
  one gigantic wheel, 164
  outstretched, whirling, ever-circling, 52
  staggering immensity of God's c, 51
  threefold, central universe, Trinity, 154
  to deny mechanism of c is to deny fact, 1303
  two-fold local universe, Son and Spirit, 154
  ultimacy of, 130
  vast c of the vibrant cosmos, 1276
  volitional c can accept or reject, 1285
  your c by Creator Son of the Eternal Son and
    Creative Spirit of the Infinite Spirit, 93
      same pair created our universe, 93
creations, administered as enormous training schools,
  417
  characterized by goodness; by potential evil, 53
  imperfections in c due to, 1159
Creative Daughter of the Infinite Spirit, a (consort of
  each Creator Son, to become local universe Mother
    Spirit), 236 (see also "Creative Spirit" and
      "Divine Minister")
  results from I S's"supreme reaction of complement",
    203
Creative Daughters, local universe Mother Spirits, 94
creative, design, pre-existent to all universe
  phenomena, 42
  desire becomes c when, 1467
  diversity, admin. uniformity, 209
  energy, stupendous eruption of, 91
  how every mortal creature can become, 1432
  only inner life of man is truly c, 1220
  opportunity on high, 508
Creative Fathers, 1304
creative imagination, liberated but controlled channels
  of, 1199
Creative Mother Spirit, 191,-97
Creative Mothers, 1304
Creative Spirit, created for every Creator Son, close
  associate, 106
  gives local universes character, 455
  gives mind, 1245
CREATIVE SPIRIT, PERSONALIZATION OF THE, 374
Creative Spirits, 1304
CREATIVE SPIRITS, THE LOCAL UNIVERSE, 203
Creative Spirits, mothers of angels, 205
  to Infinite Spirit as Creator Sons to Son, 106
Creative Spirits (Universe Mother), 203-4,-36
creativity, amazing, of American industrialism, 2081
  destructive, result oppression, war, destruction,1220

creativity (cont'd)
    evil is a partiality of c which tends toward, 1220
    haphazard or directed, controlled, 1220
    hindered by hate, fears, bigotries, 1220
    imparted by personality, which unifies activities,1227
    of inner world, most subject to your direction, 1220
    of inner world, where ideals are born, 1220
    turned to destructivity, devastation results, 1220
Creator-father (J of Lucifer), "I am your C f, can
    hardly judge you...", 1494
Creator Michaels, primary Paradise Sons, person-
    alized as M's, 234
Creator Son (represents Universal Father in lower
    u and ultimately rules u he creates, 361; Jesus
    (Michael on high) created our u, 361)
    acts instantaneously throughout his universe, 376
    Creative Mother Spirit subordinated herself to him,
      367
    has consort of same age, created for him, 203
    he who has seen a C S has seen the Father, 361
    instead of Magisterial, U, 228
    is personification of U F to local universe, 366
    Jesus, C S "made flesh", 1407
    living channel from humanity to divinity, 1281
    Michael, our C S established inhabited realms of
      Nebadon, 358
    never Universe Sovereign until experience as
      creatures...1309
    offspring of Universal Father and Eternal Son, 572
    one planet only in local universe has C S bestowal,228
    personalizes inseparability of Father and Eternal
      Son, 80
    rules supreme, 363
    sovereignty of C S passes through 6 or 7 stages, 237
    stands for Father and Son to creatures of 10 million
      inhabited worlds, 80
    viceregent before sovereign, 237-8
    when universe ready, enters into F proposal to
      create mortal man, 359
    why sometimes called "Christ-Michael", 366
Creator Sons, 162,1304
    act instantly, throughout Universe, 376
    all once born of a woman, 239
    are power-personality focalizations, ·367
    are transformative creators in cosmic sense, 1298
    become Master Sons (bestowals), 240
    choose space sites for their universes, 235
    each is fullest expression of "parents", 235
    fathers of the inhabited worlds, 28
    from capitals of, Holy Spirit, Spirit of Truth,
      adjutant mind spirits, 639
    from finite viewpoint can and do create, 1298
    grandsons of First Source and Center", 111
    how created, 88
    --Michaels, "parents", Eternal Son and
      Father, 234
    nearly million, over 700,000, 234-35
    no two exactly alike, 236
    150,000 in conclave, selected group, 234
    one planet in local U, personal bestowal, 228
CREATOR SONS, ORIGIN AND NATURE OF, 234
Creator Sons, origin of C S consorts, 203
    personalized by Father and Son, 88
    representative of Trinity only when, 1324
    Sovereign Michaels, 7-fold bestowal sons, 234
    struggle valiantly with difficulties, 39
    training of, 235
    unique, each is, 235-36, 1299
    virtually God of his own universe, 235
creator thought, invariably precedes creative action, 42
Creator(s), contact with children, 24

Creator(s) (cont'd)
    evolve in local U, 1272
    for creature to become one with, 1434
    necessary to explain U, 1260
CREATORS OF LOCAL UNIVERSES, THE, 235
Creator(s), prerogative, 1203
creatorship and God, 44
Creatorship Training, Preliminary, 203
creature, approach to Deity is sevenfold, 11
    cannot supply "living spark", 404
    can't explain existence but through Creators or
      procreators, 1260
    exists in God, God lives in, 45
creature attainments, result of individual effort and
    actual living, 361
creature character, defects of c c cured, 533
creature contribution, to evolution of finite God (S B),
    1284
CREATURE-KINSHIP SERIALS, 567
creature mind, not directly responsive to U Father, 47
Creature-trinitized Sons, 198, 243, -50
CREATURE TRINITIZED SONS, THE, 251
Creature-trinitized Sons and growth, 1280
creature volition, only areas of departure, divine plan,
    139
creature will, registered upon first act of will, 267
creature with will, has transcendant value, 138
creatures, ascending, countless already on Paradise,127
creature(s), created by Michaels, 1308
    designs and types controlled by C S, 236
    differences too numerous to narrate, 447
    discern spirit and material reality, 498
    embarked upon long...Paradise journey, 21
    how becomes one with Creator, 1434
    how becomes real in universe, 1301
    intelligent, many different types, 21
    lowest form of intelligent (mortals), 1407
    lowly, known to God directly through T A, 49
CREATURES, THE MIDWAY (see "Midway creatures",
    "midwayers")
creature(s), numerous types, 70
CREATURES OF THE CENTRAL UNIVERSE, 156
creature(s) of the conjoint creation, 205
    thousands, our imaginations can't picture, 492
    to know God, receive his love, love him, 21
    volition, 139, 1300
    "you are to become new c", 1609
credit, first commercial, 500,000 years ago, 747
credits, established for you, 315,556
    your individual c inexhaustible, 315
creed, for church, 1135
    is not a faith, 1091
    no--faith personal, 1091
Creed, The Salem, 1017
creeds, dogmas, rituals, are intellectual, 1012
    Jesus warned against c, 1592
cremation, effect on archaeology, 897
    encouraged by Nodites to reduce cannibalism, 980
    invention to prevent ghost trouble, 964
Cretaceous period, 688, -90, -92
CRETACEOUS STAGE, THE, 688
CRETE, ON THE ISLAND OF, 1436
Crete, Philistines from C taught Hebrews use of
    alphabet, 838
    12,000 B.C. brilliant Andites to C, 895
crime, adjudication simultaneous with act, 618
    and punishment, nearby planet, 818
CRIME, DEALING WITH, 818
crime, deterrent, 796, 818
    detection, atrocious methods of, 795
      early, ordeals, 795

criminal, talk with, J, 1475
criminals, efforts to control breeding of c gratifying, 818
    self-supporting on neighboring planet, 818
criminals and defectives, agricultural colonies, no breeding, 812, 818
crinoids, 681
crises, in 33, U government seized, 1251, -53
CRISIS AT CAPERNAUM, THE, 1698, 1707
crisis, how we react, 2007
    impending, 1706
    Jesus' earth life, feeding 5000 to Capernaum, 1708
    "just ahead" in apostles' lives, 1824
    man's preparation for c, 1708
    psychological, emotional upheaval, way to God, 1131
    reveals motives, longings of life-time, 2007
    way to spiritual attainment, 1096, -99
    world, J' return in, 1863
    year-long, 1708
Crispus, chief ruler of Corinth synagogue, 1471
    forward-looking Jew, 1472
    Jesus had 20 plus sessions with C, 1472
Crispus and Gaius, Paul profited from J' work at Corinth, 1473
criterion for evaluating life--time unit consciousness, 1295
criticism, to overcome habit of c of friend... 998
CRO-MAGNOID BLUE MAN, THE, 891-3
cross, center of Christianity, not central truth, 1615
    don't look at c as barbarian does, 2019
    an eternal symbol, 2018-9
    height, 2006
    high symbol, 2019
    how carried, 2004
CROSS, LESSONS FROM THE, 2017
cross, makes supreme appeal, 2018
    meaning of J' death on c, 2016
    no atonement, but significances, 2016
    not central truth of J' religion, 2018-9
    not high, feet 3 feet from ground, 2006
    not required, 2019
    symbol of triumph of love over hate, 2018
    take up his (responsibilities), 1760, -70
    to stimulate realization of Father's unending love, 2019
    world of, 229
crossbreeding, 920
cross-fertilization (planetary) of truth, beauty, goodness, 1199
crossroad, at every, Spirit says "This is the way", 383
crowds flocked to meet J, 1873
crowds knew not, Son of God, was passing by, 1935
crown of thorns, 1995
CRUCIAL YEARS, THE TWO, 1386
"crucified, let him be", 1983
CRUCIFIXION, THE, 229, 2002, -04, -06
CRUCIFIXION, AFTER THE, 2011
crucifixion, at end, all believers but 2 were women, 2010
    at end, 13 soldiers, about 15 believers, 2010
    circumstances,
        Jewish laws were ignored by Sanhedrin, 1982, -84
        Jews dominated Pilate, 1988
        Pilate was Rome's blunder, 1989
        Sanhedrin was tradition-bound, 1987
        scene of excruciating horror, 1972
        travesty, summing up of trial, 1996
    due to spiritual blindness, 1872
    earth's greatest tragedy, 1932
    Jesus' burial, 2012
    Jesus' c known on millions of inhabited worlds, 2018

crucifixion (cont'd)
    Jesus expired shortly before 3 p.m., 2011
    Jews, 1, 500, 000 in Jerusalem at time, 2014
    Jews, sacrificial system and the c, 2002
    John after 66 years, 2009
CRUCIFIXION, JUST BEFORE THE, 1997
crucifixion, learned from Phoenicians, 2005
    lessons of, 1932, -72, -99, 2016, -64
    man-managed affair, 1972, -99, 2002, -19
    method of, 2006
    natural and ordinary course of events, 1999
    natural course of events human experiences, 1969
    9:30 a.m. Friday, by 11 a.m. 1000 were present, 2008
    no connection with Passover, 2002
    not atonement, 227, 1944, 2016 (see "atonement")
    not for salvation, 2002
    not required by God, 2019
    not to influence Father, 227
    pallbearers, 2013
CRUCIFIXION, PREPARATION FOR THE, 2001
crucifixion, price of human bigotry, 1872
    proof of J' mortal nature, 1968
    records of, human, 2009
    rulers of the Jews mocked J, 2008
    scene of excruciating horror, 1972
    significance of, 2016, -18
    supreme folly of the ages, 1906
    supreme joy, no sacrifice, 1944
    unnecessary, J free to ascend to Father, 1515
    was at beginning of Passover week, 2014
    witnessed by unseen hosts of universe, 2008
    work of mortals, 1972
"crucify him, crucify him", 1994-6
cruel world, man's views of c w modified in progress by... 1306
cruelty, 1582
    atrocious c of ancient tribal wars, 784
    seeming acts of c due to limits of vision, 48
crusader, danger of, 1101
cruse of spikenard, 1879
crust of earth, about 40 miles thick, 668
CRUSTAL-SHIFTING STAGE, THE, 680
CRUSTAL STABILIZATION, 660
"cry of the needy, the Lord hears the", 1639
crystal field (see "glass, sea of")
crystallization, religious concepts, 1120

cu

cult, Christian, 965
    continence, The, 977
    dog-fetish, 778
    fosters and gratifies emotion, 965
    ghost, 958, -62
    Ishtar, 1043
    Mother of God, 984
    "musts" of, 965-6, 1005
    nature, 947
    necessary skeletal structure, 966
    new Christian needed, 966
    obstacle to reconstruction and progress, 965
    of Cybele and Attis, Phrygian, 1081
    of eternal life, after J, 1861
CULT OF MITHRAS, THE, 1082
cult of Mithras, Iranian, 1081
    of Osiris and Isis, Egyptian, 1082
    of Paul's Christianity, 1338
    of the sacrament, 984
    phallic, 962
    religious revision has to be forced upon c, 1006

cult (cont'd)
  river, 947
  spirit, 963
  star, 947
CULTISM, NATURE OF, 965
cults, ancient irrationalities understandable, 989
  of tree worship, 945
cultural
  achievements, preserved only by conserving social
    inheritance, 763
  acquirements, supernal, 494
  decadence, long period of, 719
  development, acceleration of c d...always preceded
    by invention, 907
  development, advanced religion decisive factor in,
    885
  disaster, adjustments and changes to avoid, 1086
  expansion, rate set by, 749
  immaturity, 786
  setback, most serious, 898
CULTURAL SOCIETY, 905
cultural, torch, home most important to c t, then play
    and social life, then school, 909
  velocity, 909
culture, all children must be raised in an environment
  of c, 763
  can't advance unless mind is elevated, 578
  centers--Mesopotamia, Egypt, Greece, 895
  demonstrates inherent inequality of men, 794
  driving power of c is, 908
  education, and wisdom (Rodan), 1778
CULTURE, EVOLUTION OF, 769
culture, foundation for development of, 577
  how uplifted, 910
  needs racial progression, 905
  never develops under poverty, 907
  no new sources of, 906
  one level to another, 1086
  ours is "budding", social progress "beginning", 901
  perpetuation of, religious job, 1088
  uplifted and advanced by spiritual idealism, 910
  when c advances overfast, 1302
culture, modern
  must be spiritually baptised with new revelation of
    J' life, 2084
culture, social
  strength for early s c from cooked food, 778
cultures, earliest along rivers, in East, 768
cumulative spheres, 171
cup, communion, 1938, -41, 2067
  even when a c of...water is given, 1764
  "of my remembrance", 1941
  water, "even when cup of w is given thirsty soul",
    record made of it, 1764
  while this is a bitter c", 1968
cure, of distrust and suspicion, 1575
  of plague of evil is sin-expression, 618
  rebellion, unlimited opportunity for sin-expression,
    617-8
curing by doctors better when learn more of healing
  chemicals, 735
curiosity
  aesthetic appreciation, ethic sensitivity: cosmologic
    levels of thought, 646
  purposeless, 149
  yours to be fully realized in the ages, 160
curling of lips at J, Nathaniel's (wealthy Pharisee)
  guests, 1825
currents, ascending spiritual c of the universe, 1002
  living super conductors of, 327
  of space, communication, 504

currents (cont'd)
  of spirit concept, 1778
  of time, 257
  three basic of ten energies each, 321, -23, -27, 504
  within the stream of eternity, 1285
"curses of transgression shall overtake them...", 1709
cursing, 964
curtain of cosmic destiny will draw back, 1293
CUSTODIANS OF RECORDS ON PARADISE, THE, 281
CUSTODIANS, THE TRINITIZED, 247
Custodians Trinitized
  assisted by several billion seconaphim, 248
  charge of records, plans, institutions, etc., 248
  over 10 million in Orvonton (s u), 248
custom
  spreads ideals of Eden (normally) to whole world, 587
  thread of continuity, held civilization together, 767
custom (mores)
  evolution, new ideas put forward, competition
    ensues, 768
  evolve very slowly, 927
  not able to be abandoned, but for better, 767
Cuthites, 826, 1612
cuttlefish, uses copper for oxygenation, 737

cycle of destiny ordained, man's participation
  optional, 1232
cycle of reality, completion of, 1171
cycles of cosmos, contraction, expansion, 123
cycles of space, 2 billion year expansion-contraction,
  123-4
cyclones of space, 329, 652
cyclonic transitions of a scientific era, 1090
Cymboyton of Urmia, 3 sons, 1485
  death, after, 1491
  prevailed upon J to lecture, 1485
  religious beliefs, never revealed his, 1485
CYNIC, THE, 1336
CYNICISM, 1442
Cynics, 1077, -81, -83, 1336

D

dabblings in relativity, 2078
Dagon, 1067
dairying, reorganization of Salem d projects, 1021
dairymen priests (Todas, India), 994
Dakota Black Hills, 687
DALAMATIA--THE CITY OF THE PRINCE, 743
  (Caligastia's headquarters 500, 000 years ago)
Dalamatia
  and Eden, far from Utopian societies, 764
  behind wall 40 feet high, 743
  buildings, schools, of brick, 743
  engulfed by sea, 858
  home (monogamous) dates from D 1/2 million years
    ago, 940
  ideas and ideals salvaged from days of D, 869
  in Persian Gulf region (later Mesopotamia), 743
  laws of Eden, based on other codes of D, 836
DALAMATIA, LIFE IN, 750
Dalamatia, moral law of Hap, almost 300, 000 years, 751
  Moses added 2nd commandment to D code, 969
  postrebellion era, culture of D, failing, 856
  progression by evolution, not revolution by
    revelation, 750
  remnants of ancient culture of D, 868
  successive cultures, D, Nodites, Adamites,
    Andites, 878

D

49

David Zebedee (cont'd)
  Jesus' tribute to, 1967
  kept secret his knowledge about Judas, 1932
  knew Sanhedrin's plan to kill J, 1932
  last mission, volunteer messengers of kingdom,
    2030
  majority of corps and D at 70 ordination, 1800
  married Ruth, sister of J, 2031
  peculiar minded, 2001
  safeguarding of J, 1718
  self-appointed chief of communication and
    intelligence, 2030
  sold huge camp's equipment, money to Judas, 1869
David's headquarters, Bethlehem, 1771
David's intelligence organization, 1668
David's messengers
  addressed the 26 m in Nicodemus' courtyard, 2030
  Andrew directed "discontinue service", 1869
  assembled at Nicodemus' Sunday morning, 2014
  brought good news of kingdom generally, 1833
  commotion of D m hastened J' flight, 1723
  directed Peter to Andrew, hidden in Jerusalem, 1981
  helpers in conducting pilgrim camp, 1806
  hourly reports to family of J at end, 1997
  "Jesus has risen from the dead", 2030
  Jesus on way to crucifixion, D m to 8 points, 2000-1
  Jesus thanked David for service of... 1967
  "Jesus to be crucified at behest of rulers of the
    Jews", 2001
  Jesus to Jacob, "an unseen messenger will run by
    your side", 1967
  last ones after J' death dispatched, 2011
  mobilized for Sunday's resurrection, 2001
  "most fleet and trustworthy" one requested, 1966
  operated under oath, then released from, 2030
  ordered to collect money, did, 1748
  prepared camp to care for 1500 pilgrims, 1806
  reduced to fewer than 20, 1806
  relay station at Zebedee home, 1668
  reported on believers everywhere, 1771
  responsibility of, described to J, 1720
  safeguarded J, 1718
  sent to bring his and J' mothers, 1923
  service curtailed after Magadan, 1806
  service of m started on D's initiative, 1668
  six followed J in boat to keep contact, 1723
  small camp up ravine for center, at end, 2000
  spread report J was entering city, 1881
  summonsed J' followers for council, 1720
  told J that Pharisees were at mother's house, 1743
  urgent news brought from Bethany, 1836
DAWN MAMMALS, THE, 703
dawn mammals
  appeared in Asian descendants of N.A. lemurs, 700
  appeared suddenly, 703-4
DAWN OF CHINESE CIVILIZATION, 884
DAWN OF CIVILIZATION, 763
DAWN OF INDUSTRY, 773
DAWN RACES OF EARLY MAN, THE, 703
day, Havona day 7 minutes less than our year, 153
  in Havona is moment, 271
  "is as a thousand years with God", 153
DAY OF CONSECRATION, THE, 1583
day, on Edentia, every 10th d is for relaxation,
    contemplation, 492
  Orvonton d 30 of our days, 174
DAY, ONE D ALONE WITH GOD, 1920
day, with God, John Mark in hills with J, 1920
day dream, spiritual progress not a, 2078
Daynals, do not incarnate, 232
DAYNALS, LOCAL UNIVERSE MINISTRY OF THE, 231

de

deaconesses, women teachers and ministers of early
    church, 1679
dead, believers are d if bear not fruits, 2054
  the d called to record (so-called resurrection), 409
  do not return to this earth, 1230, 1646, -80
  God of action functions and the d vaults of space are
    astir, 91   "let others bury the dead", 1801
  mortal, when will action circuit destroyed, 1230
  "risen from the d" until the Son of Man has, 1754
DEALING WITH CRIME, 818
death
  adds to experiential status, the consciousness of
    survival, 557
  Adjuster remains until mind ceases to function, 1230
DEATH, ADJUSTERS AFTER, 1231
death, Adjusters, guardians, archangels parts in d,
    1234
  advanced mortals skip sleep, go direct to mansion
    worlds at once (see "mansion worlds")
  after d, memory transcription to Divinington, 1230
  after d, T A, and soul, to morontia worlds, 1230
  after d, two nonmaterial factors of surviving
    personality persist, 1230
DEATH AND TRANSLATION, 623
death, angels after human d, 1246
  ascribed to actions of spirit world, 952
  blow to concept of J, 1865
  brain energies cease pulsations, 1230
  cessation of vital motion, 1108, 1230
  communication after d, no, 1230, 1646, -80
  end thereof is, 1566
  eternal ages after, 1961
  feared because released another ghost, 958
  first residence after d, 174
  guardian conserves 3 things upon, 1246
  "he is worthy of d...", 1983
  "he shall never taste d", if, 1797
  if at d you have attained 3rd circle... skip "sleep",
    1231
DEATH--THE INEXPLICABLE, 952
death, instead of life of Christ, 1614
  is only the beginning, 159
  Jesus', no special dispensation, 1972
  kinds, three, 1229, -31
  means of striking spiritual step with... eternity, 365
  mind and spirit survive, 141
  mind matrix etc. in keeping of seraphim, 533, 1246
  mortal has met d when mind-circuits... 1230
  mortal-mind transcript etc. in keeping of T A, 533
  natural, becomes infrequent, 571, -98
  no d on many advanced planets, 623
  no magic to achieve immediate "spirit", 541
  no messages sent back is policy throughout universes,
    1230
DEATH OF ADAM AND EVE, 851
death of Amos, J' brother, 1400
DEATH OF ELIZABETH, THE, 1499
death (of J) at any and all costs, 1909
DEATH OF JOHN THE BAPTIST, 1508, 1627
DEATH OF JOSEPH, THE, 1388
death of mind, 1230
DEATH OF ZACHARIAS, THE, 1497
death or departure, grief of those left replaced by joy,
    623
DEATH, THE PHENOMENON OF, 1229
death, pilot light in mind disappears, 1246
  precipitates man into progress toward J, 1919

defilement, 3 causes (Greeks), pork, garlic,
  menstruating woman, 936   of body, 1204
defiles man, not what enters mouth...1712-3
definitions, Jesus suggested meanings rather than
  precise definitions, 1942
  seven d or expressions of God, 4
degeneracy has disappeared on advanced worlds, 629
degenerate, defective, unfit, antisocial, disfellowship,
  585
degenerates (see "defectives", eugenics")
  church unwisely has perpetuated
  eliminated by selective reproduction, 596
DEGRADATION OF ADAM AND EVE, 845
degradation of woman, Rome, 2074
degree
  of recognition, "supreme service", 625
  of spirits' control of your soul powers, test of, 1642
  of yielding to Father, tell by, 1642
degrees, titles, men still invest in, 972
Deities, experiential, 1168
  experimental, The Supreme, the Ultimate, the
    Absolute, 1151
  in perfect unanimity eternally, 363
Deities of Paradise, personality-complemented by
  evolutionary Deities, 13
Deities of Supreme and Ultimate, evolving, 1303
Deities, order of origin of the D, 90
DEITIES, THE PARADISE, 335 (see also "God")
DEITY, action, 5
  affection is well-spring of mortal love, 234
DEITY AND DIVINITY, 2, 3
DEITY AND REALITY, 1152
DEITY, characterized by creative bestowal of
  personality, 1434
  comprehension of D helpful to cosmic orientation,
    1295
  dual in presence, 10
  eternal and actualizing, 10
  evolution, 1272, -91, -96 (see also "Supreme, The")
  existential and experimental, 10, 1268
  existential, experiential, associative, undivided, 3
  Failure to find D, 294
  four descending levels of Hindu theology, 1031
  Fragmented Entities of D, 333
  functional D of mortal creatures, 11, 1030
  grasped as unified in power, can be personalized...
    641
  impersonal, manifests regard for whole, not part,
    1305
  impersonal presence of D (Almighty Supreme and
    Paradise Trinity), 1305
  in the Book of Job, 1060
  in evolution of Jewish theology, 1053
  influenced by human will, 150
  is always singular to man, 380
  is functional on seven levels, 2
  is personalizable as God, 2
  is unity, 1138
  is universally coordinated, 637
  judgment of, 218
  level of experiential D, The, 1171
  man's 7-fold approach to, 11
  many created intelligences of, 172
  may not be divinity personality, 4
  most beautiful expression of, 1270
  no party to marriages, 929
  now factualizing, 1270
  of Supremacy, 188
  of Supremacy, sum total of the entire finite, 1279
  Original D, the Paradise Trinity, 1276
  permeating U of U, 1291, -93

DEITY (cont'd)
  personal, prepersonal, etc., never mindless, 78
  personality of D on upper...plane of Paradise, 5
DEITY PERSONALIZATION, 109
DEITY, seven-fold approach to D, 11
  seven-fold manifestation of D, 11
  the several natures of D, (7), 1294
  shares sufferings of imperfect beings, 1203
  there are 3 positive, divine personalizations of D, 110
  three personalizations of, 640
  The Three Persons of, 110
  total D function, 7 levels of, 1030
DEITY, THE TRINITY UNION OF, 112
DEITY, unifying quality of D, may be called divinity,
  2, 3
DEITY UNITY, 640
Deity Absolute, 14, 1298, 1303 (see also "Absolute(s)")
  is total Deity, 3 infinite persons required, 116
  vs. Eternal Son, 83
Deity attainment, Corps of Finality not finality of, 348
Deity destiny, personality will attain D d, man maybe,
  1232
Deity, Total, functions on seven levels, 2
Deity Unity, 640
dekamillenium (50,000 years), 390, -93
delay in writing Gospels due to, 1332
delayed, fusion not right after death, 1237
delays, mercy--are not interminable, 616
deleterious agencies, priests, holy books, worship
  rituals, ceremonials, 999
DELIBERATIVE ASSEMBLY, THE, 179
delight, supreme, of earth, service in kingdom, 1683
  of human soul, 1459
  your s d be in character of God, 1639
delinquency, cause, 941
  solved, 596
delinquents, defectives, remain in servitude, 585
deliverer
  Gabriel called J before birth, d and divine teacher,
    1345
  Jews envisaged d to come in...power, 1522
  John Baptist: "now I know you are the D", 1504
  Mary: taught sons faith in J, as the D, 1527
  "of the Jews," J, no, 1347
  of the world, J, yes, 1347
  Simeon and Anna believed J the deliverer, 1353
Deliverer
  apostles: erroneous concepts of wonder-working D,
    1754
  apostles: some truly believed J was the D, 1746
  Caiaphas: "tell us whether you are the D", 1983
  Ezra: "this Galilean cannot be the D", 1526
  Jesus, admitted fact of his divinity, 1756
    "behold, here is the D, believe him not", 1913
    "D shall be as shadow of great rock", 2035
    "I am" (the D), 1983
    "if D is son of David, how is it", 1901
    "what do you think of the D?", 1901
    "you believe D would abide on earth", 1904
  Josiah: "J, who was called the D", 1813
  Nalda: "D will declare...all things", 1614
  Philip: thrilled with assurance he had found D, 1526
  Simon and Judas: "J is the D", 1756
  temple guards: "prophesy to us...D", 1984
dematerialization, 582
democracy, dangers of, 801
  effective, 10 steps to, 802
  genuine approved (J), 1491
  not ideal for evolutionary people, 517
  of evolution, autocracy of perfection, 179
  (silly respect) (collective ignorance), 970

democracy, survival depends on,802
democratic judgments, mediocre, 970
demographic study by Gabriel B.C., 1344
demoniac possession, authentic case of, 1714
   reality in former ages, 864
demons (see "unclean spirits")
demotion, 284, 294
denarius and laborers, 1804
denial of J (Peter), 1551
Denmark, 890, -93
density, 668
   average d Urantia 5.5 times water, 668
   how it varies, 459
   one cubic inch, 6000 pounds, 458
   Veluntia, massive sun, d 1/1000 of U atmosphere,460
denunciation, J' terrible d against Jewish rulers,1905-8
denunciations, J, few d, pride, cruelty, hypocrisy,1582
   scathing rebuke bordered on ruthless d, 1910
"depart from me, I am a sinful man", 1629
departed beings return in spirit? no, 1230
departed cannot return, J explained to A, 1646
departing flash (start of transport), 438
DEPARTING FOR JERUSALEM, 1595
departure flares, 622
DEPARTURE FROM PELLA, THE, 1868
departure of J Personalized Adjuster, 2025
DEPARTURE OF JOSEPH AND MARY, 1381
DEPARTURE OF MELCHIZEDEK, 1022
departure of a seraphic transport, 436
DEPENDABLE DAVID ZEBEDEE, THE, 2000
depletion, Paradise beings incapable of, 548
deplorable, idea of perfection of Scripture, 1768
   "man's estate", 1660
depravity doctrine, hurt religion, 1091
depravity, total (bad doctrine), 1091
depression, believers immune,1739
   J' heart was being crushed, 1969
   of mind, 1836
deprivations of life here corrected, 516
depths, man can be delivered from, 1428
descend, the Gods; ascend, evolved creatures, 1278
descendants of slaves, sank civilization, 895
descending personalities, 1273
   Melchizedeks midway between highest Divinity and
     lowest creature, 385
DESCENDING SONS OF GOD, THE, 223, 335
Descending Sons
   Local Universe Sons
     Melchizedek Sons, 223, 385
     Vorondadek Sons, 223, 389
     Lanonandek Sons, 223, 392
     Life Carriers, 223, 396
   Paradise Sons, 223, 227, 232
     Creator Sons... Michaels, 223, 234, 239
     Magisterial Sons... Avonals, 223, 224
     Trinity Teacher Sons... Daynals, 223, 230-1
description of ceremonies, feast of tabernacles, 1793
desertion of the halfhearted followers, 1715
DESIGNERS AND EMBELLISHERS, THE, 506
desirable?, courage, altruism, faith, etc. 51
desire, and become, 1467
   for truth comes two ways, 1466
   God, unavoidably will be God conscious, 1288
   J' faith destroyed d, 2088
   of the heart, if supreme, 1921
   of J for simple sacrament of remembrance thwarted,
     1942
   supreme, for man, 737, 804, 1434
   to sin, not with sonship, 1683
desires, granted, 1639
   gratified, morontians, 508

D

desires (cont'd)
   intentions important, 1233
   long-cherished, have opportunity to satisfy, 508
   of the flesh, mastery of, 1610
   of the flesh, overcome by rebirth, 1610
   too much multiplication of d, modern society, 765
"desolate, your house left to you", 1908,-24
despair, whence, 2076
destination, God is man's eternal d, 67
DESTINIES, ASCENDANT, 452
destiny
   and experience, unity of, 1732
   creation of own, divine privilege, 615
   cycle of d ordained, man has option on participation,
     1232
   eternal, don't lose sight of, 2076
DESTINY, THE FINALITY OF, 1168
destiny, glorious d for material sons of space, 354
   have spiritual long view of, 1739
   man determines own, 1135, 1232, -40, 1301
   man's true d consists in, 141
   of mortals, (capsule career), 354
   picturizations of d with augmented vividness, when,
     1209
   self-determined by personality in arena of choice,
     1301
   supreme, 536
   ultimate, 1240
   your d conditioned by, 1739
DESTINY GUARDIANS, THE, 1242
DESTINY OF THE MASTER MICHAELS, 241
DESTINY OF PERSONALIZED ADJUSTERS, 1201
DESTINY, THE RESERVE CORPS OF, 1257 (see also
   "reserve corps of destiny")
destroy conflicting desire, how, 2088
"destroyers of joy and liberty", 1596
destroyers, would-be, of J (4 groups), 1905
DESTRUCTION OF JERUSALEM, 1861,-72, 1912,-15,-34
destruction, of the kingdom of Israel, 1075
   of Manotia failed despite upheaval, 606
   only when what ought to be is offered in place, 1672
deterioration, repugnant to divine nature to suffer d,137
determiners not exclusive law of cosmos, 2077
determinism present, but not alone, 2078
deterrent to crime, severity not good as certain, swift
   punishment, 796
Deuteronomy, 1071
   (epochal sermon)
   "curses of transgression shall overtake them" (this
     people), 1709
   "you shall be removed into all the kingdoms of earth",
     1709
   "shall cause you to be smitten by your enemies",1709
   "these things shall be upon you and your seed forever
     because you would not hearken", 1709
devastating calamity, planetary rebellion, 754
DEVELOPMENT OF ADJUSTERS, 1195
DEVELOPMENT OF MODERN CIVILIZATION, 900
DEVELOPMENT OF THE STATE, 800
development, overspiritual, 1209
   religious, none without effort, 1131
"devil" is Caligastia, Planetary Prince, 602,753
"devil, man is not child of devil but son of God", 1632
devil, mortal man relieved of superstition, child of the d,
   2060
   personal, fictitious idea, could corrupt minds, 753
   "still free on U", (602), 610
   that possesses my child, 1756
   too much credit, 602,-10
devils and demons, more often our own debased tendencies, 610

devils (cont'd)
  Jesus said to be with, 1746, 1892
  no more, 863, 1807
Devonian period, age of fishes, 50 million years, 678, 680
devotion, half-hearted d to God unavailing, 30
  heroic d to J' teachings "astonish the world", 1608
  on high, 271
Devouress, consigned to hell, to the D, 1045

di

dialects, conquest of d precedes spread of a culture, 908
die, commingle good and evil, you shall d, 842
  men d searching for God indwelling themselves, 1766
  most human beings d because, 365
diet, omnivorous, forward step in health, vigor, 901
difference, between evolved, revealed religion, 1101
  between religion and worldly wisdom, 1120
  between social occasion and religious gathering, 1133
  in religions of various ages, dependent on, 1127
differences desired among body of finaliters, 579
differential of creature experiences desirable, 579
difficulties, of time into triumphs of eternity, 1405
  religion is solvent for most, 2093
  stimulate true children of the Most High...556
digestion, vital energy necessary for, 778
dignity, of man, 1091
  personal, motivating influence of, 140
dilemma, mortal, man in bondage to nature, free in spirit, 1221-2
dilemmas, materialism or pantheism if deny God, 29
Dilmun, Egyptians called it Dilmat, 860
  new city of D, of Prince's staff offspring, 858
  paradise of men and God, 860
  tablets, descriptive of D, in many museums, 860
dimension, seven cosmic d of universe, 1439
dimensions of finite personality, 1226
"dinner, better a d where love is", 1674
dinner of herbs where love is, 1674
dinosaurs, 1 lb. brains, 688
  80, 000 lb. bodies, 686-7
  flying, 691
  small d was father of placental mammals, 693
direction, bodies, 379
  coordinated T A d assembled 100, 742
  made possible by force-energy, etc., Paradise, 119
directional currents, all creatures, 378
DIRECTORS OF ASSIGNMENT, 429
DIRECTORS, THE REVERSION, 339
dirt and trash "elevated" cities, 903
disagreement, angels of progress, angels of churches, (U Book), 1486
  frictions on high, 311
  religious d on what is required of man, 1127
disagreements between disciples of John and J, 1589
disappointment, arrive at Havona, d proof, 290
  becomes blessing, 555
  be fearless of, 1779
  God-knowing men not downcast by d, 1739
  hardest to bear, those which never come, 557
  on Paradise d never regarded as defeat, 294
  part of the divine plan, 258
  supreme, 250, 295
  we learn to fatten upon d, 291
  you must be fearless of d, 1779
disaster, complete secularization...lead only to, 2082
  end of world, nothing to one "saved", 1916
  godless philosophy will lead to world d, 2081
  guarantees against, 1256
  secularism leads to, 2082

disaster (cont'd)
  to avoid d cultural changes imperative, 1086
  world wide, godless philosophy, 2081
DISCERNER OF SPIRITS, THE, 313, 316
disciples, early, stumbling block, 1510
  "forsake father, mother", 1869
  over 50 who sought ordination rejected, 1801
  unwilling pay price, 1806
  vs. apostles, 1823
discipline, all must share in family d, 48
  family of God must share in family d, 48
  loving, 1608, 1931
  must be maintained by brotherhood, 1764
  of wisdom needed by children, 1923
disciplines, child doesn't understand, 1608
  love has severe, 1608
discontent, consuming thirst of mortal d, 381
discord, will plays d or melodies on mind, 1217
discouraged, "be not d by the enmity of the world", 1946
  be not d by slow progress of kingdom, 1863
  God-knowing individuals not d by misfortune, 1739
  humans d when view only transitory, 1776
  pray, and not become d, 1619
discouragement, 1776
discouraging outlooks, Old Testament, 838
discourse, about God is often divergent and fallacious, 1140
  about God vs. experiencing God, 1140
  by Nathaniel and Thomas, 1785
DISCOURSE, THE LAST TEMPLE, 1905
DISCOURSE ON ASSURANCE, THE, 1601
DISCOURSE ON JOB, 1662
DISCOURSE ON "MAGIC AND SUPERSTITION", 1680
DISCOURSE ON PRAYER, THE, 1618
DISCOURSE ON REALITY, 1433
DISCOURSE ON RELIGION, THE SECOND, 1730
DISCOURSE ON SPIRITUAL FREEDOM, THE, 1796
DISCOURSE ON TRUE RELIGION, THE, 1728
DISCOURSE ON THE WATER OF LIFE, 1795
discoveries of logical mind, 1773
discovery, greatest possible, 1731
DISCOVERY OF THE EMPTY TOMB, 2025
discovery of No. America, about 1000 years ago, 1st white man, 729
discrimination, 3 forms of cosmic, 192
discriminations ended, 2065
discussion, they loved J after d, 1380
DISCUSSIONS ABOUT WEALTH, THE, 1803
discussions, nightly, 1420
disdain of laws turns spirit ears away, 1638
disease(s), all d is result of natural causes, 990
  caused by plant-life reversion, and Adamic default, 736
  many due to lack of Adamic heritage, 851
  non-scientific treatment, 991
  of institutional religion, secularism, 1092
  prevention of d in times of Eden, 825
  scientists cure more when know chemicals, 735
  sectarianism is, 1092
disease and delinquency, problems of d d virtually solved, (normal), 596
disease-making bacteria and virus bodies, majority belong to renegade parasitic fungi, 732
disenfranchising, 1 million Sons of Paradise if God were omnificent, 1299
dish, broken d and hospitality, 787
disharmony, cosmic, for individual, 1434
  maladjustment, possibilities for will be eventually exhausted, 1292
"dishonesty, not even consistent in", 1907
disillusioned preachers, apostles, 1687

divinity (cont'd)
    fruits of d for mortal (6), 648
    humbly obedient to human mortals, 150
    indwelling spark of, 1459
    Jesus' first assertion of d nature, 1614
    known by indivisibility, 31
    never discover d except through...1116
    obedient to creature choosing, 150
    poor conception of, 1479
    tension resolved by evolution of soul, 1276
Divinity, although plural is one in human experience,380
DIVINITY AND DEITY, 2
Divinity, subordinate, 1298
"division can only...result...", family divided on
    belief, 1824
divorce, counted upon, marriage is trial, 917
    DISSOLUTION OF WEDLOCK, 928
    early d at option of man alone, 928
    Jesus refused to lay down laws, marriage, d, 1581
    Jews, man could d, trifling reasons, 1839
    on neighboring planet, 812
    politics and religion, 1930
    social safety valve for improperly prepared youths,
      929
    special dispensation for Jewish people, 1839
    wife for most trifling reasons, 1839
    will remain prevalent so long as, 929
divorcement, concerning (J), 1576, 1838
    Paradise, Trinity Sons from Paradise, on J'
      request, 1318

do

do, one thing expertly, 1779
    unselfish good (during) daily duties, 1875
    we must do as well as be, 1260
doctors, better healing when know chemistry better, 735
doctors and surgeons, early, were shamans, 989
doctrinal fetishes very bad, 969
doctrine, can't transform character, 380
    much d of depravity destroyed, 1091
    of physical humiliation, 976
    of reincarnation, 1029 (see "reincarnation")
    of renunciation unfortunately appeared, 976
doctrines, dead, powerless, 380
    theologic, apostles taught no standardized d, 1658
dodging the issue, ("salvation"), 1613
dog(s), detect approach of ghosts, howled, 964
    first domesticated animal, pet and good food, 980
    gentile d, all but Jews, 1809
    hunters had d from blue man on, 902
    "I am a believing d", Norana, 1735
    "in the eyes of the Jews", 1735
    Jesus played with, 1431
    nothing holy to, 1571
    Simon Zelotes, called woman d, 1735
dog-fetish cults, 778
dogma, 1120, -27
    due to mental laziness, 1459
    for indolent, 1120
    Occidental d has made J a white man's religion, 1032
    "reality response" saves man from d assumptions,
      191
    religious, not good to follow, 1458
dogmas of 19 centuries, 2090
dogmatic
    challenge, religionist to d unbeliever, 1127
    teachers of science and religion often too d, 1138
dogmatism, enslavement of spiritual nature, 1092
    sectarianism, diseases of religion, 1092
dogmatized, believers, No! (J), 1592

DOING THE FATHER'S WILL, 1579
dole, bad, 910
doll, first d, why, 972
DOMAIN OF POWER CENTERS, THE, 322
domains of the physical (electrochemical), 739
DOMAINS OF THE UNQUALIFIED ABSOLUTE, 130
DOMESTICATION OF ANIMALS, THE, 901
dominance over self, 2 great phases of, 1229
doom, economic order, unless, 805
    of darkness, despair, dispelled, 1118
    sealed, Jews, 1910-3, 1969
    sealed, man's d not until...64
doomed, India's budding civilization, 12,000 yrs. ago,
    881
    unevolved artificial structures, 870
door, "I stand at the door", 1765, 1829
    locked, wiseman, key, 1778
    narrow, 1828
    "stand at d and knock", 26
Dothan, at D Joseph's brothers sold him into slavery,
    1387
double personality, Christ-Michael was not d p, 1331
double tragedy, Urantia, 578
doubt, believer has only one battle, against d, 1767
doubts, are not sin, 1118
    Joseph, divine destiny for human child?, 1347
    Judas, subtle d about J' mission, 1751
    lower creatures entertain spiritual d, 361
dove, peace, 946
"doves, harmless as", 1580, -84, 1801, 1930
down-grasp of indwelling spirit, sudden, 1099
dowries, collected by prostitution, 982
dowry, origin of, 924

dragon in Revelation, Lucifer, Satan, apostate princes,
    606
dragon, symbolic of evil celestial ones, 602
dragon flies, 30 inches across, 680
drama, magnificent personality d of time, 1281
    1,000,000 actors, 1000 scenes, 501
DRAUGHT OF FISHES, THE, 1628
Dravidian, centers of culture, 881
    Deccan, stultifying belief, 1029
    India, 881
    people, Andite and native Indian stock, 881
Dravidians, so-called, were Andites, 873, 885, 1028
    superior civilization, persists in the Deccan, 882
drawn to you, people, measure of truth endowment, 1726
DREAM, JOSEPH'S, 1347
dream life, first human families had fantastic d life, 713
    illustrates fantastic speed of concepts, 503
"dreamers, drifters, do not become", 1931
dream(s), and Adjuster, 1208
    bad, J, 1379
    convinced, corrected, Peter, 1713
    convinced Joseph, 1347
    few seconds, traverse years, 503
    ghost d brought concept of supermaterial, mortal
      personality, 952
    meaning, fantastic speculation, 1681
    objects connected with d, became fetishes, 967
    ordinary d not spiritual method, 954
    regarded as prophetic by ancients, 963
drift toward materialism, 786
"drink the cup" of career incarnation, 229
drives of life, The three, 1772
drives
    innate, all normal mortals, d toward self-realiza-
      tion, 1095

drives (cont'd)
    response to d represents attitude, 1227
    three great, for good state, 803
driving force, most powerful present in world, 2063
drop of water
    holds energy of 100 H P exerted 2 years, 463
    man's union with God not as d w in ocean, 31
    non-ascender's personality as a, 1284
    one billion trillion atoms in, 463
drowning man, succor might offend a god, 947
drudgery is benumbing, 786
drumlins (gentle undulations) ice age, 701
drunken man, girl, and J, 1436
drunkenness
    gluttony, tyranny, characterize material-comfort age, 577
    looked upon as spirit possession, 968

du

dual concept, fatherhood, brotherhood, 1859
    concept of religion, the essential, 1030
    minds become triune, 1286
    nature of man, 381
DUAL-ORIGIN BEINGS, 331
dual, spirit liaison, over worlds, 379
    supervision, 370
    universe, 477
dual presence of Supreme and Ultimate, inter-
    dependently complemental in attainment of destiny,
    1294
dual spiritism, an advance, but terrible price paid, 961
dualism in ghost fear, great advance, 961
duel in place of war, 785
dueling, survival of trial by ordeal, 795
dust, composes mortal, 26, 1240
    "Lord remembers you are", 1662
    to dust, 769
    "to dust", body of J, 2023
    "we tread upon, once alive", 671
duties, even little tots had, 1394
    of cosmic citizenship, 1301
duty, first of creature, 22
    flight from d, we lose control, 1428
    folly of trying to avoid, 1428
    man's whole d summed in one commandment, 1805
    no escape, 1428, -38
    of man, 1600
    of society, 3-fold, happiness, 794
    of those who know, 1602
    perform, then accept your lot, 555
    sense of, evolutionary, 1105
    sensitivity to and acceptance of, 1284
    to man and duty to God, 1930
    transcends temporal morality, 1284
    vs. friendship, 1945
    vs. love as motivation, 1945
    worship, causation, 192

dwarf stars, 459
dwarf, white, highly condensed sphere, 464
dwelling place, erect not on bridge, 1735
dwellings of river races, how made, 902
Dyaks, primitive, 1010
Dyaus pitar, lord of heaven, Indra, Agni, 1027
Dyaus-Zeus, head of Greek pantheon, 1078
dynamics, final d of the cosmos have to do... 1263
dynamo(s), 542-3
    solar, 172   vast, 456

E

ear, divine, hears what prayers, 1639
"ear, no e open to hear", 1638
ear of human mind, almost deaf to spiritual pleas, 1213
ears, divine e open to... prayers, 95
    of spirit personalities, how turned away, 1638
    spirit e turned away, 1638
earlier ten commandments, the, 1599
earliest religious emotions, man's, 718
early Christian compromises, 2070
EARLY DAYS OF THE ONE HUNDRED, 743
EARLY EGYPTIAN RELIGION, 1043
EARLY EVOLUTION OF RELIGION, 950
EARLY EXPANSIONS OF THE ADAMITES, 870
EARLY HUMAN ASSOCIATIONS, 787
EARLY ICE AGE, 699
early land-life era, 672
EARLY LEMUR TYPES, 703
EARLY MAMMALS, AGE OF, 693
EARLY MARINE LIFE IN THE SHALLOW SEAS, 673
EARLY MOTHER FAMILY, 932
EARLY REPTILIAN AGE, THE, 685
EARLY SUNDAY MORNING, 1634
earmark of great--tolerance, 1740
earmark of religious living... sublime peace, 1101
earmarks of ideal religious philosophy, 1141
earning universe sovereignty, technique of, 238
earnings of man for year, cruse of costly ointment, 1879
earth life, our first, 1459 (see also "life, this is our
    first")
"earthen vessels, brethren, you are", 1578
earthquake, child J asked why (disillusionment), 1359
earthquakes, 662, 670, 677
    The age of, 660
    "be not perturbed by e", 1912
    frequent on new worlds, 466
    killed Andon and Fonta (42 yrs.), 713
    would shake world to pieces but for... 668
earth's core, 15 times density of water, 668
earth's greatest tragedy, 1932
easier every day to do right thing, 1740
East Indies, Andites, 873
Easter Island, 873
eastern life implantation, no contribution, 703
Eastern vs. Western Hebrew theology, 1338, -66
easy, gospel yoke is, 1766
Ebal and Girizim, 1387
Eber, the officer of the Sanhedrin, 1791-2, 1810

ec

Ecclesiastes, 1070
ecclesiastical authority, fear overthrow, 2090
    not in kingdom, 1487
ecclesiasticism against faith, 2084
ecclesiasticism incompatible with living faith (J), 2084
echinoderms, guide fossils of 200 million years ago, 680
echo of divine voice, 1205
eclipses, 946
economic
    adjustments, imperative to avoid disaster, 1086
    and political, "avoid all" (to J), 1329
ECONOMIC ATTITUDE, J', 1581
economic
    liberation, after Magisterial Son, 2-1/2 hour work
       day, 594
    life, ethical, on advanced worlds, 629
    order, how to reconstruct, 1092
       Jesus ignored e o in all his teachings, 1580

economic (cont'd)
    order, Jesus not an economic reformer, 1581
        must evolve, continue to, 804
        not business of kingdom, 1565
        not here to teach rules of trade, 1576
        profit motive must pass, 805-6
        separate spiritual realities from e o (J), 1605
        to undergo reconstruction, 1087
        value of J' teaching to, 1585
    problems, moral... spiritual... are mighty forces in
        dealing with social and e p, 1739
    realm, J ignored, 1580
economics, displaced for first time by theology, 1075
    industry, reconstruction necessary, 1092
    politics, J "no",1329
economy, doomed unless, 805
    of central universe, settled, 291
    spiritual, of the planet, 1196
ecstasy, associated with control, 1000
    emotional, J, 1000, 1807
    for God-knowing, 1985
EDEN, THE GARDEN OF, 821
Eden, the Garden of (see also "Garden of Eden")
    agriculture, no such a. before nor after, 825
    architectural plans for 1,000,000 people, 824
    brick buildings, 5000 plus, 824
    EDEN, THE FATE OF, 826
    4000 years after default, sank in ocean, 826
    if its culture had prevailed, 587
    industry and commerce, 586
    location of, 823
    moral law like Melchizedek commandments, 836
    people wished to worship Adam, 832
    second Garden, 847, 868-9, 875
    submerged, 826
    submergence of E a natural occurrence, 827
    teaching in schools of E included, 835
Eden, Gardens of
    named in honor of Edentia constellation capital, 583
    on most planets function age after age, 586
EDENIC REGIME, THE, 586
EDENIC TEACHINGS, THE (epochal revelation), 1007
EDENITES ENTER MESOPOTAMIA, THE, 847
EDENTIA, CITIZENSHIP ON, 495
Edentia, (constellation hdqtrs.) 100 times size of U, 485
EDENTIA FATHERS SINCE THE LUCIFER REBELLION,
    THE, 490
Edentia, hdqtrs. of constellation of Norlatiadek, 174
Edentia training worlds, 493
educated, the, crave knowledge of fellows, 1674
    know of lives and doings of others, 1674
EDUCATION, 806
education
    artificial, superficial, making problems, 941
    ascenders acme of e (on legislation), spheres (49),
        391
    College of High Ethics, Melchizedeks' home world,
        388   competitive on light and life worlds, 625
    divine plan, work and instruction, 412
    each generation must receive anew its e, 763
    Eden, 835
    failure of, 929
    harmonizing 2 opposite avenues of approach, 1135
    high, knowing and loving men, 1363
    higher any being's e, more respect he has for...
        others, 278
    how others live, 1674
    is business of living, 806
    is watchword of age following materialism, 577
    Jesus' real, 1363
    Melchizedek schools, 517

education (cont'd)
    methods of Eden, never surpassed, 850
    moral vs. religious, nearby planet, 811
    must be by philosophers and scientists, 806
    must change, 806
    Nebadon, 412, 417
    new systems of education grow up, 596
    normal planets, e on, 587, 835, 909
    not same as growth, 1094
    of J, 1363
    on neighboring planet, 812, 819
    Paradise, 303
    pupils become teachers, 812, 835
    purpose of, 192, 806, 2086
    purpose of all universe e, 43
    real educational growth indicated by... 1094
    rigid, stereotyped!, 1548
    schools of the morontia life, 551
    schools of the Planetary Prince, 586
    second garden, e methods never surpassed, 850
    secular e could help in spiritual renaissance, 2086
    sex and religion (Eden), 835
    should be, 1573
    students, teach immediately under J, 1658
    teach youth life planning, character progression, 2086
    work and instruction (divine plan), 412
    you are pupil-teacher all way to Havona, 279
education builders, the (morontia), 502
educational
    effort, home, center of, 931
    failure is an episode, 1780
    keynote, character acquired by enlightened
        experience, 412
    methods, must inspire intelligent patriotism, 910
    post, J offered, 1412
    spheres, surrounding hdqtrs. worlds of S U's, 278
EDUCATIONAL SYSTEM, THE, 812
educational system (Nebadon), 412
    worlds surrounding superuniverse capitals, 274
educators, true, Sethite priesthood, 850

ef

EFFECTIVENESS OF
    language, 908
    material resources, 908
    mechanical devices, 909
effort
    and decisions, vital to survival, 578
    good, of each man benefits all men, 138
    necessary for religious development, 1131
    no happiness without intelligent e, 556
efforts, material, spiritual counterparts, 1223
egg, 9x13 inches, 694
egotism, self-analysis as prevention of conceited e, 1583
    theologic, 1012
Egypt, blended colored race held forth in E, 871
    cult of Ishtar in E, called Isis, 1043
    each leader promoted his God as creator, 1044
    enriched for 30,000 years by Mesopotamians, 889
    the flight to, 1354
    great part in advancing monotheism, religion, 1048-9
    had Ikhnaton been greater... 1047
    Hebrews idea of judgment came from E, 1045
    indigo peoples overran E, wiped out green, 728
    in E (etc.) tribes assembled in cities, 879
    intellectual, moral, not overly spiritual, 1046
    Joseph's honor in E due primarily to grandfather,
        1023
    leaders taught morals before Salem teachings, 1045
    other peoples turned to mystery cult of E, 1081

Egypt (cont'd)
    overrun, inferior Arabs and blacks, 894
    political, moral tendencies favorable to Salem, 1044
    religion advanced compared with Europe, 891
    Salem missionaries had spread to E, 1042
    Salem missionaries penetrated to E, 1021
    Salem rather than E for Melchizedek because, 1018
    Salem teachings entered Europe through E, 1077
    slaves led out of E, based on Salem traditions, 1022
    the sojourn in, 1355
    son-in-law of Ikhnaton was Tutankhamen, 1048
    sought Sumerians as teachers, rulers, 876
    to Mexico, custom of blood on doorposts, 982
    transmitted revelatory religion...to Occident, 1049
    vast majority of Israel clans never in E, 1055
Egyptian
    army, first great victory, Asia, 1387
    bondage, thus began the real, 1074
    cult of Osiris and Isis, 1081
    many E administrators were Sumerians, 1044
    mystery cult (resurrected son), 1081
    nation, green man, 725
EGYPTIAN RELIGION, EARLY, 1043
Egyptian, ruler, sacrifices of, 978
Egyptians
    Amenemope wrote Psalm One of Hebrews, 1047
    believed twinkling stars represented soul's
        surviving, 1044
    burial statues improved E art, 1044
    calendar, 858
    came to believe in survival of animals, 1049
    early E believed soul and body stayed together, 953
    giant strains of green man mostly E, 725
    given to worship of nature gods, 1044
    great prophets, Amenemope, Okhban, Ikhnaton,
        Moses, 1046
    had ka and ba, 1215
    had triad gods, but not true trinities, 1143
    headquarters, most advanced culture, 894
    high concepts, 3000 years before Hebrew scriptures,
        1045
    immortality for all, too much for E, 1049
    long practiced brother-sister marriages, 918
    made human sacrifices, 980
    mainly from Mesopotamia, 894
    might have had J' "bestowal" if, 1047
    mystery religions taught death, resurrection, 1081
    only 4 great prophets in 6000 years, 1046
    origin of embalming, 1044
    preserved teachings of social obligation, 1043
    received medical knowledge from Sumerians, 992
    religion far above surrounding peoples', 1045
    Salemite physician of E, promoted Melchizedek
        teachings, 1047
    taboo on pork perpetuated by Hebraic, Islamic
        faiths, 975
    taught gentleness, moderation, discretion, 1045
    triad Justice-Truth-Righteousness, 1045
    wondrous early religion, 1047
    wrote Psalm that uses word "judgment", 1045
"Einstein formula" (?), 474, 478

el

El Elyon (God), 1015, -17, -85
    Melchizedek's Most High God, 1598
El Shaddai, Egyptian concept (God), 1053, -56, 1598
elders of Ephraim, made David king, 1073
elections, popular, right way, 802
elective bodies, Jerusem, from u school, 518
electric storms, disastrous, some planets, 563

ELECTRIC TYPES, THE (physical), 562
electrical and chemical reactions, predictable, 738
electricity, not basic energy, 456
    out of atmosphere, 543
electrified conducting regions in superstratosphere, 666
electro-chemical man, Urantian, 195, 1207-16
electro-chemical overcontrol, 1199
electrochemistry, the physical level of, 730
electron, has 10 modified forms, 476
    incredible speed, 462
    100 ultimatons constitute electron, 476
    spin, "opposite" to grosser matter, 667
electronic
    behavior, influences on, are five, 478
    boiling point, 35 million degrees plus pressures, 463
    energy particles, uncharged, 476
electrons, associations of ultimatons, 463
    energy stored as ultimatons aggregate, 475
    resist falling into nucleus, due to "no ether", 476
    ten modified forms of e, 476
ELEMENTAL TYPES, THE, 561
elementary course from pilgrim helpers, Havona, 291
elements, just 100 U, 477
    1000 on Havona, 154
    3, in universal reality, 2094
    200 on M W including 100 morontia material, 541
ELEMENTS, WORSHIP OF, 946
elephant and the horse, age of the, 697
elephants, 560, 778
    50 species at one time, only 2 survived, 697
    intelligence second only to man's, 697
    vs. mice, evolution, 560
Eleusinian mysteries of Olympic pantheon, 1079
Elihu, 1061
Elijah, 1513, 1753
ELIJAH AND ELISHA, 1064
Elijah, John Baptist was like, 1502
    our Father did speak through Moses, E...1731
    vigorous E denounced Ahab, 1074
    "why must E come first?", 1754
Elijah Mark (father of John Mark) died of brain
    hemmorhage, suddenly, 2051
Eliphaz, Bildad, Zophar--Job's friends, 1663
Elizabeth, and Zacharias rejoiced a son came, 1346
    avoided Bethlehem lest inform Herod, 1354
    childless mother of John, Baptist, 1345
ELIZABETH, GABRIEL APPEARS TO, 1345
Elizabeth, Mary foresaw visit with E, trip to
        Bethlehem, 1350
    Mary informed E of J' birth, 1351
    Mary visited by Gabriel, visited E, 1347
Elizabeth (of J' evangelistic corps) daughter of wealthy
        Jew of Tiberias, 1679
Ellanora, loyal young woman leader on Panoptia, 607
ellipse, swing of the great e, 125
elliptic symmetry of reality, 1137
Elman, Syrian, camp physician, (kingdom's hospital),
        1657-8, 1679
Elohim and Yahweh, 1856
Elohim, early Trinity concept, 1073, 1144, 1598, 1857

em

emancipation, mind, soul, 1773
embalming, origin, 1044
EMBARKING AT TARENTUM, 1470
embrace, transforming e of spiritual growth, 1002
embraced, 700,000 in same group (Mighty Messengers),
    245
EMBRYONIC STATE, THE, 800
emergence of individual, 2071

emergencies of human existence, God has foreseen all, 47

emergency regency of Urantia, Most High, 1201

emergency, 24 missions of universe e (Michael bestowal 1), 1310

EMERGENT ENERGIES, 470

emissaries, (foreign) never sent to race but by request, 749
   of same race as those being served, 749
   of social uplift, good plan, 749
   to needy tribes from Prince's staff, 750

Emmaus, two brothers, 2034

emotion, is not divine leading, 1766
   no essential part of religious experience, 1110
   not knowledge, activates man, 1090
   stirred in J, 1684

emotion designers, The, 506

emotional, activation of facts, 1090
   adjustment, lack of, 1740
   appeal, one of few J ever used, 1730
   casualties, 1773
   excitement not the ideal, 1777
   impassioned address, J, 1608-9
   instability, may come from, 1673

emotionalism, foolish outbreaks of rampant, 2062

emotionally upset, Simon, 2047
   Thomas, 2042

emotions, 1786
   alone, can't hold men together, 766
   appeal to e to arrest and focus attention, 1705
   appeals to e, 1705, -22, -30
   due to psychic climate, and environment, 1192
   earliest religions, due to, 718
   extraordinary, 1546
   human e lead to selfish material actions, 1121
   mighty, move minds, 2085
   not divine, 1766
   of love for neighbor, 1745
   origin of all art, games, contests, 766

Emperor worship, 1336, 1432

employment, means for directing people to e essential, 910
   oxen came slowly, threw men out of e, 909
   place-finding, 910

emptiness does have its virtue, for... 1281

en

enchanted age, time of J' bestowal, 1341

end, does not justify wrong way (means), 842
   foretold, J, 1531
   I will be with you to e, 1932-3 (see also under "JESUS QUOTES", also "I will be with you always")
   no such thing as, 1263
   of being, 1247

END OF JUDAS ISCARIOT, 1997

end, of the Kingdom of Judah, 1075
   of world: people will be saved, 582
   of world, when J returns, origin of idea, 1918

Endantum, 1315-6

endless quest, 1169

ENDOGAMY AND EXOGAMY, 918

ENDOR, AT, 1646

Endor, the witch of, 1646

endowment, of mind 3-fold, 192, 738
   spiritual, uniform, 63

endowments, constitutive, of man, 196
   of supermaterial world, 1228

enduring state is founded on... 806

enemies, "love your neighbors", J enlarged to... 1134

"enemies of Jesus" (see under "JESUS")

enemy, world is not an, 1579

energies, become mass, 1477

ENERGIES, EMERGENT, 470

energies, from Paradise like solar-energy to us, 1276
   harness your, 2076
   minds, spirits, 98
   near God, all 3 e, indistinguishable from him, 47
   of space, basic, divine rest essential to utilize, 506
   origins unknown to power directors, 169
   physical, 469
   physical, mindal, spiritual, 505
   redirect your e, 1738
   slowed down become mass, 1477
   superconductors, living, for over 15 e, 327
   thirty kinds of frandalanks for e, 328
   three are coordinate on Paradise, 140
   three basic, 30 subsidiary, 175, 321, 323, 327-8, 504
   three seem one near Him, 47
   (three) unification by personality, 136

energies, living, full bestowal to initial (red) race, 584

energies, spiritual, practices of believers to conserve e, 1777

energized, religionist is e by fellowship... sons of God, 1100
   we are e by urges from... mind, 1134

ENERGIZING TYPES, THE, 563

energy (is the basis of all existence, pure e is controlled by the U F), 467
   activities of unknown order, 154
   all converted to matter but for... 175
   all e and force seem encircuited, 123
   and enthusiasm, 1770

ENERGY AND PATTERN, 9

energy, and spirit are essentially one on Paradise, 104
   and spirit are one on absolute levels, 1275
   and spirit: God is source, 1182, 1275
   and spirit, suggestive of mutual kinship, 102
   assembly of e into minute spheres (ultimatons), 474
   augmenting, 1777
   available as light, 172
   can be slowed down to point of materialization, 101
   catalyzers, 471
   changes in physical e, endless, 472
   charge, 3-fold bathes all 7 super U's, 321
   circuits of living matter, 560
   circuits, 968 million years to complete circle, 175
   circuits, supply heat to arch. spheres, 174

ENERGY CONTROL AND REGULATION, 175

energy, control not complete, 1274
   control of e is a Deity prerogative, 1222
   currents for transport, 521
   decimal constitution of e, universal, 479
   direct e, control matter, to modify reality, 1222
   Dissociators, power of evolving limitless e, 328
   divine, 581
   divine, 3 original phases of, 505
   drop of water, e of 100 H P for 2 years, 463
   (Einstein's e equals mc^2), 474
   EMERGENT, 9
   eventuates from space-force, 468
   evolving e has substance, 175
   factors of pure e also present (in T A), 1182
   from space circuits, 172
   from space emanations (Adam and Eve), 834
   from spiritual communion, 1777
   God is e, 47; Father is e, 639
   giving out e, taking in e, 1777

energy (cont'd)
  governors who act as balance wheels, 322
  gravity, 470
  has substance, has weight, 175
ENERGY, HAVONA, 470
energy, indifferentiated vs. lane of e, 322
  is universally distributed, 169
  kinds, three, physical, mindal, spiritual, 504
  lanes of Grand Universe, 1276
  lines of e, 144,000 messages simultaneously, 431
  lines of 3 universally distributed, 433
  "living e has gone forth from me", 1698
  living organizations evolve limitless e, 328
  manifestations, 100 groups, 474
    64 recognized (or partially) on Urantia, 474
    succession of e particles are, 475
ENERGY MANIPULATORS, THE, 504
energy, manipulator of e Conjoint Actor, 101
  man manipulates, doesn't control, 1222
  material e of light transformed, 457
  matter dominated by Infinite Spirit, 236
  metamorphosis on cosmic stage, 1160
ENERGY--MIND AND MATTER, 467
energy, mind, and spirit (experiential synthesis), 1120
  mind, and spirit, Supreme Being, 1120
  mind circuits, 505
  misbehavior on Urantia, 458
  NETHER PARADISE, 122 (see also under "Paradise, nether")
  non-spirit e of Paradise, monota, 471
  not infinitely manifest, 468
  not in waves, 461,475   of rarest form, 464
  organization, unique, morontia, 541
  particles proceed in direct lines, 475
  pattern may configure, but not control, 10
  physical, almost endless changes, 472
  physical, one reality true to law, 139
  physical, steadfastly obedient to u law, 139
  plus vs. minus, 176
  pole, of the planet (Urantia), 438
  proceeds from Paradise, 468
  puissant e, 470,476
  pure e fashioned after...3 Gods...in one, 468
  reality, space potency to monota, 1149
  released to match control capacity, 1149
  responsiveness of e to mind action, 1275
  returns to Paradise, 468
  ripples, 860x diameters of units, 474
  secret of, 1777
  shields, while "passenger" enseraphimed, 438
  slowed down by Conjoint Creator, materializes, 101
ENERGY, SOURCES OF SOLAR, 463
energy, stream of e from sun, 460
  streams, modify course of, 2080
    like Gulf Stream, 321
  subject to mind, mind to spirit, 1292
  superconductors, living, 327
  system of 7 superuniverses, 30 phases, 470
  systems, spirit, morontia, 1216
  systems, thirty forms of physical, 175,265,321,323, 327-8,470,504
ENERGY SYSTEMS, UNIVERSAL NONSPIRITUAL, 469
energy, T A are, 1183
  three universally distributed lines of, 433
  transformers, 324,326
  transmitters, 325,327
  transmitters, living, 439
  transmutation, material metamorphosis, we study, 1138
  undiscovered on this planet, 47,325,461,467-72,-78, 469,667,902

energy (cont'd)
  unimaginable, invisible particles of matter, 172
  unique, 100 forms, Morontia Worlds, 541
  universally distributed, 169
  universe e, main streams of, 464
  unrevealed on Urantia, 851
  weight of e is relative, 175
  whence? combination of meditation, relaxation, mind contact with spirit, 1777
energy charge of the soul, 1776
energy cyclones of space, instigators of, 329
energy evolutions, vast, taking place, 263
energy-force, imperishable, indestructible, 468
energy lanes, permeate universes, to nourish and energize, 1276
energy manifestations, succession of energy particles, are, 475
  wavelike, ten groups, 474
energy mechanisms are living, 324,328-9
energy, nonspiritual, as yet unrecognized on U, 47
energy plant, tree of life, 756
energy potential unbelievably great, stellar gas clouds, 170
energy,spiritual, 505,1739,2065
  aids material achievement, 1405
  Jesus on, 1430
  Jesus to Anaxand, 1430
  Rodan on, 1777
  strength for weakness, 1777
  use for material achievement, 1405
energy wheel, 653
energy wheels, vast, 169
energy zones, in atoms, four, 478

Engedi colony, 1497,1817
England, Scotland, Wales--United Kingdom, 1490
English Coast, early Foxhall, 719
enjoyment, meaningless, 1097
  specialized techniques wanting, 942
enlightenment, scientific research, 992
"enmity between his seed and her seed", 844
enmity between Jews and Samaritans, why, 1612
Enoch, first mortal fused with T A, 514
Enoch (son of Cain and Remona) led Nodites, 849
Enoch, Book of (Bible) so-called
  inspiration to Jesus, 1390
  nearest the truth, 1390
  term, "son of Man" from, 1390
Enos, Adam's grandson, new order of worship, 850
Ensa, 212
  surrounded by 7 spheres, physical studies, 174
enseraphim, for transit to minor sector worlds, 535
  (for space travel), 535,582,1248
  like sleeping at night during travel, 430-1
  majority brought to U are in transit, 438
  planetary Adams for travel to new realm, 582
  to many worlds, finally enseconaphim, 1248
enseraphimed, transit sleep, sphere to sphere, 299
enslaved you by traditions, rulers (Jewish), 1906
enslavement to debt, through ambition, 780
enslavement vs. massacre, cannibalism, 779
entanglement, missionaries, reform instead of proclaiming truth, 1043
enter (see under "JESUS, QUOTES")
enterprise
  exquisite: home, children, culture, self-improvement, 781
  we are all part of a gigantic e, 364
enthralling epoch, moral quickening, ahead, 2082

enthusiasm, driving power of, 1773
    emancipation of mind and soul through e, 1773
    for Havona ascent, M. World #5, 537
    intelligent e, bordering on religious zeal, 1773
    may drive on into fanaticism, 1673
    Simon's, dangerous, 1524
    with e live up to responsibilities, privileges, 1770
entrapped, J never e by enemies, 1674
environment, guardian seraphim coordinates e, 1244
    handicaps of e are all overcome, 508
    manipulated continually by seraphim, 1245
    much religion helpless to change e, 1132
    no favorable e required for spiritual experience, 2064
    often mastered religion, 1132
    religion designed to change e, 1132
    religious man transcends his e, 2096
ENVIRONMENT, SPATIAL, 666
environment, too often has mastered religion, 1132
environmental
    ease, not good for progress, 1719
    effects, first few years, 1922
    stimuli, response to e s differentiated, physical,
        mental, 739
        spiritual response to e s differentiated, 739
envy, 963
Eocene period, 694

ep

EPHESUS--DISCOURSE ON THE SOUL, 1477
Ephesus, least fruitful for J' teachings, 1478
    Paul here 2 years, 1478
Ephraim, and Judah, 1798
    Israelitish, Jewish consciousness sources, 1071
EPICUREAN PHILOSOPHY, GENTILE, 1335
Epicureans, 1083
    dedicated to pursuit of happiness, 1335
    influenced Hellenized Jewish beliefs little, 1338
epilepsy, nervous malady, 1755
epileptic attack, youth, 1630
EPILEPTIC BOY, THE, 1755
epileptic boy, Apostle's failure, 1755
epileptics, and lunatics, once worshipped by the
        normal, 948
    often were priests or medicine men, 968, 986
epoch, of enthralling social readjustment ahead, 2082
    7th e of evolutionary stability, 628
EPOCHAL ANGELS, THE, 1255
epochal revelations, five, 1007
EPOCHAL SERMON, THE, 1709 (see also
    "Deuteronomy", "Jeremiah")
epochs, are born, live, and die, 365
    or phases of kingdom (5), 1862
EPOCHS, PLANETARY MORTAL, 589
epochs, seven developmental--average world, 576
    seven major religious, 1009

equal, in the spirit, yes; otherwise, no, 794, 1012
    men are not born, 774
    possibilities for spiritual progress, 63
    rights to all, no; fairness, yes, 794
    rights: weak, inferior, always contend for e r, 794
equality (see also "eugenics")
    as concept, never brings peace except, 1487
    mental and physical, no, 579, 792, 794, 906, 956, 1468
    no, on light and life worlds, 630
    of mind, Lucifer's wrong insistence, 604
    of opportunity, 906
    sex, 836

equality (cont'd)
    uniformity, not desired among finaliters, 579
    when concept fails, 1487
    would throw civilization back, 794
equilibrium (unbalanced) of energies and intellect, is
    called life, 1229
equity and justice, do prevail in universe, 373

er

ERA, THE LIFE-DAWN, 667
ERA, MAMMALIAN E ON URANTIA, 693
era, material-comfort e, 577
ERA, METEORIC, 658
era, of international harmony arriving (post-
        bestowal), 597
    of light and life ultimately, 577, 600, 621
    of planetary rehabilitation inaugurated, 757
    post-bestowal on normal worlds, vs. U, 595
eras on Urantia, start billion years ago, 672
eras, 10,000 to 100,000 years, 596
err in favor of the unfortunate, 1463
ERRONEOUS CONCEPTS OF ADJUSTER GUIDANCE,
    1207
error(s), animals, not birds, footprints, 686
    apostles stumbled into, 2059
    astronomy, 134
    Bible (see various entries under "Bible")
    bulk of David's army was non-Hebrew, 1073
    Christian, marriage not a sacrament, 927, 929
    communications, 760
    don't destroy, reform, 1076
    evil created by God?, 37, 56, 613, 1429
    evil, sin, iniquity, 765
    in finite choosing exists within evolving Supreme, 1300
    in heaven, 56, 760
    kingdom, instead of in men, is to appear, 1865
    men are equal, 794
    mischief-making e, chosen people delusion, 1005
    missionaries, 819
    not a universe quality, (a relativity), 1435
    of modern religions, negativism, 1572
    of reasoning from lower to higher, 215
    of religious leaders...reject all groups, 1076
    of teachers, supplant evolution by revolution, 1043
    Old Testament; how David became King, 1072
    Old Testament "revisers", 837, 1068, 1070-1
    on Urantia, 736, 1189
    penalty of imperfection, 1435
    rectification of, on evolutionary universes, 246
    seeing only in part, 159
    suggests, 755
    theology, 2059
    viewing matter as basic reality, 92
    viewing mind and spirit as rooted in matter, 92
    we can be cited for, 245

es

escape, can't run away, 1475
ESCAPE, TERRESTRIAL, 568
escapes narrow, man's ancestors, 705, 708
Esdraelon, plains of, 1752
Eskimos, 884
    Andonites color of present-day E, 713
    believe man has body, soul, name, 955
    believe soul stays 3 days with body, 959
    blends of Andonite and Sangik-blue, 905
    children are docile little animals, 941
    conceive everything in nature has a spirit, 954
    crime penalties decreed by wronged, 796

Eskimos (cont'd)

descendants of Andonites, 783

descended from Foxhall peoples of England, 719-20

early E seldom cannibalistic, 979

live largely by Golden Rule, 783

man has no surviving ancestry between frog and E, 732

mothers lick their babies to wash them, 940

only contact of red man before white after Asia, 723

reached No. America from Greenland, 728

sole survivors of Urantia aborigines (glacial), 700

ESSENCE OF RELIGION, THE, 1140

essence of true religion, 1950

Essenes, believed in reincarnation, expiating lives,1811

have all things in common, 1821

Jesus (Son of man) never E or Nazarite, 1535

true religious sect, 1534

essential, powers for good, how awaken latent, 1777-79

to(material success) worldly prosperity, 1779

essentials,of human existence, 764, 784, 931, 942

to spiritual work, Father's will, spiritual power, living faith, 1758

to statehood, 800

Esta, bride of James, (J' brother), 1418

et

ETERNAL AND DIVINE PURPOSE, THE, 364

eternal, estate vs. earthly state, 1649

inward plan, 63, 67, 85

ETERNAL ISLE, NATURE OF THE, 119

ETERNAL ISLE OF PARADISE, THE, 118

eternal journey, Urantia first step, 221

Eternal Mother Son, 235, 241

eternal not shown in time beginnings, 215

Eternal of Days, 155

eternal, real, the, 1123

Eternal, religionist acts as if in presence of the E, 1119-20

eternal life, can be rejected only by...1217

compatible with light-hearted, joyous living, 1206

early concept, 787

for all faith sons, 1963

gift of the Gods, 1204

independent of bestowals, 2002,-43

is, 1096

"I will give..." (J), 1963

passport to e life is...1174

progression in grace, truth, glory, 1953

to perfect man, 1953

what do to inherit?, 1809

Eternal Son, 1755 (second person of Trinity, 90; spirit bathes all creation, 78; bestows self upon all local universes through Michael Sons (J) and Avonal Sons, 1308)

ETERNAL SON, THE, 73 (see also "Son, Eternal")

ETERNAL SON, THE ADMINISTRATION OF THE, 83

Eternal Son, apostles believed J was E S, 1784

as spirit bathes all creation, 78

attained only through Infinite Spirite, 93

ETERNAL SON, ATTRIBUTES OF THE, 76

Eternal Son, beauty and grandeur of supernal personality, 79

bestowals of the, 87

bestowed self to attain Havona, 87

bestows Creator Son, 1308

bestows self in persons of Michael and Avonal Sons, 1308

confused with Michael on U, 74, 87

holds all "spirit" in his hand, 81

ETERNAL SON, IDENTITY OF THE, 73

Eternal Son (cont'd)

inspiration for all Sons, 87

in wisdom is full equal of Father, 76

is, 73-5, 88

is absolute personality

is actual upholder of vast spirit creation, 81

is coordinate with... T A presence of Father, 76

is eternal word of God, 227

is a grand and glorious personality, 80

is mercy, 94

is omnipotent in spiritual realm, 76

is omnipresent spiritually, 76

is Original Mother Son, 87

is parent of Universe Son whose presence is Spirit of Truth, 380

is Universal Mother, 79

is universal revealer, 98

Jesus had fulfilled requirements of E S, 1755

like Father, never surprised, 76

ETERNAL SON, LIMITATIONS OF THE, 77

Eternal Son

looks on all creatures as father and brother, 75

motivates the spirit level of cosmic reality, 76

ETERNAL SON, NATURE OF THE, 74

Eternal Son

not in ignoble task of persuading Father, 75

only avenue of approach to Universal Father, 93

Paul confused J with E S of Trinity, 1144

personal nature incapable of fragmentation, 86

ETERNAL SON, PERSONALITY OF THE, 79

Eternal Son, personality revelations of, 1271

ETERNAL SON, REALIZATION OF THE, 79

ETERNAL SON, RELATION OF THE E S TO THE UNIVERSE, 81

ETERNAL SON, THE SACRED WORLDS OF THE, 149

Eternal Son, seven bestowals, 87

spirit-gravity grasp of E S grand universe responds, 1276

spirit of E S is...with you and around you, 76

vs. Deity Absolute, 83

eternaliter nature, divine reality of an e n finaliter... 1271

ETERNALS OF DAYS, THE, 208

Eternals of Days (rulers of individual Havona worlds), 179, 202

each is divine equal of Ancients of Days, 208

eternity, explanation inadequate for e, 364

forward urge of e, 159

glimpse of e inspires man, 1776

historic concept of, 91

incomprehensible, 365, 1269

in e all is, 1262

is the everlasting now, 1295

of life, in a creation of love, law, unity and...1117

the one who inhabits e, 23

rugged achievement of, 1608

worship is time striking step with e, 1616

ether, absence of e prevents earth falling into sun, 476

hypothetical-group of force and energy activities, 475-6, 480

ethical, awakening on U, 597

awareness, defined, 300

consciousness necessary, 597

judgment and moral will, usually come with...590

obligations, innate, divine, universal, 616

ETHICAL PRAYING, 997

ETHICAL SENSITIZERS, 433

ethical, a society becomes e when, 577

ethics, and morals, to be truly human, 135

born, 956

highest, to love neighbor as self, 1862

E

63

ETHICS, INTERPRETERS OF, 300
ethics, J taught religion as cause, e result, 1862
   kingdom advances through <u>individual</u> believers, 1863
   of blood brotherhood, 941
   of might and right, only recently debated, 908
   a result of religion which is cause, 1862
   vs. religion, 1127, 1862
   was born, 956
etiquette, table, origin, 975
Etruscan priesthood, 1080

eu

eugenics and genetics (science of improving race and
   science of heredity)
   Adam and Eve originate violet race, 583
   Adam dismayed by defectives, degenerates, 839
   Adamic life plasm, upstepping of intellectual
      capacity, 593
   Adamic progeny never mate with inferior races, 593
   after Magesterial Son, further racial purification, 595
   biologic disfellowshipping of unfit... stocks, 585
   biologic renovation of racial stocks, 793
   brother-sister marriages, 918-9
   civilization, to flourish, antecedent racial pro-
      gression, 905
   civilizations extinguished by folly of no e and g, 719
   creativity augmented, diminished, 920
   drastic elimination of inferior, 627
   false sentiment protects defective strains, 592
   feeble-minded, parenthood denied to, 812
   finally the racial "white" of the spheres, 593
   5000 B.C. Adam's purest descendants in Sumeria, 896
   future depends on quality of racial factors, 899
   honor to be selected to mate with... 586
   hybridization secret of new, vigorous strains, 920
   idiot can't survive in warring tribal... 592
   inbreeding, consanguinous mating, 918
   India suffered, too many indigo race, 880
   indigo peoples, celestially equal, despite backward-
      ness, 725
   individuals, unfit, disenfranchised, 818
   inferior slaves deported, degenerates reduced, 813
   intelligence must supersede chance survival, 734
   interbreeding highest white, red, yellow good, 920
   limited race amalgamation ok, if... 920
   lower groups families limited, 630
   man must work out race improvement, 586
   Material Sons engraft higher creature life, 573
   mixture white and black, slight inferiority, 920
   Nodites deteriorated breeding with inferiors, 857
   not beneficial higher strains mate with lower, 586
   outmarriage and inmarriage, 918-9
   progeny of slaves deteriorated Cro-Magnons, 892
   race-improvement, task of Adamic progeny, 593
   races are purified, high state perfection, 592
   racial amalgamation <u>now</u>, detrimental, disastrous,
      726, 920
   real jeopardy is in bad strains, 921
   reasons for 3 or 6 colored races, 726
   religion needs fulcrum of sound mind, sound
      heredity, 793
   restriction on mentally defective and socially unfit,
      592
   7000 strains might have achieved humans, 734
   sex slaves polluted superior people, 776
   six races: 3 superior, red, yellow, blue; 3 races
      less endowed, 584
   subnormal man should be kept under control, 771
   survival of degenerates, defectives, due to mores, 794
   Urantia different world if... 836

eugenics (cont'd)
   volunteer adviser to purify, stabilize mortal race,
      627
   white race, blue men modified by... 725
   world helped, if lower mortal types curtailed, 592
eunuchs, modification of sacrifice, 983
Euphrates, 873-4, 889, 992, 1043
   gospel beyond, 1637, -57
   new truths, 1595
Eurasia, 878
Europe, 862, 878
   Andites driven to E by barbarians, 875-6
   Andites entered E by Caspian Sea route, 873
   Andites to E and to northern China, India, 873
   blue men scattered all over E, 869
   culture of Mesopotamia spread over E, 873
   early waves of Mesopotamian culture to E, 890
   great sex attraction between violet, blue races, 890
   modern languages derived from Asian migrants, 872
   more descendants of Adam & E than elsewhere, 871
   rapid spread of Christianity due to... 1456
   received stream of Andites, 7 major invasions, 892
   sovereignty in E, retrograde, 1489
   sudden climatic changes stopped violet men, 890
   worst cultural setback, 898
   year one, time of J', best era, 1333
European civilization, a blend of... 862, 891
EUROPEAN DARK AGES, THE, 2074

ev

evaluation demands transcendence of thing evaluated,
   1228
evaluator (personal) is child of Source of all values, 2094
evangelists, 1762
EVANGELISTS IN CHORAZIN, THE, 1726
evangelists, intimate association ends, 1741
   100 newly trained, 1666
   117 newly trained, 1668
   one-third deserted, 1715
   over 100 trained, 1658
   75 survived test, 1677
   that failed, 1677
   training at Bethsaida, 1657
EVANGELS OF LIGHT, THE, 349
EVANGELS, SERAPHIC, 552
EVE (see also "Adam and Eve")
   Adam's rib, legend of, 837
   bore Cain (father Cano, human), 843, 847
   bore 42 children by Adam after default, 834
   bore 63 children before the default, 834
   counselor, advisory, Urantia, 514
   fallen Prince tried wily attack on E, 840
   fell, first meeting with Cano, 842
   glorified E in worship of the "great mother", 895
   impatience of E brought disaster, 838
   knew chemistry and energy of nuts, fruits, 834
   mother cult, descendants of Cain, 895
   mother of violet race, 840
   no intention of betraying trust, 840
   plans laid for entrapping E, 840
   reveals her "short-cut" effort to Adam, 842
EVE, THE TEMPTATION OF, 841
Eve with Adam, 1647 pure-line descendants at default,
   834
EVENING AFTER, THE, 1634
EVENING AFTER THE CONSECRATION, THE, 1584
EVENING LESSONS, THE, 1683
EVENING OF THE ORDINATION, THE, 1576
Evening Stars, 1247 (representatives of Gabriel to all
   constellations, systems in Nebadon, 407)

Evening Stars (cont'd)
  all remained loyal to Michael, 607
  Ascendant, 407
EVENING STARS, THE BRILLIANT, 407
Evening Stars, Created, 407
Evening Stars, often are teachers in educational enter-
    prises, 517
  The Worlds of the, 408
EVENTFUL SUNDAY MORNING, THE, 1720
EVENTS LEADING UP TO THE CAPERNAUM CRISES,
  1698
EVENTS OF A SABBATH DAY, THE, 1532
events, 3 groups of e occur in life, 1830
eventuate, Transcendentalers simply, 350
eventuated children, 332
EVENTUATION OF TRANSCENDENTALS, 1159
"everlasting arms, underneath are the", 1057
everyone, do some one thing well, real life, 1779
Eveson, 834 (second son of Adam and Eve)
  became masterly leader, administrator, 849
evidence, basis of fairness, supplied by personalities
    of Spirit, 114
EVIDENCES OF RELIGION, THE, 1127

evil (unconscious transgression of Father's will, 1660)
  all things work together for good...616,1306
  almost every human has pet e, 1802
  and God, why, 1429
  and good, work for the God-knowing, 1306
  becomes sin when, 52   betrayal of trust, worst, 754
  black patches against white background, 2076
  capacity for, until spirit levels, 1458
  crystallized all of Judas' nature, 1567
  deliver us from e, 1622
  each mortal has pet e, 1802
  exalted into sin, 1429
  eye, phallic cult defense against, 962
  48 reasons for letting e run its course, 618
  futility of, 1580
  God cannot contain e, 1429
  God inclusive of all but e, and creature experience,
    1185
  "good intentioned people can do no e" (Cano), 842
  gravity-resisting, 647
  how to be cleansed of all, 1610
  how to subdue, 617-8, 1739, 2056
  inherent in this world, 1660
  iniquity, sin, error, are suicidal, 37
  is futile, 1580
  is measure of imperfectness, 1660
  is a partiality of creativity, 1220
  is a transgression of law, unintended, 1660
  Jesus not anxiously bothered by e in world, 1594
  Jesus on, 1429, 1660
  law, and rules, 555
  let us not stray into e bypaths, 1622
  men dwell upon, 2076
  mistaken judgment, 52
  need not be chosen, 1458
  nonexistent until creature mischooses, 1429
  non-resistance to e, to understand, 1950
  not created by God, 37, 613
  of church, 1864
  of national envy and racial jealousy, 597
  of rebellion resulted in good 1000 times greater...
    619   on glorified worlds also, 625
  overcome with good, don't submit, 1739, -70
  permitted, why, 615
  possibility of, necessary to moral choosing, 1458
  potential, creation characterized by goodness, 53

evil (cont'd)
  potential e inherent in incompleteness of revela-
    tion...1435
  potential e is time-existent in universe, 613
  potential e not a part of the divine nature, 36
  potential, why?, 613,1159
  proof of immaturity of self, 1435
  proof of innacuracies of mind, 1435
  reasons (48) for permitting e to run, 618
  refusal to compromise with, 1520
  sin, and good, 842
  sin, and iniquity, 1659-60
  subdue with love, faith, trust, 2056
  suggests deficiency of wisdom, 755
  tendencies, man has, 1660
  three ways of contending with and resisting, 1770
  to the truly good, e begets goodness, 1033
  willed by men, to exist, 1429
  world not fundamentally evil, 2093
evil and sin
  inevitable if creature to be truly free, 615
  origin, 1222
  technique for cure of plague of, 617-8
  why permitted, 615
evil one, "is the son of self-love" (J), 1660
  no, led astray by own tendencies, 1609
  planned to entrap Eve, 839
EVIL, SIN AND INIQUITY, 1659
evil, sin, rebellion--Gods neither create evil, nor
    permit, 613
evil (unclean) spirits (see also "unclean spirits"), 1735
  Amos believed self possessed by, 1696
  belief e s caused sickness, almost universal, 1659
  "come out of him, disobedient spirit", 1757
  "come out of him, you e s" (Simon), 1756
  demented lad, first case J cast out e s, 1713
  Elman tried to teach truth about, 1658
  epilepsy and e s (son of James of Safed), 1755
  epilepsy, not e s in young man, 1631
  "I have a son...possessed by an e s", 1757
  Jesus taught apostles to recognize e s, 1591
  Norana believed child possessed by e s, 1734
  people believed afflictions of fear due to e s, 1836
  people believed e s left Amos, entered swine, 1696
  young man taught he was possessed by, 1631

evolution

evolution (purposeful, not accidental, 401; progressing
    still throughout universe, 730,1159; never-ending
        cosmic drama, 1298)
  accelerate natural e, how to, 598
  achieves ends, 990
  ancients believed in, early Greeks clear idea of, 837
  angels act when vital link in jeopardy, 1246
  backward step in e, sea serpents, 688
  biologic principle of e, early man little self-
    restraint, 1302
  can't be artificially structured, 870
  chain of human e, links saved, 1246
  changes in plants, animals, fortuitous, 733
  changing course of e, social and otherwise, 1862
  changing idea of God, 1675
  chemistry and physics alone can't explain, 738
  climatic e changes man to farmer, 900
  comparative and advancing practical adjustment, 802
  connecting links higher animal types, no, 669
  continuing even now, 737
  cosmic e, purpose of, response to T A, 1229
  cosmic technique of growth (def.), 1097
  course of e changing, 1863
  dependent on mind ministry, 738

evolution (cont'd)
   domain of Life Carriers (phys. e), 738
   "don't interfere with" (to J), 1329
   earlier idea than "rib idea", 837
   earlier people believed in progressive creation, e, 837
   essential to economics, society, government, 804
   fact of animal e origin, no stigma, 361
   fear is necessary scaffolding for God concept, 990
   feeling, not thinking was guiding influence in e, 948
EVOLUTION, THE FOSTERING OF, 733
evolution, frogs gave rise to Reptilia, 732
   gibbons, apes (ancient) not related to man's lemur ancestors, 703
   God the Supreme is focalization of all finite e, 1304
   greatest single leap, reptile to bird, 732
   henceforth, follow growth of brain, 688
   human beings changed by Michael and associates, 1863
   human e can be delayed, not prevented, 734, 900
   human, is still in progress, 2097
   human, links of chain saved, 1246
   humans, first, 900 generations after dawn-mammals, 707
   intellectual, social, etc., dependent on mind ministry, 738
EVOLUTION IN TIME AND SPACE, 739
evolution, is purposeful, 401, 733; (150,000 proofs), 665
   land-man ratio, 768
   lemurs, Dawn mammals suddenly appeared, 700, 703-4
     established, then suddenly Primates, 700, 706-7
     human branch went forward, simians stationary, 700
     N.A., then Asiatic, dawn mammals, 700, 733
     Primates suddenly produced 2 humans, actual ancestors of mankind, 707-8
     same time, mid-mammal retrogression, simians, 700
     70 generations more, suddenly BIGGER (mid-mammals), 700, 704-5
   levels of, three, 730
   man and monkey, from same species, 706
   man appeared during ice age, no accident, 733
   man, from seaweed to lordship of earth, 731
   man upward, Adjuster downward, 1196
   man's ascent from seaweed to...731
   material inertia an effective brake, 1302
   Moses didn't attempt to go back of Adam's time, 837
   never-ending drama of cosmic e, 1298
   900 generations, dawn-mammals to humans, 707
   no organic e on Jerusem, 521
   not...accord with our present views, 560
   not perfection but practical adjustment, 802
EVOLUTION OF COMPETITION, THE, 805
EVOLUTION OF CULTURE, 769
EVOLUTION OF THE FETISH, 968
EVOLUTION OF THE GOD CONCEPT AMONG HEBREWS, 1062
EVOLUTION OF HUMAN GOVERNMENT, THE, 783
EVOLUTION OF HUMAN MIND, THE, 709
EVOLUTION OF HUMAN SACRIFICE, 980
EVOLUTION OF JUSTICE, 794
evolution of life, mechanical, mind activated, spirit directed, 1301
EVOLUTION OF LOCAL UNIVERSES, THE, 357
EVOLUTION OF MARRIAGE, THE, 913
evolution of mind, only through...738
EVOLUTION OF MORAL CONCEPTS, 1045
EVOLUTION OF THE MORES, 767
evolution of outerspace will be different, 1280

EVOLUTION OF PRAYER, THE, 994
EVOLUTION OF RELIGION, THE FURTHER, 1012
EVOLUTION OF RELIGION, THE LATER, 1003
EVOLUTION OF REPRESENTATIVE GOVERNMENT, 801
evolution, of society, greatest factor in e, 766
   of statehood, 806
   on high, 505
EVOLUTION, THE OVERCONTROL OF, 730
evolution, paper 72 to augment governmental e, 820
   physical vs. mind, 738
   plant or animal, no intervention, 733
   present culture result of strenuous, 912
   primates, 21,000 years after dawn-mammals, 707
   progressing still throughout universe, 730, 1159
   purposeful, not accidental, 401
   race e continues despite physical planet destruction, 582
   representative government, 10 stages in e of, 802
   revelational e, technique of progress, 2094
   reversion of bacteria, Adamic default, caused disease, 736
   scientific intelligence must take over, shape destiny, 734
   sequence, lifeless material to will creature, 379
   seven developmental stages civilization, 577
   7000 strains could have developed humans, 734
   slow, but effective, 749, 900, 957, 990
   spiritual and material, changes in, 1863
   spiritual: defined, 1460
   still actively in progress, Urantia, 737
   still progressing throughout...1159
   subject to sudden periodic changes, 1863
   superb attainments of mortal races justified e, 631
   tends to make God manlike, 1122
   3 distinct levels of life production and e, 730
   under perfect control, 46
   unlike we believe, 560
   unpredictable but non-accidental, 559
   vs. revelation, 66, 750, 1122
   we'll come to understand "strange doings", 590
   well defined directions everywhere, 576
   why purposeful, 401, 733
evolution, intellectual, Urantia in twilignt zone of, 973
evolution, not accidental
   adjutant mind spirits in planned advance, 709
   appearance of primitive man, ice age, by design, 733
   best strain lost, others available, 734
   ended inferior groups, appeared accidental, 733
   50,000 facts incompatible with laws of chance, 665
   integrated functioning (of...) conditions course of e, 730
   mortal men not evolutionary accident, 560
   never haphazard, nor experimental in accidental sense, 735
   processes...under perfect control, 46
   7 adjutants explain why e is purposeful, 401
   3 levels of life production and e, 730
   the universe not inevitable, not an accident, 52
"evolution of dominance", personality is characterized by a cosmic quality, 1229
evolution, organic
   a.m.s. partly condition the course of o e, 401, 730
   cell healing formula from over 100,000 phases and features, 735
   course of o e conditioned by 3 groups, 730
   how limited, 1301
   is not a cosmic accident, 735
evolution, progressive
   history of human race is one of p e, 846
   sudden changes, 1863

evolution vs. sudden transformation, 749, 758
    biologic safety brake against ruinous change, 767
    difficult, sudden revelation, 1011-2
    error of teachers to attempt too much, 1043
evolutionary
    all mortal-inhabited worlds are e in origin, nature, 559
    attainment, 7 stages of, 402
    beings can attain perfected wisdom, 180
    course dangerous on apostate planet (U), 581
    course, man can modify, 909
    Deity, 1296
    growth, source of, 1280
EVOLUTIONARY IDEA, THE, 360
evolutionary inevitabilities, 51
EVOLUTIONARY MIND LEVELS, 738
EVOLUTIONARY NATURE OF RELIGION, THE, 1003
EVOLUTIONARY PANORAMA, THE, 731
evolutionary plan summarized, 1302
EVOLUTIONARY RACES OF COLOR, THE, 718
EVOLUTIONARY RACES, THE SIX, 584
evolutionary religion, anthropomorphism highest, 67
EVOLUTIONARY RELIGION, THE NATURE OF, 1005
EVOLUTIONARY SERAPHIM, 443
EVOLUTIONARY TECHNIQUES OF LIFE, 737
EVOLUTIONARY WILL CREATURES, 564
evolutionary, worlds, normal, high destiny, 537, 599
evolutionary development
    feeling, not thinking, guiding influence, 948
evolutionary mortals, 162
evolutionary progression, Spirit begins the work of e, 379
evolutionary scheme, wisdom of e s shown by advanced worlds, 631
evolutionary will creatures, lowest level of (we are), 239
evolutionist, J was a progressive e, 1671-2
evolve, Creators do in local U, 1272, -91, -96
EVOLVING MORONTIA MINDS, 481
EVOLVING PRAYER, 995
EVOLVING SOUL, THE, 1218
evolving universe of relative perfection, 846

ex

exalt the individual, 1862
examination, self e vs. self control, 1609
example, J' e not for every life, 1425, 1585
    Jesus life not e for mortals, 1328
exchange profits at temple, enormous, 1889
excitement, does not augment energy, 1777
    is not ideal spiritual stimulus, 1777
    man wants e and adventure, 769
excommunication, among Jews, terrible penalties attached, 1814
    believers in J subject to e, 1814
    for eating with unclean hands, 1713
    or for commerce with harlot, 1713
EXCURSION AND REVERSION SUPERVISORS, 546
excursions to Paradise, 293
"excuse, (Sanhedrinists) no e for attitude", 1947
execution, cessation of existence, 37 (see "existence")
executive abodes of the Master Spirits, 150
EXECUTIVE-ADMINISTRATIVE SQUARES, THE, 527
executive, chief, of Nebadon, Gabriel, 406-7
EXECUTIVE, GABRIEL, THE CHIEF (see "Gabriel")
executive of Urantia, new every 100 years, 1252
EXECUTIVES, THE SEVEN SUPREME, 198
exhaustion from self-importance, 555
exhaustion of endowment of T A, only in eternity, 1212
exhibit areas, peripheral Paradise, 121
exhibit panorama, Jerusem, 525

existence, cessation of, 37 (see also "annihilation" and "extinction")
    creature e, the mechanism of, 483
    human e purpose of, 1174
EXISTENCE, THE JOY OF, 312
existence, new, of joy, power, glory, 2059
    science no "whence, why, whither", 1641
existential Deity, experiential Deity, 10
EXISTENTIAL INFINITE UNIFICATION, 1173
existential, Trinity vs. triunities, 1147
    unity of source of reality, 1120
EXORCISM AND COERCION, 963
experience
    all beings in sphere of Supreme must advance through e, 1195
    an e is good when... 1458
    apostles gained valuable e, though results poor, 1611
    cements together blocks in constructing wisdom, 1222
    civilization arrives when culture learns by e, 577
    doesn't yield insight, 2094
    every e is limited except the e of God, 1289
    fact of e is found in self-consciousness plus... 1123
    four steps in e of forgiveness, 1862
    God is the greatest experience in human existence, 1289
    God the Supreme is personalization of all universe e, 1304
    has no substitute, 1195, 1956
    human, what is, 1123
    importance of, 1956
    it is the e of living this life that is important, 435
    Jesus looked the man of great e in this world, 1582
    know God through e, 1453, 1856, -62, 1985
    mankind designed to evolve by technique of e, 1174
    most thrilling human, 1729
    no divine endowment can substitute for e of living, 1195
    no substitute for religious, 1728
    no worthwhile e ever happens in vain, 1200
    of any age is antechamber of more cosmic growth, 1294
    of God-consciousness remains same, 69
    of God is capacity enlarging, 1289
    of living, more important than learning, 435
    only approach to the Supreme, 1289
    on nonexistential levels, nothing is substitute for, 1185
    religion concerned with insideness of e, 1135
    religious; the tests for genuineness, 1000
    rewards of spiritual content of e, 1142
    spiritual connotation for one, not another, 451
    strange, of mysticism, inspiration, 1000
    subjective except for, 195
    sublime, 1203
    supernal, 1731-2
    supreme, 1431, -65, 1732, -37
    total, 1287
    training, universe difficulties, 1719
    unremembered, validating, 451
    when good, 1458
    with religions develops capacity for... wisdom, 1101
    without growth, 1280
experience, fruits
    Michaels have exhausted potentials of, 367
experiential attainment
    bravery, altruism, hope, faith, etc., 52
experiential (subjective) time units, 1295
experiential university, work our way through ascending levels of, 279
experiment, 34
experimental life worlds, inspected by Tabamantia, 565

experimental planet
  every 10th world is a decimal planet, 447,664
  Life Carriers devised wound healing from half
    million experiments, 735
  numerous modifications of...life patterns, 734
  outstanding episodes, two, 735
  28 features new here, useful forever in all Nebadon,
    735
  Urantia assigned to us as a life e p, 734
  Urantia is a decimal (life-experiment) world, 398
experts of communication, local universe, 505
exploitation, J against e of weak, 1803
Explorers of Undirected Assignment, 259
explosion, extraordinary double star--reached U
  1572 A.D., 458
explosions, gravity-tidal e common, 657
expression
  gift of e plus ability, recognition comes, 508
  some of e absent unless, 507
  spontaneity of e in believers, 1120
extermination of inferiors, Badonans, 720
extinction (see also "annihilation" and "cessation of
    existence"), 367
  Ancients of Days alone can decree e of intelligent
    life, 210,396
  can be decided only on superuniverse hdqtrs., 372
  final judgment on e, 3 A D participate, 210
  is cessation of creature existence, 569
  of social body, 764
  only through agencies of S U government, 372
  sentence of e confirmed, being becomes "not", 37
  sentences involving e, hdqtrs. of superuniverse, 180
  sin-identified unspiritual being, eventual e, 41
  traitors "become as though they had not been", 611
extinction, whole races
  obliterated in long, dark, bloody chapter, 589
  obliteration of peoples (orange, green), 591
  orange exterminated by red, sometimes, 585
  orange, green, indigo usually, 584
exudate, metals near surface, 668

ey

eye, for an eye, 1577,-80,1770
  "has not seen, nor ear heard", 121,269,1960
  of faith discerns spiritual values, 2078
  of spirit only will see J, 1915
  reacts to 1 octave of (100) wavelike energy activity,
    474-5
eyes, "of the Lord over the righteous", 95
  of the mind not open (J), 1466
Ezekiel, proclaimed deliverance through...1071
  taught religion reality in personal experience, 1630
  "their mouths make a show of love", 1822
  wiser than his contemporaries, 1076
Ezra, follower of John Baptist
  rejects J, 1526
  vs. Nathaniel, 1526
Ezra (Jewish tavernkeeper)
  backslidden, won by J, 1440
  built first Christian church in Syracuse, 1440

F

fabrics, morontia, mind is cosmic loom that carries...
  1217
face, Infinite shows us, is of Father of love, 1153
faces, spiritual ugliness of f of worshippers, 1378
fact, and value are unified in the Supreme, 1477
  and value have causation in Paradise Father,1477
  circle of cold f, 555

fact (cont'd)
  idea, relation (elements in reality), 2094
    reality, physical,-intellectual,-spiritual, 2094
    reason, wisdom, faith (philosophy), 2094
    science, philosophy, truth (religion says), 2094
    thing, meaning, value (celestial), 2094
  may be right as to fact, wrong in truth, 555
  meaning, value, 1299
FACT OF EXPERIENCE, THE, 1123
fact, of God vs. presence of God, 1733
FACT OF RELIGION, THE, 1105
fact, of risen Master vs. J' gospel, 2059
  unyielding, truth flexible, 549
  vs. truth, 549
    distorts, 1615,-41
fact, supernal, lowly human beings are sons of God,448
FACTORS IN SOCIAL PROGRESSION, 764
factors, of material success, 1779
  12, Urantia civilization based on, 906
factory freed woman from confines of the house, 937
facts, adjust to ideals, 1779
  and intellect, truth and being, 1641
  apparent, not always true, 2023
  don't quarrel with real faith, 2078
  individual f vs. group f, 2023
  of birth, not remedied by legislation, philanthropy,
    957
  of historic record, altered in Babylon, 1071
  right f but may be wrong as to truth, 555
  substituted for gospel, 2059
  values and reality, 1110
  vs. truth, 549,555,1615,-41,2023
  vs. value, 1471
factual knowledge, emotions, 1090
faculty, insight is f of human personality, 1105
faculty on...conservation of knowledge, 746
Fad, formulated first alphabet, 746
fail, and falter, why so many, 1199
  in progress, never, 1601
  learn to fail gracefully, 1779-80
  life a burden, unless can f gracefully, 1779
  rise indomitably to try anew, 555
  when things earthly f you shall be...1854
  you cannot f of high destiny if...64
failed "to use faith at your command", 1758
fails,when one mortal ascender f, 284
failure, a cultural experiment, 1780
  do not fear, "this is the way", 383
  an educational episode, 1780
  here, success in eternity, 1780
  in Deity adventure, 284,289
  is educational episode, may be success, 1780
  meaning of f, the, 1727,-78
  not many pilgrims experience seeming f, 294
  of Melchizedek teachings in Arabia, 1050
  on second attempt, never, 294
  overwhelming f in life may be great success, 1780
  to achieve survival, 444
  to Adjuster-fuse, not due to errors, 452
  to attain God, 284,294
  to find Deity, 294
  to heal, the Apostles' f, why, 1758
  to survive, 1199
  to win world, 1670
failures in life, apparent, 1727
Fair Havens, J and assault on girl, 1436
fair, "in appealing to men, be f", 1765
  treatment sought for races by H. Commissioners,411
fairness, civilization demands, 936
  eternal justice, divine mercy, are f, 38
fairy stories, Oriental minds delight in f s, 1352

faith

acceptance by f of merciful forgiveness, 1838
-activated soul, reaches goal of destiny, 1459
"an addition of power", 1766
admission to kingdom only by child's faith, 1536
"-adventure of establishment of kingdom", 1750
affirms religious experience, 1109
all within grasp of immediate living, 1766
Alpheus twins never lost their heart f in J, 1564
and abiding by Father's will, 1569,-83, 1829,-31
FAITH AND BELIEF, 1114
faith, and confidence in healing, 1659
   and doubt, commingled words of, 1757
   and doubt, struggle, 1664
   "and graces, sustain you", 2048
   and love, basis of beatitudes, 1575
   and love, J' new and better way to God, 1543
   and reason, unaided by mota, illogical universe, 1137
   and spiritual transformation, 1119
   and trust (among 6 virtues taught 70), 1805
   and trust, only price to pay for divine favor, 1017,
      1027,-43,-55 (see also "kingdom, price to
        enter")
FAITH AND TRUTH, 1459
faith, "...are you deficient in living f?", 1704
   as well as feeling, 1099
   assurance of absolute personal security, 2089
FAITH, ASSURANCES OF, 1118
faith, assures partaking of divine nature, 1609
   attitudes, four, (in Sermon), 1573
   "at your command, the f", 1758

b bank of f will be paying out... 2076
baptism, many Jews, not forsaking Jewish f, 2060
be righteous by f first, then do, 1584
believers died for f, gave Christianity power, 2073
bestowal of spiritual gifts limited by f", 1831
Bethany had believed in him, 1880
better science destroy superstition than f, 2078
birth of the spirit into the light of f, 1705
blind man had was slight, 1813
bowed woman believed, straightened by f, 1836
Brahman priests would not accept idea (salvation by
   f), 1028
bridges gap between It and He, 2093
brings about love of one's fellows, 1438
brings certainty, 1124
Buddhism allowed freedom, 1041
business of finding God, f only necessary, 1559
by f are you advanced, 1682
by f are you saved, justified, advanced, admitted to
   kingdom, 1536-37,-45,-69,-83-84,-86,-93,-96,
      1610,-56,-67,-82-83,1745,-66,1826,-28-29,
        1861, 2053 (see also "kingdom, nice to
         enter")
"by f become everlasting sons of God", 2054
"by f become God-conscious, reborn", 2052
by f enter kingdom now, 1861
by f every mortal may have... salvation, 1586
by f, gift of eternal life (but first "born" again), 2053
"by f in my word, fact becomes living", 2052
by f recognize indwelling spirit, 1682
by f a righteousness exceeding... slavish works (J),
   1861
by f was Abraham justified, 1682
"by f you are then born of the spirit", 2052
"by f you have become a kingdom son", 2049
"by this act she (Mary) evinces f", 1879
certainty best to deal with contention, 1126
FAITH, CERTAINTY OF RELIGIOUS, 1124

faith, (cont'd)
   -certainty, technique for dealing with non-
      believers, 1126
   change of mind by f, the new birth, 1545
   childlike but not childish, 2089
   "children of Abraham not minded to show", 1735
   children's f simple, parents should preserve, 1574
   Christian f combined with, 1083-84
   combine f with action, 1211
   comrades of J, 2084
   confidence in justice and goodness, 1580
   -contemplation, antidote for fear, 1616
   courage born of f, 1103
   courage, hope, altruism, loyalty, etc., 51
   cry of the righteous is f act of child of God, 1639
d desirable?, 51
   darkness dispelled by stretch of f, 1118
   "daughter, your f has made you whole", 1694
   decisions augmented by f, 1111
   Deity kinship must be f realized, 1289
   delivers from evils of inaction, 1438
   demoralized by panic of dread, anxiety, 1243
   destroyed every conflicting desire, 2088
   divine favor through faith, 1017,-27,-43,-55
   do not see how man can live without this f, 1453
   does f triumph over evil, sin, iniquity?, 2063
   does 6 things for knowers of divine presence, 1766
   doesn't influence ordained material laws, 1145
   -dominated persons, healing, 1658
   down through ages, f has saved the sons of men, 1683
   ecclesiasticism incompatible with living f, 2084
   effective armor against sin, iniquity, 619
   encouragement helped cure sick, 1658
   enough to lay hold of kingdom, 1603
   ensures partaking of divine nature, 1609
   enters upon limitless journey, 1141
   entrance to kingdom for any child with f, 1828
   -entrance to kingdom, 2 essentials, 1861
   expands soul's receptivity, 1621
   expectant f keeps hope-door of soul open, 2083
   "experience of the possession of living f", 1758
f fanaticism can lead to f, 2088
   far above conflicts (Faith Sons), 383
   "far better you had seen...by f", 1960
   Father responds to faintest flicker of f, 1733
   faith first, then understanding, then comprehension,
      291
   fosters and maintains man's soul, 1460
FOUNDATIONS OF RELIGIOUS FAITH, 1118
faith, gains entrance, works make progress, 1569,-83
   "gentiles able to exercise saving f", 1735
   genuine spiritual f revealed in that it:, 1108
   -gift assures eternal salvation, 1593
   gift of God, 1537
   God-knowing only by faith, 1124
   grasp of ideal values, 1091
   "-grasp the saving truth essential", 2053
   grasps fact you are sons of God, 1656
   great things happened due to f in J, 1875
   grow in grace by f, 1656
   grows out of spiritual awareness, 1138
h "has made you whole", 1828
   have f in God, in one another, 2040
   "have f in God to end of your days", 2049
   have it to yourself, 1091
   -healing, 1669,-98
   healing blind man not miracle response to f, 1812
   helped healing, 1669
   helps Adjuster, 1205-06
   how born in human heart, 1118
   humor and f of Norana touched Master"s heart, 1736

faith (cont'd)

"I do this in honor of... living f", 1757
"I have f your master can cast out demon... ", 1734
"I have not found so great f", 1648
"I know the f of your soul", 1834
ideals cannot rise higher than f, 1459
if hope to progress quickly, safely, 221
"if you are f sons, you shall never die", 2053
if you have the f to be healed, 1665
immune to disappointment, 1102
in early Buddhism, 1035
in early Taoism, 1032
in fellow man, 1574
in spittle, blind man had, 1813
in supreme values is core of religion, 1219
in time of sickness, 991
initiates man into divinity, spiritual, 1141
is... 1139
is an addition of power, 1766
is gift of God, 1610
is gift of God, price of entrance to kingdom, 1537
   (see "kingdom, price to enter")
is God-knowing and man-serving, 1114
is the insight technique of religion, 1136
is inspiration of creative imagination, 1459
is insurance, 1609
is the method of religion, 1106
is predicated on profound reflection, sincere self-
   criticism, uncompromising moral consciousness,
   1459
is the open door, 1545
is reasonable, encouraged by logic, 1137
is recognizing spiritual consciousness, 1139
is religion, 1104
is to religion what sails are to a ship, 1766
Israelites unwilling in f, 1059

j Jesus began to have f in loyalty and integrity of, 1747
Jesus enjoyed sublime, whole-hearted f, 2087
Jesus' f perfect, not presumptuous, 1102
Jesus' f-trust so great, he was devoid of fear, 2089
Jesus heard leper's words of clinging f, 1643
Jesus inspired f of the sick and suffering, 1659
John's f was strengthened by words of J, 1627
the just shall live by f, 1682
key to the door of the kingdom, 1861
"kingdom believers should possess implicit f", 1739
kingdom, to enter by f, 1861
"kingdom's doors open to all who have f", 1826
laid hold upon creative power in Master's person, 1698
last grand stretch of f, 299
leads to knowing God, 1142
leads to realization of reality of life, 1141
leads to spiritual insight, 1574
"let f reveal your light to the world", 2043
liberty of f, 1565
liberty of those conscious of sonship, 1104
liberty, sublime, magnificent, 1104
life eternal for all "who accept it by f", 2053
little f, better than great intellect, 1653
living growth, 1097
logical from inner viewpoint, 1138
"Lord I believe, I pray you help my unbelief", 1757
loyalty to J transcended f in teachings, 1612
maintains man's soul, 1460
makes one secure for the kingdom, 1656
"man can by f raise his spiritual nature", 1738
man can't possess truth without f, 1459
man is a f-son of God of love, 1460
Martha shared f but was fearful, 1845
Mary, Martha, had f in survival of believers, 1844
Master could discern f in superstition, 1875

faith (cont'd)

may appear to be quite unfounded, to science, 1138
measure of spiritual capacity of soul is f, 1740
message from J stabilized John's f, 1507
mountains of material difficulty, f will remove, 1619
must be lived, 1091
must be very near the truth of things, 1453
must dominate mode of living, 1114
must have f for prayer, 1002
"my Father will respond to faintest flicker of f", 1733

n necessary to gain truth, 1459
new birth through change of mind by f, 1545
new following, better grounded in spiritual f, 1718
newborn f smothered by church, 2085
Nicodemus acknowledged his f, claimed body, 1603
Nicodemus summoned f to gain kingdom, 1603
no influence on material laws, 1145
no kingdom admission but through child's faith, 1536
Norana, Syrian woman, f of, 1734
not creedal formulation of mortal agreement, 1091
not fasting, 1656
not predicated on reason, but is reasonable, 1137
"not receive who have not fought fight of f", 1829
"not so great in Israel", 1648
nothing atones for lack of f, 1838
"O woman, great is your f", 1735
"O you of little f", 1823
"O you of little f, wherefore did you doubt?", 1703

FAITH OF JESUS, THE, 2087
faith, of J provided for, 1112
of mortal men and women, strong and living, 1700
of those who pray, 999
often dominated by fear, 1243
one in me who can and will, 59
one struggle for kingdom, fight good fight of f, 1766
only cost of divine favor, ancient Salem, 1027
only escape from material world, 1116
only f sustains man amid problems, 1222
"only have f Martha, and (Lazarus) shall rise", 1843
only passport to eternal life, 1117
the only qualification, 1567, -86, 1796
(only requisite-price-for eternal life, salvation;
   see "kingdom, price to enter")
only through f, discover God, life eternal, 1116
opportunity for exercise of, 578
out of spiritual awareness, 1138
overcome inaction by power presence of living f, 1438
"pass from a racial f inherited", 1731

p "pass to a personal f achieved by experience", 1731
personal, beliefs may be groups, 1114
personality development predicated on f, 1266
Peter finished his declaration of f, 2050
Pharisee made public confession of his f, 1835
Pharisee spies confessed f, 1667
"possess, by f, gift of eternal life", 2053
powerful church... dared smother f, 2085
pray believing, according to f, 1620
pray with f, f will remove mountains, 1619
prevails over all, 2063
promotes spiritual vitality, righteous fruitfulness,
   1727
proof of religion, 1106
prospers religion, 1105
prostituted by smug fortunate, 1268
pure and living f had wrought the cure, 1699
"question not Father's power, but reach of your f",
   1757
"-realization... you are a son of God", 1916
-realize we are children of the Most High, 1578
reason, and logic, 1106
reason, knowledge, wisdom, 1119

faith (cont'd)

    reason, wisdom, f, highest attainments, 1141

    relation to God, 1091

    releases superhuman activities of divine spark, 1459

    religion finds values which call forth f, 2075

    religion of J a new gospel of f, 2063

    religion of spirit, participation in f, 1729

    religion validated by f, 1130

    religion without f, a contradiction, 1141

    revealed in that it: (12 things), 1108

    reveals God in soul, 1106

    reveals soul of men, 1108   rewards of faith, 1776

    right to enter kingdom, conditioned by f, 1583

    robust f of full grown man required, 1118

s salvation by f (see also "faith, salvation by" under "JESUS, QUOTES")

    Asian multitudes craved promise of, 1040

    attainment of sbf alone, 1593

    forgotten largely by time of Semite enslavement, 1055

    from Ur there was preached sbf, 1060

    Gautama came to belief in sbf, 1035

    Gautama's son grasped idea, but wavered, 1036

    gift...insures admission to kingdom, 1593

    Jesus taught (sbf) price of admission, 1545

    man gets divine inheritance by asking, 1113

    Melchizedek, news of, 1020-21

    Melchizedek warned followers to teach, 1043

    Melchizedek's gospel of sbf, 1027

    men seek, when kingdom within grasp of f, 1766

    mortals are sons of God, factual through, 2003

    passport to completion of reality, 1116-17

    Salem religion, divine favor sbf, 1017,-28,-32

    throughout universes, not dependent on bestowals, 2002

    Urantian agreement, God does everything for belief, 1020

  "salvation a free gift to those who have f", 1838

  secret of self-mastery, 1610

  securely held him (J), 2087

  "see not with eye of f", 1588

  selfish desire supersedes f, 1758

  seven stages of f in J' bestowal, 2091

  shall dominate body, mind, spirit, 1733

  Simon, Pharisee, "betwixt f and doubts", 1652

  sincere, don't fear judgment of God, 1476

  some of the rewards of f, 1117

  sons, mortals until fusion, 447-8

FAITH SONS OF GOD, THE, 447

faith, "sons shall never die", 2053

  "sonship with God, by f, is saving truth", 2052

  "spiritual destiny is dependent on f", 1739

  spiritual insight, 1574

  spiritual unity is the fruit of f, 2085

  stands for individual's relation to God, 1091

  straightened bowed woman, 1836

  struggling humanity, gospel of f for, 2063

  subdue evils by f, love, trust, 2056

  supplements logic and reason, 1125

  surely instructed only by revelation, 1137

  surety of survival, f is, 1516

  surmounted deterrents by f, 1126

  survival matter of personal experience, f in, 1641

t "take kingdom by assaults of living f", 1726, 1829

  test of f, invisible Planetary Prince, 575

  test of John's f in God, 1507

  tested prior to Havona, 290

  "...that you may have full f in the gospel", 1704

  third revival of the Apostles' f, 1753

  Thomas, you lack f, 1542

  "through f experience ennobling truth", 2052

faith (cont'd)

  through f in God, forgiveness of sin, 1545

  through J man foretastes, 1113

  through two essentials, 1861

  "to f-son of God, all work of realm sacred", 2049

  to father: "fear not, only believe", 1699

  to J, Judas was a f adventure, 1566

  to kingdom, like sails to ship, 1766

  "tranquility, patience, with f will sustain", 2048

  transcended by loyalty to J, 1612

  transformations of grace wrought by f, 1686

  translates experience into religion, 1123

  transmutes potentials to actuals, 1211

  treasures in kingdom in reach of, 1766

  triumph over doubt, assert full-fledged f, 1708

  triumph over wrong, 1580

  true f is predicated on...1459

  trust required for kingdom entrance, f for progress, 1118

  trust required of all creatures, 1326

  two basic reasons for, 1106

  unconquerable, 291

  unites moral insight, 1105

  Urantian agreement, God and Abraham, 1020-21

v validated by revelation, 1106

  vs. action, 1211

  vs. beliefs, 1205

  vs. fear slavery, 1104

  vs. theological arrogance, 1002

  victory of f over doubt, 1729

  victory that overcomes...even your f, 1601

  view from God's viewpoint, 1117

  "when great work is finished in f", 1960

  when you have f, make known...2043

  "where is your f? Peace, be quiet.", 1695

  will expand the mind, ennoble the soul, 1766

  willingness to trust, 1127

  wisdom, and experience, 1080

  "woman, great is your f", 1735

  "works of f come not at bidding of doubt, unbelief, " 1757

  you are justified by f, 1610

  "you failed to exercise the f at your command", 1758

  "you have eternal life through f", 2043

  "...your f has made you whole" (leper), 1828

  "your f shall dominate...body, mind, spirit", 1733

  your f shall save you, 1667

  "your f that saves your souls", 2053

  your soulship is grounded in f, 1610

Faithful of Days, 603

faithfulness, rewards for, 1876-77

FAITHFULS OF DAYS, 179, 207, 213

"faithless and sign-seeking generation seeks", 1714

fall, as lightning from heaven, 609

  of Jerusalem, 1075

fall of man (there has been no fom, 846; see also "original sin")

  Adam and Eve default was not fom, 845

  confused...man's degenerating to deplorable state", 1660

  fraternal creation of humans, led to theory of fom, 836

FALL OF MAN, THE SO-CALLED, 845

fall of man, tradition of Adam and Eve led to belief man fell to sorry plight, 975

fallacious teaching, environment, 956

fallacy, human inequalities due to social injustice, 956

fallible, all things human, 1768

F

false, Gods vs. things of beauty, 1600
FALSE LIBERTY AND TRUE, 613
false, "prophets", 1571
    religion or science must pass away, 1457
    theology, true religion, 1140-1
falsehood, premeditated perversion of truth, 555
falseness, in shadow of hairs turning, 555
fame widespread, J, 1668
families, all gain or lose by any member's acts, 619
    large f desired pre-affectional times, 940
    many together again on high, 532
family, all high and low, constitute Fathers, Sons, 79
    as the master civilizer, 913
    center of J' philosophy, 1581
    change from mother-f to father-f, good, 933
    church or state responsibility for f, suicidal, 941
    civilization's only hope of survival, 943
Family Commission of Twelve, 3 nominee families for
    J' parents, 1344
family, council idea, good, 941
    deserted J practically (except Ruth), 1546
    divine f of all individuals, 138
    does not survive death, 1581
    each f of Material Sons and Daughters... 515
    Eskimo children docile animals, 941
    first human, 711
    first obligation of J', 1390
    greatest purely human achievement of man, 939, 943
    importance of,
        can't run counter to Father's will, 1581
        cultural torch, home is basic to passing on, 909
        man's greatest purely human achievement, 939
        most effective of all social groups, the f, 1775
        most with lasting value has roots in f, 765
        pleasures, self-gratification, suicidal if bring
            decadence to f, 943
    insubordination in f due to protection, 941
    Jesus never again lived with his f, 1485
    large ancient f not affectional, but needed, 940
    learning arena for ethics, 941
FAMILY, THE LESSON ON THE, 1603
FAMILY LIFE AND MARRIAGE, 931
family, loyalty, most sacred trust, 1403
    marriage insures race survival, 765
    master civilizer, 913
    most effective social group, 1775
    no supernal favors for J' f, 1718-19
    of God, we are all a part of, 48
    of J felt disgraced, 1721
    of living beings, divine, 7 grand divisions, 334
    organization, transcendant pattern for, 369
    pleasures suicidal if destroy home, 943
    sex gratification, 765, 939, 942
    shift of parental responsibility... suicidal, 941
    source of most lasting values, 765
    this kingdom is a divine f, 1676
    true f founded on seven facts, 1604
FAMILY UNDER FATHER DOMINANCE, THE, 933
family, without religion multiplies difficulties, 1089
family crests, (coat of arms) origin of, 781
family life, characteristics of, 1603
    "I do not hesitate... to glorify f life", 1776
    religion, unifier of, 1089
    social achievement of prince's epoch, 591
    world of f life, stabilization of maturity, 1777
    worth any price, any sacrifice, 1776
family of Jesus,
    five members sought to interrupt solemn meeting,
        1720-21
    Jesus had little to say to group, 1484
    kept from J by pride, hurt feelings, 1587

family of Jesus (cont'd)
    received no supernatural help, 1718-19
    Ruth chief comfort of J as regards f, 1628
    Ruth refused to help f dissuade him, 1721
    start of ever-widening gulf between J and f, 1538
family relationship, better explains J' religion than
    does kingdom of heaven, 1603
famine, periodically terrible toll, 746
"famish in presence of bread of life", 1766
fanatical woman, Beth-Marion, 1666
fanaticism, convulsion of (due to T A), 1207
    disastrous threats of, 1778
    spiritual revelation may cause f, 1207
    (transient religious hysteria), 1705
fandors, 831 (see also "birds, passenger")
Fantad, 724
FAREWELL DISCOURSE, THE, 1944
FAREWELL PERSONAL ADMONITIONS (J), 1955
farewell to Abner, 1870
FAREWELL TO THE SEVENTY, 1804
farmer, victim of drought, flood, hail, pests, etc., 951
fashion unduly dominates U, 749
fast, forty days, "no", 1514, -17
fasting, 976, 1605, -56
    appropriate to law of Moses, not kingdom, 1655
    dangerous, 1574
    Jesus, day or two at a time, 1493, 1514
    not part of the gospel, 1655
    vs. believing, 1609
fatalists and materialists, 1954
fate, and chance befall them all (men), 951
    cruelty of perverse f may be means to character, 1305
FATE OF EDEN, THE, 826
fate, snares the good and the bad, 951
FATHER AND HIS KINGDOM, THE, 1855
father, -child cornerstone of gospel, 1776
FATHER-FUSED MORTALS, 448
FATHER GUIDES, THE, 294
father, human, indivisible, yet reproduces, 31
    knew everything (J thought), 1359
    loves child naturally, but child... 1676
    measure of,1471
FATHER MELCHIZEDEK, THE, 384
father, -mother concept, and childbirth, 933
    -mother concept, beginning of, 370
    (of earth) great responsibility, 1923
    of his people, 789
    significance of, 1923
Father, is the final value, the, 1781
FATHER, THE UNIVERSAL (see "God", "God, the
    Father")
Father, Universal and Mother, Universal, 1288
FATHER-WORLD RELATIONSHIPS, 147
fatherhood, "implies brotherhood", 2053
    of God, associated with truth of brotherhood, 2053
        makes imperative practice of brotherhood, 1769
    paradox, 138
FATHERLY AND BROTHERLY LOVE, 1573
fatherly love, 4 reactions of, 1573
    throughout J' teaching, 1573
fatherly vs. brotherly love, 1573
fathers, are not like judges, 1604
    tremendous responsibility on earthly f, 1923
    wise f do not punish in anger, 2017
FATHER'S BUSINESS, THE, 1659
Father's way, the, 1515
FATHER'S WILL, THE, 1971
fatlings are killed, all is in readiness, 1835
favor, divine, through faith, 1017, -27, -43, -55
favorite prayer, J', 1774

F

feelings, human, new group of, suddenly appeared, 708
feelings, strong, can't talk person out of, 1610
feelings, "that lie too deep for words", 1091
feet, washing apostles', 1938
  washing, a parable performed, 1939
fellowship, enjoyment of universe, 68
  new, brother and sister, 2067
  of believers vs. brothers, 2067
  of living as well as worship, 2067
  personal, interactions nonpersonal, 31
  with Deity, eternal goal, 1228
female, male: always, 939
females, some planets and epochs, rule males, 591
fern family, 679, 692
fern-forest carboniferous period, 682
ferns and frogs, coal age, 682
fertility, believed dependent on sex with stranger, 1043
FETISH, EVOLUTION OF THE, 968
fetish, guarded early goods for trade, 775
FETISHES, BELIEF IN, 967
FETISHES, CHARMS, AND MAGIC, 967
fetters, of life mechanism, 1302
  of materialism, 231
  of moving present, 1295   of time, 1300
feud, Abner and James, church, 1831
  between Jerusalem, Philadelphia, 1831

fi

fiat creation of race, belief perpetuated, 838
fickleness of popular acclaim, 1705, -08
fiction, David's build-up of divine kingdom, 1073
fidelity, cardinal virtue to J, 1582
"fields white for the harvest", 1615
FIFTH BESTOWAL, 1314
FIFTH DECISION, THE, 1521
FIFTH MANSION WORLD, THE, 537
fig tree, 1915   parable, 1830
fight, country folk against cities, 1065
  "I must f, but" (Rodan), 1778
fighting, early man enjoyed, 783
figs from thistles, 1571
filth test, for wife's fidelity, Bible, 795
FINAL ADMONITIONS AND WARNINGS, 1953
FINAL INSTRUCTIONS, 1538
finaliter, immortal and divine character of a f, 1284
  transcendation, technique of experience, 1286
FINALITER WORLD, THE, 509
  surrounded by receiving worlds, 509
finaliters (see also "Corps of the Finality", and "Mortal
    C of F") 249, -98, 309, -46, -52, 379, 632, -35, -43,
    1137, 1296
  as f we domicile on P, 148
  ascending mortals become f on P, 148
  called "foreign potentates" by Lucifer, 603
  children of the Supreme, 1239
  corps, and Havona natives, 221
  function in ever-increasing capacities, 628
  grand and glorious career as f, 452
  high destiny of... administrators, 216
  know eternal fusion as absolute reality, 147
  Salvington worlds of the f, 401
  we begin endless careers as f after... 298-99
  who sustain the "supreme disappointment", 250
FINALITERS' WORLD, THE, 530
finality, awful limitations of unqualified f, 29
Finality, Corps of (see "Corps of Finality")
FINALITY OF DESTINY, 1168
FINANCIAL STRUGGLE, THE, 1392
fingernails, cuttings from chief's long f a fetish, 968
finite, absonite, and absolute attitude, 113
  absonite, Ultimate, 12

finite (cont'd)
  can't comprehend Infinite, except, 1856
  exists because God so willed, 1260
FINITE FUNCTIONALS, PRIMARY ASSOCIATION OF,
    1163
FINITE GOD, THE, 1283
FINITE INTEGRATION, SECONDARY SUPREME, 1164
FINITE REALITY, PROMULGATION OF, 1158
FINITE REALITY, REPERCUSSIONS OF, 1159
finite, transcendence, 1290
  universe, finites, 468, 1260
finites, incomplete and maximum, 1162
Finns, 945
fire, and water, early fetishes, 967
  Andon conceived idea of building fire, 712
  basic human discovery, 777
  building f separated man from animal, 777
  call down f from heaven (James, John), 1553, -55, 1955
  consumes bodies, 622-3
  cremation, to prevent ghost trouble, 964
  destroyed Hebron synagogue after Sanhedrin defied,
    1718
  doesn't destroy translation temples, 622
  first educator, 777
  first f kept going for 3 days, enjoyment, 712
  first method of making f at will, 713
FIRE IN RELATION TO CIVILIZATION, 777
fire, led to metal work, steam power, electricity, 778
  made primitive society possible, 777
  mankind has worshipped f, 946
  mixed in primitive minds with magic, 947
  sin to put out, 777
  symbol of pure, wise Spirit (Zoroaster), 1049
FIRE, THE TAMING OF, 901
fire, worship of f still survives, 967
fire, animals, slaves, property (first 4 great advances,
    civilization), 901
fire worshipper, Teherma, 1592
firebrand from family hearth, 777
fireproof buildings, neighboring planet, 815
firewood, first search for on earth, 712
first, bestowal, the, 1309
  deliberate miracle, 1644
  4 civilization advances, 901
First Cause, and also a host of coordinate...causes, 1298
  an Initial Mind (Anaxagoras), 1079
  material mind demands a FC, 91-2
  of science and religion's God are one, 1106
First Father is... 23
FIRST HUMAN BEINGS, THE, 707
FIRST ISAIAH, THE, 1066
first life, this is our f life of many (see "Urantia, life,
    this is our first")
FIRST MANSION WORLD, THE, 532
FIRST OF THE HEBREW PROPHETS--SAMUEL, 1062
FIRST OR PLANETARY STAGE, 631
FIRST PREACHING TOUR OF GALILEE, 1637
FIRST SHAMANS--THE MEDICINE MEN, 986
FIRST SOURCE AND CENTER, THE, 4 (see also "God"
    and "God, the Father"), 111
First Source and Center, 22 (is Universal Father, God
    of all creation, creator, controller, upholder, 21)
  all causes are derivatives of this FSC, 1299
  exercises cosmic overcontrol of physical level, 24
  he is law, 114
  infinite, eternal, limited only by volition, 5
  infinitely complex, 1153
  is universal spirit, eternal truth, infinite reality and
    father personality, 23
  primal cause of materialization and Father of all
    spirits, 481

force control and energy regulation, by 3 groups
of living beings, 319
force charge of pervaded space, is matter for making
untold universes, 139
force, energy, power, 125
force energy transmutations, 133
force–focal headquarters, 184
force organizers, two vast orders of, 352
FORCE ORGANIZERS, ASSOCIATE TRANSCENDENTAL
MASTER, 329
FORCE ORGANIZERS, MASTER, 329
Force Organizers, Primary Eventuated Master, 329
FORCES, LIVING, 403
foreknowledge, God's, 49, 1300
Jesus', 1787
of volitional beings who elect... 1300
foreordained, trend of the cosmos, 1300
foresight, and integrity, 1854
Van's planning for promised Son, 822
foreskins, Saul required 100 f as dowry for Michal, 785
forests, man deteriorates in, 718
FOREWORD, a definitive guide, 1
forgive, "as I have forgiven you", 2047
easy for God, 38, 60
failure to f is immaturity, 1898
"them, they know not what they do", 2007
to f is Godlike, 1898
forgiven, sins are f, if you confess, 1736
forgiveness, accept through faith, 1838
automatic, but, 1630, 1861
better man understands neighbor, easier is f, 38
by Deity is renewal of loyalty relations, 985
conditioned by, 1638
FORGIVENESS, DIVINE, 1898
forgiveness, divine f is inevitable, 1898
divine, human synchrony, 1638
idea of f appeared early in religion, 976
if sins confessed, 1736; J'f implies rehabilitation, 2018
mediator not required to gain f, 41
merciful, through faith, 1838
none for blasphemy, 1714
not condonation, 2018
FORGIVENESS OF SIN, 984
forgiveness, operates unerringly, 1638
parable of king and stewards, 1763
reception of is an experience, 1862
renewal of loyalty relations, 985
sermon on, 1762
sin of eternally rejecting, 1714
technique of receiving God's f, 1861-2
through confession, 1736
through faith, 1682
through faith without penance or sacrifice, 1545
through forgiving, 1638, 1764, 1861-2, 2017-18
form fits spirit, 493, 542, 570, 1236
"form of the yet unformed"--the Almighty Supreme, 1288
formalities of your Havona arrival, 343
formalization of religion destroys, 1089
Formosa, Andites to, 873
forms: precise, "no", 1942
formulas of righteousness, Divine Spirit must breathe
upon, 380
"forsake father, mother, etc.", 1869
Fortune (youth), became Crete leader (J), 1438
fortune tellers, still patronized by the credulous, 988
FORTY DAYS, THE, 1512
FORTY DAYS, BAPTISM AND THE, 1509
FORTY DAYS OF PREACHING, 1505
forward, must go f from where (you) find selves, 2084
struggle, at every crossroad in, 383
fossilized truth, 555, 719-20

fossils,
approach transition types, man and prehuman, where,
720
beautiful ammonites, f all over world, 686
dinosaurs (locations of buried), 687
few of reptilian age, footprints however, 685
few plant f of 310 million years ago, 675
Florissant f beds of Colorado, 35 million years, 695
footprints of dinosaurs mistaken for birds, 686
Morrison beds of Colorado, fresh-water f, 687
of 35 million years ago, dogs, cats, coons... 695
oldest Carboniferous deposits, land and marine f, 681
oldest rocks containing trilobite f, location, 673
Proterozoic f, algae, coral-like plants... 670
records of 50 million year era, 693
rich f beds along coast of California, 679
small plant f missing, destroyed by bacteria, 679
that approach "missing link" in Siwalik Hills, 720
foster homes and parents, Dalamatia, 750
FOSTERING OF EVOLUTION, THE, 733
foundation, of enduring civilization, true religion, 1013
spiritual, for achievements behalf of human race, 820
foundations, gospel vs. Christianity, 2091
FOUNDATIONS OF RELIGIOUS FAITH, THE, 1118
four stages of J' life, 1749
four tones of human melody, for Ganid, 1465
fourteen aspects of personality, 1225
FOURTH BESTOWAL, THE, 1313
FOURTH MANSION WORLD, 536
FOURTH OR LOCAL UNIVERSE STAGE, THE, 634
FOXHALL PEOPLES, THE, 719
ancestors of Eskimos, 719-20

fr

fragment of Father (see also "Thought Adjuster",
Indwelling Spirit", "Mystery Monitor")
Adjusters are fragmentations of God, 1181
are known as divine gifts, 1184
dwells within human mind, a fragment of God, 17
evolves spirit soul upon mortal mind, 333
Father distributes himself to his creatures, 363
fathom what it means? f of F?, 1181
God as a person, fragments, 333
God's f would be both pure energy, pure spirit, 1182
in common with Gravity Messengers, 347
individuate portions of Infinite Spirit, 1178
mind indwelt by f possesses divine potential, 70
mysterious communion with f of F, 139
non-adjuster type, 1249
qualified absolute f of F, 1180
resides within intellect of every... mortal, 62
spirit of Son fraternizes with f of F, 1942
spiritualized personality (f of F) in creature, 141
subject to man's will, 1221
there lives within (man) fragment of infinity, 50
through presence of his fragmentized spirit, 24
whether or not indwelt by F f, 46
within each mortal... a fragment of God, 26
fragment of God, 1232
indwells, 195, 1487
fragment of living God, 62, 64-65, 78, 1487
fragmented entities of Deity, 330
fragmentized entities (T A), 1177-8
fragments, indwelling f of God, 46
of God, 1189-90
of the totality of Father's Deity, 76
fragrant, morally, 193; socially, 1089
frame in which to think, 1260
France, Somme, 715

frandalanks, are living machines, 328
    automatic in reaction, but intelligent, 327
    indicators, estimators of time required, 315
    register power pressure and energy charge, 324
    ten f on Edentia, 456
    30 kinds for basic universe forces, 328
Frandalanks, The, 324, 327
FRANDALANKS, THE, 328
FRANDALANKS AND CHRONOLDEKS, 325
fraternalism, Jew and gentile, changes necessary for, 911
fraternity with seraphim, ideal, 419
fraud, and trickery, priests, kings, chiefs, fetish men, etc., 968
    Jacob insistent resurrection a f, 2034
    trickery, shamans, 987
free, "I refer to the liberties of the soul", 1796
    if man is to be f he must be fallible, 52
    set men f to start fresh, 1583
free love, never in standing above rank savagery, 915
free society, to maintain, 798
free thinking, but not "free thinkers", 1135
free-willness, divine, 42
free-willness proved by, 616
freewill, angels do not manipulate will, 1245-6
    being, decisions unpredictable in fb, 136
    choice, but not for detriment, 552
    God never abrogates f of his children, 49
    involved in 7 things; moral decision, etc., 194
    man endowed with f, relatively final, 1300
    man in spiritual domain does have, 1134
    man must be fallible if he is to be free, 52
    mind planners on mansion worlds respect your, 553
    no universe personality can abridge f, 1246
    nothing in universe does violence to f, 1299
    only in creature realms, deviation from divine paths, 139
    participation in long struggle, 614
    personality, two phenomena; self-consciousness and f, 194
    personality volition, (f) not predictable, 155
    supreme in man, no one compels, 753
    where the spirit of Lord is there is freedom, 1135
freewills, spiritual
    God refuses to coerce or compel, 22
freedom, absolute for one, slavery for another, 1490
    and initiative, the "Father's will", 2078
    gift of civilization, 1490
    harmful unless, 802
    ideal of society, 780
    is always relative, 1490
    lost to religion of mind, 1729, -31
    none without enforcement of law, 1490
    of initiative proportional to, 2078
    prematurely taught, 759
    proportional to spirit influence, 2078
    relative nature of, 1490
    through capital and invention, 777
    to insure, must prevent, 798
    to maintain f, prevent these (12), 798
    when does more harm than good, 802
    "where the spirit of the Lord is, there is f", 1135
freedom of choice (see also "choice, free")
    approximately divine, when, 1301
freedom of speech, attempt to suppress fos led to secret writing, 1074
freedom of speech suppressed, 1074
freedoms, restraints, 1302
"freely have you received, freely give", 1801
freeze to Death, Cro-Magnon sentinels, 892
fresh beginning for all men, 1582

"Freudian ethic", religions of pessimistic despair, 2063
friction-shield (atmosphere), 660
    for transport, 438
frictions and reconciliations, 312
"friend of publicans and sinners", 1851
friendliness, characterizes spirit-born sons, 1951
    spontaneous, sincere, 1951
friendly universe,
    "entire universe is friendly to me", 1470
    filled to overflowing with assurance of fu, 1950
    "real things of world and u on your side", 1437
    real u is friendly to every child of God, 1477
friends, after death, 534, 1235
    Jesus called the Apostles f, 1745
    seeing, 343, 532, 534
    those who know God, 1431
    to make, 1438-9
    with God, 28, 1534, 1615, 1766
friendship, crowning glory of f stimulates imagination, 1776
    early man touching, crude, idea of, 714
    enhances joys, 1776
    impulse of f transcends...duty, 1945
    noblest of memories, 1779
    vs. duty, 1945
    what is essential to f, 30
    with forces of righteousness, 1854
friendship-loyalty, extraordinary human emotion, 1546
    supreme sentiment of f-loyalty held apostles, 1546
"frighten men into kingdom, don't", 1765-6
"frightened by new discovery", 1731
fringe of conflict, spirit vs. flesh, 1766
FROGS, AGE OF, 680, 685
frog(s), and Eskimos, 732-3
    into pre-reptile, 732; Africa, 683
    only species ancestor, 732-4, 695
    our ancestor f saved by 2 inches, 705
from him who has not, shall be taken away...1199
fruit, you bear much, 1945
fruits, "by their f you shall know them", 1572
    of divine spirit are, 381, 2054, -62
    of the spirit, 2062 (see also "spirit, fruits of")
    of the spirit, to bear abundant, 1602

fu

full summation of human life, 2094
fun on high, when in recess, 549
function, not person, determines providential intervention, 1305
    of Paradise, 139
FUNCTION OF PRIMITIVE RELIGION, THE, 956
functional Deity, 7-fold, 11, 1030
functions of mind, soul, spirit, closely united, 1142
FUNCTIONS OF PROVIDENCE, 1304
FUNCTIONS OF THE SUPREME SPIRITS, 205
FUNCTIONS OF THE TRINITY, 113
fundamentalism, 1768
funds, revenue, great falling off of, collapse of popularity, 1748
funeral service, origin, 959
funerals, occasions of joy, satisfaction, hope, 623
fungi, renegade, plants that lost chlorophyll-making ability, 732
FURTHER EVOLUTION OF RELIGION, THE, 1012
fuse divine Creator nature with creature, 1271
fused mortals, restrictions on, 452
FUSION, ADJUSTER, 1237
fusion, delayed, 1237
    during life consumes the body, 1212
    endowments, 1237

fusion (cont'd)
fire consumes body, 622
flash translates mortals, 624
flashes in atmosphere, worlds like ours, 622
fragment of Mother Spirit in f with some souls, 410
on earth, mortal disappears in "chariots of fire", 1212
Paradise Corps exceptions, due to f, 452
perfect on M W #5 or 6, 538
safe after, 1237-8
Spirit f vs. T A f, 717
twenty-five morontia shrines, 622
usually in mortal's local system, 1237
future, can be changed by...creativity of inner self,1221
confidence in human race, 736
energy circuits in subjugation to mind, 1292
growth, adventure, 263
holds enthralling spectacles (for us), 131
FUTURE OF THE SUPREME, THE, 1291
future, overplanning for f defeats own purpose, 1779
possibilities for disharmony, maladjustment, exhausted, 1292
spirit will have achieved dominance of mind, 1292
vastly different from present, 1293
future life, will use ideas, 734

G

Gabriel, 42, 634, 1309, 2022-23 (Bright and Morning Star, from union of Creator Son (Christ Michael) and Mother Spirit, one in each local universe, chief executive of universe of Nebadon, and of superuniverse rulers, commander in chief of the celestial hosts, 369-70)
accompanied Michael, 5th bestowal, 1314
advisory council (planetary) execs for G, 513
and angel hosts moved to "spiritual pole" of U, 2024
and celestial hosts, anxious expectancy at J' tomb, 2020
and chief rulers of universe, on U, or...2001
and J informed, J can now ascend, 1513
announcement to Mary day after conception, 1347
appealed for destruction of rebels, 609-11
appeared to Elizabeth at noon, June,8 B.C., 1345
appeared to Mary, Nov.,8 B.C., 1346
appeared to pronounce judgment on Adam and Eve,845
GABRIEL APPEARS TO ELIZABETH, 1345
Gabriel, appoints 24 one-time Urantians, manage planet, 1251
assigned Melchizedek to restatement, J' life, 1323
called J before birth, "a deliverer", 1345
GABRIEL--THE CHIEF EXECUTIVE, 369
Gabriel, chief executive of Nebadon, 370-1
chose Hebrews for Christ's birth, 1344
chose Joseph and Mary from 3 nominated families, 1344
commissions Most Highs for one dekamillenium, 390
commissions Most Highs to constellations, 390, 488
conference with, 1513
even G comprehends not method of bestowals, 1315
"final bestowal of Michael will be mortal flesh", 1316
he "shall become a great light in the world", 1347
"his life shall be the light of mankind", 1347
hosts hovered under G and T A, Gethsemane, 1969
in charge of celestial forces, 1312
informed J his sovereignty was earned, 1513
is Bright and Morning Star, 429
Jesus and Melchizedek, long conference with G, 1753
Jesus appeared beside--just above tomb, 2021
"let the dead of a U dispensation arise", 2024
local universe chief executive, 370, 407

Gabriel (cont'd)
Lucifer's first outspoken disloyalty, to, 602
Mary steadied by memory of appearance of, 1349
may deputize Melchizedek in G' name, 386
Michael, prebestowal conference with G, 1324
mistaken for Elijah by apostles, 1753
New Zealand tribe claimed concessions from G, 1005
only G excells Lanonandeks as executives, 393
presence on U necessary, J' resurrection, 2024
present at disloyal session (conclave), 604-5
rebellion, G volunteered to represent Michael, 756
received orders for special resurrection, 853
recorded first instance U resurrection...1846
regent of our universe, 371
remained on U with morontia J, 2025
renewed communication with Michael, 1513
said: "he will reveal...they are children of God",1347
seal of G on "Michael Memorial", Satania, 2015
Son of Man entrusted to G for safekeeping, 1330
supreme council of universe, on U under G, 2016
universe administration with Immanuel (elder brother of Christ Michael and his Paradise counselor), 1324
vast concourse of celestial beings under G, Lazarus' tomb, 1845
vs. Lucifer, 610-11,-16
voice of G decreed second judgment roll call, 830
worked quite alone with Michael...406
Zachariah believed of G' visit when...1345
GABRIEL'S ANNOUNCEMENT TO MARY, 1346
Gadiah, Philistine interpreter, 1428
gain, no g through impatient short cuts, 846
gain motive, was mighty civilizer, 787
gains in enlargement of living, from, 2082
Gaius met J, became supporter of Paul, 1473
Galantia, associate of Gavalia (head of superangels), 407
galaxies, clockwise, counterclockwise flow of g, 125
swinging around Paradise, 125
galaxy of saints, a spiritual menace, 2074
"Galilean, we are confounded by this G", 1882
GALILEE, APPEARANCES IN, 2045
Galilee, climate in, 1367
cost to live, 1/4 of Jerusalem, 1369
GALILEE, FIRST PREACHING TOUR OF, 1637
GALILEE, FLEEING THROUGH NORTHERN, 1725
Galilee, "glad to see you...in carefree G", 2046
last message to G, except north part, 1678
GALILEE, LEAVING, 1587
Galilee, more beautiful and prosperous district than Judea, 1369
more gentile than Jewish, 1334
GALILEE, TARRYING TIME IN, 1524
Galilee, 230 towns, 1369
"we will go into G", 1525
gall on sword of death, 1845
Gamala, 1675
Gamaliel, 1392, 2068
leading rabbi, wise counsel, "let them alone", 2067
gamble of existence, primitive man, 950
gambler, man was natural, 773
gambling, 950, 972
game, sacred and superb g of the ages, 1205
Ganid, 1422 (see also "Gonod and Ganid")
four tones of human melody, 1465
influential man, spread noble truths, 1481
Ganid's religion, 1453
gap between material, spiritual worlds, bridged, 425
GARDEN OF EDEN, THE, 821 (see also "Eden")
GARDEN OF EDEN, ADAM AND EVE LEAVE, 844
Garden of Eden, civilization was overthrown, 838
culture of G spread, produced our civilization, 877

Garden of Eden (cont'd)
GARDEN, ESTABLISHING THE, 823
GARDEN HOME, THE, 824
inhabitants destroyed Cano's Nodite settlement, 843
GARDEN, LIFE IN THE, 835
GARDEN, PLANNING FOR, 822
GARDEN, THE SECOND, 847
GARDEN SITE, THE, 823
site chosen for E, most beautiful in world, 823
three projected sites, 823
GARDEN, THE VOICES OF THE, 437
garden of your heart, water the, 554
GARDENS OF GOD, THE (50% of Edentia), 492
gardens of God, why many worlds are called, 821
gas, density can be much greater than water, 459
gas and oil, 671, 677, 690
gates, single pearly crystals, 524
gateway to soul, mind, 1705, -33
GAUTAMA SIDDHARTHA, 1035 (see also "Buddhism")
gospel of, 1036
no belief in existence of individual souls, 1035
six years of futile practice of Yoga, 1035
some day a greater G may arise, 882-3
"work out your own salvation", 1036
Gavalia, Chief of Evening Stars of Nebadon, 1308
head of the superangels, 407

ge

Gehenna, 2012
gems of beauty in diadems of glory, 504
GENERAL ADMINISTRATION (Local Universe), 371
"generation after generation, we have sent our
prophets", 1906
generation, each new, restate the J message, 2060
trend of a g determined by character, 1775
generations, dawn-mammals, seventy of, 704
mid-mammals, six hundred of, 705
900 after dawn-mammals, first humans, 707
generator, sun's interior is, 460
genes, hybridization (through dominant g)
makes for species improvement, 920 (397-98)
genetics (see "eugenics and genetics")
GENESIS OF WAR, THE, 783
GENNESARET, AT, 1705
Gennesaret, conferences, 1705-6, -41
genetics, 586, 719, 734, 836 (see "defectives", "eugenics")
Genghis Khan, 879
genius, Nathaniel, odd g of the twelve, 1558
primitive couldn't tell g from insanity, 968
geniuses, source of mutant g, 771
GENTILE PHILOSOPHY, 1335
GENTILE RELIGIONS, THE, 1336
gentile world, first century A.D., four philosophies
dominant, 1335
gentile(s), alongside Jew, 1957
GENTILES, AMONG THE, 1334
GENTILES AND JEWS, 1339
gentile(s), blood, apostles, 1548
converted many at Sidon, 1735
dogs, 1809
eagerness to hear gospel, 1737
learned much of J' teachings, 1736
Master dares even to heal g, 1735
not religions of salvation, 1336
philosophy, 1335
so-called, 1410, 1737
Tyre g interested, 1737
vengeance, days of, 1913
warmth for gospel, 1734
"gentle, be g with erring mortals", 1931
geographic center of infinity-Paradise, 126

"geography" of cosmos, 124, 129
geography of Jews, bestowal time, 1018
GEOLOGIC AND CLIMATIC CHANGES, 890
geologic errors, 670, 674, 718
GEOLOGIC HISTORY BOOK, THE, 670
geologists error, first vs. third glacier, 718
geology Urantia, 660-1, 670, 679
Gerar, Abraham to G, after Hebron and Salem, 1022
GERASA, THE SERMON AT, 1828
Gerizim, Mt. (see "Mount Gerizim")
Germany, 2 racial groups, 897
germs of true religion originate...1105
"gestalt", even in energy, sum of parts excess of
predictable, 113, 141, 1227
GETHSEMANE, ALONE IN, 1968
GETHSEMANE, IN, 1963
Gethsemane Park, The camp in, 1606
Gethsemane (see under "Jesus")

Ghats, three great rivers through Eastern G, 881
GHOST CULT, THE ADVANCING, 962
ghost cult, progressed to worship of gods, 961
GHOST CULTS, THE, 958
ghost dreams, 766
GHOST FEAR, 765, 958
ghost fear, except for gf, all society founded on...766
gave start on upgrade of religious evolution, 958
impressed men must regulate their conduct, 956
only religion up to time of revelation, 955
GHOST FEAR, SOCIALIZING INFLUENCE OF, 766
"ghost, giving up the g", 954
GHOST PLACATION, 959
GHOST-SOUL CONCEPT, THE, 953
GHOST-SPIRIT ENVIRONMENT, THE, 955
ghosts, 795, 955, 958
all tribes and races once believed in g, 961
alleged communications with, 987
and glorified g, beyond realm of ghostland, 961
notion of 2 kinds sprung up all over world, 961
reputed to have appeared, 791
techniques for frightening (7), 964

gi

giantism in races, unexpected g occurred among green,
orange, 584
giants among green and orange men, 724
gibbon raid, 708
gibbons, and apes, earlier types deteriorated the
simians, 706
beat to death, father of first humans, 709
Gibeon, Canaanite city, 1073
Gibraltar Isthmus, gave way as result of earthquake, 890
protected Mediterranean trough, 889
Gideon, J' parents recounted days of G, 1374
GIFT OF REVELATION, THE, 1007
gift(s), good, have long been in waiting, 1639
Jesus' to every mortal, 2063
material vs. spiritual", 1831
"my saving g to all nations", 1711
of eternal life through faith, 2002, -29, -43, -53 (see
also "kingdom, price to enter")
receive this g in your hearts, 1948
spiritual g depend upon capacity, 1831, 1954
to God, man's choicest, 22
gifted individuals, celestial artisans help, 507
GILBOA AND IN THE DECAPOLIS, AT, 1617
GILBOA ENCAMPMENT, THE, 1617
Gilboa, 1374 (see also under "Jesus")

Gilboa (cont'd)
  Jesus and apostles on, 1617
  Saul's tragic defeat at, 1072
giraffelike camels, 698
girl babies killed, 770
girls unwanted, exposed to death, 2073
Gischala, 1741
"give, more blessed to", 316, 1131, 1581
give up possessions, apostles and 70 only, 1803

gl

glaciers, 699-702, 718, 721
glands, ductless, 15,000,000 chemical reactions
    possible, 737
  influence spiritual receptivity, 566
glass, sea of (see "sea of glass")
gleam of righteousness in soul, 1117
glories, artistic, after we shed animal body, 507
  of Paradise, not for selfish, 1638
glorified ascendant mortals, 6 groups aid Ancients of
    Days govern, 178
GLORIFIED MATERIAL SONS, 347, 349
GLORIFIED MIDWAY CREATURES, 347, 349
GLORIFIED MORTALS, 347
"glorious inheritance of sonship", 1824
glory, augments as we ascend, 493
  foretaste of, 1754
  to glory, each life in eternity, 1953
gnats, strain at g and swallow camels, 1736

go

"go and do likewise", 1810
"go into all the world", forsaken by J' followers, 1051
goal, is God: rest: then eternity of service, 269
  of citizenry, 806
  of destiny, extinction or survival, 764
  of eternity ahead, 365
  of existence, next, quality thinking, 910
  of human happiness (altruism), 1131
  of self realization, 1096
  of time--finding God on Paradise, 557
  of transcendent service, 558
  of universe ascension, 1228
  perfection is our eternal g, not our origin, 846
  personality tastes sweetness of g fulfillment, 435
  this life, final goal the U F, 1435
  transcendent, of children of time, 21
  ultimate of human progress is, 1608
goal fulfillment, enjoyed after our first 8 lives, 435
goals, and motives in common, 1592
  easier to agree on g than on beliefs, interpretations,
    1130
  eternal, must change, 1774-5
  final, Universal Father, 1435
  first in Supreme, then in Ultimate, and perhaps
    Absolute, 1307
  great, of human existence, 140, 910, 1206, 1608
  not creeds, to unify men, 1091
  of the ages, spiritual training, essential to, 269, 867
  of all personalities is spirit, 140
  of destiny, look well to, 943
  society's two, self-control and social service, 806
  unity on g not on interpretations, 1130
  worthy needed, 1572

GOD

GOD, 2, 3
God (word symbol designating all personalizations of
    Deity, including the diverse co-ordinate and sub-
    ordinate personalizations, 2-6)
  abhors iniquity, 1676
GOD THE ABSOLUTE, 13
God the Absolute, 1168, 1201
    experiences, encounters, completion of divinity, 4
God, acts of G that disturb us, 48
  adjusts with mortals through T A, 47   affront to, 60
  age by age, to find him, 39
  aids in ascending search for G, 2062
  all men are children of G, 1091
  all things possible with, 46, 291, 1757
  alone, numberless places at one time, 44
  Ancestor (supernal) of all things, 34
  and Caesar, religious philosophy knows, 1114
  and evil, how come?, 1429
  and imperfection, 36
  and man coexist in a unified personality, 8
  and man directly related, 1187
  and man, everlasting personal connection, 28
  and man, personal relationship, 109, 195, 1187, 1304-5
  and man, united nature of, 1711
  and men need each other, 2084
GOD AND NATURE, 56
God, and Son love dominated...618
  and there is no other, 1781
  anthropomorphic? What a mistake!, 297
  appease G, J did not die to, 2016
  appeasing G, barbarous idea, 60
GOD, THE APPROACH TO, 62
God, argue about G, but experience exists above
    controversy, 30
  as Father takes precedence...618
  as Father transcends G as judge, 41
  as J taught, 1857, 2017
  as-love, as-pattern, 1154
  as man loves G he becomes eternal in actuality, 1285
  as personality, Nathaniel "sold" Rodan, 1784
  as reality, is not mystery, 27
  as seen by scientists, artists, etc., 68
GOD, ASCENDING SONS OF, 443
God, at this moment, G continues to uphold, 55
  atonement, a philosophic assault on G, 41
  attain presence of G through worship, 1641
GOD, THE ATTRIBUTES OF, 44
God, aware of all things all times everywhere, 77
b "be not deceived, God is not mocked", 37
  "becomes what you are to make you what He is", 1664
  being "friends with G", easy, 1534
  belief in, based on personal participation, 1119
  best known as Universal Father, 59
  binds up wounds of soul, 41
  blaspheme against G, no forgiveness, 1820
  "bless you", 954
  blunder to humanize, except T A, 53
  bridged gulf between self and you, 39
c "calls the stars by their names", 49
  can be contacted only through T A, 25
  can be known only by...1856
  can contact you, 62
  can make contact anytime, anywhere, 62
  cannot be proved, can be realized, 24
  cannot do the ungodlike thing, 1299
  cannot find G by searching, 39
  cannot know imperfection as experience, 36

God, Gods (cont'd)
Father, God the (cont'd)
his divine presence dwells in minds of men, 139
how He deals, 1804
how related to 6 coordinate Absolutes, 1147
idea, highest human concept of G, 2097
immediate contact with mortals, 24
in heaven loves me as F, 1378
"in Him we all live and move", 29
in him we move, live, have our being, 139
indulgent, lax, no, 1653
infinite in all his attributes, 34
initiates and maintains reality, 7
intimate touch with you, 139
is changeless, 1597
is final value, The F, 1781
is God of personalities, 70
is limited only by volition, 95
is living love, 2097
is most certainly everywhere present, 95
is not a bookkeeper, 1590
is not the G of Jew or Gentile, 1568
is source and cause of personality, 79
judges intentions, 1571, -76
know the F, worship G, 1857
knows what you have need of, 49
like earth father, 1597
looks into hearts, 1571
love of, personal, 1288, 1305
loved man before J was here, 2002

loves even erring children, 1795
loves family, and each individual, 1597
loves you, believe, 1537
man's highest concept of God, 1260, 2097
may intervene with any individual, 363
may uphold with unlimited forces, 55
mighty to save the soul, 1634
most beautiful and sublime pronouncements
   about, 1069
name is of our choosing, 22
name stands for depth of enthronement, 23
needs more than "little or no time", 1733
never compels, 1820
never does aught associates can do, 362
not always kindly and merciful, 1605
not in hiding, 62, 64   of all, 1460-61, 2064
on Paradise, we stand in recognition of, 1238
only partial revelation of INFINITY, 1153, -63
permits suffering, 1605, -32, -49, -61
   doesn't send it, 1661, -63
personal traits of the F, 53
personality bestowal, exclusive function of, 70
personality is absolutely unified, 638
personality primacy, 28
personally contactable on all levels, 1031
plan and purpose embrace all, 34
prayers, doesn't answer literally, 1639
primal member of all triunities, 1147
pure energy, spirit to time-space, 639
realizes all our experiences, 29
requires much fruit, 2054
requires we grow up by grace, 2054
reserves direct communication through T A, 1184
responds to faintest flicker of faith, 1733
revealed in dual phenomena, pure energy, pure
   spirit, 639
revealed self by nature, not name, 22
"reveals self by methods of his choosing", 1627
rules by compelling power of love, 1608

God, Gods (cont'd)
Father, God the (cont'd)
rules through his sons, 51
same as Personalized T A (J), 1522
self-limitation possible, 59
FATHER, THE SEVEN SACRED WORLDS OF THE,
   144
Father, speaks within the heart, 1664
spirit of F is in mortal men, 2097
spoke through Moses and prophets, 1721
"source of all true judgment", 1795
stands aside after having...71
"stands at head of government whose credentials
   we bear", 1565
FATHER, THE SUPREME REVELATION OF THE, 88
Father, synonymous with I AM in personality, 1152
Thought Adjuster to all who have attained F, 1181
thought of F eternalizes dually, 638
treats ascending sons as cosmic individuals, 1290
truth about, dawned upon prophet, 21
FATHER, THE UNIVERSAL, 21
universal concept of creator, controller, 21
universal primacy, 35
FATHER, THE UNIVERSE ATTITUDE OF THE, 54
Father, unsearchable nature of, 1266
"what the F desires", 1656
when you find the F, you'll be like him, 1592
without the F would not anything exist...468
working for welfare of all creation, 362
yearns for association of every being who...62
Father-Absolute, is the Father of all other Creators,
   58
Father and Son, know whereabouts of all...in
   universe, 77
Father and Sons are one literally, figuratively,
   spiritually, personally, 361
Father Creator, acme of evolution of Yahweh
   concept, 1061
Father fragment (see "fragment of Father, also
   "Mystery Monitor", "indwelling spirit", "Thought
   Adjuster")
Father fragments, 139, 145, 333, 347
Father God is primal cause, 47
Father-Infinite, 6
Father life (mortal), predicated on truth, sensitive
   to beauty, dominated by goodness, 1175
Father, Son, and the Holy Spirit, 2067
Father-Son, inseparability, 80
knowledge of F-S must be through Infinite Spirit,
   93
Father to the Eternal Son, is also Pattern to the
   Paradise Isle, 1147
Father, Universal, first great cause, 2077
is absolute of Absolutes, 1148
no perfection apart from 1781
pure energy, pure spirit, 639
ten great names, functions, 1147
Fatherhood and brotherhood, 966
Fatherlikeness, determines success of quest, 1174
spirit success proportionate to achievement of F,
   1174
Father's discipline done in love, 1946
FATHER'S ETERNAL PERFECTION, THE, 35
Father's, family, 1597, 1898
heart is...grieved when...children fail, 58
love and Son's mercy, 2062
love individualizes (absolutely) personality, 138
love, mercy, no bargaining for, 1585
FATHER'S LOVE, MINISTRY OF THE, 75
Father's love, profound and perfect, 1675

God, Gods (cont'd)
  Father's loving nature to all mankind, 1390
  FATHER'S NAME, THE, 22
  Father's, "Paradise mansions", 120
    plan, 1266
  FATHER'S PRIMACY, THE, 52
  FATHER'S SUPREME RULE, THE, 50
  Father's, universe, "many tarrying places", 1947
    Way, seven commandments, 751
    will, 1829, 1946 (see also "will of the Father")
      according to, 1706, 1869
      chief purpose of man, then peace can be, 1951
      is law, vs. your will, 1588
      man should work persistently... 1661
      your law, or your will, 1589
  Fathers, 7 to our mortal races, flesh and spiritual,
    (normally), 587
  favor with G to be had by faith, 1021
  fellowship with G results in service, 1862

GOD, THE FINITE, 1283
God, First Cause of science, 59
  "forbid we should go on doing these... ", 1894
  4 views of G, scientist, artist, philosopher, religionist, 68
  fragment of, in every normal man's mind, 62 (see
    also "fragment of Father", "fragment of living
    God", "Mystery Monitors", "Thought Adjusters")
  friends with G, 28, 1534, 1615, 1766 (see also
    "partners with God")
  from G flow flood-streams of life, energy,
    personality, 119
  functions on 3 Deity-personality levels, 3
  functions 7 ways, 111
GOD, THE GARDENS OF, 492
God, goodness, beneficence, mercy, and love of G, 1675
  goodness, mercy, wisdom, 26
GOD, THE GOODNESS OF, 40
God, goodness of G must be mated with truth of science
    and beauty of art, 43
  the great and only G, 35
  growth of the idea of (Yahweh), 1598
  "has become what you are, that he...", 1664
  hand is on mighty lever of... realms, 52
  hangs the earth upon nothing, 55
  happiness for those certain about G, 1766
  has decreed sovereignty of... mortal will and that
    decree is absolute, 71
  has embarked on eternal adventure with man, 64
  has found you, 1440
  "has made of one blood all the nations", 593
  has made "a way for the lightning", 47
  has personal knowledge of all thoughts and acts, 363
  has sonshipped you, 1733
  hears prayer unerringly when, 1638
  highest objective reality G, man's contact only
    through, 2095
  his will rules the whole, 137-8
  how perfect in imperfect universe, 31, 36
  how reveal self to men too busy?, 1733
  how to know G, 1856
  "I am the G of Abraham, Isaac", 1900
  "I am", J, 1983
  "I, the Lord, change not", 58
  idea of G as contrasted with ideal of G, 1781
  idea of G unimportant, be acquainted with ideal of,
    1783
  if G withdrew, total collapse, 55
  if man hears G, G is hearing man, 1638
  if not personal, and conscious, infrahuman, 1130
  "if this man not from G!", 1813
  impossible teach G if no desire to know, 1466

God, Gods (cont'd)
  "in afflictions he is afflicted", 29
  in every man, also transcendent--only faith, not
    logic, can harmonize this concept, 69
  in G man moves, lives, has his being, 22
  in G no variableness, 137
  in his subordinates, variation, 137
  in image of man, 29
  in lower vs. higher religions, 1781
GOD IN MAN, 1192
God, in man (variously put), 45
  in personal experience is real religion, 2084
GOD IN RELIGION, 66
God, in science, religion, philosophy, 59
  in search of lost sheep, new with J, 1770
  incarnate in J, not to reconcile angry G, 1083
  includes coordinate and subordinate personalizations
    of Deity, 4
  inclusive of all but evil and creature experience,
    1185
  increased happiness always for those certain about
    G, 1766
  indispensable to survival, 24
  infinite, universe finite, 468
GOD, THE INFINITY OF, 33
God, inhabits eternity, 23, 50
  inherently kind, compassionate, merciful, 38
  intervenes, 1305
  is absolute truth, 1125
  is all and in all, nothing, no one exists without him,
    646
  is all-wise as well as all-powerful, 58
  is approachable, 63
  is changeless, 58, 137-8, 222
  is energy, 47
  is a Father, first, last, eternally, 59
  is Father, Supreme is Mother, 1288
  is finite Deity, 1283
  is the first truth and the last fact, 1125
  is a freewill and primal personality, 138
  is the greatest experience in human existence, 1289
  is highest objective reality, 2095
  is highest universe value, 1238
  is the initiating thought, the Son, the expressionful
    word, 80
  is the law, 114
  is love, 26, 30, 38, 50, 94, 616, 1004, 1486, 1782
  is love, but love is not God, 40
  is love, Son is mercy, 75
  is man's eternal destination, 67
  is never subjected to surprise, 49
  is not a formulated hypothesis to, 2095
  is personal self-conscious being, personally present
    too in infinite number of beings, 139
  is a personality, 23
  is personality, 28, 138
  is personality of love, 2095
  is Ruler, power, form, energy, process, pattern,
    principle, presence, idealized reality, 53
  is spirit, 25-6, 30, 74-5, 1857
  "is spirit" (J), 1486, 1614
  is spirit personality, 30
  is to philosopher a hypothesis of unity, 30
  is to philosophy an idea, 30; a possibility, 1125
  is to psychology a desirability, 1125
  is to religion a person, 30; a certainty, 1125
  is to religionist, a... spiritual experience, 30
  is to science a cause, 30; a possibility, 1125
  is to scientist a primal force, 30
  is a transcendent reality, 23
  is truth, beauty, and goodness, 1279

God, Gods (cont'd)

is unity, Deity is universally coordinated, 637

GOD IS A UNIVERSAL SPIRIT, 25

God, is the universal upholder, 98

is will, 58

Jesus' childlike faith in God, 2089

Jesus' death, G not responsible for, 2002

Jesus illuminates concept, 41

Jesus' living faith in, 2087

Jesus revealed G as Father of each, 41

Job, driven to G, how, 1664

kingdom, but not a king, 1855

GOD, KINGDOM OF, 1500

God, kingdom of G vs. kingdom of good, 40

k know only by experience, 1453, 1857

-knowing, only by faith, 1124

knowledge of G supplemented through T A, 49

known by experience, not teaching, 1856

knows all things, 48

"knows our downsittings and our uprisings", 49

laid down incarnate life in devotion, 2018

last mortal rendezvous, 1935

law of, destroys sin, 41

let go of G so he may... refresh our souls, 1777

light no mortal man can approach, 25, 27

like father, J, 1769

like wise husbandman, 1946

lives in all his spirit-born sons, 64

lives within you, 39

"the living", 31

loathes hypocrisy, 1676

GOD, LOCAL UNIVERSE SONS OF, 384

God, look at G as of now, not time of Moses, 1597

"looks into your souls", 1838

lost sight of G, harvest of world wars, 2081

love and be loved, only a person, 31

love, dominant in dealings of G, 40

love G through love of men, 1727

GOD, THE LOVE OF, 38, 1304

God, love of G saves sinner, law of G destroys the sin, 41

loves each creature, 1304

loves each of his creature sons alike, 454

loves not like a father, but as a father, 41

"loves sinner, hates sin", yes and no, 41

"loves you, his sons", 2052

loving kindness automatic, 38

loving personality, 1122

loving personality can't reveal to loveless person, 30

m made and manages universe, 2080

makes man more than he is when... 1285

makes direct contact with man, 64

man can deny G, but be moral, good (graft), 1126

man feels he ought to believe in G, 1105

man must want, 1466

man should not blame G, 1661

manifests up to creature's capacity, 27

man's choicest gift to G, 22

man's comprehension of Father is personal experience, 1153

man's eternal destination, 67

man's most thrilling human experience, 1729

many personalizations, 4

many subordinates, 467

many who know G fear to assert feelings, 1126

meanings of G in U Book, 4

meanings of term, 1294

means 7 different Gods, 4

mercy to individual, impartiality to total, 137

mistake to dream of G far off, 64

God, Gods (cont'd)

the more man loves G, the greater the reality of man, 1285

the more man withdraws from G, nearer cessation of existence, 1285

more than personality, not less, 1785

most certain of all experiences, 1127

the most indescribable of all presences, 1127

the Mother, Supreme Being, 1289

much more Deity not comprehensible, 1153

must first find man, man find G, 1299

mystery, no, 27

GOD, THE MYSTERY OF, 26

God, name given to best and highest man knows, 1127

n names and concepts of, 1598

names of,

All-powerful One, 23

Creator Father (Isaiah), 1057, 1600

Divine Controller, 23

El, 1053

El Elyon, 1053, 1600

El Shaddai, 1053, 1598

Elohim, 1053, 1598

Father in Heaven, 1598

Father in Paradise, 1597

Father of Fathers, 23

Father of Lights, 23

Father of Universes, 23

Final Father, 1113

First Father, 22

First Great Source and Center, 23

First Source and Universe Center, 22

Gift of Life, 23

Havona Father, 23

Infinite Upholder, 23

Jehovah, 1053

Lord God of Israel, 1069, 1598

Most High, 1598

Paradise Father, 23, 1600

the One Universal, 1035

Spirit Father, 23

the Supreme, 1318, -24

Supreme Yahweh, 1598

Universal Center, 23

Universal Creator, 1064

Universal Father, 231, 1069

Universal Spirit Ruler, 1600

Yahweh, 1052, 1598

nature, G not the only influence in, 137

GOD, THE NATURE OF, 33

God, "near G in the mouth, far from in the heart", 1676

never ceases to bestow himself, 36

never hesitate to ask G for wisdom... 999

never surprised, 49

never wrathful, vengeful, angry, 41, 57

new concept of G, J taught, 1590, -97

a new revelation of man to, 1984

no diminution of, 49

no personal attitude toward sin, 41

no respecter of persons, 27, 1608, -62, 1731

no valid proof you've found G, 1733

non-Father manifestations (12), 1146

not a bookkeeper, 1590

not derived from good, all good from G, 2095

not a doctrine, living presence in souls, 2066

not fact of G, presence of, 1733

not functioning as blind force, 47

not hiding from men, 25, 46

not invention of idealism, but its source, 2095

not less than personality, 1119

G

God, Gods (cont'd)

Supreme Being (cont'd)

after finding G S, quest for Ultimate!, 1293
all creatures will find S simultaneously, 1290
all universe activity partially reunited by S, 1304
ascender draws upon S B for character... 1284
avenue through which creatures pass inward, 1288
avenue through which love flows outward, 1288
be characteristic of exalted rule of S B, 1324
(beautiful descriptive, definitive paragraphs),
   1278, 1304
   is truth, beauty and goodness, 1279
becomes finite synthesis of... 1279
becoming high expression of total will of G, 1278
catalyzer of all universe growth, 1283
central universe source of time-space unity, 292
complete evolutionary actualization of, 1291
correlates, Ultimate unifies, 1305
creatures could not evolve without the S, 1284
deity culmination of grand universe evolution, 1164
descent, ascent, revelatory of Deity evolution of
   G S, 1278
desire G, consciousness of S born in your mind,
   1288
enlarging sovereignty of S B in Satania, 1251
error can exist only within presence of S B, 1300
ever-present influence of S B is in Havona, 162
evolution of, will sometime be completed, 353
evolutionary unification of experiential Deity, 161
evolving as personality synthesis in grand
   universe, 1304
evolving God of time and space, 4
evolving presence of, 46
evolving two ways is one reality, 12
expanding outward in G the 7-fold, 11
experiential Deity, 1304
experiential God of evolutionary creatures of...
   4
focus of potentials on finite level, 1264
foretasting of his... activities (providence), 1305
God the 7-fold coordinating in the S B, 641
God the U, and God the A, personal repercussion
   of... 1172
growth is the nature of the S B, 1262
he does not as yet operate personally, the... 271
how G S advances one more step, 1278
if man defaults, personality becomes part of S B,
   1232
in finite cosmos, trinity unity is in G S, 1279
in Havona is reflection of Paradise Deity, 11
inability of Havona pilgrims to find G S, 188
is: 1278
is the Almighty Supreme, and God the Supreme, 11
is an actualizing Deity as are also... 10
is beauty... truth... goodness, 1278
is both creature and creator, 1271
is coordinator of all, 1305
is derived Deity, 1263
is the essence of evolution, 1283
is evolutionary-experiential self, 1294
is experiential, 1165
is expression of minds to creatures, 104
is the finite Deity, 1239, -83
is God in time, 1280
is God the Supreme, and Almighty Supreme, 1281
is the living cosmos, 1287
is mind, spirit, and the universe, 1139
is striving within us for Deity expression, 1284
is synthesis of all finite realities, 1281
is the Trinity as comprehended by man, 1292

God, Gods (cont'd)

Supreme Being (cont'd)

is truth, beauty, goodness, 1279
is unification of 3 phases of Deity reality: God the
   Supreme, the Almighty Supreme, the Supreme
   Mind, 251
is united ministration, 96   is Universal Mother, 1288
is the universe, 1139
is your divine Mother, 1288
is your universe home, 1288
less and other than the Trinity, 115
man's comprehension capacity exhausted by
   concept of S B, 1262
motion intensively inward, extensively outward,
   1265
mystery now surrounds this S B, 1239
SUPREME BEING, NATURE OF, 1266, -78
Supreme Being, of origin in Trinity, 1270
personality from the Paradise Trinity, 12
personality of non-ascender return to G S, 1284
Planetary Supervisors contribute to S B, 1251
powerizing as sovereign of supercreations, 354
reality of, constituted by, 1434
realm of Providence--S B and C A, 56
relation of man to S B, foundation for duty, 1284
Secrets of Supremacy are secrets of the S B, 149
seraphim part of mortal progression through S B,
   1245
seven phases of will of, 1325
some of your associates (and you) children of S B,
   1249
sometimes called Ultimacy of Deity, 2
sovereignty of S attained when God's rule is actual,
   1306
sovereignty of S in Nebadon, thanks to bestowal,
   1327
struggles for expression throughout grand
   universe, 1283
sum total of all finite growth, 1281
synthesis of energy, mind, and spirit, 1120
synthetic coordinator of... universe activities, 11
teaches experiential children as cosmic total, 1290
technique for finite to attain absonite, 12
through Havona you discover G S, 1296
TRINITY PERSONALITIES, THE SUPREME, 207
Trinity Ultimate is S B, plus Architects and
   Supreme Creators, 352
ULTIMATE, GOD THE, 12; the Absolute, 10, 13
the Ultimate, the Absolute in process of
   actualization, 11
UNIFIER, THE SUPREME, 643
united ministries, influence of the S, 96
vs. the Father, 1290-1   vs. the Ultimate, 1160
we live, move, have our being, within the
   Supreme, 1283
will be actualized in mind of... man, 1286
will be an end in time of growth of G S, 1280
with S B, achievement is... status, 1260

God, Gods (cont'd)

† tender nature of G best expressed in, 59
term--always denotes personality, 4
term "God" denotes personality, Deity may not, 4
theory vs. presence of, 1733
there is no power but of G, 46
things pertaining to G limited by, 48
think of G as creator, controller, upholder, 21
those who can't know G, reckoned among animals,
   1468
though cannot find by searching, be guided, 39
to find G, 1440

God, Gods (cont'd)
   to him only 2 groups of people, 1468
   to humanize, mistake, 53
   a transcendent reality, 23
   true and loving Father, only concept J taught, 2017
U understand G, no; know G, yes, 1856
   understanding of G impossible, 50, 1856
   unfair?, 47
   union with G not like drop in sea, 31
   Universal Spirit Ruler, 1600
   U of U is the work of G, 21
   upholder of all creation, 21
   Urantia people, primitive concepts of, 60
V various meanings of word G, 4
   vs. Deity, 4
   vs. Father, 1856-7
   view of science, philosophy, etc., 1125
   vision embraces highest welfare of all creation, 48
W was passing by, 1935
   we can know him in our hearts, 1453
   we cannot search out G by knowledge, 1453
   we, in presence of G in an age, 95, 1221
   we minister to G in others, 1475
   what chance without man's time to learn, 1733
   what G has joined together, 929
   what G (Ruler) is, 53
   what He is, 1965
   when man finds G, he has found everything, 1289
   when man gives G all he has, G makes man greater, 1285
   when men search for G they're searching for everything, 1289
   why confusion of certainty about G, 1140
   will does not necessarily prevail with person, 137
   will of G does prevail (not always with individuals), 1263
   will of G, doesn't prevail in part, but in whole, 137
     in any occupation, 1732
     limits God's presence, 48
     will prevail in end, 1932
   without G, no personality, 28
   without G, nothing (scientific secularism) leads to peace, 2082
   word "God" cannot be defined, 1856
   Word of G in the flesh, 1712
   a word signifying all personalizations of Deity, 3
   work of G is literal as well as spiritual, 55
   wrath of, 1597
   wrong ideas about, 59
   wrongdoer, is Father of even the, 68
   you are near G in the mouth, not heart, 1677
   you can be known as friend of G, 28
   you should not fail to accept him, 51
   your only assurance of a personal G, 1107

God-consciousness, indispensable, 1035
   is equivalent to, 2097   is inalienable, 196
   no word can designate what we call, 1130
   spirits of Divine Presence assist man to, 17
   such an experience constitutes G-c, 2097
   three varying factors of, 67
God-knowing,
   all things work...for advancement of, 616, 1306
   experience, the finality of, 2094
   man, why he tells experiences, 30
   mortals only positive proof of G, 24
God-knowing creatures, supreme ambition, 21
God-knowing mortals,
   all things, good and evil, work for advancement of, 1306

God, Gods (cont'd)
God-knowing mortals (cont'd)
   can know unity, 2096
   can't be lonely, 1291
God-man partnership, (see "partners, man with God")
God, The One, by Ikhnaton, destroyed by priests, 1048
God-seeking mind-soul, 1209
God-Son, as father, mother, 76, 79
GOD THE ULTIMATE, 12
God the Ultimate, 1168-9, 1266
   absonite spheres of G U, 1201
   in Corps of Finality, challenge of G U, 305
God unidentified selfhood, iniquity reveals transient reality of, 1301
God's, absoluteness pervades, 59
   attitude toward individual, total, 137
   conformity is volitional, 138
   doings, intelligent, wise, kind, our curtailed vision can't see, 47
GOD'S EVERYWHERENESS, 44
God's, forgiveness, 4 steps, 1862
GOD'S INFINITE POWER, 46
God's, influence, you determine for self, 46
GOD'S LAW AND THE FATHER'S WILL, 1588
GOD'S LIMITLESSNESS, 49
God's, love, 1304
     intelligent, far-seeing parental affection, 40
     man can feel, 50
   name, J enlargement of revelation of, 1965
   plan, embraces every creature, 365
   presence in soul, see it in others, 1733
   presence, thus limited because, 48
   purpose triumphs, 51
GOD'S RELATION TO THE INDIVIDUAL, 62
GOD'S RELATION TO A LOCAL UNIVERSE, 362
GOD'S RELATION TO THE UNIVERSE, 54
God's, rule, when actual, sovereignty of Supreme attained, 1306
   search for lost sheep, 1851
   separate but unified contact, the T A's, 363
   sovereignty unlimited, 52
GOD'S UNCHANGING CHARACTER, 57
GOD'S UNIVERSAL KNOWLEDGE, 48
God's, way not going to be the easy way, 1522
   will and man's will, 1431
   will prevails, widely, 51, 137-8
     not necessarily with men's hearts, 51
   will, to know, 1118
   will, ultimately, 1263
GOD'S WRATH, 1597
Gods, the, 613, 1638   are very trustful, 437
   are related to time as an experience in eternity, 1295
   forces, spirits, personalities, realities, 1160
   have attributes, Trinity has functions, 1304
   speak to their creations in laws of spirit, mind, matter, 1638

Godad, the hermit of India, advised Gautama, 1035
godless philosophy will lead to worldwide disaster, 2081
godless religion devoid of survival value, 1126
gods who came down to earth (folk tale), 856
GOING THROUGH SAMARIA, 1607
gold, Andites worked g 9000 B.C., 903
   first metal sought by man, 904
   Rome lost g to Levant, factor in fall, 2074
gold-bearing quartz, 110 million years, 689
golden age, 975
   far from realization of Utopian, 764
   myth, but Eden was a fact, 838
   of primitive man, 717

golden age (cont'd)
  penalty for is service on less advanced planet, 625
GOLDEN AGES, THE, 624
Golden Calf, Aaron and the G C (Peter), 1637
golden calf of Bedouin tribes, 1056
GOLDEN RULE,
  Andonites early taught the G R, 783
  as restated by J demands... 1585, 1771
  becomes possible put G R in operation, 596
  Buddhist, 1447
  cannot be understood as dogma or precept, 1950
  center and circumference of philosophy, 1950
  Eskimos largely live by G R, 783
  fatherly affection higher application of G R, 1573
  for men of high ideals, 1650
  great law of human fairness, 1931
  greatness through Spirit of Truth insight, 1949
  is loving, 1111
  Jesus explains 6 levels of application, 1650
  Jesus' G R demands active social contact, 1585
  Jesus instructed G R in ordination sermon, 1571
  may be an offense without spiritual discernment, 1949
  misapplied, 946, 1111, 1931, -49
  moral and ethical beings can live by, 577
  not for insects, 946
  not to be interpreted literally, 1949
  of human fairness cries out against all... 614
  older G R could be obeyed in isolation, 1585
  only moral beings live the G R, 597
  others, negative, 1585, 1771
  positive, 1771
  taught apostles, 1931
  "taught you in positive form", 1931
  unspiritual interpretation, 1949
  valid only under Spirit of Truth, 1950
  vital factor in J' religion, 2093
  when literally interpreted, 1949
  without superhuman insight... 1949
"Golden rulers", must defend selves, 804
  practical course among weak or wicked... 804
Golgotha, angry mob of infuriated Jews, 2013
  covered by many thousands crucified Jews, 2005
  flower of Jewish race died on G, 2005
  Jesus' legs not broken, but side was pierced, 2011
  Jesus on cross alive 5-1/2 hours, 2011
  Jesus quoted Scripture, 3 things audible, 2010
  Jesus started for G bearing own cross beam, 2011
  Jews didn't want bodies exposed because... 2011
  Joseph and Nicodemus claimed body, 2011
  Joseph's new tomb, little north of G, 2013
  location, 2005
  long cross timbers already at G, 2004
  many Jews hastened out to G, 2007
  Peter and John race for G, after the news, 2027
  route to, 2030
  rulers of Jews planned to throw J' body into open pit
    for animals, 2012
  Sanhedrinists on hand to see body sent to Gehenna,
    2012
  soldiers and J arrived at G before Mary, 1997
  usual route was long to G, 2005
Gonod and Ganid (wealthy Indian father and son,
    traveled whole Mediterranean world with J as
    interpreter, teacher, for a year)
  by apparent chance, J met G G, 1422
  farewell, tearful, but courageous, 1481
  "four tones", 1465   J' pay year in advance, 1423
  meeting J in Jerusalem, 1422
  never in this world, knew teacher was J, 1481
  "teacher, let's you and I make a religion", 1467
  worthy successor (Ganid) to his father, 1481

good, all g in this life, enhances future life, 1134
  all things work together for g, 616
GOOD AND BAD SPIRIT GHOSTS, 961
good, and evil, 842, 1429
GOOD AND EVIL, 1457
good, and evil,
    cosmic coordinates, no, 961-2
    cultural birthmark of ghost cults, 962
  discourse on (J), 1457
  doing g not enough, faith first, 1584
  effort of each man benefits all, 138
  evil spirits only from Caligastia to Pentecost, 962
  for evil, 1033
  from evil, 619-20
  God's workings all for the most g, 48
  highest g is unconscious, 1862
  is, 842
GOOD LUCK AND BAD LUCK: CHANCE, 950
good, more powerful than evil, 1770
  no act of g is ever wholly lost, 552
  not cosmic coordinate with evil, despite
    philosophy, 962
  of the Universe is the eternal real, 1123
  resulting from evil (Satania rebellion), 619
  "return g for evil", 1577
  sin, evil (definitions), 842
  truly g is... more powerful than evil, 1770
good luck, primitives feared a run of g luck, 950
good news, carried healing for the sick, 1595
  "of eternal life", 2043
  of kingdom, 1585, 1607, -16, -35
  of "knowing God, and yourself as a son of God", 67
  people not prepared for, 1537
GOOD SAMARITAN, THE STORY OF THE, 1809
good to others, doing,
  circumscribed at first, 1133
  enhancement of future life, 1134
  impulse to deny ego for benefit of neighbor, 1133
good works are "by products", 1931
goodness,
  and evil, proof of man's will, 1458
  choose, 1583
  correlated (everlastingly) with discernment of truth
    and beauty, 1458
  embraces... experiential perfection-hunger, 647
  friendliness, of J, 1541
  God the Supreme is the g of supreme spirit values,
    1304   is, 647   like truth, is relative (J), 1457
  men turned from... concept of isolated g, 43
  must be attractive, 1874
  quest rather than a possession, 1458
  to greatness, 317
  true g must be unconscious (right hand), 1583
  truth, beauty (see "truth, beauty, and goodness")
  without grace repels, 1874

gospel

gospel,
  about Jesus, not of, 1041, -84, 2059, -66-7
  acceptance of g improves home life, 1923
  all nations, races would embrace g, if, 1670
  as embodied with Paul's cult blended with... 1340
  assures that you will be unafraid in trouble, 1767
GOSPEL AT IRON, THE, 1643
gospel, "be aggressive in preaching g", 1931
  before family, 1682, 1722
  belongs to all who believe it, 2044
  blended with, 1340
  "but one g eternal life by faith", 2041
GOSPEL BY LUKE, 1342
GOSPEL BY MARK, 1341

gospel (cont'd)
    cardinal features of the g are... (5), 1863
    carried throughout Empire, 1596
    changed by subtle process, 2051
    changes (see "changed, religion of J" and "changes in J' religion")
    childhood in, 1736
    Christianized version of g conflict, 2069
    churches are obstacles to advance of, 2084-5
    comforting and healing, 1595
    concerned with love, service, 2053
    cornerstones of g, brotherhood, service, 1930
    custody of mere priests, not to be left to, 2044
    "dead rise" is not the g, 2054
    death of J, g not dependent on, 2002
    directed to individual, not nation, 1593, 1624, -30, 1863
    distorted by ransom idea, 2061
    doesn't stop trouble, 1767
    early, cardinal features of, 2029
    elevation of ideals, 1775
    enhancement of insights, 1775
    enrich living with 7 endowments, 1859
    exalts every mortal, materialism cheapens life, 1125
    failed nearly, due to changes, 1864
    father-child, cornerstone of, 1776
    "fear no man when you proclaim g", 2049
    first steps at changing of, 2051
    five cardinal features of, 1863
    for new age, 1595
    for weaklings and slaves?, 1607
    founded on faith, hope, love, 2063
    fresh beginning for whole human race, 1582
    friendship with G is the g, 1766
    "God is Father of all men" lost from g, 2067
    good news, 1957, -59
    "good news for liberty of mankind", 2033
    good news of g is, 1586, -98
    got blended with 3 teachings, 1340
    greatly distorted (ransom idea), 2061
    guide for all who preach the g, 1765
    a historical religion displaced J' g, 1866
    humanitarian labors no substitute for g, 1931
    in mind, vs. in heart, 1927
    in power without miracles, 1833
    infectious in its transforming power, 1766
    is friendship with God, 1766
    "is love of the Father, service of his children", 2053
    is "nothing more nor less than...", 1590
    J' g a new religion of faith, 2063
    J "my g is", 1590
    J taught about positive nature of, 1769
    J would have men godlike and solve their own problems, 1581
    Jewish writers glossed over gentiles' reception of, 1736
    joyous fellowship vs. repentance, 1584
    liberation will bring g to all nations, 1930
    like mustard seed, 1931
    like seed of the living being, 1931
    lives, give to the g, live by the g, 1823
    living truth is g, 1931
    makes one unafraid of trouble, 1767
    message to individual, not to nation, 1593, 1624, -30, 1863
    messengers, J gracefully refused to accept, 1801
    mortals are sons of God, 1957
    must be carried to world, 2053
    new, about J, 2059, -66
    new, after Pentecost (quote), 2066

gospel (cont'd)
    new, and art of living, 1778
    new g can't conform to what is, 1576
    new vs. old forms, 1542
    no part suffered such misconstruction as... 1915
    no wide acceptance until home life... 1922
    not about J, but living, spiritual reality of the g of J, 1041
    "nothing takes place of proclaiming the g", 1931
    of Gautama, the, 1036
    of individual initiative 500,000 B.C., 749
    of J, world would have embraced if, 1670
    GOSPEL OF JOHN, 1342
    gospel, of kingdom, 1865-6, -59 (see also "kingdom")
    GOSPEL OF THE KINGDOM (sermon on), 1535
    GOSPEL OF MATTHEW, 1341
    gospel, of nonresistance, lives of nonviolence, 1608
    of personal religion--sonship with God, 1338, -40
    of spiritual liberty, 1340
    peace on earth, not until g prevails, 1951
    peace to the individual, but... 1951
    "proclaim, nothing takes place of g, 1931
    "proclaim to all nations", 1824, 1913
    "proclaim to every person", 1824
    proclaimed with power, without miracles, 1833
    real, was, 1866
    "rejoice in loyalty to g and pray", 2041
    requires more love, wisdom in home, 1922
    resurrection, early faith in, 2029
    saving truth of g is, 2052
    settledness of goals, 1775
    so-called g's of Matthew, Mark, Luke, John, 1341
    social--no, 1565, 1624, 1862, 2082
    solvent for spiritual difficulties, 2060
    sonship still is saving truth of g, 2052
    spirit of positive aggression, 1609
    spread by Tyrians, 1737
    spread rapidly in peace, 2068
    struggling humanity, g for, 2063
    "suffer, for sake of my g", 1947
    teachers, only business to reveal God... 1593
    (that was the g of kingdom, lost), 1866
    to be preached to all, 1608, 1804
    trouble, g makes one unafraid of, 1767
    truths concealed in, 2061
    two truths of first import are... 1593
    ultimately will transform world, 2061
    vs. Christianity, foundations, 2091
    "vitality, g must show increasing", 1932
    what if Rome had g, instead of Greek Christianity?, 2074
    will prevail, 1913
    "will rule this world", 1608
    will some day liberate nations, 1930
    "will spread to all the world", 1807, 1913
    will triumph, 1913, 2075-6
    world has never... tried, ideas, ideals, 1863
    world would have accepted the real g, 1670
    worldwide only when home life is better, 1922
    "yoke is easy", 1766
    "you are ignorant of the g", 1996
    youth would respond to g, 2085
gospel of Jesus (changes, substitutes for),
    abandon primitive notion, God as offended monarch, 2017
    abandoned for g of Lord Jesus Christ, 2066
    Abner called Paul: "clever corrupter of J' teachings", 1832
    appeasing G through sacrifice a barbarous idea, 60
    atonement incompatible with G concept J taught, 2017

gospel of Jesus (changes, substitutes for), (cont'd)
atonement, misrepresented F in eyes of J, 1494
certain adaptations to appeal to mystery religionists, 1337
changes seemed to facilitate preaching, 2061
Christianity, much J did not teach, 1670
concealed truths will emerge, 2061
fact of resurrection in place of truth of g of J, 2061
failed establish kingdom in hearts, followers of J gradually came to establish church, 1865
fellowship of believers in J, not brothers in family kingdom of F, 2067
followers departed from his teachings, 1825
followers progressively distorted J' g, 1864
God is F of J, took place of F of all men, 2067
Jesus brotherhood became instead, a church, 2067
Jesus' life as revelation lost to ransom idea, 2061
Jesus taught G only as loving F, 2017
Jesus taught service, not sacrifice, 2017
Jesus viewed sacrifice as travesty of divine justice, 1494
kingdom concept modified by two tendencies, 1864
"kingdom now" forgotten, promised for future, 1865
led to belief J was Redeemer, 1864
lost in proclamation of risen Christ, 2066
"message not changed by my resurrection", 2052
Nathaniel, Peter, disagreed, preaching about J instead of g, 2058
a new gospel about J in place of... 2059
New Testament devoted to Paul's experience, not religious life of J, 2091
New Testament meagerly Jesusonian, 2091
not new religion, but also new order of human society, 2069
not simple spiritual appeal of J, 2069
outpoured Spirit became part of g: error, 2063
Paul compromised J' teachings, 1337
Paul created new religion, new version, 2059
Paul got atonement idea via Andonites, Moses, 716
Paul put J before J' teachings, 2092
Paul, theologic compromises, 984
Peter led in substitution facts about g, 2059
reinterpreted by Greek philosophy, 2069
religion of J became religion about J, 2051
replaced by unconsciously formulated new g, 2063
socialized in Christianity, 2069
subtle process of... changing religion of J, 2051
unintended transformation into religion about J, 2075
used living commentary on g, in place of g, 2067
Gospels, how writing of G was delayed, 1332
imperfect, brief, changed world history for 2000 years, 1342
origins:
John, 1342
Luke, 1342
Mark, 1341
Matthew, 1341
government, autocratic for planets in early career, 573
GOVERNMENT, BEGINNINGS OF, 788
government, best for evolutionary people, tri-partite, 797-8
best which coordinates most, governs least, 803
(celestial) desires only voluntary loyalty, 605
constellation, 487
disappearing on advanced worlds, 630
divine ideal is, 517, 799
don't promulgate truth through, 1931
downfall assured by ignorance, selfishness, 803
early, of planet, autocratic, 573
effective g must have power, 789

government (cont'd)
efficient tribal g, first, 716
essentials of civil progress, 803
GOVERNMENT, EVOLUTION OF HUMAN, 783
GOVERNMENT, EVOLUTION OF REPRESENTATIVE, 801
government, evolves from family to mankind, 1488
"Father is head of g whose credentials we bear",1565
form not important if... 803, 806
highest function of g is adjudication, 247
ideal form, but, 799
ideas without ideals, 1220
less is needed as civilization develops, 597
mankind g required, 1490
men assume burdens of g because, 803
GOVERNMENT, MONARCHIAL, 789
government, must continue to evolve, 804
neighboring planet, 808
not what it is, but does, determines social evolution, 803
on central universe, none, 155
GOVERNMENT ON A NEIGHBORING PLANET, 808
government, ours on U, 1258
passes from representative, to individual self-control, 599
GOVERNMENT PLANETARY, THE, 1254
government, planetary, (100,000 staff), 573, 820
prime mission of, 906
regulate social conduct only enough, 805
retrogression, 1489
rule of individual self-control, 599
sacred feature, only, 806
sector, 181
seed and secret of purposeful growth, 433
GOVERNMENT, SERAPHIC PLANETARY, 1250
government, should exercise minimum of... control, 803
social administration and coordination, 599
supporting people, J against, 1461
system administrators, 572
systems vs. constellations, 371
tri-partite, 487, 789, 806
U g seized in 33 crises, 1253
U peoples, representative!, 517
world, 1489
government, inhabited creation,
Avonals, Sons of service and bestowal, 225
closely associated with Creator Sons, 225
judicial actions and missions, 225
Creator Sons, makers and rulers of U, 234
Divine Counsellors, 281
are divine counsel of the Trinity, 216
part of fact-finding, truth-revealing tribunal, 217
totallers (unerring) of testimony, 218
HAVONA NATIVES (no. beyond conception), 221
INSPIRED TRINITY SPIRITS, a secret in the Paradise Trinity, 219
PARADISE CITIZENS, 222
Paradise Sons, administrators, 235
Perfectors of wisdom (7 billion), 215, 281
administration in superuniverses, 216
combine with ascenders (see possible wisdom), 216
personify divine wisdom, 215-6
revealers of truth to planets, 216
Sons of the Trinity embodiment of service, 230
Stationary Sons of Trinity, grand corps, 218
act in connection with evolution, 219
two billion and seventy central universe, 219
Teacher Sons, coordinating personalities, 215
Trinity Teacher Sons conduct all tests, 231
teachers of spirit personalities, 231

government,representative, highest type, 595
  10 steps to, 802
  vanishes under individual self-control, 599
governments, created for men, not opposite, 1490
  of 10 continents, inferior to best on U, 819
GOVERNMENTS, THE SECTOR, 181

gr

grace, apostles (4) grew in g, 2056
  by g attain moral heights of... human destiny, 2083
  "creation not... idleness, but progression in g" (J), 1953
  "daily grow in g" (J), 1920
  faith, g by means of living f, 1656
  grow in g by faith, 1656
  "growth in g essential", 1682
  Judas failed to grow in love and g, 2056
  kingdom is free, but g is essential to continuance in... 1682
  may enter kingdom as child, but must grow up by g, 2054
  necessary to "enter fully into joy of Lord", 1917
  of faith, ennobled by the g, 2042
  pursuit of goodness, 317
  religion's endowments immediate, but there is g, 1120
  saving, 1918
  spiritually, as children grow up physically, 1840
  thanks, 1611
  transformations of g wrought in response to... 1686
  "we grow in g, but Master had maturity at start", 1785
"graces, tranquility and patience", 2048
graciousness, 1874
GRADUATE GUIDES, 269
GRADUATE GUIDES, ORIGIN OF THE, 270
  numbers beyond comprehension, 270
grafts, humanistic, on spiritual nature, 1126
grain storage room, birthplace of J, 1351
Grand Canyon, 670
grand universe, activated by a Supreme Mind, 1303
  after perfected g u, rest, then quest!, 1293
  body likened to, 1276
  growth characterizes, hence experiential, imperfect, 1268
  is a mechanism as well as an organism, 1303
  is the present organized and inhabited creation, 129
GRAND UNIVERSE, THE LIVING ORGANISM OF THE, 1276
grand universe, ministering spirits of, 7 groups, 285
  our local u near outer borders (far-off corner), 129
  place in master universe 1-2
  seven trillion inhabitable worlds, 166
  sphere of time-space descension of Paradise personalities, 4
  superuniverses, arch. spheres, billion Havona spheres, 166
  3-fold Deity domain of... 12
  units in each level of organization, 167
  what, after entirely settled in light and life?, 636
grandchild, only civilized man loves his, 750
Grandfanda, 304
  all Gravity Messengers under G, 346
  chief of supreme body of universal assignment, 353
  first "pilgrim" discoverer of Havona, 270
  in the days of, 87, 203
  prior to times of G, 296
granite, lava layers when cooled, form g, 668
grapes from thorns?, 1571
graph method, secure intelligence in Havona by gm, 289
  used for teaching in Havona, 303

gratification of hunger for self-expression, 508
gratitude, in new group of human feelings, 708
  strangers, for gifts, give thanks, 1828
  would require centuries to express g, 304
gravita, among material organizations responding to Paradise gravity, 126
gravita domain, 175
gravitation, universe, and motion are twin facets, 482
gravitational control, all things held forever in grasp of, 47
gravity, absolute vs. linear, 125
  adjusted for each new universe, 49
  all is circuited in Isle of Paradise, 71
  anti- (see "antigravity")
  atoms, electrons, subject to g, 465
  circuits, the 4 absolute, 131
    of Isle of Paradise, 45
    presence vs. force center, 131
  competition-gravity (human), 773
  condensation, 464-5
  cosmic g is function of Isle of Paradise, 139
  energy, 470
  forces, 5
  independent of time and space, 131
  inevitabilities, 51
  is the omnipotent strand... 125
  laws of, defied?, 1519
  linear-response is a measure of, 482
  local or linear operative with appearance of... 476
  negative to, 323
  no pull on unattached uncharged... particles, 476
  omnipotent strand, 125
  Paradise is source and substance of physical g, 101
  physical, mental, spiritual g distinct realms, 739
  power control creatures, various attributes (anti-gravity), 101
  pre- and post-, 469
  presence circuits of... 176
  solar system without g like... 2075
  sole control of energy-matter, 10
  ultimatons not subject to local g, 465
  UNIVERSAL, 131
  universal lines of g converge in F, 119
gravity bodies,
  balance, stabilize, 153-4
  enormous dark, 153
  hide Havona from universes, 153
  zone unique between 2 circuits, 154
gravity-deficiency spheres, 171
gravity energy, cosmic phenomena below levels of, 321
gravity-explosion planets, 170
gravity forces (material) convergent in nether Paradise, 5
gravity-heat contention, 465
GRAVITY MESSENGERS, 346
Gravity Messengers, and finaliters, much in common, 347
Gravity Messengers, liaison between Evening Stars and G M, 145, 260, 408
  timeless technique of traversing space, 347
  under jurisdiction of Grandfanda, 346
GRAVITY, MIND, 132
GRAVITY, MIND-G CIRCUIT, 103
gravity,
  Deity fragments other than T A, don't use, 333
  85% functional in Grand Universe, 132
  of the Infinite Spirit, 155
  universal mg centered in I S, 639
GRAVITY, PARADISE, 125
gravity, Paradise,
  cosmic force, energies unresponsive to, 9
  pull is circular, not linear, 476

91

gravity, Paradise (cont'd)
   three general levels of response to, 125-6
gravity, personality, is non-computable, 133
GRAVITY, PHYSICAL, 132 (see also "gravity" above)
gravity, physical,
   determiner of non-spirit energy, 140
   how stabilized, 125
   source of, 101
gravity reaction, precise gr masses of...dimensions
   and...weight, 476
gravity researchers, conclusions as to master universe
   g systems, 132
gravity-responsive,
   force-energy is variously gr, life is not, 404
   pattern is not gr, 404
gravity, spirit,
   action of sg is measure of living energy of divinity,
      140
   automatic, 84
   is realm of Eternal Son, 139, 639
   leads back to Eternal Son, 81
   like neural circuits in body, 84
   literally pulls soul Paradiseward, 84
   of u of u, one of 7 spirits of advancing worlds, 2062
   pull is as real as physical, 139
   real as physical g, 82
   vs. physical, 140
gravity-spirit circuits, Adjusters undoubtedly use gsc
   and others, 65
GRAVITY, SPIRITUAL, 132 (same as "gravity, spirit"
   132, 139)
gravity systems, three of master universe, 132
gravity-tidal explosions, 658
gravity traversers, instantaneous velocity vs.
   seraphim, 260
GRAVITY TYPES, the (of beings), 561-2
gravity unification is universal and unvarying, 638
grazing animals, suddenly, 695
GREAT COMMANDMENT, THE, 1901
great, for even humblest to be g, 435-6
   "he who would be g", 1536, 1868, 1907
   how man is, 435
   is server of all, 1536
   men ignored, why, 1594
   men (Jesus, John Baptist), 1506, -26
   practically all early g minds Christian, 2074
GREAT RELIGIOUS LEADERS, THE, 1008
Great Sources and Centers, 165
great, things happened, because J had faith in people,
   1875
   things, to do, go do them, 1438
Great Lakes, 701
Great Mother in Phrygian cult, 1084
Great Mother, temples of (Mithraism), 1083
Great River, 1215
Great Spirit,
   Onamonalonton directed his race to worship, 513
   Onamonalonton revived worship of, 723
greater love hath no man than this, 2018-19
greatest gains--spiritual, when, 1209
greatness, and goodness cannot be divorced, 317
   badge of, 1574
   how to grow in, 317
   innate, 786
   lies in, 557
   on Urantia, shown by self-control, 317
   planetary (on Urantia), 317
   Secret of Greatness, 317
   "secret of g in kingdom", 1940
   spiritual g consists, 1758

greatness (cont'd)
   through grace, 317
   tolerance, 1740
   unselfishness and morality, 317
   "unselfishness badge of g", 1572
Greco-Roman world, affluence, poverty, no middle
      class, 1333
   great minds became Christian, 2074
Greece, most valuable strains of...white races, 895
   no priesthood, why, 1078
   Palestine, contrasted, 1079
   375 superior Adamsonites settled, 895
Greek,
   Christianity, effect on Rome if gospel of kingdom
      instead of GC?, 2074
   cities of the Decapolis, 1626
   contractor, to the, 1474
GREEK CULTURE AND FLAVIUS, 1600
Greek, part in Christianity, 2068-9
   pedant at Athens (J), 1476
   philosopher, discussion with J, 1476, 1641
GREEK PHILOSOPHIC THOUGHT, 1078
Greek, philosophy, Christianity embraced best of, 2070
   philosophy, Hebrew theology (Philo), 1338, 1433
GREEK PHILOSOPHY, RODAN'S, 1772
Greek, religion vs. art and philosophy, 2071
   scriptures (J), 1355, -59, -89
   speaking gentile, Norana, 1735
   worker and the Roman foreman, 1430
Greeks,
   among first to recognize causes of disease, 990
   and Romans favored monogamy, 927
GREEKS, APPEARANCE TO THE, 2033
Greeks, basis for mythological traditions, 895
   before Paul's message in hands of, 2068
   believed in oracular advice, 988
   believed in 3 souls in man, 955
   believed menstruating woman cause of defilement, 936
   believed weak men had weak souls, 953
   carried gospel to whole Empire, 2069
   comprehended most, 1932
   converted Stephen Barnabas, 2068
   ended peaceful period, 2068
   first with rational treatment of sick, 992
   forced Christ on Rome, 2071
   good teachings adulterated by slaves, 1077
   group of believing G from Alexandria, Athens, Rome,
      1902
   had wisdom of serpent as symbol, 946
   higher worship fell before cults, 1080
   immortality, G had believed in, 2073
GREEKS, INFLUENCE OF THE, 2071
GREEKS, THE INQUIRING, 1902
Greeks, invented Hades for weak souls, 953
   Jesus would have ordained 20 G, but for...1924
   large numbers from Alexandria, 2068
   later on had triad gods, 1143
   magnificent intellectual advancement, 1078
   monotheism but for...1078 message, make light of, 1607
   needed bigger, better God, 2071
   origin, 862
   posted an alarm, 1971
   pro-genitors of, 895
   religion based on beauty, 67
   revulsion, ethics to depravity, 1080
GREEKS, THE SALEM RELIGION AMONG THE, 1077
Greeks, science without religion, 1726
   taught descent of man, J ascent, 1660-1
   too, were overcome with awe and fear, 2034
   treated women better than...937

guidance,
    accepted, brings consciousness of divine contact, 381
    accepting g no life of ease, 1245
    for teachers and believers, 1765
    go alone to seek g, 1747
    unerring, to God, 39
guide to real insight is love, 2076
GUIDES, THE FATHER, 294
GUIDES, THE GRADUATE, 269
GUIDES, ORIGIN OF GRADUATE, 270
GUIDES, JUSTICE, 434
GUIDES, THE SUPREMACY, 292
GUIDES, THE TRINITY, 292
guiding star, religion is gs of civilization, 1013
guilt, don't harbor, 1736
    is purely a matter of personal sin, 2003
    no racial g before God: guilt is personal, 2003
    "refuse to have feelings of", 1736
    sense, mark of glory, 984
    test, marital, in Bible, 795
guilt feelings, due to conflict, ego interest, other than
    self-interest, 1134
guilt, purely personal, 2003
    matter of rebellion against F, 2003
guilt, sense of,
    from interrupted spiritual communion, 1133
    from lowering one's moral ideals, 1133
    transcendent distinction, 984
guilty ancestors? Nodites denied!, 859
gulf bridged by faith, 2093
Gulf Stream, specialized currents, power, like, 34
gypsum, indicates aridity, 685
gyroscope illustrates effect of antigravity, 101

H

habiliments of light of the celestial world, 1753
habit(s), for spiritual character, 1777
    of criticizing friend, to overcome, 998
    of worship, 1777
    repetition necessary, 1210
    strength-giving, 1777
    substitute ideals for bad h, 1739
    (temptations) how to deal with, 1738-9
    what h is to individual, custom is to group, 767
    which favor religious growth, 1095
Hades, 1855
    invented by Greeks, 953
Hagar, concubine of Abraham, 1023
"hairs of head are numbered", 419, 1682, 1820
half-breeds, chief troubles due to prejudices, 920
half-heartedness, (what's wrong with most of us), 1923
Hallel, J spoke after chanting of the H, 1795
halo, origin of, 834
Hamathites, 1612
hammer, great forward step in civilization, 768
Hammurabi, 876
Han Empire, and Roman, two great, time of J, 1487
hand, apparently cruel, killed Joseph, 1388
    left, not know, 1577, -83
HAND, THE MAN WITH THE WITHERED, 1664
    life of righteousness, 1665
handicaps, Adam and Eve faced many on U, 839
    all earthly h removed in morontia, 508
HANDICAPS, MATERIAL, TO ADJUSTER IN-
    DWELLING, 1199
handicaps, of heredity and environment are overcome,
    508
handling wealth, 1462
hands laid upon heads, 1569   Hap, 747

"happened" (circumstanced?)
    inferior groups (pre-human) eliminated, 733
    Jesus h to meet Gonod and Ganid, 1422
    Jesus h to meet Simon's family, 1375
    man appeared in ice age, not accident, 733
    North American lemurs led to migrate, 733
happiness, always for those certain about God, 1766
    and joy take origin in inner life, 1220
    and wealth, 1573
    beatitudes start with h, 1573
    ensues from truth, 42
    factors constituting human h, 794
    highest h linked with pursuit of worthy goals, 1037
    highest h linked with spiritual progress, 1098
    human, is achieved when... 1134
    increasing always, 1766
    is resulting total of... 1573
    mind h and unity from dedication to will of F, 1480
    none without intelligent effort, 556
    not from sensual, selfish, 1519
    of h man has realized little, 1098
    religion yields h, 1106
    vs. disappointment and sorrow, 42
"happy are the" (beatitudes), 1573
"happy hunting grounds" (lethal submergence), 893
happy, Jesus, 1614
happy personalities, supremely, 549
Hap's prayer, 747
harassments, deliverance from mental h, 1670
hard sayings of J, not commands, 2093
hardships, human vs. cross, 2019
harem, chief dismissed h, was killed, 927
    purpose was... 927
harlotry, badge of h, 1652
    temple h, 982, 1043
harmonics, great appreciation of h, 1 in 1000, 500
harmony, and peace not at cost of individuality, 1591
    detected in chaos, 1307
    is keynote of central universe, 301
    is the speech of Havona, 500
HARMONY SUPERVISORS, 288
HARMONY WORKERS, THE, 507
harp, Jesus', 1364, -87, -89, -93, 1402
"harp of God", morontia receiver for space communi-
    cation, 539
harvest, of ingathering, celebrated, 1793
    terrible, from seed sowing (crucifixion), 2005
HASTY FLIGHT, THE, 1723
hate, and anger, challenge evils of h by love, 2064
    habiliments of, (Judas), 1926
    how love is turned to, 1927
    "is the shadow of fear", 1632
    love can turn into actual h, 1927
    mobilization of h in Judas, 1567
"hated, even as world has h me", 1964
hates me, "who h m hates Father", 1947
hatred, Cain and Abel, 848
    unreasoning, un-Christlike h of Jews, 1909
    warning, intensifier h, 1941
Havona (perfect and divine universe, center of creation,
    1 billion spheres of enormous magnitude, which
    ascending mortals ultimately reach, 152), 136,
    178, 636, 1163
    ability to comprehend is passport to, 290
    all way in to H we are pupil-teachers, 279
    almost unbelievable mass, 152
    appeared "with" Conjoint Actor, 91, 1148
    arrival at H requires: perfection of purpose, tested
    faith, disappointment proof, sublime sincerity,
    divinity of desire, 290

he

healing (cont'd)
HEALING THE PARALYTIC, 1666
healing, phenomena, the, 1669
    prayer contributes to enjoyment of abundant health,
      999
    prayer not technique for curing real and organic
      diseases, 999
    remedial procedures aided by prayer, 999
    reserve powers stored in unconscious mind, tapped
      by prayer, 999
    under influence of strong personality, 1658
    Urantia method improved on another Satania world,
      735
    usual diagnosis, entrails examination, 991
    wound h and cell reproduction, result of over 1/2
      million experiments, 735
health, 757
    Adjusters delighted to contribute to, 1204
HEALTH, ANGELS OF, 1256
health, anger depletes the h, 1673
    early prayers, bargaining for h, 983
    good h, essential to temporal life, 1778
    goodness of soul, (Socrates), 1079
    guardians of h and life, 747-8
    humor on U, h insurance, 549
    in industry, first attention paid to, 815
    influences religious experience, 1095
    laws of h in Garden of Eden, 836
    nonscientific treatment of disease, 991
    "not the smile nor frown of God", 1831
    practical test of religion, 1000
    prayer contributes to h, 999
    primitive ideas of h at J' time, 1341
    problems of h, best solved when, 1779
    the result of material causes,1831
    sanity, happiness, truth, beauty, goodness, 43
    Sethite priests, concern with h, 850
    Spirit of Truth a tonic for h, 2065
    sunlight, h-giving, disease-destroying, 748
    taught in schools of Garden of Eden, 835
    total, arises from unification, 1097
    wisdom lost for 500,000 years, 747
    Zoroaster, subordinates and h, 1049
health resorts, primitive, 991
hearing (human) extended, 630
heart, covenant written on tablets of the h (Jeremiah),
    1071
    Father speaks within the h, 1664
    human h is deceitful (Jeremiah), 1609,-30
    in your heart Father is present, 363
    "let not your h be troubled", 1955
    a new h will I give you, 1630
HEART OF COUNSEL, THE, 312
heart,of J' religion, 1582
    of man, divine spirit within (J), 1457,-74-5
    "there was but one h", 2065-6
    water the garden of your h, 554
heart, gigantic (like), inner zone of nether Paradise,122
hearts, clean, rather than hands, 1713
hearts' desires, if God is supreme delight, 1639
hearts, J appealed to h of hearers, 1632
    "no wonder h burned within us", 2036
    spirit influence in h, 1700
heat, electronic boiling point, 35 million degrees, 463
    for pain, early discovery, 991
    from our sun, boil all oceans in 1 second, 464
    sun's interior, unbelievable 35 million degrees, 463
heathen city, so-called (Scythopolis), 1370
HEATHEN, WHY DO THE H RAGE, 1725
heathenish, to believe in fetishes, magic, ok to accept
    relics and miracles, 968

heating system, Jerusem, equable temperature, 519
heaven, first, second, to seventh, 174
    "I saw a new h and...earth" (John), 599
HEAVEN, THE KINGDOM OF, 1858
heaven, mansion worlds, 174
    of U believers, is Jerusem, system hdqtrs., 519
    "on earth", light and life worlds, 625
    wise advisers of the first h, 553
heaven of heavens, 7 levels, mansion worlds to
    Paradise, 553
heavenly helpers, 1191
heavenly life with earthly existence, 1405
HEAVENLY REPRODUCERS, 500
Hebrew (see also section "Jewish, Jews")
    concepts of God, six, 1598
    Moses' problems with H captives, 1055-8
    prophets, later, 41
    theology failed to expand, 1076
    theories, Book of Enoch nearest to, 1390
    thought, eastern and western, 1338,-66
HEBREW HISTORY, 1071
Hebrew history, 784-5, 1023,-49,-70
    converted into a fiction of sacred history, 1071
    disastrously exploited by Jewish and Christian
      writers, 1071
    distorted, by attempts to transcendentalize H
      prophets, 1071
    exploited by Jewish and Christian writers, 1071
    records altered in Babylon, high points to
      illustrate, 1071
    Saul's army 3000, priests changed to 330,000, 1072
Hebrew literature, religious culture and liturgy by
    way of Egypt, 1043
Hebrew priests, destroyed "The One God", claimed
    Ikhnaton's Psalms, 1048
Hebrew prophets, proclaimed God, Father to Israel, 41
HEBREW RELIGION, THE, 1075
Hebrew religion, based on goodness, 67
    believed in a "God of battles", 784
    clearly defined evolution of God concept, 1039
    concept: God as a vindicator of moral values, 67
    evolutionary link between evolution, revelation, 1011
    factually predicated on covenant...1052
    great mistake of the H r, 43
    influenced by Egyptian, Babylonian, Iranian concepts,
      1052
    judgment for life's sins idea from Egypt, 1045
    link between evolutionary, revelatory religions, 1011
    monotheistic, prejudiced against Trinity concept,1144
    much turns out to be profane history, 1075
    nature spirits in H r, angels of fire, water, air, 947
    of Old Testament evolved in Babylon during captivity,
      1075
    soil out of which grew Christianity, 1075
    spiritual retrogression, 1075
    3000 years before Scriptures written, great
      Egyptian triad, 1045
    transmitted much morality of Egypt, Mesopotamia,
      Iran, to Occidental peoples, 1052
Hebrew ritual, whole bloody r overthrown but for
    stubborn priests, 1067
Hebrew scribes, altered records, partly cause of Jews
    rejecting J, 1024,-71
Hebrew scriptures, editors left in telltale reference,837
    Jesus' remarks on, 1767
    Jesus renounced Messianic ideas for self, 1522
    Jesus voiced Psalms at end, 2010
Hebrews, abolished paying "blood money", 796
    Amenemope's book was H's sacred book before O.T.
      writing, 1046
    Arab ancestors, 787

H

heritage of the ages is yours, 1240
hero, valiant and courageous h--J (Joshua ben Joseph), 1013
HEROD (the Idumean) ACTS, 1353 (father of Herod Antipas, died 4 B.C., 1334)
    after H's death, holy family returned to Palestine, 1355-6
    built harbor of Caesarea, 1334
    census taken year late, 7 B.C., 1350
    died 4 B.C., son Antipas ruled later to 39 A.D.,1334
    helped make Palestine crossroads of...world, 1334
    reason for his overlordship of Judea, 1334
HEROD ANTIPAS (son of Herod the Idumean)
    apostate Jew, believed nothing, feared everything, 1717
    Asmonean Palace, stately home of Herod, Jerusalem, 1379
    at Tiberias had meeting with Sanhedrin representatives, 1717,-19
    change of heart about J, 1741
    cheated J' family, 1393-4, 1992
    discussed by Joseph and Mary on trip, 1351
    fears once more aroused by J' healings, 1633
    gave Herodias' daughter head of John Baptist, 1508
    governed Galilee and Perea J' youth to 39 A.D.,1334
    great builder like father, rebuilt Sepphoris, 1334
    imprisoned wife, buried strangled sons, 1375
    in Jerusalem dwelt in old Maccabean palace, 1992
    intrigue and murder common at court of H, 1354
    jailed John Baptist, 1502
HEROD, JESUS BEFORE, 1992
Herod Antipas, J eluded followers by passing through H's Galilee, 1759
    Jesus knew ruler would soon notice his work, 1587
    knew fair trial for J impossible in Jerusalem, 1719
    knew he had no jurisdiction over J in Judea, 1992
    many of household of H believed in J, 1647
    never recovered from killing John Baptist, 1992
    ordered all boy babies under 2 years old destroyed, 1354
    Philip, brother of H A almost follower of J, 1789
    sent spies again, was John Baptist risen?, 1633
    sent spies to check on J' quiet work, 1534
    Sepphoris, one of residences of H A, 1368
    spies sought babe J for a year, 1354
    spies reported priests of Ur went to Bethlehem, 1353
    startled by J' stately appearance, 1992
    "that fox" (J), 1393, 1872
    twelve years after search for babe, J to Jerusalem, 1374
    villages built by H, superior architecture, 1375
    was informed J' kingdom was spiritual only, 1717
    wished to be rid of J, 1872
Herodians, political party, 1535
Herodias, 1508
Herod's household, believers, 1647
heroes, man is profoundly influenced by h he honors,1013
heroism, in leadership of second garden, 869
    of the God-knowing, 1608
    Heshbon, 1868,-70
Hezekiah, King, 946

hi

hibernating in spiritual sense, Christianity, 2074
High Commissioners, one order of Universe Aids, 406, 410
high destiny, you cannot fail of h d if...64
High Son Assistants, more needed, 254
HIGH SON ASSISTANTS (250,000 in Orvonton), 243, 253

higher law vs. lower law, 137
HIGHER PERSONALITIES OF THE INFINITE SPIRIT, 264
HIGHER SPIRIT ORDERS OF ASSIGNMENT, 413
highest, function of government, adjudication, 247
    human concepts, U. Book uses, 16-17
    moral choice, choice of...will of God, 435
    mortal attainment, true self-mastery, 1610
    philosophy, based on reason, faith, truth insight,1137
    relationship, marriage, 1838
    religious concept ever, J, 1781
Hildana, woman taken in adultery, 1792-3
"him who is able to save", prayers to, 1408
Hinayana, division of Buddhism (asocial doctrine), 1038
Hindu peoples,shackled souls of H p in spiritual hopelessness, 1029
HINDU RELIGION, THE, 1031
HINDUISM, 1447 (see also "Brahmanism")
    claimed Christ was incarnation of Vishna, 1032
    four descending levels of deity, divinity, 1031
    has been usually a tolerant religion, 1031
    oldest, most cosmopolitan religion of world, 1031
    part of basic social fabric of India, 1032
Hindus, concept of the atman (like T A), 1215
    devotees of physical humiliation, suffering, 976
    food taboos, fetishism, sacred cow of H, 975
    friendly relations with house snakes, 946
    had triad gods before Trinity was revealed, 1143
    Hinduism most ancient of "now" religions, 1011
    kindle altar fire primitive way, 1004
    religion of metaphysics, 67
    Sethite priests influence persisted among H, 1009
    trinity was Being, Intelligence, Joy, 1144
Hippos, 1763
historians, primary midwayers are h, 425
historic exhibit areas, 7 trillion on peripheral Paradise,121
history, confusion in Hebrew h due to, 1070
    Hebrew (see under "Hebrew")
    miscarriage, planetary, 754
HISTORY OF THE REBELLION, 607
history, of universe, beginning of, 1158
HISTORY OF URANTIA, 651
HISTORY, SACRED AND PROFANE, 1070
history, sacred h of Jews is profane history, 1075
    what it is, has been, made by might, 908
Hittites, 896,1054
    Assyrians, Philistines, raids on Palestine, 1019

ho

Holocene or postglacial period, 702
Holy Area of Paradise, 120
holy book, oath on hb, form of refined fetishism, 969
"Holy One of Israel", is also "loving Father", 2087
Holy Spirit, comes first, then T A, 379
    effective with followers of divine leadership, 379
    in all humans, 1003
    initial supermind bestowal, 1003
    is ministering circuit of local Creative Spirit, 95
    is of Universe Daughter of Infinite Spirit, 380
    is the presence of the Infinite Spirit, 100
    kingdom of God is joy in the H S, 382
    Master Spirits may influence bestowal of, 190
    more help to those who obey, 379
    not in word only but...power and in the H S, 380
    one will return, baptize with H S (J B), 1505
    the spirit of the I and the Mother Spirit, 2062
holy water, belief in hw still survives, 967
    Mithraics dipped fingers in hw on entering temple,1083

human (cont'd)
    highest h attainments, 1141
    institutions, antagonisms, 938
HUMAN INSTITUTIONS, BASIC, 772
HUMAN INSTITUTIONS, PRIMITIVE, 772
human, institutions, 3 general classes, 772
    interassociations, suspicions and irritations of, 766
HUMAN JESUS, 1424
    Paul lost sight of, 2092; time to resurrect, 2090
human, leaders--Adjusters, 1198
    life, ancestral plasm inaugurated by Life Carriers,
        mind is gift of local universe Mother Spirit,
        ability to reproduce from Universe Spirit, 404
    life, concept inherent in Father, 405
        expression in the Son, 405
        realization in the Spirit, 405
    life, knowledge of, 1425   summation of, 2094
    limitations, awful spectacle of, 59
    living, important to find out J' beliefs, 2090
HUMAN MIND, THE EVOLUTION OF THE, 709
human, mind of J follows divine, 1522
    mortal (see also "mortals")
        character of God portrayed to... by Creator Son,233
        creature designs and types controlled by Eternal
            Son, 236
        energy-matter dominated by Infinite Spirit, 236
        mind is endowment of third Source, Center, 236
        nature of son, portrayed by Avonals, 233
        personality designed and bestowed by U Father,236
        spirit designs and types controlled by Trinity or...
            236
        teacher personality of Infinite Spirit disclosed by
            Daynals, 233
    nature, better side of h n fostered by...770
        embittered, rarely heeds divine warnings, 1567
        not inherently sinful, 1739
        no thing h n touches, infallible (J), 1768
        3 inalienables, 192
    not from monkeys or gorillas, 697,700,703,705
    outranks Adjuster, 1239
HUMAN PARADOX, THE, 1221
human, personality (see "personality"), 8-9, 29
        is the time-space image shadow cast by divine
            Creator personality, 29
HUMAN PERSONALITY AND ADJUSTERS, 1198
human, potential, in 7000 strains other than...734
    primitive, suddenly, 700
    problems, competence for solving, 1581
        solvent for, 2093
    proclivities, four strong, 780
    progress, measured by attainment and mastery of 7
        cosmic circles, 569
        revelational evolution, technique, 2094
    race, destined to know U F, 60
        heroic chapter in annals of h r, 1021
        history of h r is one of progressive evolution, 846
        homeland of, 878
        no surviving ancestry between frog and Eskimos,
            732
HUMAN RACE, RELIGION AND THE,1132
human, race, spiritual assets of, 2076
        vs. physical planet, 582
    races of Urantia, lowly... creatures, 21
    relations, 494,1430
    relationships, ideal of, 1651; important, 494,1228,-35
    religions,none ever surpassed one-time humanism of
        Nile Valley, 1045
HUMAN RESOURCES, 907
human, resources, as factor in U civilization, 907
HUMAN RIGHTS, 793

human (cont'd)
    rights, desires, practices
        duty of society to provide (man) opportunity for,794
        home embraces essential functions, 931
        few in Middle Ages, 794
        originate society, can destroy it, 764
        threat against family life, 942
        three groups function as a social mechanism,772-3
    sacrifice, "according to the word of the Lord", 981
HUMAN SACRIFICE, EVOLUTION OF, 980
human, sacrifice, maiden in molten metal for bell, 981
HUMAN SACRIFICE, MODIFICATIONS OF, 981
human, sacrifice, origin, 722
    put end to cannibalism, 983
    stopped cannibalism, 980
    virtually universal in religious customs, 980
HUMAN SELF, SURVIVAL OF THE, 1232
human, service, supreme satisfaction of (J), 1465
    society, China once head of, 1035
    species improvement, hybridization, 920
    stocks, blended vestiges of both herbivorous and
        carnivorous, 593
    stones, constitute living temple, 1747
    subject of this revelation, 1243
    tendency, to exalt teacher in place of teachings, 1413
    things: all fallible, 1768
        must be known in order to be loved, 1118
    thought, all divisions of h t predicated on assump-
        tions, 1139
    through whom this communication is made, 1208
    traits, rudimentary, appeared, 705
    triumph of, ultimate, 736
    trust, most sacred, 1403
    type of mind, 1st decision, 710
    unity, only through religion of spirit, 1732
    upreach, divine downreach, 1125
    wills that perish (J), 1431

humanism, of the Nile Valley, 1045
    religion without God, 2084
humanists, drift with current, 2080
humanists and socialists, despite these, religion
        always stabilizer of society, 1091
    many err in teaching about religion, 1091
humanitarian labors no substitute for gospel, 1931
humanitarianism, indicted, 1087
humanity to divinity, ascend, 2092
human's ancestors, 3 mutations from lemurs, 703
humans, associated due to hunger, sex, fear, vanity,
        765
    drew together--why, 765
    first, beginning 3rd glacial advance, 700
    first h full maturity at 12 years, 708
    the first h on U appear, 700,707
    first, potential life of 75 years, 708
    five original types, blended, 905
    inequality of h, mental and physical, 792
    intelligent (?) believe in good luck, evil eye,
        astrology, 973
    lowly, are sons of God, 448
    normal--drives toward growth, 1095
    on earth 2000 years ago, contribution to J' life story
        in U Book, 1343
    only 2 groups in eyes of God, of universe, 1468
    only 2 ways in which mortals may live, 1775
    perfected--in universe management, 348
    primitive, appeared suddenly, 700
    spirits do not return to earth after death, 1646

humans, not equal
  ability, endurance, skill, fortitude, 792
  eradicate inequalities through biologic renovation, 793
  if...inequalities cease to be profound paradoxes, 1268
  intellectually, socially, morally, 1468
humbled, he who exalts himself, 1838
humblest man, dispells darkness by faith, 1118
humility, before God is altogether appropriate, 1676
  early, an attempt to deceive spirits, 963
  hypocrisy of self-conscious h, 1676
  indeed, becomes mortal man, 1676
  Jesus aimed at true h toward G, 1582
  vs. hypocrisy, 1676
humor, advantages, values of, how it functions, 549
  Andonic clans, h almost absent, 714
  automatic safety valve, 549
  celestial, 547
  divine antidote for exaltation of ego, 549
  from Adamics, more of than music, art, 549
  Jesus remarked half-humorously...1744
  little h graced these early tribes, 748
  missing in Jews (J), 1736
  mortal, 548
  mortal h becomes most hearty when, 548
  Norana's h touched J, 1736   Nathaniel's, 1558
  of today derived from Adamic stock, 835
  reversion directors depict high h, 548
  spirit h never unkind or blasphemous, 547
  superhuman h quite different, 547
  Thought Adjuster on high contributes to spiritual laughter, 550
  three levels of appreciation, 547
  true religion should not destroy sense of h, 1100
  vulgar and unkind confused with h, 549
humor taste, trying to improve the ht (Joy of Existence), 312
hunger, and thirst for true righteousness, 1774
  for perfection, 1119
  "for righteousness", 1683
  "for truth", 2054
  indescribable of unspiritualized mind, 381
  march, early, 10 miles long, 768
  soul, 942
  spiritual, prevented, 381
  strikes, 796
hungry, bread of life...given only to h, 2054
  can lead only the spiritually h, 1466
  message received by h Jews and gentiles, 1806
  teacher of truth attracts only the h, 1815
  "willing hands, earnest hearts, not go h", 1577
hungry souls, famish in presence of bread of life, 1766
hunter to herder, task of P P, 742
HUNTING STAGE, THE, 768
husbandman, Godlike wise, 1946

hy

hybridization, superior and dissimilar stocks good, 920
Hydra, 732
hydrogen changed to helium, 464
hygiene, doctors need to know more body chemistry, 735
hymn of redemption of first-born (J), 1353
hypnotism, shamans, 987
hypocrisy, Jesus' few denunciations largely against h,1582
  Jesus: "My Father loathes h", 1676
  Jesus swept aside...vanity and h, 1671
  "leaven of the Pharisees, which is h", 1820
  majesty of Master, h of his enemies, 1892

hypocrites, scribes and Pharisees, 1907-8
  these h make long prayers, 1907
  why play the part of h, 1836
  you h, 1712 (see also under "Jesus, quotes")
hypocritical, J: "this sinful and h generation", 1760
  "to a h generation no sign...", 1745
Hyrcanus, John, 1612
hysteria, transient religions h (fanaticism), 1705
hysteric medicine women, 986

I

"I abhor myself" (Job), 1663
"I am a God at hand as well as afar off", 44
"I am he" (deliverer), 1614
I am (J could say) (16 things), 1965
"I am -" (the many things J could say), 1965
I AM, 1040, 1150-1, -69-70, -73
  actuality of the potentials of I AM is absolute, 1263
  as the I AM, we postulate his permeation of total infinity, 1166
  as Triune and as Sevenfold, The I AM, 1153
  "before Abraham was, I am" (J), 1750, -86, -97
  Concept of the I AM, 6
  connotes unqualified infinity, 1153
  the cosmos of the Infinite I AM is endless, 1122
  duality incomprehensible, 1261
  the Father-I AM has achieved liberation, 1266
  final conception of Buddha, sometimes I AM, 1040
  the First Source and Center, the I AM, 1139
  First Source and Center, I AM, reality's origin, 1262
  hypothesis of all that is unknowable of God, 1153
  "I know...because I am a son of--", 1127
  infinite God, 2080
  Infinite I AM is Father of Michael, 1122
  is...extension of the "infinity of will", 6
  is the God of human salvation, 1122
  Jesus so revealed this name of the Father, 1965
  LEVEL OF THE I AM, THE, 1172
  must exist before existentials, after experientials, 1174
  only the I AM is causeless, 1126
  original monotheic Creator personality, 638
  PHILOSOPHIC CONCEPT OF THE I AM, 1152
  Potential and Actual encircuited in the Original, 1263
  signifies also I WAS and I WILL BE, 1296
  a son of I AM, 1127
  synonomous (in personality) with Universal Father, 1152
  "that I AM" (J), 1965
  three spirit expressions unified in the I AM, 639
  unified before becoming Universal Father, 639
  a unity in infinity...expressed as the I AM, 1261
  Universal Father in Paradise Trinity is the I AM of the Trinity of Trinities, 1174
I have sinned...and it profited me not, 1440
"I, the Lord, change not", 58
"I will be subject to the will of my Father", 1523 (see many sayings under "Jesus, Quotes")

ic

ICE AGE, THE CONTINUING, 700
ICE AGE, THE EARLY, 699
ICE AGE, PRIMITIVE MAN IN THE, 700
ice age, 2,000,000 years plus, termination 35,000 years ago, 702
ice invasions (6), 699, 701
Iceland, 869, 1021
iconoclast, Simon an i by nature, 1565

id

idea, creature-trinitized, 254
  of God and the ideal of God, 1781
  power of, lies not in its truth, but vividness, 961,
    1005
  vs. decision, difference, 1112
ideal, conditions for gaining light, truth, 1209
  human estate, 1080
  of religious philosophy, 1141
  social order, 1087
  society prevented by weak and wicked, 804
idealism, cannot survive if idealists exterminated, 804
  great test of, 804
  is i desirable?, 51
  national, its test, 804-5
  not equal to religious reality, 2095
  of the race, essential, 911
  of statehood, by evolution, 803
  vs. necessity, 1405
idealist(s), dead, no good, 804
  extreme i and scientists at loggerheads, 1457
  financial affairs of i (J) difficult, 1566
  Jesus' life a comfort to the disappointed i, 1393
  use oars, don't drift, 2080
  vs. materialist, barren extremes, 1779
ideals, and ideas, 1740
  born only in creative inner realms, 1220
  elevate source of social stream, 909-10
  facts adjusted to i (wisdom), 1779
  highest, can't be lived up to, 1133
IDEALS OF FAMILY LIFE, THE, 939
ideals, of Jesus
    lost to ideas about, 2070
      will assert full power, 2070
  of objective cosmic reality, 1141
  of spirit reality satisfied when, 1950
IDEALS OF STATEHOOD, THE, 803
ideals, of west, mainly Socratic, 1077
  origin of, 1133
  supermortal, striving for i, always characterized
    by, 1100
  vs. ability to live up to them, 1133
  vs. ideas, 1220, 1740, -82-83
ideas, defined (J), 1478
  minds, sometimes astonishingly similar, 191
  power is in vividness of, 961, 1005
  values, meanings, 1775
  vs. ideals, 1220, 1740, -82-83
  vs. positive decision, 1113
  wrong i about God, 59
ideas and ideals of J, world has never sincerely tried,
  1863
identical in origin, nature, destiny,
  light, heat, electricity, magnetism, chemism,
  energy, matter, 472
identification, badge of natal i, 190
IDENTITY AND DIVERSITY OF THE MASTER SPIRITS,
  186
identity, arrival of T A constitutes identity, 569
  becomes as though it had never been, 37
  continuity of i proved by...1236
  equates with T A, 569
  eternalized, 1182
  is memory, insight, consciousness, 1235
  memories of past, 550
  not necessarily personal, 8
IDENTITY OF THE ETERNAL SON, 73
identity, survival of, 1182, 1232, -86
  vs. personality, 8, 10
  with indestructible reality, 1276

ideograph recorders, 503-4
ideograph techniques, "flash" learning, 503
ideographic techniques--broadcast, 431
idiots, either beaten to death or revered, 968
idleness, disenfranchisement for i, 818
  is destructive of self-respect, 1765
  should never be tolerated, 780, 803
idler, worker made slave to i, communism, 780
idol, crude, reputedly fell from heaven, 1478
idolatrous, Jesus admonished, leave on earth nothing
    potentially i, 1330
  parchment, doorpost (J' view), 1372
idolatry, distinguish from symbolism, 946
idols, are material only, 1681
  a refinement of fetishism, 969
Idumea, 1987
ignorance, and superstition, disease-breeding practices
    of, 748
  breeds suspicion, 597
  profound, "our", 47
ignorant, be patient with the i, 1931
  creatures of this world, 1570

Ikhnaton, clear concept of revealed religion of Salem,
  1047
  descendants of I. in Alexandria, respects to child, J,
    1355
  Egyptians accepted half-heartedly, briefly, 1046
  heart of I. teachings, 1st Psalm, 1047
  next to I. of Egypt, Asoka great leader, 1037
IKHNATON, THE REMARKABLE, 1047
Ikhnaton, taught in post-Melchizedek era, 1009
  through I. Mesopotamian culture to Hebrews, 1043
illegitimate children, primitive people prevented i c, 791
  wards of girl's mother, 770
illumination which inspires soul, 1774
illusions, optimistic, preclude wisdom, 1779
illustrations of spiritual faith, twelve, 1108

im

IMAGE AIDS, THE REFLECTIVE, 202
"image of God", not physical likeness, but rather gift of
  spirit presence, 1193
imagination, evil bypaths of our i, 1622   glands, 566
  stimulation of i, is glory of friendship, 1776
images and idols, 969
imbalance, between self-liberty and self-control, 1302
  intellectual and spiritual growth, Greece, India, 1078
  self-liberty and self-control, 1302
  technology vs. worship-wisdom, 1302
Imhotep, Andite architectural genius, 894
  pyramids, 894
"imitate my life, no" (J), 1953, 2091
imitation of God is key to perfection, 1221
Immanence of the Projected Incomplete, 1291
Immanuel (older brother of Christ Michael, only
    personality in Nebadon who has not acknowledged
    subordination to his brother Michael; is Union of
    Days from Paradise, 370)
  assumed u authority in Michael's bestowal absence,
    1309
  bestowal release of I., for J, 1513
  communicated with J, period of tomb, 2016
  counselled M to remain aloof from rebels, 617
  instructions to J on healing, observed, 1659
  Jesus was called "I.", said "...my elder brother",
    1409
  Jesus instructed Gabriel carry on under I., 2022

Immanuel (cont'd)
    Jesus' Paradise brother, 1311-12, -14-15, -23-24
    Jesus' Personalized Adjuster to Salvington and I.,
        2025
    messenger of I. appears to J, 1376
    Michael (J) took counsel with I. on rebellion, 605
    pre-bestowal instructions to Michael, for U, 1325,
        1594
    wanted J to finish earth career, 1515
immaterial, not safe to postulate i is always nonspatial,
    1297
immature, humanity, why, 1772, 1829
    personality, pride of, 1778
immaturity, time unit of i concentrates meaning-
        value into moment, 1295
    Urantia, why, 248
IMMEDIATE RESULTS OF REBELLION, THE, 758
immense spheres, seven, 143
immensity, staggering i of God's... creation, 51
immorality of human intolerance, 597
IMMORTALITY, THE ATTAINMENT OF, 1212
immortality (see "eternal life"), mechanism for, 12
    time, space (J on), 1438
impact, human can feel i of Father's LOVE, 50
impartiality, God's attitude to the total, 137
impatience is a spiritual poison, 557
imperfection, in the evolutionary, arises how, 1159
    limitations of, compensation for, 1159
IMPORT OF TIME, THE, 315
important, we find out what J believed, 2090
importuning, value of, 1619
impossible, nothing is i in liaison with God, 291, 1181,
    1299
impoverished souls, majority of i s are rich, 556
impregnable, spiritual sureties are i, 1096
impression or power of idea, due to vividness, 961, 1005
improvident today, depend on state, 780
impulse, strong, not sign of divine, 1766
impulses, natural,
    not given you to be frustrated, 160
    to be fully realized, gratified, 160

in

in-marriage, restrictions against i-m are purely
    taboos, 919
inaction, faith delivers from evils of i, 1438
inalienables, of human-consciousness, 195
    of human nature, 192
inbreeding, 918-19
incarnation (4 orders sonship), 584 (see "Adam and Eve",
       "Melchizedek", "Michael", 1331, "Prince's Staff
       of One Hundred")
    guide for Michael (from Immanuel), 1324
    mystery of i, more and more unfathomable, 1376
    of a Creator in the likeness of a creature, 1325
incarnations, creature i, purpose of, 1308
    making two one (God and man, J), 1331
Incas, ancestors of I., Andeans and Andites from J, 873
incense, Judas, 1567
incentives for living, three, marriage provides all, 942
incest, origin to ideas of i, 916
income tax, world of light and life, 10%, not
    progressive, 625
incomplete finites, 1162
inconsistencies in revelation, 42
inconsistency of modern mechanist, 2078
inconsistent religionists, J quoted Isaiah, "delight in
    injustice", 1656
increasing happiness, 1776

India,
    ancient I. was catch basin for migrating races, 879
    Brahmans exalted selves above their gods, 1028
    Buddha never clearly defined Nirvana, 1036-7
    Buddhist missionaries to China, 1035
    civilization of I. doomed 12,000 years ago, 881
    complex mixture, mostly green, orange, black
        races, 869
    cosmology of Buddha hurt by superstitions of I., 1040
    cosmopolitan country, days of Melchizedek, 1027
    creativity diminished, matings of inferior strata, 920
    desire and ambition virtually destroyed, 1029
    earliest race mixtures, red, yellow, and Andonites,
        879
    15,000 B.C., peoples of I. lay stagnant, 871
    gave rise to many religions, philosophies, of
        eastern Asia, 1042
    great need in I. today is...1032
    harbors blend of secondary Sangiks, 728
    Hinduism integral part of social fabric of I., 1032
    Hindus conceived atman (like T A), 1215
    Hindus devotees of physical humiliation, 976
    home of most cosmopolitan people ever, 726
    Jesus' views on caste system, 1468
    Kateri people of I. still worship a stone, 944
    "like lighthouse when you return to I.", 1432
    modern languages from people who conquered I., 872
    Mongoloid, Caucasoid, Negroid blended, 905
    much stock of red man left in I., 723
    need today for Jesusonian gospel, 1032
    no age restrictions on marriage, 916
    people of southern I. ruined budding civilization,
        1028-9
    peoples of I. sought leaders from Sumeria, 876
    philosophical framework is there, spark needed, 1032
    race mixtures in I. were blending of... 879
    rainbow thought to be gigantic celestial snake, 947
    red men passed around highlands of I., 727, 883
    rejection of Salem gospel, turning point for I., 1028
    religion in Europe, low ebb compared with I., 891
    self-torture vows today harmful in I., 977
    serpent has been revered, 968
    shamanism flourished in I., 988
    Siddhartha, prophet prince of I., 1039
    Siwalik Hills of I. fossils nearest to "missing links",
        720
    spiritual life, prostrate, helpless, 1029
    still looks for return of Buddha, 1000
    stultifying reincarnation, 1029
    thread of monotheism of I. from Adamites, 881
    to this day stone can be used as a witness, 945
    Todas tribes, 994
    tree spirits regarded as cruel, 945-6
    Trinity concept, perpetuated in Agni, 1143
    Trinity conception, compounded, 1144
    Vedic priesthood brought inertia, pessimism to I.,
        1029
    Vedic priests, 1029
    vegetarian tribes as admixed in peoples of I., 851
    vital turning point for, 1028
    west of I., established ancestry of humans, 703
India, China,
    manuscripts from all world at Alexandria, 1432
    needed a Peter, or Paul, 1430
Indians (see also "red men"),
    Central and So. America, steeped in human
        sacrifice, 980
    from China to America 85,000 years ago, 723, 727
    vital philosophic omissions in Brahmanism, 1030
indictment, J' final i of his vehement enemies, 1905

indictment (cont'd)
  Jesus' i of the rulers, scribes, etc., 1906-08
  of J by Sanhedrin court, 1985
indignation, celestial beings, 1984
  characteristic, J, 1529
indigo-black, Saharans, heavy strains of green and
    orange, 889
INDIGO RACE, THE, 725, 904 (see also "black race")
indigo race,
  blue men of Europe and mixed of Arabia drove out
    i, 728
  had desire to worship Unknown until few 1000 years
    ago, 725
INDIVIDUAL AND RELIGION, THE, 1130
individual, basic liberties, vital, 805
  emergence of, 2071
  exalt, 786, 1862
  family member may suffer material consequences of
    family mistakes, 1630
  God as loving the i, new in world, 1590
INDIVIDUAL, GOD'S RELATION TO THE, 62
individual, hope of better world is only in i, 1630
  insurance against death, premium is, 763
  Jesus' teaching for i, not state, 1580
INDIVIDUAL MORTAL, THE, 630
INDIVIDUAL MORTALS, RELATION OF ADJUSTERS
    TO, 1203
individual, pattern of i is arrangement of energies plus,
    483
  pre-eminence of, cardinal feature of gospel, 1863
  rises by choice above sin, 761
  sacredness of i, 1862-3
  sovereignty of, 1488
  truly religious i seeks...67
individual ascenders, 3 groups, take up careers on 1st
    to 7th m w, 569
individual initiative, new gospel of, 749
individual, J' concern with,
  "I am representative...to the i", 1624
  if you are in personal difficulty, come to me, 1624
  J' emphasis was on individual, not race or nation,
    1585
  J saw each soul a perfecting, separate i, 1582
  J sought each soul to develop in own way, 1582
  J was interested only in the i, not the mass, 1580
  left no books, forms, organizations affecting
    religious life of i, 1593
  made clear, teachings applied to i, 1580
  Master had profound respect for every human i, 1545
  nothing so important to J as the i human, 1546
  pre-eminence of i cardinal feature, 1863
  religion of kingdom a genuine personal experience,
    1862
  sermon, religion is personal experience, 1629
individualism, ultra, 749, 752, 786
  vast survival scheme for, 1241
individuality, characteristic stamp of one of Master
    Spirits, 190
  components of, spirit, mind, energy, 102
individuals, countless, have ascended, 2024
  countless have had personal guardians, 2024
  how destroy selves, 37
  instantly, as though "had not been", 37 (see
    "annihilation", "cessation of existence",
    "extinction")
  mandate of dissolution, 37-8
  "relate yourselves to God as i", 1630
  self-identification with iniquity, 37
indivisibility and "procreation", 31
indolence, increasing dangers of, 786
INDUSTRIAL ORGANIZATION, 813

industrial, servitude, 780
  slavery, threat of, 786
industrialism, amazing creativity of American i, 2081
  American i due to secularistic revolt, 2081
  and agriculture, weakness of both, 769
  should promote initiative, encourage individualism,
    786
  vs. militarism, modern, 786
  weakness of i, lacks excitement and adventure, 769
industry, amazing American i, due to, 2081
  and commerce--Garden of Eden, 586
INDUSTRY AND TRADE, THE COMMISSION ON, 747
INDUSTRY, ANGELS OF, 1256
industry, Dalamatian, 747-8
INDUSTRY, THE DAWN OF, 773
industry, early specialists in, 774
  emancipated women, 937
  first specialists, salt, pottery, 774
  learned through oppression, 779
  on mansion worlds, 521
  organization, efficiency, aims of modern i, 786
  perils of budding i on Urantia, 786
  serves higher aims on advanced worlds, 629
  then private property, demand government, 783
  without morality, 2086
indwell mind (soul) T A and Infinite Spirit, 1178 (see
    "Thought Adjusters")
indwelling, divine lover, 2094
  divine presence, 2093
  interpreter and unifier, 2095
INDWELLING THE MORTAL MIND, 1203
indwelling spirit (see also "Mystery Monitor", and
    "Thought Adjuster"), 62
  adjusts mind to...divine attitudes, 76
  "already does spirit of Father indwell you" (J), 1602
  and others, hover over, inspire you, to worship, 304
  "association of mind with i s of...God", 1931
  assurance of the indwelling of God's spirit, 1545
  "authority of truth is spirit that indwells", 1768
  can you realize true significance of i s, 1181
  discovery in mind by i divine s, 2095
  "Father has sent his spirit to live within" (J), 1588
  "Father sends his spirit to indwell" (J), 1536
  "finding God and knowing him in your own souls" (J),
    1732
  the God-consciousness is resident in i s, 2095
  "God dwells within you", 1664
  greatest of unfathomable mysteries, 26
  "his spirit actually dwells within you" (J), 1609
  "I will return as a spirit indweller" (J), 1953
  impulses not necessarily from i s, 1766
  J taught us God lives in man, 1777
  leading of the indwelling divine presence, 2093
  "led...by Father's spirit which lives within..."(J),
    1674
  men can suspend efforts to discover, 2095
  men die searching for God who lives within them, 1766
  men shut off...spirit that dwells within, 1672
  mind of man dwelling place of gift, 1779
  only spirit-indwelt intellect is...loving, 2094
  only spirit-indwelt man can seek fuller experience
    in...2094
  only spirit-indwelt mind sees universe friendly to
    individual, 2094
  "only uniform thing among men is i s", 1672
  revelation by i divine s, 2095
  something from God actually dwells...26
  spirit fragment of F dwells within you, 78
  spirit messengers...to indwell men...50
  spirit of F which indwells minds, 1700
  spirit of God living in the mind of man, 2078

indwelling spirit (cont'd)
  spirit of God who dwells in minds of men, 1742
  "spiritual part of...F in every faith son" (J), 1661
  this lover hails from source infinite love, 2094
  three evidences of this s i of mind, 2094
  unless a divine lover lived in man...2094
  "when (man) becomes indwelt by my Father's
      spirit...becomes divine in his destiny", 1676
  "who yields to...i s will...come to me" (J), 1711
"indwelt by Son as well as by Father", 1948
inequalities, temporal, not religious paradoxes if we
    knew...1268
inequality, of human beings, 792
  of men, Alpheus twins, 1959-60
inertia, of animal legacy, breakthrough, 1242
  of primitive man, safety brake, 767
  -resistance, difficulty, 1488
inevitabilities, the, 51
  courage, altruism, hope, faith, etc., 51
  Trinity, Master Spirits, etc., 1266
inevitable, universe was not i, 52
infallibility, only the Creators possess i, 1768
  no place for spiritual i in J' brotherhood, 2085
  nothing human nature touches is i, 1768
infant in boat on water, Sargon, Moses, Cyrus,
    Romulus, 982
infant mortality, how reduced, 934
infant-receiving-schools, 531
infants, awaken on arrival of parent, 531
  supernatural i put adrift on river, 947
inferior, degenerate strains overload races today, 920
  races, such i r as the Bushmen of Africa, 1132
  way, repugnant to divine nature, 137
inferiors, campaign for extermination of i (Badonan),720
  when 50% of civilization is i, c is doomed, 818
inequalities of men, eradicate many i through biologic
    renovation, 793
infinite,
  awesome master universe, only partial revelation
      of i, 1153
  on levels of i, present moment contains all past,
      future, 1296
  God, but finite universe, 468
  mind, is apparently a law in itself, 104
Infinite, denotes finality implied by primacy of FSC, 6
  face which I. turns to us is face of Father of love,
      1153
  how great, 1153
  is used to denote...6
  Mind, 162
  Mother Spirit, 162 (see also "Mother Spirit")
INFINITE POWER, GOD'S, 46
Infinite Spirit (Third Person of Trinity, Third Source
    and Center, Conjoint Creator of all, executive of
    united will of Father and Son, 1304, 1755)
INFINITE SPIRIT, THE, 90, 105 (see "Spirit, Infinite")
Infinite Spirit, acting in untold legions of beings, 96
  bestows ministry of mercy on our behalf, 95
  bestows non-Father personality, 106
  both Father and Son function through him, 96
  can bestow personality, 106
  children of the I S--angelic hosts, 285
  Conjoint Creator of ALL, 96
  endows vegetables, animals, then humans, 379
  eternity origin of,90
  executive of united will of Father, Son, 249
  functional family of, 107
INFINITE SPIRIT, HIGHER PERSONALITIES OF, 264
Infinite Spirit, "himself makes intercession for you", 96
  in addition to energy, physical, ministers love, 100
  indwells evolving soul, 1178

Infinite Spirit (cont'd)   I
  initiates work of evolutionary progression, 379
  is the Conjoint Actor (Creator), 96
  is mind God, was inevitable, 638
  is omnipresent, 95
    Holy Spirit is local to universe, 95
  is parent of Universe Daughter whose presence is
      Holy Spirit, 380
  is personally conscious of every intellect in all
      creation, 103
  is source of mortal mind, 80
  is "the spirit of God", 96
  is the universal unifier, 98
  labor of I S largely effected through 7 adjutants, 379
  local universe family of I S higher orders of, 413
  man can experience beneficence of, 100
  manifold agencies, influences of, 1244
  a mercy minister, 92
  mother of all angelic ministers, 205
  names of I S, other,
    Conjoint Actor, 101
    Conjoint Creator, 101
    God of Action, 101
    God the Spirit, 102
    Infinite Mind, 102
    Third Person, 102
    Third Source and Center, 101
    see many more, 92,99
INFINITE SPIRIT, NATURE OF THE, 92
Infinite Spirit, often referred to as "spirit of God", 96
  omnipresent, Holy Spirit in each local universe, 95
  only means of attaining Eternal Son, 93
INFINITE SPIRIT, PERSONAL AIDS OF THE, 268
  conservative estimate, high into trillions, 268
Infinite Spirit, personal influence on created beings, 96
INFINITE SPIRIT, PERSONALITIES OF THE, 105, 336
Infinite Spirit, personalities of I S, 3 distinct orders
    of, 418
  one of 7 grand divisions of divine family, 334
INFINITE SPIRIT, PERSONALITY OF THE, 96
Infinite Spirit, "primary eruption" in (consort), 204
  Primary or Paradise supernaphim created by, 285
INFINITE SPIRIT, RELATION TO THE, 185
INFINITE SPIRIT, RELATION TO 7 MASTER SPIRITS,
    185
Infinite Spirit, representative of the unified Father-Son,
    161
  reveals combined love of Father and Son, 94
  satisfaction of I S, as to U bestowal, 1755
  speaks to you, "he who has an ear...", 96
  spirit presence of I S referred to as "spirit of God",
      96
  supercontrol of energy and things physical, 100
  three distinct orders of personalities, 418
  trillions upon trillions beings spring from, 119
  untiring Mind Minister of time and space, 161
  untold legions of manifold beings originate in, 96
  what I S does is function of Conjoint Actor, 112
INFINITE SPIRIT, THE WORLDS OF THE, 149
"infinities of divinity", seven, 471
infinity, and numbers, 1294
  beyond mortal comprehension, 1153, 1261, -69
  concept represents the exercise of faith, 6
  diversified into 7 absolutes, 1150, -63
  is total reality, in Seven Absolutes, 1146
  is total reality, 7 phases of, 1157
  master paradox, 1262
INFINITY OF GOD, THE, 33
infinity, of reality incomprehensible, 1261
  on one hand UNITY, on other DIVERSITY, 1262
  pre-existential and post-experiential, 1163

infinity, response, 5
INFINITY, THE SEVEN ABSOLUTES OF, 1155
infirmity, woman with spirit of i, 1835
"inflation", Galilee cost of living, 1/4 of Jerusalem's, 1369
influence, J most dynamic ever, 1091
    Jesus' on 32 religious leaders, Rome, 1455-6
influenced by his chosen heroes, profoundly, man is, 1013
information, all focalized at any desired point, 105
    in 1 hr. as much as 1000 years, 289
inhabited creation, completely circled by outer rings of universes, 131
INHABITED WORLD, RECOGNITION AS AN, 709
INHABITED WORLDS, THE, 559
inhabited worlds in Satania (619), 359
INHABITED WORLDS, ORIGIN OF, 465
INHERITANCE, DIVIDING THE, 1821
inheritance, for family, 1604
inherited urges, 1572
iniquitous one, 1660
iniquity, become wholly unreal by embrace of i, 37
    destroys prayer connection, 1638
    penalties of i are inexorable, 1660-1
    suggests, 755
initiative, do not diminish, 772
    industrialism should promote, 786
    proportional to spiritual influence, 2078
injustice, be willing to suffer i, 1571
    inequity, in universe, sooner or later, you have justice, mercy, 373
INNER LIFE, THE, 1219
inner self revealed in morontia form, 1236
inner voice, there really is an, 1104
insanity, and evil spirits, 1591
    intellectual death, T A departs, 1230
    mind dead when circuits of will-action destroyed, 1230
    no prisons or hospitals for the insane, 818
    personal disintegration...border on cosmic i, 754
    practically non-existent advanced worlds, 629
    primitives couldn't tell genius from i, 968
insects, appeared 210 million years ago, 680
    born educated, 909
    using golden rule for i, error, 946
insemination, artificial (?), 742, 745
insensitivity, service, 786
insight, acquire spiritual i by faith, 1574
    approach i through love of beautiful, etc., 2076
    capacity for i from religious experience, 1101
    child of i looks for Spirit of Truth in wise sayings, 1949
    concerning i, mind can discover, recognize, interpret, choose, 2094
    connotes choice between:
        good and evil
        human and divine
        material and spiritual
        time and eternity
        truth and error, 2095
    cosmic i, spiritual discernment, 806
    defined, 1226
    experience doesn't yield universe i, 2094
    faculty of human personality which accrues...1105
    find God through leadings of spiritual i, 2076
    a gift, wisdom must evolve, 1109
    highest i of the cosmic mind, 192
    inner, spiritual communion termed s i, 1105
    into 5 things through enhancement of wisdom, 806
    is powers of prevision, 135

insight (cont'd)
    Job's i discerning at last, through faith, 1664
INSIGHT, KNOWLEDGE, WISDOM, 1121
insight, love is true guide to real i, 2076
    man is self-conscious of i, 1773
    mind can attain high levels of i because not wholly material, 2094
    of cosmic citizenship transcends sphere, 1258
    prayer is designed to expand i, 1616
    precedes foresight, 1228
    religious i, power to turn defeat into higher desires, 2096
    settle problem, accord with superhuman i, 1208
    spiritual i connotes choice between...2095
    spiritual i essential to living Golden Rule, 597
    spiritual, is religion, 1105,-07
    spiritual, only s i discerns operations of spiritual nature, 140
    superhuman i had only through religious experience, 2075
insights, God is source of man's superanimal i, 2095
    innate in endowed cosmic mind, 192
    religious i lead to unselfish acts and service, 1121
    scientific, moral, spiritual, are innate, 192
    three, for man to function...as a personality, 192
inspection trips are made, 754-5
Inspector, Associate, 413
INSPECTORS, THE ASSOCIATE, 268
inspectors, official animal i at temple, 1888
inspiration, glimpse of circle of eternity essential to, 1776
    of Adjuster, great help, 1223
inspired--how (Adjuster), 1223
instantaneously, Creator Son acts throughout his universe, 376
INSTIGATORS OF REST, 299
instinct, endowment of adjutant mind-spirits, 932
    for Deity, 1003
    maternal, 932
    never changes, mores do, 938
    precedes reasoned knowledge, 1137-8
instinctive and reflex animal behavior, result of adjutant mind-spirits, 709
institution, every i embraces personal interest antagonisms, 938
INSTITUTIONAL RELIGION, 1092
institutional religion, 1087, 1128
    leaders tend to become administrators, not ministers, 1092
    tends to establish oppressive ecclesiastical authority, 1092
institutionalization of religion, detracts from spiritual quality, but, 1083
institutions, and men on trial at bar of human needs, 1457
    embrace antagonisms, 938
    man should control i, not be dominated by, 772
    necessary to religions, 1076
INSTITUTIONS OF SELF-GRATIFICATION, 772
INSTITUTIONS OF SELF-MAINTENANCE, 772
INSTITUTIONS OF SELF-PERPETUATION, 772
institutions, worth of?, 1388
INSTRUCTION FOR TEACHERS AND BELIEVERS, 1765
instruction(s), education, 412
    Paradise 1 hr. worth 10, 000 years, 303
    three for high spiritual orders, 1179
instruction methods, Philip, effective technique of all teaching, 1557
INSTRUCTIONS TO MICHAEL ON BESTOWAL, 1327-30
INSTRUCTORS, EXTENSION-SCHOOL, 339
insubordination, children, why, 941

insurance, faith is, 1609
  in place of fictitious spirits, gods, 956
  reserves, planet in light and life, 625
insurrection, extinction of instigators of, 1326
integration, amalgamation (ok), 920
  with universe, 2097
integrity, and foresight, 1854
  intellectual i, how maintained, 1433
intellect, Absolute Mind, (Conjoint Actor) source of i,99
  achieve organization of i by decisions, 1398
  is, 1136
  powers of i unknown to mortals, 106
  relationship in i between unit of time and maturity,
    1295
  resides in pulsations of adjutant...1286
  source of local universe i is Divine Minister, 1236
  Third Source...is personally conscious of every i,
    103
  transformation in i, (lunatic), 1696
  vs. faith, 1653
intellectual, and moral suicide, 2079
  cross-fertilization on U, 597
  development evolution, necessary for religion's, 1128
  evolution, no limit to, 631-2
  living, 1114
INTELLECTUAL UNITY, 638
intellectual vs. true religion, 1780
intelligence, can't explain moral nature, 192
  circuits, of universes, like body's neural
    sensation paths, 1276
INTELLIGENCE CO-ORDINATORS, 289
INTELLIGENCE CORPS, THE, 429
intelligence, corps, of Gabriel, 429
  corps, of Prince's administration, 856
  cosmic, of universes, received by T A,
    201, 1207
  "division", David's, 1668
  grows out of, 1949
  lack of, extinction for huge reptiles, 687-88
  results of decline, 908
  universe, 7 divisions of, 160
  vast scheme of universe i, 201
  wisdom, indispensable to true culture, 908
  wisdom, truth, 1949

intelligences, splendid, to Urantia, 1 million morontia
  directors, etc., here 40 days with morontia J, 2040
interassociations of Trinity, (3 Paradise Deities), 1318,
  1324-5
interbreeding good, 920
intercession, no influence needed to get loving-kindness,
  38-9
  "Spirit himself makes i for you", 96
intercession of saints, galaxy of "saints" a spiritual
    menace, 2074
  no influence necessary with God, 38-9
  no, trouble certain for believers, 1767
interchange of strength for weakness, constitutes
    worship, 1777
interdependence throughout U of U, 1275, -90
interest, in young, 1420
  things of (1000) unknown here, 599
interest on capital, honest wealth is entitled to i, 1463-4
  man learned to live on i (flocks), 768
intergravity tensions, 476
interlude, strange (J Lazarus), 1836
INTERLUDE VISIT TO JERUSALEM, THE, 1647
intermediaries (see also "intercession")
  educated mortals delivered from i, 1013
  galaxy of "saints" a menace, 2074
  none function between T A and men, 1187

intermediaries (cont'd)
  presume to stand between man and God, 987
  shamans presume to stand as i, 986
  unnecessary, God and man are directly related, 1187
international relations--foster, 597, 908
international trade, good, 908
international unsettledness, secular revolt, too much,
  2081
internationalism, step in the right direction, 1489
internationalist, Simon "no", 908, 1565
  spiritually-minded, 1565
interplanetary travel, 546 (see also "enseraphimed",
    "transport", "transporters", "travel")
  long flight to Havona, 175
  mansion worlds to system headquarters, 430, 534
  reach Havona cleared for Ascendington, 148
  system assembly representatives, 632
interpreter in mind, part of Universal Unity, 2094
INTERPRETERS AND TRANSLATORS, 546
INTERPRETERS OF COSMIC CITIZENSHIP, 434
INTERPRETERS OF ETHICS, 300
INTERPRETERS, RACIAL, 553
intervention (see also "Most High's rule in kingdoms of
    men")
  angels rarely intervene, 1246
  coop.; seraphim, midwayers, phys. controllers,1246
  Father has right to intervene with individuals, 363
  function determines, not the individual, 1033, 1305
  in affairs of nations, upon orders, 491
  Matadormus illustration, 1802
  midwayers i only on instruction, 1361
  ordinary circumstances i only by midwayers, 1361
  to safeguard men and women of destiny, 1361
  when ordered to i, angels find a way, 1246
intolerance, 1486, 1641
  and caste, none on mansion worlds, 534
  "angels weep because of your i", 1246
  characterizes material-comfort age, 577
  immorality of human i, 597
  inimical to human progress, 803
  is mask of doubts, 1641
  narrow-minded, 1768
  no state, high development, while i exists, 803
  none on high, 534, 1486
  to combat, 803
intoxicants and drugs intrigued the primitive, 776
intoxication, 945, 1436
instrospection (see also "born again, be")
  and self-examination not in J' religion, 1583
  "if you confess your sins, they are forgiven", 1736
  no, but self-forgetfulness and self-control, 1609
  no, constant spiritual renewing of your mind, 1609
  prayer an antidote for harmful, 1621
  "refuse to harbor even the feelings of guilt", 1736
intrusion of agencies, non-spiritual, 45
intuition, result of adjutant mind-spirits, 709
INTUITION, THE SPIRIT OF, 402
intuitions, 3 cosmic i develop in thinking, 192
inundations, No. America (24), 691
invasion, divine i of soul, 2095
  of man by bestowed spirit of Father, 542
invention, due to aridity, 907
  machines, rendered slaves obsolete, 779
  post-Adamic epoch, 592-3
  precedes cultural development, 907
inventions, mechanical, benefits to be derived from,
  are inestimable, 902
invertebrate-animal age, 675
investment, wise, form of insurance (J), 1803
invincible, mortal man dedicated to God's will, 1970
invisible made visible, seraphic helpers & Melchizedeks,
    574

invisible offspring, every fourth, Adamson, Ratta, 861
invitation always: "whosoever will, come", 1820
invitation-command, astounding: "be you perfect", 290
(see also "be you perfect" under "B", and "be you
perfect" under "Jesus, Quotes")

Iowa, 875
Iran, 875
IRAN, THE SALEM DOCTRINES IN, 1049
IRANIAN CULT OF MITHRAS, 1082
iron, copper, vanadium, oxygen, 737
double role in blood cells, 737
IRON, THE GOSPEL AT, 1643
iron, soft i of immaturity to steel of character, 1305
Iron (town), 1890
Iroquois Indians, 933
federation, why failed, 800
many reforms in funeral waste, 960
why powerful, 960
irrigation ditches, artificial, provided night mist to
refresh Garden of Eden, 823
1000's of miles of, Garden of Eden, 824
irritability, freedom from after 3 days vacation, 1611
still exists on Edentia, 494

is

Isaac (son of Abraham), 1021, -24
records altered to make birth miraculous, 1023
Isaac (money lender) complicates for J, 1397
Isador, writer of Gospel of Matthew, 1341
ISAIAH, THE FIRST, 1066
ISAIAH, THE SECOND, 1068
Isaiah, referred to Jews when he wrote:, 1902
taught racial deity (and) Universal Creator, 1011
Isaiah, Jeremiah, 2nd Isaiah, Ezekiel, etc., promises
of, 1071
Isaiahs, high level of Deity doctrines of the I., 1057
Ishtar, 1042-3
Isis, 1043, -48
Isis and Osiris, 1081
Islam, 1011
overwhelmed Abnerian Christianity, 1869
prevailed in northern India over Hinduism, 1030
rise of I. overwhelmed J' teaching, 1869
start, black stone, 1051
Islamic taboo, pork, 975
Isle of Light, 118, 281
Isle of Paradise (see "Paradise")
"ism", many an "ism" has arisen from aborted T A
contact, 1207
isolated, Urantia one of most i planets, 491
isolation, about to descend on apostles, 1928
man's dislike of i resulted in civilized society, 764
"mischief and miseries of i", 2055
of personality, undesirable, 1099, 2055
personality i, to avoid, 1985
planetary i circumvented through T A, 1191
vs. friendship, 1776
why bad, 1776
Israel, 1062, -65, 1352-3
and Judah, 1072
children of I., no longer, but of God, 1629
court of, 1794
covenant with God abrogated, 1910
ISRAEL, DESTRUCTION OF THE KINGDOM OF, 1074
Israel, end of nation drew on apace, 1910
"farewell to benighted rulers of I. ", 1904
go to lost sheep of I., 1681

Israel (cont'd)
had repudiated Son of God, 1910
"I once more offered I. salvation", 1906
king of I. conspired with king of Egypt, 1074
majority in clans of I. never in Egypt, 1055
not children of I., but of God, 1629
quick history of struggle of I., 1732
repudiated by Son of God, 1910
repudiated J, plan shattered, 1910
silenced spiritual leaders, retrogressed, 1075
"witness, I have once more offered I. ", 1906
Israel (Ephraim), northern kingdom vanished, 1074
Israelite, genuine I., Nathaniel, 1527
Israelites, after Melchizedek and Abraham, children of
Israel, 1055
Amos warned I. ritual no substitute for... 1066
Moses: simple narrative of creation to I., 837
never gave up belief in stone altar, 969
issues of battle (J vs. Jews) clearly drawn, 1742
"it is better that one man die", 1847
it is my will that your will be done, 1303
IT IS, the Brahman, the Absolute, the Infinite One, 1031
itinerary, our, 1248

J

Jacob of Crete, 1597
Jacob (son of Isaac), venerated a stone, 944
Jacob, the stone mason's son, 1368
Jacob's well, where J met Nalda, 1611
Jainism, 1011
led to changes in Brahmanism, 1031
Jairus, Jesus to J: "your daughter is not dead", 1699
loyally withstood pressures of religious leaders, 1709
one of rulers of synagogue, Capernaum, 1698
resigned, aligned self with Jesus, 1718
JAIRUS'S HOUSE, AT, 1699
JAMES AND JUDAS ALPHEUS, 1563 (see under
"APOSTLES")
James, brother of Jesus, 1418
"I come to call you to the service of the kingdom",
2032
suffered later for not appreciating J, 1723
talked with morontia J, at Bethany, 2032
treasurer of church at Jerusalem, 1802
James of Safed, 1755
eloquent appeal for son's healing, 1757
JAMES ZEBEDEE, 1552 (see under "APOSTLES")
Jansad, son of Eveson, 849
Japan, 1033-34
Andites, small groups, to Japan, 873
Confucius, great influence in Japan, 1034
132 Andites in boats J to S. A., ancestry of Incas, 873
proto-Taoism known as Shinto, 1033
Shin sect, progressive, 1041
Japanese,
ancestors of J driven from Asian mainland 12,000
B.C., 884
emperor, used clay images to replace human
sacrifices, 980
had missionaries from Salem, 1021
Jaram, the Hittite, 1019
Java man, bones recently found, 719
jaws of death, John accompanied J to, 1555

je

Jebus, Salem became Jebus, then Jerusalem, 1015
worship centered in gorgeous royal chapel, 1073
Jehovah, name came to use 1500 years A. D., 1053
jelly fish, 732

jeopardy, civilization, 586, 911, 1220
  human species, 921
Jephthah and his daughter, 980
Jeramy, Nicopolis, Greek, 1471
  host to J, Paul guest of his son, 1471
JEREMIAH, THE FEARLESS, 1067
Jeremiah (J quoted in epochal sermon), "this man is
    worthy to die for he has prophesied against our
    city", 1709
  "let not rich man glory in his riches", 1822
  "man shall die for his own iniquity", 1630
  proclaimed era of inner righteousness, 1071
Jericho, Abirim and Segub sacrificed in walls of J, 981
    (see also under "Jesus")
  children of J playing with Creator of universe, 1840
  Jesus stopped at J, 1351, 1809
  mothers brought children to J, 1839
Jerusalem (see also under "Jesus")
  after destruction of J, 1861
  agitation for tax rebellion, 1396
  all Jerusalem discussing, 1910
JERUSALEM, AT, 1810
Jerusalem, "daughters of J, weep not for me", 2005
  destruction of, 1861, -72, 1915, -34
JERUSALEM, THE DESTRUCTION OF, 1912
Jerusalem, destruction predicted, 1414, 1906, 2005
  fall of, 1075
  high pitch of excitement, 2034
  "I will return", 1384
  Jesus gazed in silence, 1399
  Jesus prophesied to enable followers to save selves,
    1913
  Jesus 3 weeks in, around, city, 1494
  Jesus' unexpected appearance in, 1789
JERUSALEM, THE JOURNEY TO, 1648
Jerusalem, leaders another chance, 1809, -37, -82-83
  "never knew such a religion in J!", 1436
  O, Jerusalem, 1384, 1872-82, 1903, -06, -08 (see
    details under "Jesus, quotes")
  persecutions (of Christians), 1565
  siege of, 40 yrs. after Jesus died, 2005
  siege of, 1000s Jews died on Golgotha, 2005
  six of the apostles remained in J, 2058
  thrilled Jesus, 1375, -77
  tragic associations of fear, betrayal, death, 2046
  2,500,000 Jews from all the world for festivals, 1339
  whole city stirred up, 1883
  "worship G not at J, but where you are", 2053
Jerusem, advisory council (1900 years ago), 513
  almost 100 times size of Urantia, 509
JERUSEM BROADCASTS, THE, 522
JERUSEM CIRCLES, THE, 523
JERUSEM CITIZENSHIP, 539
Jerusem, description of, 519
  executive council, 12 members, 512
  Father's world, 610
  foretaste of Paradisiacal glory, grandeur, 521
  headquarters of Satania, 174
  intricate material economy, 521
  manufacturing, laboratory sectors, no smoking
    chimneys, 521
JERUSEM, PHYSICAL ASPECTS OF, 519
JERUSEM, PHYSICAL FEATURES OF, 520
Jerusem, spiritual, semispiritual, morontia forms, 436
  system capital, 100 times size Urantia, 509, 519, 1235
  training worlds of J surpassed by Edentia, 493
JERUSEM TRIANGLES, THE, 528
"J" listings are resumed after "JESUS" and "Jews"
  listings.

JESUS   J

Jesus of Nazareth (Michael of Nebadon), (creator of
    Nebadon, our universe, 367; a Son of the Eternal
    Son of Paradise, 74, 366)
Jesus (name is Greek form of "Joshua"), "Of all human
    knowledge, that which is of greatest value is to know
    the religious life of Jesus and how he lived it. ", 2090
Jesus,
  ABNER, AT BETHLEHEM WITH JESUS, 1798 (see
    also under "A")
  Abner, last meeting with J, 1870
  about 100 disciples who would brave Pharisees, 1717
  abrogated ceremonials, 1133
  accidents, material, 1361
  ACCIDENTS, TEACHING ABOUT, 1830
  accusers, bloodthirsty, 1990
  achieved here what takes man pre-Paradise career
    to do, 2092
  achievement before 30 years old, 1426
  acknowledgement to sources of Urantia record and
    concept, 1343
  acted as "nurse" to his ill apostles, 1718
  Adam and Eve, J' message to, 852
  Adam, Paul called J the "second" A, 1582
  added to what prophets taught, 1582
  address, most notable, of his public ministry, 1858
  address, one of his most remarkable, at Luz, 1728
  address, one of the most impassioned, 1608
  Adjuster, insensitivity of J to time, 1516
  Adjuster now Personalized, 1512 (see also "THOUGHT
    ADJUSTERS, JESUS' PERSONALIZED")
  the Adjuster that indwelt J, 1200
  admission of divinity, 1730, -46
  admonished: neglect not daily worship, 1805
  admonition: escape fear, helplessness, 1985
    escape personality isolation, 1985
    on meditation and reflection, 2047
    on preaching, 1543
    to apostles, 1533
  ADOLESCENT YEARS, THE, 1395
  adultery, woman taken in, 1472, 1793
  adventure, great and testing a. (then) to believe in
    J, 1727
  adventure of exploration (Caspian), 1484
  adversity, mission of, 1688
  advice, for one rich man alone, 1462-63
    (Immanuel's) on attitudes toward politics,
      economics, society, 1326, 1514
    seldom offered unless asked for, 1420
  affection for Ganid, 1427
  affectionate pity for spiritually blind, 1376
  afflictions, 3 forms of a. for apostles to meet, 1591
  after baptism, 40 days of adjusting self, 1512
  after Judas missing, last words to 11, 1966
  again called the apostles to order, 1953
  age at baptism, almost 31-1/2, 1512
  age, projecting plan of a new a., 1595
  aggressive child, 1366, -96
  agony, overwhelming emotional, 2011
  aimed at in his life, superb self-respect, 1582
  Alexandria, home of Philo, 1339; Rodan, 1772
    J lived in A 2 years as child, 1354
  Alexandrian proposal, the, 1413
  all men are your brothers, 1431
  alms, refused, 1414
  alone, 1634-35, -47, -59, -88, 1703, -15
    at Cana wedding, 1529
    day and night Gilboa, 1495
    Gilboa, much a. on mountain, 1618

Jesus (cont'd)

Jesus (cont'd)

AT LIVIAS, TEACHING, 1871
AT MAGDALA, THE STOP, 1679
AT NAZARETH, THE SOJOURN, 1683
AT PELLA CAMP, 1817-50
AT PELLA, LAST TEACHING, 1850
AT PETER'S HOUSE, 1761
AT PHILADELPHIA, THE VISIT, 1833
AT POOL OF BETHESDA, 1649
AT RAMAN, THE STOP, 1641
AT RIMMON, PREACHING, 1637
AT TIBERIAS, SABBATH, 1680
AT TOMB OF LAZARUS, 1843
AT TYRE, 1737
AT TYRE AND SIDON, THE SOJOURN, 1734
AT ZEBULON, THE VISIT, 1642
atonement, no, 1494, 1972, -99, 2002-03 (see also
    "atonement" under "A")
    sacrificial ceremonies swept away, 1133
attacked idea of Jewish deliverer, 1708
attacks on error and tradition, 1103
attempts to see his family, 1744
attention, scorned attracting, 1520
ATTITUDE, THE APOSTLES', 1883
ATTITUDE OF THE PEOPLE, 1670
attitude, of soul vs. behavior, 1584
ATTITUDE, POLITICAL, 1580
attitude toward commercializing... religion, 1891
attitude(s), doing the Father's will, 1579
    economic, 1581
    material problems, 1581, -83, 1624, -62
    social, 1580
    toward women, 1546, 1671, 1839
audacious boldness, 1789
audience, over 4000 each morning, 1817
authoritative, original, patient, 1672
authority, Andrew's and other human records, 1341
    behind Jesus Papers, 1319, -21
    refused universe a., 1753
    superhuman records resorted to, 1343
    taught as one having, 1571, 1630
averse to praying in public, 1620
aversion to Jerusalem's Herod-built temple, 1404
aversion to political priesthood, 1404
avoided distracting details, 1771
awful human moment for J, 1969
b babe J secreted with father's relatives, 1354
BACK IN NAZARETH, 1356
banqueters answered not J' question, 1834
banquets, many with high, low, rich, poor, 1653
baptism, 1587; and age (31-1/2) reconciled, 1512
BAPTISM AND THE FORTY DAYS, 1509
baptism, ended purely human life of, 1512
    J' b by John, noon Jan. 14, A.D. 26, 1504
    J received b not as rite of repentance, 1511
    J refused to intervene, arguments on b, 1593
    John didn't expect J in line of b candidates, 1504
    marked beginning of J' public career, 1408
BAPTISM OF JESUS, 1510
baptism, "of John, whence was it?", 1892
battle, issues of b drawn, 1742
beatitudes, 1570, -73
beauty as an influence to worship, 1840
becoming life partner with spirit, 1430
BEFORE HEROD, JESUS, 1992
before J, evil spirits could invade minds, 863
BEFORE THE SANHEDRIN COURT, 1978
began his work with the poor, neglected, 1594
beggar, J refused to teach him, 1440
BEGINNING THE SUPPER, 1937
beginning to have faith in his apostles, 1747

Jesus (cont'd)

BEGINNINGS OF THE CHRISTIAN CHURCH, 2066
"behold God and man!", 2000
belief in triumph of righteousness, 1739
believed to be the Eternal Son, (by apostles), 1784
believers, 50,000 down to 500, 1705
    healthy growth started, 1718
    regarded prayer as magic, 1946
    thousands saw J, 1789
birth time--Mediterranean world one empire, 1332
beside himself, apostles near believing J was, 1546
    Capernaum, group believed J "bh", mad, 1720
    many believed J "was bh", 1537
    Peter, James, John, "J possibly bh"?, 1594
    Pharisees told Mary J was "bh", 1721
best revelation, 33
BESTOWAL COMMISSION, THE SEVENTH, 1325
BESTOWAL, THE FIFTH, 1314
BESTOWAL, THE FIRST, 1309
BESTOWAL, THE FOURTH, 1313
bestowal here was for whole universe, 1326, -28,
    1424, 1514
bestowal instructions, 1325
BESTOWAL LIMITATIONS, THE, 1327
BESTOWAL OF MICHAEL ON URANTIA, THE, 1323
BESTOWAL OF THE SPIRIT OF TRUTH, 2059
BESTOWAL, THE SECOND, 1310
BESTOWAL, THE SEVENTH AND FINAL, 1316
BESTOWAL, THE SIXTH, 1315
BESTOWAL, THE THIRD, 1312
BESTOWAL, THE TIMES OF MICHAEL'S, 1332
bestowal was for universe, 1749, 2003
BESTOWALS OF CHRIST MICHAEL, THE, 1308
BETHANY, THE MESSAGE FROM, 1836
BETHANY, ON THE WAY TO, 1838
BETHANY, SABBATH AT, 1878
BETHESDA, AT THE POOL OF, 1649
Bethlehem, much of October (A.D. 29) in, 1788
BETHLEHEM, THE TRIP TO, 1350
BETHSAIDA, BACK IN, 1703
BETHSAIDA HOSPITAL, 1658
BETHSAIDA, LAST WEEK AT, 1665
BETHSAIDA, RETURNING TO, 1677
BETRAYAL AND ARREST OF JESUS, THE, 1971
BETRAYAL, LAST HOUR BEFORE THE, 1966
betrayal, not required, 1940
betrayal of J, church in commerce, politics, 2085
betrayed, just before J was, 1966
BETRAYER, LAST WORDS TO THE, 1940
"beware the leaven of the Pharisees...", 1820
beware of the support of the multitude, 1927
bigoted, professed followers of J, 1909
BIRTH AND INFANCY OF JESUS, 1344
birth--conceived, born, like all other babies except,
    1317
    date, noon, Aug. 21, 7 B.C., 1351-52
    Gabriel's appearance to Mary, only supernatural
        thing about J' b, 1347
    lineage was nobility of the common people, 1344
BIRTH OF JESUS, THE, 1351
birth, "ordained by heaven... call him Joshua", 1346
bitter cup, anticipated, 1522
"blessed are those in the ages to come...", 2042
BLESSING THE LITTLE CHILDREN, 1839
BLIND MAN AT JERICHO, THE, 1873
boat builder, designer (of Capernaum), J was,
    1419-20, -24, -92, -95, 1535
boat built by J' own hands, 1628
body (almost 36 years old) left in tomb, 2021
body in tomb day and a half, 2012, -14-15
body in tomb, morontia J out, 2021

Jesus (cont'd)

body, mortal, not raised, 2023, -43
body of J, sought by Archangels, 2022
bold appearance in Jerusalem, 1789, -93
books, laws, none left behind, 1593
born a babe of the realm, as any other baby, 1405
"born again, be", (see under "B")
both men and women loved him adoringly, 1403
bought family repair shop on "time", 1399
bread of life, 1712
break bread with all, 1541
BREAKFAST WITH THE PHARISEES, 1833
bridges, burned all behind him, 2093
brothel keeper and J, 1651
brotherhood, before the church, 2067 (see also
    "brotherhood" under "B")
brotherhood, not church, 2067, -85
brothers and sisters, ages 7 to 18 (J was 22), 1409
    better relationship, 1371
    5 brothers and 3 sisters, 1373
brought new method of living to U, 2018
BUDDHISM, 1446
building (now) temple of human stones, 1747
burden of J' message was, 1460, 1514, -19
BURIAL OF JESUS, THE, 2012
burial, why hasty, 2013
burned all bridges behind him, 2093
by arrival, monogamous world, 927

C cabinet maker, was, 1410
Caiaphas thought J great man, 1422
calamities, accidents, not divine acts, 1671
came during a revival of spiritual thinking, 1332
came to set things in order, 1661
CAPERNAUM, BACK IN, 1531
CAPERNAUM, THE EPOCHAL SERMON, 1709
CAPERNAUM, EVENTS LEADING UP TO C CRISIS,
    1698
CAPERNAUM, FOUR EVENTFUL DAYS AT, 1628
CAPERNAUM, LAST DAYS AT, 1717
CAPERNAUM, SATURDAY NIGHT IN, 1719
CAPERNAUM, THE VISIT TO, 1527
Capernaum, why J moved to, 1398
caravan conductor, was, 1484   c repair shop, 1410
CARAVAN TRIP TO THE CASPIAN, THE, 1484
carpenter, was, 1410
Caspian, caravan trip to (nearest J came to Orient,
    1484)
    Damascus
    Lake Urmia (through Assyria)
    Media
    Parthia
    Urmia (ancient Persian city)
casually did good, 1875
celestial being, the first to appear to J, 1376
CELSUS' GARDEN, IN, 1758
CENTURION'S SERVANT, THE, 1647
ceremonial hand washing, 1825
ceremonials abrogated, 1133
ceremonies vs. reality, 1825
CHALLENGING THE MASTER'S AUTHORITY, 1891
chance (?) meeting, Gonod, Ganid, 1422
chance (opportunity) another for Jews,
    "even now I offer you...", 1908
    "I have once more offered Israel and her rulers",
        1906
    "I would give these teachers another...", 1809
    "one more and last chance to hear gospel", 1883
    to feast, to give Sanhedrins and leaders...1810
change in the Master's teaching tactics, 1714
changed much, 1494-95, 1527

Jesus (cont'd)

changes in J' religion (see "changes in J' religion"
    under "C")
changing course of human evolution, 1863
character sketch of J (beautiful), 1101
charge to John, J', 2009
charmingly, beautiful life, 1579
cheerful, unusually, despite solemn occasion, 1720
child, J taken to Egypt, why, 1047
    most human beings like lost c, 1465
    rearing, Mary and Joseph, 1358
    training, J was positive in, 1401
childlike faith in God, J', 2089
children, J fairly well got along with, as boy, 1368
    J loved little c, 2076
    J missed c, 1421
Chinese merchant, to the, 1475
chooses his apostles, 1524, -26, -39
chose time of his death, 1818
chose to ascend through experience to Trinity, 1323
chose to be guided by human mind, 1723
chose to end work, 1818, 1920
chose Urantia 4000 years ago, 486
Christianity and the Jesus gospel, 1865 (see
    "Christianity" under "C")
church, if espoused Master, would attract youth,
    2085 (see "church" under "C")
    J did not found, 2085
    J has fostered, 2085
    should learn anew from J, 2086
churches, obstacles to J' teachings, 2085
circles of mind-understanding, achieved, 1493
civil laws, observed all, 1580
clean hearts vs. hands, 1671
combat, personal, none, 1368-69, 1469
come to proclaim joy, 1541
COMFORT, LAST WORDS OF, 1953
comforted hungry minds, ministered to thirsty souls,
    1875
COMMANDMENT, THE GREAT, 1901
COMMANDMENT, THE NEW, 1944: "love...as I have
    loved you" (see also under "Jesus, Quotes")
commandment, new--no new burden on souls, 1944
commended (J) what to his Father?, 2015
comments on anger, 1673
commerce swept from temple in 5 minutes, 1890
communal life for J' followers, no, 1581
communion, J really present at, 1942
    unbroken, with God, 2089
    with Father, 1493, 1527
compassion boundless, 1874
    sympathy, J taught, 1580
completed task of incarnated life, 1494
compliments the irate husband, 1470
compromised (Greeks not ordained), 1924
conceived, 1346; day later, visitation from Gabriel,
    1347
CONCEPT OF GOD, THE, 1598
CONCEPT OF THE KINGDOM, JESUS', 1859
CONCEPT, THE NEW, 1748
conception ordained by heaven, 1346
CONCEPTS OF THE EXPECTED MESSIAH, 1509
concepts of J (U Book) from minds of men for 2000
    years, 1343
concern was for individual, not mass, 1580
concerned only with...man's spiritual life, 1580
condemned by Pilate, 1996
condemned criminal, to the, 1475
condemned to death, 1871
condition of J, carrying crossbeam, 2005

Jesus (cont'd)

conference, important, 1531
conference with Gabriel, 1513
CONFERENCE WITH JOHN'S APOSTLES, 1624
confesses divine nature, 1614, 1983
confidence, profound, in universe, 2089
conflict, supreme c as a child, 1373
conformed but didn't consent (13th year), 1384
conformed with reasonable laws of Moses, 1905
conformed with traditions of Israel, 1905
Confucianism (Ganid's summary), 1452
confusion in younger days, 1390, -93
CONGREGATION AT PHILADELPHIA, THE, 1831
conquest, by sacrifice, of pride, selfishness, 1590
conscious of pre-existence, 1395
consciousness of divinity and destiny, 1386
CONSECRATION, EVENING AFTER THE, 1584
consistently uncommunicative, 1418
contact, personal, with all peoples but red, 1485
contact with his chief u administrators, 1659
contentment, on, 1674
contrived to detach episodes of his life, 1413
coordinated faith with experience, 2088
copartnership, man with God, 2002
CORINTH, PERSONAL WORK AT, 1474
Corinth, 2 months stay in, 1476
cornerstone of J' religion, 1769
could have saved self, 1975
could help because he loved, 1874
could see snow-capped Mt. Hermon from Nazareth, 1363
couldn't make internationalist of Simon, 1565
"councils of Men", not directed by, 1412
COUNSEL AND ADVICE, FURTHER, 1329
counseled hungry souls, too many for this record, 1476
COUNSELING THE RICH MAN, 1462
COUNTING THE COST, ON, 1869
courage, heart of teachings, 1582
court, J pleaded for poor man in, 1462
COURT OF SANHEDRISTS, BEFORE THE, 1982
courtship of parents began with cup of water, 1349
cousin of John Baptist, 1345, 1503-04
craved confidential friend, 1391
created this universe of Nebadon, 24
    actual c of this u of things, beings, 1372
    creator and organizer of all... 1367
    direction of universe of own making, 1318
    in reality, incarnated Creator of a universe, 1408
    life to instruct u of his creation, 1999
    maker of the heavens and earth... 1409
    Sanhedrists in judgment on righteous Creator of u, 1984
    selected site for u building, 654
creator, our, 1573
Creator Son, Michael, acts today, 376-77
CRETE, ON THE ISLAND OF, 1436
criminal, advice to condemned, 1475
crisis, J reacted lovingly in c, 2007
crisis time in earth life--from feeding of 5000 to Capernaum synagogue, 1708
Crispus, chief ruler of synagogue, 1471
CROSS, LAST HOUR ON THE, 2010
CROSS, LESSONS FROM THE, 2017
CROSS, MEANING OF THE DEATH ON THE, 2016
cross, not required by God, 2019
CROSS, THE THIEF ON THE, 2008
crossbeam, carried, not cross, 2004
CRUCIAL YEARS, THE TWO, 1386
CRUCIFIXION, THE, 2004, -06 (see also "crucifixion" under "C")

Jesus (cont'd)   J

crucifixion delay, due to 2 thieves, 2001
CRUCIFIXION, JUST BEFORE THE, 1997
CRUCIFIXION, PREPARATION FOR THE, 2001
crucifixion, result of natural events, no plan, 1969
Cymboyton and J, 1485
CYNIC, THE, 1336
CYNICISM, 1442
CYPRUS, THE SOJOURN AT C--DISCOURSE ON MIND, 1479

d DAMASCUS EPISODE, THE, 1412
Damascus road, J on the, 2091
Damascus scribe, 1423, -56, -59, -68, -92
danger, greatest to J, Jerusalem religious leaders, 1647
dangers in Jerusalem, 1788
DANGERS OF THE VISIT TO JERUSALEM, 1788
Daphne, Grove of, repellent to J, 1480
daring, amazing, J' use of women, 1678
date of baptism reconciled, 1512
David: J denied being of house of D, 1348
DAVID ZEBEDEE, THE DEPENDABLE, 2000
David Zebedee, farewell of, 1967
    later life of, 1869
    relieves Judas of the "bag", 1933
DAY AT CAMP, THE, 1923
day by day (13th year) thinking through his problems, 1380
DAY OF CONSECRATION, 1583
death, creature experience of, 1969
    decreed by supreme court of Jews, 1909
    died natural d on cross, 2015
    illustrated mortal survival, 2017
    J elected to suffer d of human, 2020
DEATH, JESUS', IN RELATION TO THE PASSOVER, 2002
death, man's plan for J, not God's, 1572, -99, 1971 2002, -19
    not fact of d but way he met it, 2017
    not Father's will, cruelty of evil men, 1972
    of Amos, 1400
DEATH OF ELIZABETH, THE, 1499
DEATH OF JOHN THE BAPTIST, 1508
DEATH OF JOSEPH, THE, 1388
DEATH OF ZACHARIAS, THE, 1497
death, outworking of events, 1972, -99, 2002
    penalty, facing, 1475
    price of human bigotry, 1872
    result of prejudice, spirit blindness, 1872
    sentence without trial, 1910
    submitted to d of free will, 2004
    supreme folly of ages, killing J, 1906
    to accomplish many things, 1872
    true significance of, 2016
    unnecessary, 229, 1513
DECAPOLIS CITIES, IN THE, 1626
DECAPOLIS, IN THE D AND AT GILBOA, 1617
DECAPOLIS TOUR, THE, 1762
decided Messianic references not to him, 1522
decided trust his Father (Adjuster) for details, 1523
DECISION, THE FIRST GREAT, 1516, -23
    through sixth (during the 40 days)
declines u authority, 1753
deference to Father's will changed John's character, 1555
defiles, what d man, 1712
Deity, called only 2 names by J: God and Father, 1856
"Deliverer, son of the living God", 1746
Deliverer, whose son is he?, 1901
denial of J by Peter, 1551, 1980
denounced belief in... superstition, 1681

113

Jesus (cont'd)

denounced spiritual disloyalty of Jewish leaders, 1932

denounced unjust Jewish divorces, 1839

denunciation, last, of bigoted rulers, 1905

denunciation of Jewish rulers, 1905-06, -08, -10-11

denunciations against pride, cruelty, oppression, hypocrisy, 1582

DEPARTURE FROM PELLA, THE, 1868

DEPARTURE OF JOSEPH AND MARY, 1381

Departure of the Personalized Adjuster, 2024

DEPENDABLE DAVID ZEBEDEE, THE, 2000

describes his approaching last ordeal, 1871

description of his acme of religious living, 1101

DESCRIPTIONS OF J (see also "Apostles, drawn to J for"), 1101, 1389, -95, 1400, -5, -15, 1527-28, -44, 1546, -66, -82-83, 1589-90, -94, 1671-72, -74, 1702, 1785-87, 1874, 1954-55, 1984, -99, 2087

DESIRE FOR PREFERENCE, THE, 1936

desire for supper's symbolism thwarted, 1942

desired to travel, 1381

despite being on his guard, "many similar events" (wine at Cana), 1531

destroy actions like fasting, afflicting soul, 1512

destroyed what was, only when offering better, 1672

DESTRUCTION OF JERUSALEM, 1912

details, avoided distracting, 1771

did not fast for affliction of his soul, 1512

did not teach improvidence, idleness, indifference, 1822

did not teach negative submission, 1770

didn't countenance indifference to one's family's needs, 1822

didn't despise Pharisees, but their systems, 1893

didn't teach religion as man's only pursuit, 1583

died naturally, 2008

died, not to save man, 2002

died royally--as he had lived, 2011

differentiated repentance, change of mind by faith, 1545

disappeared for 40 days, 1504

disappeared from their sight, 2054 (see also "vanished" under "Jesus")

disappointment, spiritual values of, 1688

disciples, did not part with "wealth", 1802

early, stumbling block for, 1510

most outspoken were former Sanhedrists, 2013

only about 100, 1717

required to believe with him, not in him, 2089

vs. apostles, needs, 1823

discipline, J used wise d early, 1401

disconcerting disillusionment, child J, 1359

discourse, confused in minds of apostles, 1915

DISCOURSE ON REALITY, 1433

DISCOURSE ON SONSHIP AND CITIZENSHIP, 1929

DISCOVERY OF THE EMPTY TOMB, 2025

DISCUSSION AT THE OLIVE PRESS, 1975

discussion of good and evil, 1428

disillusioned by inner temple, 1377

disillusionment, parents not all-knowing, 1359

dispatching the runner to Abner, 1966

DISPENSATIONAL RESURRECTION, THE, 2024

DIVERSION AND RELAXATION, 1610

divested religion of magic, 1141

DIVIDING THE INHERITANCE, 1821

divine and human, 2092

DIVINE FORGIVENESS, 1898

divine, messenger to the world, 1347

nature, his first pronouncement of, 1614

DIVINE NATURE OF JESUS, THE, 1785

divine, or fraud, 1785

Jesus (cont'd)

divine (cont'd)

spark, the, 1472

truly, 1408

truth, 1733

vs. mortal mind (Lazarus), 1844

divinity announced,

to apostles, 1746, -48

to Jews and the world, 1790

to Nalda, Deliverer, "I am he", 1614

to Sanhedrists, "Son of God", "I am he", 1983

divinity attained, still human, 2092

divinity attainment, 7 stages, 2091

divinity, clearcut recognition of, 1748

growing awareness of, 1408

J' first admission of, 1614

proof of, 1968

self-realization of, slow, started, 1408

DOING THE FATHER'S WILL, 1579

domain of J, universe of Nebadon, 601

dramatic possibilities, undramatic handling, 1543

drawing power in bestowal, 2018

dreamer, J no illusions of, 1881

dreams, revolting, of slaughter, 1379

drunkard and J, 1436

DURING THE SABBATH DAY, 2014

dust to dust, body of J, 2023

duty to family, performed, and more, 1539

didn't countenance indifference to needs of one's family, 1822

e EARLY CHILDHOOD OF JESUS, THE, 1355

EARLY HOME LIFE, 1921

EARLY MANHOOD, JESUS', 1407

early tried to avoid a religion about him, 1413

earth mission exclusively spiritual, 1839

EARTH PARENTS, JESUS', 1348

earthborn Jew, declined aggrandizement, 1522

easy to love J, 1541

Eber and his fellows, J talks to, 1792

ECONOMIC ATTITUDE, 1581

economic theories, formulated none, 1581

economics, J no concern with, 1565, -76, -80-81, 1605

economics, politics, "no" (Immanuel), 1329

educated, J highly e, 1363

educational post, offered, 1412

effort to win Jews, 1905

egotism, prevention of, 1583

Egypt, the sojourn in, 1355

why parents took J to E, 1047

EIGHTEENTH YEAR, JESUS', (A.D. 12), 1398

EIGHTH YEAR, JESUS', (A.D. 2), 1364

elevated morality to majestic levels, 1585

ELEVENTH YEAR, JESUS', (A.D. 5), 1369

Elohim and Yahweh, 1856

embalmed, Joseph and Nicodemus e J' body, 2013

emotion, indignant in intense e, 1384, 1890

spoke with marked, 1609

swept by e in Nazareth, 1684

emotional appeal, made, 1730

emotional ecstasy, moment of, 1807

emotions, appeal to e first, 1705

thoughts, of J recorded, 1844

emphasis on "first making the tree good", 1582

emphasis on 2 truths of first import, 1593

employed symbols because. . . 1942

emptied self of prehuman existence, 1408

encampment at Bethsaida, a model, 1657

end of purely human life, 1512

end, saw from the beginning, 1594

ends gained by compromise and diplomacy, no, 1520

Jesus (cont'd)

endured great anguish, 1969

enemies, and idlers went to witness crucifixion, 2004
  apostles demoralized when J crucified by e, 2066
  "be not downhearted when believers join e", 1946
  brought into J' presence, woman of evil repute, 1792
  "contend with bitter, self-deceived e", 1801
  "crucify him! crucify him!", 1994-95
  declared J' teachings impractical, 1720
  defeated in efforts to trip up J, 1899
  discourse intended as last appeal to e, 1905
  followed by 50 friends and e, 1838
  "friends and e, I am the true shepherd", 1819
  hesitated to denounce him openly, 1790
  hired debased men to make trouble, 1686
  hired numerous rough men to harass him, 1684
  hostile in Nazareth, 1684
  hour has come, Son betrayed into hands of e, 1968
  J made clear had not feared to confront, 1736
  J never dealt ignobly with e, 1674
  J never disposed to take advantage of e, 1892
  Lazarus becoming big problem to e, 1878
  "a man's foes may be of his own household", 1722
  marvelled at his teaching, 1790
  minded to have J put to death, 1993
  mob cried for blood of J, 1995
  no hero to populace when in hands of e, 1993
  only e noted no washing of hands, 1834
  poured out with others to welcome J, 1882
  reckoned whole movement had broken up, 1741
  ruffians laid hold upon J, 1687
  "since some of you (are) my bitter e", 1818
  soldiers mocked J, e had gone their way, 2001
  Son of Man prepared to face e, 1970
  "sufficient e among the religious leaders", 1704
  taxes supported activities of sworn e, 1743
  "things our e plan in secrecy", 1820
  troublemaker for J, wife forced to prostitution, 1793
  unfriendly Pharisees sought to entrap J, 1838
  were industriously spreading the rumor, 1719
  were taken aback by his appearance in Jerusalem, 1789
  "when our e bring you before rulers", 1912
  why do we flee from threats of e, 1728
  "will be put to death at instigation of his e, chief priests and rulers of the Jews", 1967

enjoined silence about glory because, 1754
enjoyed pleasure of others, 1495
enlarged revelation and name of God forever, 1965
enlarged scope of "neighbor", 1134
enlargement of the revelation...1963-64
ENMITY OF THE WORLD, 1946
Enoch, Book of, nearest to truth of Hebrew theories, 1390
entanglements with the economic, etc. "no", 1327
enthralled, thrilled, first view of Jerusalem, 1375, 1381, 1882
EPICUREAN, THE, 1335
Epicurean teacher, to the, 1474
EPILEPTIC BOY, THE, 1755
epileptic, the young, 1630
epochal sermon, 1709
epochs in life of J, extraordinary, 1492
escaped Bethlehem massacre, 1354
escaped the clamoring multitudes, 1646
essence of teaching, 1008, 1593
essentials of success, 1739
ESTABLISHING THE REMEMBRANCE SUPPER, 1941

Jesus (cont'd)

estimating the soul's worth, 1739
Eternal Son, J not, 366
ethics and morals, J no concern with, as such, 1862
evaluated, no generation has e J and actions, 1699
EVANGELISTS IN CHORAZIN, THE, 1726
  (see also "evangelists" under "E")
evening conferences at Zebedee home, youths, 1421
EVENING LESSONS, THE, 1683
EVENTFUL SUNDAY MORNING, THE, 1720
EVENTS OF JESUS' SIXTH YEAR (1 B.C.), 1359
EVENTS OF A SABBATH DAY, THE, 1532
everything has its time, 1436
evil, J refused to advertise, 1582
EVIL, SIN, AND INIQUITY, 1659
evil, 3 ways to contend with, 1770
evil, why not bothered by, 1594
evils of Pharisees, 1714
evolutionary religion alone until baptism, 1112
evolutionist, progressive, not revolutionist, 1672
exalted the individual, not the group, 1862
EXAMINATION BY ANNAS, 1978
example for anyone, no, 1425
example no, inspiration yes, life of J, 1328
execute J as violator of Jewish law, 1673
executive experience, 1485
exemplified a new and original plan of life, 1594
existence, the path of normal earthly, 1518
expects results from us (fruits), 1931
experience (wisdom of) with faith, 2088
experiences, all phases of human, 1392
experiences, most enthralling of e, 1424
extraordinary events (7) in bestowal experience, 2091
Ezra, the backslidden Jew, 1440

f fables, allegories, advised against (parables ok), 1692
face shown with glory, 1523
faced death, little concern with trials, 1999
fact vs. presence of God, 1733
FAITH AND TRUTH, 1459
faith, childlike but not childish, was J' f, 2089
  destroyed J' every conflicting desire, 2088
  devoid of fear, because of heights of trust, 2089
  is gift of God, 1537
  is price of entrance to kingdom, 1537 (see also "kingdom, price to enter" under "K")
  is the only requisite, 1537,-45,-67,-69,-83-84,-86
  J had f in men, 1875
FAITH OF JESUS, THE, 2087
faith, of the sick, J inspired the, 1659
  people, confidence in J because of his f in them, 1875
faith, salvation by,
  "by faith are you saved", 1682 (see also "kingdom, price to enter" under "K")
  "know...saved by faith", 1610
  one of two truths of first import, 1593
  "salvation is the reward of f", 1802
faith, securely held him, 2087
  wholly free from presumption, 2090
"false Messiah", (Ezra), 1526
false teachers and bigoted rulers, 1905
fame as a healer, 1671
FAME, THE WIDESPREAD F OF JESUS, 1668
familiar to J, man's total experience, 1425
family, admonition to, explained, 1723
  another visit with f precluded, 1743
FAMILY ARRIVES, JESUS', 1721
family, at Bethany, 1997
  center of J' philosophy, 1581
  characterizations, 1401

Jesus (cont'd)

family (cont'd)

confused, 1396
confusion, consternation, 1724
could not comprehend Father's business, 1722
discussion, 1401
experience of farm life, 1394
faithfully provided for care of his f, 1555
feared dishonor through J, 1721
feared for own safety, 1721
financial struggle, 1392
great trial to J, 1546
"gulf" begins, 1538
in turmoil (zealots), 1397
income from doves, milk, 1391
gave it up, why, 1581
J tried to meet with f, 1743
FAMILY, THE LESSON ON THE, 1603
family, meeting in Capernaum, 1494
neglect of f needs not countenanced by J, 1822
no special gift others didn't receive, 2065
not at teaching camp, 1657
not without its recalcitrant child, 1417
supposed disgrace, 1721
wished to stop his preaching, 1721
farewell address, 1929
farewell admonitions to apostles, 1955
FAREWELL DISCOURSE, THE, 1944
FAREWELL PERSONAL ADMONITIONS, 1955
farewell, public address of mercy, 1905
to Abner, 1870
to aged Simon of Bethany, 1897
to apostles, 1944
to Gonod and Ganid (A. D. 23), 1481
FAREWELL TO THE SEVENTY, 1804
farm, first experience on, 1357
fasted day or two at a time, 1493, 1514
fasting and self-denial, J didn't teach, 1605
FATEFUL SANHEDRIN MEETING, THE, 1909
father, J is our universe, 1405
Joseph angered by J, 1371
FATHER AND HIS KINGDOM, THE, 1855
Father, is living love...the, 2095
J never tried to prove the, 1855
may be known by experience, not by mind, 1856
only concept of F J ever taught, 2017
fathers and mothers sought his help, 1671
Father's business, 1403, -05
FATHER'S BUSINESS, THE, 1659
Father's business, alone "about the F b", 1659
(at 14) alternated between worldly affairs and F b,
1386
family could not comprehend F b, 1722
"I will be about my F b, for we...", 1625
kept J too preoccupied to think of marriage, 1403
"time to be about your F b" (13th year), 1376, -89
"tomorrow we must be about the F b", 1634
what Scripture prophecies applied?, 1390
Father's way, the, 1514
FATHER'S WILL, THE, 1971
Father's will, always subject to, 1417, -24
J saw religion in terms of, 2088
favorite means of teaching love of Father, 1853
favorite means of teaching man's neighborliness, 1853
fear, and pride, destroyers of joy and liberty, 1596
free from f, conscious of spiritual invincibility,
2088
helplessness, to avoid, 1985
"fear not", J' watchword, 1582
"FEAR OF THE LORD", THE, 1675
fear of, vs. love of, the Lord, 1675

Jesus (cont'd)

feared care of sick would deter spiritual mission, 1634
feast, great, for J, 1560
FEAST OF THE DEDICATION, 1809
FEAST OF SPIRITUAL GOODNESS, 1656
FEAST OF TABERNACLES, AT THE, 1788, -93
FEAST, PARABLE OF THE MARRIAGE, 1894
feasts, make f for the poor, 1580
features underwent rapid, multitudinous changes, 1659
FEEDING THE FIVE THOUSAND, 1700
fellowship extended to all men of all ages, 1593
fickleness of popular acclaim, 1705
FIFTEENTH YEAR, JESUS' (A. D. 9), 1389
FIFTH YEAR, JESUS' (2 B. C.), 1357
FINAL ADMONITION AND WARNINGS, 1953
FINAL APPEARANCES AND ASCENSION, 2052
final purely human act, baptism ceremony, 1511
finally conscious of pre-existence, 1528
financial affairs of idealist, (J), difficult, 1566
FINANCIAL STRUGGLE, THE, 1392
FIRST AND SECOND DAYS IN THE TEMPLE, 1381
FIRST APPEARANCE TO THE APOSTLES, 2040
first pronouncement of his divine nature, 1614
FIRST SERMON IN THE SYNAGOGUE, 1391
FIRST TEMPLE TALK, 1790
first Urantia religion to...1112
fishes, cooked 7 for the 10, J served John Mark, 2047
FISHES, THE DRAUGHT OF, 1628
fishes, f with shekel in mouth, 1744
5000 people, 2 dried fishes!, 1701
153 large ones, no miracle, 2046
Peter's friend, several baskets of f for tax, 1744
fisherman, J was expert, 1369
fishing, first experience, 1364
five women, the, 2025
flashing eye, swift words of rebuke, (for Peter), 1760
Flavius and J, 1596, 1600
fled Cana, too much sensation, 1645
FLEEING THROUGH NORTHERN GALILEE, 1725
FLIGHT, THE HASTY, 1723
flight to Egypt, the, 1354
floodtide of spiritual illumination swept over J, 1376
follow J, means to, 2090
sure way to trouble, 1767
followers, J expects them to strive, 1573
shrank, 1 month, over 99%, 1705
take up own responsibilities, 1770
force, approval of f to protect majority, 1891
forced by course of natural events, 1388
forecast own death, 1714, -54, -59, -89, 1966-67
foreknowledge, last night with apostles, 1928
forethought, not against f but anxiety, 1579
formulated program to establish kingdom, 1523
"forsaken me, why have you", 2010
FORTY DAYS, THE, 1512
forty days, and no man saw J again for fd, 1504
FORTY DAYS, BAPTISM AND THE, 1509
forty days, decisions, not temptations, 1515
FORTY DAYS OF PREACHING, 1505
forty days, reason for, 1512
told apostles about, 1588
founded the religion of personal experience, 2092
founder of religion, only one, supermaterial acts, 1671
FOUR MONTHS OF TRAINING, 1533
FOURTEENTH YEAR, JESUS' (A. D. 8), 1387
fourth and last stage of human life, 1749
fourth (last) phase of earth ministry, 1751, -59
fourth stage of life in the flesh, 1749
FOURTH YEAR, JESUS', 1357
"freely accept" fatherhood, brotherhood, 2053
frequent trips from home, 1360

Jesus (cont'd)

friction with Joseph and Jude, 1372
friend, J best in all the world, 1546
"friends", called apostles, 1945
friendship, J the ideal of, 1785
from "not good" to "sinless", 2092
fruits of acceptance, (J), religion derives authority
    from, 1730
functioned in executive capacity, 1485
FUTURE, THE, 2084

g GABRIEL APPEARS TO ELIZABETH, 1345 (see
    also "Gabriel" under "G")
Gabriel, J met in wilderness, 1513
GABRIEL'S ANNOUNCEMENT TO MARY, 1346
Galilee, climate in, 1367
GALILEE, FIRST PREACHING TOUR OF, 1637
GALILEE, LEAVING, 1587
GALILEE, TARRYING TIME IN, 1524
games, athletic, young J' response to, 1370-71
garments to soldiers, at crucifixion, 2007
genius for dealing with adversaries, 1892
GENTILE PHILOSOPHY, (J' time), 1335
GENTILE RELIGIONS, (J' time), 1336
GENTILES, AMONG THE, 1334
Gerizim, on, taught great truths, 1616
GETHSEMANE, ALONE IN, 1968 (see also
    "Gethsemane" under "G")
GETHSEMANE, IN, 1963
Gethsemane, 1963
    camp for remainder of J' life in flesh, 1897
    J and apostles spent time living in G, 1606
    (Park), the camp in, 1606
    tents overlooking public camping park, 1895
    tents pitched at G, to avoid crowds, 1648
gift of his Greek scriptures to avoid taxes, 1393
gift to every mortal according to capacity, 2063
GILBOA ENCAMPMENT, THE, 1617
girls of J' family educated, 1396
given Greek Hebrew scriptures by Alexandria friends,
    1355
"God" and "Father", use of, 1856
God and man, J was both forevermore, 1331
God, incarnate in man, always, 1331
    J alone with G for 6 weeks, 1492
    a living reality in life of J, 2087
    of perfection, J revealed, 1604
    only concept of G J ever taught, 2017
    revealed in man and man uplifted to God, 1906
    terms J used for G, 1856
God-knowing, proof of, 1733
God-man, 7 men getting used to J, G-m, 1534
GOD'S LAW AND THE FATHER'S WILL, 1588
God's will and man's will, 1431
GOD'S WRATH, 1597
"Gods, the", J used the term, 1430
GOING INTO JERUSALEM, 1878
GOLDEN RULE (see also "GOLDEN RULE" under "G")
    demands action, 1585
    negative rule works in isolation, 1585
    plus, 1651
GOLGOTHA, ON THE WAY TO, 2004
Gonod and Ganid, J met in Jerusalem, 1422 (see also
    under "G")
GOOD AND EVIL, 1457
good, J went about doing g, 1770
good news, we proclaim, 1766
GOOD SAMARITAN, STORY OF, 1809
good tidings emphasized, 1535
goodness, on, 1458
gospel (see also "gospel" under "G")

Jesus (cont'd)

GOSPEL BY LUKE, THE, 1342
GOSPEL BY MARK, THE, 1341
gospel, illuminated more by J' life than death, 2002
    J listened to objections to, 1607
    "my g is", 1590
    new religion, Rodan, 1775
GOSPEL OF JOHN, THE, 1342
GOSPEL OF MATTHEW, THE, 1341
gospel spread assured, J could die, 1807
government supporting people, J against, 1461
grace, J was full of g and truth, 1874
    of personality, matchless, 1534
grasp of the affairs of men, 1810
GREAT COMMANDMENT, THE, 1901
great day in life of, 1632
GREAT SUPPER, PARABLE OF THE, 1835
greatest victories, triumphs, over fears of
    personality isolation, 1985
greatest of all works in J' earth ministry, 1844
greatest Urantian, out of humble circumstances, 1200
Greek contractor, to the, 1474
Greek Scriptures, J given, in Alexandria, 1355
Greek worker and the Roman foreman, the, 1430
Greeks, group sought J, 1902
GREEKS, INFLUENCE OF THE, 2071
Greeks, thirty entered kingdom, 1903
greetings to each apostle, at end, 1897
grew in favor with man and God, 1387
grew up, like any other child, 1355, 1407
groaned at Lazarus' tomb, 1844
growing awareness of divinity, 1408
guards (Roman) faltered at sight of J, 1954
guidance for all ages, 1583
guidance, for all who preach gospel, 1765
guide for those who teach truth, 1765
guided by human mind, 1723
had not where to lay his head, 1723, -50, 1801
had won the world... by submission to F's will, 1522
"hairs of your head are numbered", 1820
handicap to his work, 1584
"happened" to meet Gonod, Ganid, 1422
"happened" to meet Simon's family, 1375
happy and God-revealing life, 1614
hard sayings, demands on self, 2093
    not commands, 2093
hard to explain his own non-resistance, 1579
harp (see "harp" under "H")
harpist, skillfull at 11, 1364, -87
has promised F all his sheep will be brought into
    one fold, 1819
"has risen from the dead. His tomb is empty", 2030
he despised no man, 1594
he vanished from their (apostles') sight (see under
    "Jesus, vanished")
headquarters of this Universe is Salvington, 366
healed blind man at Jericho, 1873
HEALING (see also "healing" under "H")
healing, apostles, J could have instantly healed, 1718
HEALING, AT SUNDOWN, THE, 1631
Healing at Sundown,
    astonished, J was the most astonished, 1633
    great day in the life of a universe, 1632
    J made physician, much as a teacher, 1633
    J slept little, night of this healing, 1634
    narrator of paper was present, 1633
    sick, ailing, J gazed on almost 1000, 1632
    spiritual kingdom not advanced by, 1633
    thrilling spectacle to celestial onlookers, 1633
    unintended demonstration, 1633

Jesus (cont'd)

Healing at Sundown (cont'd)
vast retinue of seraphim, others, descended, and in a moment...1633
Zebedee yard, 683 persons healed, 1633
healing the believer, 1834
HEALING THE BLIND BEGGAR, 1811
healing, commonplace difficulties, afflictions, 1718
demented lad, 1713
desired for its spiritual benefits, 1669
epileptic son of James of Safed, 1757
for faith-dominated persons, 1658
for repeat of J' healing J would have to be present, 1700
hemorrhage, healed woman of, 1698
"I perceive that life has gone forth from me", 1669
"I perceive that power has gone forth from me", 1669
incidental, not part of J' plan, 1633
inspired faith and confidence, 1659
J frequently delivered victims of fear, 1836
J suffered men self-healing by powerful faith, 1670
kingdom's first hospital used material and spiritual methods, 1658
lepers, "were not 10 cleansed? Where then, are the other 9?", 1828
leprous man at Iron, 1643
lunatic of Kheresa, 1695
might interfere with J' mission, 1633
mind and spirit, transformations of, 1658
multitude aroused to emotional frenzy by h, 1645
nine ungrateful Jews and one grateful Samaritan, 1827
Norana's daughter, 1735
100 beneficiaries of unconscious h, 1669
HEALING THE PARALYTIC, 1666
healing, paralytic, "sins, your s are forgiven", 1667
phenomena, the, 1669
place no limitation on possible exhibition of Master's spiritual power, 1700
powers unlimited, timeless, 1669
profound human faith in h, 1669
reconstructive power of immense faith, 1669
result of 3 powerful influences, many cases, 1669
spittle, to encourage using material methods, 1813
spontaneous or unconscious, not understood by midwayers, 1669
taught followers of all ages not to despise material means, 1813   Titus and afflicted son, 1644
transformations, banish fear, anxiety, 1658
unconscious h by J, beneficiaries of, 1669
use material and spiritual practices, 1658
vast retinue healed throng, 1633
why apostles failed (physical and spiritual), 1758
with spittle and clay, 3 reasons, 1812
HEALS THE BOY, JESUS, 1757
heard leper's words of clinging faith, 1643
heart of man, spirit within, 1457
heart was being crushed, 1969
hearts, put into h, don't take out of, 1592
heathen, why do the h rage?, 1725
Hebrew, J was master of early, 1362
HEBREW RELIGION, THE, 1338
helper, the promised, 1948
helpless babe, average and normal infant, 1346
HERALDS OF THE RESURRECTION, 2029
here to make clear two ideas, 1590
HEROD ACTS, 1353
HEROD, JESUS BEFORE, 1992
hidden with Joseph's relatives, 1354

Jesus (cont'd)

high levels of conscious contact with T A, 1421
HIGH PRIEST'S PALACE, ON THE WAY TO, 1977
HINDUISM, 1447
Holy One of Israel, 1788
HOME AT NAZARETH, THE, 1349
honor, J refused proffered, 1413
hostile to no man, 1893
HOSTILITY OF THE RELIGIOUS LEADERS, 1672
"hour has come", 1495, 1504, -35, 1789
HOUR OF HUMILIATION, THE, 1984
house finisher, J was, 1410
house owner, J was unknowingly, 1422
how can God...create evil?, 1429
how lifelong family friendship began, 1375
human, and divine, "as he yet is", 2092
HUMAN AND DIVINE MINDS, JESUS', 1787
human, heart longed for escape, 1969
humiliation of the h J, 1968
HUMAN JESUS, THE, 1424
human race, fresh beginning for whole, 1582
human, taken from men by religion, the h J, 2090
was h, 1594
humanity, proof of, 1968
humanly assured, mission of revelation (A. D. 7), 1373
humble one's self to be exalted, 1582
HUMILIATION, THE HOUR OF, 1984
humor and sagacity in questions, 1383
humor, Norana's touched J, 1736
hurry, never in a h, 1874
hypocrisy, denunciations...against pride...1582
"how can you justify such h?", 1907
leaven of the Pharisees...is h, 1820
my Father loathes h, abhors iniquity, 1676
of...humility is childish, 1676
out of false humility springs much h, 1676
swept aside pretensions of vanity and, 1671
hypocrites, these h make long prayers, 1907
"well did Isaiah prophesy of you h", 1712
"why play the part of h?", 1836
"woe upon you, scribes, Pharisees, h!", 1907-08
hypocritical, even now F would receive these h leaders, 1905
this sinful and h nation, 1760
to h nation no sign shall be given, 1745

i

idea of contention, slaughter repugnant to J, 1522
ideal concept largely failed, but, 1865
ideal of the mortal creature, 2000
ideal religious life, lead, 1329
ideals compromised by C leaders, to save ideas, 2070
ideals of J, reinterpreted, challenged West, 2073
still latent, will assert power, 2070
ideas and ideals never tried seriously, 1863
ideas on politics, science, philosophy freely expressed, but not as authority, 1421
identified with business, laboring men, publicans, politicians, patriots, 1565
if your mind does not serve well, exchange it for mind of J, 553
ignored "great men" (why), 1594
ignored Jewish traditions, flouted dogma, 1340
imitate life, no, 2061; but share his faith, 2091
"imitate my life, no", 1953
immoral woman, Nalda, 1614
in all points tested, 1313-14
"in him were hidden all the treasures of wisdom and knowledge", 1417
in potential possession all power in heaven and on earth, 1522
in touch with directors of universe affairs, 1659

Jesus (cont'd)

incarnated and lived as mortal man, 80
INCARNATION, THE, MAKING TWO ONE, 1331
increasingly self-conscious, 1376
indictment of J by Sanhedrin court, 1985
indictment of Jewish rulers, 1905
indignant, mildly, 1821
indignation, characteristic, 1528
individual, emphasis on i, 1597, 1629-30
  for emergence of, 2070
  most important to J, 1546
  salutations to the twelve, 1897
  teaching for i, not state, 1580
  vs. community, 1862-63
indolent, made no appeal to, 1590
indulged in many reminiscences, 1684
influence, most dynamic ever on earth, 1091
  of the Greeks, 2071
influence on, talks with
    (see also "teaching Ganid, Gonod" under "Jesus")
  Anaxand, on influencing foreman, Caesarea, 1430
  Angamon, leader of Stoics, 1456
  boy, fruit vendor in Messina, 1440
  Chinese merchant, 1475
  Claudius, slaveholder, 1461
  Claudus, preached in Rome and Spain, 1440
  condemned criminal, 1475
  courtesans of Corinth, 1472
  Crispus, rabbi at Corinth, 1471
  Epicurean teacher, Corinth, 1474
  Ezra, backslidden Jew, 1440
  first Christian church in Syracuse, 1440
  Fortune, who became Crete leader (son of Simon
    who carried J' cross piece), 1438
  Gadiah (Simon later), 1428
  Gaius of Corinth, 1473
  Greek contractor and builder, 1474
  Greek philosopher, 1476
  Greek physician, 1471
  homesick Phoenician, 1478
  judge on behalf of poor man, 1462
  man beating his wife, 1470
  Marcus, speaker at Roman Forum (successor to
    Peter), 1461
  Mardus, leader of Cynics, 1457
  miller at Corinth, 1474
  mistress of Greek inn, 1475
  Mithraic leader, Corinth, 1474; Rome, 1459
  Mithraic priest, Carthage, 1439
  Mongolian, influence on Taoism, 1430
  Nabon, Greek Jew, Mithraic, 1459
  prostitutes, 1472
  Roman centurion, 1474
  Roman judge, Corinth, 1474
  Roman rich man, 1462
  Roman senator, 1461
  Roman soldier, 1461
  Romans (500), 1461
  Rome's religious leaders, 1455-56
  runaway boy, 1475
  Stephen, 1411, -56
  Swiss father and Son, 1466
  thinker at Ephesus, 1478
  thirty-two religious leaders, 1456
  traveler from Britain, 1475
  young man who was afraid, 1437
infuriated man, and J, 1436
inheritance of parental traits, 1348
inherited a vast universe, 1574
inherited traits of his parents, 1348

Jesus (cont'd)

innocent, yet in trouble, 1397
INQUIRING GREEKS, THE, 1902
instructed 70 in what to teach, 1804
INSTRUCTION FOR TEACHERS, BELIEVERS, 1765
instruction, ideal principles of living near God, 1579
instruction methods, 1456, 1875
  conscience appeal, mind appeal, 1722
  difficult to get men to disown the past, 1722
  emotion's appeal, then mind, gateway to soul, 1705
  get man in kingdom first, then... 1592
  lead, drive out error, news, persuade, 1592
  on use of fables, allegories, parables, 1692
  refrain from taking out of hearts, 1592
  repeatedly: don't become dogmatized, 1592
  school plan of learning and doing, 1658
  show perfected vision vs. part vision of past, 1592
  studiously avoided negative, 1582
  technique of social contact, 1460
  three parables and what they illustrated, 1853
  used cream of scriptures, 1769
  used positive note even in prayers, 1771
instructions on alms (charity), 1580
instructions to the Seventy, 1804
intellectual power, J was, 1589
interest in, art and beauty, 1600
  people great, 1412
  planets and stars, 1360
interested supremely in one thing, 1383
interpretation of man to God, revelation of God, 1328-29
interpreter, teacher, for Indians, 1423
interviewed 150 young people in Jerusalem when 12, 1380
intimate contact, all races but red, 1485
intimated on his return, will be seen only by eye of
  faith, 1919
intimidated, could not be, 1999
into such a generation of men, J was born, 1338
introspection, not required in J' religion, 1583
invincibility as a mortal man, 1970
invited to live in India, 1436
is man's Creator, his Universe Father, 1573
"is not dead, he has risen!", 2032
is really present, (Lord's supper), 1942
"it is better that one man die...", 1847

j Jacob, of Crete, 1597
Jacob, the stone mason's son, 1368
Jairus resigned synagogue, joined J, 1718
James (brother of J), head of the family of Joseph, 1418
  never again gave up faith, 1495
  to Passover with J, 1399
  vs. Abner, 1831
Jeramy at Nicopolis, Greek, Paul in same home later,
  1471
JERICHO, THE BLIND MAN AT, 1873
JERICHO, WORKING IN, 1595
JERUSALEM, THE DESTRUCTION OF, 1912
JERUSALEM, GOING INTO, 1878
JERUSALEM, INTERLUDE VISIT TO, 1647
"Jerusalem, Jerusalem, O", 1384, 1872, -82
Jerusalem, J not accredited in, 1422
JERUSALEM, LAST APPEARANCE IN, 2055
Jerusalem leaders closed synagogues to, 1643
JERUSALEM, MONDAY IN, 1888
JERUSALEM, ON THE WAY TO, 1867
Jerusalem schooling, J indifferent to, 1370
JERUSALEM, THE SITUATION IN, 1910
JERUSALEM, THE START FOR, 1880
JESUS' FAMILY ARRIVES, 1721
JESUS' HUMAN AND DIVINE MINDS, 1787
"Jesus, Jesus, have mercy upon me" (Bartimeus), 1873

Jesus (cont'd)

Jesus of Nazareth (Christ Michael), 1325
Jew, "one who thinks something besides racial
superiority", 1477
JEWISH PEOPLE, THE, in J' time, 1333
JEWISH RULERS, QUESTIONS BY THE, 1899
Jewish traditions, antagonism to, 1655
Jewish tutor of son of Indian merchant, 1472
JEWS AND GENTILES, 1339
Jews and Gentiles both, banquet, 1903
JEWS AND THE SAMARITANS, THE, 1612
Jews, another chance, last, 1906
one more, 1811
one more chance to hear... receive, 1883
purpose, give Sanhedrin and leaders another
chance, 1810
Jews, answer to J' last appeal, 1909
J and associates were, 1788
J gave them personal religion, 1629
J had pity and love for, 1386
lacking in humor, 1736
rebuke to all, 1810
"seek to kill me because", 1791
JEWS, STATUS OF INDIVIDUAL, 1909
Jews, stumbling block, 1510
jobs offered, more than 12, Rome, 1461
John (Apostle), ordered from trial room, 1984
JOHN THE BAPTIST, 1496 (see also under "J")
John, great, but those of new way greater, 1509
J thought much about, 1539
last word to J, 1507
"tell John he is not forgotten", 1626
tribute to, 1627
John Mark, and the lunch basket, 1920-21
JONAH, AT JOPPA--DISCOURSE ON, 1428
JOSEPH AND MARY, 1344
Joseph and Nicodemus before Pilate, 2012
JOSEPH'S DREAM, 1347
JOSIAH BEFORE THE SANHEDRIN, 1813
Joshua ben Joseph, 1344; J' earth name, 1317
Joshua (Jesus) (Greek form), 1351
journey, last with twelve (to upper room), 1934
journey over world, unknown to world, 1483
JOURNEY TO JERUSALEM, THE, 1374
JOURNEY UP THE COAST, THE, 1736
JUDAISM, 1444
JUDAS (ISCARIOT) AND THE CHIEF PRIESTS, 1924
JUDAS, THE END OF, 1997 (see under "Apostles")
Judas, a faith adventure for J, 1566
final decision, 1910
JUDAS IN THE CITY, 1972
Judas, J tried but could not save, 1941
JUDAS'S DOWNFALL--CAUSES OF, 2055
JUST BEFORE THE CRUCIFIXION, 1997
justice and mercy, 1468, 1577, 1638
Justus, the merchant, 1472
k kept apostles in service-contact with people, 1000
kept his work before Sanhedrin, 1811
KHERESA, THE K LUNATIC, 1695
KHERESA, THE VISIT TO, 1694
kindly look and sympathetic smile, 1470
KING-MAKING EPISODE, 1702
kingdom (see also "kingdom" under "K")
and J' return, not tied together, 1860
concept of J' slumbers, 1866
declaration to build k based on, 1748
an evolutionary experience, 1603
instruction on the, 1568
is in three essentials, 1585
KINGDOM, J' CONCEPT OF THE, 1859
kingdom, J never gave precise definition of, 1862

Jesus (cont'd)

kingdom (cont'd)

KINGDOM, J' TEACHING ABOUT THE, 1862
KINGDOM, LATER IDEAS OF THE, 1864
kingdom, new, instruction on, 1588
not as good illustration as family simile, 1603
KINGDOM OF GOD, THE, 1500
KINGDOM OF HEAVEN, THE, 1858
KINGDOM OF HEAVEN, CONCEPTS OF, 1858
KINGDOM, THE TALK ABOUT THE, 1746
kingdom, teachings of, 2 things, 1593
two truths of first import, 1593
kingdoms of earth, paltry to J, 1522
kissed kneeling young man, 1802
knew Mary, Martha, Lazarus as children, 1375
knew the methods of the world, 1520
knew self as Creator, 1409
knowledge was self-limited, 1408
"lads, have you caught anything?", 2046
laid his hands upon heads of 70, 1801
LANDLORD, PARABLE OF THE ABSENT, 1893
languages, Aramaic and Greek, J spoke at 7 years
of age, 1362
Aramaic, Greek, Hebrew (fluent), 1358
Indian, 1427
LAST DAY AT THE CAMP, 1929
LAST GROUP PRAYER, THE, 1963
LAST HOUR BEFORE THE BETRAYAL, 1966
LAST HOUR ON THE CROSS, 2010
last journey with the twelve, 1934
last mortal rendezvous with apostles, 1935, -37
last Passover with any of his family, 1416
LAST SOCIAL HOUR, THE, 1927
LAST SUPPER, THE, 1936
LAST TEACHING AT PELLA, 1850
LAST TEMPLE DISCOURSE, THE, 1905
LAST VISIT TO NORTHERN PEREA, 1825
last word to John (Baptist), 1507
LAST WORDS OF COMFORT, 1953
LAST WORDS TO THE BETRAYER, 1940
last year of settled life, 1421
last year with freedom to play (11), 1370
LATER ADULT LIFE OF JESUS, THE, 1419
LATER CHILDHOOD OF JESUS, THE, 1366
LATER DISCUSSION AT THE CAMP, 1916
LATER IDEAS OF THE KINGDOM, 1864
later ministry and death of Abner, the, 1832
LAW, LIBERTY, AND SOVEREIGNTY, 1490
lawful to give tribute to Caesar?, 1899
laws, conformed with reasonable laws, 1905
lawyer who professed faith, 1901
layman, greatest religious teacher was, 2091
LAZARUS, AT THE TOMB OF, 1843
Lazarus (prescience?), 1836
LAZARUS, WHAT BECAME OF, 1849
learn to be faithful even in prosperity, 1931
lectures at Urmia on "Brotherhood of...", 1485
lectures "kingdom of God", "kingdoms of men", 1485
led men to feel at home in the world, 2093
left behind no books, laws, human organization, 1593
left final untangling of situation to F, 1532
left home unceremoniously, 1419
left without eating breakfast, 1826
legend of the shepherds, 1352
legislative, judicial, authority in group, 1764
lens, J is spiritual, 1857
LEPERS, THE TEN, 1827
LESSON REGARDING CONTENTMENT, 1674
LESSONS FROM THE CROSS, 2017
"let's you and I make a new religion", 1467
liberty, through recognition of truth, 1594

Jesus (cont'd)

life after baptism not required of J, 1513
LIFE AND TEACHINGS OF JESUS, THE, 1323
life, example no, inspiration yes, 1425, 1585
  how narrative of life was gathered, 1332
  ideal for all worlds and all mortals, 1585
  ideal revelation personality of God, 30
  inspiration for entire universe, 1585
  J' life, not his teachings, assist most, 1582
  J' life provides fixed point for anchor of time, 2063
  J valued the whole life, 1582
  more illuminating than death, 2002
  not an example, but an inspiration, 1328
  not example to follow, 2061; but share his faith, 2091
LIFE OF A SHEPHERD, THE, 1497
life, revelation of Father, 1543
  saved as infant, 1354
  story of J, thanks to Midwayers, 866
  to instruct entire universe, 1999
  was lived for every person of every age on every world of a far-flung universe, 1585
lifetime, what man does in ages J did in lifetime, 2092
light (clear) did not come to J (13th year), 1383
"light" of the world, 1795, 1903
lighthearted and joyful, 1528
"like any other child", permitted to grow up, 1355, 1407
little was premeditated, in Master's ministry, 1875
lived, and worked with gentiles, 1410
  as a man, would die as a man, 2008
  doing services for people, 1461
  for a whole universe, 1999, 2017
  a religion of service, 67
  a revelation of God, 1855
lives life anew in all believers, 2062
living faith in God, 2087
living J should be in churches, 2090
lodging changed, too much "publicity", 1735
loneliness, terrible feeling of human loneliness, 1968, 2006
looked a King, 1702
looked with commingled pity and love, (Peter), 1981
Lord's prayer, origin of, 1389
  part of spoken by J, 1511
LOST SON, PARABLE OF THE, 1850
love, for ignorant mortals, 2000
  for Martha, Mary, Lazarus, 1404, 1837
  greater than any hitherto on earth, 2019
  J' love for children ended killing, 2073
loved, all manner of men, 1424
  by all at Zebedee's, 1421
  devotedly, J was, 1403
  truly, each individual, 1874
  with superhuman affection, 1672
loves the Jews still, 1909
lowest ebb in popularity, 1718
loyalty, and fealty challenged, 1397
  not sacrifice, J demands, 1945
  to Father above all, 1521
Lucifer rebellion, end of the, 1493 (see "Lucifer rebellion" under "L")
Lucifer, Satan, Caligastia vs. Jesus, 602
m MAGADAN, THE RETURN TO, 1771
MAGDALA, THE STOP AT, 1679
majestic appearance, 1979, -82-84, -90, -92
"make him king", 1702
makes open break with Pharisees, 1813
making the tree good (emphasis), 1582
malice, none toward chief priests and rulers of Jews, 1907

Jesus (cont'd)

MAN, THE, 2090
man, afraid to understand J, 1736
  among men, 1407-08, -13, -25, 1573, -94
  J came to create in m a new will, 1583
  J was the perfection of, 1604
  mistreating his wife, 1470
  most truly religious, ever, 2090
  not hungry for the truth, 1466
  of sorrows, J falsely called, 1954
  valiant, courageous, 1013
  whole, union of body, mind, spirit, 1590
MAN WITH THE WITHERED HAND, 1664
mankind, wanted to leave to m memory of... 2008
man's creator, 1572
"many... teachers are blind guides", 1713
marriage and divorce, 1576-77, -81, 1838-39
marriage, James', 1418; Miriam's, 1418
marriage of Simon, marriage of Jude, 1484
martyr, did not seek to become m, 1756
MARY, MARTHA, AND LAZARUS, 1375
Mary, Martha, Lazarus loved J at 12 as if brother, 1380
Mary (mother of J), (see also under "M")
  avoided J, 1628
  J and M got along better, 1401
Mary (sister of Lazarus), (see also under "M")
  anoints J' feet, 1879
Master, J called, 1515, -18-19, -39, -41-43, -46-47, 1551, -57, -64, -67, -69, -76
  apostles soon called J M, 1549
  J first called M at Zebedee's, 1421
master philosophy of life, 1572
Master Son, 239-40, 316
MASTER'S ARREST, THE, 1973
MASTER'S ASCENSION, THE, 2057
MASTER'S SECOND COMING, THE, 1914
MATERIAL BODY OF JESUS, THE, 2022
MATERIALISM, THE VULNERABILITY OF, 2078
mathematics for several years, J studied, 1364
MEANING OF THE DEATH ON THE CROSS, 2016
meanings, large, put into small expressions, 1771
measure of social institutions and usage of religion, 1388
measure of validity of religion, 1572
meeting after sermon, 3 hours, 1711
MEETING OF THE SANHEDRIN, 1847
meetings, family, employees, 1421
MEETINGS OF JESUS AND JOHN, 1503
meets Stephen, 1411
memories soothed and strengthened J, 1969
men, all, J' brothers and God's children, 2093
  high value placed on, by J, 2093
  J would make Godlike, 1581
  what m must be, not do, 1584
mental distress, suffered great, 1372
mental harassments, sought by victims of, 1671
merchant from Mongolia, the, 1429
MERCY AND JUSTICE, 1468
mercy, "may be lavish, justice is precise", 1469
MESOPOTAMIA, IN, 1481
message, Christianized, 2069; restate every generation, 2060
MESSAGE FROM BETHANY, THE, 1836
message, his saving, 1670
  if not changed, all would have embraced gospel, 1670
  solvent for spiritual difficulties, 2060
  taken too literally by followers, 1577

Jesus (cont'd)

natural laws, accidents, 1830
   no abridgment of, 1517,-19
nature, laws of, not violated, 1530
   of J' mission, 1390, 1635
NAZARETH, BACK IN, 1356
NAZARETH, THE HOME AT, 1349
Nazareth, opinions...unfavorable to J, 1684
NAZARETH REJECTION, THE, 1686
Nazareth, return to, 1483
NAZARETH, THE SABBATH SERVICE AT, 1684
NAZARETH, SCHOOL DAYS IN, 1362
NAZARETH, THE SOJOURN AT, 1683
Nazareth, synagogue ceremonies better, 1377
Nebadon, the sovereignty of, 1494, 2057
NECESSITY FOR LEAVING, THE, 1951
negative denunciations, few, 1655
never again in universal favor (Capernaum), 1398
never again in universe, any being like J, 1699
never argued about fatherhood or brotherhood, 2091
never belittled self "proving" the father, 1855
never called to himself "all who are dreamers", 1590
never ceased loving the Jews, 1909
never entrapped by enemies, 1674
never hurt present good motivations, 1428
never meddled with temporal affairs, 1821
never premeditated anything dramatic, 1882
never without power if he chose, 1326
new and living religion of the Spirit, 1893
new and living way, man to God, J is, 1426
new commandment (see under "Jesus, Quotes")
new following after defections, 1718
new gospel about J, 2059
new religion of J' needs...966
new revelation of man to God, 1984
NEW SCHOOL OF THE PROPHETS, A, 1657
New Testament meagerly Jesusonian, 2091
next to family loved family of Lazarus, 1404
night before Bethlehem massacre, taken away, 1354
NINETEENTH YEAR, JESUS' (A.D. 13), 1401
NINTH YEAR, JESUS' (A.D. 3), 1366
no emphasis on struggle between soul and body, 1749
no longer necessary to go "out" to teach, 1808
no man saw J again for 40 days, 1504
non-resistance,
   and nonviolence, heroic believers will astonish
     mankind, 1608
   compensated by loyal friend Jacob, 1368-69
   did not teach negative submission, 1770
   hard to explain his n-r to apostles, 1579
   not if attacked by creature lacking moral judgment
     and spiritual reason, 1469
   not a rule of J' family, 1401
   to all selfish reaction to universe, 1950
   unwillingness to fight for his rights, 1368
normal child, 1359
normal life, lived, 1407,-13,-25
not afraid to identify with all kinds, 1565
not anxiously bothered by evil in world, 1594
not even angry when...2000
not even a moral reformer, 1582
not heard before Jewish court, 1990
not a militant revolutionist, 1671
not vanquished, merely undefending, 1988
not what you may obtain, but may give, 2039
NORTHERN PEREA, LAST VISIT TO, 1825
nurse, gentle and adept with Ganid, 1479

O O Jerusalem... (see under "Jesus, Quotes")
obedience to natural law, 1519

Jesus (cont'd)

objective, J had one only, 1522
OCCIDENT OF THE FIRST CENTURY AFTER
   CHRIST, THE, 1332
occupations, work,
   boat designer, 1419-20
   boat maker, 1419,-24,-92,-95, 1535
   cabinet work, 1410
   caravan conductor, executive, 1484-85
   carpenter, 1410
   fisherman, 1369, 1420
   housefinishing, 1410
   interpreter, 1423
   lecturer, 1485
   miner, 1643
   repair shop, 1410
   scribe, 1423,-56,-59,-68,-92
   smith, 1368, 1410   tentmaker, 1456
   tutor, Jewish, 1423
   worker in canvas and leather, 1387
   yoke maker, 1367,-87
occupied with single task, 1520
of morontia, after resurrection, 2022
offensive, assumed the, 1708
older persons, J liked company of, 1369
omitted thanks at breaking bread, 1611
ON COUNTING THE COST, 1869
on cross of mortal existence 25 years, 2018
on earth "to comfort minds, liberate spirits, save
   souls", 1576
ON THE ISLAND OF CRETE, 1436
ON THE WAY TO NAPLES AND ROME, 1440
"one altogether lovely" was J, 1403, 1566
ONE DAY ALONE WITH GOD, 1920
one look, you knew J was man of experience, 1582
one more chance,
   another chance, Sanhedrin and Jewish leaders, 1810
   even now I offer you, 1908
   for people of Jerusalem, 1883
   opportunity (teachers in Israel), 1809
   your last c to come forward, 1906
one of Creator Sons, 1145
one-third believed, at Capernaum synagogue, 1537
one world in ten million, a Creator Son (J), 596
"only begotten Son personalizing 611, 121st universal
   concept of divinity and infinity", 366
only religion founder who performed supermaterial
   acts on earth, 1671
only supernatural event about birth of J, Ardnon was
   told, 1317
only supernatural occurence, Mary's conception,
   J' birth, was Gabriel's appearance, 1347
opened up understanding of Scriptures, 2036
opposition to J had subsided, 1741
ordained for followers, gather to do something, 1091
ordained the twelve, 1568
ORDINATION OF THE 70 AT MAGADAN, 1800
original thinker, 1368
our brother, friend, sovereign, father, is J, 1405
"OUR RELIGION", 1453
our religion is throbbing with new life, (J), 1766
p pagan, the thoughtless, 1466
   was not dissatisfied with himself, 1466
paid no attention to public opinion, 1594
"pallbearers" for J, 2013
papers, Jesus, in U Book, authority behind,
   human records (Andrew's too), 1341
   superhuman records resorted to, 1343
papers, how prepared, sources, concepts, resources,
   1343

Jesus (cont'd)

PARABLE OF THE SOWER, 1688
PARABLES, MORE ABOUT, 1691 (see "parables" under "P")
PARABLES, MORE BY THE SEA, 1693
Paradise Son personalized as a Michael, 234
parents, J noted, had opposed views, 1372
    were average people, 1317
partiality, none for family, 1719
partially in Christianity, ideas, ideals of J, 2072
participated in no sacrificial service, 1936
partisan, J would not be even today, 1581
passed test of civilized man, 1521
PASSOVER AT JERUSALEM, 1596
Passover, bloodless, 1648
PASSOVER, J' DEATH IN RELATION TO THE, 2002
Passover, visit to Jerusalem, 1404
    with James at the P, 1399
    with Joseph at the P, 1409
    with Jude at the P, 1415
    with Simon at the P, 1411
path of normal earthly existence, 1518
patience with Jude, 1416
patiently dealt with Nalda, 1613
Paul confused J with Eternal Son of Trinity, 1144
Paul vs. Jesus, gospel, teachings (see under "Paul")
pearl of great price, 1583, 1694
pearls, "guilty of casting our p before swine", 1585
    "neither cast p before swine", 1571
    "uselessness of casting p before swine", 1999
PELLA CAMP, AT THE, 1817
PELLA, IN CAMP NEAR, 1626
PELLA, LAST TEACHING AT, 1850
PELLA, MOVING THE CAMP TO, 1806
PENTECOST, AFTER, 2069
PENTECOST SERMON, THE, 2060
PENTECOST, THE SIGNIFICANCE OF, 2060
PENTECOST, WHAT HAPPENED AT, 2062
people were made better for life, 1484
perceived end of one dispensation, beginning of
    another, 1903
PEREAN MISSION BEGINS, THE, 1817
PEREAN TOUR, THE, 1870
perfect life, evaluated on high, 1330
perfected, human personality, 1425
    human soul, T A left, 1511
    man of a universe, 1103
    specimen of self-control, 1609
persecution of Lazarus, J foresaw, 1844
person of J submerged the kingdom, 1864
personal, attitude, indifferent to tragedy, 1932
    encounter, nearest to, 1436
    greetings to apostles, 1897
PERSONAL MINISTRY, 1460
personal, ministry trip (Caspian), 1484
    morality and group loyalty, 1373
PERSONAL RELIGION, 1581
personal, salutation to each apostle, 1897
    sovereignty throughout broad domains, 1328
    talks in Corinth, 1474
personality, appealed to disparate people, 1589-90
    isolation, to escape, 1985
    J made clear high worth of human p, 2076
    preparing for, change in attitude, 1484
    of J awake during death, 2016
    of J strong and forceful, 1589
    perfection and symmetry, 1101
    unique in symmetry, 1101
personality-control achieved, 1493
Personalized Adjuster, 1341, 1511, 2020, -22, -24 (see
    also "Thought Adjuster, Personalized")

Jesus (cont'd)

Personalized Adjuster helped Urantia Book, 1341
pessimistic views, Paul's, not shared by J, 2093
PETER AND JOHN AT THE TOMB, 2027
Peter, and Simon and the 100 swords, 1871
PETER CALLS A MEETING, 2057
PETER IN THE COURTYARD, 1980
PETER'S CONFESSION, 1745
Peter's confession, beginning of final period, Son of
    God, 1749
Peter's confession of J, 1746-47
PETER'S HOUSE, AT, 1761
PETER'S PROTEST, 1759
PETER'S QUESTION, ANSWER TO, 1824
Peter's wife's mother, 1631
Pharisee and the publican, the, 1838
Pharisees and scribes, good and bad, 1386
PHARISEES, BREAKFAST WITH THE, 1833
PHARISEES AT RAGABA, THE, 1825
Pharisees, confounded the, 1655
    criticized, 1540
PHILADELPHIA, CONGREGATION AT, 1831
Philadelphia, J arrived with 600, 1833
PHILADELPHIA, THE VISIT TO, 1833
PHOENICIA, ON THE WAY TO, 1728
PHOENICIA, THE RETURN FROM, 1741
physician as much as preacher, 1633
picture on the floor, the, 1366
pictures of J most unfortunate, 1590
Pilate, Pontius, 1987
PILATE, J APPEARS BEFORE, 1989
Pilate, J really pitied P, 1999
    "on trial before J", 1999
PILATE, THE PRIVATE EXAMINATION BY, 1991
PILATE'S LAST APPEAL, 1994
PILATE'S LAST INTERVIEW, 1995
PILATE'S TRAGIC SURRENDER, 1996
pitcher, man with the p, 1933
pity and love for Jewish people deepened, 1386
pity, seldom indulged in, 1874
plan of a new age, the, 1595
planning, wise and thoughtful, 1410
PLANS FOR PUBLIC WORK, 1514
plans, three pondered, one elected, 1748
plea to the Jews, last temple discourse, 1905
plot against J, entangling questions, 1901
POLITICAL ATTITUDE, 1580
political, other ideas, freely expressed (unauthor-
        itatively) at Zebedee evening meetings, 1421
    prestige, J wouldn't gain pp, 1521
    social, economic attitudes, instructions on, 1580
    social, economic problems, 1839
POLITICAL SOVEREIGNTY, 1487
politics, economics, trade, not Father's will, 1576, -79
    forbidden, 1580, 1605
pool of Bethesda, 1649
poor and wealthy, J' attitudes toward, 2093
poor man, falsely accused, to the, 1462
poor usually sincere and pious, 2093
portrayed love of heavenly Father, 2016
possessed matchless grace of personality, 1534
post-bestowal status, 1317
POUNDS, PARABLE OF THE, 1875
power, and glory, J will return in, 1603
    J aware of potential, 1416
    never without, if he chose, 1326
    over life and death, 1837-38
    possessed unlimited, 1543
    spiritual, through J; no limitation on, 1700
powerful extended arm held man away, 1436
practical as well as idealist, 1393

124

Jesus (cont'd)

    prayed, for wisdom and judgment, 1634
      in hills, because no room, 1635
      in tones of majesty, 2050
      Judas would love brethren, 1897
      never as duty, 2089
      often in ravine, 1968
      "this cup, if it is your will", 1968
    PRAYER AND WORSHIP, TEACHINGS ABOUT, 1616
    PRAYER, THE ANSWER TO, 1848
    PRAYER, THE BELIEVER'S, 1619
    PRAYER, THE DISCOURSE ON, 1618
    prayer, last group, 1963
    PRAYER, MORE ABOUT, 1620
    PRAYER, OTHER FORMS OF, 1621
    prayer, primarily for disciples, 1620
      supercommunion with Supreme Rulers, 1621
      was to J expression of attitude, 2089
      whole nights at p, 1620
    prayers, answers to questions on p, 1848
      from other worlds, 1621
      trouble with boy J about his p, 1360
    praying was done silently, 1621
    "preached" in synagogue,
      enemies present for open "warfare", 1707-08
      first sermon, 1391
      first sermon after baptism, 1532
      religion is a personal experience, 1629
      six Jerusalem spies on hand, 1665
      ten days after John's imprisonment, 1535
    preached, not against wealth, property, 1581
      repentance, followed by good tidings of joy, 1509
      temperance and taught consistency, 1673
      that religion is a personal experience, 1629
    PREACHER, THE STRANGE, 1764
    PREACHING AT RIMMON, 1637
    preaching tour, first public, started Sunday, Jan. 18,
      A.D. 28, 1636
    preaching tour of Galilee, 1637
    PREACHING TOUR, THE SECOND, 1668
    PREACHING TOUR, THE THIRD, 1678
    PREFERENCE, THE DESIRE FOR, 1936
    prehuman experience recalled, 1424
    PREPARATION FOR THE CRUCIFIXION, 2001
    PREPARATION FOR THE LAST MISSION, 1808
    prepared, followers for impending dispersion, 1717
      openly to assume role of...Son of God, 1749
      thirty Romans for leadership, 1456
    "prescience" of J (swords), 1871
    present in hearts of man, 1700
    PRESENTATION IN THE TEMPLE, THE, 1352
    priests, from Ur visited babe, 3 weeks old, 1352
      righteous resentment of, 1386
    Prince of Peace, 1536
    PRIVATE EXAMINATION BY PILATE, THE, 1991
    problem, momentous, occupied with, 1707
      skipped food, ate little, 1707
    problems, had all conflicts, confusions, 1393,-95
      human, to solve, 1581
      non-religious, J ignored, 1581,-83, 1624
      not spiritual, no voice, 1839
      three recurring in ministry, 1523
    proclaim joy to moral captives, 1541
    prodigal son, told many, many times, 1853
    profound respect for every human, 1545
    PROGRESS OF THE PREACHING TOUR, 1673
    progression, J requires, 1782
    progressive evolutionist, a, 1671-72
    progressively self-conscious of divinity, 1327
    prohibitions, rebukes, won't suppress animal urges,
      1582

Jesus (cont'd)

    "...promise me that these my sons..." (Salome), 1867
    promise to return (morontia), 1962
    PROMISED HELPER, THE, 1948
    promised, to U by Melchizedek 2000 yr. B.C., 1024
      two things after ascension, 1918
    pronouncements, detracted from Scriptures, 1767
      new and startling, 1341
      not shocking if, 2093
      two greatest, 2084
    proofs of his mortal nature, 1968
    proves truth and faith vindicated, 2063
    prophecy, fall of Jerusalem, 1882, 1906, -12-13, 2005
      Judas in great danger, 1715
      Lazarus' death, to glorify God, 1836
      Peter, three denials before cock crow, 1962
      some of you put to death, 1584
    prophesies, his "rising", 1871
      own death, 1759, 1824, -68, -70, 1904
      to the Jews, 1709
    "prophesy to us who struck you", 1984, 2000
    protested not, when called "Lord of Glory", 1408
    PROVIDENCE, FUNCTIONS OF, 1304
    prudence and foresight, J did not forbid, 1579, 1854
    psychologist, vs. J, 1437, -79, 1610
    psychology of J with young man, 1437
    public appearance, nearest to (early), 1462
    public baths, J refused to go to, 1472
    public career, beginning of, 1408
      first real sermon, 1536
    public women, the two, 1472
    PUBLIC WORK, BEGINNING THE, 1587
    punishment, God punish a nation for sin of individual,
      no, 1630
      of criminals, yes, 1579
    PURPOSE OF AFFLICTION, THE, 1661
    purpose, of the trip to Rome, 1424
      one great, 2090
      two-fold, 1388, 1407, -17, -23, -25
    put positive action into passive Jewish, 1769

q qualified to rule as representative of Trinity, 1323
    question, and answer sessions, 1420; for apostles,
      1546
      first he asked about himself, 1745
      J didn't fully answer, 1469
    question mark, J was one, 1358
    question, on mission always answered, 1999
      one supreme q about J, 1708
    questions, asked of rabbis at 12, 1382
    QUESTIONS BY THE JEWISH RULERS, 1899
    questions to apostles, believe in me?, 2049
      love me?, 2047
      obey me?, 2049
      serve me?, 2048
      trust me?, 2048
    quoted Isaiah first sermon, 1391

r "Rabbi", J was called, 1534
    rabbis' school, J indifferent to, 1370
    races, all, receptive to J' message, 1485
    raised Lazarus because villagers believed, 1880
    reactions of the individual apostles, 2037-39
    readings, took advanced courses of, 1387
    Reality, 5
    REALITY, DISCOURSE ON, 1433
    really great man, a true hero, 2009
    really understood men, 1874
    rearing the children, 1401
    reason, wisdom, and faith, 2094
    reasons for enemies wanting J' life,
      Pharisees, four, 1911; Sadducees, three, 1911

Jesus (cont'd)

REBECCA, THE DAUGHTER OF EZRA, 1402
rebel, a, 2007
reborn, being (see "born again, be" under "B")
rebuked, apostles, 1788, 1867
    James and John, 1525
    Mary, 1529
    the sons of Zebedee, 1788
rebukes Judas, 1879
recital of life, necessary to show fellow Jews
    rejected him, caused ignominious death, 1909
recognition of the equality of women, 1671
reconciles man and wife, 1470-71
records, (Gospels) changed history for 2000 yrs., 1342
RECORDS, PREVIOUS WRITTEN (life of J), 1341
recreational pleasures, last, 1402
recurring situations (3), 1523
Redeemer, J erroneously made the R, 1864
redeemer, ransomer, no, 2017
redemption of J, firstborn, 5 shekels, 1352
redemption rite, "go before the Lord to establish his
    kingdom", 1353
referred to Deity by 2 names (God and Father), 1856
reformer, economic, no, 1581
    J not a moral r, 1582
    political, no, 1580
refuge for adolescents, all ages, worlds, 1395
refused, narcotized wine on cross, 2007
    offer of Sanhedrists, believing (go to 70), 1811
    to be submerged by the ailing, 1644-45
regard for every human, 1545
regard for J at lowest ebb, 1718
registered self as "skilled craftsman", 1420
regretted necessity of using term "kingdom", 1856
regular about working hours, 1504
rehabilitation implied in J' forgiveness, 2018
rejected by, Jews because, 1024
    Nazareth, Jerusalem, Capernaum, 1880
RELATION TO RIGHTEOUSNESS, IN, 1861
relationship to take precedence over all others, 1593
relatives, no close, as apostles, 1538
release from life, didn't seek, 2063
relentless, inexorable against sin, rebellion, 1766
relics; J wished none left behind, 2008
relieved the tension among apostles, 1747

religion

religion, about J, 2091
    acquire compassionate character, do will of the
        Father, 1582
RELIGION, DISCOURSE ON TRUE, 1728
religion, is a personal experience, 1629
    nature of, 1769   never passive, 2064
RELIGION OF JESUS, THE, 2091 (see also "religion"
    under "R")
religion of Jesus (not "about" J)
    and service of man, 1769-70
    apart from Christianity, 2086
    based wholly on living his... life, 1593
    brotherhood, no church, 2067
    can never be higher concept than r of J, 1781
    changed to "about---", 2051
    Christianity not r of J but about J, 1084
    civilization would drastically change, 2090
    compared to others, 67
    cornerstone of, 1769
    creates highest type personality, 2063
    cross not central truth of r from... teachings of J,
        1615
    demands, 2083

Jesus (cont'd)

religion of Jesus (not "about" J), (cont'd)
    demands experience, 1782
    described, 2063
    divorced from force by Pentecost, 2064
    dogma never should come from, 2084
    drastic changes civilization if r of J should
        supplant... 2090
    essence is not social service, 1770
    evolutionary till J baptised; evolutionary,
        revelational, till crucifixion; morontia after
        resurrection, 1112
    Father's will, and unselfish service, 2090
    for everybody, 1583
    fosters highest type civilization, 2063
    founded as r of personal experience, 2092
    heart of, 1582
    high spiritual concept... revival of teachings, 1866
    in this brotherhood no place for... 2085
    inherited Jewish fetters, 2064
    is destined to conquer empire of... secularism,
        2082
    is for everybody, 1583
    J distinguished between his teachings and possible
        r about him, 1543
    J early recognized r about him might compete with
        gospel, 1413
    joy and peace for man NOW, 2063
    living hope for every real religion, 1583
    living r, should supplant theologic r, 2090
    most dynamic influence in history, 1091
    most powerful unifying influence, 2065
    must be lived, about can be preached, 2091
    needs new, appropriate symbolism, 966
    new gospel about J in place of fatherhood...
        brotherhood, 2059
    new gospel of faith, a, 2063
    no religious introspection, 1583
    not merely believing, but actually doing, 1769
    one of valor, courage, heroism, 1582
    opiate to people, no!, 2063
    opposite of Judaism, what man must be, not do, 1584
    or Paul's, 2069; vs. Paul's, 2095
    peace... during which gospel about J spread, 2068
    positive nature of, 1769
    powerful unifying influence, most, 2064
    r about J complicated Master's teachings, 1487
    religion of love, a, 2095
    requires new symbolism, 966
    sect was growing, 2067
    simple spiritual approach, 2069
    social service is a certain effect of, 1770
    sum and substance of, 1769
    to conquer an empire, 2082
    transcendent spiritual summons, 2083
    transcends all former concepts, 1781-82
    unique, 1112
        Golden Rule (see under "G" and in this section)
        introspection, self-examination, no, 1583
        stands apart from all r, 1583
        teachings suitable all ages, all worlds, 1583
        true goodness must be unconscious, 1583
    untouched by modern science, 2076
    U waiting for reality of gospel of J, 1041
    vs. others, 67
    wholly based on... 1593
    will not be bankrupt, 2076
    will triumph, 2075-76
    world would have embraced, 1670

Jesus (cont'd)

religion, personal experience, Paul's, 2091; J, 2092
RELIGION, SECOND DISCOURSE ON, 1730
RELIGION, THE SUPREMACY OF, 2093
religion's mission, not social, political, 2093
religions of authority (assent), on, 1729
religious leaders of Rome taught by J, 1456
religious living, acme of, 1101
religious man, no desire to produce just rm, 1582
"remember me when you come into your kingdom",
    (thief to J), 2009
REMEMBRANCE SUPPER, ESTABLISHING THE,
    1941 (see also under "R")
rendezvous, last mortal, 1935
reorganization for last year, 1742
repairman, was, 1410
repeatedly dashed...hopes of his A, 1548
repetition, J found it necessary, 1831
represented only the Father, 1856
repudiated part of a Scripture, used part, 1769-70
rescue human J from dogmas, 2090
respect for every human, 1545
respect, outward show of, for J, 1747
rest, 3 days with 3 apostles, 1593
restful season of labor, 1605
RESURRECTION, THE, 2020
RESURRECTION, THE DISPENSATIONAL, 2024
RESURRECTION, HERALDS OF THE, 2029
resurrection not material, 2020,-23 (see also
    "resurrection" under "R")
RESURRECTION OF LAZARUS, THE, 1842,-45
retaliation, abhorred, 1770
return from 40 days in hills, 1505
RETURN FROM ROME, THE, 1468
RETURN OF MICHAEL, THE, 1918
return of Michael, 226
    "(after) long winter of material mindedness", 1915
    Avonal bestowal here complicated by promised
        roM, 227
    be ready to welcome him on earth, 1919
    believers (laid) fast hold on promises to return,
        1914
    explicit promise of Creator Son, 1025
    "I promise I will sometime return to this world",
        1914
    "I will return...to receive such a kingdom...as
        is now denied me", 1876
    import to roM added by fact of archangel activities
        here, 409
    Jesus, lives...he is coming again, 2067
        on numerous occasions declared intention, 1918
        promised sometime to come back in person,1863
        stated definitely... revisit this world in power
            and glory,1603
    little change in U government seen until roM, 1259
    Melchizedek too? upon roM, 1251
    most misunderstood of J' teachings, 1918
    natural to one of his nativity spheres, 1918
    not in mortal flesh with (divine attributes), 1699-
        1700
    one of two promises of J, 1918
    "only the eye of the spirit" will behold (M) on
        earth in his own name, 1915
    (perhaps) to be seen only with spiritual eye, 1919
    second advent of tremendous sentimental value,
        1919
    Son of Man rejected now, but in another age, will
        be received, 1876
    times of roM known only in Paradise, 1915
    U "out of step", account of promised, 598

Jesus (cont'd)

return of Michael (cont'd)
    we believe Michael will come in person, 1919
    "when the fullness of the age has come to pass",
        1915
    when he returns, all the world will likely know,
        1919
    "(when) spiritual springtime (comes) summertime
        of new visitation draws near", 1915
RETURN OF THE SEVENTY, 1806
return to Jerusalem when he prepared to leave world,
    1816
returned to John's group, 1505
returned to status of supreme sovereignty on
    Salvington, 2057
RETURNS TO PILATE, JESUS, 1993
revealed God as Father of each human, 41
reveals divine nature, 1746
revelation (see also "revelation" under "R")
    of God, J was a, 1856
    of man to God, 2000
    of man to himself, 196
    was a new one, 1542
revelations, essential, revealed in J, 1593
revenge, J made no allowance for, 1579
revolutionary idea, J' most (attitude to women), 1671
revolutionist, J not a militant r, 1671
rewards, next world, eternal life, 1593
    only, for his children, 1593
    spiritual joy, divine communion, 1593
RICH MAN AND THE BEGGAR, THE, 1854
RICH MAN, COUNSELING THE, 1462
rich usually wanton and irreligious, 2093
RICH YOUNG MAN AND OTHERS, THE, 1801
riches, J used no influence of, 1520
richest experiences, one of J', 1461
richest period of life, 1461
RIGHTEOUSNESS, IN RELATION TO, 1861
RIMMON, PREACHING AT, 1637
"rising from the dead", talk about, 1754
Rodan and J' gospel, 1775 (see "Rodan" under "R")
Roman centurion, to the, 1474
Roman judge, to the, 1474
Roman senator, to the, 1461
Roman soldier, to the, 1461
Roman trip (cities, places, in sequence visited), 1427

Joppa, 1428	Corinth, 1471
Caesarea, 1429	Athens, 1476
Alexandria, 1432	Troas, 1477
Lasea (Crete), 1436	Ephesus, 1477
Cyrne, 1438	Rhodes, 1479
Carthage, 1438	Cyprus, 1479
Malta, 1440	Paphos, 1479
Syracuse, 1440	Salamis, 1480
Mycena (Messina), 1440	Antioch (Syria), 1480
Naples, 1440	Sedon, 1481
Capua, 1441	Damascus, 1481
Rome, 1455	Mesopotamia, 1427, 1481
Switzerland, 1466	Ur, 1481
Tarentum, 1468	Susa, 1481
Nicopolis, 1471	Charax, 1481
	Babylon, 1483

Roman trip, known as Damascus Scribe, 1423
Rome, friends loved J, 1468
    group meetings, J' friends, 1468
    influence upon the religious leaders, 1455
    J departed without farewells, 1468
    J uplifted about 500, 1461
ROME, ON THE WAY TO, 1427

Jesus (cont'd)
  Rome (cont'd)
    purpose of the trip to, 1424
    ROME, THE RETURN FROM, 1468
    Rome, 6 months in, 1456,-61
    <u>ROME, THE SOJOURN AT</u>, 1455
    ROME, TRIPS ABOUT, 1466
  ruffians hired to harass J, 1684
  rugged Galilean fishermen called him Master, 1590
  RULE OF LIVING, 1650 (see also "GOLDEN RULE"
    this listing, also under "G"; also "whatsoever
    you would" under "Jesus, Quotes")
  rule of power, reign of glory, no, 1544
  ruler of universe, 852, 1376
  rulers (see also "chief priests, rulers of Jews")
    benighted r of Israel, 1904
  rulership of his universe, unqualified, 1407
  rumors, enemies of J spread, 1719
  runaway lad, to the, 1475
  Ruth, chief comfort to J, 1628
S SABBATH AT BETHANY, 1878
  SABBATH AT TIBERIAS, 1680
  Sabbath observance modified, 1402
  sacrament, J established only one, 1942
  sacrifice, J and, 1945
    J did not die as, 2003
  sacrificer, ransomer, no! saviour, yes!, 2017
  sacrifices don't help prayer, 1640
  saddened at times, never discouraged, 1594
  SADDUCEES AND THE RESURRECTION, THE, 1900
  safe until hour he was ready, 1920
  SAFEGUARDING THE TOMB, 2014
  safeguarding of J, 1718
  sagacity and humor in questions, 1383
  salvation by faith alone, truth of first import, 1593
    (see also "salvation, by faith" under "S"; "faith,
    salvation by"; and "kingdom, price to enter")
  <u>SAMARIA, GOING THROUGH</u>, 1607
  SAMARITAN REVIVAL, THE, 1615
  sand, writing on s only, 1514
  Sanhedrin, another opportunity for, 1809 (see also
    "chance (opportunity) another for Jews"
    under "C") (see "Sanhedrin" under "S")
    "believers", profound talk to, 1810
  <u>SANHEDRIN COURT, BEFORE THE</u>, 1978,-82
  Sanhedrin Court, last day, first meeting, 1982
    last day, second meeting, 1985
  Sanhedrin, J extolled by Josiah before, 1814-15
  SANHEDRIN, MEETING OF THE, 1847
  Sanhedrin's charges against J, 1850
  sat at no man's feet, 1388
  Satan and Caligastia with J, 1493
  SATURDAY EVENING, THE, 1715
  saved, few or many? (Pharisee), 1823
  saved? what shall we do to be, 1682
  savior, correct to refer to J as, 2017
  saw men as weak rather than wicked, 2093
  saw self as he was prior to earth, 1512
  SCHOOL DAYS IN NAZARETH, 1362
  school of thought, allied to none, 1535
  scorned attracting attention, 1520
  scourged, before condemned, 1995, 2004
  scourging of J, the, 1995
  scribe of Damascus, 1423,-56,-59,-68,-92
  Scriptures, how he read, 1399-1400
    J used positive half of a...1769-70
  SCRIPTURES, TALK WITH NATHANIEL ON THE,1767
  Scythopolis episode, the, 1370
  seaside meetings, 3 a day, 1717
  season of quiet meditation, 1513

Jesus (cont'd)
  second Adam, the, 1025
  second appearance, to Mary Magdalene, 2027
  second arrival of Melchizedek (with J?), 1251
  second coming (see "return of Michael" in this section)
  SECOND COMING, THE MASTER'S, 1914
  SECOND MEETING OF THE COURT, THE, 1985
  secret of his unparalleled religious life, 2089
  SECULAR TOTALITARIANISM, 2081
  sees into heart of God, and man, simultaneously, 1603
  "seeks no glory for self", Thomas, 1636
  self-consciousness of mission, 1368
  self-control, J perfected specimen of, 1609
    not self-denial, 1609
  self-denial, fasting and, no, 1605
    not in J' religion, but self-control, 1609
  self-examination, not in J' religion, 1609
    not required, 1583
  self-forgetfulness, J' splendid, 2088
  self-mastery instead of self-denial, 1609
  SELF-MASTERY, LESSON ON, 1609
  self-respect, superb, 1582
  sensual urges, how not repressed, 1582
  sent John from room, terrible hour, 1984
  send word to Abner of death and resurrection, 1966
  SERMON AT GERASA, 1828
  SERMON, EPOCHAL, 1709
  SERMON, FIRST IN SYNAGOGUE, 1391
  sermon, first pretentious, 1536
  SERMON ON FORGIVENESS, 1762
  SERMON ON THE GOOD SHEPHERD, 1818
  SERMON ON THE KINGDOM, 1535
  SERMON ON THE LIGHT OF THE WORLD, 1794
  SERMON ON THE MOUNT, 1570,-72
  SERMON, THE PENTECOST, 2060
  SERMON, THE SABBATH S AT PELLA, 1819
  sermon, would stop a s to help a person, 1875
  served John Mark breakfast, 2047
  seven stages, divinization of J, 2091
  SEVENTEENTH YEAR, JESUS' (A. D. 11), 1396
  SEVENTH YEAR, JESUS' (A. D. 1), 1361
  seventy, the (see under "S")
  severe with men because he loved them, 1875
  sex attitudes, 1574
  SHINTO, 1451
  shocking words, not if, 2093
  shortcuts, J used no, 1520
  show of outward respect, not wanted, 1747
  showed what apostles must <u>be</u>, not do, 1584
  SHREWD STEWARD, PARABLE OF THE, 1853
  sick, J visited all, at camp, 1658
  sickness should be banished (sermon), 1632
  silent and much changed (Mt. Hermon), 1494
  silent receptivity after prayer, 1641
  similitude of creature, J in, 1536
  Simon from Cyrene, 2006
  SIMON PETER'S NIGHT VISION, 1703
  SIMON THE PHARISEE, VISITING, 1651
  simple spiritual appeal of J, lost in "pretension",
    2068-69
  sin and forgiveness, 1861   sin, Norlatiadek, 490
  sincerity, J placed great value upon, 1582
  single thought for bestowal, 1514
  singleness of purpose, 1594
  sinners came to call, 1537
  "sit not down in the chief seat...", 1834
  SITUATION IN JERUSALEM, THE, 1910
  sixteen years of age, was over 6 ft. tall, 1497
  SIXTEENTH YEAR, JESUS, (A. D. 10), 1395
  SKEPTIC, THE, 1336

Jesus (cont'd)

skeptic, J not a moral, 2093
skilled craftsman, registered as, 1420
skillful teacher, 1368-69
slaughter, sacrifice, "why?" (J), 1375
smiled on man, helped with problems, 1875
smith, worked as, 6 months, 1368, 1410
social advancement, no rules for, 2093
SOCIAL ATTITUDE, 1580
social behavior, J taught no rules of, 1576, 1610
social brotherhood and spiritual brotherhood, 1864
social, economic, political reforms "not the
    business of the kingdom", 1565
social evils, due to indiscriminate kindness, 1580
SOCIAL HOUR, THE LAST, 1927
SOCIAL MINISTRY, 1465
social parasites, professional alms-seekers, 1580
social situations, taught patience, tolerance,
    forgiveness, 1580
socialization of religion, little on, 1643
sociology, discussed at Zebedee home meetings, 1421
soil from which soul grows, on, 1738
SOJOURN AT ROME, THE, 1455 ────── (see also:
SOJOURN AT TYRE AND SIDON, 1734   Amathus,
SOJOURN IN EGYPT, 1355   Cyprus,
SOJOURN ON MT. HERMON, THE, 1492 Nazareth)
sole concern of J, 1576, -80
solitary wanderings, 1492
solution to human problems, 1581, 1611
some ideals of J sacrificed in building Christianity,
    2074
Son, Eternal, J not, 74, 366   Master Son, 239-40
Son of God, J admitted he was, 1408 (see under "S")
"Son of Man", the, 1390
son, "this is my beloved s", 1506, 1754-55
soothed self, how, 1969
sorrow upon sorrow, plight of J, 1969
sorrowed by rejection at Nazareth, 1688
sought permission confer with Satan, 1493
sought to avoid unfair tax, 1393
sought to restore man's dignity, 1091
soul, each to develop in its own way, 1582
soul healer and spirit liberator, 1345
sources of Urantia Book, about, 1341
sovereign of our universe, 89, 1112
sovereignty, completion of universe, 1513
SOVEREIGNTY--DIVINE AND HUMAN, 1486
sovereignty earned, 1454-55, 1513
sovereignty of Nebadon, 1494
speaker at the forum, to the, 1461
spear pierced left side, 2011
spies, 6 appointed to watch J, 1654 (see "spies" in "S")
spirit channels, J' ascension through, 2057
spirit of J, alongside T A in men, 1700
    fraternizes with Father fragment, 1942
SPIRIT OF TRUTH, THE, 1594, 1949 (see also under
    "S")
spirit progress in J' lifetime on U equal to man's
    in whole pre-Paradise career, 2092
spirit triumphed over flesh, 1970
"spiritual appeals only, for unity among men", 1672
spiritual invincibility, conscious of, 2088
spiritual stronghold, J was, 1589
SPIRITUAL UNITY, 1591
spit upon, 1983-84, -95
spoke, authoritatively on religion, not on secular
        subjects, 1421
    directly to mens' souls, 1594
    in tones of majesty, 2050
    to consciences and souls, 1632

Jesus (cont'd)

spoke (cont'd)
    with authority, 1545
    with emotion, 1844
    with supreme authority, 1571
stages of J' life in the flesh, four, 1749
standard of living, J' family declined, 1400
stands ready to welcome you in heaven, 1919
"Star of Bethlehem", the, 1352
START FOR JERUSALEM, THE, 1880
startling announcements at Caesarea-Philippi, 1750
statements on "Magic and Superstition", 1680
status and progress, address on, 1653
status of the personality of J, 2015
Stephen, meets J, 1411
    stoned to death by irate Jews, 1411 (see also
        under "S")
stirred, J was s within his spirit, 1591
STOIC, THE, 1336
stone which the builders rejected, the, 1894
stopped sacrifice, 1133
storm on sea of Galilee, 1694
straight and narrow way, the, 1828
strange doings, to understand, 1423
strange, periodic, indignant emotions, 1890
strategy, J resorted to public, 1397
strode majestically, 1890
struck, was, 1979, -83-84, -99
students crafty, hypocritical, asked questions, 1899
students of J life, mistake of, 2092
study, caused his apostles to, 1533, -35
    intense, 1420
stunned apostles early about "end", 1531, -44
subject to Father's will, 1523
subjected apostles to rehearsals in disappointment,
    1708
subjects of J in training 24: sympathy, cooperation,
    tolerance, 1624
sublimation, teachings to apostles, 2047
success with young people, secret of, 1420
SUDUANISM (JAINISM), 1450
suffering and sorrow, terrible plight of, 1969
SUFFERING, MISUNDERSTANDING OF, 1662
summary, admonitions to apostles, 2047
summation about J (wonderful), 1578-79
summation of much of J' teaching, Emmaus, 2034-35
summoned, J had been, 1752
SUNDAY MORNING WITH THE APOSTLES, 1880
supernatural ministration to his family, no!, 1719
SUPPER, BEGINNING THE, 1937
SUPPER, ON THE WAY TO THE, 1934
supreme, mission, 1406
    personality to us, 367
    requirement, "follow me", 2089
    (universe) sovereign on Salvington, 2057
surmised majority of Jewish leaders not accept
        gospel, 1811
surprised at own miracle, 1530
surrender of man (J) to God, 1972
swept away all... sacrifice and atonement, 1133
swine, pearls (same with subnormal minds), 1440
    (see also "swine" under "S")
Switzerland, visited, 1466
swords, no comment on, 1871, -80
symbol of remembrance, bread, 1942
symbols, instead of experience, 1728
    J used, why, 1942
synagogue, Capernaum, closed to J, 1717
    Hebron s defied Sanhedrin, burned, 1780
    (see also "synagogue" under "S")

Jesus (cont'd)

SYRIAN WOMAN, THE, 1734
system of positive religious ethics, 1329
systematic teachings on Urantia, 1485
t TALK ABOUT ANGELS, THE, 1840
talk on woman and wife, 1471
talked all night with the 12, 1578
talked till after 2 a.m. with apostles, 1656
TALKS TO THE APOSTLES ON WEALTH, 1823

TAOISM, 1451
TARENTUM, EMBARKING AT, 1470
TARRYING AND TEACHING BY THE SEASIDE, 1688
task of weaving mortal, divine natures into one, 1405
taught (see also "instruction methods")
    about the whole man, 1590
    apostles by questions, answers, 1546
    apostles to seek for true causes, 1812
    "be perfect, even as the Father in heaven is
        perfect", 1091, 1583-84, 1784 (see also "be you
        perfect" under "B" and under "Jesus, Quotes")
    by asking questions, 1383
    character building "no", growth "yes", 1583
    compassion, sympathy, 1580
    for all ages (in time), 1576
    forgiveness, 1580
    from life more than from law, 1672
    God is a Father, not a bookkeeper, 1590
    little about God, 1857
    man is ascending, 1660-61
    of God, 2 things, 1857
    patience and tolerance, 1580
    pure sympathy, compassion, 1580
    religion as cause, ethics as result, 1862
    sensual urges not suppressed by religious rebuke
        or legal prohibitions, 1582
    spirit easy victor in man's "internal" warfare, 1749
    voluntary conformity to God's will, 1582
    what men must be, not do, 1584
tax collectors, balked, 1393
teacher, not a preacher, 1594
    of man's spirit, but through the mind, 1594
    play, a born t even in play, 1369
    was not a systematic t, 1672
    was a positive, 1482
TEACHING ABOUT ACCIDENTS, 1830
TEACHING ABOUT THE FATHER, 1590
TEACHING ABOUT THE KINGDOM, 1593, 1862
teaching, about marriage, 1839
    apostles, questions and answers, 1546
TEACHING AT LIVIAS, 1871
TEACHING AT TYRE, 1737, -39-40
teaching, changed, 2051
    dynamic, 1590
        self-denial, no, 1605; will prevail, 1720
    followers distorted teachings, 1864
    for individuals, not state, 1580
    Ganid, Gonod
        about Buddhism, 1466
        about man not hungry for truth, 1466
        on animals, souls, 1431
        on career of Ganid, 1465
        on caste system, 1468
        on man and animal, 1479
        on mercy and justice, 1468
        on Plato's teachings, 1433
        on subnormal beggar, 1441
TEACHING IN SIDON, 1735
TEACHING IN SOLOMON'S PORCH, 1815
TEACHING IN THE TEMPLE, 1596

Jesus (cont'd)

teaching (cont'd)
    methods, techniques, (see "teaching methods of J"
        under "T")
    mind vs. heart, 2052
    Pella, 1817; last at P, 1850
    public, parables and short discourses, 1546
    requires spirit progression, 1782
teachings, and life, heritage of all peoples, 1330
    apply to individual, not state, 1580
    behind gains in living, 2082
    change, new significance in, 1749
    help man solve complex problems, 2086
    heritage of all peoples, 1330, -47
    heritage of all religions, 1330
    identified with no t of, 1580
        political theory, economic theory, social
        system, industrial system
    ignored civic, social, economic realms, 1580
    J vs. followers, 1749
    knowledge, wisdom, faith, truth, love, 1112
    necessary to reiterate, 1831
    never tried on large scale, 1720
    of J, culminated in Pentecost, 2065
        overwhelmed by Islam, 1869
        vs. about J, 1543
    rediscovery of J and life due, 2083
    restated, modern language, 1598, 1620, -38, -80, -92,
        1739, -65, -72, 1929
    seventy, last talk with, 1804
    (this Book) from 2000 individuals, 1343
    to become heritage of all religions, 1330
    understand his t by his life, 1581
    what to BE, no DO, 1584
technique of helping, 1875 (see also "teaching methods"
    this section)
techniques of teaching, 1592
Teherma, the Persian, 1592
TEMPLE, CLEANSING THE, 1888
TEMPLE, THE FOURTH DAY IN THE, 1383
temple talk, first, (last year), 1790
TEMPLE TAX COLLECTOR, THE, 1743
TEMPLE, TUESDAY MORNING IN THE, 1897
TEMPLE, VISITING ABOUT THE, 1883
temporal affairs, never meddled in, 1821
tempt not the angels of your supervision, 1931
temptation, lead us not into, on, 1738
temptations, of J, what they were, 1493-94
    one of greatest, 1412
    puerile symbolisms, 1514
tempted, no, 1515
tempted to release John from prison, 1539
TEN LEPERS, THE, 1827
tensions, solution for, 1610
TENTH YEAR, JESUS' (A.D. 4), 1368
tentmaker of Antioch, 1456, -92
terrible denunciation of Jewish rulers, 1910
test, for religion, for institutions, 1388
    J passed, of civilized man, 1521
    of every institution and usage, 1388
tested, followers, 1708
    "in all points like as you are", 1403
    in all things, 1407
tests, no material, for spiritual problems, 1523
text for graduation: Isaiah, 61:1
thanks, neglected to give (verbally), 1611
thanksgiving on up to worship, 1640
thanksgiving too scarce, 1640
that we all might have life, more abundantly, 1749
theme, J often emphasized, 1592

Jesus (cont'd)

theologians, dishonest, 1386
THIEF ON THE CROSS, THE, 2008
thing, meaning, and value, universal reality, 2094
think of his righteousness, not sinlessness, 68
THIRD DAY IN THE TEMPLE, THE, 1382
THIRTEENTH YEAR, JESUS' (A.D. 7), 1373
THIRTIETH YEAR, JESUS' (A.D. 24), 1483
THIRTY-FIRST YEAR, JESUS' (A.D. 25), 1492
thirty pieces of silver, the, 1998
THOSE WHO SAW THE CRUCIFIXION, 2008
Thought Adjuster (see "Thought Adjusters", also
    "Thought Adjusters, Personalized, J")
T A prepared by indwelling Melchizedek, 1511
thoughtless crowd jeered at J on cross, 2007
thoughtless pagan, 1466
threatened with stoning, 1797, 1815-16
three concerns, 372
three-fold prayer in garden, 1972
three stories at same time, liked to tell, 1852
three talks to 24 in 3 weeks training, on... 1624
three weeks to Passover at 23, longest layoff since
    13, 1411
thus did expose folly of rabbinic rules, regulations,
    1713
TIBERIAS CONFERENCE, THE SECOND, 1719
Tiberias, secret trips to, 1647
time, and space, J' Adjuster on, 1516
    couldn't be limited by J, 1516
    miracles, many, 1530
    of J Palestine and Syria enjoying peace, prosperity,
        1333
TIME OF THE TOMB, THE, 2012
TIME OF WAITING, THE, 1494
"time to be about your Father's business" (age 12),
    1376, -89
time vs. space (miracles), 1516
titles of evening lessons, 1683
to apostles, "refrain from discussing", 1545
told John Z. he expected to travel extensively, 1421
tolerance, passive, no, 1579
tomb, appeared above t with Gabriel, 2021
    J emerged from at 3:02 a.m., 2021
        body of J remained in tomb, 2021
        Pilate's seal unbroken, 2021
    Michael active while J' body in t, 2016
    of Joseph of Arimathea, 2013
took for granted men believed in Father, 1855
tore apostles' hopes of personal exaltation, 1548
torn by opposing courses, 1515
torture, slow death, for J, 2006-07
TOTALITARIANISM, SECULAR, 2081
"tough", could be, 1825, -93, 1901
tour of (Roman) world, 1427
traditionalism, attacks on, 1103
traditions, violates, 1825
tragedy gave J family responsibility, 1373
training as perfected God-man, 1421
TRAINING EVANGELISTS AT BETHSAIDA, 1657
TRAINING THE KINGDOM'S MESSENGERS, 1538
trance prophet from Bagdad, and J, 1666
TRANSFIGURATION, THE, 1752
TRANSFIGURATION, MEANING OF THE, 1755
transfiguration sustained J at end, 1872
TRANSITION YEARS, THE, 1483
transits through morontia stages, 2041
transplantation of J' teachings from Jewish to
    gentile soil, 1864
travel, thought about distant cities, 1411
traveler from Britain, to the, 1475

Jesus (cont'd)

travels, purpose of, 1424
travels unknown to apostles, 1456, -83
treasurers (all) of wisdom and knowledge hidden in J,
    1417
treatment, inhuman, unnecessary, 229
    of public women, astonished Ganid, 1472
TRIAL BEFORE PILATE, THE, 1987
trial, summation of, 1996
"tribulation, through t, many enter kingdom", 1533
tribute to Caesar, lawful?, 1899
tried to substitute terms for "kingdom", 1861
tried to teach apostles fickleness of religious
    hysteria, 1705
tried to teach "will of God" place of "kingdom", 1860
Trinity, J not of the infinite T, 1145
TRIP TO BETHLEHEM, THE, 1350
trips of personal ministry, adventure, 1484
triumphant in BOOK OF JOHN, 2092
triumphed over all, 1494
TRUE VALUES, 1456
truly loved people, 1399
trust Father (Personalized T A), 1523
TRUTH AND FAITH, 1459
truth, embraced always, 1390
    for an entire age, 1594
    unerring recognition of, 1390
truths, new and advanced, 1593
    two most important, 1593
TUESDAY EVENING ON MOUNT OLIVET, 1912
TUESDAY MORNING IN THE TEMPLE, 1897
tumult ended discourse, 1797
TWELFTH YEAR, JESUS' (A.D. 6), 1371
TWENTIETH YEAR, JESUS' (A.D. 14), 1403
TWENTY-EIGHTH YEAR, JESUS' (A.D. 22), 1421
TWENTY-FIFTH YEAR, JESUS' (A.D. 19), 1415
TWENTY-FIRST YEAR, JESUS' (A.D. 15), 1407
TWENTY-FOURTH YEAR, JESUS' (A.D. 18), 1413
TWENTY-NINTH YEAR, JESUS' (A.D. 23), 1423
TWENTY-SECOND YEAR, JESUS' (A.D. 16), 1409
TWENTY-SEVENTH YEAR, JESUS' (A.D. 21), 1419
TWENTY-SIXTH YEAR, JESUS' (A.D. 20), 1416
TWENTY-THIRD YEAR, JESUS' (A.D. 17), 1411
"two and two to teach", why, 2055
two celestial visitations, 13th year, 32nd year, 1408
TWO CRUCIAL YEARS, THE, 1386
two natures in one, 1407
TWO SONS, PARABLE OF THE, 1893
U unable to finish discourse, 1797   unafraid, 1955
uncle, favorite, 1385
"Uncle Joshua, tell us a story", 1416
uncommunicative, 1418, 1707
uncontending, 1985
UNDER THE ROMAN EMPIRE, 2073
understanding comrade, J was, 1546
understood the minds of men, 1670
unfairness of sitting in judgment, 1764
unforgettable look at Peter, 1981
unfortunate believers overlook man J, 1013
unification, J only hope for, 2085
unified (splendidly) human personality, 2088
uninfluenced by praise, 1594
union of human and divine, basis of "church", 1748
union of 2 natures, stumbling block, 1510
unique, never again, 1699
united to discredit J, 3 groups, 1899
unity, not uniformity, desired by J, 1965
unity, spiritual, faith union with J, 2085
universal sovereign, 377
universality of J' religion, 2064

Jesus (cont'd)
    universe administrators, J in contact with his, 1659
    universe Sovereign, 2000
    unostentatious majesty, 1999
    Urantia Book, J' Adjuster helped UB, 1341
    URMIA LECTURES, THE, 1485
V valiant and courageous hero, 1013
    value, political, economic, social of J' religion, 1585
    values, spiritual, come first, 1581
    VALUES, TRUE, 1456
    vanished (in an instant) from their sight, 2032, -36,
      2039-40, -42-44, -50, -53, -57
    vanquishes adversaries, 1892, -99, 1900-01
    vast host with J unseen, unused, from 40 days
      forward, 1516
    vast retinue of (helpers) around, 1632
    vast store of information about J and teachings, 1343
    versatile and aggressive, 1461
    versatile worker, 1387
    versus 2nd person of Trinity, 1144-45
    victory eventually, 1904, -14, -30-33, 2075
    views of J in Capernaum, 1719
    VIEWS THE TEMPLE, 1378
    VINE AND THE BRANCHES, THE, 1945
    vineyard laborers, parable, 1804
    visit of Elizabeth and John, 1400
    visit to Annas, 1596
    VISIT TO CAPERNAUM, 1527
    VISIT TO PHILADELPHIA, THE, 1833
    VISIT TO ZACCHEUS, THE, 1873
    visit with John at Jerusalem, 1494
    VISIT WITH MARTHA AND MARY, 1797
    VISIT WITH NICODEMUS, 1601
    visit with Ruth, 1628
    visited by Gabriel and Melchizedek, 1753, -55
    visited sick of encampment, 3 times a week, 1658
    VISITING ABOUT THE TEMPLE, 1883
    visits Jerusalem, 1421
    visits planets during much of his time, 367
    voice, fascinating, 1382, 1796
    voice was sonorous, 1506
    VULNERABILITY OF MATERIALISM, THE, 2078
W walked, leisurely across Italy on Appian way, 1468
    on water--no, 1519
      too fast (criticism) to synagogue, 1684
        (but)never in a hurry, 1874
    walking on water (Peter's dream), 1703
    walks through angry mob, 1687
    wanderings, Palestine and Syria, 1492
    wanted, heart belief, 1413
      no intellectual surrender, 1413
      to leave memory of a...life, 2008
    wants fruits for revelation, 1931
    warned against creeds, 1592
    warning, about prayer, penance, sacrifice, 1640
      against religion about self, 1543
      of the friendly Pharisees, 1872
    was, and is the new and living way, 1113
      believed to be Eternal Son, 1784
      full of grace and truth, 1874
      given to man's hungry soul, 2070
      God and man, always and forevermore, 1331
      a Jew, but...a mortal of the realms, 2002
      "Jewish tutor", 1423
      Michael before Urantia life, 1323
      a miraculous person, 1331
      a mortal of the realms, 2002
      never in a hurry, 1874
      a new revelation, 1542
      a revelation of God, 1856

Jesus (cont'd)
  was (cont'd)
      supremely interested in all...men, 1557
      truly a master of men, 1589
      unable to continue the discourse, 1797
    washed feet of apostles (no kiss), 1939
    WASHING THE APOSTLES' FEET, 1938
    wasted little time upon trifles, 1495
    wasted no effort on those who couldn't perceive, 1440
    the way, the truth, and the life, 1593
    we mortals will appear before J, 1238, -48
    we will amplify the address of, 1858
    weak men, rather than wicked, J' view, 2093
    "weaklings, do you resemble?", 1608
    wealth (and the kingdom), 1801, -21-23, 2093
    WEALTH, TALKS TO THE APOSTLES ON, 1823
    wealth vs. what it causes, 1581
    weaning of his family, 1410
    weary, did not grow, in teaching, 1590
    WEDDING AT CANA, THE 1528
    WEDNESDAY, THE REST DAY, 1920
    WEEK OF COUNSEL, A, 1717
    WEEK OF REST, A, 1718
    welcomed at tomb by morontia personalities, 2022
    "went about doing good", 1875
    wept at 12, over his spiritually impoverished
      people, 1381
    wept, due to family neglect, 1587
      (Lazarus' tomb), 1844
      over Jerusalem, 1882
      (13th year) over Jerusalem, 1381
    WHAT BECAME OF LAZARUS, 1849
    what did J commend to the Father's hands?, 2015
    WHAT HAPPENED AT PENTECOST, 2062
    WHAT MUST I DO TO BE SAVED?, 1682
    what others could do, J did not, 1668
    what prayer meant to J, 2089
    what took place with J, never evaluated, 1699
    what will they do with J, 1910
    "who is my mother...?", 1722
    why, blessed poor, condemned rich, 2093
      he came (to comfort and succor), 1663
      indignant at temple, 1890
      J' doings were strange and secretive, 1423
      Jews rejected, 1024, -71
    WIDESPREAD FAME OF J, 1668
    widow with 5 children, 1465
    widow's mite, the, 1883
    will return to Urantia, 1319
    will, strong w required to believe as and what J did,
      2090
    wine NOT a miracle, 1530
    wisdom of the brotherhood, prevail, 1764
    wise counsellor, had only one, 1397
    wish of J will abridge time (bang), 1517
    with, James at the Passover, 1399
      Joseph at the Passover, 1409
      Jude at the Passover, 1415
      Simon at the Passover, 1411
    "woe upon you, scribes, Pharisees, hypocrites!", 1907
    woman married 7 times, 1900
    WOMAN OF SYCHAR, THE, 1612
    WOMAN TAKEN IN ADULTERY, 1792
    WOMAN WITH THE SPIRIT OF INFIRMITY, THE, 1835
    women, equality with men, 1839
      J accorded equal rights, 1546
      J' attitude toward, most revolutionary, 1671
    WOMEN'S EVANGELISTIC CORPS, THE, 1678
      (see also under "W")
    words wasted on those who can't perceive, 1440

Jesus (cont'd)
work, beginning public, 1587
identical as if only Son of God, 232
later, of spiritual depth, 1808
limited by "associate on high", 1594
"work" he was to undertake, 1513
worked as miner, 1643 (see also "occupations of J"
this section)
WORKING IN ZEBEDEE'S BOATSHOP, 1495
works well known to all Jewry, 1791
world ministry, 2 ways to go, choose, 1515
world most needs J now, 2084
world's most whole-hearted religionist, 2093
WORLD'S RELIGIONS, THE, 1442
worship of himself permitted on earth, 1409
worshipping, no; personal communion with Father,
yes, 1618
would have ordained 20 Greeks, but...1924
would make all men Godlike, 1581
would win by tact and tolerance where others would
fight, 1778
wouldn't cramp spiritual imagination, 1942
written charges of the Sanhedrist, 1990
wrong, don't only condemn, 1765
wrote upon the sand, 1793
years 13th to 32nd, no thing supernatural or superhuman, 1408
yielding spiritual fruits, 1945
yoke maker, expert, 1367, -87
"you...cleanse the outside of the cup...", 1908
YOUNG MAN WHO WAS AFRAID, THE, 1437
young people, secret of success with, 1420
younger generation jealously resented J' fame, 1684
youth and J, 1920-21
ZACCHEUS, VISIT TO, 1873
Zealot episode, the, 1396
Zebedee of Capernaum, 1419
ZOROASTRIANISM, 1449

JESUS, on

"One of the most important things in human living is
to find out what Jesus believed, to discover his ideals,
and to strive for the achievement of his exalted life
purpose." 2090

Jesus, on (see also "Jesus, teaching Ganid and Gonod")
accidental riches, 1464
accidents and events, 1830
achievement vs. direction of progress, 1653
adultery, 1576
AFFLICTION, 1590-91, 1649, -61-62, -64, 1831
ages for progressive attainment, 1961
all things are sacred, 1732
angels, 1841
for his deliverance if he desired, 1975
anger, 1673
animals and souls, 1431
anointing, anticipation of J' death, 1879
answer to prayer, 1848
anxiety for material things, 1823
apostles' failure to heal, 1758
apostles, lambs among wolves, 1584, 1800 (see
section "Apostles")
appeals to human feelings, 1705
appearances vs. inner souls, 1826
approaching Father as child of God, 1629
arithmetic (sheep-shearing), 1476
ASSURANCE, 1601, -41, -74
"astrology", 1680

Jesus, on (cont'd)
authority, from the Father, 1819
of truth, 1768
b baptism, 1593
beatitudes, 1570
beautiful teachings in Scriptures, 1769
beauty and art, 1600
becoming, as one with the Creator, 1434
life partner with spiritual energy, 1430
like child, 1761
server of all, 1907
being, positive: not eye for eye, 1770
human, 1739
reborn (born of the spirit), 1438, 1576, -92, 1602,
1660, 1731, -38 (see also "born again, be")
saved, 1682
unafraid, 1767
valiant, 1931
bestowal of spiritual gifts, 1831
bidding the poor to banquet, 1834
blasphemy, 1714
blindness and sin, 1812
bravery, 1608
bread of, earth vs. bread of life, 1710-11
heaven, 1712
life, 1822, -29, 2054
the broken bread, 1942
business of the kingdom, 1565
c caste system, 1468
catastrophes--of little matter to believers, 1916
certainty about kingdom, 1641
character, 1572
of the Father, 1597
of the kingdom, 1605
characters, well-balanced, 1673
children, 1597, 1608, -19, -62, -75, -61, 1831, -98,
1906, -48, -52, -63, 2045
of the house, taking blessings for granted, 1828
CHILDREN, BLESSING THE LITTLE, 1839
chose to terminate his work at high point, 1818
citizenship and sonship, 1929
cleanliness, external vs. internal, 1826
cleansing the "outside", 1825
coming end of Jewish nation, 1906
commercializing practices of religion, 1891
commonplace toil and labor, 1960
CONCEPT OF GOD, 1598
conflicts, wasteful and weakening, 1738
confused men and women, 1472
consequences of sin, error, 1630
CONTENTMENT, 1674
controversy, defense of truth, 1932
cosmic disharmony, 1434
courage, 1641
and faith, dangers of, 1673
covetousness, 1821
crime, to criminal, 1475
criticism, 1641
cultural familiarity with life, 1674
cup of wine, 1938, -41
cynicism, 1765
d danger, postponing entrance to kingdom, 1829
dangers of courage and faith, 1673
dealing with timid and fearful souls, 1765
dealings with civil rulers, 1930-31
deceitful human heart, 1609, -30
dedicate life to kingdom, real needs will be supplied,
1823
defense of the truth, 1932
the Deliverer, 1614

Jesus, on (cont'd)
despising the revelation of the Father, 1826
destroy this temple, 1895
destruction of Jerusalem, 1912, -15
devoting one's self to work, 1823
devotion to nonviolence, non-resistance, 1608
difference between his teachings and life, 1543
divine forgiveness, 1898
divine spirit in every human, 1472, -74-75
divorce, 1576-77, 1581, 1838-39
doing the Father's will, 1579
doing good on the Sabbath, 1665, 1834
door, straight and narrow, 1828-29

e easy way vs. difficult, 1730
economic attitude, 1581
educated persons, 1674
elevating drudgery, 1475
the end of his bestowal, 1759
endowing spirit helper (Spirit of Truth), 1947-48, -54,
2035, -57 (see also "Spirit of Truth" this section)
enlarging cosmic conceptions, 1439
error, 1435
essentials, of material success, 1739
to faith entrance to kingdom, 1861
estimating soul's worth, 1739
eternal ages for... becoming perfect, 1961
evil, 1435, -58
and the evil one, 1660
EVIL, SIN, AND INIQUITY, 1660
spirits, 1591, 1646, 1713, 1807

f facing life like a man, 1437
failure of apostles to heal, 1758
faith, 1459, 1609, -19, -41, -53, -56, -98, 1715, -31, -33,
1735, -45, -66, 1802, -12, -23, -28, -31, -34, -38,
1916, -35, -54, -60, 2040-41, -43, -48-49, -52-53
(see also section "Faith" under "F")
and salvation, 1682
attitudes (4), 1573
price of entrance to kingdom (see "kingdom" this
section, also "kingdom, price to enter"
under "K")
-quickened mortals are the sons of God, 1957
sincerity, 1861
vs. fasting and affliction of soul, 1656
faithfulness, 1854
false guides of a nation, 1908
false prophets, 1571
false sympathy, self-pity, 1766
FAMILY, 1603
farewells to apostles, 1955
fasting and prayer, 1655-56
fate of, the disobedient Jewish people, 1913
Jerusalem, 1872, -82, 1934, 2005
FATHER, 1590
Father-child relationship, 1585, 1898
Father, no respecter of persons, 1468, 1608, 1831, 1958
fatherhood of God, brotherhood of man, 1603
FATHERLY AND BROTHERLY LOVE, 1573
Father's requirement of his children, 1917
fear, 1437-38, 1571, -96, 1610, -16, -32, -99, 1710, -14,
1726, -67, 1820, -59, 2042, -49 (see also "fear"
under "F")
and doubt, 1824
evolving into love, 1675
of authority of Scriptures, 1768
of the Lord, 1675
vs. faith, 1745
feed my lambs, 2047
fickleness, superficiality, of crowds, 1927
finding God, 1440

Jesus on (cont'd)
focusing attention, 1705
force vs. righteous causes, 1765
forgetting self (Peter), 2039
forgiveness, 1545, 1638, -82, 1714, -36, -62-63, 1861, -98
forthcoming tests in Jerusalem, 1871
freedom, 1490
freely giving, 1764
freewill beings and power, 1487
friendship with God, 1766
fruits of divine spirit, 2054
future of the apostles, 1912

g gentile faith, 1648
giving each all he will receive, 1954
"giving eternal life to faith sons", 1963
God, 1857
and mammon, 1577
the Father, 1590
-knowing individuals, 1739
values man, 1682
GOD'S WRATH, 1597
going on from glory to glory, 1953
the golden rule, 1571, 1650, 1931, -49-50
good, and evil, 1457
and evil (Godiah), 1429
Samaritan, 1810
the GOOD SHEPHERD, 1818
goodness, 1458
gospel (see also "kingdom")
and trouble, 1767
cardinal features of, 1863
for all men, 2044
making men unafraid, 1767
yoke, 1808
THE GREAT COMMANDMENT, 1901
growing concept of God, 1598
growth of living truth, 1917

h handling temptation, 1738
handling wealth, 1462
happiness, 1570, -73
and contentment, 1674
"hard times are just ahead of us", 1959
harvest plentiful, 1800
hate, fear, revenge, 1632
he who is not against us, 1764
he who would be great, 1940
healing vs. teaching, 1635
health, 1831
hearing with mind, not hearts, 2052
heathen that rage, 1725
Hebrew Scriptures, 1767
heeding the invitation, 1829
his, coming death, 1871
coming death and resurrection, 1952
mission, 1390, 1466, 1576, -78, -90, 1608, -35, -75,
1710, 1824, 1903, -55, 2033-35, -41-42
own prophecies, 2052
rejection by Jews, 1903
return, 1876, 1915
teachings, 2035
home life of children, 1921-23
home's influence on life, 1921
honorable wealth, 1821
"how can you justify such hypocrisy and dishonesty?",
1907
how to be saved, 1682
human melody, four tones, 1465
human wills, 1431
humor, 1736
hungry souls (spiritually), 1766

Jesus, on (cont'd)
poor and rich and the gospel, 1830
poor widow's mite, 1883
potential evil, 1435
PRAYER AND WORSHIP, 1616, -18-20, 1860
prayer, answer to, 1848
thanksgiving, worship, 1638
preferment and service, 1939
pride, warning, 1808
problems, dealing with, 1739
prodigal son, 1851 (see under "P" for many
"parables")
profit, 1464
PROMISED HELPER, THE, 1948
prophecies of troubles to come, 1912
punishment, 1630
purpose, of affliction, 1661
of this gospel, 1765
r REALITY, 1433
rearing children, 1401
rebellion against Father, 1766
rebirth in kingdom, 1592, 1602, -76, 1731, 2052-53
(see also "born again, be" under "B")
reckoning the cost, 1869
refusing the supper invitation, 1835
rejection of revelation of God to man, 1906
relationship, man and God, 1898
son to Father, 1604
religion, as personal experience, 1624, -29
(long discourse), 1737
of mind vs. spirit, 1729
stagnated, tradition, 1727
true, 1728-30
religions, of assent vs. r of spirit, 1729
of authority, 1729, -32
religious teachers, moral cowards, 1769
remembrance sacrament, 1941, -43
repentance vs. change of mind, 1545
resistance to attacks, 1469
rest, and relaxation, 1610-11
for his human associates, 1543
resurrection of the dead, 1900
retaliation, 1579
returning good for evil, 1770
revelation of the spirit, 1747
rewards of faith, 1766
rich entering kingdom, 1803
riches, 1464
and kingdom, 1803
righteousness, 1576, 1683, 1714, -26, -70, 1826, -62-61
rock of spiritual reality, 1747
RULE OF LIVING (GOLDEN RULE), 1650
rule of the Most Highs, 1488
rulers, of Jews using misrepresentations of Scriptures, 1768
scribes, Pharisees, 1907
running away from duty, 1428, -38, -75
s sacrament, remembrance supper, 1941, -43
sagacity needed with aggressiveness, 1958
salt and savor, 1870
salvation, and faith, 1682
as free gift, 1838 (see also "kingdom, price to
enter")
by faith, 1593, 1610, 1802, -28, -61, 2054
grace of, 1850
matter of personal choosing, 1828
terms of, 1838
through (3) only, 1947
sarcasm, 1765
Satan falling from heaven, 1807

Jesus, on (cont'd)
SCIENCE, 1476
SCRIPTURES, 1767
Scriptures, consistent with enlightenment of their
times, 1767
gathered in recent times, 1767
misrepresentative of Father, 1768
use of, 1769-70
searching for those lost, 1851
second coming, 1914 (see "return of Michael", under
"Jesus")
second commandment, 1901
security of the kingdom builders, 1916
self as a man of sorrows, 1766
self-deceit, 1609
self-defense for himself, 1469
self-denial, self-control, 1609
SELF-MASTERY, 1609
self-respect, 1729, -40, -65
self-righteousness, 1826
serpents, doves, 1580, -84, 1801, 1930
service and preferment, 1939
service trails and happiness highways, 1437
serving, 2048-49, -53-54
seventy, ordination of, 1801
sheep not of my fold, 1815, -18-19, -29
sickness, affliction, 1649
sifting of the kingdom, 1715
signs, 1744
sin, and blindness, 1872
of the Jewish rulers, 1906
sincerity and discretion, 1961
sitting in judgment on courtesans, 1472
social attitude, 1580
sons and daughters of God, 1686
SONSHIP AND CITIZENSHIP, 1929
soon-to-be death and resurrection, 1967
sorrow and the wicked, 1674
SOUL, THE, 1477-78, 1738 (see also "soul" under "S")
soul-conflict, 1478
soul, refreshing the, 1739
SOVEREIGNTY--DIVINE AND HUMAN, 1486-87, -93
SOVEREIGNTY, POLITICAL, 1487
space, conceptions of, 1439
speaking to those in distress, 1570
SPIRIT OF TRUTH (promised helper), (see also
"Spirit of Truth" under "S") 1536, 1642, 1930, -47
1948-49, -51, -54, -57-61, -64, 2032, -35, -41, -43,
2044, -57
spirit, unity's implications, 1592
within you, 1438
spirits, of the dead, 1646, -80
unclean, 1541
spiritual, destiny, 1739
evolution, 1460
SPIRITUAL FREEDOM, 1796
spiritual, greatness, 1758
liberty, 1591
problem solving aids material, 1662
progression, 1736
religion and science, 1727
SPIRITUAL UNITY, 1591
spiritual value of disappointment, 1688
state's right of self-defense, 1475
status and progress, 1653
stewardship of wealth, 1463
still small voice, 1664
stone which the builders rejected, 1894
stream of divine ministry, 1638
success, essentials of material, 1739

Jesus, on (cont'd)

suffering, 1662,-64
supreme, adventure, 1608
   experience, 1732
   folly of all the ages, 1906
   joy, "crucifixion", 1944
   reactions of fatherly love (4), 1575
survival, 2054
sympathy, 1766
tarrying (stopping) places in Father's universe, 1947
teaching, gospel, 1456,-60,1592-94,1692,1705,-65,
   1769,-71
   truth, 1765
teachings of Son of Man, 2035
temptation and human nature, 1738
test and trial, 1824
thinking before speaking, 1962
three essentials of kingdom, 1585
three kinds of events in life, 1830
TIME AND SPACE, 1438-39
time for everything, 1436
trade, barter, profit, 1464
traditional barrenness of Jews, 1732
traditions, of fathers, 1712
   vs. God's commands, 1712
treasure, 1821,-23
triumph over...intellectual doubting, 1961
true believer, 1740
TRUE RELIGION, 1728,-30
true values, 1456-57
true vine, 1945
trust, 2048
   and spiritual preparedness, 1820
   in riches, 1803
truth, 1917
   and faith, 1459
   hunger,1861
truths of being, 1641
two viewpoints of all mortal conduct, 1577
unclean spirits (see "evil spirits")
unconcern with material things, 1821-22
unification, unity, 1732
unity in cosmic universe, 1477
universe progress, 1460
value of, proper home training, 1921-22
   status with God, 1653
values, true, 1456
victory for united efforts, 1904
vine and the branches, 1945
vipers, offspring of, 1908
walking in light, not darkness, 1904
walls (of stone, of prejudice), 1879
war, 1487, 89-91
warning, when to depart Jerusalem, 1913
wasting words, 1441
watchful servants, 1824
WATER OF LIFE, 1795, 1820,-29, 2054
water of the living spirit, 1613
way to, eternal estate, 1642
   the Father, 1947
   goal of destiny, 1437,-60
wealth, 1803,-21,-23
   (one man's), 1462
what defiles man, 1712-13
what Deliverer will be, 2035
when you stand before judges, 1912 (see "Josiah,
   blind man", 1812)
whited sepulchres, 1908
"why do you leave us?", 1951
why no record of gospel teachings, 1768

Jesus, on (cont'd)

why rulers sought to kill him, 1790
why they want to kill me, 1791
wicked, the w and sorrow, 1674
wisdom, 1481
   discretion, courage, 1958

JESUS, Quotes

"One of the most important things in human living is to find out what J believed... Of all human knowledge that which is of greatest value is to know the religious life of J and how he lived it. " 2090

"a man of faith, courage... service, for God's sake",
   1438
"a man's foes may be those of own household", 1951
"a man's gift makes room for him, and brings him
   before great men", 1478
"a new spirit will I put within you", 1630
"a part of every father lives in...child", 1898
"a servant is not greater than his master", 1939
"a spiritual incarnation in souls of believers", 1953
"a wise parent never takes sides", 1589
"a woman is sorrowful in her travail, but", 1952
"abomination, such practices are an", 1653
"about the Father's business", 1659
"about to commit supreme folly of the ages", 1906
"about to go where you cannot come", 1792,-95
"accept fatherhood...implies...brotherhood", 2053
"accept theory of God, fail realize presence", 1733
"accidents of time, victims of", 1830
"account for all this righteous blood", 1908
"accounting may be...this very generation", 1908
"acquire spiritual attitude of sincere child", 1733
"acts suicidal to all moral growth", 1653
"add love to your philosophy", 2049
"adversity, I will go through, with you", 1767
"affliction is not frown of God", 1831
"afraid, arise and be not", 1754
"after all this be killed and raised from dead", 1759
"after I have received sovereignty of my domain",1948
"all Jerusalem has heard that which I have spoken",
   1979
"all kingdom believers better world citizens", 1930
"all men are my brothers", 1541
"all men are the sons of God", 1585, 2053
"all men will reject you" (Jews), 1882
"all power...presently in my hands", 1544
"all shall be resurrected in a more glorious form",
   1846
"all sickness...taken away from you", 1629
"all soul conflict...lack of harmony...", 1478
"all that pertains to flesh of little profit", 1715
"all things are possible to him who...", 1757
"all things are sacred in lives of...spirit led", 1732
"all things have become sacred", 1960
"all upright work is sacred", 2049
"all who desire my presence, am with", 1948
"all who find Father, first find me", 1947
"alms, when you give", 1577
"alone, not good for man to be", 2055
"also be prepared for trouble", 1533
"always is provided authority of leadership", 1959
"always respect the personality of man", 1765
"an abomination in sight of the Lord", 1653
"an unseen messenger will run by your side", 1967
"Andrew, do you trust me?", 2048
"angelic hosts are a separate order", 1841
"angels keep worlds in touch", 1841

Jesus, Quotes (cont'd)

"but the hour has come", 1789

"but who say you that I am?", 1746

"by faith are you eternally advanced", 1682

"by faith become (eternal) sons of God", 2054

"by faith (belief) are you saved" (justified, advanced, given eternal life, enter kingdom), (see also under "Faith") 1536-37, -45, -69, -86, -93, 1610, -67, -82, 1683, 1745, -66, 1826, -28-29, 2053

"by faith every mortal... salvation", 1586

"by faith you have become a kingdom son", 2049

"by loving and serving you, I have been God-revealing to you", 2053

"by their fruits you shall know them", 1571-72

c "Caesar, render unto", 1474, 1580, 1740, 1899, 1929, 1957

"Cain went to Nod and got self a wife", 1660

"call you offspring of vipers", 1908

"called to be light of the world" (Jews), 1906

"camel to go through... needle", 1803

"can you not watch with me?", 1968

"cannot compel men to love truth", 1713

"cannot run away from... God and self", 1475

"cannot worship God and... serve mammon", 1577

"capacity to forgive... is Godlike", 1898

"carry on until I come", 1917

"carry the pack a second mile", 1770

"cause walls of prejudice...hate, to crumble", 1879

"cease to fear men", 2049

"cease to trifle with my words", 1613

"challenge the unrighteous stranger", 1770

"character can be improved", 1572

"cheek, turn the other", 1571; (meaning of), 1770

"chief purpose in living mortal life", 1951

"child, as a little" why used,1676

"child, dependent on parents" (early concepts), 1922

"childlike and darkened minds of my people", 1404

children, "become as little", 1585

"born of spirit... masters of self", 1610

"can't see corrective affection", 1597

"their immaturity can't penetrate to discern..." 1597

"choose you this day whom you will serve", 1710

"cities whose builder is God", 501, 1935

"city whose builder and maker is God", 1474

"city whose foundations are righteousness", 1474

"cleanse the outside of the cups" but, 1826

"cleanse yourselves, not duty but privilege", 1610

"cleave to... wife, two... become as one", 1839

"the cock will not crow until you... ", 1962

"come, all ye who labor", 1590, 1627, 1808

"come, not to call righteous, but sinners", 1541

"come out of him, disobedient spirit", 1757

"come out of it", 1631

"come (not) to judge... rich nor poor",1822

"come to me, all who are indolent", J never said,1590

"come to me all you who labor", 1590, 1627, 1808

"come to proclaim spiritual liberty", 1591

"come to put love in place of fear", 1675

"comfort minds, liberate spirits, here solely to",1576

"comfort the anxious", 1543

"commandment, new"

"become the apostle of the nc", 1955

"learn to love men as I have loved you", 2047

"love all men as I have loved you", 2041

"love men with the love wherewith I have loved you", 2057

"love the flock as I have loved you", 2048

"love one another even as I have loved you", 1944, 1945, 1961-62

Jesus, Quotes (cont'd)

"commandment, new" (cont'd)

"love one another with a new and startling affection, even as... ", 2044

"loving men and serving them, even as I", 2043

"provided you have kept my nc", 1951

"which I will presently give you", 1939

"commandment, there is but one", 1901

"commissioned to save, not judge, men", 1571

"commit your way to the Lord", 1639

"common, have things in", 1577

"common people hear my words gladly", 1893

"companionship, I crave your", 1968

"compel your lower nature to obey higher", 1461

"concerned, be not c what ye shall say", 1820

"concerned not by what can gain, but give", 2039

"confess your sins, they are forgiven", 1736

"conform with authority", 1906, -24

"conform with letter of Moses' law, but souls steeped in iniquity", 1908

"confused by doctrines of perfection of Scripture", 1768

"consider the lilies, how they grow... ", 1823

"constant... renewing of your mind", 1609

"controversy only when forced on you", 1932

"cooperate with these elders in Israel", 1906

"corrupt tree bears evil fruit", 1571

"courage, may your c atone for your ignorance", 1579

"create in me a clean heart", 1640, 1769

"creation not rest... but progression in grace... ", 1953

"Creators only possess infallibility", 1768

"creature may crave infallibility, but... ", 1768

"cup, emblem of bestowal of Spirit of Truth", 1941

"cup, even when a c of water is given", 1764

"cup, I am ready to drink this last", 1955

"cup of my remembrance", 1941

"cup, take this, all of you... drink of it", 1941

"cup, take this, and drink it... ", 1938

"cup, while this is a bitter c", 1968

"curses of transgression shall overtake them (Jews)", 1709

d "daily grow in grace", 1920

"danger to... postpone entrance", 1829

"darkness, your d shall be as noonday",1656

"daughters of Jerusalem, weep not for me... ", 2005

"dead, let others bury the... ", 1801

"dead of an age entered... eternal ascent", 2053

"dead rise is not the gospel", 2054

"dead, talk about rising from the... ", 1754

"deadly conflict (now)" with Jewish religion, 1730

"death, man shall never taste", 1797

"death, Son of Man will be put to", 1759

"deeds, good, do in secret", 1577

"delights of bestowal of... affection upon men", 1944

"deliver keys of the outward kingdom", 1747

"delivered of her child... forgets anguish", 1952

Deliverer (see "Deliverer" under "D")

"den of robbers, (Temple) you have made it", 1890

"depart from us", 1829

"desire to see my children... whole", 1633

"despise not one of these little ones", 1241, 1761

"despise not the chastening of the Lord", 1662

"destined to lead mean life if... ", 1739

"destroy, I have not come to", 1576

"destroy the prejudice engendered by ignorance",2043

"destroy this temple", (pointed to body), 1895, 1982, 1985

"destroying consequences of iniquity are inexorable", 1661

Jesus, Quotes (cont'd)

"did it to one of the least", 1727
"difficult for (wealthy) to enter kingdom", 1803
"difficulty whets ardor of truth lover", 1740
"discerned the true meaning of parables", 1691
"discipline to save your ease-drifting souls", 1931
"discover God in your soul, then in other... ", 1733
"discretion defers anger", 1673
"disobedient people will fall by the sword", 1913
"divine forgiveness is inevitable", 1898
"divine truth, don't discount because source is
    human", 1733
"do good to those who hate you", 1571
"do it in remembrance of me", 1943
"do men gather grapes from thorns?", 1571
"do not destroy... self-respect", 1765
"do not doubt the love of the Father", 1662
"do not indulge in sarcasm at expense... ", 1765
"do not love souls of men... love men", 2043
do not "only condemn wrongs", 1765
"do not overmagnify your office", 1558
"do not strive with men", 1577, -93, 1932
do not "take something out of hearts", 1592
"do not wound the self-respect of... souls", 1765
"do to all men that which you know I would do... ",
    1651
"do your good deeds in secret", 1577
"dogs, present not that which is holy to d", 1571
"don't allow (not understood) to crush you", 1897
don't "approach Father as a child of Israel", 1629
"don't be side-tracked, teach gospel", 1543
"don't build cult about my beliefs", 1543
"don't permit self to believe Scriptures... ", 1768
"don't seek to advance truth by governments or laws",
    1931
"don't try to prove you have found God", 1733
"door, I stand at the", 1765
"doubt, wherefore do you?", 1753, 1845
doves, "harmless as", 1580, -84, 1801, 1930
"draught of the living water", 1613
"duty of man, two great privileges", 1600
"duty of man, whole", 1600, 1805
"duty to man and duty to God", 1930

e "ear for four tones of human melody", 1465
"easier for a camel to go through", 1803
"effectiveness of... desire to do will... ", 1586
"elevate the drudgery of your daily toil", 1475
"Elijah has already come", 1754
"emotionally men react individually", 1672
emphasis, "make the tree good", 1582
"endeavor to talk with spirit of own soul?", 1475
"endowed with power from on high", 2057
"endowed with power of performance", 1609
"energy, living, has gone out of me", 1698
"enjoy a fourfold satisfaction in life", 1465
"enter into glorious inheritance of sonship", 1824
"enter into the joyous fellowship of the sons of God",
    1584
"enter joyfully into your spiritual inheritance", 1820
"entrance to kingdom free, but... ", 1682
"ennobled by... faith to love unbelievers", 2042
"the entire universe is friendly to me", 1470
"equal capacity for reception of material", 1831
"even as I have loved you (5 times), love", 1944-45
"even as the world has hated me", 1964
"even good thought must be modulated", 1961
"even he to whom I gave the sop", 1941
"even if I bear witness about myself", 1795
"even now I offer you mercy", 1908
"even now is the kingdom at hand", 1569

Jesus, Quotes (cont'd)

"even now would I gather your... ", 1908
"even though heaven and earth shall pass away", 1736
"even to the end", 2049
"even to the end of the ages", 2044
"even to ends of the earth", 2033
"even where a cup of... water is given", 1764
"everlasting arms, underneath are the", 1662
"every day, easier to do right... ", 1740
"every man who looks upon a woman", 1576
"every plant... shall be rooted up", 1713
"every tradesman deserves wages", 1464
"evil forces of darkness have conspired", 1940
"evil is futile", 1580
"except a grain of wheat falls... ", 1903
"except a man be born from above", 1602
"except a man be born of the spirit", 1602
"except through me, no man... ", 1947
"except you become... like this child", 1761, 2089
"experience the joy of knowing we are his Sons", 1928
f "faith adventure, (Father's) kingdom in hearts of
    men", 1750
"faith at your command, failed to exercise", 1758
faith, "by f, sup with me in kingdom", 1943
    "... dominate... body, mind, spirit", 1733
    "Father will respond to... ", 1733
    "... have not of yourselves... is gift", 1610
    "in a living experience save you", 1745
    "the just shall live by", 1682
    "made you whole", 1698
    "none so great in Israel", 1648
    "not affliction nor fasting", 1656
    "... partakers of divine nature", 1609
    "small, better than great intellect" (dead), 1653
    "your f shall save you", 1667
"faith-quickened mortals are the Sons of God", 1957
faith, salvation by (see same heading under "F")
    "alone will pass you, but... ", 1569
    "believe it, " and have, 1593
    "believe this gospel of kingdom... ", 1682
    "by f are you eternally advanced... ", 1682
    "by f are you justified, by f are you saved", 1682
    by f believer enters the kingdom (J), 1861
    "by f was Abraham justified", 1682
    "by faith... you are born... of eternal life", 2052
    "by f you have become a... kingdom Son", 2049
    door open to any who by f seek Father through
        Son (J), 1828
    doors of kingdom, opened to all with f to enter (J),
        1826
    "down through ages, this f saved... men", 1683
    enter the kingdom of heaven (J), 1596
    "gift of eternal life... men receive by f", 2041
    "the gift of God, price of entrance to kingdom", 1537
    "good news... by faith become... everlasting Sons",
        2054
    "good news of gospel, every mortal... ", 1586
    "is the open door for eternal love of God", 1545
    "kingdom, f will pass you through", 1569
    kingdom within grasp of all with living f (J), 1766
    made apostles secure in the kingdom (J), 1656
    "possess by f, gift of eternal life", 2053
    "right to enter kingdom, conditioned by", 1583
    "s bestowed upon all who accept it by f", 2053
    "s is the free gift of God", 2054
    "s is gift of God to all who believe they are his
        sons", 2053
    "s is reward of f, not merely of works", 1802
    simple childlike belief, key to door (J), 1861
    sincere seekers glad to hear tidings of (J), 1593

go "not to love souls of men but...men", 2043
"go on in the joy...of the kingdom", 1652
"go on trusting, for I will not fail you", 2048
"go on until spiritually perfected", 1953
"go tell my apostles and Peter", 2027,-39
"go tell that fox (I) preach in Perea", 1872
"go to lost sheep of...Israel", 1681
"God and mammon, cannot serve", 1577,1854
"God, be merciful to me a sinner", 1838
"God...his spirit lives within hearts of men", 1475
"God is likewise seeking to find you", 1850
"God is spirit", 1856
"God...leads men into...repentance", 1610
"God loves you...as individuals", 1629
"God, none is good but...", 2092
"going to place to which...you cannot come", 1944
"good, return for evil", 1739,-70
"goodness of God leads men into repentance", 1610
"gospel belongs to all who believe it", 2044
"gospel belongs to...Jew and gentile", 2044
"gospel directed to individual not the nation", 1630
gospel, "good news of g is", 1586
"gospel is a living truth", 1931
"gospel is teaching friendship with God", 1766
"gospel is to be preached to all", 1608
gospel, "my g is nothing more nor less than", 1590
"gospel never fails...peace to individual", 1951
"gospel...not to custody of mere priests", 2044
"gospel (this) will triumph over all enemies", 1913
"grace, growth in, essential", 1682
"gradual divorcement, politics and religion", 1930
"grapes from thorns?", 1571
"greater love can no man have", 1944
"greater love has no man", 1575
"the Greeks have exalted beauty", 2043
"group relationships, we provide leadership", 1959
"grow by grace to full spiritual adulthood", 2054
"grow in ability to feel the presence of God", 1733
"grow in grace by means of that...", 1656
"grow to full stature, spiritual adulthood", 2054
"grudges, vengefulness, proportion to ignorance",1898
"gruelling bondage of institutional religion", 1731
"guilt, refuse to harbor...", 1736

h "had not where to lay his head", 1723
"hairs of your head are all numbered", 1682,1820
"hand to the plough", 1801
 "the...handicaps of evil are inherent", 1661
"hands, Father into your h", 2011,-15
"hanker not after meat which perishes", 1710
"happiness, increasing h if certain about God", 1766
"happy are the", 1570
"harmony and peace, not at cost of social harmony,
    spiritual peace", 1591
"harvest is plenteous, but laborers few", 1681,1800
"hate is the shadow of fear", 1632
"have called upon you...be born again", 1731
have "chosen to go through full life", 1753
"have come to show the Father to your...eyes", 1952
"have eternal ages before you" to progress, 1961
"have faith in God", 2049
"have faith in God...in one another", 2039
"have made my house a den of robbers", 1890
"have revealed to you mysteries of heaven", 1934
"having finished my life in the flesh", 2022
"having rejected...you will not find", 1639
"he has become what you are...to make you what he
    is", 1664
"he shall never taste death", 1797
"he shall surely give you the sincere desires of your
    heart", 1639

"he was not rich toward God", 1821
"he who betrays me is at hand", 1968
"he who has an ear, let him hear...", 96
"he who has seen me has seen...", 1750,1857,1947,
    1960
"he who has seen the Son has seen...", 1855
"he who hates me hates my Father", 1947
"he who is not against us is for us" vs. "he who is
    not with me is against me", 1764
"he who is small in kingdom is greater", 1627
"he who loves father or mother more than this
    gospel", 1682
"he who...loves his life, may lost it", 1903
"he who rules...self is greater than...", 1609
"he who walks in the darkness", 1904
"he who will not work shall not eat", 1579
"he who would be greatest", 1868,1906-07,-40
"head, I have not where to lay my", 1750
"health not smile of heaven", 1831
"hear O Israel, the Lord our God", 1901
"heard my words without comprehending", 2052
"heart, create in me a clean", 1769
"heart is deceitful above all things", 1630
"heart, neither let it be afraid", 1955
"heart, my h aches for my people", 1903
"hearts, clean hands vs. clean", 1713
"hearts, don't take something out of", 1592
"hearts, let not your h be troubled", 1575,1947
"hearts, refrain from taking belief out of", 1592
"the heathen are not without excuse", 1725
"heathen concentrate their energies...", 1725
"heavens were opened" for vision, 1511
"help these women get a new start", 1473
"help you think before you speak", 1962
"hen, even as a h gathers her brood", 1872,1908
"henceforth, men may enjoy...art", 1600
"here am I, send me", 1805
"here...is the truth you committed to us", 1918
"hereafter, a ceaseless progression in grace", 1953
"herein is the danger" in postponement, 1829
"hid his life in...surety of eternal kingdom", 1916
"the Hindus preach devotion", 2043
"honors me with lips, but", 1712
"hour has come", 1495,1504,-29,-35,1789
"the hour has come, I...go to the Father", 2055
"hour has not yet come", 1399,1409,-14,-17,-21,
    1494-95
"hour, until the (his) h comes", 1533,1791
"house is left to you, desolate", 1908
"house, not broken into if", 1824
"house to be broken into", 1824
"how can Satan cast out Satan?", 1714
"how can you...ask God for consideration", 1764
"how can you justify hypocrisy, dishonesty?", 1907
"how can you reject the light of God?", 1979
"how carefully you cleanse...cups", 1826
"how could you doubt?", 2032
"how long before you believe and obey?", 1845
"how long shall I bear with you?", 1704
"how long will you tarry in valley of decision?", 1820
"how so unable discern signs of times?", 1745
"how will your rabbis justify themselves?", 1907
"human heart is deceitful", 1609
"human interest is fostered by...", 1956
"humility becomes mortal man", 1676
"hypocrites, hypocrites, hypocrites", 1656,-76,
    1712,-45,-60,1907-08

i "hypocrites, why play part of", 1836
"I abhor myself " (Job), 1663

"I always stand near",1808
"I am... (16 appellations), 1965
"I am all that you say, but more", 1711
"I am Alpha and Omega", 1408
"I am, before Abraham was", 1750
"I am the bread of life", 1942
"I am concerned with... religions", 1624
"I am constrained to... unfold to you", 1759
"I am" (Deliverer, S of G), 1983; I am in the F", 1948
"I am intolerant of iniquity", 1766
"I am the light of life", 1795
"I am the light of the world", 1795, 1812, 1903
"I am the living way", 1281
"I am the new and living way", 1829
"(I) am offered up as price of bigotry and...
    prejudice and spiritual blindness", 1872
"I am on earth solely to... ", 1576
"I am ready to drink this last cup", 1955
"I am representative of F to the individual", 1624
"I am ruthless with sin, intolerant of... ", 1766
"I am saddened... grieved, ... disappointed", 1867-68
"I am" (Son of God, the Deliverer), 1983
"I am the (that) door", 1828-29
"I am this bread of life", 1711
"I am to continue to serve through you", 1942
"I am the true vine", 1945
"I am the way, the truth, the life", 1947
"I am with you always", 2042, -44, -53-54
"I bear no malice toward these" (rulers), 1907
"I become spiritual incarnation in souls", 1953
"I beheld Satan falling as lightning", 1805
"I came forth from God", 1750
"I came to show the Father to your... eyes", 1952
"I could command... legions of angels", 1975
"I crave your companionship", 1968
"I declare to you as... the whole duty of man", 1600
"I desire that you depart from this place", 2009
"I enacted for you a parable", 1939, -44
"I forewarned you of my betrayal", 1941
"I give each of you all you will receive", 1954
"I give (gifts) each... all you will receive", 1954
"I... glorify family life", 1776
"I go to lay down my life", 1868
"I have arisen", 2027
"I have better worlds where you shall work", 2049
"I have called and you have refused to hear", 1639
"I have called upon you to be born again", 1731
"I have come to bring peace, but", 1944
"I have come to call sinners", 1537, -41, 1750
"I (have) come to give you a personal religion", 1629
"I have come to judge neither the rich nor... ", 1822
"I have come to seek... save... who are lost", 1750
"I have lived with you, then will live in you", 1948
"I have meat to eat you know not of", 1615
"I have no mother, I have no brothers", 1722
"I have not come to legislate but to enlighten", 1576
"I have not found so great faith", 1648
"I have not where to lay my head", 1750, 1801
"I have offered Israel salvation", 1906
"I have other and better worlds", 2049
"I have revealed God as your Father", 2052
"I have sheep not of this fold", 1819
"I have sought to heal them of their unbelief", 1903
"I have taught you by word of mouth", 1961
"I... help you carry out the spirit... of your
    decisions", 1625
"I, if I am lifted up, will draw all men", 1190
"I knew... these evil plottings", 1941

"I know the Lord will save his anointed",2010
"I know not whence you are",1829
"I know that not all (Jews) have failed me", 1903
"I leave your house to you desolate", 1924
"I long to show my brethren the glory... ", 1965
"I look beyond the act... ", 1576
"I look... to uncover the motive", 1576
"I marvel at the belief of the gentile", 1648
"I need no defense by the hand of man", 1934
"I now go... to lay down my life", 1868
"I perceive that life has gone forth from me", 1669,
    1698
"I pray for all who... hereafter believe", 1964
"I received such authority... even before this world
    was", 1819
"I represent the Father to the individual", 1624
"I require... life of loving service for your brothers",
    2043
"I return as spirit indweller of each", 1953
"I... return to these worlds of light", 1947
"I send you forth as sheep" (lambs), 1584, 1800
"I send you forth to love men", 2043
"I send you forth to proclaim... ", 1570
"I shall presently leave you", 1569
"I speak boldly concerning these mysteries", 1750
"I speak farewell to chief priests... ", 1904
"I speak to... benighted rulers of Israel", 1904
"I stand at the door and knock", 1765, 1829
"I... stop at nothing to restore self-respect", 1765
"I tell you the Father and I are one", 1750
"I thirst", 2008, -10
"I told you... I would rise from the grave", 2052
"I want to set men free", 1583
"I who speak to you am he (Converter)", 1614
"I will be about my Father's business", 1625
"I will--be clean" (leper), 1643
"I will be put to death by chief priests and rulers of
    the Jews", 1967
"I will be subject to the will of my Father", 1523
"I will be (am) with you always (even to the end)",
    2033, -42, -44, -49, -53-54
"I will be with you to the end", 1932-33
"I will come again", 409
"I will come back... for a little while", 1962
"I will go apart by myself", 1753
"I will go before you", 2054
"I will go before you... to uttermost parts of the
    earth", 1961
"I will go on with you to the very end", 1957
"I will join you in a... period of rest", 1610
"I will not hesitate to lay down my life in the service
    of his manifold flocks", 1819
(I) "will not meet expectations of the Messiah", 1750
"I will petition (for) your real needs", 1639
"I will pour out my spirit", 1954
"I will pour out upon all flesh", 1904 (see also
    "pour(ed) out" in this listing)
"I will present my teaching in a parable", 1818
"I will return" (see under "Jesus", "return of
    Michael")
"I will return to cleanse yonder temple", 1384
"I will return to deliver my people from bondage",
    1384
"I will return to my place among you", 1309
"I will return to you as a spirit indweller", 1953
"I will rise to be with you", 1967
"I will send you a spirit helper", 1947
"I will sometime return", 1914
"I would change your name to Peter", 1525

Jesus, Quotes (cont'd)

"I would do one more mighty work for these Jews", 1837

"ideal of my life...doing Father's will", 1953

"idleness is destructive of self-respect", 1765

"if a man walks in the night", 1837

"if any man thirst, let him come to me", 1795

"if believers bear not fruits, they are dead", 2054

"if dedicate...your real needs...supplied", 1823

"if faith sons, you shall never die", 2053

"if I am a son of destiny...", 1403

"if I be lifted up...in your lives", 1904

"if I do not wash your feet", 1939

"if I lay down my life...take it up again", 1819

"if I will...what is that to you?", 2048

"if the blind lead the blind", 1571, 1713

"if you are anxious about your bread...", 1823

"if you are not fruitful, he will...cut away branches", 2054

"if you fail to reckon the cost", 1869

"if you have the faith to be healed", 1665

"if you know what you are doing you are blessed", 1655

"if you love me, prepare...for supreme sacrifice", 1750

"if you truly want to find God", 1440

"if you will not stumble in fear", 1823

"if you will trust me...will help you to be kind", 2048

"if you would be first in the kingdom", 1761

"if you would be made whole", 1827

"if you would be my messenger", 1802

"if you would be triumphant over temptations", 1739

"if you would only believe", 1845

"if your brother sins against you", 1762

"if your neighbor smites you...", 1571

"ignorance, may your courage atone for your i", 1579

"imitate my life", no, 1953

"important, what you are becoming, not what you are", 1653

"in accordance with truth committed to...", 1918

"in fellowship of kingdom, all men are equal", 1958

"in gospel...Father goes...to find", 1762

"in kingdom, neither rich nor poor", 1679

"in kingdom, there shall be neither Jew nor gentile", 2033

"in...kingdom, you are to become new creatures", 1609

"in me is the way now open still wider", 1604

"in my...universe are many abodes", 1934

"in perfect peace whose mind is...on God", 1731

"in rejecting me, (Jews) reject Him who sent me", 1902

"in spirit your citizenship is in heaven", 1740

"in the sight of God...all men are equal", 1958

"in time of testing...soul is revealed", 1824

"in...universe are...tarrying places", 1947

"in your hearts you fail to comprehend", 2052

"inasmuch as you did it to...", 1727

"iniquity, I am intolerant of", 1766

"injustice, passive reaction to", 1770

"innocent victims of accidents of time", 1830

"intellectual pride precedes...downfall", 1940

"intelligent children do not fear...", 1675

"into your hands I commend...", 2011

irony ("that service you have done me") ("brought me to witness...self-righteousness"), 1826

"is it not lawful...to do what I will with my own?", 1804

"it is finished", 240, 2011

"it is from the heart...evil thoughts", 1713

"it is more blessed to give...", 1581

Jesus, Quotes (cont'd)

"it is the Father's will that I drink this...", 1975

"it is your faith...saves your souls", 2053

j "Jerusalem...a religion of authority", 1729

"Jerusalem (shall) be trodden down", 1913

"Jew and gentile are your brethren", 2049

"Jewish people called to become light of world", 1906

Jews, another chance (see also under "Jesus")

"about to lose your position in world", 1906

"am now offering you your last c", 1906

"even now I offer you mercy, forgiveness", 1908

"I have once more offered Israel and her rulers...", 1906

"I would give these...an opportunity to see the light", 1809

"Jews at least know whom they worship", 1614

"the Jews have extolled goodness", 2043

"Jews? where then are the (cleansed)...", 1828

"John, do you love me?", 2047

"John is dead, Herod has beheaded him", 1627

"John preached repentance, you proclaim joyous fellowship", 1584

"joy of consciousness of sonship with God", 1905

"joy of the Lord, enter fully into", 1917

"joy of sonship to God", 1931

"joy over one sinner who repents", 1841

"Judas, his love grew cold", 2055

"Judas, hope you will always be loyal", 1542

"judge as you would be judged", 1475

"judge, come to j neither rich nor poor", 1822

"judge not", 1580

"judge not" outwardly, 1791

"judge not, that you be not judged", 1580

"judge of the earth shall require an accounting", 1908

"judgment on souls (no, but) maintain temporal order", 1763

"justice, honesty, fairness, will guide", 1464

"justice makes a nation great", 1462

"justice shall swiftly descend upon (Jer)", 1912

k "kept all save...the son of revenge", 1964

"kill, leaders seek to k me", 1791, -96

"kingdom" (see also "kingdom", and "kingdom of heaven" under "K")

"believers hunger for righteousness", 1683

"by assaults of faith", 1829

"...consists in 3 essentials", 1585

"divided against itself", 1714

"entrance to, is free", 1682

"have revealed mysteries thereof", 1934

"of God has come near to you", 1801

"of God is within you", 1861, 2084 (probably J' greatest pronouncement)

"kingdom of heaven is", "at hand", 1801

"consists in these 3 essentials", 1585

"a divine family", 1676

"even now among you", 1536

"family fellowship with G the F", 1861

"God within you", 1569

"like...", 1693-94

"like a leaven", 1694

"like a merchant seeking pearls", 1694

"like a seed growing", 1536

"like a sweep net", 1694

"realization of God's rule in hearts", 1588

"a realm of order", 1959

"righteousness, peace, and joy in the H.S.", 1536

"spiritual brotherhood of man", 1808

"a spiritual kingdom", 1605

"a spiritual relationship between God and man", 1486

"to be an everlasting dominion", 1568

"within you", 1859, -61, -67

"kingdom of heaven, seek first", 2088

kingdom of heaven, various terms for k used by J, 1861

"kingdom of life", 1861

"kingdom... shall break down every barrier", 1569

"kingdom... taken away from you",1894

"kingdom, this hour of the k has come", 1568

"kingdoms, have not come to reform", 1576

"knock and it shall be opened", 1619

"know not divine way, you are unfortunate", 1655

"know the Father by experience, not teaching", 1856

"know the truth regarding gratitude", 1827

"laborer is worthy of his hire", 1584

"laborers together with God", 1934

"lads, have you caught anything?", 2046

"lamp of the body is the eye", 1577

"last shall often be first", 1804

"law and teachings, not before Abraham", 1767

"law, observe the essentials of the", 1906

"law of human fairness", 1931

law of the universe: "ask, receive, seek and you shall find", 1838

"law relieves crafty children of responsibility", 1712

"laws of fruitfulness" (fig), 1830

"laws of relation to Father's will", 1660

lawyer, "not far from the kingdom", 1901

"lay down my life, take it up", 1819

"lay not this sin to their charge", 2018

"lay up treasurers in heaven", 1577

"Lazarus, come forth!", 1846

"Lazarus has fallen asleep", 1837

"Lazarus is dead", 1837

"lead you to Father... not without your consent", 1820

"lead your spirits into the truth", 1951

"leaders of Israel will not have" (peace), 1905

"leaders of my people... blinded their eyes", 1902-03

"leaders of my people hardened their hearts", 1903

"leaders plan murder", 1826

"leaders... the supreme folly of the ages", 1906

leadership, authority of where "will creatures" cooperate, 1959

"learn how also to feed the soul", 1440

"learn to love, forgive, one another", 1762

"learn to set a guard upon your lips", 1962

"learn to step aside from rush of life", 1739

"leave your house to you desolate", 1908,-24

"leaven... hidden in three measures of meal", 1694

"leaven, put leaven of new truth in old beliefs", 1932

"lesser matters of life should give way", 1798

"let all mankind benefit from your ministry", 1931

"let down your net for a draught", 1628

"let faith reveal your light to... world", 2043

"let not your heart be troubled", 1947,-54-55,-66

"let others bury the dead", 1801

"let the roll call of planetary resurrection begin", 2024

"let... souls be valiant", 1934

"let unruly member become an outcast", 1763

"let us create the sight of this blind...", 1812

"let us go into Samaria", 1612

"let us go to John", 1504

"let your light so shine", 1571

"life eternal, what would a man give", 1760

"... life has gone forth from me", 1669

"life more abundant in the spirit", 1902

"life more abundantly", 1558,1819

"life, no man can take away my", 1819

"light of the world, I am the", 1795,1903

"light of the world, you are", 1570,-72

"like a treasure hidden in a field", 1694

"lilies, how they grow", 1823

"lips honor me but hearts far from me", 1712

"little ones, despise not one of these", 1761

"live, and love, and serve", 2084

"live by teachings, (not) imitate my life", 1953

"live individual lives of originality and freedom",1591

"live the righteous life fearlessly", 1571

"live to make known the glory of God", 1934

"lives, be not anxious for", 1577

"lives of originality and freedom", 1591

"living faith increasingly manifests", 1916

"living, only purpose in" (do will of the Father),1602

"living water, shall never thirst for", 1613

"loaves and fishes. bring me the", 1701

"loose the colt and bring it back", 1881

"Lord hears the cry of the needy", 1639

"Lord is my shepherd", 1769

"Lord... satisfying your soul... renewing your strength", 1656

"lose his life shall find it", 1134

love, "add love to your philosophy", 2049

"love admonished by wisdom, guided by intelligence", 1922

"love all men as I have loved you", 2053 (see also "commandment, new" this listing)

"love... does make the old world new", 1945

"love for God and man whole duty", 1600

"love for others measures self-respect", 1740

"love God and learn to do his will", 1676

"love God supremely", 1560

"love is the ancestor of all spiritual goodness", 2047

"love is... dangerous trait" (in parents), 1922

"love is founded on understanding", 1898

"love is the greatest relationship", 1615

"love is the greatest thing in the world", 2047

"love is never self-seeking", 1739

"love is nurtured by unselfish service", 1898

"love is the outworking of", 1898

"love is perfected in wisdom", 1898

"love is supreme reality... when...", 1922

"love is the very spirit of religion we proclaim",1730

"love the Lord your God", 1805,1901

"love men as I have loved you", 2041,-43,-47-48, 2053,-57

love, "my love overshadows you", 2057

"love not the souls of men, but men", 2043

"love of riches", 1802-03,-21-22

"love one another", 1932,-45,-51,-55,-61,1962,2044 (see "love all men", later teaching)

"love one another even as I have loved you", 1944

"love with a new and startling affection", 2044

"love your children as God loves you", 1471

"love your enemies", 1571,-80,1909

"love your neighbor as yourself", 1769-70,1862,1901, 1944,-50,2054

loves, "whom the Lord loves he corrects", 1662

"lower nature, compel it to obey higher", 1461

"loyalty to... convictions, heroism", 1608

Lucifer, "downfall of L, the iniquitous one", 1808

m "maintain living spiritual connection with me", 1945

"make haste, Zaccheus, and come down", 1874

"make no denunciations of Caesar", 1542

"make no record of teachings... lest", 1768

(make) "sure know about your heavenly inheritance", 1822

"make sure truth abides in your lives", 1920

"make sure you daily grow in grace", 1920

"making the tree good", 1582

"man...can bear the noble fruits", 1738
"man from worm...to a divine destiny", 1676
"man is ascending surely up", 1661
"man...is not a child of the devil", 1632
"man is only defiled by that", 1713
man is the son of God,
    "all are equally the sons and daughters of God",
       1679
    "approach the Father as a child of God", 1629
    "cry of the righteous...the child of God", 1639
    "God is your Father...you are his son", 1590
    "God is your Father, you are his sons", 1593
    "the good news--the Fatherhood of God", 1608, -16
    "grace that grasps fact that you are son of God",
       1656
    "guidance...becoming in reality a son of God",
       1603
    "he is in reality a son of God", 1592
    "heed the call to acceptance of sonship", 1608
    "highest privilege of (you) liberated sons of God",
       1676
    "honor (God) as Father of your spirit youth", 1676
    "how to become truly the sons of God", 1797
    "in truth are you the sons of God", 1601
    "know that you are a son of God", 1600
    "man is the son of God, not a child of the devil",
       1632
    "none...detracts from fact that man is son of
       God", 1660
    "peacemakers, shall be called son of God", 1570
    "religion...brotherhood of man, sonship with
       God", 1603
    "saving truth that man is a son of God", 1681
    "spiritual brotherhood of the sons of God on
       earth", 1702
    "teaching mortal man that he is a son of God",1808
    "trust...God of truth, whose sons you are?", 1730
    "ultimate goal, Fatherhood of God", 1608
    "universal Fatherhood of God", 1808
    "worship (God) as loving all-wise Father of your
       mature appreciation", 1676
    "yes, Simon, all men are sons of God", 1585
    "you are therefore sons of God", 1642
"man laid up treasures...on earth", 1821
"man shall not live by bread alone", 1578
"man, what defiles", 1712-13
"man's miseries not a personal visitation", 1664
"man's whole duty this one commandment", 1805
"many abodes (stations), in Father's (house)", 1947,
    1951, -53
"many delightful stopping places for...", 1475
"many false teachers will arise", 1913
"many lives to prepare you for one ahead", 1953
"many mansions, in my Father's house", 341
"many, many stations to prepare you", 1953
"many who are first shall be last", 1804, -29
"marriage to be desired by all men", 1839
"the Master of truth will require a reckoning", 1918
"the Master sends greetings...the hour has come",
    1966
"masters, no man can serve two", 1854
"Master's yoke is easy", 1590
"material affairs of this world?" (no), 1821
"matter of clean hearts rather than", 1713
"may not deny state the right of defense", 1475
"may your courage atone for your ignorance", 1579
"may your wisdom equal your zeal", 1579
"maybe you are the salt", 1430
"measure of spiritual capacity", 1740

"...the measure of your immaturity", 1898
"the measure of your truth endowment", 1726
"meat (my) is to do the will of Him who...", 1615
"meat to eat you do not know about", 1615
"meet a man bearing a pitcher", 1933
"men, all are sons of God", 1585
"men are living...sons of...Father", 2053
"men evil, not necessarily sinful", 1660
"men owe it to selves to make best their lives", 1672
"men set free to start afresh", 1583
"men, twelve commonplace", 1569
"the men you chose from the world" (to Father), 1964
"merchant is entitled to his hire", 1464
"mercy may be lavish, justice is precise", 1469
"message, your m not changed by my resurrection
    experience", 2052
"messengers, my m must not strive", 1577
"methods of power in material world", 1940
"mighty stimulus to powers of personality", 1931
"mile, carry the pack a second", 1770
"mind bravery is a higher type", 1608
"minister to one of the least of these", 1916
"minister to the sick", 1590, 2033
"minister to sick in either mind or body", 1801
"misfortune, not discouraged by", 1739
"misinterpretation of...sacred writings", 1768
"mission, my m will not bring peace", 1824
"money cannot love", 1398
"moral nature can be modified", 1572
morality not rules, but living, 1585
morality of J always positive, 1585
"more abundantly enjoy good things", 1541
"more blessed to give than to receive", 1581
"more joy in heaven over one sinner", 1762
"mortal craves to be a complete person", 1573
"mortal man cannot see the spirit Father", 1952
"mote out of your brother's eye", 1571
"mother, who is my", 1722
"motive determines morality", 1585
"motive, I look to uncover the", 1576
"motive, it is the m that counts", 1571
motives, two, post baptismal mission, 1578

"mouth, not that which enters into", 1712
"move not from house to house", 1801
"much has been given to you", 1824
"much of man's sorrow is born of", 1674
"my beloved son", 1504, -06, -11
"my brethren, you are earthen vessels", 1578
"my Father...is no respecter of persons", 1608, -62
"my Father loathes hypocrisy, abhors iniquity, 1676
"my Father will respond...flicker of faith", 1733
"my friend arise! stand up like a man", 1437
"my hour has come", 1495, 1504, -29, -35, 1789
"my hour has not yet come", 1103, 1414, -17
"my house...a den of robbers", 1890
"my kingdom is not of this world", 1543, 1750, -58,
    1870, -81, 1914, -91, 2035
"my kingdom is not to come with noise and glamor",
    1533
"my (little) children", 1543, 1605, -75, 1908, -49, -59
"my love overshadows you", 2057
"my mission is to live a life...", 1466
"my mission will not bring peace in...", 1824
"my mother, how could you?", 1397
"my one purpose...to reveal the Father", 2052
"my peace I give to you", 1954
"my peace I leave with you", 1575, 1966, 2040, -42,
    2050, -53-54

Jesus, Quotes (cont'd)

"my peace shall abide upon you", 2057
"my people... strain at gnats and swallow camels", 1736
"my rebellious son" (to Lucifer), 1493
"my sheep hear my voice", 1815
"my son, arise! come out of him", 1757
"my soul is distraught by that...ahead", 1903
"my spirit, just like me except for body", 1949
"my spirit shall be upon you", 1932
"my spirit shall dwell within you", 2049
"my Spirit of the Truth...shall guide you", 1914
"my spirit upon you, now and to end...",1932
"my spirit will illuminate (for you)", 1951
"my words of truth shall not (pass away)", 1736
"my work for you is done", 1908
"mystery of salvation within your own soul", 1474
n "nation only better through individual", 1630
"need, your Father knows your", 49
"needs a loaf, give him a stone?", 1619
"needs will be supplied if", 1823
"neither cast pearls before swine", 1571, -85, 1999
"neither did this man sin, nor his parents", 1812
"neither do I condemn you", 1793
"never dare to compel mens' minds", 1931
"never endeavor to frighten men...into kingdom",1766
"never grow up in spirit perception?", 1605
"nevertheless, your will be done", 1640
"new and better way, I proclaim the", 1537
"new commandment I shall...give you", 1939 (see "commandment, new", this listing)
"new dispensation of grace and truth", 1941-42
"new kingdom is like a seed growing", 1536
"new law endows you with...self-mastery", 1609
new life, "when enter the kingdom, reborn", 1592
"new light of the gospel", 1768
"new message of self-forgetfulness", 1609
"new revelation...no man can take away", 1952
"new teaching, don't attach to old", 1914
"new way" of self forgetfulness, self-control, 1609
"next revelation of eternal progression", 1915
"no labors take place of proclaiming gospel", 1931
"no longer child of Israel, but child of God", 1629
"no man can serve two masters", 1577, 1803
"no man goes to the Father except through me", 1947
"no man has taught me truths I declare", 1790
"no man a stranger to one who knows God", 1431
"no mention...of our trials and troubles", 1610
"no one will lay hands upon me... ", 1920
"no place of preferment at my table", 1940
no "spiritual work in absence of s power", 1758
"no such thing as common labor", 1960
"not come to legislate but to enlighten", 1576
"not everyone who says 'Lord, Lord' ", 1569
"not good for man to be alone", 2055
"not my will, but yours be done", 1514, 1774, 1968
"not one stone...upon another", 1882
"not required one should betray me", 1940
"not the righteous but sinners", 1540
"not seven but to seventy times seven", 1763
"not a sin to have honorable wealth", 1821
"not so guilty since you are ignorant of gospel", 1996
"not so much by words as by lives", 1569
"not that which enters into the mouth", 1712
"not...to teach rules of government, trade,or social behavior", 1576
"not too late to welcome the Son of Man", 1905
not "what you may obtain, but...can give", 2039
"not yet proclaim (I) am Son of God", 1750
"nothing hidden that shall not be known", 1682

"nothing takes place of human experience", 1956
"nothing to do to earn...salvation", 1838
"now has my hour come", 1940
"now I take leave of you", 1908
"now offering (Jews) your last chance", 1906
o "O faithless and perverse generation", 1757
"O Jerusalem...even now would I gather your children... ", 1908
"O Jerusalem...what slaves you are...victims of your own traditions", 1384
"O Jerusalem...which kills the prophets...how often I would have gathered your children... ", 1872
"O Jerusalem...your enemies shall utterly destroy you", 1882
"O woman, great is your faith", 1735
"O you of little faith!", 1823, 1960
"obey law until" rulers overthrown by Most Highs,1906
"of citizens of kingdom, more is required", 1570
"offered sonship to all the Jewish nation", 1905
"offering sacrifices commanded by Moses", 1643
"old order is bringing itself to judgment", 1904
"on earth to comfort, liberate, save", 1576
"on these two commandments hang... ", 1901
"once more do I warn you", 1894
"once more offered Israel salvation", 1906
"one commandment, greatest of all", 1901
"one more day to do the Father's will", 1928
"one of the least of my brethren", 1917
"one of you...in grave danger", 1715
"one sows and another reaps", 1615
oneness of J' matchless life, 1866
"only business, reveal God to individual", 1593
"only the Creators possess infallibility", 1768
"only have faith, Martha", 1843
only J saw apparition (T A), 1511
"only one thing is really worthwhile", 1798
"only our brethren, the Jews, seek to harm us", 1612
"only the soul that sins shall die", 1630
"only uniform thing...indwelling spirit", 1672
"organize under Andrew", 1544
"our Father is changeless", 1597
"our Father who is in heaven", 1620, 1923
"our kingdom is a realm of order", 1959
"out of the mouths of babes and sucklings", 1890
"outpouring of Spirit of Truth", 1943
outsmarts Sanhedrin agents, 1793
"overanxious, be not", 1640
"overcome evil with good", 1739
"overspecialized, become not", 1726

p parable(s), (see under "P")
"parting of the ways, you have come to the", 1710, -14
"pass through many abodes in Father's universe",1951
"Passover, this is the new", 1943
"patient, strive not, be", 1592
"peace, and have it more abundantly", 1954
"peace be to (upon) you", 2032-33, -40-41, -43-44, 2046, -50, -52-55
"peace, can't be p between light, darkness", 1905
"peace, can't be p between truth, error", 1905
"peace, he will be kept in perfect", 1731
"peace more abundantly", 1954
"peace of God...passes all understanding", 1627
"peace on earth and good will", 1569
"peace on earth" when "Father's will" observed,1824, 1951
"peace which passes all understanding", 1627
"peacemaking is the cure of distrust and suspicion", 1575

"Satan, falling as lightning from heaven", 490, 1807
"save his life (selfishly), shall lose it", 1760
"saving faith...is the gift of God", 1610
"score of men, members of Sanhedrin", 1903
"scriptures are sacred because...", 1768
"scriptures are faulty and altogether human", 1767
"scriptures, look for beautiful teachings", 1769
"secret of greatness in spiritual kingdom",1940
"secret of the mastery of self", 1610
"secretly (take) widow's houses", 1907
"secure title to mansions of eternity", 1474
"secure work for those without" it, 1765
"see me, when you again", 1952
"see with eyes of the spirit", 1602
"seek and you shall find", 1619
"seek first the kingdom of God", 1569, -77-78, 2088
"seek for spiritual food", 1710
"seek the greater, lesser will be found...", 1823
"seek in life, the glory of God", 1907
"seek the Lord while he may be found", 1850
"seek no unearned recognition", 1740
"seek only that which belongs to you", 1740
"seek to have his will of love dominate your life",1598
"seek to live peaceably with all men", 1930
"self-control, enjoyable and ennobling", 1610
"self is more than sum of sensations", 1479
"self-mastery, heights of...attainment", 1610
"self-mastery...measure of man's...", 1609
"self-respect, I will stop at nothing to restore",1765
"self-respect, purpose of gospel to restore", 1765
"selfish desire for worldly preferment", 1758
"sell, go and s all that you have", 1802
"send to me...most fleet messenger", 1966
"send you as lambs among wolves", 1800
"send you forth as sheep in midst of wolves", 1584
"separate spiritual from all other problems of the
    age", 1605
"serious things of life only" (no!), 1558
"the servant is not greater...", 1946
"serve the Lord, your God", 1629
"serve your fellow men", 2049
"set a watch before my mouth", 1640
"seventy times seven", 1763
"shadow of a great rock in a weary land", 2035
"the shadow sure to follow the substance", 1823
"shall cheer and comfort me all...my life", 1403
"shall endow you with power", 2055
"shall find spiritual rest for your souls", 1808
"shame on those false religious teachers", 1731
"she has anointed my feet", 1652
"she has done a good thing in her heart", 1879
"sheep belong not to my fold", 1815, -18
"sheep, go to lost s of Israel", 1681
"sheep in the midst of wolves", 1584
"sheep, my s hear my voice", 1815
"sheep not of this flock", 1577, 1841, 1959
"shepherd will be smitten and the sheep scattered
    abroad", 1962
"should we sit in judgment...?", 1827
"show what great things God has done", 1697
"sickness and health, matters of", 1831
"sickness is really not to the death", 1836, -42, -44,
    1848
"sickness shall be taken away from you", 1629
"sifting of kingdom distresses you", 1715
"sin...an experience of creature consciousness",1898
"sin, I am ruthless with", 1766
"sin...is not a part of God's consciousness", 1898
"sin not essential to survival", 1661

"sin, which of you convicts me of", 2092
"sincerity most serviceable...wedded to discretion",
    1961
"sinful pleasures vs. righteous realities", 1745
"sinner, joy in heaven over one", 1762
"sins forgiven if you confess", 1736
"smites cheek...turn the other", 1571, 1770
"so shall Jerusalem be trodden down", 1913
"so will I dwell in everyone who believes", 1816
"so you have said", 1979-80
social behavior, trade, government, "not come to
    teach", 1576
"social harmony" not at price of "free personality",
    1591
"society (nation) only better through individual", 1630
soft answer to "unbelievers, and live", 1958
"soil of the evolving soul is human", 1738
"some day all nations (through gospel) freedom,
    liberty", 1930
"some of you...are as vipers", 1714
"someone touched me", 1698
"sometimes bid the poor", 1834
"Son...be killed and raised from dead", 1759
"son, fear not...faith shall save you", 1667
"Son of Man, lord even of the Sabbath", 1655
"Son of Man now enters upon last phase", 1759
"the Son of Man...shall rise again", 1759
"Son of Man a spiritual incarnation in...believers",
    1953
"Son put to death...shall rise again", 1759
"son, to be s receive God as Father", 1601
"sons, do the s of the bridechamber fast?", 1653
"sonship, citizenship, not incompatible", 1929
"sonship with God, by faith, the saving truth", 2052
"soon we will send the Spirit of Truth", 2057
"sorrow will not help us", 1400
"sorrows, your teacher is not a man of", 1766
"soul, my s is distraught", 1903
"soul, thirsty, cup of cold water to", 1764
"souls are steeped in iniquity", 1908
"souls, here solely to save s of men", 1576
"sour grapes and the children's teeth", 1630
"source of all life, the Father", 1820
"sparrows sold for 2 pennies", 1682, 1820
"speak not hearsay", 1545
"speak, out of the abundance of evil in your hearts",
    1714
"spirit helper, I will send you", 1947-48
"spirit is willing but the flesh is weak", 1968
"spirit, it is the s that quickens", 1715
"spirit, my s will be upon you", 1932
"spirit, my s will dwell with you", 2054
"spirit of my Father indwells you", 1584
"Spirit of Truth, live with you, in your hearts", 1949
    (see also "Spirit of Truth, poured out" under "S")
"Spirit of Truth shall be poured out", 1642
"Spirit of Truth will comfort you", 1947-48
"Spirit of Truth will lead each of you...to labor", 1957
"spirit realities, love is the greatest of", 1608
"Spirit...will endow you with power", 2055
"spirit will speak through you", 1584
"spirits, our, into the minds of men", 1807
"spiritual destiny controlled by longings", 1739
"spiritual food vessels filthy", 1826
spiritual force, break through resistance, 1829
"spiritual gifts limited by capacity", 1831
"spiritual gifts limited by...faith", 1831
"spiritual greatness consists in...", 1758
"spiritual incarnation in souls", 1953

"the tree is known by its fruits", 1714
"trial discloses what is in the heart", 1824
"trials and difficulties to prepare him", 1466
"tribulation, but be of good cheer", 1954
"troubles from fear soil of his heart", 1674
"true, the just shall live by faith", 1682
"true light which lights every man", 1181
"true not only of this world", 1819
"true praying is... reaching heavenward", 1618
"trust and confide in one another", 2055
"trust in Him who is able to sustain the body", 1682
"trust my teaching, believe in God", 1576
"trust therefore, and confide in one another", 2055
"truth compelled by secular laws", no, 1931
"truth, illuminated by love of", 1739
"truth, my words of t will not pass away", 1736
"the truth shall make you free", 1796
"turn back, you may even now", 1577
"turn the other cheek", 1571, 1770
"two things can't run away from", 1475

u "ultimate goal of human progress is", 1608
"unafraid of life, honest and consistent", 1740
"unbelievers, minister loving service to u", 1930
"underneath are the everlasting arms", 1662
"universe, in my Father's u are many abodes",
  1934, -47, -51, -53
"universe is truly fatherly", 1573
"unless you are born again", 1829
"unseen messenger will run by your side", 1967
"unselfishness... badge of human greatness", 1572
"untaught people are accursed", 1792

v "vale of tears", this is not, but "a vale of soul
  making", 1675
"vengeance, the days of gentile", 1913
"vengeance savors not of kingdom... ", 1788
"victims, these folks innocent v of time", 1830
"victory overcomes all uncertainty", 1601
"victory shall eventually crown our efforts", 1904
"vigorously defend the truth" (spiritual), 1932
"vipers, call you offspring of v", 1908

w "walk in the light... become liberated", 1904
"walls of prejudice, self-righteousness, hate", 1879
"war any more, neither shall nations learn", 1769
"wars and rumors of wars", 597
"watchman, only the w must keep vigil", 1495
"water of life, the divine spirit", 1712
"water your souls with traditions of men?", 1796
"the way is straight and narrow", 1828
"the way of the Father's service for mankind", 1916
"the way... to eternal life is... narrow", 1828
"the way, the truth, and the life", 1593
"we are beholden to do will of the Eternal", 1649
"we have other realms beside this", 1625
"we piped for you and you did not dance", 1627
"we pray for strength to sustain us", 1963
"we were not fellow servants in ministry", 1829
"we will send our spirits into minds of men", 1805
"weaklings?, do you resemble", 1608
"wealth is unenduring", 1822
"wealth, whence came this?", 1462
"weep not, your son is not dead", 1645
"welfare of soul is more than food... ", 1823
"well done, good and faithful servant", 1917
"well of water... everlasting life", 2035
"were not 10 cleansed? where are the... Jews?",
  1828
"what do you want me to do for you?", 1867, -73
"what has (disaster) to do with believer", 1916
"what is it you seek as evidence of my mission?",
  1710

"what is new and true... accept", 1656
"what profit you... gain world... lose your soul", 1822
"what shall it profit a man... ?", 1581
"what were you disputing about?", 1757
"what will they do with J?", 1910
"what you have decided to do, do quietly", 1941
"what you will not learn (one way) trouble", 1962
"whatever comes between you and... truth", 1804
"whatsoever you would that men... ", 1571, 1650, 1931
"wheat, a grain of w falls into the earth", 1903
"when the blind lead the blind", 1907
"when enemy smites... one cheek", 1770
"when enter the kingdom, you are reborn", 1592
"when the Father's will becomes your will", 1589
"when the fullness of the age has come", 1915
"when I return, it shall be with power", 1915
"when power from Spirit of Truth has come", 2043
"when the Son of Man is lifted up... ", 1795
"when to pray, I will not say", 1640
"when unbeliever attacks you, stand in vigorous
  defense of truth which has saved and sanctified
  you", 1932
"when the wind blows, you hear", 1602
"when you (are) competent, I will ordain you", 1668
"when you... ascended to me in my universe", 1947
"when you enter kingdom, you are reborn", 1592
"when you pray, go apart by yourself", 1577
"where are the other 9, the Jews?", 1828
"where believers are... I am in midst", 1763
"where have you laid him?", 1843, -44
"where I go, you cannot come", 1792, -95
"where I go, you shall presently come", 2049
"where is your faith? peace, be quiet", 1695
"where two or three believers are gathered", 1763
"where two or three of you agree", 1763
"where you (science) leave off, we begin", 1641
"where your treasure is... ", 1822-23
"wherefore do you doubt?", 1753, 1845
"wherefore do you fall asleep?", 1968
"which is greater, the gold or the temple?", 1907
"which of you convicts me of sin?", 1797, 2092
"who attains... this united nature... shall live
  forever", 1711
"who commits sin is the bondservant of sin", 1796
"who do men say that I am?", 1745
"who enters kingdom, shall never perish", 1642
"who exalts himself, humbled", 1834
"who hates me hates the Father", 1947
"who is my mother, who are my brothers?", 1722
"who of us is competent to judge his brother?", 1558
"who refuse to grow old gracefully", 1740
"whom do you seek?", 1974
"whom the Lord loves, he corrects", 1662
"whoso humbles himself... exalted", 1907
"whoso stops his ears to the cries of the poor... ",
  1639
"whosoever drinks shall never thirst", 1613
"whosoever loses his life shall save it", 1760
"whosover will, let him come... ", 1820
"whosoever will save his life shall lose it", 1575
"whosoever wills may enter", 1829
"whosoever would be great among you", 1868
"why are all of you so filled with fear?", 1695
"why are you troubled by trifles?", 1798
"why do the heathen rage?", 1725
"why do you call me good?", 2088, -92
"why do you halt between two opinions?", 1820
"why do you languish in futile yearning?", 1726
"why have they come to besiege us?", 1635

"why have you fasted?", 1656

"why have you forsaken me?", 2010

"why play the part of hypocrites?", 1836

"why should Jew or gentile (not) accept the good news?", 1820

"why should you live in fear?...fear not", 1820

"why so downcast...?", 1437

"why...transgress...by laws of your traditions?", 1712

"why waste words upon one...", 1440

"why were you afraid?", 1753

"wicked flee when no man pursues", 1674

"willful unbeliever, when the w u attacks you", 1932

"will be with...who desire my presence", 1948

"will of the Father, do, then never fail", 1601

"the will of the Father" (Sermon), 1629

"will of God will prevail in the end", 1933

"will pour out Spirit of Truth", 1948

"will remove mountains in path of spiritual", 1619

"will save souls of poor who seek him", 2035

"will spit upon and scourge" (me), 1871

"will stop at nothing to restore self-respect", 1765

"wind blows, hear rustle, do not see the wind", 1602

"wisdom embraces discretion", 1958

"wisdom, may your w equal your zeal", 1579

"wisdom, that you may love", 1870

"wish to kill me" (murder), 1791,-95, 1820,-26

"with God all things are possible", 1803

"woe upon all of you lawyers", 1826

"woe upon all who despise the revelation", 1826

"woe upon all who shun justice...reject truth...", 1826

"woe upon the light-rejecting inhabitants", 1807

"woe upon you, false guides of a nation", 1908

"woe upon you hypocrites", 1907-08

"woe upon you Pharisees...", 1826

"woman, behold your son", 2009

"woman, great is your faith", 1735

"woman, if you would only believe", 1836

"woman, where are your accusers?", 1793

"woman, your faith has saved you", 1652

"the word of life is very near to you", 1686

"words, why waste w upon one who...", 1440

"work, he who will not w not eat", 1579

"world is filled with hungry souls who", 1766

"world is only a bridge", 1735

"...world knows very little of you" (Father), 1965

"world will stumble--my words", 1533

"worlds whose habits...righteousness", 1935

"worship God where you are, as you are", 2053

"wounded in the house of a trusted friend", 1677

"a wrong is not righted by vengeance", 1580

y "yes, David, I know all about it", 1933

"yes, I am such a king", 1991

"yoke, take my y upon you", 1808

"yoke, take upon you the divine", 1627

"you and all...men are sons of God", 2043

"you are all the children of light", 2042

"you are all fools and blind", 1907

"you are commissioned to save men, not to judge them", 1571

"you are expected to believe with a whole heart", 1733

"you are ignorant of the gospel", 1996

"you are justified by faith", 1610

"you are the light of the world", 1570-72

"you are like whited sepulchres", 1908

"you are not far from...the kingdom", 1901

"you are not of my fold", 1829

"you are not to attack the old ways", 1932

"you are the salt of the earth", 1570,-72

"you are the sons of the living God", 1661

"you are teaching friendship with God", 1766

"you are then born of the spirit", 2052

"you are to remain unmoved by fear", 1610

"you belong not to my fold", 1815,-18

"you cannot buy salvation", 1683

"you cannot compel men to love truth", 1713

"you cannot earn righteousness", 1683

"you cannot serve God and Mammon", 1854

"you cannot talk men out of their perplexities", 1610

"you cannot worship God and serve mammon", 1577

"you charge me with blasphemy", 1816

"you chose" (apostles) "I have chosen", 1964

"you do well to be meek...", 1676

"you failed to believe me because...", 2052

"you garnish the tombs of the righteous", 1908

"you have a common goal of existence", 1592

"you have said", 1940

"you knew not the time of your divine visitation", 1882

"you know not what you ask", 1867

"you know who I am; come out", 1713

"you know your fathers rejected...prophets", 1894

"you make proselyte worse than...heathen", 1907

"you may also ask in my name", 1952

"you must account for all of this righteous blood", 1908

"you must be led by the spirit", 1738

"you must be reborn", 1576

"you must be righteous in order to do the work", 1584

"you must let others bury the dead", 1801

"you now plan to kill those who come", 1826

"you shall abide in my love", 1945

"you shall all be taught by God", 1711

"you shall also survive mortal death", 2054

"you shall ascend the universe of universes", 2052

"you shall be baptized with the Spirit", 1593

"you shall be unafraid when trouble...", 1767

"you shall...be with me in Paradise", 2009

"you shall be with me in person", 1947

"you shall come to my joy", 1935

"you shall know the truth and...", 1594, 1796

"you shall love the Lord your God...", 1901

"you shall love your neighbor...", 1901

"you shall not covet", 1822

"you shall receive your sight", 1873

"you shall see greater things than this", 1754

"you shall then see the Father himself", 1952

"you should call no man Father in the spiritual sense", 1907

"you should learn to love one another", 1762

"you, sons of God on earth", 2052

"you think to stone me", 1815

"you too, shall serve with me in...kingdom", 1967

"you wicked reprobates", 1908

"you will be indwelt by the Son", 1948

"you will...discover God in other...souls", 1733

"you will go forth to become fishers of men", 1544

"you will seek...but will not find me", 1944

"you will then seek and not find me" (Jews), 1872

"your enemies shall utterly destroy you", 1882

"your faith has made you whole", 1698, 1873

"your Father knows what you have need of", 49

"your fellow men will then seek after you", 1726

"your house is left to you desolate", 1908

"your kingdom come, your will be done", 1860, 2088

"your leaders seek to kill me", 1796

"your life is eternally secure in the Father", 1916

JEWISH, JEWS

"The fact that the spiritual leaders and religious
teachers of the Jewish nation...rejected...Jesus
and conspired to bring about his cruel death...should
not cause...followers of the Christ to be prejudiced
against the Jew as a fellow mortal. " 1909

Jews (cont'd)

conscience, not bothered in c at all, but scrupulous in ceremony, 1987

considered all others heathen, 1340

contact with gentiles, trial to apostles, 1610

contempt for gentiles, 1339

contributed least to comprehension of, 1076

contribution to spiritual understanding, small, 1076

corrupted Noah's flood story, 874

could cheat gentiles, 775

could have foreseen J, 1510

credit given, 1011, -76, 1732

"crucify him! crucify him!", 1994-96

cruelty, 779, -84-85

curse of, 1709, 1872, 2005

customary Wednesday weddings, 1528

d darkened minds of Moses' day, 1560

Davidic dynasty, depradations equalled by gangster nobility in Samaria, 1074

days of barrenness, 1732

death scene of a nation, 1999

deliverer idea, clung to, 1837

denunciation, last of bigoted leaders, 1905

derision incited at cross, 2007

determination to destroy J, grim, 1932

"determined to spurn the kingdom", 1903

discrimination, unjust, women, 1377

dispensation ends, 1903

dispersed by commerce or oppression over world, 1339

divine destiny could not fulfill, 1340

"dog in the eyes of the Jews", Norana, 1735

doom, Jews had sealed their, 1910-13, -69

e education, scriptures only till 12, 1362

effrontery of subject citizens seeking crucifixion, 1989-90

end, inglorious, 1906, -99

enter no gentile building...1987

established and fossilized religion, 1730

ethics with gentiles, 775

evaded own law forbidding execution, 1989

evil, out of abundance of e in your hearts, 1714

excommunicated believers in J, 1814

excommunication for eating with unwashed hands,1713

executed a drunk gentile, 1382

expected miracles of power, 1509

f fables, 1068

facial appearance, whence?, 896

failed to know God in spirit, 1466

faith in Universal Father, kept, 1075

false charges, to Herod, 1992
to Pilate, 1990

false pride of descent, 1339

family stability, strong, 939

family status better than gentiles, 1335

"farewell to benighted rulers of Israel", 1904

Father and Son love the, 1909

feared Roman stop to uprising, 1891

feared to molest bold apostles, 2060

feeding 5000, appealed to, 1708

fire destroyed defiant synagogue, 1718

first to the Jews, then to the gentiles, 1584

fitted eminently, to receive J, 1332

"fixed" theology, 1339

flower of race, died on Golgotha, 2005

follies of rabbinic system, 1713

"folly, supreme--of all ages", 1906

forced teachers out to ends of empire, 2068

from human standpoint, J was a Jew, 1594

g Gabriel predicted Jews would hardly receive J, 1347

Jews (cont'd)

gentile city would defile, 1374

"gentile dogs", all others than, 1809

gifts to Nazarites, 1497

girls given little education, 1396

God, as King over all, 1590
growing concept of, 1598
"in mind, but not spirit", 1467
loved by, 1909
sans a philosophy, 1467
think they will be serving, 1951

God's expectations for, 1536

Golgotha, 1000's upon 1000's Jews died on, 2005

gospel, carried all over Empire, 1596
movement, believed crushed, 2045
writers glossed over, 1736

greatest feat in evolutionary religion, 1075

Greeks, Romans, 2043

guards at tomb, seized with terror, 2023

h had not expected Messiah, a "Son of God", 1748

had peculiar regard for number 70, 1806

hard to govern, 1988

harm us, "only the Jews seek to", 1612

hated by Pilate, 1988

"He (God) repented that...he had...made man", 1510

"he who hates me, hates Father", 1947

"he who is not with me is against me", 1714

healing on Sabbath, criticized J for, 1836

health, couldn't seek h on Sabbath, 1631

held in bondage by priests and, 1340

Herod to Jews "J can preach in Perea", 1742

"his blood be on us and on our children", 1996

history (altered), 838, 874, 1023, -68, -70-72

hope, material, never to be realized, 1521

hungry (spiritually), and gentiles, 1806

hypocrisy of J' enemies, 1892

"hypocritical leaders", 1905

i "I know that not all have failed me", 1903

"if we do not stop...the world will go after him",1882

Ikhnaton, Egypt, 1047

immortality, belief in, no, 2073

impossible to fulfill divine destiny, 1340

"in rejecting me, they will reject Him", 1902

incited crowd against J, 1993

influenced by Zoroastrianism, 1050

infuriated, wanted body of J, 2012

"iniquity, filled up cup of their", 1912

insincerity of leaders, 1892

insisted Romans conform as to "images", 1988

interviewed J secretly, 1596

irate--killed Philip's wife, 1558

Israelite, genuine, 1527

j Jerusalem, bitter persecution by, 1616

Jerusalem leaders influenced Tiberias, 1647

Jerusalem, 1, 500, 000 in Jer time of crucifixion, 2014

Jerusalem--vs. Philadelphia, 1831

J' death, no cause for prejudice against Jew as fellow mortal, 1909

J' indictment of Jews, 1905-08

J' last appeal to, 1905

J' love and pity for Jews deepened, 1386

J' "personal religion in place of racial", 1629

J' promise to rise, Jews fearful over, 2014

J put to death by chief priests and rulers of the Jews, 1967

J, when he appeared among, 2033

J' work well known to all Jewry, 1791

Jewish, expectations, "no" to, 1523
idea of serving God, 1583
people, be discreet about (to apostles), 1580
tutor (J), 1422

Jews (cont'd)
    Joseph, racial strains, 1344
    journey of 1000 yards, 1654
    (Judahites) sought always to defame Israelites, 1072
    Judaism is Melchizedek teachings of Kenites
       modified by Jews, 1444
    judges, thirty prejudiced and tradition-bound j, 1984
    "killed heaven-sent teachers", 1906-08
    "King of the Jews", 1994-95, 2000, -05, -07
    kingdom, ideas, − combined, confused, 1858
       to the − was Israelite community, 1865
       − would not give up idea of, 1868
    knew God in mind, 1466
    lacking in humor, 1736
    last appeal to, 1905
    last offer of mercy to rulers of −, 1910
    laws ignored, 1982, -84-85
    lax and unfair divorce practices, 1838
    leaders, blinded by fears, prejudices, 1672, 1714, -26
       conference with Herod, 1719
       frantic, well nigh, 1672
       hired ruffians to harass J, 1684, -86
       incited derision at cross, 2007
       overawed by J' entry, 1891
       ". . . reject me, . . . reject Him", 1902
       religious, dangerous to J, 1647
       representatives lied to Herod, 1717
       secret meetings about J, 1654
       spies, 6 secret, appointed, 1654
    learned that their secular Messianic idea led to their
       destruction, 1913
    lepers − and Samaritan, 1828
    Levantine race, Oriental and Occidental, 1332
    liberties curtailed short time, 1339
    loathed Judas, 1997
    long continued national desolation, 1500
    looked upon all gentile ways with contempt, 1339
    "Lord shall cause you to be smitten by your
       enemies", 1709
    lost motion of religious evolution, 1340
    malice and hatred of −, 1993
    man could divorce for trifling reasons, 1839
    many thousands banished from Rome, J' time, 1339
    Matadormus, member of Sanhedrin, 1802
    men will reject, 1882
    military valor in ancient times, 1077
    mission spiritual, not political, 1334
    misunderstood Moses, 1560
    not under leadership of Sanhedrin, 1994
    Moses' efforts with, 1058
    "Most High. . . finally overthrow this nation. . . ", 1906
    murderously intentioned, 1843
    nation, end of − drew on, 1910
    national egotism and false faith, 1075
    necessary to show certain fellow Jews rejected J,
       caused ignominious death, 1909
    new and relentless persecutions by the Jews, 2068
    new concept of destiny devised in Babylon, 1075
    no longer approach God as children of Israel, 1629
    northern vs. southern, 1072
    of old, famed for theologic peculiarities, 1077
    often buried the comatose, 1837
    "one more chance", 1809, -11, -37
    "one more mighty work for these", 1837
    "one who talks something besides religion", 1477
    "one who thinks something besides racial super-
       iority", 1477
    only, sought J harm, 1612
    orthodox − "J walked too fast", 1684
    overcharges, 1889-90, 1354

Jews (cont'd)
    overhonored ancestors, 1581
    paid in full as a nation, 1909
    parties and sects of the, 1534
    Passover, no connection crucifixion, 2002
    Paul's changes to please Jews, 1831-32
    persecutions, new and relentless by, 2068
    Pharisees, against J, 1826
       established and fossilized religion, 1730
       judged selves by lowest standard, 1838
       Sadducees, antagonistic, 1605
       Sadducees, Herod's men, 1708
    Pilate's tragic surrender to, 1996
    pitiful and pathetic (atonement ritual), 1494
    plan to make − light bearers shattered, 1910
    politically appointed priesthood, 1386, 1404
    power over Pilate due to blunders, 1988
    power to feed, power to rule, 1702
    prayers, had 25 or 30 set, 1620
    prejudiced villagers, against −, 1788
    prevented work in Judea and Galilee, 1617
    priests, false claims, 838, 1068, -70
    profits, exorbitant, from people, 1889
    prominent, allegiance to J, 1910
    prophecy to the −, 1709
    Psalms, "let us break bonds of mercy", 1725
    punished J without a verdict, 1996
    questions by rulers of the −, 1899
    quick history of struggle, 1732
    quieted down considerably, 2045
    rabbis, 500 passages, Messiah, 1509
    rabbis, "who is my neighbor", 1580
    realm of order, 1959
    rebuke to all, 1810
    refusal of J' spiritual concept of Messiah, would mean
       direct conflict with Rome, 1913
    refused to see mission as spiritual, 1334
    "reject, all men will r you", 1882
    rejected J because, 1024, -71
    rejected Moses, Isaiah, (J), 1075
    rejected Paul at Corinth, 1472
    rejected wonderful story of God, 1075
    rejection, apparent or not, 1455
       in J' eyes, go to gentiles, 1957
       of J prophesied, 1347
       of J, why, 1071
    religion, humor would have prevented Pharisee's r,
       1736
    religion involved in tax agitation, 1397
    religion of, 1339, 1509, -45, 1726, -29
    religion of authority, 1729
    religion without science, 1726
    religious communities everywhere, 1333
    religious leaders very antagonistic, 1617
    removed from Perea, 1817
    repudiated Son of God, had, 1910
    ruffians hired to harass J, 1684, -86
    rulers of, concerned about J, 1596
       decreed Lazarus' death, 1849
       instigated crowd against J, 1994
       J' body to wild beasts, 2012
       mocked J on cross, 2008
    sacred history of − is ordinary profane history, 1075
    sacred law of the, 1713
    Samaritans, and the −, 1610, -12
       avoided dealing with, 1374
    schools in Capernaum "tops", 1548
    scribes destroyed every record to "raise" their
       leaders, 1024
    scripture changed, 1599

John the Baptist (cont'd)
    faith tested, 1507
    famed throughout Palestine, 1503
    fashioned self after Elijah, 1499
    flowing hair and peculiar dress (like Elijah's), 1497
    great kingdom concept not in JB's teachings, 1860
    great things for JB after earth, 1507
    "heard JB thunder this parable", 1854
    Herod, fear of JB after death, 1717
    Herod wondered if J was JB risen, 1633
    heroic but tactless preacher, 1502
    imprisoned at Machaerus, 1508
    in order to understand his message, 1500
JOHN IN PRISON, 1506
John the Baptist, intellectual uncertainty, 1503
    J came to earth from heaven, 1507
    J said "tell John he is not forgotten", 1626
    J tempted to free JB from prison, 1539
    J thought much about, 1539
    "John is dead, Herod has beheaded him" (J), 1627
JOHN JOURNEYS NORTH, 1503
JOHN JOURNEYS SOUTH, 1506
John the Baptist, Judas asked J, why JB not got out,1542
    kingdom concept JB taught, 1858
    "the kingdom of heaven is at hand", 1502
    like Elijah, 1502
    Mar. A.D. 25, John started preaching, 1501
    message to J from prison, 1626
    "much more than a prophet", 1627
    natural outworking permitted, John's career, 1507
    Nazarite, went forth from colony, 1605
    noble character, 1497
    "parable not according to gospel we preach", 1854
    parted with J, 1506,-26
    prayer, his, for disciples, 1618
    preached only 15 months, 1502
    preaching concerned Herod, 1534
    preaching had many meanings, 1501
    proclaimed kingdom in advance (J), 2041
    prophet, accepted as, 1501
    "repent and be baptized", 1510
    rulers afraid to release or execute him, 1617
    so much vice, believed end of age, 1498
    soil of his heart, suggestive seeds (spiritual), 1346
    strong man, noble character, 1497
    tended to believe end of world near, 1498
    "this is my beloved Son, in whom...", 1504-06
    uttered prophecy, 1507
    visited J' family with his mother, 1400,-97
    visits Nazareth, 1400
    was taught J was the true Messiah, 1498
John the Baptist's apostles, liked courage J displayed
    at Jerusalem, 1798
John, Gospel of, "dictated" by John at age 99, 1556
    story of its writing, 1342
John's (Baptist), apostles, J' conference with, 1624
    religion vs. J, 1609
    separation from J' apostles, 1648
John Hyrcanus, 1612
John Mark, 1923, -63,-71, 2047
    crucifixion, prior to, 1963
    followed, joined apostles, 2045
    homecoming sad, 2051
    knew what was coming, 1967
    lunch basket, and the, 1920
    "mighty messenger of kingdom" (will be), 1921
    near by always, 1921
    silent, 1927
    summoned apostles after cross, 2014
    upper room, house of, 1933
    welcomed 13 to father's home, 1935

John Zebedee, Apostle, 1553 (see under "Apostles")
Jonah, 1767
    discourse on Jonah with Nathaniel, 1767
    J on Jonah at Joppa, 1428
Joppa, 1411, -28, -92
Jordan crossing, John baptised at, 1501
Jose, renowned Nazareth teacher, 1372
Joseph, a believer, of Tyre, 1737, -44
Joseph (brother of J), born A.D. 1, 1362, 1720-21
    "maybe our strange brother is coming king", 1527
Joseph (earthly father of J), adopted by descendant of
    David, 6 generations B.C. 1347
    and Jacob, partnership, 1389
    and Zebedee, partnership, 1405
    carried many non-Jewish racial strains, 1344
    convinced by dream, 1347
JOSEPH, THE DEATH OF, 1388
Joseph, family involved in evolution of religion, 1344
    how could mortal offspring have divine destiny?, 1347
    not in David-Solomon line, 1023, 1344, -47-48
    surprise of his life, J and athletic games, 1370-71
    untimely death, 1348, -72, -88, 1992
Joseph of Arimathea, 1810
    and Nicodemus, asked Pilate for J' body, 2012
    attended meeting to hear J, at Nicodemus', 1810, 1924
    boldly acknowledged faith, claimed J' body, 1603
    morontia J appeared at home of, 2033
    really believed J would rise from dead, 2013
    turned back from seeing J through fear, 1606
    with apostles, Greeks, others, to hear J, 1905
    women to embalm J, at home of, 2014
Joseph (son of Abraham), principal reason for honors in
    Egypt, 1023
Joseph and Mary, chided each other gently, 1381
    children (chronologically)

Jesus B.C. 7, 1351	Simon A.D. 2, 1365
James B.C. 3, 1357	Martha A.D. 3, 1350, -67
Miriam B.C. 2, 1357	Jude A.D. 5, 1370
Joseph A.D. 1, 1362	Amos A.D. 7, 1373
	Ruth A.D. 9, 1389

    chosen by Gabriel, 1344
    confused by J, 1387
    educated, good teachers, religious views differed,1349
    evolution of religion, 1344-45
    family dwelling in Nazareth, location of, 1350
    fled with J just in time, 1354
    furniture, furnishings of, 1350
    genealogies of, constructed late, not factual, 1348
    good teachers, 1349
    married   March 8 B.C., J conceived Nov., 1345
    nominated by Family Commission of Twelve, 1344
    one night in clean stable, three weeks in inn, 1351
    selected from three nominee families, 1344
    started for Bethlehem Aug. 18, 7 B.C., 1350
    two years in Alexandria, 1354
    were poor, 1350, -54
Joshua, (see also "Jesus"), Caleb and, 1828
    "epochal sermon": "choose you this day whom you
        will serve", 1710
    name meaning the human J, 1351
Joshua ben Joseph, the human Christ,
    Gabriel to Mary, son, call him J, 1346
    Ganid called on J when in religious trouble, 1471
    historic fact of JbJ part of Christian belief, 1084
    "I sometimes think J is a prophet", 1467
    J born, circumcised, named Joshua, 1351
    J conferred with Satania enemies as human, 1493
    the Jewish baby, 1317
    never knew (on U) J was Jesus, (Ganid, Gonod), 1481
    Personalized Adjuster guided J while he was, 1200

Joshua ben Joseph, the human Christ (cont'd)
    successor to Moses, 1059, 1710
    the teacher, 1482
    "Uncle J, tell us a story", 1416
    unfortunate, believers overlook the hero, 1013
JOSIAH BEFORE THE SANHEDRIN, 1813
Josiah, blind man, 1812
    cast from synagogue, associated with Creator of
       universe, 1816
    destroyed corrupt politicians, 1074
    the healed blind beggar, 1812-13, 1873
    preacher, became life long, 1816
    spoke well for J, 1814-15
Jotapata, 1638, 1744
JOTAPATA, AT, 1638
JOURNEY UP THE COAST, THE, 1736
journey while you slumber, 431
Joy of Existence, The, 312
joy, hearts filled with j, J' followers, 1766
    highest of Paradise existence, 304
    in this world and eternally, 1537
    of spirit, consciously experienced in life, 2065
    returned manyfold for price...kingdom, 1537
    supreme, crucifixion bestowal of affection, 1944-45
       in existence, 312
       yielding spiritual harvest, 1945
    you cannot have real j by yourself, 1220
joys, independent of material, 381
    of living, divinely watered souls don't need environ-
       ment for, 381
    of loving activities, 1437
jubilee, celebrates light and life, 202
jubilees, seven, last at beginning of eternity service, 305
Judah, added (not true) to list of tribes in battle, 1072
    AND EPHRAIM, 1073
    AND ISRAEL, 1071
    end came suddenly, people taken to Babylon, 1075
    four miles west of Jerusalem, in the hills, 1346
    Jewish consciousness, origin in Judah, 1071
    tribe of, more gentile than Jewish, 1072
    undoing of, 1071, -74-75
Judahite editors (error), 1073
Judahites, always sought to defame Israelites, 1072
Judaism (religion), 1444
    mistake of, 43
    renaissance of, from Greek translation, scriptures,
       1338
JUDAS ISCARIOT (Apostle), 1565 (see under "Apostles")
JUDAS'S DOWNFALL, CAUSES OF, 2055
Jude (brother of Jesus), 2008
    all year family affairs smooth, but for, 1417
    and James, accompany J to John Baptist, 1504
       defended selves, 1401
       feared for own safety, 1721
    and others arrived after J on cross, 2007
    and Simon wished to marry, postponed, 1484
    born A. D. 5, 1370
    Capernaum synagogue, 1421
    conscientious, not, 1417
    jailed, 1415
    judgment not to be feared if, 1476
    kept promise, 1418
    marriage, sober senses after, 1417
    Mary, James, Joseph, Ruth responded to hasty call,
       1720
    patriotic outburst, unwise, 1416
    retained faith but let pride interfere, 1721
    sister-in-law heard alarming report, 1720
    trouble at Passover, 1415
    wanted to be fisherman, J helped, 1417

Jude (brother of Jesus) (cont'd)
    went with Mary and Ruth to J at end, 1997
    "you are mighty man of God", 1532
    zealots, 1415
judge (magistrate) sacred duty of a j, 1462
judge, not on basis of single unfortunate episode, 1739
    of all the earth, accounting, 1908
judges, appointed for life, and confirmed, 809
    choose only those wise by replete experience, 798
    hold degrees in statesmanship, 816-17
    integrity of, an index to civilization, 797
    one set of chiefs, were also teachers, 789
    when stand before j be not anxious beforehand, 1912
judgment, evaluate in light of enlightenment and
       conscience, 1115
    for all of us, 1918
    individual may be warped, 1764; distorted by
       passion, 1764
    is work of Stationary Sons of the Trinity, 114
    man presumes to sit in j on God, 1984
    mistaken (evil) becomes sin only when, 52
    of Deity, 218
    of man, based on "good servant", 274
    of mortal's life after death, 1231
    of this life in next world, 1918
    others' religions by your standards of truth, no, 1115
    we stand in presence of, 1915
judgment day of a new epoch, deceased sleep until, 341
judgment-decisions, how mind functions to exercise, 1295
judgments, 3 basic j or choices of mind, 2094
    self-judgment--moral choice
    social judgment--ethical choice
    God judgment--religious choice
JUDICIAL ACTIONS, 226
judicial mechanism of Nebadon, 372
judicial trusts, government, teaching, both sexes, 625
judiciary, should be of highest, most noble types, 247
Jupiter, planet, moons of, 656-57
Jupiter was a reveler, 773
Jurassic epoch, 688
jurisdiction, Pilate, Herod, 1992
jurors of Orvonton, the Supreme, 247
just, the j shall live by faith, 1682
Justa, J and apostles at home of, 1737
justice, administered by Trinity, 1146
    and equity prevail, 373
    and ideals, concepts of, powerful, 1302
    and mercy, 1638
JUSTICE AND RIGHTEOUSNESS, 36
justice, basic law, 1638
    "civil government is founded on j" (J), 1462
    delay, reasons for, 617
    evidence, judgment, 114
JUSTICE, EVOLUTION OF, 794
justice, function of j, performed collectively by Trinity,
       1146
    great nation, j for humblest citizen, 1462
    group function, not personal act, 1146
    it always is a plural function, 114
    it is never a personal act, 1146
    it is the Trinity attitude of love, mercy, ministry, 114
    makes a nation great (J), 1462
    may be slow...but it is certain, 616
    mercy, discourse, 114-15, 1468
    must be administered by brotherhood, 1764
    nature provides but one kind, 794
    never personal, group function, 1146
    not fairness but disposal of case, 797
    punishment is for groups, 1469
    slow but certain in universe, 616

justice (cont'd)
    supreme j can act instantly, 616
    sure and swift, 818 (see "police")
    tempered by mercy (Orvonton), 182
JUSTICE, TIME LAG OF, 615
justified by faith (see also "salvation by faith")
    saved, 1682
    "you are", 1610
Justus, devout merchant, host to J and Paul, 1472
    J took public women to Justus' home, 1472

K

ka and ba, Egyptians and Africans, 1215
Kaaba Stone, 967
    to Arabs, what Yahweh to Jews, 1051
kaleidescopic adjustments, pilgrims make k a in
    meanings, values, 428
Kanata, 1765
kangaroo, 732
Karkar, 1074
karma principle, close to truth of, 1030
Karuska, J at home of, Sidon woman, 1734
Kateri people, India, 944
Katro, ancestor of Moses, 1016

Kenites, 1024
    Hebrews knew of Trinity from K, 1144
    Melchizedek teachings, modified by Jews is
        Judaism, 1444
    Moses advances partly due to K traditions, 1058
    non-Hebrews, as were Calebites, Jebusites, 1072
    revered Salem teachings, 1052
Kentucky, volcano, 675; (coral, 678)
Keturah, concubine, not wife of Abraham, 1023
key to, perfection is imitation of God, 1221
    rebirth, 1602
keys of, kingdom, 1756, are (sincerity), 435
    outward kingdom, 1747
KHERESA LUNATIC, THE, 1695, 1765
KHERESA, THE VISIT TO, 1694, 1723, -41

ki

Kidron valley, 1912, -33
kindness, indiscriminate, 1580
    (wrong) makes social evils, 1580
kindred spirits, 71, 191, 1088
    not wholly a figure of speech, 82
king, "become our", 1580
    every inch (He) looked a k, 1702
KING-MAKING EPISODE, THE, 1702
"King of the Jews", 1994-96, 2000,-05, -07
King Pepi, 1045
King Saul, 1495
    and the witch of Endor, 1646
king, wise man is k (Stoics), 1991
"kingdom idea", not best way to illustrate, 1603
    why J used, 1603
KINGDOM OF GOD, 1500
kingdom of God (see also "kingdom of heaven")
    believe Father loves you, you are in, 1537
    "come with power, will", 1760
    has come near to you, 1801
    in hearts, 1193
    is not meat, drink, but righteousness, joy, 382,
        1536-37
    kingdoms of this world about to become, 1500
    memorable sermon of J on, 1536
    Urmia lectures (J), 1485

kingdom of God (cont'd)
    vs. kingdom of good, 40
    why this term, 1855
kingdom of God, new,
    apostles further instruction regard to, 1588
    apostles, work with him establishing, 1524
    I would learn all about the, 1524
    "my Father is about to set up in hearts...", 1568
KINGDOM OF HEAVEN, THE, 1858
kingdom of heaven (in this list, "kingdom" and "kingdom
    of heaven" are treated as one)
    Abner, to end, faithful teacher of... 1832
    Abnerian vs. Pauline Christianity, 1869
    "acceptance of divine sonship", 1727
    "act as ambassadors of my F's", 1571
    admission to, 1802 (see also "kingdom, price to
        enter")
    advanced not, by mass healing, 1633
    all welcome, 1541
    all who truly desire eternal life, 1829
    ambassadors of spiritual k receive real rewards in
        another world, 804
    anger, not a part of the, 1725
    at hand, 1901-02
    begins with and centers in, 1859
    being divested of lukewarm, half-hearted, 1715
    being righteous by faith, must precede doing
        righteousness, 1584
    believe in F, status in heavenly citizenship sure, 1601
    believer enters k now, by faith, 1861
    believers, now better world citizens, 1930
    birth of spirit into light of faith, 1705
    brotherhood of k, 1803
    "builder, true believer is", 1740
    built on truth of union (human and divine), 1748
    business of, 1565
    cannot stand still in k, 1917
    cardinal features of, 1863
    chosen apostles, set apart for service of, 1577
    church humanized shadow of J' intended, 1865
    church, vs. k, 1866
    come only through much sorrow, 1687
    comes through change in hearts, 1533
    concept of k changed to cult of eternal life, 1861
KINGDOM, CONCEPTS OF THE, 1858
kingdom of heaven, consists in three essentials, 1585
    continuance therein, how, 1682
    a divine family, 1676
    the divine government, founded on... 1486
    doctrine of J, k never been tried, 1863
    double nature of, here, in heaven, 1860
    earth never tried ideals of, 1863
    endows human living with 7 things, 1859
    enter, to, 1861
    entrance free, 1682 (see also "kingdom, price to
        enter")
    essentials to enter by faith, 1861
    establish in own soul, 1863
    "established by unselfish service", 1725
    evolutionary experience, 1603
    experience man can't contain, 1862
    failed, has largely, on earth, 1866
    failing to establish k, J followers set it off into
        future, 1865
    "faith adventure, Father's k in the hearts of men",
        1750
    faith gift which insures admission to, 1593
    faith only required, 1537, -45, -59, 1656 (see also
        "faith")
    faithful to k in prosperity, be, 1931

kingdom of heaven (cont'd)

KINGDOM, THE FATHER AND HIS, 1855

kingdom of heaven, first k, all else added, 1536, -69, -78
    five phases or epochs of, noted by J, 1862
    "founded on love", 1725
    four distinct groups of ideas, 1859
    four steps of inner righteousness, 1862
    from earth up through stages to Paradise, 1603
    future, set off in k, why, 1865
    "gentiles, shall be taken by the g", 1735
    "God is your Father, you are his sons", 1593
    "gospel messengers have forsaken all to proclaim",
        1801
    gospel vs. Christianity's, 2091
    great day of the k judgment, 1571
    has largely failed on earth, 1866
    heavenly citizenship, 1829
    idea distorted, 1864
    ideas, embraces four distinct groups of i, 1858
    "if you'd enter, have a righteousness...", 1576
    in Christian era, four groups of ideas, 1859
    in coming k no negative, restraints, 1600
    in heart of believer, death blow to this concept, 1865
    in hearts, 1525, -44, 1634, 1730, -50
    in hearts of men, coming, 1544
    in, if faith in F's love, 1537
    in service of k, lay not up treasures, 1577
    inner, true religion of k, 1862, -67
    "is at hand" (John Baptist), 1502, -06, -37
    is brotherhood of citizens born again, 1568
    is an exclusively spiritual brotherhood, 1088
    is family of God, 1860-61
    is life of service, 1536
    is personal, fruits are social, 1862
    is a spiritual relationship, God and man, 1486
    "it is your Father's k you seek to enter, 1585
    J' concept now slumbers, 1866

KINGDOM, J' CONCEPT OF THE, 1859, -65

kingdom of heaven, J explained koh an evolutionary
        experience, 1603
    J knew koh was overthrow of evil in, 1522
    J never gave a precise definition of, 1862
    J regretted necessity of using word "kingdom", 1856
    J' return not connected with, 1860
    J taught always, man's personal experience... 1859
    J taught dual concept of, 1859-60
    J taught was personal experience, 1860

KINGDOM, J' TEACHING ABOUT THE, 1862

kingdom of heaven, J' various terms for, 1861
    John (Baptist) thought it was due to dawn, 1498
    keys of, 435
    last year's preaching, more spiritual phases of k,
        1704

KINGDOM, LATER IDEAS OF, 1864

kingdom of heaven, lesser things should give way for,
        1797
    life hidden in security of, 1916
    life, new, in the, 1592
    life of righteousness and joy in service, 1536-37
    like a mustard seed, 1583
    many nominally accept k, 1931
    Master taught many new, advanced truths of, 1593
    "mighty messenger of the" (John Mark), 1921
    modified by two tendencies, 1864
    my k is not of this world, 1536, -43, 1750, -58, 1870,
        1881, 1914, -91, 2035 (see also under "Jesus,
        Quotes")
    "my k is a spiritual dominion", 1991
    mysteries of k, have taught, 1934
    naught of material, 1605

kingdom of heaven (cont'd)

    new concept of double nature of k, 1860
    no admission without faith of little child, 1536
    no man can close door in face of hungry soul, 1541
    no matter price you pay, manyfold joy, 1537
    not best way to illustrate relation to God, 1603
    not of this world (see "kingdom is not of this world"
        under "Jesus, Quotes")
    not "a rule of power or reign of glory", 1544
    not to come with noise and glamor, 1533
    now, 1861
    now among you, 1536
    of the Father, 1571
    of good, 40
    of spiritual pre-eminence, 1862
    (on high) a realm of order, 1959
    only a divine koh built on so mediocre... 1564
    open, for faith to enter, 1826
    open to all, 1541, -68
    overthrow of evil in mens' hearts, 1522
    pathway to trouble, 1767
    Persian teaching of, 1858
    price of admission (part of) pet evil, 1802
    privileges of ambassador, 1981
    "proclaimed in mercy", 1725
    prophetic forecast of k in ages to come, 1864
    realm of order, 1959
    rule of living within the k, 1596
    search for new koh in your hearts, 1525
    seek first the, 1578

SERMON ON THE KINGDOM, 1535

    since God is a spirit, k is spiritual, 1486
    so "near at hand", 1597
    social, economic, political reforms not business
        of the, 1565
    sons of k double responsibility, 1930
    sons of k third and sacred obligation, 1930
    sorrow, would come only through s, 1687
    spiritual, not grasped, 1579
    steps (4) of human righteousness, 1862
    steps of inner righteousness, 1862
    take it by spiritual assault, 1726
    the talk about, 1746
    task of J, 1520
    term should have separated it from earthly, 1858
    these Monitors become koh within you, 1193
    this k is a divine family, 1676
    three essentials, 1585
    to be built on combined nature of J, 1748
    to enter the k, 1861 (see also "price, to enter
        kingdom", "faith", and "faith, only requisite")
    to gentiles became Church, 1865
    to J was believers, 1865
    to Jews meant, righteous state, Messiah, 1500
    to Jews was Israelites, 1865
    training messengers of, 1538
    "treasures of, within reach of faith", 1766
    two truths of first import in teachings of, 1593
    unfortunate use of word k, persecution, 2072
    various terms J used for k, 1861
    vs. kingdoms this world, 1929
    vs. "trust in riches", 1803
    way of light which leads to the entrance, 1710
    wealth and the k, 1802-03
    whatever price you pay, receive manyfold, 1537
    when John Baptist finished will proclaim, 1532
    when k comes, approaching age of improved human
        relations, 1862
    which of five phases, 1863
    why put off in future, 1865

kingdom of heaven (cont'd)
will be proclaimed to ALL, 1864
"within you", 1193, 1861, -67
worth the price, 1537, 1761
would come by sorrow, 1687
"you are in koh when Father's will... yours", 1589
you who believe... are sons of God, 1601

KINGDOM OF ISRAEL, 1070
vanished, 1074
KINGDOM OF JUDAH, 1070
end of, 1075
"kingdom of life" (J often said), 1861
kingdom of light, Judas' passage from k to darkness, 1567

kingdom, price to enter (see also "choosing", "faith,
    salvation by", "salvation")
"ask and you shall receive", law of universe, 1838
become as little children, 1585
believe... accept forgiveness... by faith recognize
    spirit of God, 1682
believing, by simple, sincere faith, 1584
by faith, born again, children of eternal life, 2052
by faith, every mortal may have... salvation, 1586
by faith in fatherhood, you may enter, 1596
"cannot earn righteousness, salvation is gift...", 1683
change of mind by faith, the new birth, 1545
Creator bestows favor in response to faith, 1032
dedication to doing Father's will, 1829
desire to enter k, take it by spiritual assault, 1726
divine favor for nothing, by faith, 1017
divine inheritance but for the asking, 1113
door... wide open... (price) faith of one who comes,
    1567
enter by faith, progress by works, 1569, -83
faith alone pass you through its portals, 1569
faith and trusting dependence of child, 1536
faith, the connection between... and enduring reality,
    1116
faith gift... insures admission to k, 1593
faith is key to the door, 1861
faith only necessary in finding God, 1559
faith, passport to eternity of life, 1117
faith, the saving truth of gospel, 2052
faith... which leads to life everlasting, 1796
for divine favor, trust in... God, Salem, 1027
"I will give eternal life to all who will become faith
    sons", 1963
"if you believe it, is your eternal salvation", 1593
J taught, by faith believer enters k now, 1861
k... result of believing the good news, 2054
new birth, required as admission, 1545
"possess by faith, gift of eternal life", 2053
repaid manyfold, 1537
salvation, favor with God, by faith, 1021
salvation is by regeneration of the spirit, 1610
"salvation is the free gift of God", 2054
"salvation is a free gift to all who have faith", 1838

salvation out of faith-realization of child-father, 1585
"salvation... those willing to receive such gifts", 2019
salvation through faith, 1028
"survival dependent on being born of the spirit", 2054
treasures of k within grasp of faith, 1766
wholly free, but growth in grace, to continue, 1682
"whosoever will may come" price is faith, 1567
you are justified by faith, 1610
you have eternal life, as gift, through faith, 2043

KINGDOM'S MESSENGERS, TRAINING THE, 1538
kingdoms of earth, paltry things, 1522
Kingdoms of Men, Urmia lectures (J), 1485
kings and queens, origin of idea, 632
kings say "love, let us cast away the cords of", 1725
kinship, of divine spontaneity in all personality, 71
    to Deity resists against disharmony, confusion, sin,
        361
    with Deity, faith realized, 1289
Kirmeth of Bagdad, 1666
Kish, 1043
kiss, embrace, traitorous, 1974
kiss, J washed apostles' feet, did not k, 1939
kissing, origin, saliva, 787

knotted cords, (beads?), 1681
know, God as your Father, man as your brother, 1091
    how do you k that I don't k, 1125
    how shall we k, 1601
    most important thing to, 2090
    yourself as angels k you (help to), 553
knowledge, 557
    accumulation of protoplasmic memory material, 1111
    activated emotionally!, 1090
    and wisdom, 908, 2076
    culture, and wisdom, do not confuse, 1780
KNOWLEDGE, THE CUSTODIANS OF, 301
knowledge, disconcerting, a little k is, 2076
    the faculty on dissemination and conservation of, 746
KNOWLEDGE, GOD'S UNIVERSAL, 48
knowledge, in k alone, no certainty, but religionist
    knows, 1120
    insight, needs k of religion, 2076
    is an eternal quest, 1120
    is possessed only by sharing, 280, 557
    is relative, 42
    leads to placing men, social strata, castes, 1122
    a little k is truly disconcerting, 2076
    living accumulation of all k, 302
    mere pursuit of, despair, 2076
    most valuable of human k, J, 2090
    never k of absolute truth, 1120
    of greatest value (J), 2090
    of religious experience, is superhuman, 1142
    only antidote for so-called accidental ills, 957
    partial k is potentially evil because, 42
    religious, certainty of, superhuman k, 1142
KNOWLEDGE, SCIENTIFIC, 907
knowledge, seven million subdivisions, 302
KNOWLEDGE, THE SPIRIT OF, 402
knowledge, time is required to gain k, religion's endow-
    ments are "now", 1120
    unearned, premature, proscribed, 1109
    vs. truth, 1435, -59
KNOWLEDGE, WISDOM, AND INSIGHT, 1121
knowledge, wisdom, insight, science, philosophy,
    religion, 1122
    wisdom, needs interpretation of w, 2076
    wisdom, religion, revelation, 1122
    withheld from local u personalities, 410
    without character, 2086
knowledge and truth, not till show you can impart it, 280

Kopet Dagh, east of south end, Caspian, 862
Kopet mountains, 868
Koran, 917, 962
Kung Fu-tze (Confucius), 1034
Kush, 1048

L

labor, all earthly labor a service to Father, 1960, 2049
  becoming more honorable, 814
  "come all ye who labor", 1590, 1627, 1808
  division of, first result of organization, 773
  early specialization of, 5 divisions, 773
  efforts of design, 773
  is ennobling, drudgery is benumbing, 786
  lessened effort, shortened days, social progress, 907
  no secular, 1960
  no such thing as common, 1960
  production of lower levels of labor, control, 771
LABOR, THE SPECIALIZATION OF, 773
labor, compulsory,
  abolished usually upon Adamic arrival, 585
  common laborers used as are horses, cattle
    585
labor, stormy, childbirth or spiritual birth, 1130
laboratories, cosmic evolutionary, 740
"laborers are few", 1800
ladder, living, whereby man climbs from chaos to
  glory, 107
Lake Van, 1021
  and Caspian Sea region "mighty men of old", 822, 860
  still exists, 860
lakes and streams-Edentia, 485
lamb, 946
"lambs, as lambs among wolves", 1800
Lamech's exultation, 1764
"lamp of the body is the eye", 1577
"lamps burning before the throne", 378
Lanaforge, 511; (system sovereign), 808, 853
  upon arrival of L archrebels dethroned, 609
land, yield reduced, struggle follows, 770
land animals, suddenly, 680
land bridges, Bering Strait (see "Bering Strait land
  bridge")
  connecting E.W. hemispheres disappear, 683
  Sicilian, to Africa, 826, 891
LAND-EMERGENCE STAGE, THE GREAT, 678
land-life period, the vegetative, 678
land-man ratio, 768-70, 887, 908
land masses, separated, 663, 668
  still connected, 683
land of Nod, 758, 837, 849, 859
land plants, suddenly, 689
LAND STAGE, THE NEW CONTINENTAL, 693
LAND TECHNIQUES — MAINTENANCE ARTS, 768
landing and dispatching fields, Paradise, 721
landscape of time, from perspective of broadened
  horizons, 1296
language, and alphabet, mechanisms and mind, 2080
  and civilization, 630, 908
  as factor in U civilization, 908
  can't express reality of infinity, 1261
  differences, barrier to peace, 908
LANGUAGE, EFFECTIVENESS OF, 908
language, greatest, most serviceable thinking tool, 908
  handicap, inadequate to explain, 32-33
  impossible to depict religious experience, 2096
  little needed, central U, 503
  ours, gross and limited, 501
  peace rarely attained before common language, 594
  symbolic of concepts, 630
  universal, 807
    lost hope due to Lucifer, 746
    promotes peace, culture, happiness, 908
languages, modern, from early central Asian tribes, 872

languages, (con't)
  three prevailed in Palestine, time of J, 1338
  universe, etc., 537, 546
LANONANDEK RULERS, THE, 393
LANONANDEK SONS, THE, 392
  Satan, 754
LANONANDEK WORLDS, THE, 394
Lanonandeks, Primary, 392
  Secondary, 392
  Tertiary, 392
Lao-tse, 1009, 1339
LAO-TSE AND CONFUCIUS, 1033
Lao-tse, never taught error, seeing, doing, thinking
  nothing, 1034
  taught "faith in God will remake the world", 1034
Laotta, 843, 847
Lapland, 893
Lapps and Eskimos, 905
larval stage, church is in larval s of J' teachings, 1866
LAST ANDITE DISPERSIONS, 873
LAST DAYS AT CAPERNAUM, 1717
last is first, least becomes greatest, 466
LAST SUPPER, THE, 1936 (see also "communion" and
  "remembrance supper")
latent powers for good, 1777
LATER EVOLUTION OF RELIGION, THE, 1003
laughter, primitive man smiles, knew no, 714
  spiritual laughter in survival, 550
launching, enseraphimed, 438
lava bed, sub-crustal, stabilized U, 662
law, and love interrelationship through Trinity, 1145
  and the Trinity, 114
  at first always negative and prohibitive, 796
  cannot advance morality, 193
  a covenant, took place of luck, 983
  -directed subjects vs. privileged sons, 1588
  divine ordinances, violation, 1662
LAW FORECASTERS, 432
law, "great, long known to us", 1669
  inexorable, impersonal, equivalent to providence, 137
  the intellectual foundation of justice is, 432
  is life itself, not the rules, 555
  is unchanging reaction of an infinite, perfect, divine
    mind, 137
LAW, LIBERTY AND SOVEREIGNTY (J on), 1490
law, libraries, living and circulating (Technical
  Advisers), 414
  nation passing from negative to positive, 818
  new, endows you with liberty of self-mastery, 1609
  new law of spirit vs. old law, 1609
  "observe the...law" (J), 1906
  of God destroys the sin, 41
  of human fairness (G.R.), 614, 1931
  of human society, 769
  of justice, basic for selfish, 1638
    mercy can't circumvent, 1638
  "of love, supreme", 1560
  of the spirit, 1689
  of the universe: ask and you shall receive: seek and
    you shall find, 1838
  Oriental--stern and arbitrary, 2072
    Greek--was fluid, artistic, 2072
    Roman--was dignified, respect-breeding, 2072
  population, land arts, standard of living, 769
  Roman, 2072
  spoken law higher authority than written, 1340
  universal, recognize reality of Paradise Deity as
    u law, 1145
lawgiver, there is only one, 46
LAWS AND COURTS, 796

laws (cont'd)
    civil, J observed all, 1580
    disdain of laws turns spirit ears away, 1638
    divine transgressed, unintentional, deliberate, 1660
    few in ideal state, 803
    first negative,   then positive, 796, 803
    game, first, 781
    govern large number, not an individual, 478
    great, 1633, -39, -69
    in spirit world, reliable as material, 505
    maintain order, 1763
    natural, cosmic technique of Paradise, 468
    of the Garden, 836
    of God are habits of God, 137, <u>1222</u>
    of human society, 769
    of living, two fundamental:fatherhood, brotherhood,
       1603
    of nature, laws of God, 2072
       seem dual realms, physical, spiritual, in reality
       are one, 481
    of relation to Father's will, 1660
    of spirit, mind, and matter, God speaks in, 1638
    spirit law real, as physical, 82
    spiritual, reliable as material, 505
    unchanging, are habits of an unchanging God, 1126
    uniform, world, universe, 1736
lawyers, 1833
    have taken key of knowledge from people, 1826
    near kingdom, 1901
    rebuked, 1826
    to entangle J, 1809
    "woe upon you", 1826
layman, J, 2091
    world's greatest religious teacher was, 2091
Lazarus, 1415, 1606, 1837, 2058, -71
LAZARUS, AT THE TOMB OF, 1843
Lazarus, died on Sunday, resurrected Thursday, 1846
    fled to Philadelphia, 1869, -97, 1927, -32, -34, -76
    hasty flight from Bethany, 1849, 1932
    "if you had been here, L would not have died", 1842-43
    J advised L to flee, 1880, -97
    J foresaw persecution of, 1844
    J said farewell to L, instructed him to flee, 1897
    Jewish leaders decreed L' death, 1849, -80
    loved J after discussion, 1380
    Martha, Mary, 1375, -80, -99, 1404, 1595
    persecution, harassment, 1869
    raised because villagers already believed, 1880
<u>LAZARUS, THE RESURRECTION OF</u>, 1842, -45
Lazarus, second death of L in Perea at 67, 1849
    T A of L detained on U, 1844
LAZARUS, WHAT BECAME OF, 1849
lazy ethically, socially indifferent, 1457
lazy peoples, compelled to work by slavery, 779

le

lead only hungry to God, 1466
lead, two weights of, 474
"lead us not into temptation",why?, 1738
LEADERS, THE GREAT RELIGIOUS, 1008
leaders, great, why? (T A), 1198
    ignorant religious leaders of J' time, 865
    must come from, 786
    needed, 2082
LEADERS OF REBELLION, THE, 601
leaders, religious, great mistake, 2077
    thanks to Adjusters, 1198
    to discover leaders society must turn to...786
leadership, always for group, 1959
    and inspiration in spiritual renaissance, 2083

leadership (cont'd)   **L**
    as factor in U civilization, 911
    call to, 2082
    dependent on, 1739
    effective and wise, 911
    in all group relationships, 1959
    (on high) for groups, 1959
    religion does need new, 2082
    wise leadership has never exceeded 1%, 911, 1008, -90
leadings, divine, 379
    unconscious, 1475
Leah, daughter of Philip, prophetess of Hierapolis, 1858
learn to fail gracefully, 1779
learned men, in love with J, 1810
learner, if you are willing learner Spirit will lead, 381
learning, how to live, 1548
    is discovering, 1573
    less important than experience, 435
    100, 000 years learning in one hour, 503
    "pride of unspiritualized learning is treacherous",1433
"leave system of religious ethics" (to J), 1329
"leaven, put leaven of new truth in old beliefs", 1932
LECTURES AT URMIA (24), 1485
led astray by own natural tendencies,1609
left hand not know, 1577, -83
LEGEND OF CREATION, THE, 836
legislation, cannot secure social growth, 1097
LEGISLATIVE AND EXECUTIVE FUNCTIONS, THE
    (local u), 373
legislative function ceases when...633
legislative, judicial, authority, 1764
leisure, for self improvement and planet advancement,
    595
    from machines good if used for valuable tasks, 909
    Havona, after arrival, 343
    must have ambition, 907
    must produce, 803
    necessary to civilization, 907
    required to build civilization, 769
    to think essential to civilization, 902
    unearned leisure may be greatest of human
       afflictions, 1305
lemur, ancestors of human species from N. A., 733
    N. A. types' migrant descendants, dawn mammals!,
       700
    present lemur not ancestor to man, 703
LEMUR TYPES, THE EARLY, 703
lemurlike (our) ancestor, narrow escapes, 706
lemurs, true lemurs sprang from ancestors (in N. A.),
    696
lemurs' ancestors appear, 696
"lend, but you shall not borrow" (Moses), 1058
leper, first miracle intentionally performed, 1644
    healing, 1643-44
lepers, ten, only Samaritan thanked J, 1827-28
leprosy, 1827
lesson, important, teamwork, 312
LESSON ON SELF-MASTERY, 1609
LESSON REGARDING CONTENTMENT, 1674
lessons, evening, titles of J', 1683
LESSONS FROM THE CROSS, 2017
"let us make mortal man in our image", 78
"let us now go forth to take the kingdom", 1579
lethal submergence, drowning of Cro-Magnons, 893
"let's go", Thomas, 1562
Levant, Caucasoid and Negroid blended, 905
    Graeco-Romans turned to mystery cults of L, 1081
    peoples consummated marriage by sex act, 924
    peoples' religion was modified by Sethites, 1007
    peoples settled on coast and up rivers, 885

Levant (cont'd)

peoples' taboo, never ate apples, 967
spiritual revival and recognition of monotheism, 1078
was homeland of faiths of Occidental world, 1042
Levantine, mystery religions, degraded, 1081
Levantine race, Jews, part Occidental, part Oriental, 1332
Levantines, Jews, eminently fitted to receive J, 1332
part Occidental, part Oriental, 1332
level of experiential Deity, the, 1170-72
level of the I AM, the, 1170,-72-73
level of three Trinities, the, 1170-71
levels, cosmological (3), 646
of cosmic evolution reflected in 3 ways, 1210
of decisions (7), 1650
of deity function, seven, 1030
of functional activity (7), 1162-63
of mind reality, 192, 195
LEVELS OF REALITY, UNIVERSE, 1162
levels, of wisdom, 806
three of cosmologic thought, 646
lever, God's hand is on mighty lever of realms, 52
Levites, 1794, 1810
and priests, 1502
"hear what children of the L say?", 1890

Ii

LIAISON STABILIZERS, 544
"liberate man's spiritual nature" (to J), 1328
liberties, liquid liberties of enlightened sonship, 1728
natural, 614
will increase under world government, 1491
liberty, after gaining, men must prevent: (12), 798
Liberty, Declaration of (Lucifer Manifesto), 603
liberty, false and true, 613
false, the assumption of self-assertion, 614
finality of, only for finaliters, 435
highest form, 2060
human, through truth, 1594
into license, primitives, 758
must be, disciplined by wisdom, 1923
motivated by loyalty, 1923
restrained by love, 1923
subject to group regulation, 906
needs compensation by liaison with spirit, 1302
of children in modern homes, not restrained, etc.,
1923
of faith, 1565
of living vs. license of sinning, 1655
"of mankind, gospel is good news for", 2033
of self-mastery, 1609
self-destroying technique when, 613
self-motivated liberty an illusion, cruel deception, 613
spurious personal liberty, Lucifer, 601
suicidal when, 613
taught prematurely, bad results, 759
LIBERTY, THE THEFT OF, 614
LIBERTY, TRUE AND FALSE, 613
liberty, true liberty is fruit of self-control, 614
without conquest of self is a figment of...613
vs. fear, 1609
"where spirit of Lord is, there is", 2063, -65
without restrictions is dream, 906
libraries, J visited Greek, Latin, in Rome, 1455
living, 7 million divisions of knowledge, 302
library, Alexandria, J and Ganid visited greatest in
world, 1432
living...technical adviser, 280
license is forerunner of abject bondage, 613
licking evil, overcome it with good, 1770

life, adjudication, 314
after death (see "eternal life")
aimless without worthy goal, 1572
all creature life beset by inevitabilities, 51
LIFE AND TEACHINGS OF JESUS, 1323, PART IV of
URANTIA BOOK (see also "Jesus" sections)
life, "as all life is in your hands", 1964
as such, constitutes...404
believers must learn to escape the rush of, 1739
bestowal of life, result, self-perpetuation, self-
propagation, self-adaptation, 1301
biological unit of, 560
celestial--at least 70 major divisions, 487
cheap or dear depending on land-man ratio, 769-70
chief purpose of, doing F's will, 1951
circuits of system, attuned to, 742, 745
continues because, 1459
cult of taking no life arose, 1029
"dedicated to gospel, needs met", 1823
-determining trio (on high), 396
differs, 560
does not originate spontaneously, 396
Edentia, 10 divisions of material, 492
efforts, to multiply fruits, 1778
equilibrium of energies and intellect, 1229
essence of, is spirit, 467
essentials of temporal (Rodan), 1778
LIFE ESTABLISHMENT ON URANTIA, 664
life, eternal voyage of discovery, 159
events, 3 kinds, 1830
everlasting, 1096, 1459, 1900
existent, because, 731
expectancy, 25 to 500 years, 564
fabricated from energies and material, 730
Fatherlike life, predicated on, 1175
final goal of, 1435
500,000 years to establish life new world, 400
force-energy is gravity responsive, life is not, 404
forms of (10), 492
formula, experiments, 735
four stages of, 1748
full summation of life (3 things), 2094
fully resistant to amazing flood of space rays, 667
future, 532
groups, 7 basic on Havona, 156
"has gone forth from me", 1669
has a universe function, 1459
human, can't end--why, 1460
human, an instant of time, 1232
ideal life for each human foreordained pattern by T A,
1204
ideal life of loving service, not fearful apprehension,
1206
implantations on Urantia (why 3), 668
impossible except for atmosphere's "blanketing"
effect, 666
LIFE IN DALAMATIA, 750
life, in flesh to life in the morontia, 2020
LIFE IN THE GARDEN, 835
LIFE IN HAVONA, 158
LIFE IN MESOPOTAMIA, 849
life, inherent capacity for...universal energy, 457
initiated, but lacking 2 essential attributes, 404
initiated only one way, 568
LIFE, THE INNER, 1219
life, innocent sometimes suffer this first life, 1663
intelligent, universe pattern, 173
intelligent, who can decree extinction, 396
inward readjustment, is to U too, 1438
is an adaptation, 1434

life

life (cont'd)

Life Carriers (cont'd)
LIFE CARRIERS, MELCHIZEDEK, 400
Life Carriers, not allowed to influence moral creatures, 400
LIFE CARRIERS, ORIGIN AND NATURE OF, 396
Life Carriers, papers by, 651-730
  petition of, 1312
  planned new type mortals to be teacher-leaders, 856
  request administrative head for planet, 572
  three independent implantations, U, 731
  through when will appears, 400
  two resident on U, 500,000 years ago, (722),742
life-carrying bundle (24 pattern units), (our scientists say "23"), 398
life-creation era, 204
life currents, Satania, on U, 857
LIFE-DAWN ERA, THE, 667
life "defined": constitutes the animation of some pattern-configured...system of energy...404
  endless change of factors of life unified by...1235
  essence of life is spirit, 467
  existence of...equilibrium of energies and intellect, 1229
  a process which takes place between the organism... and its environment, 1227
life-determining trio, local universe: Gabriel, Melchizedek, Nambia, 396
life endowment, added to association of energy-matter plus "breath of life", 404
life eternal, all who believe in Son, 1711
  "ceaseless progression in grace, truth, glory", 1953
  "for all who follow", 1815
  is gift, 1802,-38 (see "eternal life", "salvation")
  is gift of the Father's living spirit, 1642
  glorious progression, 1604
  to gain,
    believe gospel, accept forgiveness, have faith,1682
    give up pet evil, 1802
    love Lord God, and neighbor, 1809
life eternal plan (salvation)
  Bestowal Plan, 85,454
  Plan of Mercy Ministry, 85,95
  Plan of Perfection Attainment, 54,85,645
  The Salvage Plan, 39,85
LIFE-EVOLUTION VICISSITUDES, 736
LIFE, EVOLUTIONARY TECHNIQUES OF, 737
life experiment, unique features on U, 735
life implantation, American, produced human's ancestors, 703
  central, eastern, western, 667
life (like Father), predicated on truth, sensitive to beauty, dominated by goodness, 1175
life machine, evolution has provided you a life machine (body), 1216
life mode, can't radically modify, 749,767
life-modification world, unforeseen development, Nodites, 857
life-modifications, U, serviceable to all Nebadon, 735
life, natural, is wholly transient as to individualities, 1106
life, new orders of
  angiosperms, fig trees, tulip trees suddenly, 689
  appear suddenly (don't evolve), 669
  flowering plants, suddenly, 691
  natural genetic biologic mutations, 669
  true scorpions, air breathers, suddenly, 678
life, order of, beyond range of human imagination, 328
life, our first, this is, 26,158,221
  birth sphere of spirits of Paradise ascension, 1675
  first link in chain through...ages, 435

life, our first, this is (cont'd)
  initial life of material existence, 158
  initial life of mortals, always a struggle, 578
  innocent often suffer in this first life, 1663
  present mortal state but a vestibule, 1225
  second generation of soul is...1459
  U is starting point, 1225
life patterns on U, in cooperation with spiritual powers, 667
life plasm of Andon descendants transplanted, 742
life requisites, 1616
  worship, alternate with service
  work, with play
  religion, balance with humor
  philosophy relieve by poetry
  strain, relax by worship
  insecurity, antidote by faith...
lifeless instead catalyzed by vital spark, 399
life's function is finding God, 1459
life's struggles, three, 910

light, and electricity--not basic energies, 456
  children of light, all will see J, 1919
  clear light did not come to lad J, 1382
  has weight, 173,460
  highly explosive, 460
  "his life shall be the light of mankind" (Gabriel),1347
  "I am the light of the world", 1795,1903
  is real, 460
  is a real substance, 172
  let your light shine, 1571,1692
  Material Sons saturated with celestial light, 581
  of life, divine spirit personality, 118
  of life, or temporal prince, Messiah?, 1382
  "of the world, I am the...", 1795,1903
LIGHT OF THE WORLD, SERMON ON THE, 1794
light, "of the world, you are the", 1570,-72
  on Jerusem, system capital, 519-20
  pilot light in human mind, when disappears, 1246
  proof that light has weight, 172
  spiritual, produces celestial harmony, 499
  succession of energy particles, 475
  three-fold, for Paradise and Havona, 149
  three kinds in universe: material, intellectual insight, spirit luminosity, 9
  true light that lights every man, 1104
  waves, no, 461
  without heat, 47,143,172,174,323
light and life, 1291-92
  achieved despite natural history of a planet, 600
  achieved personally by J on U, 636
  Adams usually prevail until, 584
  admission of planet to light and life marked by temple, 622
  advanced stages of world settled in, 629
  "believers passing from...judgment to light and life", 1649
  competitive activities prevail, 630
  connection with Mother (Creative) Spirit, ages of, 204
  education, competitive, for mastery of truth, beauty, goodness, 625
  end of: idleness, friction, poverty, social inequality, degeneracy, 629
  era of light and life is 7th, final, developmental e, 577
  evolutionary ages to light and life, 1000 years or more, 598
  evolutionary goal of planet, 232
  first stage only before one language, one religion, 626
  first to seventh stage of, 627
  future spiritual age, epoch of kingdom, 1863

166

light and life (cont'd)
    government financed by tithing, 625
    in era of light and life many exempted from death, 570
    J personally achieved status of, 636
    life is refreshingly simple, 630
    local universe in circuits of light and life when, 177
    marks of universe ready for circuits of, 177
    natural resources are social possessions, community
        property, 625
    near perfection, System Sovereign proclaims, 599
    not one superuniverse even approaches, 635
    one language, one religion, one race, 624-25
    peace is threshold to utopian ages of, 820
    planets of light and life go on for eternity, 621
    race can be purged of detrimental, 627
    seven stages in unfoldment of era of, 621
LIGHT and LIFE, THE SPHERES OF, 621
light and life, stages of light and life as worlds achieve
        them, 627
    sublime foreshadowing of divine worlds, 630
    superuniverses will sometime attain to status of, 1163
    techniques, advanced, feasible when settled in, 1302
    Trinity Teacher Sons departure, then era of, 600
    universes will be settled in, 1290
    when U is settled in, 1025
light-energy, electron in collision gives up particle of,
        475   for mortals thro vegetative incarnation, 286
    particles of light-energy added or lost by electron
        orbital shifts, 475
light-rejecting cities, 1807
"light, true, which lights every man", 447
light years, activity 50 million light y beyond outer space
        level, 130
    beyond grand universe, area energy increasing 25
        million light years, 130
"lighted by the true light", 590
lighthouse, of Pharos, 1432   lightouses, suns are, 459
    "you will be like this lighthouse" (to Ganid), 1432
lightning, "God has made a way for the", 47
    (Satan) fall as, 490, 1807
"lilies, "consider the, how they grow", 1823
lily, roots in slime, 1737
    "white, like man" J, 1737
limestone, formed 2 ways, 661
limitation is "mechanism of universes", 1303
LIMITATIONS OF THE ETERNAL SON, 77
LIMITATIONS OF REVELATION, THE, 1109
limitations on (Creator Son) Universe Father, 236
limitless space on Paradise, 121
limits of mortal destiny, 116
linen coat, John Mark, 1963, -75
link, missing, nearest transition types, India, 720
"lips honor me, but hearts far from me", 1712
liquid liberties, from frozen religious forms (J), 1728
liquors, intoxicating, from plants, plants worshipped,
    945
list of antitheticals, courage, altruism, hope, etc., 51
literature, first of man, salt ad, 775
    oratory, flourish, 630
lithographic stone, Germany, 687
littleness not scorned, 1564
live, according to the trend of the universes, 1306
    divinely, means to live the will of God, 1175
    forever, united nature, God-man, 1711
    just two ways mortals may live together, 1775
    long as can on earth for kingdom, 1958
    more intensely in the present through maturing, 1295
    move, and have our being in the...Supreme, 1283
    or die by mind, (moral decisions), 1216
    peaceably, 1930

lives, "be not anxious for your lives", 1577   L
    many, succession of personality manifestations, 1459
    noble, above success, 2096
    "not to be worldlike", 1946
    of disciples, lead to believers, 1593
    three groups of events can occur in , 1830
LIVIAS, TEACHING AT, 1871-72
living, and dead, adjudication, 567
LIVING, THE ART OF, 1775
living, art of living must be remastered often, 1772
    efficient living comes from, 43
    enrich living with endowments of new life (7 things),
        1859
    for others, strength in, 1776
LIVING FORCES, 403
living, ladder, 107
    library, 302
    machines, 328
    making a living requires religion...for ideal
        solution, 1778
    mirrors, 308
    near God, 1579
    newspapers, 289
    noble, rewards spiritual, 2056
    one of most important things in, 2090
LIVING ORGANISM OF THE GRAND UNIVERSE, 1276
living, religion of J vs. theologic r, 2090
    right, spiritual prize, 2056
    rule of, 1650
    successful, 1773
    supreme experience of, 1431
    things strive for perfection, 373
    three incentives for living, 942
    two fundamental laws of, 1603
living death, persistence of material momentum,
        Adjuster gone, 1230
"living epistles", superaphic custodians of knowledge, 301
living law libraries, Technical Advisers, 280
living mirror, wisdom, philosophy, 311
living organisms (without vital spark) lack mind endow-
        ment and reproductive powers, 404
living religion of J should supplant religion about J, 2090
living spark of life, whence, 404
"living water, draught of the", 1613

Io

loathes, my Father loathes hypocrisy, abhors iniquity,
    1676
loaves and fishes, 1710
    elimination of time and visible life channel, 1702
"local" negative effects on God's plans and laws, 56
local self-interests, disintegrate society, 911
LOCAL SYSTEM ADMINISTRATION, THE, 509
local system description, 519
LOCAL SYSTEM HEADQUARTERS, THE, 519
LOCAL UNIVERSE, THE
    PART II of URANTIA BOOK, 357
LOCAL UNIVERSE, ADMINISTRATION OF THE, 366
LOCAL UNIVERSE CENTERS, 320-21
local universe, circuits, 177
    concerns: creation, evolution, maintenance,
        ministry, 372
LOCAL UNIVERSE CREATIVE SPIRITS, 203
local universe, denied right to pass on eternal life or
        death, 372
LOCAL UNIVERSE, GOD'S RELATION TO, 362
LOCAL UNIVERSE GROUPS, OTHER, 416
LOCAL UNIVERSE, MINISTERING SPIRITS OF THE, 418
LOCAL UNIVERSE MINISTRY OF THE DAYNALS, 231
LOCAL UNIVERSE MOTHER SPIRIT, THE, 374

local universe (cont'd)
    100 constellations, 166
    1/100,000 energy charge of Super U, 169
    ours not in settled order, 177
LOCAL UNIVERSE, PERMANENT CITIZENS OF THE,
    414
LOCAL UNIVERSE, PERSONALITIES OF THE, 406
local universe, something of everyone except F, 361
LOCAL UNIVERSE SONS OF GOD, 384
LOCAL UNIVERSE SOVEREIGNTY, 237
local universe time, 372
local universes, creators of the, 235
LOCAL UNIVERSES, EVOLUTION OF, 357
locations of races, after Adam and Eve, 868
locked door, seek the key, don't destroy, 1778
logic, and mathematics, not always reliable, 1476
    is attempted technique of philosophy, 1106
    is (faith and reason), 1139
    is the synthetic...1139
    is the technique of philosophy, 1138
    realization of religion, not dependent on, 1107
    recognizes First Cause as It; soul affirms First
      Cause as He, 2093-94
loneliness, and spirit of truth, 2061
    escape from, 1985
    J felt, 2006
    J, terrible feeling of human, 1968
    tremendous sense of loneliness, bore down, Adam
      and Eve, 839
lonely, God-knowing can't be, 1291
longevity, early Sumerian kings vs. later, 857
    errors, 900 years actually 70, 858
longings, and ambitions, mortal satiated, 508
    spiritual, noble, 508, 2069
loom, cosmic, is material mind that carries morontia
    fabrics, 1217
Lord, God of Israel, 1598
    "God omnipotent reigns", 46
    "I believe...help my unbelief", 1757
    "I believe" (Josiah), 1816
    "(the) L does not afflict willingly", 1662
    "the L our God is one God", 115
    "whom L loves, he corrects", 1662
Lord's Prayer, origin, 1389, 1620, -40
    part of, 1511
Lord's Supper, celebrated correctly, fellowship meal,
    then cup, 2067
    truce between ego and altruistic urge of T A, 1133
losing self, intelligent self-surrender, 2065
loss, cultural loss due to no hdqtrs schools, 587, 588
    of existence, greatest punishment for wrongdoing or
      rebellion, 37 (see also "annihilation" and
      "cessation of existence")
lost, "have come to seek and save the", 1750
    nothing of survival value is ever lost, 1197, 1200-01
    record of Apostle Andrew, used in U Book, 1341
Lot, 1019, -59

love

love, about Father's, 1289
    accept freely, 1740
    "all men as I have loved you", 2053 (see "command-
      ment, new" under "Jesus, Quotes")
    all true love is from God, 1289
    amazing discoveries of new and greater, 1289
    ancestor of all spiritual goodness, 2047
    and civilization, 1124
    and law in time space creations, 1145
    and psychology test, 1140
    and wisdom, more required in home, 1922
    and you forgive, 1898

love (cont'd)
    believe Father's love, to be in kingdom, 1537
    brother as yourself, 1603
    brotherhood, only, prevent aggression by strong, 805
    brothers more through sympathy, service...1956
    brothers, supreme experience, 1431
    Caligastia, in love with himself, 742
    can never be captured, 1289
    can turn into actual hate, 1927
    can't weigh in a balance, 2095
    character, not without genuine, 1775
    concept of love, generates superanimal effort, 2096
    conditioned by wisdom, qualified by loyalty, how, 43
    constantly reinterpreted, 1950
    dangerous and semiselfish trait in parents, 1922
    dead, when love is once really d, 1941
    defined, 41, 648
    "devote your life to proving love greatest", 2047
    "doesn't stop difficulties", 1945
    -dominated, the Father and Son, 618
    early, father loved Primate twins, 709
    enemies, 1134
    essence of religion, 1124
    "even divine love has severe disciplines", 1608
    experiment in thoughtless brotherly love, 2067
    fatherly, 1575, 1676
      vs. brotherly, 1573
    Father's, central truth of Universe, 2108
      is eternally creative, 2018
      is truly contagious, 2018
      real to man only by passing through him, 1289
    fellow men, love of, test of spirit, 1642
    finite being can feel impact of F's love, 50
    for cattle, not for wives (primitive), 769
    for ever-changing highest cosmic good of the loved
      one, 1950
    for God will be outpoured for fellow men, 1306
    fraternal, transcendental civilizer, 598
    genuine though man can't explain, 1140
    God's love overshadows each creature...time and
      eternity, 1304
    greater love hath no man, 2018
    greatest of all spirit realities, 1608
    hate, how love is turned to, 1927
    high order of love conditioned by wisdom, 43
    highest motivation, 2096
    home life requires more love and wisdom, 1922
    how to love people, 1098, 1419
    how to love your brothers more, 1955
    humanitarian fellowship, 2094
    is all-embracing of truth, beauty, goodness, 67
    "is the ancestor of all spiritual goodness", 2047
    is the desire to do good to others, 648
    is dynamic, 1289
    is the greatest thing in the universe, 648
    "is the greatest thing in the world", 2047
    is guide to true insight, 2076
    is infectious, more catching than hate, 1098
    is not God, 40
    is nurtured by service, 1898
    is only born of...understanding of...1098
    is perfected in wisdom, 1898
    is the secret of beneficial association between
      personalities, 141
    is sum total of truth, beauty, goodness, 648
    is supreme reality of universe when...1922
    is the supreme relationship, 1608
    J' a greater love than any hitherto on earth, 2019
    J loved men who sat in judgment on him, 1984
    "the Lord God", 1809

love (cont'd)
    a love that eclipses all other facts, 454
    make love of God real by loving others, 1949
    "makes old world new", 1945
    man can feel full impact of F's, 50
    man can't imprison God's love in own heart, 1289
    man may love, but explain?, 1140
    man receives divine love as he bestows love, 1289
    man who doesn't love might explain better than
        lover, 1140
    manifest fatherly love rather than brotherly, 1573
    measure of spirit guidance, 1642
    "men as I have loved you", 2041, -43, -47-48, -53, -57
    men because of their value, 1098
    men, not souls, 2043
    most truly divine, 1203
    must be restrained, 1923
    natural result of brotherly, 1862
    none apart from personality, 1183
    objective lure instead of subjective gratification, 1094
    of the Father, 38, 1288, 1305
       and Son, different, 76
    of a home, required for child to develop normal
        character, 1775
    of Master implies rehabilitation, 2018
    of neighbor and self-respect, 1740
    of people, 1412
    of a T A, most truly divine affection in creation, 1203
    of truth, desirable?, 51-52
    of wealth, 1802-03, -21-22
    "one another, even as I", 1944-46, -51, -55, -61,
      2042-44, -57 (see also "love all men", later
      teaching)
    "one another, through vicissitudes", 1932
    one more human each day, 1098
    only civilized man loves his grandchild, 750
    only God-knowing man can love another person as
        himself, 196
    others as self, possible only for, 196
    overwhelming sense of, 2009
    persons can only love and hate other persons, 44
    poor word for love of God, 40
    proof of liberty, 1609
    psychic illusion when, 2096
    "receive freely, and give", 1740
    receive freely regardless of your deserts, 1740
    redefined, must be, in progress, 2096
    result of being loved, 39
    search for God is unstinted bestowal of love...1289
    secret of beneficial association between persons, 141
    selfish quality of love, eliminate, 1096
    sentiment only, when, 2096
    sentiment--or real?, 2096
    sermon, on Mount, based on love, 1575
    should be admonished by wisdom, 1922
    spiritual deception when, 2096
    spiritual growth, inverse to selfish qualities of, 1096
    spiritual reality, greatest, 1608
    steps to, 1098
    supernal term needs to express God's love, 40
    supplies soil for religious growth, 1094
    supreme relationship, is, 1546, 1608, -15
    sweeps irresistibly through soul when...986
    through service, 1419
    to love others, bestow self as them, 1419
LOVE, THE TRIUMPH OF, 618
love, true love destroys hate, 2018
    true religion is a living love, 1100
    truly love, cannot through act of will, 1098
    turns sacrifice to joy, 1945

love (cont'd)
    turns to hate, 1927
    unselfish, and spirit endowment, 1228
    unselfish, is contagious, 1098
    urge to love vs. desire for salvation, 2017
    validity of, not judged by lover's capacity to explain,
      1140
    vs. duty (as motivation), 1945
    vs. mercy, 2018
    with startling affection, 2044
    without truth, beauty, goodness, only a
        philosophic distortion, 2096
        psychic illusion, 2096
        sentiment, 2096
        spiritual deception, 2096
    word painful to use due to mortal use of, 40
    yields supreme subjective gratification, 1094
    "your enemies", 1571, -80
    "your love a stumbling block for me", 1760
    your neighbor as yourself, 1445, 1769-70, 1862, 1901,
      1944, -50, 2054
    your neighbor, meaning "do good to", 1950
    your neighbor to respect self, 1740
love and marriage, need fullest examination, 929
love, divine, "and inner urge of life", 1898
    cannot be self-contained; must be unselfishly bestowed,
      1739
    forgives, then destroys, wrongs, 2018
    is outgoing in its satisfaction-seeking, 1739
    not shortsighted affection, 1304
love of God, casts out all fear, 552
    divine, destroys wrongs, 2018
    like Father, of Son like mother, 76
    operates directly in heart, independent of other
      humans, 1305
    relationship is personal, man and God, 1305
    revealed by divine Sons, 92
    saves sinner, 41
    second to nothing in divine nature, 2017
    to realize the, 1950
love-saturated soul, 1874
loved, human things must be known to be loved, 1118
loved ones, babies, 516, 533, 570
lover, divine, lives in man, 2094
lover's insight into nature of love may be faulty, 1140
loving, God more, 1955
    "one another, even as I am loving", 1949
    very much a response to being loved, 39

lower social orders, no longer abjectly ignorant,
    helpless, 1087
loyal devotion, will of creature, amazing acts of, 757
LOYAL SERAPHIC COMMANDER, A, 606
Loyalatia, great seraphim, 419
loyalty(ies) (see also "oath", and "trust")
    advantages, disadvantages, 1488
    amazing acts of loyalty to will...of F, 757
    apostles' for J, 1612, -17
    "as you rejoice in loyalty to gospel", 2041
    bred by education, 2072
    business of, create, sustain, loyalty, 1089
    children impressed only by loyalty, 1094
    cosmic morality, interactions of liberty and loyalty,
      435
    demands (requires) struggle, 1097
    desirable?, 51-52
    disloyalty, heinous crime (nearby planet), 815
    doing good to neighbor, idea expands, 1133
    fairness, tolerance, love, 1372-73
    forgiveness of sin is renewal of loyalty relations, 985

L

loyalty(ies) (cont'd)
    friend, terrible be wounded in house of trusted f,1676
    great power in mutual loyalty to a cosmic Deity, 1776
    group r activities to dramatize loyalty of r, 1092
    hard to change, 1488   like gratitude, 435
    living experience of the loyalty of love, 1012
    love-loyalty, one of three mighty drives, 803
    makes evolution difficult, 1488
    most sacred trust, 1403
    must be loyal to Sovereign Son of God, 177
    must motivate love, 1923
    new cult must promote loyalty, 966
    not sacrifice, but loyalty, that J demands, 1945

    only with perfection of loyalty, the finality of liberty,
      435
    profound loyalty to forms of r, 1745
    sacredness of all human loyalty (5), 2088
    Spirit consort's charge of fidelity and loyalty, 204
    spiritual disloyalty of Jewish leaders, 1932
    supreme loyalty to spiritual ideal, 1803 to duty, 2076
    to Father above all, 1521
    to God, loyalty to others, 1474
    to J, prayer was declaration of soul loyalty, 2089
    to one's flesh and blood, most sacred trust, 1403
    to supreme ideals, gradual or sudden, 1099
    to transcendent object, religion, 1092
    transition from old r loyalties to emerging new
      meanings and values, 1089
    transform emotions into higher loyalties, 1730
    true measure of self-mastery, character, 315
    universal appeal to loyalty, 1780
    what is loyalty?, 435

lu

Lucifer, adjudication of L, soon restore Satania
    system, 529
    administrative cabinet of L rebelled, 604
    beautiful message of, acceptance of Life Carrier's
      work, 710   betrayal handicaps man, 58
    blasphemous pretensions of L...child of light, 1327
    confined on Satania prison worlds (we can visit), 510
    deceptions involved angels, 1841
    disrupted "governor" that restrains premature, 1302
    elevated Caligastia to his personal staff, 741
    emissaries of L "tempted" J, 1493-94
    fallen, deposed Sovereign of (System) Satania, 600
    falsifier, self-exaltation, not in the truth, 754
    folly of, 614
    heed that "majorities rule" that "mind is infallible",
      605
    "I will exalt my throne above the Sons of God", 490
    "the iniquitous one", 1808
    litigation 2-1/2 seconds after crime, 618
    "secession", 489
LUCIFER MANIFESTO, THE, 603
Lucifer, not on U since...611
    pleased by Judas' betrayal, 1938
    prisoner on F's world satellite, 611
    proposed "Declaration of Liberty", 754
    rebellion, on a neighboring planet, 808
    sin of L, prostituting God-given abilities, 1519
    specious proposals to J about bestowal, 1494
    successor is Lanaforge, system sovereign, 511
    system sovereign in Nebadon, 601
    turned face away, 1972
    understand fall of L, shun spiritual pride, 1808
    why apprehension, judgment delayed, 619-20
    "you who dared to confuse the worlds", 601
LUCIFER REBELLION, THE, 601

Lucifer rebellion (200,000 years ago), 701,725,1251,-53
    1513
    about 200,000 years ago, 604,611
    Adam and Eve not involved in, 583,828
    adjudication of affairs of Lr not completed, 529
    after adjudication, luminaries on U?, 1025
    all who joined, detained until adjudication, 1247-48
    almost a free course for 200,000 years, 604-05
    Amadon and 143, outweighed harm of, 762
    brought inglorious end to progress, advancement, 576
    end of, 1494
    ever since Lr, special care over U, 491
    good from can't be outweighed by evil of, 762
    government of U, unique due to, 1250
    midwayers, 40,119 out of 50,000 defected, 863
    more than 1/4 of lower seraphic orders lost, 434
    over 7 Planetary Adams lost in Lr, 581
    Satania worlds under ban 200,000 years, 578
    Satania's Father's world satellites, interned of, 510
    self-assertion was battle cry of, 604
    sophistry of unbridled personal liberty, 434
    superphysical history altered by this calamity, 754
    system of Satania, last, greatest of all, 511
    36 more rebellion-isolated worlds in Satania, 1252
    thousands of Morontia Companions lost in, 545
    untangled by J, 1317,1417,1752-53
    virtually settled by J on Mt. Hermon, 1494
    Zoroaster influenced by traditions of, 1049
luck, 958,994
LUCK, CHANCE, GOOD AND BAD, 950
luck, superstition, 1681
    a term coined to cover the inexplicable, 951
    what man calls good luck may be bad, 1305
lucky, number 4, from compass, 968
    numbers, 3 and 7, 968
LUKE, Acts of the Apostles, 1342
    alone recorded "son" of Nain, 1646
    gospel according to Paul, 1342
LUKE, GOSPEL BY (year 82), 1342
    warped social teachings, 1581
Luminous Persons, 271
luminous worlds, seven, 143
LUNATIC, THE KHERESA, 1695
lunatics were worshipped, 948
lungs evolved from swim bladders in arthopods, 680
lure, love objective--not subjective gratification, 1094
    of a great ideal needed, 1773
lures, 1772   of known vs. unknown, 1782
LURES OF MATURITY, THE (Rodan), 1777
lures, of truth, beauty, goodness, 1092
Lut, 747,757
Lutentia, System Sovereign, rebel, 1311
"Luther", why (inelasticity of Christianity), 1010
Lutheranism, justified, 1010
luxury, in ascending career are Morontia Companions,
    547
    tremendous overload of (today), 765   vices of, 786
Luz, remarkable address by J near L, 1728
Lydda, through L enroute to Jerusalem, 1404
lynch law, vigilance societies, 792
lynching and duelling represent...796

M

Maccabean revolt, Essenes originated during, 1534
Maccabee, Judas, exploits of deliverance by JM, 1334
    Mosaic services restored by JM, 1360
Maccabees, inroad of Stoicism in Fourth Book of M,1338
    J resolved no repeat of M disappointment, 1521
    Mary's ancestry tied with M activities, 1349
    worship of Yahweh on Mt. Gerizim till time of M,1612

machine, body is a life machine, furnished by
     evolution, 1216
   cannot cherish goodness, 2077
   cannot hunger (thirst) for righteousness, 2077, -79
   cannot know, let alone know truth, 2077
   can't be conscious of value of another, 2079
   man is a m, a living mechanism, 1301
machine age, mastery of, 807, 814
machinery, benefits from m are inestimable, 902
machines, do not think, create, dream, aspire, 2079
   have begun to displace men, 909
   have no motivation, 2079
   if men were m, no personality, 2077
   living, frandalanks, 328
MACHIVENTA INCARNATION, THE, 1014
MACHIVENTA MELCHIZEDEK, 1014 (see also
   "Melchizedek, Machiventa")
MACHIVENTA MELCHIZEDEK, PRESENT STATUS OF,
   1024
Madagascar, some tribes destroy children, 770
Madon, J and apostles fared poorly at, 1644
MAGADAN, ORDINATION OF THE SEVENTY AT, 1800
Magadan Park (near Bethsaida-Julias), 1761, -99
   Abner and followers to join J at MP, 1798
   almost 100 awaiting J at MP, 1762
   entire corps assembled at MP, 1771
   J and apostles encamped at MP, 1744-45
   "on the morrow we return to M" (J), 1759
   16 days instruction at MP, 1800
   10 days in council at MP, 1806
MAGADAN, THE RETURN TO, 1771
Magdala, 1527
MAGDALA, THE STOP AT, 1679
Magi,
   story of M beautiful myth, 1352
MAGIC, 970
magic, and hygiene, 971
   and superstition, J on, 1680
   black and white from black and white smiths, 774
   black art practitioners, magicians, 987
   devotee of m forgets many failures, 947
   embraced in witchcraft, 987
   father of science, 972
MAGIC, FETISHES, AND CHARMS, 967
magic, the practice of, 972
   prepared way for religion, 1141
   search for true causes turned magic into medicine,
     901
   sorcery, impossible divorce evolved religion from,
     1004
   sorcery, necromancy, object was twofold, 970
   struggle between devotees of m and...773
MAGICAL CHARMS, 971
MAGISTERIAL MISSIONS, 226
Magisterial Son, 587
   arrives from Paradise when time is ripe, 594
   extends revelation of truth, 594
MAGISTERIAL SONS, 224
Magisterial Sons-Avonals, 88
   are bestowal sons, 229
   assisted by Melchizedeks and Archangels, 225
   "parents" Eternal Son and Infinite Spirit, 224
magnitude, Antares, 458
   central Isle of Paradise, 118
   Havona, 152
   immensity beyond grasp of mind, 128
   of organizing matter, 169
   Paradise peripheral area, 121
   space, 458
   spheres in constellation, 485
   suns, 458

Mahayana, gospel of Buddhism, 1039
   teaching ("Great Road"), 1038-39
Mahayanists, 1038
maiden vs. virgin, 1348
maidens for sex gratification, earliest peace missions,
   768
MAINTENANCE ARTS--LAND TECHNIQUES, 768
MAINTENANCE OF CIVILIZATION, 906
MAJESTON--CHIEF OF REFLECTIVITY, 199
Majeston, focalized the cosmic presence of Supreme
     Mind, 1272
   49 liaison personalities, marvelous, 201
   Paradise center of reflectivity, 206
   reflectivity phenomenon personalized in M, 162
   Supreme Being is father of M, 11
   true person, not in catalogue of...personalities, 200
major, problems, 2 of life, 1778
   religious epochs, 1009
   sector, about 1/10 of superuniverse, 181
     100 minor sectors in ms, 166, 181
majority, animal urge, 1773
   opinions, 970
   vote "changed" history, 859
Malachi, from Moses to, ideational growth (God), 1062
maladjustment, possibilities for m will be exhausted,
   1292
male, desire for sex gratification led to home, 765
male, female
   equality of sexes on advanced worlds, 564
   even in morontial, spiritual careers, 939
malice, none, J, 1907
maltese cross (cross section of space), 124
Malvorian, first Graduate Guide, 270
mammalian, affection of high order, 708
   era, 672
MAMMALIAN ERA ON URANTIA, THE, 693
mammals, the age of advanced, 695
   the age of early, 694
   assume domination, 695
   dawn-m, suddenly appear, 700, -03
   destroyed reptilian ancestors, 695
   earliest non-placental, failed, 686
   5 advantages for survival over others, 693, 733
   lemurs' ancestors, suddenly, 696
   mid-m, suddenly appear, 700, -04
   non-placental, 686, 693
   placental type, suddenly, 693, 733
mammon vs. spiritual loyalties, 1803
Mamre, plains of M, celestial beings appeared, 1021
man (see also "man's", "men", "mortal", "mortals")
   acts, the Supreme reacts, 1286
   among men, J was, 1407-08, -13 **man**
   ancestors not monkeys, gorillas, apes, 697, 700, 703,
     706
   ancestors, 3 mutations from lemurs, 703
   and ape, how related, 706
   and God are directly related, 1187
   and God, as vine and branches, 1846
   and God, distance equalized by T A, 1176
   and Simians, same species, different "parents", 706
   and wife? (on high) as Mighty Messengers, 245
   and woman, dissimilarity (mental), 938
MAN AND WOMAN, THE PARTNERSHIP OF, 938
man, and woman, superiority of combination, 932
   appearance reveals inner m, 1236
   as against animals (see "animal vs. man")
   as moral being inexplicable unless, 53
   assurance of Deity Kinship must be faith realized, 1289
   augmenting vision modifies views, 1306
   becomes spirit, never sudden, evolutionary, 541

man (cont'd)

beginning to unlock the storehouse of secrets of...
1306

"behold the m!" (said of J), 1101

can be delivered from depths, 1428

can cause his Creators sorrow, 58

can feel full impact of Father's LOVE, 50

can never decide temporal issues unless, 1093

can never transcend selfishness unless, 1093

can transcend nature, 1221

cannot destroy the supreme values of existence,
but...1285

can't hope to live up to his highest ideals, 1133

can't monopolize ministry of...2065

can't suddenly accept advanced truth, 1012

central universe is m's established destiny, 163

chemically, electrically, controlled, 1207,-16,1301

chief devotion to development and ennoblement, 1519

child of the devil is superstition, 2060

chooses, determines own destiny, 1232

chose most agreeable work, let women drudge, 774

civilized, great test of, 1521

consciousness rests on electro-chemical mechanism
below, delicately touches spirit-morontia system
above, 1216

constitutive factors of m: science, morality,
religion, 196

contrasted to Havona creatures, 52

craves belongingness, 1227

"craves to be a complete person", 1573

created out of...potential of energy, mind, spirit,
1284

created out of the potentiality of the Supreme, 1283

creates religion out of fears, by means of illusions,
944

crucial test of, trust, 314

dawn mammals, mid-mammals, Primates, then
human beings, 700

dawn races of, 703

dedicated, becomes what he wants to, 1467

defiled not by that which comes through eyes and
ears, 1713

defiled only by evil originating in heart, 1713

depravity of m, no!, 1091

descendant of fighting animals, 714

"descended" from N.A. mammals, 733

destination, 67

determines own destiny, 734,1232

discerns the fact, law, and love of God, 846

discouraged with the transitory, 1776

discovers Father in his own heart, 1290

discovers Supreme in hearts of all other men, 1290

a disposition to bargain with Deity, 965

divine in destiny, m becomes, 1676

doesn't naturally relish hard work, 1120

don't become panicky about spiritual assets of...
race, 2076

doomed, not until, 64

dual nature of, 381

each will-creature irreplaceable in all eternity, 138

early m enjoyed human flesh, 979

early m mightily gripped by custom, 767

early m no time for thinking, 901

-eating, a sacrament, 980

educated by fact, ennobled by wisdom, saved by
faith, 2094

electrically, chemically controlled, 1207

energized by urges from source in mind, 1134

ennobled--to learn good impulses are from internal,
1134

man (cont'd)

every m belonged to someone else, Middle Ages, 794

every m craves to be complete,1573

expands, grows, somewhat in way of Supreme, 1282

experiences ministry of Spirit...when, 379

faint hold upon religion, 1137

faith son of God, 2060

fall of m, no, 846

feared ghosts but believed they could be tricked,958,959

fears religion, 2083

fears what J' religion will do to him, 2083

few of days, full of trouble, 1664

finds God in self, 62

first ancestors described, 703-04,707

first appeared with ice age, 733

first experiences ministry of spirit...379

foolish, failed lay up treasures in heaven, 1821

forgets, Midwayers remember, 866

freed by secularism, then enslaved by it, 2081

from m to God (J showed way), 1426

functions on animal level when...193

-God communication channel, 1638

MAN, GOD IN, 1192

man,-God, J never again on earth as, 1699

God-knowing, Father beside him, he traverses
Supreme, 1291

God makes m more than he is, 1285

-God partnership, 1299,1467

good m who denies God, is grafted branch fed by
roots, 1126

good, not through government, 1931

great challenge to, 2097

has evil tendencies, 1660

has existed from eternity, 2002

has in keeping T A and fraction of Supreme, 1285

has right to be most certain about God, 1127

has worshiped everything on earth, 944

hears God speak, God hears prayer, 1638

help for, 381

how defiled, 1712

how he is great, 435

how identified as spiritual being, 1228

if ethically lazy and spiritually indolent, 1459

ignorant but spiritually hungry, 1st century A.D., 1337

illuminated m has a religion, 2096

image of God, 1281

imitate J, no; share his faith, yes, 2091

in control powers of truth, or opposite, 1428

"in our own image", 78

incomplete grasp of science, 1137

increasingly learns to subordinate his life machine
to...1301

indestructible reality and, 1276

individual m set off from the average, 579

"indwelt becomes divine in destiny", 1676

"indwelt by Son as well as Father", 1948

insulated from absolute levels by time and space,1303

insults what he can't achieve or attain, 1984

intended to be masterpiece, 57

intense conflicts in, 382

internal struggle, spirit easy victor (J), 1749

invincible, dedicated to God's will (mortal J), 1970

inwardly illuminated by worship, 1175

is afraid of the unknown, 1459

is architect of own destiny, 1135

is a machine, a living mechanism (and more), 1301

is a material fact, 2079

is the son of God (see under "Jesus, Quotes")

it is not good for m to be alone, 283,1775,2055
(paraphrased, 647)

man (cont'd)
    it was m, not God, who executed J, 2002
MAN, JESUS--THE, 2090
man, J, as a m, achieved light and life, 636
    J taught what m must be, not do, 1584
    judge m on potentials in eternity, 1727
    "judged by intentions", 1571
    languishes in isolation, 1776
    last 4 evolutionary mutations to m, 700
    learned to live on interest of capital (flocks), 768
    "let us make mortal m in our image", 78
    like angels, 1243-44, -48
    low levels of work ok for lowest humans, 771
    many metaphysical dilemmas of man due to, 1298
    mature vs. immature, 1778
    midwayer, cherubim, Morontia Companion, 545
    million years on earth (999, 419), 707, 718
    modern m readjustment task, 1013
    modifies physical reality to extent he has, 1222
    moral, why, 1431
    mortal, cannot see Father, 1952
    mortal, invincible, 1970
    must be fallible if he is to be free, 52
    needs cosmic perspective, 1092
    needs scrutinize charts of morality, 1086
    new creature, 1103
    next age of, increased spiritual living, 1863
    "no m is a stranger to one who knows God", 1431
    "no man lives unto himself", true, 1227
    no m now sees the Father except the Son, 1750
    no matter how humble, m is great when, 435
    normal, is the backbone of civilization, 771 (not
        "average", but "normal"-Ed.)
    normal, source of mutant geniuses, 771
    not an evolutionary accident, 560
    not God, planned death, killed J, 2002
    not inherently sinful, 974, 1222, 1739, 2003
    not to be equal, but "differentiated", 579
    not to think of God as like himself, 57
    of sorrows, J not, 1766, 1954
    1,000,000 years on earth, 700, 703, 1009
    perceives time by analysis, space by synthesis, 1297
    perfect at start, then degenerating, no!, 1660
    perfected control of life, only with T A, 1303
    persuade his mind, don't compel it, 1931
    philosopher, philanthropist, scholar, businessman,
        one m can be all, 1465
MAN, POST-ADAMIC, 592
MAN, POST-BESTOWAL SON, 595
MAN, POST-MAGISTERIAL SON, 594
MAN, POST-TEACHER SON, 598
MAN, PRIMITIVE, 589
man, profoundly influenced by his chosen heroes, 1013
    proposes but God disposes, 1046
    realization of God inalienable in m, 196
    relation to Trinity, 66
    religion of each m unique and wholly different, 1130
    religious, consumed with...righteousness, 2096
        escapes limitations through insight of love, 2096
        transcends his environment, 2096
    responsive to spirit guidance, 1276
    roots are in physical world of energy, 1301
    saved by religious faith, 2094
    saved from any depths, 1428
    self-conscious of insight, 1773
    semi-civilized m of today (1934), 1306
    served by Spirits of the Trinity, 380
    seven-fold approach to Deity, 11
    "shall cleave to his wife", 1839
    should control his institutions, 772

man (cont'd)   M
    should not be dominated by his institutions, 772
    should not blame God for, 1661
    should not complain of...1661
    should recognize his Creators are divine and finite,
        1268; that Deity is evolving, 1268
    sick with dropsical condition, 1834
    simians, descended from same tribe, 706
    sits in judgment on God, 1984
MAN, THE SO-CALLED FALL OF, 845
man, social consciousness not inalienable in m, 196
    Son of God the Father, and God the Mother, (Supreme
        Being), 1289
    spirit helps (7), 2062
MAN, THE SPIRIT IN, 380
man, spirit nucleus in, 142
    spiritualized after constellation socialization, 174
    still pins hope on outward show of piety, 958
    subnormal, should be kept under control (breeding),
        770
    summation of life, 2094
    technique changes, disposition remains same, 777
    terribly afraid of the unknown, 1459
    three constitutive factors of m, 196
    to become more realizing, 1616
    to become more than he is, give God all he has, 1285
    to enrich and unify his evolving self, 1284-85
    to m, Deity is singular, always one, 380
    too busy, he thinks, 2077
    too busy to grow, 1094
    touchingly beautiful relations between m and his
        Maker, 2002
    transcendant distinction for, 984
    traverses the Supreme, walks with Father, 1291
    treasures on earth, but not rich with God, 1821
    true destiny consists in...141
    truly is architect of own eternal destiny, 1135
    trusts and loves only a good God, 40
    union with God by progressive communion, 31
    union with God not as drop of water in ocean, 31
    universe integration of m, insight plus experience,
        1306
    unspiritualized, indescribable hunger, 381
    uplifted by extraordinary faith J has in him, 2093
    usually has chosen easier path (vs. women), 934
    vs. animal (see "animal vs. man")
    vs. the cosmos, (early) one-sided struggle, 964
    vs. an energy system, 1232
    vs. institutions, 772
    way seems right to a m, 1566
    western lemur ancestry, 703
    "what to BE, not DO", 1584
    whole duty of, 1600, 1805
    why on animal level, 192
    willing to be born again?, 1782
    (with will) 993, 408 years (to 1934) on U, 710
MAN WITH THE WITHERED HAND, THE, 1664
man, without personality, just energies...9
    -woman combination best, 932
    work, m does not naturally like, 1120
    worm of the dust by nature, 1676
MAN, WORSHIP OF, 948
man, young, who was afraid, and J, 1436

man, primitive
    appearance of not accident, 733
    constant dread of unknown, 950
MAN, PRIMITIVE, IN THE ICE AGE, 700
man, primitive, never considered anything as accidental,
    952

man, primitive (cont'd)
  requires restraints (fear, hunger), 1302
  small self-restraint, principle of biologic evolution, 1302
  sought supernatural explanations for the natural, 901
  two things in mind, food and revenge, 714
  thought only when he was hungry, 765
  "who is tormenting me?", 951

mana, the impersonal (in evolving religion), 1132
  practices, oudah beliefs, manitou superstitions, 994
management, this universe, Creator Son and Mother Spirit, 368
Manasseh, boy king, 1074
mandate, no offspring on planet for bestowal Sons, 1330
  revelatory m (U Book) of superuniverse rulers, 16
manger, J born in grain storage room, then laid in m, 1351
  men of God visited babe J in m, 1317
Mangus, a centurion, his servant, 1647
manifestations, of non-Father infinity, 1146
  universal, infinite function, 1146
MANIFESTATIONS, WAVE-ENERGY, 474
MANIFESTO, LUCIFER (DECLARATION OF LIBERTY), 603
manipulate, angels do not m the will of mortals, 1245
  environment, seraphim, 1245
MANIPULATORS, THE ENERGY, 504
manipulators: physical-energy, mind-energy, spiritual-energy, compound (all three), 504-05
mankind, all, same indwelling spirit, 1732
  brotherhood only by...1672
  designed to evolve by technique of experience, 1174
  divided into 3 classes, intellectually, 1241
    subnormal minded
    average, normal minded
    supernormal minded
  divided into 3 classes, skeletal structure, 905
    Caucasoid
    Mongoloid
    Negroid
  does not ascend effortlessly, 1284
  from American life implantation, and Eurasian-African, 703
  must learn anew, every 10 generations, 1772
  new and blended order of, 585
  on the march, 807, 1086
  parents of all, 717
  racial guilt before God, no, 2003
  ripening for real religion, 1004
  spiritual approach only can unify, 2065
  unlovely, 1573
manna, ate m in the wilderness, 1518, 1710
Manotia, (loyal) Satania's 2nd in command, 606-07
man's, ancestor not yet appeared, (end of Pliocene), 699
  ancestors, from N. America, 733
    lemurs, dawn mammals, 703
    twins migrated by choice, 708
  appearance, no accident, design, 733
  authority over woman (J on), 1471
  constitutive endowments, 196
  deplorable estate, 1660
  divine spirit, shown by 3 phenomena, 1108
  evolutionary destiny in own hands, 734, 1232
  evolutionary m supreme endowment, religion, 1121
  faith revealed 12 ways, 1108
  great universe adventure, 1303
  greatest adventure, 2097
  help from God (divine influence), 46
  high forms of thought (besides religion), 2075

man's (cont'd)
  highest human attainments, reason, wisdom, faith, 1141
  ideas, enlarging cosmic concepts due to, 1439
    enormously expanded, 1439
  life exhibits, control attributes of mind, 2079
    creative qualities of spirit, 2079
  loss, in acceptance of religions of authority, 1729
  magnificent reach for final reality, 2096
  moral will, the personality, 1458
  nearest approach to God, love, 50
  progress recorded, 1284
  seven-fold approach to Deity, 11
  sole contribution to growth, 1097
  spiritual jeopardy, 1090
  supreme duty, 1560
  supreme experience, 2096
  supreme gesture, religion, 2096
  terrestrial orientation...enhanced by, 1162
  thought, five high forms of, 2075
  threefold spiritual endowment, 2061-62
  total powers mobilized m faith, 1097
  true destiny consists in, 141
  urge for Paradise perfection creates divinity tension in living cosmos, 1276
  weakness, 610 whole duty l commandment, 180
  wisdom no higher than his faith, 1459
man's Creators, divine but finite, God evolving non-absolute Deity, 1268
man's evolution (see "evolution"), lemurs, dawn mammals, mid-mammals, primates, humans, 705-07
Mansant, great Post-Planetary Prince teacher, 726
mansion world, an epoch, awakening on mw, 1248
MANSION WORLD, THE FIFTH, 537
MANSION WORLD, THE FIRST, 532
MANSION WORLD, THE FOURTH, 536
MANSION WORLD, THE SECOND, 534
MANSION WORLD, THE SEVENTH, 538
MANSION WORLD, THE SIXTH, 537
MANSION WORLD STUDENTS, 340-41
MANSION WORLD TEACHERS, 413, 550
Mansion World Teachers, 406
  number beyond comprehension of mortal, 413
MANSION WORLD, THE THIRD, 535
mansion worlds (7), 1247 (man's first post-mortal residence) (some sojourners exempted, 288)
  Adam and Eve promised return to mw, 853
  are among 49 satellites of Jerusem's (system capital's) satellites, 174, 509
  are architectural, created for specific purposes, 509
  are 7 satellites of transition world one, 509, 530
  awaken on mw, transformation great, 1235
  before leaving, all mortals have seraphic guardians, 1248
  cared for, maintained by spornagia, 509
  children, few under 16 on, 532
  complete unification of personality, 494
  countless individuals gone to, 2024
  described, one through seven, 532-540
  1st, 2nd, and so on, through 7th heaven, 174
  first study on mw, 2 languages, 546
  glorified teacher cherubim beyond number, 413
  glorious awakening, 1248
  great confusion on the mw (Lucifer), 605
  heat and light, 520
  "heaven" as conceived by prophets, 553
  human relationships survive, 1235
  infant-receiving schools for deceased children, 531
  lose function as light and life progresses, 547
  lowest of the "heaven of heavens", 553

marriages (cont'd)

MARRIAGES, PLURAL, 925

Mars, sub-breathers, if any inhabitants, 561

Martha (sister of Andrew), 1679

Martha (sister of J, born A. D. 3), 1367, 1418, -20

Martha (sister of Lazarus)
  feared dead Lazarus not presentable, 1845
  needless tasks, trivial cares, her disposition, 1798
  rebuked by J, 1845

Martha and Mary (sisters of Lazarus)
  at public banquet of J and Lazarus, 1878
  different attitudes after message to J, 1842
  father had been Bethany's leading citizen, 1842
  great event for J to be in home, 1595
  J and James visit at Passover, 1399
  J' entire family waiting at home of, 1997
  J wanted to see M & M and Lazarus, 1404
  Jude asked family to gather at house of, 1976
  Martha busied herself, Mary no, 1798
  message to J "he whom you love is sick", 1836
  reactions to "take away the stone", 1845
  runner dispatched to family of J, 2011
  sold all, traveled to Philadelphia, 2031

MARTHA AND MARY, THE VISIT WITH, 1797

Martha and Mary, wealthy, vineyards, orchards,
  private tomb, 1842

Martha, wife of Justus, and the courtesans, 1473

Mary Magdalene, 1679, 2008, -13, -25
  became most effective teacher, 1680
  discovered tomb empty, 2026
  J appears to, 2026
  spokesman for women's corps, 2029
  witnessed four of first five of J' morontia
    appearances, 2033

Mary (mother of Jesus), 2045
  adventurous and aggressive person, 1350
  after Cana, high spirit sank low, 1534
  ambitious mother, 1529
  and brothers of J deeply hurt, 1722
  and Ruth move to Capernaum, 1484
  and T A, 3 stages, 1177
  average woman, 1317
  Bethsaida, after resurrection to, 2031
  blond, well nigh, brown-eyed, 1349
  ceremonially purified after childbirth, 1352
  closed mind, 1396
  composed, courageous and fairly wise, 1348
  "the conception within you is ordained of heaven", 1346
  cult, 895
  dancing with glee, 1530
  David sent for M at end, 1923
  died year after crucifixion, 2010
  disappointed J, 1529
  disciplinarian, 1360
  disillusioned, 1386
  family involved in evolution of religion, 1345
  had more of Davidic ancestry than Joseph, 1347
  hastened away to avoid J, 1628
  heritage from illustrious females, 1345
  "I believe your hour has come", 1529
  "I cannot understand him", 1529
  "I know I could influence my son if...", 1721
  in error, 1385
  in group to hear Peter's report of J' farewell
    message, 2058
  J denied M's stories to family, 1396
  J, 29, spent visit time mostly with M and Ruth, 1482
  lived last year with John (Zebedee, apostle), 2010
  "the Lord of all the earth shall overshadow you", 1346
  maintained long constant vigil, 1355

Mary (mother of Jesus) (cont'd)
  mind couldn't be changed, 1396
  "mother's smile might help", J, 1400
  names of her feminine ancestors, 1345
  nearly despaired of son, 1534
  not Jew, more Syrian, Hittite, Greek, Egyptian, 1345
  persistently held wrong ideas, 1396
  Pharisees camped on M's doorstep, 1743
  prepared J for throne of David, 1385
  purification from uncleanness of childbirth, 1352
  rebuked by J, 1529
  sensed wine miracle, 1530
  sunshine of maternal delusion, 1386
  thought J beside himself, 1391
  thrilled with expectation, her son supernatural king,
    1528
  to Cana in spirit of queen mother, 1528
  torn between love and fear, 1721
  upbraided J mildly, 1384
  wavered constantly, 1538
  -worship, origin of, 895

Mary and Joseph, different views of law and prophets,
  1349

Mary (sister of Lazarus) (see also "Martha and Mary")
  precious ointment on J' feet, 1879

Maryology, Danubians became mother worshippers, 897
  mother cult from Crete, 895

mask, intolerance is m of doubts, 1641
  revenge is m of cowardice, 1632

mass, and energy are one, 1477
  central creation m exceeds 7 sectors, 129
  central universe vs. grand, 129
  in matter, increase of m is equal to, 474
  is energies slowed down, 1477
  responsiveness of m to order-producing mind, 1274

"mass" (?), reduces symbolism to precise formula, 1942
  spirit conjuring comparable to, 987
  supper, not a sacrament, 1942

"Master... bid fire come down from heaven...", 1788

"Master declared that he would rise", 2044

Master (J called "Master"), 1515, -18-19, -39, -41-43,
  1546-47, -51, -57, -64, -67, -69-70, -76-78, 1672
  early called M by 12, 1549
  first called "M", 1421

Master Architects of creation, 480
  set limits within which will operates, 1300

MASTER FORCE ORGANIZERS, 329, 469-70
  not same as power directors, 352

Master Mathematician, "whence vast universe of
  mathematics without MM", 2077

Master Michaels, 234; unlimited power, 240-42

MASTER MICHAELS, DESTINY OF THE, 241

MASTER PHYSICAL CONTROLLERS, 181, 324, 627

MASTER PHYSICAL CONTROLLERS, CIRCLES OF THE,
  523, 526

MASTER SERAPHIM OF PLANETARY SUPERVISION,
  THE, 1254

Master Son, 513 (see "Son" and "Sons" under "S")

Master Sons, 422
  after 7 bestowals, 238, 240
  perfect communication with their bestowal worlds, 241

MASTER SONS, RELATION TO THE UNIVERSE, 240

Master Sons, result of bestowals, 240

Master Spirit of Orvonton, 188-89, 1236, -72

MASTER SPIRITS, THE SEVEN, 184

Master Spirits, Seven, 180, 268, 274, 291, 642
  are apparently Trinity inevitabilities, 1266
  are mind-spirit balance wheel of u of u, 150
  are primary personalities of the I S, 184
  are sevenfold source of cosmic mind, 191

materialism (cont'd)
    vs. secularism, 2081
MATERIALISM, VULNERABILITY OF, 2078
materialism, world sway of mechanistic m will be
    overthrown, 2082
    worst over, 2076
materialist, 1228, 1779
    culture a menace to civilization, 1457
    doubting m should not disturb certainty of
      religionist, 1140
    idealist, extremes, 1779
    mind disproves materialism, 2078
    secular panic, 2076
    spiritual darkness, 1118
    stoics, optimists, 1954
    unbelieving, pitiful hopes and views, 1118
    view of life, 2076
materialistic age, passing episode, 2076
materialistic mammon, spiritual loyalties incompatible
    with, 1803
materialistic tendencies, 2075
materialists, automaton conceive philosophy of auto-
    matism?, 2080
materialization of Melchizedek, 1015
materialized energy, basic units of are...473
materials woven into mortals' bodies by morontia
    supervisors, 543
mathematical level of u, no survival seen in, 1116
mathematics, and volitional, divorce attempted, 1136
    beset with qualitative limitations, 1294
    not index of action, influences, 1476
    of force, energy, power, must be reckoned with, 1146
MATING INSTINCT, THE, 913
mating, instinct, tricks selfish man, 914
    is universally natural, 915
    with higher animals, early man, 946
    with inferiors, Andonics deteriorated their stock, 719
    with lower races, no, 586
matter, all m form, on order of solar system, 477
    and energy...same cosmic reality, 467
MATTER AND ENERGY TRANSMUTATIONS, 472
MATTER, ATOMIC, 477
matter, basic units are ultimatons, 472-73
    can't love mercy, 2077
MATTER, CLASSIFICATION OF, 471
matter, depends on, 471
    energy circuits of living m, 560
    energy hardly known on U, from m less known, 328
MATTER, ENERGY — MIND AND, 467
matter, error, viewing m as basic reality, 92
    exists only by cosmic technique of Paradise, 468
    for untold universes now circulates, 139
    force, and energy, are one, 123
    gravity and (cold) organize and hold m together, 176
    heat and antigravity disrupt m, 176
    identical everywhere, except...471
    in path ordained by the Infinite Personality, 472
    in space bodies, ten grand divisions of, 471-72
    is orderly, dependable association of various
      energies, 477
    is shadowy physical body, spirit is soul of creation, 82
    is skeleton of morontia, 2021
    is time-space shadow of...648
    living, is chemical, electrical and other basic
      energies, 560
    maximum possible organization of m in Nebadon (100
      atomic materializations), 477
MATTER, MIND, AND SPIRIT, 139
matter, mind, spirit, 647, 1120
    morontia, spirit, 3 levels of true unity, 1477

matter (cont'd)
    originates in space, 170
    a philosophic shadow cast by mind, 140
    physical properties determined by, 471
    relative integrity of m assured by, 474
    shadow of spirit reality, 2021
    10 grand divisions of m, 471
    transmutations, 472
    true to the circle of eternity, 472
    uniform but for mind, spirit, 2078
    units of primary m, revolutions modified, 541
    units so stable and so efficiently flexible, 480
    work it can perform, 474
MATTHEW LEVI (Apostle), 1559 (see under "Apostles")
Matthew, (Book of M), also Mark, Luke, partly
    Jesusonian, 2091
Matthias, chosen to take place of Judas, 2045, -58
mature, human being looks upon all others with tender-
    ness, tolerance, 1773
    men view immature as parents view children, 1773
    personality, 1774
MATURITY, THE BALANCE OF, 1777
maturity, defined, 1295
    direct relationship between m and time consciousness
      in intellect, 1295
    emotional, intellectual, social, if not spiritual m, 159
    evidence of, 1774
    intellectual, emotional, social (Havona), 159
    leads to tenderness, tolerance, 1773
MATURITY, THE LURES OF, 1777
maturity, of any religion, 28
    of personality, 1094, 1774
    proportional to...1094
    relates to unit of time in man's mind, 1295
    social, human, 1773-74
maximation of all creature reality, the Supreme, 1304
maximum, finites, 1162
    light and truth, conditions for, 1209
    of being, 1123
    organization of matter, 100 distinguishable material-
      izations of space energy, 477
maximums, primary and secondary (perfect and
    perfected reality), 1158
    tertiary (neither perfect nor perfected), 1158
May Day, sex unlimited, 915, 972
Mazda-Ahura, head god, Iranian, 1049, -82
maze of living, fearless mind can lead through, 1773

me

meals, two a day, custom in Palestine, 1830
meaning is...102, 1097
meaning, "new, don't attach to old", 1914
    of God, vs. of Father, 1856
MEANING OF THE TRANSFIGURATION, 1755
meaning, six levels of (Golden Rule), 1650
meanings, from recognition and understanding, 1220
    known, values felt, 1219
    new, in old facts, is religion, 1105
    of existence changed by sense of guilt, 984
meanings, eternal, how art and philosophy inviegle man
    into realities and values of, 67
meanings and values, animals communicate no mv, 1775
    ascending pilgrims make kaleidoscopic adjustments
      in, 428
    certainty when mv, approached by faith, 1124
    concentrated into present moment by immaturity, 1295
    concerning insight, recognition of mv, 2094
    fact of God's becoming man changed all mv, 1228
    Father, universal source of, 73
    finite dimensions of personality, length determines
      m, depth signifies v, 1226

meanings and values (cont'd)
    if no value in soul, life is without m, 1219
    in soul, not contributed by mind and spirit, 1218
    insight into m of reality, mobility of v, 806
    m changed from temporal to eternal, v elevated
        from human to divine, 984
    mind knows quantity, reality, meanings--but
        quality (v) is felt, 1219
    new are emerging, 1089
    new realization of...m, new synthesis of...v, 1288
    nonexistent in wholly material world, 1220
    paramount in religion, moral values and social
        meanings, 1132
    perceived only in inner spheres, 1220
    personality imparts v of identity, m of continuity,1227
    plus things, are realities, 2094
    scrutizine m, insight which yields, spiritual v, 193
    Supreme is truth of m, goodness of v, 1278
    a surviving cult must recognize m, glorify v, 966
    thus m changed to eternal, v elevated to divine, 984
    truth, m are...goodness, v are... 648
    v unique element, m can be modified, 1261
means to an end, "all" non-spiritual things, 1228
measure of, man's spirit, self-consciousness, 1471
    planetary greatness, 317
    righteousness, 1726
    self-respect, 1740
    society's advance, 802
    spirit, human strength (and capacity), 1740
measurement, art of, 193
"meat, I have m to eat you do not know", 1615
"meat, my m is to do will of Him who", 1615
Mecca, Kaaba stone, Islamic start, 1051
mechanical, age can prove disastrous only when...909
    contrivances, animals, culture of soil, 527
MECHANICAL CONTROLLERS, 324-25
mechanical, devices as factor in U civilization, 909
MECHANICAL DEVICES, EFFECTIVENESS OF, 909
mechanical, non-teachable types of response, 738
mechanism, can deteriorate, not progress, 2079
    creation is a (living), 1303
    if universe were only a m, 2077
    man is a living m, and more, 1301
    moves on majestically...364
    of creature existence is...483
    of spirit intelligence and communication channels,391
    of time and space, 1303
    of the universes, 1303
    present, but not alone, 2078
mechanisms, all the nonvolitional patterns of plan of
        God, 1303
    are innately passive, organisms inherently active,
        1227
    are the products of mind, 1303
    basic universe m, in response to will of God, 1303
    indicate presence of creative mind, 483
    living, in grand universe (entities), 329
    mind acting on cosmic potentials, 1303
    of Paradise correlated with personality of...Son,1303
    "of the universes", impose limitations, 1303
    purposiveness of m is in origin, not function, 1303
    result of creative mind acting on (in) cosmic
        potential, 1303
MECHANISMS, UNIVERSE, 481,1303
mechanisms, universe, not mindless, 482
    vast, of material nature used, 323,328
    vs. systems, 1227
mechanisms, cosmic, conceal presence of indwelling
       mind, 482
mechanisms, entities, intelligent and living, 329

mechanist, inconsistency of m is, 2078
    concept is non-material, 2079
mechanistic materialism, blindness of, 141
mechanistic naturalism, world sway of mn will be
    overthrown, 2082
mechanistic philosopher, 53
mechanistic philosophy, intellectual suicide, 2079
mechanistic sophistries of a material philosophy, 1118
mechanistic theory (automaton) foolish, 2080
mechanize idea of "God", great blunder, 53
mediation of mind, makes meaningful, 1227
mediation of mind, through spirit conquest of energy
    matter, 1281
mediator, none needed to secure Father's favor, 41
    not required to gain Father's love, forgiveness, 38-39,
        41
medicine, early, 990
    means "mystery" in magic, 972
MEDICINE MEN AND PRIESTS, SHAMANISM, 986
medicine, no government in m, neighboring planet, 815
MEDICINE UNDER THE SHAMANS, 990
medicine, women, hysteric, 986
medicine men, 986
    powerful check on the kings, 790
    vs. smiths, 774
mediocre individual, into personality of power through
    dynamic religious living, 1094
mediocre judgment multiplied, arbiter, 970
mediocrity, dominance of m means downfall, 818
    dullness of overconservative, 1673
    twins were examples of m, felt good about it, 1563
meditation, 1774, 2047
    and devotion, man needs, 2077
    essential to decisions, 1093
    good, but loving service better, 1000
Mediterranean, and adjacent peoples,
    crude ideas concerning...1341
    an enchanted age when J came, 1341
Mediterranean, basin race, highly blended, 869, 871
Mediterranean, J' tour of, 1428
    lands, one empire, 2073
    trip,1424
        from Indian Ocean, 728
        purpose, 1427
        secret, 1483
    world, society of 5 well defined strata 1st century,
        1335
    world unified, year 1, 1332
mediums, mediumship, midwayers not connected with,
    865
medley works out to glory of God, 56
meek, "happy are the m", 1574
meekness,no, but superb self-respect, 1582
    not fear, 1574
    of spiritual origin or self-righteous superiority, 1676
meeting, such as never before on this world, 2058
Meganta, school of Rodan, 1787
Megiddo, J would gaze upon M, 1387
    to Jerusalem by way of M, 1404
Mek, leader of a council, time of Caligastia, 748
melanin, skin coloring substance, 713
Melchizedek (M Son, local universe offspring of a
    Creator Son, like J, with Universe Mother Spirit.
    Ms are superteachers, midway between highest
    Divinity and human mortals, 384-85. Widely known
    as emergency Sons, 1014)
Melchizedek, a
    authored the following papers in the U Book: 38, 39,
        45, 49, 66-72, 90, 92-106

Melchizedeks (cont'd)
  supermaterial government of U continued, but no
      contact with U races, 852
  teach: good from rebellion 1000 times sum of evil,
      619
  train Morontia Companions, 2 types, 545
  upheld Manotia at time of rebellion, 606
  were visible to A&E (also midwayers, angels), 851
  wide metamorphic range, even to physical person-
      ality level, 1014

melodies, the will play m or discord on mind, 1217
melody, has power a whole world to transform, 500
  human, four tones: business, study, philosopher,
      philanthropist, 1465
  measurements of Infinity, 2080
  of thought, 499
membership in Super Universe, requisites for, 177
memorial to Michael, staff of 1 million (Jerusem), 525
memorials, on high, 525, 2022
memories, J soothed self with, 1969
  noblest of all, 1779
memory, 535, 550, 1235
  experiences of spiritual value alone survive, 451
  mortal m survives death, 450
MEMORY OF MERCY, THE, 314
  living trial balance, statement of account, 314
memory, recall for pleasure, 1779
  reconstruction, techniques of, 451

men (see also "man")
  all are not born equal, 63, 774, 1468
  "all are sons of God", 1585
  all, innate drives toward growth, 1095
  and angels in space, 260
  and women on one job, 625
  and women, partners, 938
  and women, spiritual careers, 939
  are blessed if...1655
  are in and of the Supreme, 1280, -83, -87
  are like the lost child, 1465
  "are living spirit sons of eternal Father", 2053
  at worship, all equal, 1468
  beasts of burden, 100,000 owned by ruler, 902
  blame politics, social injustice, etc. for
      inequalities, 956
  breakers of the law if, 1655
  can change, 1572
  can realize ennobling truth (Sons of God), 2052
  "cannot compel m to love truth", 1713
  cocreators of themselves, 1273, -79
  a cosmic total to the Supreme, 1290
  differentials among men provided for, desired, 579
  difficulties are training, 1719
  disown the past, difficult, 1722
  divine privilege, creating own destinies, 615
  electrically and chemically controlled, 1207, -16
  equally influenced by J' ministry, 1485
  evil, not necessarily sinful, 1660
  evil, wicked men (Jewish rulers) death of J (God out
      of it), 1972
  evolutionary sons of God the Father, God the
      Mother, 1289
  gave up ghosts as explanation of luck, 956
  hunger and love drove m together, 766
  individuals to the Father, 1290
  intellectually in 3 classes, 1241
  loved J, 1672, 1810
  mighty, of old, 856, 862
  minority, shrewd, wicked, use force against, 1891

men (cont'd)
  monkeys, 704, 706
  must arrive at own decisions, 1802
  not equal, differential abilities, etc., 579, 1468
  numbers, countless, on Paradise, 127
  only 2 ways can live together, 1775
  only uniform thing about, 1672
  only unthinking m panicky over spiritual assets of
      race, 2076
  primitive (on series 1 worlds) few elect eternal life,
      1197
  primitive, T A of p m gains experience for another
      indwelling, 1197
  react emotionally, individually, 1672
  reflective, moved mightily by Christianity, 2085
  science sorts m, religion loves m, 1122
  should have wide range of familiarity with life, 1674
  sincere, unafraid of examination, 1641
  "snared in an evil time when it falls...upon them",
      951
  still invest in titles and degrees, 972
  "thank you (God), I am not like other m", 1838
  to live together in complex ages, need religion, 1139
  to maintain freedom, prevent these (12), 798
  two great classes, those who know God, those who
      do not, 1468
  uniform in spirit only, 1012, 1672
  vanity and ghost fear held m together, 766
  what chance has God to reveal self?, 1733
  what they must be, not do, 1584
  who can fly, 561
  why many falter, serving 2 masters on U, 1199
  why turn away from religion, 43
  with ideas--not ideals, 1220

men and women, difference never obliterated in future,
      939
  need each other here, and in future careers, 939
men, equal no, except in spirit, 1468, 1672
  all human beings are not born equal, 774
  despite differences, J loved them like brothers, 1012
  error, belief that all men born equal, 794
  in the spirit all men are equal, 1012
  J recognized difference in men's endowments, 1102
  "men of Jericho, hear me" (Zaccheus), 1874
menial work, none in spirit world, 273
men's inequalities, not due to social injustices, 956
men's lives too great for success, 2096
menstruation, meditation, men, 936
mental, attitudes, habitual, 1708
  currents, T A can sometimes arrest, 1199
  depression, physical result, 1836
  disharmony, corrected on M Worlds, 535
  disorders, hundreds healed, 1645
  distress (soul conflict) consists in, 1478
  evolutions, sudden when...740
  harassments, J sought by victims of mh, provided
      them deliverance, 1671
  healing, 1650
  healing, thought physical healing, 1645
  poisons--fear, anger, envy, jealousy, suspicion,
      intolerance, 1204
  vs. physical disorders, 1836
mentality destroyed, 1204
mentation, morontia worlds' treasure gems of, 503
menu, last supper, 1940
merciful, "God be m to me, a sinner", 1836
  "happy are the m", 1575
Mercury, same face always to sun, 657
mercy, 38, 315

mercy (cont'd)
MERCY AND JUSTICE (J on), 1468, 1577
mercy, characterizes God's attitude to individual, 137
   credit, of lavish proportions for each creature, 314
   credits, far in excess of ability to exhaust, 315
MERCY, THE DIVINE, 38
mercy, endless, 1469
   is applied love, 75
   is justice of the Paradise Trinity, 38
   is justice tempered by wisdom, 38
   J' last offer of m to Jewish rulers, 1910
   may be lavish, justice is precise (J), 1469
   ministry always individuals (J), 1469
   not a contravention of justice, 38
   not to be thrust on those who despise it, 315
   not to be tramped on, 315
   of God depicted by divine Spirit, 92
   proferred Lucifer, 603
   "show m to those who abuse...", 1932
   steps to m: just, fair, patient, kind, 315
MERCY TIME LAG, THE, 615
mercy, to receive, must show, 1639
   "trampled by rebels of time", 315
   true m comes only as climax, 315
   vs. love, 2018
MERCY, THE VOICE OF, 430
mercy, when m can't circumvent justice, 1638
Mesopotamia, 751, 838
   Abnerian Christianity, 1869
   Aden (strange preacher) in Ashtaroth, 1765
   all women...submit to embrace of strangers, 1042-43
   climate, decisive factor civilization at M, 900
   contributions to
      Cyprus, 896
      Egypt, 894
      Europe, 892
      Greece, 895
MESOPOTAMIA, THE EDENITES ENTER, 847
Mesopotamia, from M Adamites sent progeny to world,
   868
   headquarters of Planetary Prince, 743
   Hebrews inclined toward M creation story, 838
   how Sumerians appear so suddenly in M, 860
   India not out of touch with M, 10,000 years, 881
   J in, 1481
   John Baptist's followers, 1526
MESOPOTAMIA, LIFE IN, 849
Mesopotamia, Nathaniel preached in lands beyond M, 2058
   overrun by barbarian horsemen, 875-76
   reached by Melchizedek missionaries, 1021
   remnants of ancient days of Dalamatia, 868
MESOPOTAMIA, SALEM RELIGION IN, 1042
Mesopotamia, second Garden between rivers in M, 847
   seven chief deities, 1042
   similarities, M and China, due to trade, 886
   1000s of years, Adamites grew wheat, barley, 901
   Zoroaster learned of Caligastia...at Ur, 1049
mesotrons, found abundantly in space rays, 479
Mesozoic Age, 672, 692
message, between Michael, Immanuel, 2016
   burden of J', 1460, 1560-61
   from Bethany, 1836
   J', all nations and religions would have embraced,
      1670
   J' saving m, 1670
   new, after Pentecost (apostles), 2066
   of J, each new generation, restate, 2060
   sending, evolution of, 775
   that replaced the gospel, 2066
messages, from the departed? no!, 1230

messenger, gone almost 1 million years on a mission,
   259
MESSENGER HOSTS OF SPACE, THE, 273
Messenger Hosts of Space, 107, 411, 1241
messenger, service (see "David's messengers")
Messenger, Solitary,   authored papers 107-112 in the
   U Book
"messenger, unseen will run by your side", 1967
messengers, David's, 40 or 50 (intelligence service)
   (see also "David Zebedee")
MESSENGERS, GRAVITY, 346
Messengers, Mighty (see "Mighty Messengers")
Messengers of the Havona Circuits, 258
messengers, "of heaven, they have destroyed these" (J),
   1908
   of the kingdom (today) parable of sower applies to,
      1693
Messengers of the Local Universes, 259
Messengers of the Paradise Trinity, 258
Messengers of the Superuniverses, 259
MESSENGERS, SOLITARY, 256, 413
MESSENGERS, THE TERTIARY SUPERNAPHIM, 288
Messiah, after wine at Cana, all thought J was M, 1531
   all parties and sects believed M coming, 1535
   apocalyptic about M, written by Selsa, 1915
   apostles couldn't escape Jewish concept of M, 1952
   apostles preached a risen M, 2060
   "are you the M, the Son of God?" (woman), 1986
   carpet of honor for donkey bearing M, 1882
   "expect M but appearance will be in mystery", 1791
   expected, 1334, -39, -47, -49
   Ezra, "let us be aloof from this false M", 1526
   false, at Gerizim, 1989
   a future hope, kingdom with appearance of M, 1858
   hoped for M with show of power, glory, 1994
   J, at point to forbid regarding self as M, 1521
      attempted prevent followers calling him M, 1523
      couldn't remove idea of M ruling at Jerusalem, 1867
      "gives up on M", 1532, 1748
      knew he was not to become Jewish M, 1396
      knew ideas of Jews concerning M, 1515
      knew Jews wanted miracle-working M, 1521
      never be accepted by Jews as M without "wonders",
         1520
      pondered on matter of M, 1391
      started public work as Jews expected M, 1509
      would not fulfill wonder-working concept, 1754
   Jews, couldn't understand a suffering M, 1872
      expected M free them from bondage, 1509
      feared sin might prevent coming of M, 1511
      thought their history ran Abraham to Moses, 1509
   John Baptist, in prison tempted to doubt J, 1507
      new and certain notes about M, 1505
      parents of JB convinced J would become M, 1351-52
      settled he was to be herald of the M, 1499
   kingdom righteous state God (M) would rule, 1500
   Mary, convinced son was to become M, 1365, -90
      resurrected all her hopes J as M, 1527
   "Messiah is the Son of David" (scribe), 1901
   not Jewish concept M would be divine, 1347
   Peter made mistake "selling" J as M, 1552
   Psalm changed to refer to Abraham, not M, 1902
   reappearing of M, result in New Jerusalem, 1913
   secular idea of M led to Jews' destruction, 1913
   Simeon, Anna, singers, longed for M, 1353
   views of Jews on M "not with eye of faith", 1588
   would be a stem arising out of the vine, 1946
   "you claimed to be M, true?" (Annas), 1979
Messianic, 1385, -90, 1509, 1902
   difficulties, clean sweep of, 1522

Messianic (cont'd)
  prophecies
    applied to J after the fact, 1347
    J thought over, 1881
metal, red hot, terrorized early man, 748
metals, Garden of Eden, 823
  heavy sank toward planet's center, 668
  widespread early use, 903
metamorphoses, endless m of universe making, un-
    making, remaking, 176
  of the I AM, 1154
  of space, energy factors into cosmic potentials, 37
metamorphosis, butterfly out of caterpillar? !, 480
  of energy and matter, never-ending, 473
metaphysical, many m dilemmas caused by... 1298
metaphysics, confusing, 536, 1136, -39-40
  futile gesture of, 1139
  has proved a failure, 1136
  human substitute for revelation, 1139
  man's vain attempt at substitution for mota, 1136
  muddle of reason-developed m needs revelation, 1136
METEORIC ERA, THE, 658
meteorites, 563
Methusaleh (900 years were 70), 858
Mexicans, origin, 727
Mexico, Alaska, M, Cape Horn, long range formed, 689
  blood smeared on doorposts, ancient custom, 982
  greatest crustal deformations in millions of years,
    689
  later civilizations mixed 4 colors, 884
  Mother of God cult in M, 984
  Proterozoic fossil-bearing ridge, Alaska to M, 670
  source of civilizations of M, Central & So. America,
    727
  340 million years ago, Pacific arm over M, 675

mi

Micah and Obadiah, 1067
mice reproduce fast, elephants evolve fast, 560
Michael (Creator and Master Son of Nebadon, universe
    father and sovereign head of all personality in
    Nebadon, 406. Creator of this universe, 1317.
    Bestowed on this planet as Jesus of Nazareth, 1308.)
    (see also "Jesus", and "Christ Michael")

  active in universe while J in tomb, 2016
  all ranks of angels subject to his sovereignty, 422
  and associates, changing course of evolution, 1863
  babe of Bethlehem born on U, 1316
  bestowal of M, 611; 121st of an Eternal Son upon
    Universes, 1309
MICHAEL BESTOWALS, 239
MICHAEL BESTOWALS, THE, 1308
Michael, bestowals about 150 million years apart, 1309
  billion years for bestowal career, 1318
  born a creator, earned sovereignty, 1318
  certain unworthy children of M, 1331
  chose U, 1325, -44
  concerned only with creation, sustenance, ministry,
    372
  could hardly come to U until, 1053
  creator of all this universe of things and beings, 1317
  Creator Son, also member of... Trinity Ultimate, 1318
  earth name, J, 1084, 1316-17, -25
  Eternal Son of Trinity, the original M, 87
  5th bestowal, one stage of mortal evolution, 1315
  1st bestowal, 1 billion years ago, 1309
  in universe, became J (Christ Michael) on earth, 1325
  incarnation guide for, 1324
  known to U as the Christ, 1084

Michael (cont'd)
  Memorial, on first mansion world, 2015
  number 611, 121, at liberty to ascend, 1513
MICHAEL OF NEBADON, 366
Michael, of Nebadon (Master Son) universe name of Son
    who became J, 33-34, 372, 1084, 1309, -23
  the original, 234
  the original first-born Creator Son, 87
  the original presiding head of primary Paradise Sons,
    234
  the original was Original Mother Son, 87
  our Universe's creator, 1315
  personal creator of this universe, 24
  personal sovereignty combines... 1324
  ready for first bestowal billion years ago, 1309
  ruler of U of Nebadon (and its creator), 1317
  safe conduct for his created sons of Nebadon, 1325
  2nd bestowal took deposed Lutentia's place, 1311
  selected disintegrating nebula for universe building,
    654
  sovereign on world of secession and rebellion, 1312
  spends much time visiting... planets, 367
  Spirit of Truth creates consciousness of, 2061
  vs. Supreme, 1288
Michael Son, consort, prepersonal, then personal, 203-04
  to us is God, 66
Michael's bestowal on U, 409
MICHAEL'S BESTOWAL, TIMES OF, 1332
Michael's message to A&E, 852
Michaels (Creator Sons) (Paradise Sons), 234
  experientially earn sovereignty, 237
  have exhausted potentials of... finite experience, 367
Michal, daughter of Saul, 785
microscope, spiritual joy can't be put under, 2095
micro-size, volume of proton, if big as pin head... 477
Middle Ages, 801, 2077
  every man belonged to someone else, 794
middle class, the small mc, Mediterranean society,
    1st century A.D., 1335
"midgets", 562
MID-MAMMALS, THE, 704
mid-mammals, 700
  subdued their corner of creation, 705
mid-mind (evolving soul), 1218
midnight transport dispatch (from U), 439
midsonite worlds, where Melchizedeks function as life
    carriers, 400
midsoniters, the, 400, 565, 632
  parallel for mind what Adams do biologically, 633
mid-space zones, incapsulate space reservoirs, 124
MIDWAY CREATURES, THE, 415, 424 (see also
    "Midwayers" following)
MIDWAY CREATURES, THE, 855
midway creatures, (see also "midwayers")
  aid seraphim manipulate environment, 1244
  become ascending Sons of God, 248, 444
MIDWAY CREATURES, GLORIFIED, 349
"midway creatures", Havona Servitals, 273
Midwayer Commission, The, authored the Part IV papers
    in the U Book (excepting Paper 120) numbered 121-196
midwayers: (after this listing see "MIDWAYERS,
    THE PRIMARY", and "MIDWAYERS, THE
    SECONDARY")
  ably assist angels on U, 1250
  achieve use of entire energy gamut, 425
  Adamic vs. primary, 864
  after m, cherubim, (MC) most like us, 545
  almost 10,000 loyal m offset evil pair, 823
  and others assumed custody of tree of life, 756
  are not men, nor angels, are planetary sentinels, 864
  are our nearest of kin, 545

midwayers (cont'd)
Beelzebub, leader of disloyal m, 602
both groups of rebel m now held in custody, 863
can attain double velocity, 372,560 mps, 260
can help seraphim in rare human contact, 1246
can use entire energy gamut, 425
Midwayers, Chief of Urantia, authored paper 91 in the U Book
midwayers, contact "material things" at will, 865
contact T A in favorably constituted mortals, 1258
depart planets when light and life achieved, 349,444
descendants of Material Sons (Adam), 583
differ greatly universe to universe, 349
difficult to classify, 415
exalted m are interpreters, early light and life, 627
first group of permanent inhabitants, 865
40,119 of primary m joined Caligastia, 756
further cause of planetary civilization, 425
guarded settlement of loyalists day and night, 756
guardians of the human mind, 863
have definite powers over things and beasts, 865
have 150,000 facts, incompatible with "chance creation", 665
how serve T A in some minds, 1258
large numbers lost to Lucifer cause, 608
largely direct work of spornagia, 528
many are translated, achieve Paradise, 248
many of U m interned, 584
midway between Materials Sons and us, 415
must pass through parenthood experience, 516
offspring of Material Sons and Daughters, 583
1000 only to each couple, 856
1-2-3 the First, leader of loyal m, 514
1-2-3 served as governor general of U, 866
only m can intervene in material conditions, 1361
only intelligent group who remain on sphere, 415
origin of, 745
partly compensated for absence of Planetary Prince, 1254
problems involving m decided by...1254
qualified administrators on planets, 626-27
MIDWAYERS, THE REBEL, 863
midwayers, rebel m prisoners by order of Most Highs, 864
rebellious, uncontrolled, made "demon'-possessed, 1755
rebellious, under control, 1646
release of, 629
remain continuously on own sphere, 415
rolled stone from J' tomb, 2023
saved Peter after Herod killed James, 865
second advent of Michael, and m, 1919
spironga on Jerusem what m are here, 523
MIDWAYERS, TRANSLATED, 444
midwayers, transported A&E faster than birds, 832
ultimately become ascenders to Paradise, 425
unique, always appear on decimal planets, 424
MIDWAYERS, THE UNITED, 864
motto of, 866
midwayers, use undiscovered energies in their work, 325
valuable services in preparing for crises, 1257
Van was commander of loyal m, 760
views, 1787
voluntary union of m at Pentecost, 584
we can see them in light and life stages, 627

MIDWAYERS, THE PRIMARY, 855
midwayers, primary
50,000 created by Prince's staff, 424,745

midwayers, primary (cont'd)
first from PP's corporeal staff, 745
for ages sum total of spirit world to evolving mortals, 745
intelligence corps and celestial entertainers, 425
planetary historians, portray on system hdqtrs, 425
resemble angels more than mortals, 424
UNITED MIDWAYERS, THE, 864

MIDWAYERS, THE SECONDARY, 862
midwayers, secondary, 414,1332,-43,-57
almost 2000, 861
are grandsons of Adamson, 861
don't confuse with primary, 583
electrically energized, 862
help in subjection of insubordinate subversive minorities, 583
mischief after Adamson, 863
more like humans than angels, 424
1984 in 8 subgroups, 862
produced every 70 days by sex and nonsex liaison,862
semispiritual work on U, 864

MIDWAYERS, TRANSLATED, 444

"mighty man of God": Jude to J, 1532
in kingdom (Philip), 1558
mighty men of old, 822
mighty messenger of the kingdom, (John Mark),1921
MIGHTY MESSENGERS, THE, 245
Mighty Messengers, 243,619
all phases of universe activities, 245
almost one trillion our superuniverse, 245
are a class of perfected, tested mortals, 245
are Trinity embraced in classes of 700,000, 245
authored the following papers in U Book:

22	52
28	54
30	55 and co-authored 56
32	115
34	116
40	117
42	118

Jerusem citizens, loyal, became eligible to be MM, 619
of the revelatory Corps of Orvonton, 255
official observers of A D, 246
serve Perfections of Days (the 210 administrators over 70 major sectors), 210
MIGHTY SUPERNAPHIM, THE, 286
migration, the last great mammalian, 698
Milcha, cousin of Apostle Thomas, 1679
mile, second, 2084
militant J, last address in Capernaum synagogue, 1715
militarism, disintegrates the vanquished, 786
is autocratic and cruel, savage, 786
militarists, Andites best ever on U, 872
military organization, followed from capital, 776
MILITARY PREPAREDNESS, 818
milk, not after 1 year, Eve's children, 834
of black cow highly magical, 971
taboo, excreta esteemed, 968
Milky Way galaxy, vast numbers of former nebulae, 170
millenium, not for a m serene social order, 1086
miller, J advised Corinth m, 1474
mimicry believed strong in magic power, 972
mind, 8,9,403
ability to coordinate things, ideas, values, is supermaterial, 140
abnormal, no capacity for sonship, 1441

mind (cont'd)

MIND, THE ABSOLUTE, 102

mind, adjudicating, of Universal Censors, 218
    Adjuster, and will, 1217
    all is circuited in Conjoint Actor, 71
    all we have of reality subject to our will, 1216
    alone, can never fathom reality, 1641
    always reaches out towards 7 things, 483
    and brain capacity, 670
    and matter are experiential variables, 140

MIND AND MATTER — ENERGY, 467

mind, and spirit, man should develop, 1519
    and spirit, prevent universe from becoming uniform, 2078
    and will, yours and T A's, 1205
    animal and human m gifts of local Mother Spirit, 404

MIND ARENA OF CHOICE, THE, 1216

mind, attainment, ultimate of, 806
    automatically prepared for T A when... 379
    awareness required, of thing, meaning, value, 1120
    basic judgments of mortal m (3), 2094
    becomes dual, triune, 1286
    becomes mediator between material and spiritual, 1779
    becoming divine, 1205
    between 2 systems, above, below, 1216
    body minus volitional m, no longer human, 1230
    can control, dominate its level in universe, 1222
    can dominate physical level, 1222
    can portray synthesis, energy, mind, spirit, 1120
    can profit from experience, 738
    cannot create values, 2094
    cannot survive this life without spirit, 565
    can't comprehend eternal, 73
    can't stand conflict of double allegiance, 1480
    can't understand Son, 78, 80
    choices, three, of mortal m, 2094
    chooses a moral judgment, is religious experience, 1131
    circuit of, 103, 1230-32
    conflict of double allegiance, good and evil, 1480
    connotes presence-activity of living ministry, 481
    consciousness, the idea of God, 69
    constant spiritual renewing of your, 1609
    coordinates the universe, 482

MIND, THE COSMIC, 191, 481, 1269

mind, cosmic, determines freedom, initiative, 2078
    creature m not directly responsive to Father, 47
    death, (intellectual death), 1230
    defined, 142
    dependent on brain capacity afforded by, 670
    derives only from pre-existent mind, 403
    destined to become increasingly material or spiritual, 26
    differences, degree, not quality, 951
    discourse on, J, 1479
    disruption, may come from unresolved conflicts, 1480
    distributed forever, no impoverishment of source, 50
    divine, knows thought of all creation, 48
    divine lover lives in m, 2094
    does not control energy, a Deity prerogative, 1222
    does not create real values, 2094
    dominant influence on planet, 482
    dominant over matter, 740
    double allegiance, doesn't stand, 1480
    early manifests supermaterial qualities, 1480
    emancipation of, 1773
    endowment of superuniverses derives from 7 Master Spirits, 102
    endowment, three-fold, 192, 399, 738
    energy and spirit, 1120

mind (cont'd)

    evaluator dwells in m, 2094
    ever confronted with... refereeing contest...1134
    evidences (3) of spirit indwelling, 2094
    evolution, 709, 738
    evolutionary m is able to, 2096
    evolving animal m, not inherently God-knowing, 482
    evolving morontia, 481
    exchange your m for m of J of Nazareth, 553
    exists around spirit nucleus, 142
    eye of m perceives fact, eye of intellect discerns values, 1435
    first m of will dignity on u; celebrated, 710
    focalizations of Third Source and Center, 1270
    forces, are convergent in I S, 5
    fully stable only when, 1217
    gateway to soul, 1705, -33
    God is in man's, 62, 64

MIND-GRAVITY CIRCUIT, THE, 103

mind, -gravity circuit, focalizes in T S C, 103
    gravity, progeny of A&E dependent on mg, 581 (see also "gravity, mind")
    gravity, universal, centered in Spirit, 639
    growing, adjusts to broader... 92
    has response, as to gravity, 192
    has 3 basic choices, 2094
    high levels insight because, 2094
    how functions to exercise judgment-decisions, 1295
    human, J' mastery of, 1414-21, -24-25, -84
    illuminated, possible sometimes, see potential personality, 1199
    immortal, must be able to worship, and crave survival, 403
    in spiritual choosing, 756
    increasingly material, or spiritual, 26
    Infinite Spirit is source of mortal m, 80
    innate endowments of, 192
    insight, can attain, why, 2094
    interpreter lives in m, 2094
    invents origins (incorrect), 1260
    is always creative, 483
    is bestowal of (Daughters of) Infinite Spirit (Conjoint Actor), 45, 103, 564
    is cosmic instrument, will plays discord or melodies, 1217
    is creation of, 639
    is different on each Havona world, 161
    is encircuited in Holy Spirit, 1187
    is functional endowment of I S, 103, 638
    "is infallible", Lucifer, 605
    is infinite in potential, 638
    is the technique whereby spirit realities become experiential, 140
    is unity, 1120
    is your ship, T A your pilot, will is your captain, 1217
    it is by m that you live or die, 1216
    J' m, exchange your m for, 553
    J talked to Ganid about m, 1479
    knowledge is a possession of the m, truth an experience of the soul, 1435
    let this m be in you which was also in Christ J, 1123, 1408

MIND LEVELS, EVOLUTIONARY, 738

mind, liberated when modified by spirit, 140
    loaned to man, 1216
    lowest of all, human, 482
    makes spirit realities experiential, 140
    manifestations of m below level of cosmic, 53
    man's m, dominant influence on planet, 483
    material, cosmic loom, carries morontia fabrics, 1217

mind (cont'd)

material, mid-mind (evolving soul) and cosmic, 1218
no moral values, 1480
not wholly, 2094
matrix, 533
matter, spirit, all equally real, 141
mechanical-nonteachable, one world in Nebadon, 738
mechanism for communication between spirit and
matter, 1110
mediation of m aids spirit, 140
mediator between material, spiritual, 1779
Mind Minister of time and space (I S), 161
"minister to sick in either m or body", 1801

MIND, THE MINISTRY OF, 102

mind, ministry, of ams, essential to intellectual, etc.
evolution, 738
moral decision indicated in 7th mind adjutant, 1186
mortal m limited capacity of, 33
much about m is unknown, 104
must overcome evolution's restraining barriers, 1302
mysterious, quick reactions due to adjutant spirits,
739
naturally God-seeking, not God-knowing, 482
never ceases to progress, 1269
a new m, Mystery Monitors labor for, 1191
no normal m subject to rebel spirits, 863
nonmechanical-teachable organismal response, 739
not immortal when without spirit insight, 403
"not men, but will of God", 1760
not normal, 1230, 1440-41
of God, no mystery to know, 1123
of universe mechanism is creative spirit mind, 482
on U indwelt by 15-mind T A, whole world gains, 1198
on U is a compromise, 103
only brave person will face what logical m discovers,
1773
only man m that submits to spirit, can, 484
only purposive, progress towards unity, 482
over matter, 1222, -75
perceives only mind phenomena, 30
personal energy system around... 142
phenomena are not predictable, 155
Planners, 553
respect your newborn morontia will, 553
preadjutant spirit m, 480
presence of the Infinite Spirit, 1288
principle ministry of, 1181
proof of presence of m in planning cosmos, 665
pure, discerns God, 1105
the pure m hears the Adjuster, 1105
pure m is subject to universal gravity grasp... 104
purposive and dominant, effects evolution, 482
purposive and dominant, makes progress toward
harmonious unity in cosmos, 482
quickened, gateway to soul, 1705
reaches out towards, 483
realities of cosmos, three basic, 195
referees between emotional impulse and moral
growth, 1134
reinforcement for, 1205
relative values vs. religion's supreme v, 2075
religious experience, never fully understands, 69
responsive to overcontrol of spirit, 484
sans spirit, no survival, 565
ship, pilot, captain, 1217
slothful animal m rebels at, 1097
soul, m, and spirit closely united when, 1142

MIND, THE SPIRIT, 78

mind, spirit and m when fully united, 757
spirit lives in m, 1705

mind (cont'd)

Spirit of Truth stimulus for, 2065
spirit values of m flash on high, 84
spiritual dominance of m, 2 conditions, 1216
staggered by unrevealed infinity of Father--I AM,
1169
strengthened in soul by spiritual renewing of m, 1609
subconscious vs. super-conscious, 1099
subnormal, no capacity for sonship, 1441

MIND, THE SUPREME, 1268

mind, supremely happy, is the one... 1480
technique whereby you use mind of J, 1123
temporary intellect system loaned for a lifetime, 1216
thinking, feeling, perceiving mechanism, 8
transformation of J' m finished, 1495
transit of mortal m from mechanical statics to
spiritual dynamics, 1303
trust all matters of m... to T A, 1207
unifying m is supermaterial, 140
unity of m from consciousness sorter, 1480
universal urges of m (two), 1218
universally dominates matter, 484
vs. physics, chemistry, 738
we distort by useless anxiety, 103
we mar by insincerity, unrighteousness, 103
we subject m to animal fear, 103
what m desires to comprehend more important than,
1216
what m is striving to be like more important than,
1216
when m chooses right moral judgment, a religious
experience, 1131
"which was in Christ be also in you", 1123, 1408
working model of human's m studied by waiting T A,
1186
you can exchange yours for that of J, 553
yours, to receive reinforcement of T A's mind, 1205

mind and spirit relationship, results in new universe
value, the soul, 1218

mind, cosmic (see "cosmic mind"), 481

mind-energy manipulators, 504

mind judgments, result in moral values, 2094

mind laboratory, billion worlds of Havona are m laboratories of creators of cosmic m, 161

mind of God, as sure of consciousness of m of G as of
man, 1123
no mystery to know, due to T A, 1123

mind-spirit, balance wheel of u of u, 150

mind-spirits, adjutant (see "adjutant mind spirits")

Mind, Supreme, strives for mastery of energy-matter,
1276

MINDS, ADJUTANT-SPIRIT, 481

minds, deep-thinking 3 intuitions, 192
difference between m, savage and man, 951
evolving morontia, 481, 1205
human, channels of astonishing similarity, 191
inferior will spurn culture, 578
modern, advancing, expanding, 2085
of men, spirit indwells, 1536
persuade, don't compel, 1931

MINDS, PREADJUTANT-SPIRIT, 480

minds, troubled, minister to, 1591
two made one in J, 1425
vs. hearts, 2052
when included in spiritual circuits, 379

mingling, value of m with diverse groups, 526

minister, as you pass by, 1875
to God, we when we help, 1475
to the sick, 1590

MINISTERING RESERVES, 555

ministering (cont'd)
MINISTERING SPIRITS, THE, 285
ministering spirits, authorities, powers, of Infinite
    Spirit, 418
MINISTERING SPIRITS OF THE CENTRAL UNIVERSE,
    285
MINISTERING SPIRITS OF THE LOCAL UNIVERSE, 418
Ministering Spirits of the Local Universes, 286
MINISTERING SPIRITS OF THE SUPERUNIVERSES, 306
ministering spirits of time, 107, 285, 306, 411, 418, 1241
Ministering Spirits of the Universes, 286
ministering spirits to mortals, 1003, 1241
ministers, define God instead of direct worship, 993
    of experiential mind (7), 402
MINISTERS, SON-SPIRIT, 427
MINISTERS, TRANSITION, 439
MINISTERS, UNATTACHED, 429
ministrations, divine, 3 initiate growth of evolutionary
    religion, 1003
ministries, circuits of energy, mind, spirit, not
        permanently ours, 1286
    correlated (seraphim, Adjuster, Holy Spirit, Spirit
        of Truth), 1245
    divine Spirit source of continual m, 380
    fortuitous conspiracies, 55
    from three persons of Trinity, 380, 639, 2061-62
    manifold circuits of cosmic ministry, 1287
    spirit m become more and more coordinate, 380
    spiritual, gradual always, 739
    through all the helper hosts, you reach Havona, 290
ministry, four-fold, 1245; three-fold, 1003; augmented,
    1003
    many spiritual influences, all as one, 95
    mostly unconscious of this inner m (T A), 1207
    no longer can man monopolize m, 2065
MINISTRY OF THE DAYNALS, LOCAL UNIVERSE, 231
MINISTRY OF THE FATHER'S LOVE, 75
ministry, of guardian angel, unifies influences, 1244
    of merriment, 549
MINISTRY OF MIND, THE, 102
ministry of mind, principal, 1181
MINISTRY OF THE PRIMARY SUPERNAPHIM, 298
MINISTRY OF THE SECONAPHIM, 317
MINISTRY OF THE SPIRIT, 379
ministry of Spirit, conspiracy within you of s forces, 381
    descends to meet you as you are, 380
    part of divinely correlated unity of m, 1245
    water of life, prevents consuming thirst of mortal
        discontent, 381
ministry, ours, to believers, unbelievers, 1930
    personal, public, 1424
    stream of divine, 1638
    to man from savagery forward, 1003
    to man, 7 higher spirit influences, 2062
MINISTRY, UNITED, OF THE PARADISE SONS, 232
MINOR AND MAJOR SECTOR STAGES, THE, 635
minor sector, million systems, billion inhabitable
        worlds, 181
    100 local universes, 166
    rotational center of our ms in Saggitarius, 168
    training spheres, 212
minor space bodies, 172
minorities, insubordinate subversive m, midwayers
        help overcome, 583
    must suffer, 927
    unfair, unjust m, entrenched behind power, 1891
minute regulations of conduct dominated Jews, 1340
Miocene period, 698
miracles, 987, 1633 (see also "healing")
    after Cana, 1644

miracles (cont'd)
    after 40 days, J' miracles only abridged time, 1517
    age of m to age of machines, upsetting, 2077
    and religion, 1128
    apparent healing m explained, 1669
    approach m through J, not vice versa, 1671
    belief because of, 1340, 1531, -33, 1644, -53, -58, 1704
    believed in as commonplace, J' time, 1341
    centurion's servant healed, miracle?, 1648
    challenge to Sanhedrin, 1813
    cleansing of leper first m, deliberately performed,
        1644
    curing Peter's mother-in-law, no m, 1631
    deliberate, 1633, -44, -65, -67, 1702
    "don't teach expectation of m", 1804
    draught of fishes not a m, 1629
    enemies, in response to challenge of, 1665
    epileptic in synagogue, no miracle, 1631
    everyone believed in, 1340
    feeding the 5000, 1700, -04
    few, most intriguing are incarnational bestowals, 1331
    first and only nature m, preplanned, 1702
    first deliberate m, healing leper at Iron, 1644
    HEALING AT SUNDOWN, THE, 1631
    heavy catch of fishes, not a m, 1629
    in protest against dogma, 1665
    in response to challenge of enemies, 1665
    J explained boy was not dead, no m, 1645
    J would not transcend, only accelerate natural law,
        1518
    Lazarus' resurrection, 1842
    leper, cleansing the, 1643
    natural law, 1517-18, -20, -30, 1631, -44-45, -48-49
    not for proof, 1128
    not to tempt, 1834, -46, -80
    1000 afflicted, cured or helped, not m, 1658
    Pharisees compelled to notice m, 1813
    philosophic m when finite discerns God, 27
    protest against bondage of dogma, 1665
    so-called, gave J trouble, 1634
    space assembly of chemical ingredients, 1530
    strangest of all the Master's m, 1812
    superhuman agencies, 1530
    "take up your bed and walk"--no m, 1650
    we labor for a generation of sign-seekers, 1533
    wine at Cana, in no sense a m, 1530
    would call forth only outward allegiance, 1520
miraculous phenomena, to repeat today, 1700
Miriam (sister of J), birth, 1357
    belle of family, 1402, -18
mirror, defeat is true m for self, 1741
mirrors, living, primary seconaphim, 307-08
misadaptation of life, cosmic disharmony, 1434
misbehavior, fraternal consequences of m, 619
miscegenation, highly disastrous, 726, 920
    jeopardize all civilization on U, 586
    no, 586
    when no, 920
mischief in their hearts, warned against those with, 1677
misconduct, never by anyone in Havona, 155
miseries, "not a personal visitation of...judgment", 1664
misery, avoid fellowship in, 1766
    much could be overcome, 1661
    not a divine judgment, 1664
MISFORTUNES OF CALIGASTIA, 752
"missing link", 700, 704, 720
missing links never existed, 669
MISSION, THE ADJUSTER'S, 1191
MISSION AND MINISTRY OF THOUGHT ADJUSTERS,
    1185

mission (cont'd)
  of J (see "mission" under Jesus)
  of Joshua, the teacher (yearlong Mediterranean
    tour), 1482
MISSION OF THE PRINCES, 572
mission, of religion, paramount, 1086
  of revelation, to censor religions of evolution, 1007
  of T A, 1185, -92, 1205
missionaries, Buddhist, Asoka sent forth 17,000, 1037
  Christian, early failures, 1051
  Eden's emissaries, 850, 870
  first, Alexander's path, 2068
  foreign m never sent out but by request, 749
  mistakes, Africa, 750
  neighboring planet, 819
  world's first (Onagar's), 716
missionary work in reverse, 743
mis-steps, not surprising ms occur, 846
mistake, confusing teachings of J with the mysteries,
    1337
  don't make m...of failing establish kingdom in own
    life, 1863
  early Christian teachers neglected Asia, 1432
  great, changing J' message to gospel of person, 2067
  greatest, 2092
  in communications on high, 760
  not the soul's worth, 1739
  of Judaism, 43
  of modern religion, neglects truths of science, 43
  of students of J' life, 2092
  serious, of any revealed religion, 2064
  study of J, either human or divine, 2092
  to dream of God far off, 64
  to identify J with any political, economic...1580
  to regard religious dogma, superstition, as super-
    natural sedimentation, 1071
  trying to prove you've found God, 1733
mistakes, about J' teachings, 1670
  and misdeeds of Sons, 1632
  Christian leaders, early, turned to west too much,
    1430-32
  forget, have long view of things, 1739
  great in enthusiasm for gospel, 2067
  none ever made in Havona, 155
  "of all who labor on U", 1189
  2 great m early Christianity, 1670
  you don't forget here, will forget in eternity, 1739
misunderstanding, evidences fact and act of personality
    (vs. mechanism), 846
  led to 2nd bestowal, 1311
MISUNDERSTANDING OF SUFFERING — DISCOURSE
  ON JOB, 1662
misunderstandings, avoid unnecessary social m, 1740
  J seldom corrected m, 1594
mites, widow cast two into trumpet, 1883
Mithraic, cult arose from sun veneration, 947
  cult, blood-drinking, 1082
  group in Rome and J, 1455
Mithraism, 1050, -82, 1340, 1459
MITHRAISM AND CHRISTIANITY, 1083, 2070
Mithraism, competitor of Paul's cult of Christianity, 1337
MITHRAS, THE CULT OF, 1082
MIXED RACES, THE, 904

mo

mob, discerning, 1993
  J walks through, 1687
  score of well-trained guardians can restrain, 763
  spirit aroused, 1687
mobilization, in Judas, hatred, etc., 1567

mobilization (cont'd)
  of wisdom, 1776
MODERN CIVILIZATION, DEVELOPMENT OF, 900
modern phraseology, (J' teachings), 1428, -57, -59, -76,
    1479, 1598, 1620, -38, -80, -92, 1739, -65, -72, 1929
MODERN PROBLEM, THE, 2075
modest home vs. better one, 1801, -05
modesty, restraint, origin, 963
modifications of human sacrifice, 981
modifiers, (three) of man's views on "cruel" world, 1306
Mohammed, 1008, -11
Mohammedanism, degrades women, 937, 1010
moment, is a day, 271; panorama of life in m (Nalda), 1615
momentum, mortals to Paradise by rebound m, 639
MONARCHIAL GOVERNMENT, 789
money, and trade global regulation, peace, 1491
  "cannot love", J, 1398
  changers, 1889-90, 1905
    fees on more than 20 sorts of money, 1889
    percentage went to temple treasury, 1891
    profit on changing m for sacrifices, 1889
    30 to 40% fee (doubled) temple tax, small coins, 1889
  lender, Isaac, complicated J' problem, 1397
  universal language of modern trade, 787
Mongolian, sons Taoist priests, heard J, 1429-30
MONGOLOID RACES, THE, 905
mongrel (and mixed) peoples, 836
Monitor, J had aid of M organizing intellect, 1398
Monitors, Mystery, (see also "Thought Adjusters")
  deserted, due to human failure, 444
  "kingdom of heaven within you", become, 1193
monkey and gorilla, common ancestor of m&g extinct;
  neither specie connected with human's ancestors, 697
monkeys, simians, result of retrogression in mid-
  mammals, 700
MONMATIA, ORIGIN OF OUR SOLAR SYSTEM, 655, 658
monogamy, best for children, 927
  matchless association, 586, 781
MONOGAMY — PAIR MARRIAGE, TRUE, 927
MONOTA, 471
monota, energy reality from space potency to m, 1149
  living nonspirit energy of Paradise, 471
monotheism, all largely from Melchizedek, 1442
  arose as philosophic protest, 1145
  emerging, transmigration ended it, 1029
  expressions of, 1052
  Melchizedek, Abraham, Moses, Zoroaster, 1061
  Moses to John the Baptist, 1076
  origin, 1442
  revival of m in Egypt, 1078
  vs. polytheism in Egypt, 1044
  won over polytheism, 1065
monotheists, great m, Hebrews and Mohammedans, 1144
monotheistic, ideal suffered with passing of Ikhnaton,
  1048
monotony, 555
  and adventure, 159
  immaturity, 159
  multiplies troubles, 1611
  of human contact, 1611
moon, earth growth faster 2 billion years ago, 659
  how it will end, 657
  Neanderthalers sacrificed men for m to shine, 722
  nearing present mass 1-1/2 billion years ago, 659
  no air, 561, 659
  same face to earth always, why, 657
  "why go to?", (creative mind reaches out), 483
  will disrupt, shatter, distant future, 657
  worship preceeded sun worship, 947

moons, about size of U, almost ideal for habitation, 559
  cores formed, moons grew, 658
Moqui tribe of redmen, 968
moraines, 701
moral, and intellectual suicide, 2079
  and spiritual adjustments can be made on spur of
    moment, 911
  can be m, deny God, thanks to graft, 1126
  captives, 1541
  choice, highest, 435
  choosing, usually accompanied by moral conflict, 1131
  code, Hap's, 751
  code of Dalamatia, 751
  commandments, the, 1036
MORAL CONCEPTS, EVOLUTION, 1045
moral, concepts without effect, unless, 380
  conduct, never the whole of religious experience, 68
  creatures, two, quadruple, 495
  decision, T A can't invade mind prior to m d, 1187
  delinquency, J said little about, 1582
  despair, true religion is cure, 1078
  emotions, mighty, move men, 2085
  evolution, not all from revelation, 1045 (see "social
    morality")
  immaturity, evidence of, 1773
  impulses, first have to do with ministry, 1131
  infirmities, healed of, 1649
  life and ambition destroyed, 1029
  movements come from leaders, 1008
  must be m before being immoral, 2079
  only m and spiritual adjustments can be made "fast",
    911
  person before immoral acts, 2079
  power, economic problems, 1739
  quickening, on brink of, 2082
  reaction to temple harlotry, 982
  standard too high fails, 1043
  values become intellectual possessions, how, 2094
  values, can't measure, 2095
moral bank, run on the, 2076
moral choice, ability to choose between emerging
  values, 1187
moral consciousness, is just a name applied to
  emerging values, 1115
moral convictions, as real as mathematical deductions,
  2077
moral majesty of J, designing hypocrisy of his enemies,
  1892
moral nature, can be modified, 1572
  first promptings of, 1131
  how man unfolds, 1862
  impotent without...193
  is super-animal, 2096
  measure of man's, 1609
  origin of social consciousness, 1131
moral quickening, U on brink of amazing, enthralling
  mq, 2082
moral standard, Melchizedeks raised ms too high, 1043
moral values, how mv become intellectual possessions,
  2094
  no state can transcend mv of people, 803
morality, 193, 1585, 2096
  and religion, 1115, 2095
  and religion not necessarily the same, 1780
  and unselfishness, greatness, 317
  cosmic, foundation for, 1284
  determined by motive, 1585
  essential to social system, 2075
  ethics, minus God, no survival value, 1126
  fails to provide for survival of own values, 2096

morality (cont'd)
  from relation to God, 1585
  has origin in reason of self-consciousness, 68
  human, can't provide survival of own values, 2096
  interactions of liberty and loyalty, 435
  is the enlightenment of reason, 196
  is wholly evolutionary, 68
  never by law or force, 193, 1931
  never the whole of religious experience, 68
  not from nature of man, but from his relationship to
    God, 1585
  not necessarily spiritual, may be human, 2096
  predicated on spiritual realities, 2075
  pre-existent soil of God-consciousness, 2096
  realization of Adjuster's presence, 2096
MORALITY, QUICKENERS OF, 435
morality, realization of Adjuster's presence, 2096
  religion provides for survival of m, 2096
  social, not determined by religion, 1005
  traditional m just slightly superanimal, 135
  true, family life is progenitor of, 941
  without God, humanistic grafts, 1126
  without religion, 2096
  would rehabilitate self if...43
morality, cosmic
  interaction of liberty and loyalty, 435
morally fragrant persons, 193
morally unprogressive, low standards, 1457
morals, and ethics, first European religions of, 1338
  and ethics, retarded so recently as Sodom,
    Gomorrah, 1021
  and personality, 192
  religion, not the same, 1780
MORALS, VIRTUE, AND PERSONALITY, 192
morass, Christianity drains many a barbarian m, 2083
mores, always few suffer under advancing m, 927
  become traditions, traditions conventions, 772
  bring social adjustment, 937
  can't be abandoned but for better m, 767
  change, but instincts never, 938
  institutional religion has always lagged behind m, 1128
  never imposed by a superior race, 749
  new are emerging to stabilize marriage, home, 939
  no society endures loss of m except for better m, 767
  reforming m defeated noble cause, 1043
  religion and ghost fear stabilized m, 767
MORES, RELIGION AND THE, 1004
mores, sanction for low practices, 982
  survival of society depends on evolution of its m, 767
Morning Star, the Bright and M S, 369 (see "Bright and
  Morning Star")
Morning Stars, sang together, 87
morontia (term for level between material and spiritual), 9
MORONTIA ACHIEVEMENTS AND MORTAL ASPIRA-
  TIONS, 507
MORONTIA APPEARANCES OF J, 2029 (see also
  "appearances, morontia", under "Jesus)
  J did not appear to his enemies, 2031
morontia, awakening, 1230
  beauty of spheres increases inward to central Isle,
    174
  bodies, described, 2029
  career, last animal traits eradicated by, 551
    of J on U, 40 days, 2057
    overcomes all handicaps of U, 508
  changes, ascending
    8 in system, 71 in constellation, 491 Salvington, 542
  changes (less and less Material)
    570 to reach Salvington, 542
    8 in system, 71 in constellation, 542
    491 on spheres of Salvington, 542

189

mortals (cont'd)

all must have experience, evolve from lower groups, 1195

ascendant m on Jerusem, 606

187, 432, 811 on Jerusem, withstood Lucifer, 609

MORTALS, THE ASCENDING, 340

mortals, ascending, 443

become bilingual, 537

guests of Spirit-fused residents, 411

become Mighty Messengers, 454

born, live, die in relative instant of time, 1232

children of the Supreme God, 1240

chosen as protectors of planetary destiny, 1257

classified by Adjuster types, 445

comfort, no help from T A for, 1192

confronted with climbing from animal...to higher levels, 382

countless have reached Paradise, 127

countless individuals gone to mw, 2024

devoid of courageous decisions, 1207

differ greatly in...63

disqualified for survival give virgin T A experience, 1198

don't be discouraged by discovery you are human, 1739

dual nature of, 381

educated m delivered from intermediaries, 1013

encounter God on 7 successive levels, 11, 1270

erring, be gentle with, 1931

extremely fortunate on quarantined worlds, 578

faith sons before fusion, ascending sons after, 447, 449

MORTALS, FATHER-FUSED, 448

mortals, few are real thinkers, 1213

from 7 viewpoints, 565

adjustment to planetary environment, 565

brain-type series, 566

spirit-reception series, 566

planetary-mortal epochs, 567

creature-kinship series, 567

Adjuster-fusion series, 568

techniques of terrestrial escape, 568

fused with Adjusters during earth life, 570

GLORIFIED MORTALS, 347

"go on from glory to glory until", 1953

how we handicap, thwart, T A, 1199

if on Havona, would be blind, deaf, etc., 154

in future ages may be revelators, 247

intended to recognize these 7 fathers, 587

last (lowest) link of those called "sons of God", 445

learn to live more naturally, effectively, 595

linked by force and power to Deities, 100

little lower than the angels, 1248

low level of comprehension, 1232

lowest order of intelligent and personal creation, 447

lowly animal-origin m races of U, 21

many on U have attained their circles, 1212

never return to native planet, 436

no ancestry on earth between frog and Eskimos, 732

no two alike, personality is unique, 1129

no two can interpret alike the indwelling spirit, 1129

no vital spiritual deprivation due to sin of others, 762

numerous differences, planet to planet, 447

MORTALS OF TIME AND SPACE, 445

mortals, only 2 kinds in eyes of God, 1468

only 2 ways can live together, 1775

Paradise bound, delightful stopping places (J), 1475

perfect in infinite sense, can't be, 22

plan for perfecting, 54

MORTALS, PLANETARY, 340

mortals (cont'd)

MORTALS, PLANETARY SERIES OF, 565

mortals, privileged to seek communion with indwelling spirit, 63

provide for Adjuster-expression, 2078

resurrected in a more glorious form, 1846

resurrected without memory (Spirit fused), 451

room for all in Paradise, 121

saved, and on Paradise (countless), 127

sequence of ascendant steps, 354

sex-deficient, 516

short and intensive testing, 1237

should not prejudge fellow creatures, 419

MORTALS, SON-FUSED, 449

mortals, Son, Spirit, and Father relation to, 445

sons of the Paradise Father, 1240

MORTALS, SPIRIT-FUSED, 450

mortals, spiritual opportunity equal, 63

surviving m on Paradise, countless, 127, 2024

surviving, trained in universe management, 348

swayed by preacher's eloquence, 1722

three classes, accordance with Adjuster relation, 445

time-penalized but not eternity jeopardized, 761

two groups, know God and don't know, 1468

unsalvable, don't give them sympathy, 592

Urantia m entitled as sons of God because:, 448

Urantia m, intense conflicts, material and spiritual natures, 382

virtually disqualified for survival by...ancestors, 1198

who desire Caligastia's curse may join him, 610

who obey divine leadings, more ministry help, 379

why chosen for planetary service, 1257

why falter, fail, succumb, in struggle, 1199

worlds of the spirit-fused, 411

Mosaic, divorce statutes, 1838

services, 1360

Moses (founder of the Hebrew religion, 1009) 747, 778, 1354, 1513, -92, 1643, 1767, -93, 1855, 1905, -07, -25, 2013

aided by violent eruption, Mt. Horeb, 1057

"along with M, I declare..." (J), 1900

because M combatted idolatry, don't frown on beauty, 1600

built upon Salem traditions, 1022

"conform with letter of M' law, but souls steeped in iniquity" (J), 1908

creation story (6 days) credited to M, 838

dead 1000 years before creation story written, 838

denied God spoke to "people" in dreams, 954

don't view God as M saw him, 1597

Egyptians rejected M as prophet, 1046

"enjoins you, 'you shall not kill' ",1790

even M delayed in passage to mansion worlds... 596

"fasting appropriate to law of M, but..." ", 1655

"Father (God) did speak through M", 1731, 1814

followers, childlike Bedouins, 60

forbade "foundation sacrifices", was disobeyed, 981

forty years of waiting, 1436

founder of Hebrew religion, 1009

gave the law, Jews would not compromise, 1340

genius leader of Levantine Bedouins, 1009

great prophet, Egypt rejected, 1046

greatest man between Melchizedek and J, 1047

greatness was in wisdom, sagacity, 1009

had Melchizedek tradition (family), 1016

"hear, O Israel, the Lord our God is one God", 1009

Hebrews rejected M' story of God, 1075

J told Ganid of M, 40 years of waiting, 1436

Jewish feasts established by M, 1379

Moses (cont'd)
  Jewish tradition crystallized about M, 838
  joint gift of Hebrew race and Egyptian royal family, 1047
  Judas returning to teachings of M, 1925
  law of M says: "an eye for an eye", 1577
MOSES, THE MATCHLESS, 1055
Moses, member of current U Counsel, 514
  Mother royal Egyptian, 1047, -55
  a mourner, yet greater than Samson, 1575
  murderer should be put to death, 796
  negotiated for freedom of fellow Semites, 1056
  not since M such profound influence, 1338
  one of seven greatest human teachers, 1339
  organized Hebrew worship, 1058
  presented Deity as holy and upright, 1063
  promulgated 10 commandments in name of Yahweh, 1057
  so-called 5 Books of M, 1900
  sought to combat idolatry, 1600
  spurious document about M' teachings, 838
  successors to M adulterated his monotheism, 1009
  superb leader, but also meek, 1575
  supreme teacher of the Hebrews, 837
  taught first-born son is Lord's, 1352
  taught monotheism... "our God is one God", 1009
MOSES, THE TEACHINGS OF, 1057
Moses, teaching vs. J, 1404, 2016
  "those who sit in M' seat", 1906, -24, -32
  too wise for sudden reforms, 969
  tried to control fetish worship, 969
  was disobeyed, Jews used human sacrifices, 981
  "we are disciples of M" (rulers), 1814
MOST HIGH ASSISTANT, 406, 409
MOST HIGH OBSERVER, THE, 1253
Most High regencies, 1253
Most Highs, Adamic children, many, wards of MH, 861
  ambiguous use of term, U records, 488
  are Vorondadek Sons, Constellation Fathers, 488
  Edentia is seat of MH of Norlatiadek, 485
  Gabriel with MH, decided to command... 605
  greetings of MH, on new mind circuit, 710
  house of System Sovereigns replaces legislature, 633
  Lucifer in counsel with MH often, 601
  may intervene anytime on inhabited world, 1253
  Melchizedek was priest of the MH, 491, 1024
  message followed by Lucifer's, 710
  observer can seize U government in a crisis, 1253
  observer has seized U government 33 times, 1253
  observer holds veto power over U Counsel, 1254
MOST HIGHS OF NORLATIADEK, 488
Most Highs, petition to MH asking for biologic uplifters, 821
  post-Adamic age, begin to rule... men, 594
  present MH observer is 23rd on U, 1253
  rebel midwayers prisoners by orders of, 864
  rotation of MH on Edentia suspended, 490
  rule for greatest good of greatest number, 1488
  "rule in the affairs of men" Daniel, 488
  rule "in the kingdoms of men", 51, 491, 1255, -58, (1906)
  rule, some day civil rulers will learn, 1488
  rulings suggest Melchizedek may take place of Caligastia, 1025
  sent shrub of Edentia to U, tree of life, 745
  serve on headquarters, 150, 000 U years, 390
  sustained orders for special U roll call, 853
  a Vorondadek observer on U for MH, 1253
  were petitioned for way to maintain truth on U, 1014
Most Holy Sphere, 148

MOTA, MORONTIA, 556
mota, 554, 1139
  morontia m, need for, 1136
  a reconciliation between science and religion, 1136
  with m man sees truth, beauty, goodness, in world, 1137
"mote, out of brother's eye", 1571
Mother, divine, is Supreme Being, 1288
mother, sacrificed for child, ancients, 940
  "your m and brothers are outside", 1721
mother cult, 1078
  priests of mc submitted to castration, 976
MOTHER-FAMILY, THE EARLY, 932
mother force of space, 122
mother love, factor in founding early home, 765
  is instinctive, 932
  overcame mores, saved children, 770
  proportionate... 932
Mother of God cult, 895, 984, 1080
Mother Son, Eternal, of Paradise, 235, 1755
Mother Son, Original, 88
  was son of Eternal Son, 87
Mother Spirit (is Creative Spirit, Divine Minister, Universe Spirit, coordinate in divinity with Michael, co-creator of local universe of Nebadon, 406)
  acts for Master Spirit of Orvonton, 197
  and Creator Son are Father-united for adventure of universe creation, 204
  consort of Michael, Creator Son, 203
  Creative Spirit, Divine Minister (are one), 455, 1145
  discharges Master S administration responsibility, 197
  the Divine Minister of Salvington, 406
  elevated to co-sovereignty with Creator Son, becomes his equal, 204
  fragment of MS fuses with some souls, 410
  functions while Creator Son absent, 237
  furthers effect of gigantic mirror, 275
  has full endowment of antigravity, 375
  is Creative Spirit, Son consort, personalized by I S, 204
  is erstwhile Creative Daughter of the I S, 236
  is parent of Bright and Morning Star, 376
  is personalized presence of I S, called Divine Minister, 375
  jointly sponsors creatures with Creator Son, 162
MOTHER SPIRIT, THE LOCAL UNIVERSE, 374
Mother Spirit, mind spirits of MS, the 7 adjutants, 2062
  next, 7 higher spirit influences, 2062
  PERSONALIZATION OF THE CREATIVE SPIRIT, 374
  six phases of career of local MS, 203
Mother Spirit, Universe
  cocreator of each local universe, 162
  supplies essential factor of living plasm, 399
mother wheels of suns, 169
motion, absolute m, relating to unmoving Paradise, 133
MOTION AND SPACE, 133
motion, space m, 4 types, 133
  twofold, of the Supreme, 1265-66
motions and Urantia, seven, 168
"motivation", consciousness of achievement transcends material reward, 435
motivation, discover their m, to love men, 1098
  love is highest, 2096
  of bestowal, 1423
  of men shows their value, 1098
  overmastering, realization of... supreme destiny, 536
motive, it is the m that counts, 1571
  measures righteousness, 1862
  not status, and prayer, 1639

motive (cont'd)
   profit (see "profit motive")
motives, angels can unerringly discern, 313
   determine morality, 1585
   for living, major three, 942
   inscrutable, 2008
   transcendent, are 3, 805
   vital, morality determined by m, 1585
motto of United Midwayers, "what M undertake, they
   do", 866
mounds of stone, tribal competition, 724
MOUNT ASSEMBLY — THE FAITHFUL OF DAYS, 489
Mount Carmel, Elijah prophet of, 1497
Mount Gerizim, in camp on, 1612, -15
   Samaritan Temple to Yahweh, 1612
Mount Gilboa, 1351, 1788
Mount Hermon, 1751-52
   at MH, J' mission complete, 1494
   celestial pageant on, 1755
   the great temptation, universe trial occurred, 1493
   mount of J' trial and triumph, 1745
MOUNT HERMON, SOJOURN ON (J), 1492
mount, most holy, 489
Mount of Olives, 1875, -96, 1923, -81
   J sat...foretelling death of Jewish nation, 1910
   J wept over the city below, 1375
   view gave J his life's greatest purely human thrill,
      1375
MOUNT OF ORDINATION, ON THE, 1568, 2050
MOUNT OF TRANSFIGURATION, THE, 1752
Mount Olivet, 1895-96, 1933, 2057
MOUNT OLIVET, TUESDAY EVENING ON, 1912
Mount Olympus, happy-go-lucky gods of, 1078
Mount Sartaba, 1351
   three days on, 1611
Mount Tabor, 1367
MOUNTAIN, COMING DOWN THE, 1754
MOUNTAIN STAGE, THE MODERN, 696
mountain top of intellectual thought, on every, 1778
   relaxation for mind
   strength for soul
   communion for spirit
mountains, how formed, 662, 689, 691-92
   of material difficulty, 1519
   oldest in world in Asia, 692
"mourn", happy are they who, 1575
mourning, origin, 959
   outward, 1844
mouth, "out of m that defiles", 1712
"movies" on high?, 501, 504

mu

"much given, much required", 1824
mulattos, excellent humanity, slight inferiority, 920
multiple motions (7) revolutionary, confuse star
   observers, 168
multitude, beware the support of the, 1927
   heard J' denunciation, 1910
   one heart and soul, 2065
mummies, why, 953
museum, J and Ganid spent much time in m
      (Alexandria), 1433
   Sumerian records rest on dusty shelves, 860
music, 2080
   barbarous monotony, 500
   can't know through mathematics, 141
   Eden, 835
   harmony is the speech of Havona, 500
   less m from Adamics than humor, 549
   lessons, J, 1387

music (cont'd)
   low on U, 500
   neighboring planets, better, 500
   of space, 499
   one musician could change course of world, 500
   rhythm recorders, 504
   singers, the, 501
musician, one, could change world course, 500
   Simeon, singer, Jerusalem temple, 1353
MUSICIANS, THE CELESTIAL, 497, 499
must do as well as be, 1260
must unify divine law and love, 1222
"musts" for cults, 966
mutations, angiosperms suddenly: figs, magnolias, 689
   animal life exhausts capacity for prehuman m, 734
   mental and spiritual too, 740
   Sangik, 735
   new species appear suddenly, 669
   nothing supernatural about genetic m, 669
   prolific fern family appeared suddenly, 679
   sudden appearance, true birds, 691
   sudden wholly new biologic species, natural, 669
   suddenly family of flowering plants, 691
mutations, animal, sudden
   cephalopods, larger molluscs, 15 ft. long, 677
   dawn mammals, from lemurs, 700, 703
   first Nodite generation, 857
   fishes, first animal vertebrates, 679
   frog and salamander, 732
   frogs and their many cousins, 682
   hoofed animals, grazing species, 695
   human beings, primitive, from Primates, 700, 707
   humans, first true, 993, 419 years before 1934 A.D.,
      707
   humans from descendants of lemurs, 703
   land animals, first, 680
   mid-mammals from dawn mammals, 700
   one thousand plus strains fostered, 734
   placental type mammals, 693, 733
   Primates, 3rd vital m, 700, 706
   protozoan animal type, 732
   reptiles in full-fledged form, 686
   Sangik family, Badonite, superior children, 722
   scorpions, actual air breathers, 678
   sea urchins, outstanding m, 688
   simians and humans from lemurs, 703, 706
   six colored races, 701, 722
   suddenly first multicellular animals, 673
   twins of dawn mammals, superior, 704

my

"my hour has come" (J), (see under "Jesus, Quotes")
"my hour has not yet come", (see under "Jesus, Quotes")
"my (little) children", (see "children, my")
"my ways higher than your ways", 1068
my will that your will be done, 1221, 1303
mysteries, beings close to us, 147   essential to cult, 966
   impenetrable m of reflectivity known on Spiritington,
      145
   "kingdom, have revealed m thereof", 1934
   of incarnation unfathomable, 1317, -76, 1787
   of intimate high spirit interassociations, 146
   of Seraphington, closely related beings "we" can
      almost comprehend, 147
   one of most perplexing of u, 147
   secret of divine Sons' incarnations, known on
      Sonarington, 145
   seven universal m of secret spheres of P, 200
   there are still other Sonarington m, 145
   thousand always remain, 302

mysterious phenomena to explain, more and more, 278
mystery, about this stone (builders rejected), 1894
  and magnitude of God, don't let these overawe you, 139
    appears when realities of spirit... 27
    bestowal of Creator Sons, 87
    continues forever, 302
MYSTERY CULTS, THE, 1079, -81, 1337
mystery, the divine m consists in... 26
    futile to attempt to elucidate Trinity m, 112
    God resides one place, in contact with countless, 139
    "I will ceaselessly try to solve" (Divine Counselor), 221
    in persons of Trinity, 92
    in universal force-charge of space, 169
    incarnation technique of Paradise Son, 228
    incarnations of Michael on bestowals, 1313
    making man and God one, 1237
    of Deity incarnation (J) will remain unsolved, 1317, 1376, 1407
    of evolution, 147
    of life, vital spark from U Mother Spirit, 399
    of mysteries, 26-27
    perplexing, evolution of immortal soul in human mind, 147
    secrets of Seraphington involve three-fold m, 147
    technique of Trinitization to nontrinitized, 146
    the Thought Adjusters are a m of God the F, 145
    universal, how Son of God can be born of woman, 145
Mystery Monitors, 46, 64, 1180, -95, 1238 (see also "Thought Adjusters", "Fragment of Father", "indwelling Spirit")
    activities connection with MM centered on Divington, 1179
    are eternally uniform in divine nature, 1178, -88
    associated with material circuits is puzzling, 1182
    assurance you will occupy your morontia form, 1234
    chief of has close associate, Master Spirit One, 186
    chiefly concerned with future life, 1191
    constitutes soul growth and survival potential, 70
    Father indwells his children as, 1176
    Father spiritually represented by, 360
    Father's presence in minds and souls, 1190
    helped adjust mistakes of all... on this confused planet, 1189
    if deserted by mortal associate, 1200
    impossible task, reveal nature of God to creature, 1290
    indwell the thinking centers of mind, 379
    inscrutable spirit work by, 1191
    ministers higher phases of men's minds, 1203
    mission not to smooth feelings, 1192
    never able to classify MM, truly Godlike, 1182
    never arbitrarily influence you, 1204
    no limit to spiritual ascent of one with, 361
    not thought helpers, but thought adjusters, 1191
    one MM on U, a most useful, potent force, 1198
    patiently indwell for life everlasting, 364
    presents a value, exudes flavor of divinity, 1130
    secret circuits of, 177
    unlimited ability to communicate with each other, 1181
MYSTERY OF GOD, THE, 26
mystery religions, built on myths, 1338
    characterized by, 1337
    diversion, excitement, entertainment, 1081
    of T A and spirit, 1376
    prepared way for vastly superior Christian r, 1337
    promised salvation, 1337
    rites sometimes gruesome, revolting, 1337

mystic occurrences, possibly due to self-acting or Vanished Adjuster, 1178, -96, 1207
mystic phenomena, favorable conditions for mp, but J used none, 1100
    genuine?, 1000
    J never resorted to such methods, 1100
    subconscious delusions, superconscious illusions, 1100
mystical, beware, 1000
    state, characteristics of, 1099
      why not good, 1100
    T A detached during sleep?, 1196
MYSTICISM AND CONVERSIONS, 1098
MYSTICISM, ECSTASY, AND INSPIRATION, 1000
mysticism, gravitates to sub, not super-conscious, 1100
    great danger in, 1099
    may become technique of reality avoidance, 1099, 1121
    often a retreat, 1121
    sometimes has been means of spiritual communion, 1099
"mystics, passive, do not become", 1931
myth, becomes tradition, and then "fact", 1352
    moral obligation to die for state, 800
mythology, Greek m more aesthetic than ethic, 1078
    origin of much, 743, 758, 856, 895

N

Nabobad, leader of school at Kish, 1043
Nabon, Greek Jew, leader of Mithraism, Rome, 1459
Nahor, of a Jerusalem academy, 1019, 1365
Nahor, young evangelist, 1686
NAIN AND THE WIDOW'S SON, 1645
naked, all things are open and n to God, 49
Nalda, 1612
    J' morontia appearance before, 2053
    told J' story to John (Apostle), 1614
Nambia (first Life Carrier of Nebadon), 396
name, new n after perfect fusion, 538
names, for God in other worlds, 23
    of deity, confusion about, on Urantia, 1
Nanak (Guru), religious teachers from Onagar to, 1009
Naomi, marriage at Cana, 1528
Naples, J had no outstanding experience in N, 1441
narrative of J' life, whence, 1332
narratives, these n, 16th proscription on, 351
Nasanta, daughter of Elman, Syrian physician, 1679
Nathan wrote "Gospel of John" at Ephesus, 1342, 1555
NATHANIEL, HONEST (Apostle), 1558 (see under "Apostles")
Nathaniel, wealthy hypocritcal Pharisee of Ragaba, 1825
nation (also see "state")
    advanced, on a neighboring planet, 808
    better, only in progress of individual, 1630
NATION, THE CONTINENTAL, 808 (on another planet)
nation, death scene of a n, the Jews, 1999
    endurance of n depends upon courts, 1462
    essentials to national life, 800
national sovereignty, no divine right, 1491
    unlimited, n g, 1487
nationalism, 1048, -57, 1491
    barrier to peace, 2082
    essential to social survival, 803
    intense, post-planetary prince epoch, 591
    Moses, 1057
    needed, Egypt, 1048
    paradox of, 2082
    (pride) is sin-breeding, 1223
    Rome overcame tradition, 2073
nationalist cause, rejection of, 1397

N

nebulae (cont'd)
  some giving origin to 100 million suns, 169
NEBULAR STAGES, THE, 652
nebular wheels, 170
NECESSITY FOR LEAVING, THE, (U), 1591
Necho, overthrown by Nebuchadnezzar, 1075
Necho's mighty army, 1074
necklace, first one was umbilical cord, 968
need, is sufficient to insure Father's mercies, 38
  of world today, 380
"needle's eye, camel", 1803
needs, Father will care for, 1578, 1640
  "met, if life dedicated to God", 1823
  of soul, elemental, 1771
  society topheavy with supposed human n, 765
  will be supplied (seekers), 1823
needy, favor the, 1463
negative "local" effects on God's plan and laws, 56
negativism, error if religious, 1572
Negro, origin in orange, green, indigo races, 905
NEGROID RACES, THE, 905 (see also "black race",
  "indigo race")
neighbor, better a man understands n, easier to forgive,
  38
  idea of "benefit for n" circumscribed at first,
    expands, 1133
  "if your n smites you", 1571
  son of God if truly love n as self, 1600
  understand n and you become tolerant, 1098
  who is my?, 1809-10
NEIGHBORING PLANET, GOVERNMENT ON A, 808
neighbors, can't love by act of will, 1098
Nepal, birthplace of Gautama Siddhartha, 1035
Nephilim (name for Nodites), 856
nepotism, family of J received no supernatural help,
  1718-19
  J planned "no close relatives" as apostles, 1538
Nerites, final eruption of Caspian group, 877
nerve circuits, like spirit gravity, 84
nervous disorders, healed by the 70, 1807
  hundreds healed, 1645
NETHER PARADISE, 122 (see also "Paradise, nether")
neutrons, 477
never again in Nebadon, man and God in one, 1699
"New Age", no signs of appearance of, 1860
new, "and living way", Son establishes (J is), 596, 1426
  "and true, have faith to accept", 1656
  birth (see also "born again, be", and under "Jesus,
    Quotes"; see "be born of eternal spirit", "be
    reborn", "born again", and "born of the spirit")
    the change of mind by faith, 1545
    essential to deliverance, 1660
    is baptism of the spirit, 1660
  commandment (see also under "Jesus")
    "Master, if you have a nc" (Peter), 1576
NEW COMMANDMENT, 1944
NEW CONCEPT, THE, 1748
new, creatures, become in kingdom, 1609
  gospel about J, 2059
  heavens and the new earth, 1914
  message, self-forgetfulness and self-control, 1609
  order, believe and rejoice, not fast and pray, 1609
  revelation, 2086
NEW SCHOOL OF THE PROPHETS, A, 1657
new, social order, 4th mansion world, 536
  spirit, create in man a ns, 1583
  teacher, so you can judge wisely, 1951
New Testament, almost all Paul (exceptions), 2091
  authors believed in J' divinity, 2092
  Christian document, superb, 2091

new (cont'd)
  New Testament (cont'd)
    distorted, 1040, 1860
    little of human J because...2092
    not the inspiring life of J, 2091
    only meagerly Jesusonian, 2091
    why human experiences of J omitted, 2092
  new, truth, teachers of nt attempt revolution, too much,
    1043
  "New Way, The", Andrew taught, 1629
  new way vs. old, 1584, 1609, -30, -42
  New Zealand tribe, altered Christianity, 1005
  news, in Havona, 289
    in Havona gathering, reflectivity, 201
    took 1000 years to spread, 743
  "newspapers, living" (Intelligence Coordinators), 289
  NEXT AFTERNOON, THE, 1748
  next age of social development, 910

ni

Niagara Falls, 677
Nicaea, Athanasius vs. Arius, 2070
Nocodemus, 1976, 2012, -14, -20, -30
  after crucifixion, group at N' home, 2025
  apostles and David hid with N, 2001
  believed J would rise, 2013
  bewildered, big man but...1602
  body of J, N claimed, 1603, 2011
  disciple, outspoken at end, 2013
  educated believer, 1590
  fearful of his fellows, 1602, -06
  home of N, J profound talk with Jewish leaders, 1810
  J with, 1601
  morontia appearance, home of N, 2052
  "rabbi, no mere man could so teach", 1602
  refined, egoistic, altruistic, but...1602
  Sanhedrin member, 1601
  secret believers met at N' home, 1910
  turned back from J in fear, 1606
NICODEMUS, THE VISIT WITH, 1601
Nocopolis, visited on Roman trip, 1471
night, long, of Western civilization, 2075
Nile, Abraham and Lot to N for food, 1019
NILE, THE ANDITES ALONG THE, 894
Nile, center of civilization shifted to, 894
  civilization moved westward to N, 874
  Egypt reached lowest...15000 years ago, 889
  few penetrated beyond N headwaters, 873
  Sahara peoples deteriorated early N civilization, 889
  some Adamites, westward to N valley, 870
Nineveh, love of God for, 1767
Nirvana, 1041
  never clearly defined by Buddha, 1037

no

"no man lives by himself", 647
no original sin, 1222
no return by mortal to native planet, 436
Noah, 874
  son of, 830
  story of N and ark, priests' invention, 875
  true story of, 860, 874-75
nobility of the common people (Joseph's family), 1344
nobility, unconscious growth, 1095
noble, character required to "turn about", 1981
  Jerusem band of faithful mortals, 609
  to be, requires struggle,
nobleman, Titus the, 1644
Nod, leader, staff of Planetary Prince, 747
  defected in Lucifer rebellion, 757

NODITE CENTERS OF CIVILIZATION, 859
Nodite priests, in second garden reverted to pre-
   Adamic standards, 848
NODITE RACE, THE, 856
Nodite, racial and cultural term, 8th race Urantia, 822
Nodites, 822, 861, 868, 875, 895, 926
   accorded women increased recognition, 937
   Adamites admixed with N (25,000 years ago), 870
   and Adamites made mixed Andites, 859
NODITES AND THE AMADONITES, THE, 821
Nodites, and Sangiks (with Adamics) known as Andites,
   868
   Andites and N blend: Caucasoid, 905
   arose out of... transplanted life plasm, 857
   augmented Nile valley culture, 1044
   beginning of warfare, N vs. Adamites, 844
   central or pre-Sumerian, 860
   clay tablets of Sumerian descendants of N, 857
   culture declined 25,000 years till Adam, 859
   descendants of disloyal Dalamatia staff, 758,821
   deteriorated greatly, breeding with inferiors, 857
   early N thought man was soul and body, 955
   Eden dwellers contact with N from first, 840
   eighth race to appear on U, 857
   Elamite N led by Cain's son, Enoch, 849
   entered the then fertile Turkestan, 872
   Eve feared no danger, visits with N Serapatatia, 840
   family life not much until N, 940
   founded Dilman, Bablot (Babel), 858
   if leader could be born to N, by Eve, 841
   inhabited Eden after Adam's departure, 826
   in-marriage, over 150,000 years, 918
   internecine conflict over Babel dispersed N, 859
   Melchizedek resembled N and Sumerians, 1015
   monogamy wholly natural to N, 927
   mutant traits due to life-maintenance circuits, 857
   not cannibalistic, 979
   plus ordinary races plus violet: Andites, 871
   pure-line N a magnificent race, 857
   religion of Nile valley augmented by N, 1043-44
   Russia and Turkestan, Adamites mixed with, 871
   strains and Andonite in white races, 889
   superior N and Adamite strains, best Andites, 874
   10,000 years after rebellion, traditions held, 821
   3 centers after Bablot: Syrian, Elamite, pre-
      Sumerian, 859
   tower proposed, memorial to N history, 858
   traditional enmity between N and Amadonites, 822
   "tree of life" did them no good, 826
   used cremation, discouraged cannibalism, 980
   why failed of a great pre-Adamic culture, 859
non-ascender returns, as drop of water returns to sea,
   1284
non-ascenders, personality of na returns to the Supreme,
   1284
   realm of the unrealized, 1285
non-breathers, 446
   certain planets, 328
   close to U, 564
   non-Adjuster fusion types, many, 446
   nutrition and energy, 5th order of, 563
   separate order of, 561
NONBREATHERS, WORLDS OF THE, 563
nondoable, omnipotence no power to do, 1299
non-interference, celestial personalities, 1361
   rebellion, 605
nonmechanical-teachable types of response, 738
nonpersonal corporate entity, father, son, grandson
   (crude Trinity), 112   non-religionist, grafts, 1126
non-resistance, 1368-69, 1401, -69, 1579

non-resistance (cont'd)
   and J (see under "Jesus")
   and lives of nonviolence, 1608
   J did not teach negative submission, 1770
   to evil, before you can understand, 1950
      cannot be understood as dogma, 1950
      valid only under living Spirit of Truth, 1951
non-resistant to selfish, 1950
nonspatial, not safe to postulate immaterial always ns,
   1297
   true spirit levels of reality are, 482
NONSPIRITUAL ENERGY SYSTEMS, UNIVERSAL,
   PHYSICAL ENERGIES, 469
   MATERIAL MIND SYSTEMS, 480
nontemporal place, Paradise area is only, 135
nonviolence, lives of, 1608
nonviolent expression, control of personal behavior and
   state, 802
NOONTIME MEAL, AFTER THE, 1932
Nordics, 946
   Scandinavians, Germans, Anglo-Saxons, sired by
      Andites, 893
NORLATIADEK, THE MOST HIGHS OF, 488
Norlatiadek, 70 satellites of socializing training, 174
normal, developmental epochs (7), 576
   education, 587
   man should be fostered, 771
   planet, course of events, 7 epochs, 789
      no color problems, nations of one blood, 594
      would seem like heaven to us, 598
   state of cooperation between planets, etc., 177
North America, about as now, 95,000,000 yrs. ago, 689
   discovery of N A, 1000 years ago, 729
   early ice age, N A, mastodons, mammoths, horses,
      camel, deer, tigers, sloths, etc., 699
   -Europe connections disappear, 683
   future of determined by races, 899
   South America, drifted westward, 663
   temporarily isolated, 683
North American future, racial factors will determine, 899
northern lights, 520, 666
NORTHERN PEREA, LAST VISIT TO, 1825
nostalgia, ascenders leaving Nebadon, 428
nothing (of value) is ever lost, 1197
now, the everlasting n is eternity, 1295

nu

nucleus, endowed with 3-fold possibility of manifestation,
   477
   of atom, not held together by gravity nor electric
      force, 479
number, of Urantia, 182, 559
   (take census), Israel and Judah, 1599
numbers, celestial beings have, 1243
NUMBERS, SOME (a small selection of figures, giving
      some idea of wonders of our cosmos. See also
      "velocities")
   angels, 1 billion on U, 1250
   Antares, 450x diameter our sun, 458
   Assigned Sentinels, 7 billion, 268-69
   atom, 1/100,000,000 plus of inch in diameter, 477
   billion spheres of central universe, 156
   calcium atom, juggles electron between orbits,
      25,000x a second, 462
   commissions in Orvonton, 18 trillion, 278
   concept recorders, more knowledge in hour than
      100 years U, 503
   concept symbols (alphabet) billion plus characters, 503
   cubic inch of star, 6000 pounds, 458
   drop of water contains over one billion trillions of
      atoms, 463

numbers, some (cont'd)

Edentia sea of glass, crystal, 30 miles deep, 100 in circumference, 487

875 billion years ago, Andronover nebula initiated, 652

electron, 1 million orbits in 1/1 millionth of second, 462

energy, one drop of water equals 100 plus horsepower continuously 2 years, 463

energy transformers, number unbelievable, 326

frandalanks, Satania alone, beyond count, 328

graduate guides, beyond mind to grasp, 270

ideograph recorders, 100,000 years U language in hour, 503

I S, personal aids to, high trillions, 268

Jerusem, almost 100x size of U, 509

exhibit panorama, 5000 miles circumference, 525

7 walls, 50 to 150,000 gates in each, great pearly crystals, 524

Jews, 2.5 million visit Jerusalem, 1339

Life Carriers, 100 million in Nebadon, 396

lines of energy, 144,000 messages simultaneously, 431

local systems, billion in s u, 157

major sector, each, 100 billion inhabitable worlds, 181

Mansion World Teachers, billions upon billions in Satania, 550

Material Sons, Daughters, 161,432,840 on system capitals, 515

Michael memorial, Jerusem, over 1 million on staff, 525

Mighty Messengers embraced in group, 700,000, 245

millions upon millions, meteorites, Urantia atmosphere daily, 563

Morontia Companions in Nebadon, 70 billion, 545

Nebadon, over 70 billion Morontia Companions, 545

Nebadon, 10 million inhabited worlds in prospect, 416

Nebadon types of life, too numerous to catalog, 416

nebulae, some give origin to many as 100 million suns, 169

987 billion years ago, space conditions reported favorable for materialization phenomena, 651

North America, about as now 95 million years ago, 689

1 world in 10 million, a Creator Son bestowal (J), 595–96

oratory in 30", subject matter of lifetime on U, 503

Orvonton, 18 trillion commissions, 278

61 trillion advisers, 279

warmed by over 10 trillion suns, 172

our sun, life for 25 billion more years, 465

weight 2 octillion tons, 459

Paradise, area for existing universes 1 to 4%, total area for these activities, 1 million times that required, 121

chance meeting communicates more than U language in 1000 years, 503

1 hour instruction equals 10,000 years U methods, 303

residential units (each unit 1 billion workers), 121

1000 units, a division

100,000 divisions a congregation

10 million congregations an assembly

1 billion assemblies a grand unit

7 grand units make a master unit

7 master units a superior unit   *(21,707 fol-

7 make a supersuperior unit   lowed by

7 make a celestial unit   33 zeros)

7 make a supercelestial unit

7 make a supreme unit

(uses less than 1% of space)*

numbers, some (cont'd)

personalities (and others) constitute well-nigh limit-less number, 330

projected, 500 billion architectural worlds, 175

seconaphim, mirrors effective over 100,000 light years distance, 308

several billion super-u Orvonton, 248

seraphim, 501,234,619 pairs on U, 1250

operating organization, 71,663,616 individuals, 421

12 legions plus at J' command, 1516

servitals, 138 billion on 490 satellites, 274

700,000 Lanonandeks of Lucifer's type, 601

7 trillion space reservations, only 4% of area, 121

snow, 20,000 ft. deep, 699

solar heat, 35 million degrees, 463

Solitary Messenger, million year journey, 259

Solitary Messengers come to U, leave, at 841 billion miles per second, 261

space respiration, 2 billion year cycle, 124

spornagia, live 40 to 50,000 years, 528

Stationary Sons of Trinity, 37 billion plus, 218–19

study worlds of central creation, 1 billion, 156, 221, 228

sun density, one ton per cubic inch, 460

sun in Orvonton, 300 million miles diameter, 460

sun, our, 6 billion years old, go for 25 billion more, 465

superuniverse, 250,000 light years radius, 359

Supreme Power Centers, 10 billion, 322

Technical Advisers in Orvonton, 61 trillion, 278

temperature, interior our sun, $35,000,000^o$ F, 463

10,000 systems inhabited worlds in Nebadon, 601

thought reduced to record, rate of 500,000 words or thought symbols per minute, 503

Universal Censors, exactly 8 billion, 217

Uversa concept symbols, more than billion characters, 503

Uversa energy circuits, over 968 million years to go round s u, 175

Veluntia, sun, density 1/1000 density of our atmosphere, 460

worlds with people 30 inches high, other worlds, 10 ft. high, 562

zone of energy, increases for over 25 million light years, 130

nursery (probationary), 569

NURSERY, THE PROBATIONARY, 531

nurses, J' time, 1658

nutrition, omnivores, step forward, 901

six kinds of animal and mortal, 563

O

"O Jerusalem" (J), 1384, 1872, –82, 1908

"O tenderhearted...assist the blind", 1811

oars, idealists use o, don't drift, 2080

oath, finaliter (implies oaths customary?), 349, 1292

finaliter o, only Father-fused take fo, 343

importance of, 238

Michael Sons and sovereignty, 238

of allegiance, Eden, 828, 830

on holy book, 969

originated Dalamatia, 797

status finaliters, 349

to Trinity (Son's), 1308

Trinity o of eternity, 351

Trinity o of eternity, Corps of Finality, 305

oaths, David's messengers released from, 2030

Obadiah and Micah, bold, brave prophets, 1067
obedience to natural law, 1519
obey, the divine leadings, help Holy Spirit, 379
   those who o are helped, 379
objects, of art, J comments to Flavius, 1600
   2 are organization, 3 are a system, 1227
obligations, duties, 1301
   high, holy vs. trifles, 1987
obliteration, eternal, 529 (see also "annihilation", and
   "cessation of existence")
obscene of today, part of religion of our ancestors, 1004
observer, cannot be the thing observed, 1228
observers, system, one to another, 371
obstacles to reality perception, time, space,
   experience, 1171

oc

OCCIDENT, MELCHIZEDEK TEACHINGS IN THE, 1077
OCCIDENT OF THE FIRST CENTURY AFTER CHRIST,
   THE, 1332
Occidentalizing of J' teachings, lost appeal to all men,
   1084
occult, (mystic phenomena) genuine?, 1000
   result of T A detached during sleep?, 1196
occurrences, on worlds, not all doings of F, 48
ocean of force-energy contains all spheres, 476
oceanic nursery of life, 684
oceans, all boil in 1 second, heat of our sun, 463
   all continents tend to creep into, 669
odor, artists of (symphonies, spiritual grandeur), 506
offerings, greatest of all o, consecration of will, 2088
oil, of reconciliation, 312
   use of anointing o by John's apostles, 1678
ointment, (costly bread for 5000) Mary (sister of L),
   1879
   costly, used to anoint J' feet, 1879
Okhban, great Egyptian prophet, murdered, 1046

old, and true, new and false, 1656
   grow o gracefully, 1740
   "old, old story" people with good motives can do no
      evil, 842
   religion, self-examination, self-denial, 1609
      vs. new (Jesusonian), 1951
   "things are passing away", 631
OLD-AGE INSURANCE, 814
Old Testament (see also "Scriptures")
   amazing barbarism kept in sacred writings, 795
   at variance from Hebrew history, 1070
   creation account dates from long after Moses, 837
   deals with women as a form of property, 917
   doesn't record great battle at Karkar, 1074
   Egyptians' teachings sacred to Hebrews before O T
      written, 1046
   en masse editing in Babylon, 1023
   Jewish religion of O T not genuine, was evolved in
      Babylon, 1075
   marital guilt test (Numbers 5:11-31), 795
   new record made O T, Hebrew records then des-
      troyed, 1070
   sayings distorted to apply to J, 1348
older religion of ceremony, authority, 1893
Oligocene period, 696
olive oil lamp, J' boyhood home, 1350
Olivet (see "Mt. Olivet")

om

omissions, Bible, (N.T.), 2092
OMNIAPHIM, THE, 307
omniaphim, solitary, 1310

omnificent, God is not o (does not personally <u>do</u> all),   O
   1299
omnipersonal beings, 1201
   Personalized Adjusters, 1201
OMNIPOTENCE AND COMPOSSIBILITY, 1299
OMNIPOTENCE AND OMNIFICENCE, 1299
omnipotence, does not imply power to do the nondoable,
   1299
   no power to do the ungodlike, 49
   omnipresence, omniscience, 76-77, 1160
omnipotent, God is truly, but not omnificent, 1299
Omnipotent (the transcendental Almighty), 1297
OMNIPRESENCE AND UBIQUITY, 1296
omnipresence of God, 45
OMNIPRESENT SPIRIT, THE, 100
omniscience, among realities, with transcendental
   level, 1160
OMNISCIENCE AND PREDESTINATION, 1300
omniscience, "God knows all things", 48, 105
   Son, Father, Conjoint Actor, Supreme Being, 77
   through reflectivity, 105
omniscient, Trinity members all o all the time, 77
omnivores, great forward step, 901
Omri, King, tried to buy Shemer's estate, 1073

on

ON COUNTING THE COST, 1869
ON THE ISLAND OF CRETE (J), 1436
ON THE MOUNT OF ORDINATION, 2050
ON THE WAY TO BETHANY (J), 1838
ON THE WAY TO GOLGOTHA (J), 2004
ON THE WAY TO THE HIGH PRIEST'S PALACE (J),
   1977
ON THE WAY TO JERUSALEM (J), 1867
ON THE WAY TO NAPLES AND ROME (J), 1440
ON THE WAY TO PHOENICIA (J), 1728
ON THE WAY TO ROME (J), 1427
ON THE WAY TO THE SUPPER (J), 1934
Onagar, the first truth teacher, 715, 717, 1009
Onamonalonton, Hesunanin (Amerind leader), 1008
   far distant leader of red man, 513
   high civilization before 35,000 B.C., led by O, red
      man, 884
   lived to 96, hdqtrs. in great redwoods California, 723
   some red men preserved O teaching, 789
one, Deity is always o to man, 380
   -eyed person, no perspective, 1434
One High in Authority, authored in the U Book, paper
   25, and co-authored 31
ONE HUNDRED, EARLY DAYS OF THE, 743
one hundred, the o h of Caligastia, 742
ONE HUNDRED, ORGANIZATION OF THE, 745
one, in me who can, 59
   language, religion, philosophy, essential to
      progress, 626
   "more chance" to believe, 1837
   race, one language, one religion, post-bestowal age,
      597
   who can't do one thing expertly, 1779
onlookers, celestial, 1409, 1972, -84, -95, 2008, -11
only begotten Son, 109
only begotten Son is Eternal Son, 73

open door, faith is the, 1545
   in early Roman state, for talent, ability, 1335
operation, early, Andonite life-plasm to the hundred, 742
Ophel, 1794
opiate of the people, not J' religion, 2063
opinions, minority, none among councils of perfection,

opportunities, on high in ages to come, good ideas
  wanted, 734
opportunity, ability, 1876
  creative, on high, 508
  for service, we make by trustworthiness, 316
  Matadormus missed, 1802
  must wait for, 1300
  universe unfailing in equalizing, 624
opposites, universal: spirit, material manifestations,
  140
oppression, 1464, 1582
optimism, and pessimism, 2079
  for U, ultimate evolutionary triumph, 736
optional routes to Havona, we choose, 538, 552

or

"oracle from God in everybody", 1216
oracles, Latin peoples consulted, 1080
ORANGE MAN, THE, 723
orange race wiped out, 724
oranges in space, 458
oratory, flourishes on advanced worlds, 630
  half-hour equal to U lifetime, 503
  promoters of, 503
  rare treats ahead, 503
  to record thought, 503
orbital movements vary, solar system, 657
orbits, modified circles to extreme ellipses, 667
ordained Greeks, J almost, 1924
order, maintain temporal o, 1763
  natural o of U upset by rebellion, 1661
  "of Michael", 234
  old, fast and pray, new, believe and rejoice, 1609
orders of survival and ascension, 568-70
ORDERS, UNCLASSIFIED AND UNREVEALED, 333
ORDINATION, THE, 1569
ORDINATION, THE EVENING OF THE, 1576
ORDINATION OF THE SEVENTY, 1800
ORDINATION OF THE SEVENTY AT MAGADAN, 1800
ORDINATION OF THE TWELVE, THE, 1568
ordination of the twelve reenacted, 2050
ORDINATION SERMON, THE, 1570
ORDINATION, THE WEEK FOLLOWING THE, 1578
Ordovician period, 676
organic unity in universe, 56
organism, living and material penetrated by intelligence
  circuits, 1276
organisms, neither vegetable nor animal, 731
  preintelligent vs. mind ministry, 738
ORGANIZATION AND ADMINISTRATION (Thought
  Adjusters), 1188
organization, first result of o was division of labor, 773
ORGANIZATION, INDUSTRIAL, 813
organization, none, just J' brotherhood, 2067
  of book, 215
  of local system, 509, 559
  of planets, systems, constellations, etc., 166, 182
  of political power, family to mankind, 1488
ORGANIZATION OF THE SUPERUNIVERSES, 165, 182,
  208 (see also "Urantia in cosmic organization")
ORGANIZATION OF THE TWELVE (apostles), 1547
organization, Orvonton, 18 trillion commissions, 278
  Orvonton, huge staff, 198, 246, 279
    61 trillion advisers, 279
ORGANIZATION, POLITICAL, 809
ORGANIZATION, SERAPHIC, 421
organization, space levels around Paradise, 129
  the superuniverses, 164, 182, 208
  under God, 467
  universes, 167

organizations, physical, passing out of existence, 167
organized space, various forms energy and matter
  circulate, 461
ORGANIZERS,   THE MASTER FORCE, 329
ORIENT, ANDITE EXPANSION IN THE, 878
ORIENT, MELCHIZEDEK TEACHINGS IN THE, 1027
Orient, no go, divided Christianity, 2084
Oriental salutation, wasted time, 1805
Orientals, delight in fairy stories, 1352
  religion of J vs. about J, 2086
orientation, 182, 379
ORIENTATORS, UNIVERSE, 428
ORIGIN, A-B-C first, etc., midwayers, 862
  Adam & Eve, original, each local system, 415
  adoption of children, 960
  agriculture and transportation, 902
  all night wake, 958-59
  all reality in the I AM, 1262
  alphabet (first) and writing, 746
ORIGIN AND NATURE OF THOUGHT ADJUSTERS, 1176
origin, Andites, 868
  animal forms of life, 731
  Arabs, 727
  astronomy, 901
  baptism as part of Christianity, 1626
  basis of relational reaction of the Gods, 314
  basket making, 902
  Being, Intelligence, Joy (Hindu trinity concept), 1144
  belief in reincarnation, 953
  belief in relics, 968
  belief in the stone altar, 969
  belief: return of J meant end of world, 1918
  bird family, 732
  blood-bond concept of relationships, 932
  bone relics, saints, 968
  Brahma, Siva, Vishnu, 1144
  bronze, 904
  brown men, 727
  Buddha accepted Godless concept of salvation
    through faith, 1035, -37
  Buddhism, took o in a person, not a myth, 1036
  burial of the "great" in places of worship, 852
  camels and llamas, 696
  candles in rituals, 947
  cannibalism, 978-79
  capital accumulation, 776
  carrier pigeons, 746
  chance as revelatory of will of gods, 987
  chemistry, 901
  child adoption, 960
  child marriages, 916
  Christian church's errors, 2066
  Christian version of "Lord's Supper", 984
  Christmas-tree, Maypole, 946
  church burials, 852
  circumcision, 791, 982
  civilizations, South and Central America, 727
  cock as a weathervane, 964
  colonization, 982
  commercial credit, 747
  commercialized prostitution, 791
  common fear, 766
  "commons" (like Boston commons), 782
  communion service, 978
  comprehension of Paradise trinity, 1143
  cornerstone concept, trinkets, etc., 981
  courtesy, 963
  cremation, 964, 980
  Cro-Magnons, 890
  cult of taking no life, 1029

origin (cont'd)

    dance, early form of military drill, 785
    dependability, moral dignity, 983
    depreciating compliments, 963
    dipping fingers in holy water, 1083
    divining rod, 946
    doll, 972
    domesticated animals, dog, 778
    domesticated horse, 902
    domestication of animals, 902
    dove, symbol of peace, 946
    dowry, 924
    ear piercing, 982
    early belief "Son of God" would come, 852
    early beliefs in white and black magic, 774
    early caste of priests, 774
    embalming the dead, 1044
    ethics, 956
    evil and sin, 1222
    evolution of Greek gods, goddesses, 1078
    faltering, failing, succumbing to struggle, 1199
    father-family vs. mother-family, 933
    flag as national symbol, 970
    flag musn't touch ground, 970
    folk tales of gods who came down, mated women, 856
    frog and salamander, 732
    funeral service, 959
    "God bless you" upon sneezing, 954
    "golden age", "fall of man" hypotheses, 838
    gospels, 1341
    government, beginnings of, 788
    Greek mythology, 895
    Hades, for anemic souls, 953
    halo encircling head, 834
    hammers, clubs, 768
    handshaking, 748
    happiness and joy, 1220
    harem, why, 927
    head hunting, 960
    Hebraic concepts of Divine Creator, 1055
    highest happiness, 1098
    holy water, 964
    home as an institution, 940
    human institutions (three classes), 772
    humility, 963
    idea of heaven and hell, 953
    idea of human soul, primitive, 953
    idea that men are born equal, 794
    ideals, 1133
    identical in o, nature, destiny--light, heat,
      electricity, magnetism, chemism, energy
      matter, 472
    incest (ideas of), 916
    industrial organization, food-gathering lines, 768
    inns, public lodging houses, 774
    intellectual selves, 1216
    intermarriages, tribal, 788
    Islamic religion, 1051
    "isms", 1207
    J' papers in this book, 1343
    Jewish story of Noah, 860
    kings, 776
    kissing, 787
    legends of Adam and Eve (rib), 743
    "Lord's Prayer", 1389
    lucky number "four", 968
    making of eunuchs, 983
    man's, in a "special creation", 975
    many new "isms", religions, aborted T A contacts,
      1207

origin (cont'd)

    Mary worship, 895
    medicine, 901
    metaphysics, 1136
    Mexicans, 727
    midway creatures, 744-45
    midwayers, 1000 "born" to each of 50 couples, 855-56
    military organization, 776
    Mithraism, in Persian sun veneration, 947
    modern forms of divine worship, 978
    modern science,(birth of), 901
    modern writing in trade records, 775
    monotheism, 1442
    Moses, reputed teachings of, 838
    mother cult, 895
    mourning costumes, 959
    mythology, much, 743
    Neanderthal race, 720
    nebulae, 1216
      (10 different forms), 169
    Nodites, descended from Prince's staff, 821, 857
    non-flesh diet, 744
    oath, 797

ORIGIN OF GRADUATE GUIDES, THE, 270
ORIGIN OF IDEALS, THE, 1133
ORIGIN OF INHABITED WORLDS, 465
ORIGIN OF LIFE CARRIERS, 396
ORIGIN OF MATERIAL SONS OF GOD, 580
ORIGIN OF MONMATIA (the Urantia Solar System), 655
ORIGIN OF SERAPHIM, 418
ORIGIN OF SOLITARY MESSENGERS, 256
ORIGIN OF SPACE BODIES, THE, 170
ORIGIN OF THE SUN, 655
ORIGIN OF THOUGHT ADJUSTERS, 1177
ORIGIN OF URANTIA, 651

origin, one face of planet always to another, 657
    paying "blood money", 796
    peace tendencies, 765-66
    phallic cult, 962
    philosophy, 1135
    physical sciences, various, 1135
    pioneer "professional" class, 774
    placental mammals, 733
    pointing is bad manners, 990
    political parties, 792
    politicians of primitive society, 774
    potential evil, 1159
    pottery by baking, 902
    preachers, 992
    preference for out-marriages, 919
    prenatal marking of children, 962
    primitive industry, 773
    private ownership of land, 782
    private property, 746
    professional prostitutes, 918
    racial o determined by skull vs. skeleton, 904
    reincarnation (recurring incarnations), 953
    religion born of fear, awe, dread, 950-51
    religious traditions, 1727
    Reptilia, 732
    retrograde motion in astronomic system, 657
    rib myth, Adam and Eve, 837
    rights (are social), 794
    ritual, pageantry, 2070
    royal marriages, brother and sister, 835
    Sabbath-day tradition, 832
    sacramental services, 984
    sacrifices as part of worship, 716, 974, 977
    sacrificial system, 974, 977
    sanctuary, 775

origin (cont'd)
 scalping, 955
 schools, 791
 science, 901, 972-73
 secondary midwayers, 861
 secret societies, 790
 secularism, modern, from 2 influences, 2081
 seraphim, 418
 serfdom, 779
 seven-day week, 751
 "seven" fundamental in scheme of things, 184
 sex laxity, 982
 Sikhism, 1012
 sin, original, 952, 974, 1222, 1339
 six colored races of U, 735
 slavery, 585, 774, 778
  near-s for women, 768
 social ceremonials, 992
 social classes, 792
 solar system, gravity explosion, 170-71
 solemn style in prayer, 965
 space bodies, 170
 spheres, hundred modes of formation, 172
  majority, 10 groups, 170
 spies, secret police, 792
 spittle as a healing agent, 1044
 sponges, 731
 striving for spirituality, 766
 suicide as ancient social vogue, 790
 Sumerians, 200,000 years ago, 860
 sun of our solar system, 655
 sun, ours, usual origin, 653
 swearing, profanity, 992
 table etiquette, 975
 taboo on man-eating, 981
 taboos, 974
 tatooing, 983
 theology and metaphysics, 1135
 theory of struggle between higher and lower natures, 1131
 Thought Adjusters, 1177
 tombstone, 945, 964
 toy, umbilical cord, 968
 trading counter, 775
 tradition of "900 year" old man, 858
 triad religious beliefs (evolutionary), 1143
 trials, 1143
 tribal government by clever, farsighted, 987
 Trinity, First Christian concept, Antioch, 1144
 true religious impulse, 1132
 unusual o of our planetary family, Monmatia, 655
 Urantia Book (see "Urantia Book")
 Urantia, dual origin, 170-71, 466, 651, 656
 use of ambassadors, 834
 veiling of women, 962
 violet race on inhabited worlds, 583
 wedding ceremony, 924
 wedding customs, 924-25
 wedding presents, 916
 wheel, 746
 women sharing honors with men, 831
 worship, 944
ORIGIN AND NATURE OF THE MATERIAL SONS OF GOD, 580
ORIGIN AND NATURE OF THOUGHT ADJUSTERS, 1176
ORIGIN OF IDEALS, THE, 1133
ORIGIN OF MONMATIA--THE URANTIA SOLAR SYSTEM, 655
ORIGIN OF RELIGIOUS TRADITIONS, 1727
ORIGIN OF SPACE BODIES, 170
ORIGIN OF URANTIA, THE, 651

ORIGINAL, ACTUAL, AND POTENTIAL, 1261
original Michael, bestowals of, 87
original sin, 971, 978
 ascribing death to spirit world led to doctrine of, 952
 mankind has no such racial guilt, 2003
 no inborn moral guilt or atonement, 2003
 Paul's doctrine of o s partially Mithraic, 1339
 phases of Paul's teachings of o s, original, 1339
 soul looked upon as under forfeit, 974
originality, each world of Havona unique (billion spheres), 159
 society should foster, 786
 yes, but not eccentricity, 1673
origins, consider, take note of the man, in what manner was he born?, 314
ORIGINS OF SACRIFICE, 977
ORIGINS OF WORSHIP, THE, 944
ORIGINS, THE SIGNIFICANCE OF, 314
Orlandof, great teacher of blue race, 725
"orphanhood" of man destroyed (Spirit of Truth), 2060
Orphic brotherhood, best of the cults, 1079
Orvonon, 725,
 (our s u, one of the seven s u), 129, 182, 359
 commission sent to U, 1
 conciliating commissions, 18 trillion, 278
 conclaves, great c take place, 199
 corps of truth revealers, 1
 day equals 30 of ours, 174
 illuminated, warmed, by over 10 trillion blazing suns, 172
 not one cool planet in 40 for life like ours, 173
 over 10 billion administrators, 246
 staff, numbers beyond comprehension, 196
 suns in, vast majority like U origin, 653
ORVONTON, THE SUPERUNIVERSE OF, 167
Orvonton, watchlike, elongated-circular grouping, 167

O S

Osiris, 1045, -48, -67
OTHER FORMS OF PRAYER, 1621
other-mindedness, 1123
OTHER NATIONS, THE, 819
ought to believe in God, 1105
"Our Father who is in heaven", 1103, 1923
our real business on earth (J), 1466
"OUR RELIGION" (Ganid), 1453
OUR STARRY ASSOCIATES, 458
OUTBREAK OF THE REBELLION, THE, 755
outcast, let unruly brother become an, 1763
outer space, development, 129-30
 levels, 129
  first and second, 130
  fourth and outer, 130
 mobilizing universes of, 129-31
 new system of universes organizing in, 354
 universes now nonspiritual, 132
 universes of, 351
 unorganized realms of, 2015
outlook, of heathen small and narrow, can concentrate energies, 1725
outlying organizations, more space between, 168
outmarriage was a peace promoter, 919

over-care, peace based on, 1954
over-conscientious, in the o c, conflict, 383
OVERCONTROL, CONTROL AND, 1301
overcontrol, electrochemical, and heredity, handicap T A, 1199
OVERCONTROL OF EVOLUTION, THE, 730
OVERCONTROL OF SUPREMACY, THE, 115

overcontrol (cont'd)
OVERCONTROL, UNIVERSAL, 135
overpopulation, comparatively cheapens human life, 770
over-revelation, bad, 330
OVERSEERS, CELESTIAL, 412
overseers, regional, 7 groups, 179
over-soul, cosmic (great Supreme), 1285
OVERSOUL OF CREATION, THE, 1285
overspecialization, J deplored, 1673
over-teaching, over-enlightenment, 750
over-world unchanging, underworld changing, 1297
Ovid, Phoenician teacher, 1019

ownership, of land, private, out of agriculture, 782
   private, increased liberty, enhanced stability, 782
oxen, slow adoption of o, due to unemployment, 909
oxygen, copper, vanadium to purify. . .737
oxygenation by copper, iron, vanadium, 737
ozone layer, over 40 protective operations similar to,
   666
ozone plus 24 other protectors, 665

P

Pacific Ocean, 660
pagan cults, 1336
pagan, the thoughtless p, and J, 1466
pageant, celestial, on Mt. Hermon, 1755
pain, suffering, essential to progressive evolution, 951
Paleozoic era, 672, 684
Palestine, and Syria, prosperous in times of J, 1333
   Antioch, J said "(near) P, may be I shall come back
      sometime", 1480
   Augustus' religion flourished except in P, 1081
   central group from Sahara to Nile and P, 890
   chosen by Melchizedek for own bestowal, 1018
   climate ranged from frigid to torrid, 1367
   dark days in P, idea of God, 1060
   end of April, one vast flower garden, 1367
   family devotion, affection, (Jews')transcended gen-
      tiles', 1335
   great highways of antiquity passed through P, 1333
   Greece, contrasted, 1079
   hard to explain fully why P chosen for J, 1344
   home of Terah's superior offspring, 1018
   Jerusalem center of worship for Eastern and Western
      Jews, 1339
   J chose P for public career, 1483
   location of P influenced Melchizedek and C M
      bestowals, 1018
   secret of survival, was in Roman policy, 1334
   serpent was revered in P, 968
   survival of P as state, thanks to Rome, 1334
   three languages in J' time, Aramaic, Hebrew, Greek,
      1338
   tribes of central P constantly raided, 1019
Palisades, Hudson River, 685
"pall bearers", (J'), 2013
Palonia, system of, rebel Lutentia, 1311
paltry things, earthly kingdoms to J, 1522
Panama Isthmus, 693-94
pandemonium, did (should) He (Father) move, 119
Pandora, 935
panic, materialist--secular, will be over, 2076
   materialistic, due to scientists,2076
panicky, don't be, about spiritual assets of human race,
   2076
panoply of space, moving, 1117
Panoptians, didn't join L rebellion, 607, 610

PANORAMA, THE EVOLUTIONARY, 731   **P**
panorama, humans in endless unfolding of infinite p, 1194
panoramic depiction, Jerusem history, 528
Pantheism, omnificence, 1300
Pantheon of gods, 1027-28
paper, (No. 9, U Book) revealed on U by Divine
   Counselor, 107
papers (U Book) (see also "Urantia Book")
   life of J, by former midwayer attached to Andrew,
      1332
   put into English, by mandate, 354, 648
   (Series of 5) presenting narrative of Universal
      Father, 72
   technique authorized by superiors, A. D. 1935, 1319
   these, fleeting glimpse only, 144
parable, conduces to forcing thought through hearing,
   1692
   each can take what finds reception in his heart, 1818
   enacted by J, 1939, -44
   enemies less cause for offense, 1693
   if not one, used another, 1590
PARABLE, INTERPRETATION OF THE, 1689
parable, J' favorite, 1850, -53
   Job, wonderful, unique, 1662-63
   Nathaniel's summary of teachings, 1876
   of brotherly love, (enacted), 1938
   of John Baptist, not as our gospel, 1854
   one feature of each p to teach, 1672
   referred to Jewish nation, 1894
   sower, interpretation of, 1689
   speak not a p to you, 1759
   to reject truth of p requires mind action, 1692
   tried another, 1590
   value of using p in teaching, 1692
   vs. (fables) allegory, 1672, -90-92
   virtues of, 1691

PARABLE OF THE ABSENT LANDLORD, THE, 1893
parable of the, bread, living, 1711
   carpentry, 1738
   children of the house,
   cornerstone, 1694
PARABLE OF DIVIDING THE INHERITANCE, 1821
parable of the, door to kingdom, 1828
   fig tree, 1830
   flesh not bread, blood not water, 1712
   foolish carpenter, 1738
   foolish rich man, 1821
PARABLE OF THE GOOD SAMARITAN, 1810
parable of the, good shepherd, 1818
PARABLE OF THE GREAT SUPPER, 1835
parable of the,"harvest plenteous, laborers few", 1800
   high place at table, 1834
   householder, hired laborers, 1804
   Job, 1662
   judge and widow, 1619
   king and his stewards, 1763
   kingdom of heaven, treasure, 1694
   laborers in vineyard, 1803
   leaven hidden in 3 measures of meal, 1694
   lily rooted in slime and muck, 1737
   lord, servant and the, 1824
   lost piece of silver, 1851, -53
   lost sheep, 1850-51, -53
PARABLE OF THE LOST SON, 1850
parable of the, marriage feast, 1824, -34-35, -94
   meat which perishes, 1710
   merchant and pearl, 1694
   money lender and two debtors, 1652
   mustard seed, 1693

203

Paradise (cont'd)

is absolutely at rest, but is not in space, 1156
is an eternal and exclusive existence, 126
is from eternity, no record of origin, 118
is home, Havona the workshop, playground, of
    finaliters, 163
is nucleus of ultimaton, 467
is only nontemporal place, 135
is source of the physical universes, 7
is universal stabilizer, 98
Jerusem, step to supernal perfection of P, 523
J visits, 367
large enough for activities of infinite creation, 121
magnificence of physical perfection, 118
master pattern of universal material reality, 8
material sphere and spiritual abode, 118
mechanism of, 1303
messengers of P carried exhortation "be you
    perfect", 21
Michaels volunteer from, 1308
mortals ascent to P bypassing morontia, 570
mortals, countless m have already reached P, 127
most gigantic...body of cosmic reality, 118
Most Holy Sphere of P, beauteous grandeur, 120
mysteries (7) of secret spheres of P, 200
neither time nor space on, 1173
no royal roads to, 551
no shortcuts, to, 551
nonpersonal and extraspiritual, 8
nonpersonal self of Father, 126
not all who reach Salvington reach P, 449
not a creator, a unique controller, 7
not part of universal creation, 126
not upward, but inward, 209
nuclear Isle, 152
    of light and life, 118
of single constitution, 637
on P necessary to direct, control, expression of
    worship, 304
one may reach P with companion of earth, 283
only stationary thing in universes, 7, 1156
organization of space energy, absolutum, 120
our ultimate arrival assured, 1781
Personal Aids flash to and from uttermost...268
personalities at resurrection, 2021
personnel of P undergoing reorganization, 263
plan, 867
pre-energy not responsive to P gravity, 329
presence circuits, gravity circuits, 45
primal origin and final goal, 126-27
problems of residence on P take time, 296
pronounced Michael head of U, 1317
pull, all transformations of force subject to, 139
realities, 2096
responds to all physical metamorphoses, 29
river of energy and life outpouring from, 468
satellites of P give forth light without heat, 174
satellites (21), 143
selective techniques of P not arbitrary, 247
seraphim advance by guiding souls to P, 1249
sometimes engulfed in spiritual tide, 304
Son, Spirit, each has realm, 140
source and substance of physical gravity, 101
source of all material universes, 637
space cycle, 2 billion years, 149 (see also "space
    respiration")
PARADISE, SPACE FUNCTIONS OF, 124
Paradise, space is a bestowal of P, 124
    space potency, 120 (see also "space potency")
    spirit and energy, one, 104

Paradise (cont'd)   P
spirit comes from P through Havona, 1164
spirit realities, revealed in...639
super-mortal conceptions of Deity on P, 1260
supernal opportunity to attain, 443
three domains of activity, 119
thrill of all time when first pilgrim arrived, 270
time and space are non-existent on P, 2
time is non-existent on P, 739
trail of divinity pursuit and...127
twenty-one worlds of associated activities, 351
unique controller, not a creator, 7
PARADISE, THE UNIQUENESS OF, 126
Paradise, universal headquarters, all personality
    activities, 127; and source-center all energy
    manifestations, 127
until P goodness more quest than attainment, 1458
up to P glory from spiritual darkness, 304
values concealed within facts, 2078
warm welcome awaiting you on P, 283
will-creatures have embarked upon P journey, 21
worlds, Father's circuit of, 144, 1231
worship is the refreshing play of P, 304
"worthy capital" of cosmos, 119
you find God as a person on P, 1296
"you shall some time be with me in P", 2009

Paradise Avonals, 223, 225, 427, 587, 594, 596 (see also
    "Avonal Sons" and "Magisterial Sons")
Paradise bestowal Sons, in every phase...are God and
    man, 217
Paradise Central Shining, personal contact with, 271
Paradise Corps of Finality, ascendant beings, trained
    in...348 (see also "Corps of the Finality")
Paradise Deities, "I go to do the will of the PD" (Michael
    billion years ago), 1309
Paradise Deity, Trinity, existential
    experientially evolving in 2 Supremacy phases which
    are unifying as Supreme Being, 11
Paradise-Havona day, 153
PARADISE-HAVONA SYSTEM, 129, 152
Paradise Master Spirits, cosmic mind of the, 45
Paradise Michael (Creator Son, J Christ), lives and dies
    only once as lowest order, 239
PARADISE, NETHER, 122
Paradise, nether, source of all physical-energy and
    cosmic-force circuits, 122
    unfailing energies emanating from, 1276
PARADISE, PERIPHERAL, 121
Paradise, peripheral, seven trillion space reservations,
    only 4% of area thus assigned, 121
Paradise Personality center, all creation circles
    eternally around, 47
Paradise pilgrims of eternity, 291
PARADISE, SACRED SPHERES OF, 143
Paradise Son, why must be bestowed on sphere, 227
PARADISE SONS OF GOD, THE, 223
PARADISE SONS OF GOD, THE, 87
Paradise Sons of God, bestowal, final, member of
    racial group which, 239
PARADISE SONS (of God), BESTOWAL OF THE, 227
PARADISE SONS, UNITED MINISTRY OF, 232
Paradise Spirits (see also "Master Spirits")
    every intelligent creature bears stamp of 1 of 7, 190
PARADISE TRINITY, THE, 108 (see also "Trinity")
Paradise Trinity, and Deity, no limit to potential, 200
    diverse associations (7) of the persons of the, 1324
    of three beings is in reality one Deity, 1331
PARADISE, UPPER, 120
Paradisiacal area, origin of man in, 703

205

paradox(es), due to finite divinity, 1268
PARADOX(ES), THE HUMAN, 1221
paradox(es), in finite comprehension, God...69
    inseparable from temptation, 1222
    J stated, 1134
    religion always characterized by p, 1121
    religious, to understand, 1268
    spirit and thought, 1121
    time, space, experience, 1173
PARALYTIC, HEALING THE, 1666
paralyzed by fear, 1745
paranoiac, some earliest priests were p, 986
parasites, social, 1580
parasitic fungi, (bacteria) renegade, retrograde, 732
parchment and paper, 500,000 B.C., 746
pardon, our God will abundantly p, 39
parent-child relationship, 40
parent, true p continuous service-ministry, 941
    wise p refuses take sides in petty quarrels, 1589
parental, experience, 516
       required, 531
    love, 1921; selflessness is inherent in, 41
    procreators and Creator, 942
    responsibility essential, 516
    responsibility, shifted to church or state suicidal, 941
    schools, nearby planet, 811
parents, and deceased children, 516, 569
    can understand "mercy time-lag", 616
    copartners with Makers of heaven and earth, 1839
    delinquency of own offspring, 1653
    follies, children suffer too, 843
    J inherited traits of his parents, 1348
    loved son so much, denied him blessed experience
      with J, 1922
    of all mankind, 717
    of re-created you, soul, 1193
    over-indulgent, 1653
    rewarded by excellence of children, 804
    wisdom as well as love, 1922
"parks", preserves, natural state areas, Jerusem,
    grandeur of, 520
Parsees, dog came to be sacred animal of P, 967
    fearful, 1050
    fire persists in symbolism of P, 778
    perverted Zoroaster's teachings, 1050
PART AND THE WHOLE, THE, 137
part, suffers or benefits with whole, 138
    to whole--relative velocity, 138
partaker of divine nature through rebirth, 1609
Parthian, kingdom, 1487
    states, Jews trading in, time of J, 1333
partial, approaches to reality, 1090
    progress, greatest spiritual jeopardy, 1090
    to perfect, J showed way from, 1426
particles, invisible, unimaginable energy, 172
partner, of enthralling adventure, 1430
    of spiritual energy, divine truth, 1430
    your faithful p, God the Adjuster, 1193
partners, in eternity, 245
    two moral creatures, quadruples potential, 495
partners, man with God
    Adjuster can achieve...union of God and man, 1176
    Adjuster-man p, a most amazing cosmic phenomenon,
      1238
    after fusion, supernal p factualized, 1239
    and woman, cooperate to create...immortal souls,
      1471
    character, man can perfect, 2000
    choice of God in face of alternative, 1431
    eternal liaison with faithful partner, God the
      Adjuster, 1193

partners, man with God (cont'd)
    experiential growth implies creature-Creator
      partnership, 1268
    in liaison with God, absolutely nothing is impossible,
      291
    J transcendant exhibition of copartnership, 2002
    man can work in liaison with God, 1279
    material life partner with spiritual energy and
      divine truth, 1430
    no limit on destiny of such a partnership, 1181
    no limitation on possibilities, 1299
    revelation discloses man's capacity for p, 1122
    soul is co-creative partner in own immortalization,
      1282
    sublime partnership with...source of all wisdom,
      1119
    time lag permits creature to be, 1159,-64
    when man in p with G, great things happen, 1467
    who does Father's will, partner of time-space
      Creators, 614
PARTNERSHIP OF MAN AND WOMAN, THE, 938
party government, first, 792
party, joyous, wine, 1540, 1627
paschal lamb, 1399
    childlike, meaningless ritual (J), 1404
passions, bridle your, 2076
passive, J opposed, 1770
passivity, creatures do not attain perfection by, 1284
Passover, 1521, 1793
    ancient P commemoration, morally ignorant multi-
      tudes assembled for, 1376
PASSOVER AT JERUSALEM, THE, 1596
Passover, at P J met "by apparent chance" Indian
      travelers, 1422
    crucifixion no connection with, 2002
    end of winter, 1793
    first bloodless feast, J and 12, 1648
    first without lamb, 1404, 1648
    J and Apostles, 1596
PASSOVER, J AND THE, 1379, 1404
Passover, J' first P (103 from Nazareth), 1374
    J takes James to, 1399
    J takes Joseph to, 1409
    J takes Jude to, 1415
    J takes Simon to, 1411
    Jews scrupulous avoiding gentile building day before
      P, but intrigued for judicial murder of J, 1987
    no relation between J' death and P, 2002
    supper, purification necessary for Jews if...1987
    "this is the new" (J), 1943
    vs. new remembrance supper, 1942
passport, eternal p to endless possibility of infinity, 1174
    from human limitations to finality of divine...1200
    to eternity, attainment of Universal Father is, 294
    to Paradise, ability to comprehend is...290
past, difficult for men, break with p, 1722
    "forget, go forward" (J), 1736
    hard to persuade men to disown, 1722,-36
    is unchangeable, only future can be changed, 1221
pastoral life made possible by animals, 768
PASTORAL STAGE, THE, 768
paternalism, too much, Rome, 2074
Path, Eightfold of Buddhism, 1036
paths of differential conduct opening, closing, 1300
patience, A&E would have succeeded with more p, 840
    cannot function independently of time, 617
    "cultivate", 2048
    J', 1672
    J had p with apostles' human shortcomings, 1760
    J had p with Nalda, soul was hungry, 1613

patience (cont'd)
 J' untiring p enabled him serenely to endure, 1401
 J' with Jude, 1416
 never will you gain by circumventing divine plan, 846
 no manifestation of impatience will help, 1436
 real families are built upon tolerance, p, forgiveness, 1604
 Serapatatia lacked p, hence default of Eve through
   Cano, 841-42
 striving...increases p, forbearance, fortitude,
   tolerance, 1100
 transcended by forbearance, 1295
patient, "always be", 1593, 2082
 be p with the ignorant, 1931
 be p, your opportunity ahead, 734
patriotic, outbursts, unwise, Jude, 1416
 vs. nationalistic (not the same), 1385
patriotism, intelligent p, one of three mighty drives of
   ideal state, 803
 necessity for, 910
pattern and person, new relationship evolving between,
   1303
PATTERN AND FORM--MIND DOMINANCE, 483
pattern, aspect of living being, 483
PATTERN, ENERGY AND, 9
Pattern, FSC is P to the Paradise Isle, 1147
pattern, is a master design from which copies are
   made, 10
 J knew men were different, no set p, 1582
 of an idea--the reality--does it occupy space?, 1297
 reality of any p consists of, 10
 units of life in sex cells, 24 result in 24 basic orders
   psychic organization, 398
patterns, 10, 398, 1263
 vs. relationships, 127
paucity of language (can't describe force and energy), 469
Paul, 976
 and atonement, failed in this, 1339
 and others, deathblow to J' ideas, 1865
 and Stoicism, 1336
 and women, 977
 before P, leadership of believers in Greek hands, 2068
 built up progressive society, 1865
 carried message to gentiles, 2069
 changed brotherhood, 2092
 China and India ready, needed a P, 1430
 "Christ and Him crucified", 2071
 Christian religion, much of P's personal views, 1084
 church of P, substitute for kingdom, 1864, 2092
 clever corrupter, 1832, 2091
 compromised J' teachings, 1337
 confused J with Eternal Son of Trinity, 1144
 converted Crispus, rabbi at Corinth, 1472
 cult of continence, celibate priesthoods, 977
 cult of P blended Greek philosophy, mystery cult
   teachings, and morality of Jewish religion, 1340
 deathblow to church, 1865
 didn't dream his letters would be called "word of
   God", 1084
 doctrines influenced by Philo, Plato, Stoics, 1340
 drew spiritual lessons from sprouting grain, 945
 early Christian doctrines based on religious experience of Philo, J, and P, 68
 encumbered Christianity, 984, 1339
 ended doctrines of redemption through human
   sacrifice, 984
 Ephesus, 2 years, 1478
 fearless denunciation of Peter, 1551
 followed error of Peter, substitution, 2059
 found Corinth ripe, 1473

Paul (cont'd)
 friend of Justus, friend of J, 1472
 great organizer, 2070
 his compromise of J' teachings superior to
   mysteries, 1337
 "I am persuaded that neither death...", 1101
 "I speak this by permission", 977
 if followed, end of human race, 977
 in Athens, 2071
 in principle, preserved doctrine of sacrifice (atonement), 716
 keen theologic trader, 2071
 learned of existence and reality of morontia, 542
 lost sight of human J, 2092
 Luke based Gospel on P's story, 1342
 Luke was a gentile convert of P, 1342
 made adaptations of J' teachings, 1337
 made it difficult for woman, 937
 Mark associated with Peter, later P, 1341
 one of seven great teachers, 1339
 one of three factors in spread of Christianity, 1456
 pessimistic view of humankind, 2093
 philosopher, if not sole founder, of Christian religion,
   1412
 rejected Jewish practices, 2064
 religion of faith, hope, charity, 2095
 Roman, Hebrew culture, Greek tongue, 1332
 sole founder of Christian religion?, 1412
 Stephen, P saw him stoned, 1411
   death of S led to winning Saul (Paul), 1456
 sudden and spectacular conversion, 1099
 superiorities of Paul's compromised Christianity, 1337
 teachings, compromises, 1637
 tentmaker, lecturer of Ephesus, 1478
 theories partially Mithraic in origin, 1339
 Titus sent to Crete by P, 1436
 transformed new gospel, 2091
 "the Unknown God", 2071
 vs. Philo, atonement, 1339
 viewed ascendant mortals on Jerusem, 539
 went forth to build progressive society, 1865
 why he prolonged stay in Corinth, 1474
 with Philo and J, greatest teachers, 1010
 women, poor recognition of, 1679
 writings not intended as J' teaching, 1670
   much J did not teach, 1670
Pauline, Christianity, 2070
 vs. Abnerian Christianity, 1869
Paul's, errors: original sin, hereditary guilt, innate
   evil, atonement, 1339
 new religion of Christianity, 1083
 "rising cult of Christianity", 1337-39
 theology of Christianity, 1342
 writings, 1430, 1670, 2091
Paul's vs. J' gospel, teachings
 Abner parted with P on theology, philosophy, 1381
 Antioch became hdqtrs. of "Pauline Christianity",
   1869
 atonement idea, wrong, 1339 (see "atonement" under
   "A")
 church became substitute for J' kingdom, 1864
 "clever corrupter of teachings of J" (said of P), 1832
 continence not part of J' gospel, 977
 deathblow to J' concept of divine kingdom, 1865
 Hebrews rejected J' gospel and P's, 2069
 J did not share P's low view of mankind, 2093
 J' life from lowly levels to divinity was real message
   of Christianity, 2092
 J, a religion of love; P, religion of faith, hope,
   charity, 2095

Paul's vs. J' gospel, teachings (cont'd)
    J' religion of personal experience, P's worship of
        J and brotherhood of believers, 2092
    made certain adaptations of J' teachings, 1337
    P led to belief J was Redeemer, 1864
    P lost sight of valiant human J, 2092
    P made Christ (not his teachings) a religion, 2092
    P made his Christian teachings easier to accept, 1637
    Pauline Christianity Hellenized won pagans, 2070
    P's Christianity not simple spiritual appeal of J, 2069
    P's church socialized shadow of J' intended kingdom,
        1865
    P's compromise superior to best in mysteries, 1337
    P's Hellenized Christianity, 2073
    P's version later so paganized Constantine was won,
        2070
    P's was Christianized version of J' message, 2069
    Philadelphia, hdqtrs. of Abnerian (J) kingdom
        religion, 1869
    religious and social organization, instead of J'
        gospel, 1864
    some of P's teachings, original with himself, 1339
    started new Christian cult on blood...of covenant, 984
    theory of original sin, partially Mithraic, 1339
    women, difficult time, Pauline doctrines, 937

pe

peace, 1824
    accepted when, 786
    and J, 597
    barriers to, two, 908
    "be upon you" (J), 2032, -41, -43-44, -46, -50, -52-55
    "believer, peace in own heart", 1824
    cannot be between truth and error, 1905
    for world, not until, 1489, 1824, 1951
    from faith in Father's overcare, 1954-55
    from religious living, 1101
    "gospel brings p to individual", 1951
    "he will be kept in p", 1731
    "I leave with you" (J), 1966, 2040, -42, -50, -53-54
    in religious world, 1090
    in this life, subject will to Father, 1221
    J' kind, 1575
    many languages, barrier to, 908
    materialists', 1954
    measures civilization's advance, 783
    mission, king rides ass, 1881
    missions, earliest--maidens given for sex, 788
    "more abundantly", 1954
    "my mission will not bring", 1824
    no other way p can be realized, 1491
    none between life and death, light and darkness, 1905
    "none for the wicked", 1674
    not natural, 437, 766, 783, 966
    not a question of armament or...1490
    not to bring p, but a soul-struggle, 1782
    not without God, 2082
    of mind, 1192
    "on earth and good will among men", 437, 597
    "on earth" not "until all...believe", 1489, 1824
    on earth, only when, 1490-91, 1951
    only in mutual recognition of supersovereignty, 1487
    promotion by trade, 787
    races blended, one language, first, 594
    religions, to achieve, 1487
    religious, 1486
    religious, when, 1487
    social yardstick, 783
PEACE, THE SOULS OF, 437
peace, speak p, but mischief in hearts, 1676

peace (cont'd)
    stoics and fatalists,
    sublime, from religious living, 1101
    sublime in difficult, rugged life, thanks to T A, 1192
    superb, bestowed by Son on brethren, 1954
    "think not that I have come to bring...", 597
    three kinds, 1954
    to achieve in this life, 1221
    when men believe it best for material welfare, 786
    world-wide under law, 820
    world-wide, usually Post-Adamic period, 594
peace chiefs, through motherline, war chiefs fatherline,
    788
peace on earth, only world government, and not until
    then, 1489
peace tendency, acquired, more especially from J, 766
peace which passes all understanding
    after vision of God, there follows a, 1663
    amazing earmark of religious living, 1101
    is cosmic poise, absence of all doubt and turmoil, 1101
    spiritual growth yields joy, p, etc., 1098
    take...the divine yoke, and experience, 1627
    this is indeed, a p, etc., 1955
peaceably, seek to live p with all men, 1930
peaceful relations terminated (J brotherhood and
    Pharisees-Sadducees), 2068
"peacemakers, happy are the", 1575
pearl of great price, 1583, 1694
pearls before swine, 1571, -85, 1999
    (related idea, 1440-41)
pearly gates, 524
peat beds, 681
Pella, camp--almost 4000 in residence, 1868
    departure from P for last Passover, 1865
    encamped, over 1200 people, 1817
    4000 followers gathered at P, 1817
PELLA, IN CAMP NEAR, 1626
Pella, in Perea, 1801, -06, -08
    Isador wrote Matthew at P, 1342
    J' last sermon at P, 1858
PELLA, LAST TEACHING AT, 1850
PELLA, MOVING THE CAMP TO, 1806
penalty for golden age, 625
penance, and sacrifice, primitive, 60
    negative form of...renunciation, 976
    no, faith yes, 1545
peninsula in Mediterranean, first Garden of Eden, 823
Pentecost, 863-64, 866, 962 (see also under "Jesus")
    beginning of summer, 1793
    call to spiritual unity, 2065
    designed to loose J' religion from dependence on force,
        2064
    end of belief in sacred families, 2065
    feast of, 1379
    great festival of baptising, 2060
    proselytes' time for fellowshipping, 2060
    significance of, 2060
    "Spirit of Truth" sent to indwell all men (see "Spirit
        of Truth")
    teachings of J culminated in P, 2065
    what happened at, 2062
Pentecost, after
    all racial fetters broken, 2063
    end of special priesthoods, 2065
    man had power to forgive, 2064
    no "unclean spirits" on U, 1591, 1646
    obliteration religious discrimination, 2065
    self-assertiveness lessened, 2065
    spectacle of God seeking man, 2065
    Spirit of Truth, universal world influence, 2065

Pentecost, after (cont'd)
  spiritual experience disassociated from environment, 2064
  U mortals may proceed upon death, 596
  women stood before God equal with men, 2065
Pentecost's spiritual endowment of man, 2064
people, advanced,on a neighboring planet, 808
PEOPLE, ATTITUDE OF THE, 1670
people, chosen p, mischief-making error, 1005
  clamored for 3 things for years, 1523
  common, will respond again, 2090
  good qualities of a p reflected in statehood, 806
  government supporting p or vice-versa, 1461
  hundreds mentally healed, 1645
  J' interest in p great, 1412
  look upon their potentials, 1727
  make a civilization, not vice-versa, 854
  most die because, 365
  non-breathing, near U, 564
  of world, Spain to India (feast of tabernacles), 1793
  physical types on planets, 560
  rank and file lean to material, why, 2076
  some worlds, can fly, 561-62
  supporting government, not vice-versa, 1461
  ten feet tall, 562
  two and one-half feet tall, 562
  uncultured p irritate, offend each other, 714
peoples, best regulated by balanced tri-partite government, 797-98
  superior, red, yellow, blue, 584
perception, 3 distortions of, 1137
Perea, 1741,1808
  beautiful, 1817
  last visit to Northern P, 1825
  Lazarus fled to P, 1849
  3 months tour of all P, 1808
Perean mission, 1771
PEREAN MISSION BEGINS, THE, 1817
Perean tour, 1870
perfect, and imperfect are truly interrelated, 637
  be you p (see under "be you perfect" and under "Jesus, Quotes")
  "be you p even as I am p", command of UF, 295
  "eventually be p, even as I am p", 1537
  man craves to be, 1573
perfect beings, inhabitants of billion Havona worlds, 52
perfection, attainable, 1192
  compensations for limitations of inherent p, 1159
  creatures do not attain p by passivity, 1284
  evolutionary, implies other-than-perfection, 1159
  in next life achieved in spirit now, 1221
  innate striving for, 737
  is a progressive attainment, 36
  key to, 1221
  Nebadon Corps of Perfection, 411
  not possible here, 1101
  order of p gone, with humans given "power of choice", 277
  our goal, not our origin, 846
  seek for p in the love of God, 1610
  seek through service, 1536
  seven conceivable types, 3
  we arrive at Havona, with one kind of p, 290
  "you await...final touches of...", 297
perfection-hunger, experiential, 647
  leads to faith paths, 1118
PERFECTIONS OF DAYS, THE, 179,210
Perfections of Days
  corps of assistants to superuniverse directors, 210
    are in turn assisted by...210
  rule as vicegerents of Ancients of Days, 210

Perfector of Wisdom, authored the following papers in the U Book, 11, 12, 13, 14, 20, 21, 26, 27
PERFECTORS OF WISDOM, THE, 215
Perfectors of Wisdom, one billion serve Ancients of Days, 178
"perform greater acts of love", 1944
perils of budding industry on U, 786
period, third, personality reassembly, 1232,-34
PERMANENT CITIZENS OF THE LOCAL UNIVERSE,414
PERMANENT CITIZENS OF URANTIA, THE, 865
PERMANENT CITIZENSHIP, THE CORPS OF, 334,337
permanent recognition as you ascend inward, 498
Permian period, 684
permit evil to run its course, reasons, 617-18
permitting evil to run its course, 618
Perpetua (Peter's wife), fed to wild beasts in the arena, 1808
perplexities, many are nonexistent, 1611
  many handled by being forsaken, 1611
  monotony may multiply p, 1611
perplexity, of such high beings as Divine Counselor, 55
"persecuted, happy are they who are", 1575
persecutions, dispersed apostles, 2045
  early, drastic, 2073
  new, relentless, by Jews, 2068
  powerful church p of truth bearers, 2085
  why, 2072
Persia, 751,947,1049,1143
Persian, concepts of eternal life, 1865
  doctrines of good and evil, 1864
  teaching of divine kingdom, 1858
Persians, freed Jews from Babylon, 1075
persist in praying to change your attitude, 1619
PERSISTENCE OF TRUE VALUES, THE, 1200
person, every p craves perfection, 1573
  mediocre, how to become personality of idealistic power, 1094
  religionist, socially fragrant, 1089
PERSONAL AIDS OF THE INFINITE SPIRIT, 268
personal, communion, Father desires with all, 63
  efforts effect advancements, 508
  experience, 1641,1916
  God and man, 1305
  God, controls all pure energy, 467
  in all that is p, matter is skeleton of morontia, 2021
  liberty unbridled, always trouble, 833,846
  memory breaks in continuity of p in end, 540
  ministry, 1460,-74
  morality and group loyalty, 1372-73
PERSONAL PHILOSOPHY OF RELIGION, A, 1113
PERSONAL REALITIES, 141
personal, a p religion, 1629
PERSONAL RELIGION, 1581
personal, transit forms, not until Paradise, 430
  what is p is through direct act of Father, 70
  work, 1545
personal act, inferior p a repugnant to divine nature, 137
personal evaluations (of meanings and values) results when, 1094
personal God, your only assurance of a G, 1107
personal guardian angel, soon as third circle attained,569
personal religious experience, consists in two phases, 2095
  God-consciousness, 17
personalities, from highest realms, self-directing, 410
  goal of existence of all p is spirit, 140
  happy, supremely, 549
  inerrant p of Havona, 52
  insignificant, 1543
  judge on potentials, 1727
  lowest finite p of time (we mortals), 587

personalities (cont'd)

manifold p throng the universes, 417

material, morontia, absonite, spiritual (all), 637

PERSONALITIES OF THE GRAND UNIVERSE, 330

PERSONALITIES OF THE INFINITE SPIRIT, 105, 335–36

personalities, of the Infinite Spirit, 3 orders, 418

PERSONALITIES OF THE LOCAL UNIVERSE, 406

personalities, respect, 1765

some forwardlooking p and T A, 1258

subordinate, are not God, 60

PERSONALITIES, THE SUPREME TRINITY, 207

PERSONALITIES, THE TRANSPORT, 289, 310

personalities, contact

are mobilized in reserve corps, 1258

excepting less than 20 c p, reservists unaware of their role, 1257

human subject used in this...1243

such as used for U Book, "set up" by midwayers, 865

through one such, these revelations...materialized, 1258

personality, 29, 80, 261, 846

active, golden rule demands a p, 1585

active, no real religion apart from highly a p, 1120

PERSONALITY, ADJUSTERS AND, 1183

PERSONALITY, ADJUSTERS AND HUMAN, 1198

personality, after death, 1234

all is circuited in Father, 71

and individuality, 1227

and power, union of, expression...in Supreme, 1275

PERSONALITY AND REALITY, 1226

personality, ascends levels of the u, 1439

aspects of, fourteen, 1225

assurance, faith, truth, insight, 1111

attains Deity, regardless, 1232

awakening, enters morontia form created for it, 1234

awareness, dependent on other awareness, 196

becomes part of Supreme Being if...1232

bestowal of p results: self-determination, self-evolution, self-identification, 1301

bestowed by Father, 8–9, 70, 77, 79–80, 106, 109, 138, 194–96, 236, 334, 363, 448, 640, 1201, -25–26, -32

can destroy individuality, 1283

can unify identity of living energy system, 1225

can't perform in isolation, 1227

"can't undertake to define p", 194, 1225

cause of events, 135

changeless

in the presence of, 1225

one part of you remains unaltered, 1225

Original Personality is, 1434

permanence in the presence of change, 1140

reality (only one) in everchanging experience, 9

unaltered forever, 1225

characterized by, 106

characterized by "the evolution of dominance", 1229

chief purpose development of balanced p, 2086

circuit

all responding to p c "we call personal", 9

"bosom of the Father" refers to p c, 64

Father has knowledge of all...through p c, 363

Father, remote, but nearest to you...445

moral creatures in grasp of, 196

of God, far-flung, 25

Spirit-fused mortals are in p c, 450

transmits worship to Father, 71

PERSONALITY CONCEPT, SPIRITUAL VALUE OF THE, 31

personality, continues, 247, 1236

control, iniquity indicative of vanishing p, 755

cosmic circles of p growth must be attained, 1233

personality (cont'd)

cosmic scheme of p identity, 142

creation is dominated by p, 846

creative and unifying presence of, 1275

(creature) distinguished by 2 phenomena, 194

credits, we are rich, refuse to believe it, 556

decisions unpredictable, 136

"defined" (impossible), 8, 29, 31, 70, 194, 1218, -25

denies man is machine, 2077

designed by Universal Father, 236

destiny of divine perfection and service, 1096

development, never exhausted, 1169

dimensions of finite, 1226

disagreement evidences fact of p, 846

distinguished by 2 phenomena, 194

divested of corporeality, 29

double p, J was not, 1331

each is individual, 138, 1225

energy-matter dominant except in p, 1275

energy-positive, energy-negative, cherubim, 422

enshroudment in flesh on U, 1235

Eternal Son is the pattern personality, 10

eternal vs. potential, 1237

ever-ascending, evolving, on levels of...1175

every p and the Supreme, 1283

express actively, courageously, 1770

expression, only through T A, 1303

extinction of, 26, 37, 41, 367, 529, 612 (see also "annihilation", and "extinction")

Father bestows, forever maintains personal relations, 109

Father fragment achieves p only by, 1201

Father is secret of reality of p, 8

Father, p of, 27

Father's bestowal of p throughout universe, 79

finite p has 3 dimensions, 1226

follows types, but is always unique, 1220

form connotes arrangement of energies, 483

forms, human and spirit, 483

fourteen aspects of, 1225

free, preserve, 1591

God as p, Nathaniel "sold" Rodan, 1784

God cannot be plural to, 640

God gives by his own free will, 1232

God is, 28

God is a being surcharged with p, 138

God is destiny of, 27

God is father p, 79

God is a freewill and primal p, 138

God is source, bestower, cause, of p, 79

God-circuit, 71

God not less than p, 1119

PERSONALITY, THE GOD OF, 70

personality, God's love real to man only by passing through his, 1289

gravity-circuit, 133, 195

gravity of U Father, 176

groups, composite, 337

guardian is custodial trustee of survival values, 1247

Havona home of every pattern of p, 162

identifiable regardless of changes, 194

identity, cosmic scheme, 142

identity, reality of, 1232

immature, proud, 1778

impersonal everywhere, responsive to p, 1183

impossible science comprehend p, 1215

in Deity, demands other equal, 1145

in p spiritual transcends material, 1863

PERSONALITY IN THE UNIVERSE, 29

personality, independent of, antecedent to T A, 194

210

personality (cont'd)

    individualized absolutely, by Father's love, 138

    Infinite, 472

    Infinite Spirit can bestow p for Father, 106

    integrating insight of, 1297

    intercourse with the personal God, 31

    irreplaceable meaning-value in the finite, 1284

    is diverse, original, exclusive, 194

    is divinely stable that...1303

    is a level of deified reality, 8

    is recognizable identity, 194

    is responsive to gravity, 131

    is superimposed upon energy, 8

    is unifier of components of individuality, 102

    is unique, absolutely unique, 138, 1225

    is uniquely conscious of time, 1226

    isolated, executed, becomes part of Supreme, 37

    isolated (Judas), 2055

    isolation, J triumphed over all fears of, 1985

    isolation, to avoid, 1985

    J' p remarkable for perfection and symmetry, 1101

    J splendidly unified human p, 2088

    knowledge of Father's p through Son, 109

    loving p can't reveal self to loveless p, 30

    majestic, is purpose of education, 2086

    man develops p because, 1775

    manifestation, dual phases, 938

    man's moral will, (synonym), 1458

    mature, 1777

    maturity of, 774, 1774

    may eternalize by choosing will of the Father, 1295

    morality (virtue) indigenous to human, 192

PERSONALITY, MORALS, VIRTUE, AND, 192

personality, morontians resemble, but have distinct p, 545

    mortal self is a personal self, has p, 1205

    must transcend space, vanquish time, 1096

    never a second identical expression of p, 1284

    no entity has p unless endowed by God, 334

    no love apart from, 1183

    non-Father, 106, 266

    none apart from God the Father, 70

    not body, mind, spirit, or soul, 9

    not definable, but 14 things known about, 1226

    not necessarily a concomitant of mind, 325

    of causation is changeless, 1434

PERSONALITY OF THE ETERNAL SON, 79

PERSONALITY OF GOD, THE, 1783

personality, of God, goodness is part of, 40

PERSONALITY OF INFINITE SPIRIT, 96

personality, of J preparing...1484

    "of man, always respect the", 1765

    of man with p of U F, relationship, 138

    of non-ascender returns to Supreme, 1284

    of power, how, 1094

    of religionist, 1120

PERSONALITY OF THE UNIVERSAL FATHER, 27

personality, only, can transcend material, 1439

    only, foreknows its acts, 193

    pattern, mind, 3 absolute actuals, 1151

    performance on cosmic stage, 1160

    perpetuated on higher level of progressive existence, 1459; potential power constantly indwelling you, 1199

    potential p of moral being centered in... Father, 5

    powers of, 1031, -97

    powers, stimulus to, 1931

    pressure may deform the p, 1135

    presumptuous to attempt to define, 194, 1225

    pride (Caligastia) falling in love with self, 742, 752

    primacy, 28

personality (cont'd)

PERSONALITY REALITIES, 8

personality, reality is proportional to divinity relationships, 613

    reassembly of constituent factors of, 1247 (see also "reassembly")

    reassembly of p is reunion of Adjuster and soul, 1230

    recognition, independent of memory, on high, 451

PERSONALITY REGISTER, THE UVERSA, 334

personality, relationships in p, spiritual is predominant, 274

    relative to physical, mind, spirit systems, 1275

    released from handicaps of time, space, 740

    religion of J creates highest type of p, 2063

    remains intact after evolutionary worlds, 535

    results of isolation of (Judas), 2055

    righteousness not automatic, 238

    satisfaction, in unity, 1120

    secrets, 7 spheres, 144

    seeks new achievement, all p, 422

    seeks personality association, 1147

    self-destruction, 1301

    seven potential dimensions, 1226

    Solitary Messengers, prerogatives of...261

    Son is absolute p, 79

    soul (as synonym), 1459

    source of, 1225

    sovereignty of, 1729

    spiritualized p, shadow on...mind, 141

    spiritualizing your p, (how), 1098

    stability of p experienced only by those who...1775

    stabilizes endless change of factors of human life, 1235

    stable and permanent when it knows God, 1303

    stagnation, 786

    stagnation of p never, 316

    stimulus to all inherent powers of p, 1931

    strong, unified, possible to all, 1101

    study of, difficulties, could be avoided if, 1227

    subject to infinite diversification, 8

    subject total p to...1774

    superhuman p, union of mind and spirit, 29

    superimposed upon energy, 8

    supernal p of Eternal Son, 79

    supernal, unique, firstborn to parents of a new universe, 369

    supreme p of the u's, 1285

PERSONALITY SURVIVAL, 24, 1225 (see also "salvation")

personality, survival of p dependent on choosing, 69

    survival, optional to man, 1232

    survival, T A standard of, 1457

    survival yes, (identity), 1232

    survives through soul, 195

    term "God" always denotes p, 4

    third phase of p existence, 731

    Third Source bestows non-Father p, 106

    T A is focal point for, 1479

    T A is identity of p in future, 1247

    time-space shadow, 29, 648

    to p spirit is soul of creation, matter is shadowy... body, 82

    to transform, 1094

    total powers mobilized--faith, 1097

    transcendency of spiritual over material in p, 1863

    transports, 121

PERSONALITY UNIFICATION, 639, 1227-29, 1572

personality, unification, in absence of, altruistic drive may overdevelop, 1132

    unification of mind, soul, spirit, 66

    unified, possible for every mortal believer, 1101

    unifier of spirit, mind, energy, 102

personality (cont'd)
unifies matter, mind, spirit, 66, 137
unifies mind...spirit, 140
unify (see also "unify personality")
unifying and creative presence of p results in, 1280
unique (Gabriel and others, 369), 138, 1283
unique is, 138, 369, 1129, 1284
unique p of a non-ascender returns to Supreme, 1284
unique when bestowed, there are no duplicates, 1225
unity defies analysis, 1238
unity of p, requires guiding sense of...1480
universal p circuit, 196
unpredictable decisions, 136
unsolved mystery of the universe, 70
PERSONALITY, URANTIA, 193-94
personality, vs. non-personal, 193
virtue is volitional with p, 238
volition is not predictable, 155
where upon death?, 1234
why can function rationally, 192
will attain Deity, 1232
but identity may not, 1232
wisdom-action of every p aids evolution of Supreme, 1283
worth of, 2076
personality form, made ready awaiting mortal, mansion world, 1232
personality gravity, noncomputable, 133
personality volition, all creatures of v seek new achievements, 422
PERSONALIZATION OF THE CREATIVE SPIRIT, 374
personalizations of Deity, 3
PERSONALIZED ADJUSTERS, 444 (see "Thought Adjusters, J' Personalized")
PERSONALIZED ADJUSTERS, DESTINY OF, 1201
PERSONIFICATION OF CHANCE, THE, 951
persons, at tremendous velocities (S M), 261
become more real as they ascend, 1210
God (Father) is truly no respecter of p, 1468, 1608, -62
J no respecter of, 1564
morally fragrant, 193
PERSONS OF DEITY, THE THREE, 110
persons, prepared for Christianity by J, Rome, 1456
socially fragrant, 1089
those who cannot know God, reckoned among animals, 1468
perspective, none for the one-eyed, 1434
true, from study of origin, history, destiny, 215
true, of any reality problem, 215
persuade your fellows (for you) to succeed, 1774
Peru, Andeans and Andites from Japan, ancestors of Incas, 873
traces of Andite blood reached P, 884
pervaded, super-universes, by Master Spirits, 275
Nebadon by Creative Spirit, 455
pervades, all creation; divine energy, 468
Nebadon, space presence of Divine Minister, 455
perversion of principle, falseness, 555
PETER, SIMON CALLED, 1550 (see also under "Apostles")
Peter, "I will not stumble over anything you do", 1962
sermon on "Aaron and the Golden Calf", 1637
petrified forests, epoch of 150 million years ago, 686

ph

phallic cult, origin, 962
Pharaoh(s), 1019, -73
pharisaic practice, strict, 1825
Pharisee, Abraham (converted P) gave goods to J, 1666
and the publican, the, 1838

Pharisee (cont'd)
ruler of synagogue at Philadelphia, unfriendly P, 1836
seat of honor, 1833
sneering P comprehended, was baptized, 1835
thank God "not born a woman, leper, or gentile", 2065
"thank you I am not like other men", 1838
unfriendly P headed Philadelphia synagogue, was deposed, 1836
PHARISEE, VISITING SIMON, THE, 1651
Pharisees (see also under "Jesus")
almost convinced J should be charged, blasphemy, 1713
and publican, 1573
and Sadducees, pronounced antagonism to J, 1605
apostles frightened by determination of P, 1715
astonished by J' words of discernment, 1655
at Livias, friendly, told J, "flee", 1872
PHARISEES AT RAGABA, THE, 1825
Pharisees, began to crystallize accusations, 1850
beware leaven of the P, 1745
PHARISEES, BREAKFAST WITH THE, 1833
Pharisees, called on Mary, waited for J, 1743
criticized J for his part in carefree affair, 1540
criticized P before believer Ps, 1820
"...declare you have come...from heaven?", 1711
desired J' death for 4 reasons, 1911
disciples of John comforted, P confounded, 1656
discourse of J intended last indictment of P, 1905
failed to entrap J, 1902
53 P and Sadducees to start warfare on J, 1707
"fossilized religion defended by P" (J), 1730
"give us a predetermined sign...", 1714
had systematic, dogmatic theology, 1672
"heal blind man, give P reason to accuse", 1812
hearing people talk, resolved to act, 1791
"how can you give us...blood to drink?", 1712
"hypocrites", 1908 (see also "hypocrites")
Jesus, at temple answered questions of P, 1796
didn't vehemently denounce P, 1582
had great respect for sincere P, 1386
held hypocritical P in contempt, 1386
"Isaiah did prophesy of you hypocrites", 1712
knew many P honest of heart, 1582
preached on "Good Shepherd" before P, 1818
reproached P at Nathaniel's home, 1825
way to proclaim open break with P, 1813
Magadan, Sadducees and P, tried to trap J, 1744
man with dropsy, and, 1834
"many persistent in refusal to see light", 1826
messengers sent recalling 6 spying P, 1666
moral, thoroughly, though spiritually blind, 1792
much given to acquirement of riches, 1854
occupied with false progress, 1653
of Sanhedrin, believers in J, 1978, -85
one charged J in league with devils, 1714
one condemned J at Zaccheus home, 1874
100 disciples would brave opposition of P, 1717
particular in 3 things, 1827
passed death sentence without trial, 1910
peaceful relations with P terminated by Greek preachers, 2068
persecuted Lazarus after resurrection, 1869
quarreled while questioning Josiah, 1814
reaction of bitter resentment, 1910
religion, couldn't come to people with humor, 1736
resentment against P and Sanhedrin, 1741
scribes and rabbis, in many ways progressive, 1534
sought to convince Mary J demented, 1721
spent week vainly searching for J, 1724
"such honors the P seek", 1940

Pharisees (cont'd)
  synagogue closed to J, instigation of P, 1717
  taunts couldn't alter J' decision, 1520
  this is prophet P long sought to kill, 1790
  upon Lazarus' resurrection, P alarmed, 1847
  vaingloriously paraded righteousness of slavish
    works, 1861
  warning of the friendly P, 1872
  "we are confounded by this Galilean", 1882
  wealthy P devoted to almsgiving, 1651
  who heard, some entered the kingdom, 1826
  "woe upon all of you lawyers", 1826
  "woe upon you P", 1826, 1908
  would kill J for 4 reasons, 1911
  zealots, unlike P, impatient for Messiah, 1396
Pharisees, Sadducees, religious parties, not sects, 1534
Pharos (lighthouse of), 1432
Phasaelis, Archelais, new cities, 1607, -11
phase dangerous, of modern society, now, 765
phases of instruction (Paradise requirements), 3 phases,
    each has 7 groups, 12 minor divisions of 70 sub-
    sidiary groups, each subsidiary, 1000 classifica-
    tions, 291
Phenix, J was told way to P, 1437
phenomena, amazing partnership of man and T A, 1238
  medley of works for good, 56
  of natural and spiritual worlds, falsely so-called
    sciences and religions, 1137
  psychic (?), unrevealed spirit helpers "closely
    related", 147
PHENOMENON OF DEATH, THE, 1229
Philadelphia, 1411-12, -91, 1769, 2029
  and Antioch, 1869
  church, held closer to J' gospel, 1430
PHILADELPHIA, CONGREGATION AT, 1831 (see
  "Abner, head of church at Philadelphia")
Philadelphia, hdqtrs. of early church in south and east,
    1831, -69
  morontia J at P, 2041
PHILADELPHIA VS. ANTIOCH, 1831
PHILADELPHIA, THE VISIT TO, 1833
philanthropy, 777
PHILIP THE CURIOUS (Apostle), 1556 (see under
  "Apostles")
Philip (brother of Herod-Antipas)
  almost a follower of J, 1789
  half-hearted believer, 1741, -45
Philistine, Saul required 100 P foreskins as dowry, 785
Philistines, 1370
  could not have defeated Saul but for David, 1072
  refugees from Crete, 838, 1023
Philo (wealthy educated Jew of Alexandria), 1339, 1811
  adaptation of Plato to Hebrew theology, 1637
  and Paul of Tarsus, greatest teachers 1st century,
    A.D., 1010
  brother was a banker of Alexandria, 1433
  difficult task, harmonizing Greek philosophy, Hebrew
    theology, 1433
  doctrine of atonement, wiser than Paul, 1339
  doctrine of contrast, temporal and spiritual, 1865
  glimpsed T A, 1339
  harmonized, systemized Greek philosophy, Hebrew
    theology, 1338
  helped mitigate some Greek objections to Judaism,
    2073
  led way for Trinity concept, 1339
  Peter, Paul, 68, 1010-11, 2073
  possessed Amenomope's Book of Wisdom, 1046-47
  teachings of J supplemented by ideas of P, 1864
philosophers, greatest error, 42

philosophers (cont'd)
  Paradise, 302
  superaphic, 620
PHILOSOPHIC CONCEPT OF THE I AM, 1152
PHILOSOPHIC COORDINATION, 1135
philosophic, dilemmas, if God not personality, p d
    materialism or pantheism, 29
  dynamics, in spiritual insight, 1120
  mazes of material and morontial worlds, 1286
  proposition of master universe, the major, 638
PHILOSOPHIC THOUGHT, GREEK, 1078
philosophy, and brotherhood, epoch of, 577
  and metaphysics fail, revelation affirms, 1106
PHILOSOPHY AND RELIGION, 1140 (see also "philo-
    sophy" and "religion")
philosophy, assertions of attitude are essence of p, 1457
  attempts unification of experience, 2096
  balance with poetry, 1616
  barren extremes of, 1779
  begins to attain unity when, 1477
  beliefs of p are unproved, 1127
PHILOSOPHY, BRAHMANIC, 1030
PHILOSOPHY, BUDDHIST, 1038
philosophy, can't be built on either materialism... or
    spiritism, 1136
  chief pursuit of citizens, ultimately, 806
  cosmic p must accelerate to keep pace, 1146
  difference between a religious and non-religious p,
    1114
  founded on facts, soul of p is spiritual insight, 1120
PHILOSOPHY, GENTILE, 1335
philosophy, is observation of man's observation of
    material world, 1228
  is search for wisdom, 1122
  man's attempt to unify human experience, 2096
  many-sided problems in cosmic equity and spiritual p,
    620
PHILOSOPHY, MASTERS OF, 302
philosophy, materialistic, denied by H2O, 141
  most intriguing question in finite, 1281
  mota, more than a superior p, 554
PHILOSOPHY, NATURAL, 479
philosophy, never can attain satisfactory comprehension
    of soul, 1215
  of the Eightfold Path, 1036
  of life, a master p, 1572
  of life vs. religious authority, 1098
  of perfection available, Paradise, 303
PHILOSOPHY OF RELIGION, 1129
PHILOSOPHY OF RELIGION, A PERSONAL, 1113
philosophy, of survival, attunement, 437
  of universe can't base on so-called science, 480
  proper, 1135-37
  reformation of p must go on, 1092
  religion, science, in unity, 1080
  religious p, 4 phases in development of, 1114
  settle in your p, "God is approachable", 63
  should be relieved by rhythmic poetry, 1616
PHILOSOPHY, THE SOUL OF, 311
philosophy, strives for brotherhood of wisdom, 1122
  technique of, 1106, -20
  three assumptions, 1110
  three distortions, 1137
  to be of moral value to man, 1140
  to solve problems, 302
  vs. religion, 1080
  yields unity, 1106
philosophy, godless
  leads to unhappiness, unrest, war, disaster, 2081

picture on the floor, the, 1366
pictures, creation of new p out of old facts, 555
    of J, bad, 1590
    of mind, sometimes work of T A, but...1207
picturization techniques, 100,000 years knowledge,
    1 hour, 503
piety, man still believes show of p will deceive an
      omniscient God, 958
    springs from, 1785
pigs, giant, became extinct, 696
Pike's Peak, 692
Pilate (see also under "Jesus")
    "behold the man!", 2000
    believed J an innocent fanatic, 1991
    caption for cross-beam, 2005
    charge of blasphemy no weight before P, 1985
    cowardly Roman judge, 1996
    crucify him immediately, order to soldiers, 2001
    deep seated hatred of Jews, 1988
    false charges to P, 1990
    guard for tomb of J, 2014
    illegally scourged J, 1995
    J heard no charges until before P, 1986
    moral coward, 1987,-96
    never recovered from part in crucifixion, 1989
    "on trial before J", 1999
    one more attempt to save J, 1994
    reprimand from Caesar, 1996
    Sanhedrin officer sought use of Roman guards from
      P, 1973
    Sanhedrin sought to justify P in a death sentence, 1983
    sealed tomb, 2014
    seals unbroken, J "out", 2021
    suicide, 1989
    tragic surrender to Jews, 1996
    trembling with fearful emotion, 1995
    troubles with Jews, 1988
    unjust, fear-ridden judge, 1994
    "was afraid of a tumult or riot", 1996
    washed his hands, 1996, 2001
    why his disfavor with the Jews, 1988
    wife Claudia helped spread gospel, 1989-90
pilgrim discoverer of Havona, 270
PILGRIM GUARDIANS, 545
PILGRIM HELPERS, THE, 291
PILGRIM RECEIVERS AND FREE ASSOCIATORS, 546
PILGRIMS, THE ASCENDING, 340
pilgrims, 800 lodged in camp, ready for, 1500, 1806
    from all regions of Empire, 1806,-08
PILGRIMS, HAVONA, 343
pilgrims, of time advance life to life, world to world,
    417
    to Jerusalem, 20 kinds of money to change, 1889
pilot, yours is T A, mind is ship, will is captain, 1217
pilot light, instant p light in mind, disappears...1246
pilot worlds (Havona)
    after work on first finished, the next, 291
    ascending, descending pilgrims, mingle, pass, on
      p w, 288
    of circuit 3, momentous "milestone", 294-95
    of Havona circuits, "schools of the 7 circles", 280
    pilgrim lands on p w with perfection of purpose, 290
pilot worlds (local universe), home world of Melchi-
    zedek Sons, 387
Pindan, poet, 1079
pint can never hold a quart, 556
Pisces, conjunction in, 1352
Pitcairn experiment of blending races, 920
"pitchers, broken, of ceremonial service", 1796
pity, (J) affectionate p for spiritually blind, 1376
    sympathy, consolation--extend, withhold, 1766

"placate wrath of unbelievers, rather than die", 1958
place (job)-finding devices, as factor in U civilization,
    910
placental mammals from reptilian dinosaur, 733 (see
    "mammals")
plague of evil, sin; technique for cure, 618
plan, aborted, Urantia mortals were to have natures
      more spiritually responsive, 382
    all part of immense, 364-65
    ascendant, give out truth as soon as gained, 339, 342
    awry, 382, 884
    crystallized, J, 1748
    divine p prevails, in destiny of a planet, 51
    Edenic would have helped us, 586-87
      world administration is usual p, 588
    Father's, 36, 365, 1266
    for each mortal's life, 365, 1183
    for future ages, 553
    for a life, T A brings model careers, ideal lives, 1204
      (see "Thought Adjusters")
    for mortals, concern of 7 super-U, 54
    for mortal's universe career, 340
    J' p changed twice, 1748-49
    of God, opportunity, progress, endless life, 365
    of J upset, 229
    of mercy ministry, 85
    of a new age, J projecting, 1595
    of perfection attainment, 3-fold, 85
    of progressive attainment, 85
    of Salvation, 645
    racial, 884
    to foster spiritual types and conserve, on U, 1207
    to make Jews bearers of truth, shattered, 1910
plane of life, may be of joy and ecstasy, 1773
planet (see also "solar system", and "Urantia")
    doomed, mortals carried away, 582
    each has its own scale of life, 560
    ends, life removed, 582
    fifth of our solar system, now asteroids, 658
    -forming era, the, 657
    in conduct and destiny of p divine will prevails, 51
    normal, early purge of retarded, defective, 839
    ours is Urantia, 1
    seven stages on a, 627
PLANETARY ADAMS, THE, 580
PLANETARY ADMINISTRATION. 573
planetary age, at end, lower achieving mortals arise,
    1247
planetary, amphitheater, 606
    celestial service, 1257
    chief executive, mortal, elective, 628
    circuit establishment, initial, 710
PLANETARY COUNCIL ON ART AND SCIENCE, 748
planetary, crises, emergency governments (33x), 1253
PLANETARY CULTURE, 578
planetary, commissions, plan to train, then social
    uplift, 749
PLANETARY CUSTODIANS, 544
PLANETARY ENVIRONMENT, ADJUSTMENT TO, 565
planetary evolution, almost 100 modes of p origin, 172
PLANETARY GOVERNMENT, THE, 1254
planetary, government, 820
    of U unique in all Nebadon, why, 1250
PLANETARY GOVERNMENT, THE SERAPHIC, 1250
PLANETARY HEADQUARTERS AND SCHOOLS, THE,
    575
PLANETARY HELPERS, 436
planetary, historians, 425
    history, 1/4 Paleozoic, 250,000,000 years, 684
PLANETARY LIFE, THE, 559
Planetary Midwayers, 337

planetary (cont'd)
  ministers, may cause subjection of insubordinate
    minorities, 583
PLANETARY MORTAL EPOCHS, 589
PLANETARY MORTAL EPOCHS, 565, 567
PLANETARY MORTALS, 340
PLANETARY PHYSICAL TYPES, 560
planetary pole, space communication, 710
PLANETARY PRINCE OF URANTIA, 741
Planetary Prince of Urantia, 764, 846, 1327 (see also
    "Caligastia", and "Prince", "Prince's")
  arrived 500,000 years ago, 701
  arrived half million years "late", 735, 741
  authorized reproduction of midwayers without
    restriction, 855
  Caligastia early sought to be PP, 741
  culture of PP, only among Nodites and Amadonites,
    821
  half of human history since arrival of PP, 718
  intercommunication usual, 372
  is usually invisible, but Material Son & Daughter
    usually visible into age of light and life, 584
  made task of A&E difficult, hazardous, 830
  Melchizedek probably to take place of fallen PP,
    1025
  on most worlds welcomes Creator Son, 584
  100 modified Andonites used tree of life, 826
  people near PP lived in comparative harmony, 725
  Ratta, descendant of PP married Adamson, 861
  red man's ancestors in touch hdqtrs. of PP, 723
  staff made pottery 500,000 years ago, 903
  tree of life in courtyard, Father's temple, 826
  unique title carried by J, 1919
PLANETARY PRINCES, THE, 51, 572
Planetary Princes, become Planetary Sovereigns, 577
  directed by Lanonendeks, 393, 742
  invisible to mortal beings, 575
PLANETARY REBELLION, THE, 754 (see "Lucifer
  Rebellion")
planetary, receivers, 1024
  resurrection, 2024
  roll calls of the dead, first, second, third, 2024
  rulers on their worlds, 1025
PLANETARY SERIES OF MORTALS, THE, 565
PLANETARY SERVICE OF THE DAYNALS, 231
planetary, supervision, 1255
  supervisor, name withheld: why, 1252
PLANETARY SUPERVISORS, THE BOARD OF, 1251
planetary, systems, myriad, made to be inhabited, 21
  tours, Universe of Nebadon, 407
planetesimals to enormous solid spheres, 172-73
planets, cooperate, 177
  grow, 658
  for habitation can start from collisional debris, 171
  habitable, 3 in our solar system's twelve, 173
  in our solar system (12), 172, 656
  inhabited, elsewhere, 47, 52, 559, 1621, 2018
    hard for our astronomers to see, 172
    hard to detect, 172
    most important planets of creation, 172
    7 trillion potential, 129
    small, nonluminous, 172
  the more ideal p for intelligent beings, 173
  non-breathers' close to U, 564
  not result of solar revolution, 657
  of the loan order, T A gain experience, 1212
  others, know of us, 2016, -18-19
  place of spiritual polarity, 2024
  small, dark, best for habitation, 259
  small p may accumulate in space, 171

planets (cont'd)
  subduing of by Post-Adamic man, 593
  why inhabited? for "family" love, 21
PLANNING FOR THE GARDEN, 822
planning, wise, essential to worldly prosperity, 1779
plans, T A's lay p for man's career, 1183
plant, evolution, most important step (chlorophyll), 737
  world, red men appealed to sex passions of, 972
plants, all had same ancestors as bacteria, 732
  and all else modified for spiritization of ascenders,
    543
plasm, germ, energy activities of space no effect on, 667
plasm, living, Universe Mother Spirit supplies essential,
    399
platforms, teaching (at Temple), 1888
Plato, 1009, -79, 1338, 1433, -76, 1637, 1811
  contributed to Paul, 1340
play builders, 502
play, recreation, 1543, -58, -62
  playground, Havona is the p of finaliters, 163
  plea to the soul, an Adjuster's, 1213
pleasure, adventure, avoid useless, 149
  desirable?, 51-52
  escape, from the pain potential, 52
  have, but... 943
  is augmenting content of life, 905
  meaningless, border on evil, 1097
  most exquisite, 303
  selfish, 1097
  suicidal if succeeds in destroying property, 943
  supreme, presence of U Father, 32
  unwise pursuit of, 942
    human institutions shot through with, 942
  without restraint, 2086
pleasures, man entitled to physical p, 1096
  physical p cannot satisfy soul's hunger, 942
pledge, imposed by Melchizedek about churches and
    priests, 1077
  to monogamy, 586
pledges, harmful, extreme, religious p, India, 977
Pleistocene period, (last completed), 702
Pliocene period, 699
plot, fill day with entangling questions to J, 1901
"plough, if he turns back", 1801
plunging forward, human society, 912

poems of harmony, planets of light and life, 1306
poetry, 2080
  rhythmic p should balance philosophy, 1616
pogrom, Caesarea, 1430
poise, cosmic, absence of all doubt, turmoil, 1101
poison meant power, early rulers, 790
poisoned weapons, early in history of race, 785
poisonous emanations from sun, 666
poisons, physical and mental interfere with T A's effort,
    1204
pole, energy p of planet, "launching pad", 438
Pole Star, 1045
poles, magnetic, 662
police, armies, none on advanced worlds, 630
  celestial, agents of Ancients of Days, took Lucifer, 611
  night, 791
  1/10 force of 50 years ago (neighboring planet), 815
political, J' attitude, governments, 1421, 1576, -80, 1839
  machine, King David's corrupt, 1073
  optimism, an illusion without God, 2082
  order, not business of kingdom, 1565
  order, value to p o in J' teaching, 1585
POLITICAL ORGANIZATION, 809

political (cont'd)
  other ideas, expressed (unauthoritatively by J) at
    Zebedee evening meetings, 1421
  panacea, 2077
  prestige, J would not gain, 1521
  science, duty of, 1092
  science must reconstruct economies and industry,
    1092
  social problems, J aloof from, 1576, -80, 1839
    J expressed opinions, not as authority, 1421
POLITICAL SOVEREIGNTY, critical stage, 1487
political, spoilsmen, 803
  wisdom vs. selfish sagacity, 598
political regime or system,
  none that denies God can contribute, 2084
political sagacity, selfish p s is ultimately suicidal, 598
political, social, economic problems,
  J would have men solve their own, 1581
politics, and religion, 1581
  and religion, divorce, 1930
  commerce, not for church!, 2085
  without principles, 2086
pollute, unkind to T A to p physical body, 1204
polyandry, (plural husbands), 926
polygamy, 781, 926
  passing because it doesn't pay, 779
polyglot city, Antioch, Daphne's shrine of shame, 1480
polygyny, rare (plural wives), 926
polytheism, inconsistency, 1145
POOL OF BETHESDA, AT THE, 1649
Pool of Siloam, 1812
pool of water, called Bethesda, 1649
poor, and oppressed, religion passive to, 1087
  "he is the hope of the p", 1662
  J began his work with the p, 1594
  loser, Judas, 2056 (see "Apostles, Judas")
  man, falsely accused, J and the, 1462
  "poor in spirit--the humble, happy are the", 1573
  "when you give banquet, bid the p", 1834
  "why was not this ointment sold for the p?", 1879
  "you have the p always", 1879
popularity, collapse of p of J with masses, 1748
population, control, 599
  control fosters better men, 770
  500,000 years ago, 1/2 billion, 741
  laws of, 769-70
  polyglot, Tyre, 1737
  quantity vs. quality, standard of living, 770
  reduction fosters better side human nature, 770
  stabilization, 599, 630, 908
  surplus unceremoniously eaten, 979
pork, garlic, menstruating woman (causes of defilement), 936
pork, taboo on p perpetuated by Hebraic, Islamic faiths,
  975
Porshunta, 724
positive, action to save wrongdoer, 1770
  determination required for religious growth, 1131
  injunctions always, J, 1401
POSITIVE NATURE OF JESUS' RELIGION, THE, 1769
possessed by demons, a reality in former ages, 863-64
possessions, are needful, 1536
  no sin in, 1600
"possible, all things are p to him...", 1757
POST-ADAMIC MAN, 592
postbestowal ages, 204
POST-BESTOWAL SON MAN, 595
post-Havona Trinities, Ultimate and Absolute, 16
POST-MAGISTERIAL SON MAN, 594
postmoral human development, religion unfailingly
  exhibited, 68

"postoffice" failure, celestial, 760
POST-PLANETARY PRINCE MAN, 591
postponement, danger of, 1829
  is not avoidance, 551
POST-TEACHER SON MAN, 598
postulate of human survival due to H S, 1003
potency, space (see "space potency")
potential, is supreme over actual, 1123
  reality as meaningful as actual, 1296
potentiality, 3 absolutes of, 55
potentials, for finite growth, exhaustion of, 1306
  of function of master universe, 144
pottery, art lost for 150,000 years, 903
  origin, 902
"pour out upon all flesh" (see "Spirit of Truth, poured
  out")
Poutaenus, Christian teacher, followed Nathaniel to
  India, 2074
poverty, accompanies defectives, 803
  all but vanished (light and life), 629
  and dependence can't be eliminated if... 803
  and family of Joseph, 1360
  became so abhorred that... 776
  competition-gravity brings, 773
  culture never develops under p, 907
  man's natural, tyrannical estate, 773
  people courted p (in error), 976
  remains even on worlds of light and life, 629
  shall your believers court poverty?, 1603
  should not be tolerated, but, 803
  unfortunately taught in many religions, 976
  world leaders, p-stricken (ideals), 1220
power, and achievement "through renewing of Spirit", 380
  atomic, prophecy (?), 780
  center, physique of a, 1276
POWER CENTERS, THE DOMAIN OF, 322
POWER CENTERS, THE NEBADON, 455
power, centers, never play or relax, 323
POWER CENTERS, THE SUPREME, 320
power, centers, 10 billion, 322
  controlled through mind by spirit by virtue of...
    personality, 1280
  currents, specialized, like Gulf Stream, 321
  early was expected to be used selfishly, 797
  essential to government, 789
  explanation of term, 9
  final fruits of finite growth, controlled p, 1280
POWER, GOD'S INFINITE, 46
power, "gone forth", 1668-69
  initial political p family, then government, 1488
  J aware of his potential, 1416
  mighty p in new spiritual affection, 1739
  none but of God, 46
  not in word only, but also in p, 380
  -personality synthesis, under Supreme Being, 11
  political, consummate p of mankind, 1488
  of Christianity, service and faith, 2073
  of an idea lies in vividness of appeal, 1005
  omnipotence implies no p to do the undoable, 1299
  rules, as conditioned by patience (Orvonton), 182
  superhuman, religionist aware of contact with, 1100
  techniques vary planet to planet, 457
  that deprives others of natural liberties, 614
  there is no p but of God, 46
  universe, 9, 470
  universe, electronic organization of p, 321
  without conscience, 2086
POWER DIRECTORS, ASSOCIATE, 325
power directors, ignorant of origin of energies they
  handle, 169

power directors (cont'd)

POWER DIRECTORS, SEVEN SUPREME, 320

power directors, 3 billion in a superuniverse, 319, 325

POWER DIRECTORS, THE UNIVERSE, 319, 336

POWER SUPERVISORS, MORONTIA, 337, 542

powerful, driving force, dynamic influence, J' message,
    1091, 2063, -71

    most p unifying influence in world, J' religion, 2065

powers of intellect, wholly unknown to mortals, 106

Powers of Paradise, attain presence of, 304

pr

PRACTICE OF MAGIC, THE, 972

praetorium, trial of J before the, 1987

"pragmatism", wrong way to achieve righteous ends,
    bad, 842

Prajapati, deity-father principle, 1028 (see also
    "Brahman")

pray, and be not discouraged, 1629

    as children, 555

    "especially for Peter", 1703

    for divine wisdom, 1640

    for extension of kingdom, 1640

    for gifts of spirit, 1639

    (for) "a new and greater love for your brethren", 2041

    "for strength to sustain us", 1963

    "for those who despitefully use you", 1571

    "go apart by yourselves, use not... repetitions,
        meaningless phrases", 1577

    human will be strengthened by divine, 1969

    in the light of scientific facts, 999

    in secret, 1640

    in spirit of thanksgiving, 1640

    that you may be strengthened, 999, 1927

    to near at hand alter ego (T A), 997

    transform emotions into higher loyalties, 1728

    urge to p often is often from angels' influence, 1245

prayed, in tones of majesty, 2050

    with words of power, 2050

prayer (see also under "Jesus")

    after p, silent receptivity, 1641

    all spirit-born p certain of answer, 1849

    all supplications belong to realm of E S, 65

    always a socializing, moralizing, spiritualizing
        practice, 997

PRAYER AND THE ALTER EGO, 996

prayer, and personal effort, 1639

PRAYER AND WORSHIP, TEACHINGS ABOUT, 1616

prayer, and worship, unbroken communications with
    God, 2066

    answer is often in own changed attitudes, 1307

PRAYER, THE ANSWER TO, 1848

prayer, answer to p depends on, 1639

    answered not literally, 1639

    answers are often unrecognizable, 1848

    antidote for harmful introspection, 1621

    approach to reserve powers, 999

    approach to T A contact through unselfish p, 1099

    "ask also in my name", 1952

    "ask what my spirit wills", 1945

    beneficent ministry to the soul, 1621

    "breath of the soul", 1619

    can be an abomination, 1638

    chief agency of religion, 995

    city, nation, can be (have been) helped by, 998

PRAYER, CONDITIONS OF EFFECTIVE, 1002

prayer, connection destroyed, 1638

    connection, spirit circuits, 1638

    dangers in perversion of, 995

prayer (cont'd)

    declaration of soul loyalty (J), 2089

    delay of answer often betokens a better answer, 1848

    designed to expand insight, 1616

    digs channel for divine bestowals, 2066

    discourse on, 1618-20, 1860

    diseases, not for curing real, 999

    divine plan for making over that which is, 1621

    early p of Andonic peoples, 716

    early p was a bargaining petition, 983

    effective (J') because he believed, 1408

    effective technique, 997

    effort of finite to approach infinite, 1848

    elevates man because... 1002

    enlarges spirit capacity, 1640

    enlightened p must recognize T A, 997

    even perverted p elevated mores, 995

    every honest attempt counts, 1475

PRAYER, EVOLUTION OF, 983, 994

PRAYER, EVOLVING, 995

prayer, five requirements of effective, 1620

    for material, ok for immature minds, 998

    for one's fellows, beneficial, 1621

    formal, no, 1618

    function of spirit-born believers, 1946

    gradually displaced magic, 972

    group prayer good, 998, 1001

    Hap's 500,000 years ago, 747

    has been the ancestor of many good things... 998

    "He (J) prays like a man, performs like a God", 1786

    introspection, p is antidote for harmful, 1621

    is... 1848

    is great unifier, 1460

    is sublime-thinking, 1616

    J and family, 1389, 1401

    J' p was for wisdom and judgment, 1634

    J, talked to Father, 1360, -65

    J' threefold p in garden, 1972

    J' warning about "fancy", 1640

    J, what p meant to, 2089

    John Baptist's p for disciples, 1618

    last group p, 1963

    laws of prevailing petitions, 1002

    leads up through thanksgiving to worship, 1640

    "let spirit move you to", 1640

    like recharging batteries of the soul, 1621

    little associated with animism, 995

    look what he did (the Master), 2088-89

    "Lord's", 1620

    may be many things, 1001

    may enrich life, worship illuminates destiny, 1123

    mental, nervous ailments, cure for numerous, 999

    mighty promoter of social evolution, moral progress,
        spiritual attainment, 995

    mobilization of soul powers, 2089

PRAYER, MORE ABOUT, 1620

prayer, morning and night, (J' quoted Sc), 1640

    motive of p gives it right of way to divine ear, 1639

    must be the "desire of the soul", Adam, 836

    must observe, not disdain, laws, 1638

    natural to children of light, 1655

    "nevertheless your will be done", 1640

    no sincere p denied an answer except, 1848

    no substitute for ministry, 1639

    not better with fasting, penance, sacrifices, 1640

    not dependent on intellect, social or cultural status,
        1000

    "of identification", 204

    of soul is a personal matter, 1640

    of thanksgiving, healthful attitude, 1100

prayer (cont'd)
    often can be answered only in eternity, 1848
    one appropriate for all God's children, 1640
    only in trouble, is thoughtless, misleading, 1640
    overemphasized, worship neglected, 1123
    perversion, prostitution, distortion of, 995
    positive note in J' p, 1771
PRAYER, PRIMITIVE, 994
prayer, private, danger in overmuch, 1001
    process of changing human will for divine, 1621
PRAYER, THE PROVINCE OF, 999
prayer, psychic (psychological) always, sometimes
        spiritual, 995, 997
    receptivity for Spirit of Truth determined by p, 2065
    record of J' words about p wrong, 1946
    right p recognizes internal and external Divinity, 997
    secondary agencies, N G, 999
    seeking wisdom, forgiveness, better than confes-
        sions, petitions, 998
    should be directed to Son, 66
    silent receptivity after, 1641
    sincere, a mighty force, 999
    sincerity of p determines its being heard, 1639
PRAYER, SOCIAL REPERCUSSIONS OF, 998
prayer, socializing, moralizing, spiritualizing, 994, 996
    solemn style (ancient mores), 965
    spiritual value in p seized... 84
    splendid way to elevate ego, 997
    spontaneous outburst of God-consciousness, 1002
    subjective gesture, contacts objective realities, 1002
    substitute for action, no, 997
    supreme magic, p not, 1946
    technique that institutionalizes religion, 999
    thanks, "with all your p, give t", 1443
    thanksgiving, too little in p, 1640
    thanksgiving, worship, Nathaniel confused, 1638
    things deleterious to, 999
    T A, "filters out" and forwards adoration, 65
    to make man more realizing, 1616
    triumph of love over hate: "Father forgive them",
        2018
    true, 1001-02, 1616, -18
    true p appears when, 995
    truest is communion with Creator, 996
    tuning soul to catch broadcasts of U F, 1621
    two functions of, 997
    unethical, 997
    urge to p is often from seraphim, 1245
    use of set, 836
    vs. magic, 995-96
    vs. worship, 65, 1616, -21
    what p was to J, 2089
    when an abomination, 1638
    when will aligned with Father's, 1946
    wise father does not answer...literally, 1639
    words are valueless; motivation, spirit content
        count, 85
    words, irrelevant, God answer's soul's attitude, 1002
    words, phraseology, unimportant, 1640
    worship reaches F through His personality circuit, 65
    wrongly emphasized by modern religions, 1123
prayer time, 1401
prayer wheels, prayers hanging on trees, 983

prayers (see also below "prayers, answers to")
    answers will be on deposit, awaiting...1849
    channel for transmitting, 84
    except adoration, worship, concern local universe, 65
    from other planets, 1621

prayers (cont'd)
    Hebrew Sc J' approved most: 1640
        "create in me a clean heart"
        "set a watch,...keep the door of my lips"
    if dedicated, are answered, 1639
    J' answers to apostles' p questions, 1848
    J: two most important for: 1640
        knowledge of Father's will
        divine guidance
    reach "personalities" concerned, 84
    seized by universal circuit of spirit gravity, 84
    selfish, material requests, fall dead, 84
    spirit born petitions are all certain of answer, 1849
    usually do not proceed out of local U, 65
    worship to Father through personality circuit, 84
prayers, answers to
    are in spiritual terms, 1848
    await capacity for receptivity, 1848-49
    delayed, often betokens a better answer...1848
    depend on, 1639
    none without faith, 1849
    not material, 1849
PRAYING AS A PERSONAL EXPERIENCE, 1001
PRAYING, ETHICAL, 997
PRAYING, PRIMITIVE, 994
praying vs. rejoicing, 1609
preach, can p religion about J, but must live religion of
        J, 2091
preacher, Peter outstanding p but at front or rear in
        following J, 1551
PREACHER, THE STRANGE, 1764
preachers, all believers (Spirit of Truth for all), 2063
preacher's eloquence, people swayed by, 1722
preaching, about J' teaching, p, 1771
PREACHING AT RIMMON, 1637
preaching, instruction, 1765
    persistent p of gospel, some day bring all nations
        unbelievable liberation, 1930
PREACHING TOUR, FIRST, OF GALILEE, 1637
PREACHING TOUR, THE SECOND, 1668
PREACHING TOUR, THE THIRD, 1678
PREADJUTANT-SPIRIT MINDS, 480
precious ointment, Mary (Lazarus' sister), on J' feet,
        1879
PREDATORY ANIMALS, ADVISERS REGARDING, 746
PREDESTINATION AND OMNISCIENCE, 1300
predestination, "yes", but human may reject, 1300
predict, why physicists, scientists, religionists can't p,
        56
predictable, everything physical or spiritual (mind no),
        155
pre-energy, not subject to p gravity, 329
pre-existentials and post-experientials, 1163
pregnancy, early man didn't connect with sex, 931
pregnant Reflective Spirits, result in servitals, 275
prejudice, 1774, 1827, -97, 1995
    against individual Jews, no!, 1909
    and ignorance, inhibitors of growth, 1094
    and the recognition of truth, 1773
    "blinded by", 1672, 1714, -26, -45
    blinds the soul, 1774
    bondage of p, 1792
    eliminate selfish p, how, 1774
    engendered by ignorance, 2043
    hate, fears, hinder creativity, 1220
    historical recital not cause for p, 1909
    inseparably linked to selfishness, 1774
    interferes with work of T A, 1199
    J, none, 1671
    Samaritans p against Jews, J' time, 1788

preknowledge, example of J', 2046
   J often resorted to, 1645
PRELIMINARY INSTRUCTION, 1568
prelude to true worship, 1133
premarital disillusionment to temper idealization, 930
pre-matter, sevenfold electronic organization of, 479
prenatal marking, evil eye, superstitions about, 962
PREPARATION FOR THE LAST MISSION, 1808
preparedness, military defense, security through p, 793
   national survival demands p, 804-05
   without religion p means war!, 805
prepersonal channels to God, 65
PREREQUISITES OF ADJUSTER INDWELLING, 1186
prerequisites of progressive government, 807
prerogatives of the U Father, 468
presence embellishers, the, 506
PRESENCE OF GOD, THE, 64, 95
presence of God, and Son, 76
   consciousness of (how), 2089
   lower beings wouldn't know, 62
   vs. fact of God, 1733
presence vs. force center circuits, 131
PRESENT STATUS OF THE REBELLION, 610
present, to illuminate the, 1295
   trivial divorced from past and future, 1776
PRESENTATION IN THE TEMPLE, THE, 1352
presentation, this, 2075
preservation of representative government, provisions
   for, 802
pressure, core of earth, 25,000 tons per sq. in., 668
   hope for church that removes creedal p, 1135
   let p develop stability and certainty, 555
   may deform the personality, 1135
preuniverse, physical supervision of Nebadon P, 456
prevention of diseases, Garden, 825
PREVENTION OF TRANSITIONAL BREAKDOWN, 911
PREVIOUS (to U Book) WRITTEN RECORDS, 1341
prevision (insight), 135
price, "but are we willing to pay the p...?", 1782
   Jews paid terrible p for rejecting J, 1909
   to enter kingdom (see "kingdom, price to enter")
pride, forgive injury to, 1590
   "goes before a fall", true, 1223
   greatest danger to spiritual integrity, 1223
   in family, nation, good--if not carried too far, 1558
   is deceitful, intoxicating, sin-breeding, 1223
   kept family from J, 1587, 1721
   man's great weakness, 1596
   misled by, 1714
   much sorrow from wounding of, 1674
   obscures God (Shinto), 1451
   of immature personality, 1778
   shun all forms of spiritual p, 1808
   vainglorious, suicidal, 1223
   warnings against, 1808
pride, honor, ambition, vanity,
   gave origin to all art, games, contests, 766
priest, not occurred to people p should lead moral life,
   1338
priesthood, altered record, 1067
   pro, con, 993
   special, end of, 2065
   tyranny, Hebrew, 1075
   Vedic, black flood of pessimism, 1029
priesthoods, special, ended by Pentecost, 2065
priest-ridden Hebrews refused accept J, 2069
priests (see also "chief priests, rulers of the Jews")
   alterations of Scripture, 1023, -70, -75
PRIESTS AND RITUALS, 992
priests, China emancipated from p, 1033

priests (cont'd)
   early, paranoiacs, 986
   evil Egyptian, 1048
   false claims in Jerusalem, 838
   from Ur, the 3, 1352
   gospel not to custody of mere p, 2044
   greedy, overcharged, 1889
   have delayed science, 993
   intervene between religionist and "god", 986
   millstone about neck of the races, 993
   no custody of religion, 2063
   (rabbis) politically appointed, 1386, 1404
   retained bloody ritual, 1067-68
   stubborn, Jews, 1067-68, -70, -75
   virgins, had all v first, 935
   washed feet, made water holy, 964
   what to do?, 1596
priests (Babylonian exile),
   destroyed records of Hebrew affairs, 1070
   many times failed to "cover" their profane changes,
      1072
priests (rabbis), money,
   changing m, tremendous profits, 1889
   childbirth, mother must be purified by sacrifice
      payment, 1352
   desired: J' death, his zeal struck at their revenues,
      1911
   firstborn son, 5 shekels tax, 1352
   greedy p charged "week's labor" for pair of doves,
      1889
   J' attitude toward profiteering disclosed, 1891
   money changers paid % to temple, 1891
   perfect sacrifices rejected to compel temple pur-
      chases, 1888
   profane profiteers overthrown by J, 1890
   profiteering desecration of national house of worship,
      1889   profits (family) enormous, 1888
   rabbis were judges also, 1891
   redemption of firstborn, 5 shekels, 1352
   sacrifice (payment) for purification, 1352
   temple pens for sacrifices, enormous profits, 1888
   30 or 40% to 100% commission for changing money,
      1889
   treasury $10 million while poor paid unjust levies, 1889
   two young pigeons, purification cost, 1354
   violent argument over alleged overcharging, 1890
   were exempted from paying temple tax, 1889
   "will be deprived of authority over that to which... 1791
"priest's title" to land, 781
PRIMACY, THE FATHER'S, 52
Primal Father, 480
PRIMARY AND SECONDARY CAUSATION, 1298
PRIMARY ASSOCIATION OF FINITE FUNCTIONALS,
   1163
PRIMARY ASSOCIATORS, 325, 328   (slavish creatures)
primary, eventuated master force organizers, 329
PRIMARY LANONANDEKS, 392
PRIMARY MIDWAYERS, 424
PRIMARY MODIFIED ORDER OF ASCENSION, THE, 570
PRIMARY NEBULAR STAGE, THE, 652
PRIMARY SECONAPHIM, THE, 307
primary spheres of Salvington, 387, 391
PRIMARY SUPERNAPHIM, MINISTRY OF THE, 298
PRIMATES, THE, 706
primates, human type of hand and foot, 707
Primates, 700
   mother of first pair, died for them, 708
prime minister, origin of, 790
PRIMITIVE CLUBS AND SECRET SOCIETIES, 790
PRIMITIVE HUMAN INSTITUTIONS, 772

primitive (cont'd)
  justice, 795, 797
PRIMITIVE MAN, 589
PRIMITIVE MAN IN THE ICE AGE, 700
PRIMITIVE PAIR ASSOCIATIONS, 931
primitive, planetary atmosphere, 659
PRIMITIVE PRAYER, 994
primitive, races, antisocial, 764
     intoxication and drugs intrigued p r, 776
  religious experience, 1131
  society, four divisions: industrial, regulative,
     religious, military, 777
     owns children (Communism), 787
     rose through fire, animals, slaves, property, 777
primitive man,
  an animal with self-consciousness, 1479
  believed intoxication rendered one divine, 945
  feared a run of good luck, 950
  golden age of, 717
  short lives in the flesh (Adjusters), 446
PRIMORDIAL FORCE, 469, 638
primordial, force behavior, suggests our postulated
    "ether", 476
  force-charge of space, 122
  relationships, three great classes, 1157
Prince Caligastia (see also "Caligastia")
Prince of Peace, (J, Son of Man), 1536
  Jews paid in full, price of rejecting, 1909
Prince of Salem (Melchizedek), 389
Prince's administration, gains all lost within 10,000
  years, 821
PRINCE'S CORPOREAL STAFF, THE, 574
Prince's corporeal staff, 100 chosen from 785,000
  Jerusem volunteers, 742
PRINCES, MISSION OF THE, 572
PRINCE'S REIGN, THE, 749
PRINCE'S STAFF, THE, 742
Prince's staff, corporeal and relatively human, 744
  from Jerusem, rematerialized here, 742
principalities nor powers, 1101
principle, perversion of p is falseness, 555
principles vs. rules, 1584
printing, without p very hard to perpetuate truth, 1022
printing press, 907, 912
prison worlds, 510
  of spiritual darkness, 611
  Satan now detained on, 611
PRIVATE PROPERTY, 780, 901 (see also "ownership")
private property, after communism failed, 782
  brought increased liberty and stability, 782
  the great advances that grew up around, 782
  has been stabilizer of marriage, 917
  land ownership came with agriculture, 902
  led to industry, industry to government, 783
  love of wealth, 1802
  pleasures suicidal if destroy property, 943
  resulted in all government, law, civil rights... 782
  "those who put their trust in riches", 1803
  "what should a man do with his wealth?", 1462
privilege, divine, creation of own destinies, 615
  exalted, cleansed of all evil, 1610
  group p demands group service, 906
  not duty, to cleanse mind and body, 1610
privileges, two great, 1600
prize, the eternal, supreme goal, 1096
probation, is possible, extension of time to prove self,
  1233
  nursery of Satania, 516
PROBATIONARY-DEPENDENT ORDERS OF
  ASCENSION, THE, 569

PROBATIONARY NURSERY, THE, 531
PROBLEM, THE ADJUSTER'S, 223 (see also "Thought
  Adjusters")
PROBLEM, CHRISTIANITY'S, 2082 (see also
  "Christianity")
problem, effective solution of any, 1773
  the great p of life, 1199
PROBLEM, THE MODERN, 2075
problem, of equilibrium, difficult because of growing
    cosmos, 1274
  solution demands mind free from... 1773
  solving, 215, 311, 1723-24, -39, -77, 1204
  solving, efficacy of rest and relaxation in, 1611
  solving, greatest method, worshipful meditation,
    1773-74
PROBLEM, THE URANTIA, 839
problematic situations and achievement, 1719
problems, attempting to solve universe p, 302
  best-solved religious standpoint, 1779
  between self, others, not solved in lifetime, 1134
  contribute mightily to development, 1719
  economic, social, use spiritual energy, moral
    power, 1739
  for p of life, logic and math not infallible, 1476
  major, of Urantia (5), 626
  men Godlike, then can solve, p, 1581
  new, for religionist, 1133
  new universes, 254
  no escape, 1428
  non-religious, J ignored, 1583
PROBLEMS OF GROWTH, 1097
PROBLEMS OF THE LUCIFER REBELLION, 613 (see
  also "Lucifer rebellion")
PROBLEMS OF RELIGION, THE SOCIAL, 1086
problems, of self-realization, as we master, 1284
  only religion can sustain man amid, 1222
  perspective, comes from study of... 215
  religion solvent for most human p, 2093
  requiring consummate wisdom, 311
  solution of p requires courage, sincerity, 1773
  "spiritual, our mission...", 1660
  to overcome, a great ideal, 1773
  to solve, courage, sincerity, 1773
  "to solve some p, forsake them", 1611
  two major are, 1778
  unsolved p of eternity on Paradise, 303
processional of spheres, 164
proclamation of coming kingdom, first, 1593
PROCLAMATION OF YAHWEH, THE, 1056
proclamations of advancing jurisdiction (3), 1312
procrastination, dedication to will, 1829
procreation, non-sexual, result, midwayers, 855
  not predicated on culture, nor is salvation, 70
prodigal son, illustrates father's love for erring child,
  616
  J' favorite parable, 1850, -53
producer, be, as well as consumer, 1779
profane profiteers (temple), 1890-91
professional alms-seekers, 1580
profit and J, 1465
PROFIT MOTIVE, THE, 805
profit motive,
  abuses attendant upon misuse of capital, 777, 780
  base and unworthy of an advanced society, but
    indispensable in evolution, 805
  economy doomed unless augmented by service m, 805
  gain m is mighty civilizer when augmented by desire
    to serve, 787
  is to service m what fear is to love, 805
  passing of p m will give education new level of values,
    806

profit motive (cont'd)
    social order, change slowly, and for better, 782
    trade and barter entitled to legitimate p, 1464
    200 years ago dominant, now being displaced, 813
    under capital system highest degree of freedom
      ever, 777
profiteering, J' attitude on p at expense of poor, 1891
profits, enormous, (priestly families), 1888
    temple, systems of exorbitant overcharge, 1889
program for expanding civilization, 12 parts, 804
progress, all effected by revelational evolution, 2094
PROGRESS, ANGELS, THE, 1255
progress, civil, essentials of, 803
    dependent on knowledge and wisdom, 740
    divine evolutionary plan alone works, 830
    educational does not mean intellectual, 1094
    effort necessary, 1131, 1861
    essential in spirit affairs, 1916-17
    essentials of civil, 803
    finite, predicated on, 1266
    from leisure with ambition, 907
    from secularism, 2081
    growth by, 1749
    in grace, essential, 1682, 1745
    in quest of Infinite, proportional to Fatherlikeness,
      1174
    indispensable to human p, ethics and morality, 1107
    is technique of revelational evolution, 2094
    man acts, Supreme reacts, thus p, 1286
    mortal can forsake will of F anytime, 1219
    no time limit set on p of ascending, 288
    not speed, but certainty!, 1653
    occurs suddenly when, 740
    of each augmented by achievement of all, 1094
    of individual, for better nation, 1630
PROGRESS OF THE PREACHING TOUR, 1673
progress, or retrogress, 1736
    ordained, 99
    religion ministers to p of all through p of individual
      and p of each is augmented by p of all, 1094
    social factors in, 764
    to p quickly, need revelation, 221
    towards...unity, only by purposive mind, 482
    valueless without growth, 1097
    watchword of universe, 54
    which concerns 3 or more persons, 432
    with Adjuster, 1206
progress in light and life,
    one language, religion, philosophy required, 626
progress, spiritual,
    possibilities for s p equal to all, 63
    predicated on, 1095, 1118
progression, depends upon knowledge, wisdom, survival
    doesn't, 740
    fact of p when man acts, and Supreme reacts, 1286
    science, philosophy, religion, 1228
    spiritual, 63, 1118
    this transaction constitutes p, 1286
    to eternity, not only spiritual, 412
progressive, aggressive souls, only on earth, 2063
PROGRESSIVE CIVILIZATION, 576, 804
PROGRESSIVE RELIGIOUS EXPERIENCE, 1111
PROGRESSORS, MORONTIA, 342, 557
prohibitions, refrain from oppression, condemnation,
    vanity, 1656
project, eternal, we are all a part of a, 364
projects which are futile or unreal, no time for, 149
proletariat, free, Mediterranean society, 1st century,
    A. D., 1335   Prometheus, 901
promise, "all your real needs shall be supplied", 1823

promise (cont'd)
    "ask for the heavenly, the earthly shall be included",
      1823
    "I shall give you rest", 1808
    proved by countless thousands, 1808
    "salvation is a free gift", 1838 (see "salvation")
    (see also "Jesus, Quotes")
promised land of spiritual reality, 364
promised Son (Adam), 3000 volunteers to prepare for,
    822
promises, J' 2 p not linked together, 1863
    of J have been tested, 1808
PROMOTERS OF ORATORY, 503
PROMULGATION OF FINITE REALITY, 1158
pronouncements, two greatest J ever made, 2084
proof, cannot produce p you have found God, 1733
    demonstrations you know God, but no p, 1733
    no, but 2 demonstrations you are God-knowing, 1733
    none in mortal state, science or religion, 1139
    of J' humanity, mortal nature, 1968
    of much of J' divine nature, 1968
    of superconsciousness, 1095
    of T A in man, only to man of indwelling, 1139
    partial p for science, religion, on morontia level,
      1139
    spiritual reality not demonstrable to world, 1139
propaganda, department of missionary p, 1021
    insidious p of personal liberty to Eve, 846
propagandist, Matthew a very efficient, 1559
property (see "private property")
    agriculture; genesis of private ownership of land, 782
    and capital, distinct social advance, 780
    community (natural resources), 625
    disputes, early handling of, 797
    earliest was preserved food, 746
    in successful Roman state, private p, 801
    marriage, family life, home, civilization's only hope
      of survival, 943
    personal, essential, 802
    pleasures suicidal if...destroy p, 943
    private p essential to modern national life, 800
    private p necessitated government, 783
    regarded as a spiritual handicap, 976
    responsibilities of wealth, 1462
    right to p is social, not absolute, 782
    spiritual values come first, 1581
    10 methods of amassing wealth, 1462
    1000's of believers sold, 2067
prophecies, Messianic,
    figurative passages misapplied to J' mission, 1348
    most altered to apply to J long afterward, 1347
prophecy, astronomers will see...130
    better methods will disclose 10 grand divisions of
      Orvonton, 459
    Christianity will triumph, 1866
    coming, social readjustment, moral quickening, 2083
    coming, spiritual enlightenment, 2082
    forecast of kingdom in ages to come, 1864
    future appearance of teachers of truth, 1010
    Gabriel predicted Jews would hardly receive J, 1347
    generations on earth will grasp J' teachings, 1616
    gigantic struggle, religion of J will triumph, 2075-76
    "I will return to cleanse yonder temple" J (12), 1384
    Jeremiah's p read into J' sermon, 1709
    Jerusalem, destruction of, 1906, -12-13, -15, 2005
    Jerusalem, "they shall utterly destroy you", 1882
    J on his return "in the spirit", 1915
    J prophesies own death, 1759, 1824
    J to John, "likely outlive...apostles", 1955
    "Jewish nation will come to an inglorious end", 1906

prophecy (cont'd)
Judas (in great danger), 1715
last world war (year 1934), (more terrible destruction to come), 2082
Lazarus' death, to glorify God, 1836
man will someday achieve relative mastery of, 1306
Melchizedek, future occupation of Canaan, 1020
mind-reading (mind-energy manipulators?), 504
mind will see synthesis of the Supreme, 1120
new revelation at some future time, 1863
new telescopes will reveal...130
Peter's triple denial before cockcrow, 1962
physicists will detect ultimatonic rays, 474
religion of J destined to conquer, 2082
religions on earth, will realize a unity, 1012
shattering of the moon, 657
"so numerous shall your seed be", 1020
some of you put to death, 1584
"soon-coming persecutions" of gospel, 1931
spirit indwelt man, prevision, 135
(spiritual agencies) will continue forever, 1003
supernatural sovereignty of planetary government, 1490
teacher Sons will appear here after...231
telescopes will reveal...375 million...130
"they will hardly receive him" (Gabriel), 1347
to the Jews, from Deuteronomy and Jeremiah, 1709
today and future, men who know him, love J, 1672
true prophets vs. shamans, 988
true teachers will continue to appear, 988
Urantia, quivering on brink of enthralling epoch, 2082
will be days of gentile vengeance, 1913
world sway of...materialism...be overthrown, 2082
worst materialism is over, 1118, 2076
wrest new secrets from elemental storehouse (1934), 780
Zechariah's--followed by J, 1881
prophesy, "to us who struck you", 1984, 2000
prophetic, forecast of kingdom, age to come, 1864
vision, true, is a superpsychologic presentiment, 1000
vision, visitations, such, not hallucinations, 1000
prophet(s), 988, 1062
attempts to transcendentalize the p, 1071
dimly saw the Father, 1738
Egyptian, 1046
exalt ideals, scientists assemble facts, philosophers coordinate ideas, 1110
false, 1571
Gautama, real, 1035
"give up quoting", 1731
PROPHETS,
Hebrew (see also under individual names)
Amos and Hosea, 1065
Elijah and Elisha, 1064
First Isaiah, 1066
Jeremiah the Fearless, 1067
Micah and Obadiah, 1067
Samuel--First of the Prophets, 1062
Second Isaiah, 1068
prophet(s), killed the heaven-sent (J to Jews), 1872, 1906, -08
PROPHETS, A NEW SCHOOL OF THE, 1657
prophet(s), not end of God's ministry, 1731
not without honor, 1538
"stop praising heroes of Israel", 1731
supposed, 1666
taught with then light, 1597
Teuskwatawa, Shawnee, early 19th century, 988
usually advance of people, theologians hold them back, 1128
vs. theologians, 1128
will continue to appear and teach, 988

propitiation, 974, 978 (see also "atonement")
proselytes, Christianized Greeks, Judaism, 2074
gentile, "devout men", 1420
gentile, J talked to, 1411
prosperity, and success, augmented by circle attainment, 1211
learn to be faithful even in p, 1931
not sign of God's favor, 1662, 1830
the one thing essential to worldly, 1779
prostitute became life-long member of Corinth church, 1473
prostitutes, addressed, helped by J, 1472
origin, 918
prostitution, temple, 965, 982, 1065
protective, operations vs. sun's rays (over 40), 665
practices, make habitual, 1777
PROTECTIVE SOCIALIZATION, 763
Proterozoic era, 670, 672
protest, patriotic, false, 2009
vs. progress, 1565
proton, if magnified to head of pin, pin would be...477
protoplasm cell, association of...560
protoplasmic memory material, knowledge accumulation of, 1111
Protozoa, 670
prove, do not try to p God, 1733
proved, nothing is, 1139
Proverbs, basis of P was Amenomope's book, 1046
providence (see also "circumstanced")
amazingly fortuitous conditions due to...Supreme, 1305
amazingly fortuitous coordination of the unrelated, 56
apparent "accidents" of cosmos part of finite drama, 56
becomes increasingly discernible, 1306
celestial artistry, manipulating forces and energies, 507
confused medley works out p for good of men and angels, 56
cosmic, inexorable law equivalent to function of p, 137
discerned to extent one perceives evolution's purpose, 1305
discoverable to extent of capacity to perceive, 1305
does not mean G had decided for us, 1304
doesn't intervene for person, but for some total, 1305
Father has right to intervene with any individual, 363
Father's hand many times in human affairs, 1071
PROVIDENCE, FUNCTIONS OF, 1304
providence, is a function extending up through transcendental realms, 1304
is not whimsical, fantastic, nor magical, 1307
is partial and unpredictable, 1307
is a real and emerging p in finite realm, 1305
is sure and certain march of galaxies and personalities, 1307
is Trinity motivating cosmic panorama, 1307
materialistic, 1058
most of what we call providential is not, 1305
of God, interlocking activities celestial beings, 54
often imagination, 1305
an organic unity in universes, underlies events, 56
a real and emerging p in finite realm, 1305
seraphim coordinate, manipulate, unify environment, influences, 1244
6th century B.C., coordination of spiritual agencies ...truth unfolded, 1033
Social Architects bring working groups together, 432
spirit personality in action for spiritual economy of planet, 1196
unpredictable due to creature attitudes, 1307

providence (cont'd)
    V Son on orders intervenes in mens' affairs, 491
    wealth, if given up, probably re-entrusted to
        Matadormus, 1802
Providence, be not dreamers trusting in fictitious P,
    1931
    Ecclesiastes, reaction to overoptimistic belief in P,
        1070
    Moses was a believer in P, 1058
    "mysterious dispensations of P", 944
    realm of S B and C A, 56
PROVINCE OF PRAYER, THE, 999
provincial jealousies disintegrate society, 911
"provocation, be forbearing under p", 1931
prudence, foresight, integrity, 1854
    forethought, 1579

ps

Psalms, Amenemope, to Isaiah, believers in Salem
    religion, 1060
PSALMS AND THE BOOK OF JOB, 1060
Psalms, by Salem teachers, not Jews of Babylon, 1043
    cover great range of time, 1060
    falsely claimed by Hebrews, 1043, -48
    from shepherd boy (23rd), 552-53
    J recited P at end, 2010
    last supper, sang 118th P, 1943
    130th, Nazarenes sang, 1377
    one written by an Egyptian mentions "judgment",
        1045, -47
    origin, 1043, -60
    wealth of devotional and inspirational ideas, 1060
    work of a score or more authors, 1060
pseudo elopement, transition between capture and
    courtship, 923
pseudo seance, 791
"psychiatry", health, 1097, 1438, 2093
    moral, spiritual, adjustments (at once), 911
psychic circles, have to do with...1209
    many mortals on U have attained their, 1212
PSYCHIC CIRCLES, THE SEVEN, 1209
psychic circles, seven cosmic levels, 1210-11
    traversal of c demands harmony, entire personality,
        1209
psychic function, inherent in circuits of evolving mind,
    1207
psychic mobilization, partial,
    leads to partial-spiritual reality in conversion, 1099
psychic organization, 24 basic orders of p o due to
    "bundles", 398
psychic phenomena (?), spirit servers unrevealed to
    us (too closely related), 147
psychic speculations, danger in, 1099, 1208
psychologic projection,
    spiritual forecasts of T A, not p p, 2078
psychologists of first heaven, 553
psychology, of J with young man, 1437
    personality, 1227
pterosaurs, flying, 688
Ptolemais, down coast from Tyre, 1741
Ptolemy, 838

pu

puberty ceremonies, taught, leave other mens' wives
    alone, 791
public, builders, 502
    opinion, education of, 802
        has always delayed society, 802
        not necessarily right, 970
        retards social evolution, preserves civilization,
        802

public (cont'd)
    opinion (cont'd)
        to be of value must be nonviolent, 802
    revenue, the first, 796
    servants, representative government must guide and
        control p s, 802
    women, the two, and J, 1472
    work of J begins, 1587
publicans and sinners, 1540-41
publicity spokesman, 1559
publicized for 35,000 years, U as choice for bestowal,
    1316
PUISSANT ENERGY, 470
pulsations, rhythmic p of adjutant mind spirits, 1286
    three kinds, mid-zone, 122
punish, God does not, 1661, -64
punishment, greatest, loss of existence, 37
    J approved of p of evildoers, criminals, 1579
    litigation for Lucifer in 2-1/2 seconds, 618
    of wrongdoers, yes, 1579
pupil-teacher, you will be all way to Havona, 279
pupils become teachers, nearby planet, 812, 835
PURCHASE AND DOWRY, 923
"pure in heart, happy are the", 1574
PURE SPIRITS, ADJUSTERS AS, 1182
purest spirit reality, T A, 1216
"purgatory?", 541
purification, confession,
    meaningless ceremonies, 976, 984
purification of mortal stock (light and life), 627
purification of mother, paid for, presence
    unnecessary, 1352
Purim, feast of, 1379
purpose(s), and results, 951
    become fixed, no change in, 1295
    capacity to discern universe p is attainment, 1305
    divine and single, despite appearances, 637
    divine, is, 557
    education, civilization, religion, personality, 192
    erecting monument to experiential wisdom, 615
PURPOSE, THE ETERNAL AND DIVINE, 364
purpose(s), glorious, eternal, 364
    great and glorious p in march of the universes, 364
    number ceases to have meaning, regard to creature's
        p, 1295
PURPOSE OF AFFLICTION, THE, 1661
PURPOSE OF THE CENTRAL UNIVERSE, THE, 160
purpose(s), of cosmic evolution, 1229
    of each superuniverse different, 181
    of education, civilization, life experience, religion,
        personality, 192
    of education, fourfold, 806
    of group religious activities, 1092
    of human existence, 1174
    of human struggling, 1574
    of J, two, 1388, 1407
    of life, 1459
    of ministration, 381
    of morontia career, eradicate animal traits, 551
PURPOSES OF THE SEVEN SUPERUNIVERSES, 181
purpose(s), of superuniverse development (7), 1163
    of the trip to Rome, 1423-24
    of universe, 1329
    one great, J, 2090
    one, of true believer, 1946
    real business on earth (if we know God), 1466
    supreme, 2086
    to achieve universe value, 1238
    u of u, to duplicate Havona everywhere, 614
purpose in living, only to do the will of the Father, 1602

purpose of living, supreme p deepen by...contact with
divinity, 1774
pursuit of happiness, 630
putting off decision, danger in, 1829
puzzle, many a p in mind domain, 1297
pygmies, 764, 994, 1010
no marriage institution, 914
pyramids, 894

Q

Qualified Vicegerents of the Ultimate, 1291
quanta, relation to stability of matter, 474
quantity is fact, quality is values, 1477
quantum, 474-75
quarantine (due to Lucifer rebellion, U and other
planets in Satania were isolated, cut off, 318, 578,
756 (see also "Lucifer", "Lucifer rebellion")
development here as on other isolated worlds, 578
one possibility of interplanetary communication,
through Adjusters, 1190-91
planetary q limits this revelation, 578
suddenly no outside counsel, advice, 755
system circuits severed, U isolated, 755
system of Satania isolated, in q from sister
systems, 756
U retarded in intellectual, spiritual, progress, 578
quarantined, planets--majority to protect selves, 46
planets, why, 46
worlds, 1191, 1252
QUARTAN INTEGRATION, ULTIMATE, 1166
quartz from sandstone, 674, 676
QUASI-MORONTIAL EXISTENCE, THE USUAL MID-
PHASE OF, 730
Queensland, cannibals today, 979
quest, eternal q is for divine coherence, 42
QUEST FOR THE SUPREME, THE, 1287
quest(s), final q of eternity is endless exploration...1174
for God is endless, 1169
the four, 196
question, one supreme: why did J turn back tide of
enthusiasm?, 1708
quiescent mid-space zones, 124-25
quinine, raw cocoa, used early, 991

R

"rabbi", how title was achieved by teachers, 1891
rabbinic system, follies of, 1715
rabbinic teaching, women low, 1671
rabbinical alterations, 1023-24, -70-71, -75
rabbis, ruled synagogues, 1471 (see "Sanhedrin")
taught ignorant, not pious, 1545
were judges, 1891
race, after amalgamation, "racial white", 593
amalgamation, limited, ok if, 920
and color, none, (Post Magisterial times), 594
authority to purge r of detrimental, 627
commissioners very active on Urantia, 1253
efforts to purify and stabilize human r, 627
eighth to appear on Urantia, 857
for eternity about over, 295
for perfection is on, 365
human, fresh beginning for whole, 1582
if "lower" r can't rule, won't serve, is doomed, 723
improve a r must, 586; how, 630
improvement plan wrecked on Urantia, 586
is not to the swift...951
of superior potential, highlands of S.A., 728
problem not solved by mating, but adaptation and
control, 586

race (cont'd)
purification, U peoples have not even yet undertaken
r p, 592
spiritual assets of human r (don't discount), 2076
races, admixture now, disastrous, 726
and nationalities, all, at camp, 1657
are of one blood, 593-94
authority to purge r of the detrimental, 627
blue men superior ("white race"), 584
colored, 564, 718, 723, 904 (see "Sangik")
commissioners, 411
early r superior to later, 584
early, trash and dirt abounded, 903
evolution continues, 582
failure of plan here makes hard understanding, 584
five basic, 904
green and yellow suffered, assimilation of indigo, 880
higher r of U complexly admixed, 1223
if do not blend, one race may be doomed, 723
keen, laudatory rivalry among r of men, 575
many on U do not preclude progress, 626
RACES, THE MIXED, 904
races, modifications of r through colors desirable, 584
mortal primitive appear in order of spectrum colors,
589
no competent judges on U to decide fitness, 585
no pure, 919
normally purified early, 592
not equal, 584
not mix on U with lower strains, 586, 592, 719, 726, 920
RACES OF URANTIA, THE SIX SANGIK, 722
races, pass through seven developmental epochs, 576
present-day overloaded with inferior and degenerate
strains, 920
primary, many respects superior, 919
primitive, don't undertake sudden uplifting, 749, 767
no sudden uplift, 749
purification, 592
red and yellow, war for over 200,000 years, 883
red, green, orange, destroyed themselves, 727
red, orange, yellow, green, blue, indigo, 589
remnants of 9 human r commingled on U, 1255
secondary could have enhanced primary, 919
six basic, order of spectrum, 564, 584, 589
RACES, THE SIX EVOLUTIONARY, 584
races, those usually missing or exterminated, 584
three white, 897
usually backward r are laborers, 585
violet, ninth to appear on U, 850
we should disfellowship unfit, degenerate, etc., 585
what dooms a race, 723
where located after Adam & Eve, 868
Rachel (cousin and wife of Jacob), 944
Rachel (sister-in-law of Jude), 1679
RACIAL AMALGAMATION--BESTOWAL OF THE
ADAMIC BLOOD, 585
RACIAL AND CULTURAL DISTRIBUTION (Violet Race),
868
racial, antipathy, early, 726
contacts, 1485
cultural distribution 35,000 years ago, 868
development, interbreeding, 585
differences, do not survive death, 567
epochs, 567-68
faith vs. personal, 1731
fetters, broken by J on day of Pentecost, 2063
hatreds, lack of ideals, 1220
RACIAL IDEALS, 909
racial, ideals as factor in U civilization, 909
interbreeding, good and bad, 920

racial (cont'd)
  interbreeding not so bad as multiplying inferior, 921
  intermarriage, 726
RACIAL INTERPRETERS, 553
RACIAL MIXTURES, 919
racial, origins, determining by skull vs. skeleton, 904
  softness, undesirable, 786
  uplift, inferior and unfit usually eliminated before, 585
  uplift, superior individuals mate at Garden with violet, 586
  uplifters, Adamic, 764
"radar" for Solitary Messengers, 257
RADIATION, SOLAR, 460
radiations, diverse, accompanied by space-energy unknown on U, 667
radiations, flood-tides of...energy, 667
radical human adjustment, mother-family to father-family most, 933
radio broadcasts, long distance transmissions due to, 666
radium, negative particles, velocity of light, 477
radium clock, 659
rain making, 987-88
"rain to fall on the just and unjust", 39, 1830
rainbow, 947
Ramah, at, 1741
RAMAH, THE STOP AT, 1641
ransom, and atonement, J no, 2017
  J' life became a new gospel of r, 2061
  wrong idea of r took over gospel, 2061
Rantowoc, received 1st guardian angel to U, 1242
  wise man of red race, 1242
Rantulia, nearby system, 606
rarest form of energy from collisions, 176
Ratta married Adamson (120-20), 861
"ravens, consider the", 1823
"raw eaters", a term of derision, 778
rays of radiant energy, affect inheritance plasm, 667
rays, ultimatonic, shower in upon U, 474
rays (wavelike manifestations) (10 groups), 474

re

react with good for evil, not submission, 1770
reactions to existence, 951
readjustment, inward, is to u too, 1438
readjustments of human values, more in generation than in 2000 years, 1013
readjustments, vital r of attitudes essential...1774
ready, be r for J, 1919
real, the eternal r is the good of the u, 1123
  growth, 1094
  mind, matter, spirit, equally r, 141
REAL NATURE OF RELIGION, THE, 1104
real, to become, 1301
  trouble, disappointment, serious defeat...only when, 142
realest thing in mind and soul--the T A, 1105
realities, are three, 1434
    causation in physical world
    self-consciousness in intellectual world
    progressing selfhood in spirit world
  associated with transcendental level are 10, 1160
  "eternal and spiritual", 1641
  eternal r are rewards of striving, 1859
  forces, spirits, personalities, 1160
  Judas fleeing from, 1567
  of celestials, thing, meaning, value, 2094
  of philosophy; reason, wisdom, faith, 2094
    physical, intellectual, spiritual r, 2094

realities (cont'd)
  of religious consciousness; science, philosophy, truth, 2094
  only r worth striving for are, 1096
REALITIES, PERSONAL, 141
REALITIES, PERSONALITY, 8
realities, righteous vs. sinful pleasures, 1745
  spirit r experiential through mind, 140
  three basic mind r of the cosmos, 195
  "which are central in kingdom", 1615
  which never entered the concept of human minds, 269
  worth striving for, 1096
realities, morontia,, mind and spirit, potential for creation of, 757
realities of heaven, essential to stabilize society, etc., 2075
realities, Paradise spirit, emanations of Son, influences of Spirit, and T A, 639
reality, absolute, (7 absolutes), 5
  Absolutes: 3 persons of Deity, Paradise, and 3 Absolutes, 115
  actual and potential, 7
  all absolute r is from eternity, without beginning, 1153,-55
  avoidance, dreaming, 1099
  chronological origins of r, lead to 7 Absolutes of Infinity, 1154
  comprehension of (God), 2094
  conditioned and limited by, 1163
  contests, higher r wins, 37
  cosmic, distinct realms, physical, mental, spiritual, 739
  cosmic, finite, 140, 1096, 1261,-75
    energy and matter, one, 467
  cosmic, three levels: finite, absonite, absolute, 1260
  creative, 1301
  deified r, all of infinite Deity potentials, 7
REALITY, DEITY AND,1152
reality, designated as finite, absonite, absolute, 1260
REALITY, DISCOURSE ON, 141, 1433, 2094
reality, divisible from time, space, viewpoint as...7
  existential and experiential, 7
  expression of personality, energy, spirit, etc., 1148, 1149
  fact, idea, relation, 2094
  the Father initiates and maintains, 7
  finite, infinite, eternal, 43
  finite, new, exists in two phases, 1158
  finite, three functioning levels of, 140
  the 4 levels of universe r on U, 8
  God is absolute in r, 48
  God the Supreme is maximation of all creature r, 1304
  grasped only through God, 31
  highest objective r is God, 2095
  I AM postulated as primal source of all r, 1157
  infinite, total, existential in 7 phases, 7 coordinate Absolutes, 4
  interassociated r, difficult of identification, 7
  is relative (except Absolutes), 1266
  J on, 1433
  levels of r, absolute, transcendental, finite, 1031
  levels of r, limited by, 151, 192, 1162, 1260
  manifest in humans on 4 levels, 8
  manifestations, local universe are 3, matter, morontia, spirit, 1136
  manifold existents and latents, 1162
  many forms and phases of, 1162
  maximum of, 1096
  mind, 192, 195
  never in u was God such a living r as in human J, 2087

reality (cont'd)
    no ideals of r, values of perfection, apart from God, 1781
    none, but for God, 55
    not grasped by logic, math, 31
REALITY OF GOD, THE, 23
reality, of God denied, system no good, 2084
REALITY OF HUMAN CONSCIOUSNESS, 195
reality, of personality, Father is secret of, 8
    of presence of God is most certain, 195
REALITY OF RELIGIOUS EXPERIENCE, THE, 1129
reality, of religious experience, transcends other achievements, 1142
    of the Supreme, defined, 1434
    oversimplified, supreme philosophical blunder, 215
    partial approaches to r, 1090
    personal and impersonal, 7
    personal r is spirit, 141
REALITY, PERSONALITY AND, 1226
reality, personality r, Center of, proper approach to study man, 215
    physical, spiritual, personality r, in cosmic mind, 196
    possible unlimited integration of r, 1171
    problem, perspective to be had only from study of origin, history, destiny, 215
    promulgation of finite, 1158
    realization, three levels of, 69
    realizations, 4 latent and inherent in self-consciousness, 196
    repercussions of finite, 1159
    "response" negates a priori assumptions, 191
    science, politics, society, religion, 1436
    source of universe r is the Infinite, 1434
REALITY, SOURCES OF SUPREME, 1263
reality, spirit levels of r are independent of space, 482
    spiritual possibility is potential r, 2096
    supreme r of Universe, love, 1922
    three elements in universal r: fact, idea, and reaction, 2094
    three functioning levels of r, 140
    three primal phases on many levels, 6
    time, space, experience, obstacles to r perception, 1173
    to modify-control matter, direct energy, 1222
    total is functionalized through triunities, 1147
    totality, 1152
    two actual phases of, 126
    undeified, deified, interassociated, 6-7
    unified 3 ways, absolutely, functionally, relatively, 1160
    universal, qualities manifest on 4 levels, 8
    universal r has relative meaning, 1439
REALITY, UNIVERSE, 6
REALITY, UNIVERSE LEVELS OF, 1162
REALIZATION OF DEFAULT, THE, 842
REALIZATION OF THE ETERNAL SON, 79
REALIZATION OF GOD, THE, 58
realize eternal destiny, compatible with joyous life, 1206
"realm of the unrealized", (failure to survive), 1285
realms of pre-energy, prespirit, and personality, 99
reap "men r what they sow" (J of Job), 1663
reason, alone can't validate values of religious experience, 1116
    exhibits wisdom when...1142
    faith, logic, 1106,-39
    faith, knowledge, wisdom, 1119
    faith, mota, 1136
    grows out of material awareness, 1138
    introduces man to facts, things, 1141

reason (cont'd)
    is the method of science, 1106
    is the understanding technique of the science, 1136
    "together, come now, let us r t", 1445
    vs. finite experience, 1146
    wisdom, and faith, 2094
reasoning, 4 errors of r, likely when start with lower, proceed to higher, 215
    technique of time-space r used to reach us, 5
reasons for triumph of Christianity in the Occident, 2069
reassembly (morontia), Adjuster and soul are r of personality, 1230
    if transitory personality experiences no r, 553
    of lower achievers, end of planetary age, 1247
    of memory, insight, and...identity, 1235
    of personality factors, a resurrection, 341
    of personality invokes 3 things, 1234
    personality r on identification world, 431
    repersonalization on morontia worlds, 1230
    seraphim are indispensable to r, 1230
    thanks to guardian seraphim and T A, 1247
    unites identity and personality in eternal manifestation, 1230
    we reconsciousize at morontia awakening, 1230
    your T A present at r, 1234
REBECCA, THE DAUGHTER OF EZRA, 1402,2008,-13
Rebecca, faithful, life long, 1403
Rebecca (daughter of Joseph of Arimathea), 1679
rebel, J a r, 2007
REBEL MIDWAYERS, THE, 863
rebel personalities, used sophistry and deception to lead subordinates astray, 1313
rebellion, action to prevent r greater value than loyalty in a r, 245
    advantages to U from the, 578
    "against the righteous rule of heaven" (J), 1664
    against tradition, 1404
    brought sin to this world, 1660
    by Planetary Prince instantly isolates planet, 394
    can occur only if permitted, 1326
    cannot accelerate social evolution, 830
    "cannot occur during your (J) absence", 1326
    changes world so much, no idea of what's normal, 591
    don't half cure...or hide hideous visage of rebels and r, 617
    end to direct translation to m w, 596
    free course for r uproots sympathy, 617
    handicap of, 578
REBELLION, HISTORY OF THE, 607
REBELLION, THE HUMAN HERO OF THE, 761
REBELLION, IMMEDIATE RESULTS OF, 758
rebellion, instigators, instant extinction, 1326
    invested with automatic seed of defeat, 1326
    J relentless against sin, r, 1766
    let r pursue a natural course of self-obliteration, 617
REBELLION, THE LUCIFER (see under "Lucifer")
rebellion, Lucifer, adjudication ere long, 529
    Lucifer, one of 3 system sovereigns in all Nebadon history to rebel, 393,511,605
    Nebadon, several times in, 572-73
    non-interference, superiors defied, took no note, 605
    none in absence of Michael on U, 1326
    one of worst in Nebadon, 511,1311
    only 3 in 10,000 systems, 601
    outbreak can be controlled?, 1326
REBELLION, OUTBREAK OF THE, 604,755
rebellion, over 700 sons, local u, 393
    periodic outbreaks of r against tradition, 1404
REBELLION, THE PLANETARY, 754
REBELLION, PRESENT STATUS OF THE, 610

rebellion (cont'd)
  rare, 10,000 systems, 3 Sovereigns in r, 601
  terminated, J (Michael) authority for future, 1513
  13 planetary Adams lost in Satania, 581
  thirty-seven worlds in Satania, 609
  this was a Lanonandek rebellion (Lucifer a L Son), 607
  vast majority in r repented, 758
  why, 393, 572
  worlds isolated by r, primary supernaphim take command of... 298
rebellion-isolated worlds, 36 beside U in system, 1252
rebellion-sin, 361
"rebellious attitude, no answer", 1639
rebels, interned, status unchanged for 1900 years, 611
  planetary staff of 100 r, degraded to mortal levels, 757
  wrong-thinkers, plan for rehabilitation, 38
rebels against God, advocates of "self-assertion and liberty", 602
rebels and rebellion, cure through unlimited sin-expression, 617-18
  nothing to be done to half cure or hide, 617
  there will come an end for, 529
reborn (see also "born again, be", and under "Jesus, Quotes" see "born")
  born again (meaning of), 1576
  citizens, 1568, 1930
  evidence is sincerely love one another, 1601
  first, before advanced teaching, 1592-93
  inner, to outer also, 1438
  when you enter kingdom, 1592
  you, for God's sake, 1438
  you must be, 1576
rebuke, sudden and scathing r of Jewish rulers by J, 1910 (see also "rebuked", and "rebukes" under "Jesus")
RECENTS OF DAYS, 179, 211
Recents of Days (21,000), concerned primarily with physical problems, 211
reception, millions upon millions at r for J(Michael), return to Salvington, 1316
receptive, man most r in worship, 1641
recess, vacation, rest, 1610, -77
recession, decreased earnings; capital, management, labor, all share alike, 813
recession of spheres--only apparent, 134
reciprocals, evolutionary, experiential r, Supreme and grand universe, 1278
  evolutionary r, Supreme Being, grand universe?, 1281
reckoning required of us all, 1918
RECOGNITION AS AN INHABITED WORLD, 709
recognition... essential to development of character, 1775
recognition, understanding, and meanings, 1219-20
recognize, we can r people forever, 498
reconciliation between Abraham and Melchizedek, 1020
reconstruction, of economics and industry required, 1092
  social, religious part, 1092
record, Father's messengers r service of love, 1764
  made by Cedes, available for Luke's Gospel, 1342
recorded, all of significance in inhabited creation, 281
  emotions and thoughts of J, 1844
RECORDER-TEACHERS, 554
RECORDERS, THE CELESTIAL, 281, 433, 436, 439, 503, 554
RECORDERS, THE CHIEF, 288
RECORDERS, THE (Seraphic Hosts), 429
recorders, 431, 433, 436, 439
  some born fully developed, 429
recording angels, 554, 1243

record(s), all occurrences, 281; all naked souls, 313
  complete on every individual, 409
RECORDS, CUSTODIANS OF, ON PARADISE, 281
record(s), 500,000 words one minute, 503
  formal of the Universes, 201, 281
  Jewish r altered, rewritten, 838, 874-75, 1023-24, 1068, -70, -72, -74-75, 1348, 1599
  live vs. dead, preserved in living minds, 201
  material, morontial, spiritual, 436
  mortal, on high, 2015
  "of every service of love", 1764
  of J' human emotions and divine thoughts, 1844
  of life of spiritual value, 201, 1231, -43
  Reflective Spirits and seconaphim, 200-01
  spiritual, reflectivity, 201
  superhuman on high--J' life, 1343
recreation, 511, 1370-71, 1402, -29
rectangles, 1000 on Jerusem for lower native life, 527
RECTANGLES--THE SPORNAGIA, THE, 527
red and yellow races, 200,000 years warfare, 883-84
red man, 885, 905, 907, 960, 1010 (see also "Indians")
RED MAN, THE, 723
red man, always monogamous, 723
RED MAN AND YELLOW MAN, 883
red man, Blackfoot Indians, descended from Onamonalonton, 723
  children tractable, docile little animals, 941
  dispossessed of Asiatic homelands 50,000 years before Adam, 884
  driven from Asia 50,000 years before Adam, occupied America, 869
  driven out of Asia 85,000 B.C., 869
  entered America over 80,000 years ago, 723, 728
  Eskimo contact 5000 years ago, Hudson Bay, 728
  far above indigo-black-race, 584
  4000 years after Eskimo contact, white man, 729
  highest sex code of evolutionary races, 913
  Iroquois, 938
    made reforms in funeral waste, 960
    matriarchal idea kept I from statehood, 933
  isolated 15,000 B.C., 871
  killed off mastodon, 702
  no r m ever returned to Asia, 723
  Onamonalonton 65,000 years ago, revived "Great Spirit", 723
  predominant in civilizations of Mexico, Central America, 884
  recent prophet (1800s) Teuskwatowa, 988
  supreme in Eastern Asia 100,000 years before yellow tribes arrived, 883
red men, American r m never attained statehood, 800
  Amerinds, expected return of Onamonalonton, 1008
  among mixed peoples, Mexico, Central, South America, 727
  believed selves descended from coyotes, 837
  buffalo dance to ensure hunt's success, 972
  cannibals, Central America, 979
  concept of Great Spirit, hazy concept, 1007
  could have had Adamite blood, but too far away, 890
  devoted to plant theory of universal remedies, 991
  did not enslave, 779
  first in Asia, N.E., 11 tribes, 7000 people, 727
  first mortal to achieve personal guardian, Rantowoc, 1242
  first to develop elaborate weddings, 924
  first to receive full bestowal of living energies, 584
  first, usually, to attain human levels, 584
  forsook Asia, 11 tribes, 7000 persons, 727
  ("Great Spirit", see also)
  hazy tradition of war with archer people, 887

red men (cont'd)
  held "Caligastia 100s" teachings longest, 1007
  J, intimate contact all races but r, 1485
  leaders good as Abraham, but geography wrong, 1018
  missed developing great civilization, 723
  Moqui tribe revered serpent, 968
  N.A. r m thought ancestors were animals, 837
  often had war chiefs and peace chiefs, 789
  overspread fertile hunting area of N.A., 907
  retrogression in America, lost early traditions, 723
  struggle for 200,000 years with yellow men, 883
  suffered from too much warfare, 887
  superior, with blue and yellow, to secondary races, 919
  supreme, Eastern Asia, 100,000 years, 883
Redeemer, J' kingdom teaching submerged into mystic R idea, 1864
redeemer, J no r, but savior, yes, 2017
Redeemer-Creator, Jesus, mystic conception not J' Christianity, 1864
redemption, always opportunity at end for, 615
REDEMPTION AND COVENANTS, 982
redwood trees, in California, hdqtrs. red man 65,000 years ago, 723
  replaced fern forests by end of Cretaceous period, 692
  (Sequoias in Greenland)?, 696
"reflectible" order of sonship, 309
reflections (sound) of naked spirit, souls, 506
REFLECTIVE IMAGE AIDS, THE, 179,202
Reflective Mother Spirits, 202
  synchronize superuniverse governments, 206
REFLECTIVE SPIRITS, THE, 200,452
Reflective Spirits, mother-makers of marvelous angelic hosts, 205
reflectivity, and universe rulers, 105
  appears to be omniscience, 105
  from local U to superuniverse, and vice versa, 201
REFLECTIVITY, MAJESTON--CHIEF OF, 199
reflectivity, Michael acts timelessly by r, 377
  most complex "phenomenon"...in all creation, 105
  nature, character of R Spirits one of 7 universal mysteries, 200
  news gathering and decree disseminating, 201
  power to see, hear, sense, and know all as it transpires in superuniverse, 105
  progression of creature and Supreme evolution observed by A D, 1284
  a service mortals, ascendant, don't contact, 202
  services described, 201
  spiritual records preserved by r, 201
  superuniverse r service used by Mighty Messengers, 245
REFLECTIVITY, UNIVERSE, 105
reflectivity, universe r mechanisms serve Ancients of Days, 1284
  vast r mechanism serves minded universe, 328
reflex, conditioned, spiritual, 1095
reform, don't destroy all ritual, 1076
  of institutions must be accelerated, 1086
  of mores is not proclaiming truth, 1043
  (social gospel) vs. proclaiming truth, 1043
refrain from oppression, condemnation, vanity, 1656
refreshment of our souls, 1777
refuse, 1000s of years to learn to burn r, 748
regime, no r that denies reality of God can...2084
region of motion, elliptical, quiescence around, 125
REGISTER, THE UVERSA PERSONALITY, 334
registration of T A on Uversa, 119 hours required,1186
regression (retrogression), bacteria exhibit a degree of r, 732

regression (retrogression) (cont'd)
  cultural advances, but biologic retrogressions, 892
  from fairly kind to woman, r to shameful treatment, 778
  Life Carriers, purposefully eliminated...733
  many, many r in struggle of U civilization, 768
  Neanderthals r for 250,000 years, 721
  nearly doomed red man, 723
  Onagar's descendants reverted to raw flesh, 716
  when material progress outruns worship-wisdom, 1302
REGULATION, ENERGY CONTROL AND, 175
rehabilitate, to r religion, morality, 43
rehabilitation, in Master's love, and forgiveness, 2018
  of Christianity, 2075
  of Lucifer rebellion followers, 759
  planetary, 758
  rebels, 38
  through love, 2018
reign, 50,000 years, Constellation Father, 488
reincarnation, 1037 (see also "Eternal Life", "body, morontia", "lives, many", "transmigration", "worlds", "morontia changes")
  belief came from Adam's mansion worlds, 953
  custom of naming children after others, 953
  danger of r, deliverance from, 1037
  doctrine of, 1029
  Essenes believed in r, 1811
  fetishism may impinge on r, 967
  from the Dravidian Deccan, 1029
  from primitive doctrine, 953
  Gautama fought valiantly against belief in r, 1035
  highly spiritual personalities, life to life, 361
  J had difficulty teaching no r, 1811
  J let John be "Elijah" to the apostles, 1754
  lingering belief in r, 1811
  monotonous round of repeated transmigrations, 1029
  mortals survive, progressive universe existence, 1459
  new morontia body each world, 534
  no resurrections, new bodies, after system hdqtrs., 539
  orange race especially had belief in r, 953
  philosophically debilitating teaching, 1029
  primitive doctrine, recurring incarnations, 953
  "resurrected in more glorious form", 1846
  Spornagia only creatures that experience r, 528
  step by step, life by life, goal...attained, 295
  stultifying belief in transmigration, 1029
  transitional culture worlds, 509
  we experience 570 morontia changes, progressive, 542
  we, progressively more spiritual, 542
rejection, general at Chorazin, 1644; Capernaum, 1715
  of Christianity many lands, why, 1051
  of J, Jews--why, 1071
  of survival, 1179,1218
    deprives the Supreme, 1283
rejoice and believe, 1609
"rejoice in Him who has power to", 1820
re-keyed on morontia worlds, 544
relation, man to God, J changes, 1675
RELATION OF ADJUSTERS TO INDIVIDUAL MORTALS, 1203
RELATION OF ADJUSTERS TO UNIVERSE CREATURES, 1195
RELATION OF THE ETERNAL SON TO THE INDIVIDUAL, 84
RELATION OF THE ETERNAL SON TO THE UNIVERSE, 81
RELATION OF THE INFINITE SPIRIT TO THE UNIVERSE, 98

relation (cont'd)
RELATION OF THE SPIRIT TO THE FATHER AND THE
  SON, 93
RELATION OF THE SUPREME TO THE PARADISE
  TRINITY, 1264
RELATION OF THE SUPREME TO THE TRIODITES,
  1265
RELATION TO CREATURES (Seven Master Spirits), 190
RELATION TO THE UNIVERSE, 54
relationship, every true r an end in itself, 1228
    sublime only between personalities, 31
    with J, takes precedence over all, 1593
relationships, and systems, distinction between, 1227
RELATIONSHIPS, FATHER-WORLD, 147
relationships, primordial-unity, duality, triunity, 1157
relativity, faintly glimpsed findings of, 2078
    in completeness of knowledge, 42
RELATIVITY OF CONCEPT FRAMES, 1260
relativity, of reality, 1435
relaxation, 1293, 1611,   a backward glance, 550
    determines capacity for spiritual receptivity, 1777
    every 10th day, one of r, 492
    of the ages, 297
    rest, vacation, 1610, 1677, 1718, -71
    vital, 1777
    whence, 1774, -77
    worshipful practice which renews the mind, 1774
relic worship, superstitious, 968, 2008
relics, 1080   relics and miracles, 968
relics, belief in, outgrowth of fetish cult, 968
relief map of planet Jerusem, in pearly observatory, 521

religion

religion, achieves highest ministry when... 1086
    achieves realization of love, 986
    activation of, is superemotional, 1090
    acts unwisely often, 1121
    adjusted to mores, 1005
    always and ever dynamic, does something, 1121
    ancestor of ethics and morals, 1104
    and animism often separate origins, 995
    and citizenship, 1929
    and cults, 965
    and experience, 1140
RELIGION AND THE HUMAN RACE, 1132
RELIGION AND THE INDIVIDUAL, 1130
religion, and making a living, 1778
RELIGION AND MORALITY, 1115
RELIGION AND THE MORES, 1004
RELIGION AND REALITY, 1119
RELIGION AND THE RELIGIONIST, 1088
religion, and science (see at end of "religion")
RELIGION AND SOCIAL RECONSTRUCTION, 1086
religion, arises, how, 1004
    arose, how, 957
RELIGION AS MAN'S LIBERATOR, 1116
religion, association with secular handicaps, social
      ministry, 1086
    assumes 3 things, 1139
    at its best (J), 1782
    authority and sovereignty, 1487
    avoid secular work, in social reconstruction, 1087
b balance with humor, 1616
    barrier to outmarriage, 918
    becomes institutionalized by prayer, 999
    becoming real because, 141
    before J, not personal, 1336
    begins where facts stop, 1641
    best time for progress, 100-200 A. D. , 2074
    beware of reforming mores, 1043

religion (cont'd)
    birth of primitive r, 708
    "birth day" of r in individual, 1130
    brotherhood, worship, service, 1769, 2053
    business of, 1089
    called "Christianity" at Antioch, 2068
    can always triumph over... logic of unbelieving mind,
      1104
    can function on 3 levels, 1095
    can never be observed, or understood, from the
      outside, 1107
    cannot grow unless, 1088
    cannot reconstruct self until, 1087
    can't advance fast, 1004-05
    can't develop in advance of intellectual... 1128
    can't judge r by accompanying civilization, 1127
    can't spread, fettered by national culture, 2064
    central truth of, 1127
    certitudes from entire personality, 1119
    characteristic earmark of r, social fruits, 1126
RELIGION, CHARACTERISTICS OF, 1107
religion, charges against, 1006
    children give rise to "struggle" idea, 1131
RELIGION, THE CHRISTIAN, 1083 (see "Christianity")
religion, Christian, is (paragraph summary), 1011
    Christianity's strength due to, 1079
    clash between new and old, 1893
    clean hearts vs. hands, 1671
    commercialized, 1891
    complex concepts of life now and hereafter, called r,
      944
    concepts of purpose of (various), 67
    concerned with insideness of experience, 1135
    connotes progression in spiritual ascension,
      expansion, 2080
    conservator of morals, 1091
    consists in... 1107
    controversy, r and science, 2076
    "cooperate, until the Most Highs overthrow this
      (rejecting) nation", 1906
    core of, 1219
    couldn't save great empire from (10 things), 2074
    culminates in worship, 2075
    cure for soul hunger, moral despair, spiritual
      disquiet, 1078
d danger: serves church, not God, 1092
    dares to criticize civilization and progress, 1128
    deals with origins, science with phenomena, 2077
    deeply concerned with scientist, 2076
religion,
    definitions of: (presently over 500 definitions of r,
        1129) (see also "religion, true")
    consists in sublimity of the soul's trust, 1107
    exclusively spiritual experience of soul of God-
        knowing, 1739
    friendship with God, 1534, 1615
    individual's experience with spiritual realities,
        1780
    is the conviction-faith of the personality, 1104
    is devotion to what one believes of supreme value,
        1100
    is divine embrace of cosmic values, 2080
    is the ennobling transformation of material facts
        of life, 2080
    is exclusively spiritual experience of soul of God-
        knowing man, 1739
    is an impulse for... soul for dynamic service, 1096
    is an independent realm of response to life
        situations, 68
    is living, dynamic experience of divinity attain-
        ment predicated on human service, 66

religion (cont'd)
  grounded always in personal experience, 1128
  growing r must conserve adherents' moral values,
    1038
  growth provided for, 2064
  guiding star of all civilizations, 1013
h handicapped by racial, social, economic fetters, 2064
  harmonizes the rivalrous, 2082
  has become a nominal influence only, 2081
  has double origin, 1728
  has mighty forces in social, economic situations,
    1739, 2085
  has to do with experience, 1140
  hastens planetary evolution, 1129
RELIGION, THE HEBREW, 1075, 1338
religion, Hebrew, great mistake of, 43
  Hebrew, survives, conserved moral values, 1076
  helpless to change environment because e has
    changed r, 1132
  highest concept, 1128, 1781
  highest evidence of reality of r, 1127
  highest yet revealed in universe of Nebadon (J'), 1128
RELIGION, THE HINDU, 1031
religion, humanism only until God, 2084
i ideal, r of the, 1780
  if spiritual, never disturbed by physical science, 1727
  imbalance between r and intellectual, 1078-79, 1302
  immature, 1775
  implies spirit world responsive, 40
  implies undiscovered ideals, 1781
  important all collective movements, 1089
  impulse of r is in spirit influences activating will to
    be unselfish, 1132
RELIGION IN HUMAN EXPERIENCE, 1094
religion, in r, J followed method of experience, as
    science pursues technique of experiment, 2076
  in schools, 1089
RELIGION, IN TIBET, 1038
religion, independent of theology, 1141
  indispensable source, superior civilization, 883
  individual defines r in own terms, 1129
  individual experience, (J' mission), 2093
  inner response to outer condition, 2095
  insideness of human experience, 1135
  inspires to live joyfully, 1093
  instinctive longing for, 1008
RELIGION, INSTITUTIONAL, 1092
religion, institutional, in stalemate of vicious circle,
    1087
  institutional, lags behind mores, 1128
  institutionalization of r, 1083
  institutionalized, power wanes, 1092
  intellect, and r must balance, 1128
  intellectual earmark of r is certainty, 1126
  intellectual factors of r important, (overdevelopment
    bad), 1121
  intellectual foundation of r, 647
  intellectual philosophy vs. true r, 1780
  intermediaries unnecessary, 1013
  invented as insurance, 975
  is based on experience and r thought, 1130
  is beginning and ending of... existence, 68
  is cause, ethics result, 1862
  is imperfect, 1115
  is inspiration of man's evolving nature, 1104
  is sustained by faith, 1137
  is valid only when... 1572
  is a way of living as well as thinking, 1013
  isolate as part of life, can't, 1124
j J' attitude toward commercializing, 1891

religion (cont'd)
  J brought the philosophy of r down to earth, 1771
  J defines, 1641
  J exemplified what he taught, growth by technique of
    living progress, 1749
  J followed method of experience, 2076
religion,
  J', future of, 1569
    after animalism, materialism, new spiritual age
      initiated, 231
    apostles grasped few teachings, other generations
      will (grasp all), 1616
    J, lifted up, will draw all men, 2084
    kingdom of brotherhood will (triumph), 1866
    kingdom will yet be proclaimed... to every
      individual, 1864
    much will be revealed... as mortal religion
      ascends... 1003
    a new and fuller revelation of J' religion is
      destined to conquer... 2082
    rejected now, in another age will be received, 1876
    religions some day will realize a unity in worship
      of F, 1012
    revelation... in and through J, shall not fail, 2097
    Teacher Sons, even now visit U planning projected
      sojourn, 231
    to become heritage of all r, 1330
    true teachers will ever continue to appear, 988
    U waiting for... 1041
    when present superstition r is over... J' gospel
      will persist gloriously, 2082
    will not be bankrupt, 2076
    will triumph, 2075-76
  J' life revealed new, higher type of r, 2087
  J' new r, 1730, -42, -74-75, -78
  J on r to Gonod, 1436
  J' r bequeathed for guidance of all ages, worlds, 1583
  J taught a r, but (due to error) became a, 2092
  Jewish vs. Greek, 1079
  joyful living, 1093
  judge civilization by its r, 1127
  keep r free from unholy secular alliances only by (5),
    1089
l language cannot depict it, 2096
  last thing to perish or change in a race, 1004
RELIGION, LATER EVOLUTION OF, 1003
religion, leads to increased social service, 1121
  leads to serving men, ethics, altruism, 1122
  letters, and, 1127
  lever, 793
  live up to responsibilities with energy, enthusiasm,
    1770
  lives in spite of contamination, 1107
  living experience of divinity attainment, 66
  the love for God is r, 1122
  loveless zeal is always harmless to r, 1089
  lower (social gospel?) vs. higher, 1781
  loyalty to transcendent object, 1092
  magic replaced by morals, 1132
  magical and mythological parentage of, 1141
  makes its endowments available, 1120
  man creates r out of fears, by means of illusions, 944
  manifestations of nature and function, 1115
  mankind ripening for real r, 1004
  man's liberator, 1116
  man's most effective institution, 1006
  man's supreme endowment, 1121
  man's supreme gesture, 2096
  material things, no concern with, 2076
  maturity of, 28

religion (cont'd)

method of r is faith, 1106

mighty lever that lifts civilization from chaos, 793

ministers to all through progress of individual, 1094

miracles, r has nothing to do with, 1128

a mode of reacting to situations, 1780

modern, error of, 1572

moral mandates, not organic involvement, 1087

moral stability and, 1086

morality, science, outlive civilizations, 196

morals and r, not the same, 1780

more and more to separate from politics, 1075

more you have, more certain you are, 1119

most unyielding of human institutions, 1004

a motivation that... makes life truly worth living, 1100

must act as cosmic salt that... 1087

must adapt quickly to change, 1086

must adapt self, 2073

must be influence for moral stability, 1086

must be more than an idea, 1120

must ever be, 1013

must have unselfish, loving service motivation, 1090

must possess moral energy, 1466

must possess spiritual driving power, 1466

n natural, only two things modify it, 1006

natural r, from superanimal endowment, 1003

RELIGION, NATURE OF EVOLUTIONARY, 1005

religion, nature of (Paper 101, 1104), 1770

needed most NOW, 1090

needs new leaders, 2082

needs redefining, 1013

never advanced by appeals to so-called miraculous, 1128

never becomes scientific fact, 1012

never content with mere thinking, feeling, 1121

never mere intellectual belief or philosophic reasoning, 1780

new, about J, 2068

and spiritual meanings in facts, 1105

art of living and r, 1778

challenge of a new age now, 2075

from aborted T A communications, 1207

in place of Christ's, 2059

mature, 1775

pays price of compromise, 1626

Peter inaugurated, 2091

philosophy plus gospel, 1774

r, Father goes forth to find man, 1762

r, not a r in present meaning of that word, 1730

r "of" J, changed to "about" J, 2051,-59,-66,-75

r of maturity, 1775

teachers of, to ends of empire, 2068

teaches self-forgetfulness, 1951

vs. old, 1951

way, transformed by Spirit... 1609

no civilization without, 1006

no longer is r only an idea when, 1121

no organic involvement in secular work!, 1087

no theological shelter, 1733

none real without active personality, 1120

none without determinations, 1131

normal and natural to man, but optional, 69

not alone for weaklings, 1583

not a "child" of culture, 1119

not a function of life, a mode of living, 1100

not grounded in science or morality, 68

not invalidated by false beliefs, 1130

not passive, 1770

not safeguarded by common sense, 1768

religion (cont'd)

not submissive, 1770

not to be used as shelter to avoid life, 1733

o of authority, 1729-32   of beauty, 67, 2095

of faith, hope and charity, 2095

of fear vs. of love, 1090

of Hebrews, Greeks, Paul, J, 2095

RELIGION OF THE IDEAL, THE, 1780

religion, of Jesus (see under "Jesus", also above "religion, J', future of")

of J, for weaklings?, 1607   of J vs. others, 67

of love, 2095   of mind vs. of spirit, 1729-30

of moral sublimity, 2095

of personal spiritual experience, 1732

of spirit means... vs. of mind, 1729

of the spirit (not mind) requires exertions, 1729

of spirit of freedom, 1731

of spirit of God, 1742

of spirit vs. mind, 1729-32

often acts unwisely, unreligiously, but it acts, 1121

often mastered by environment, 1132

ok but theology false, 1140

old way, suppress, obey, conform, 1609

Olympian, why it perished, 1078

on neighboring planet is, 811

one central truth of every r, 1127

opiate to the people, not J', 2063

organized cult is crystallized r, 1330

organized, is, 1616

organized r (is) conservatively tardy, 1128

orthodox, puerile, 1399

others not moral and ethical, 1338

others vs. Christianity, 1781-82

our highest r the life of J, 1128

p pagan cults, 1336

paradox in finite comprehension, 69

paradoxical necessity, r labors under, 1121

paramount mission of, 1086

Paul's new r of Christianity, 1083

perception of r subject to ignorance, superstition... 1119

persists in absence of learning, 1107

personal experience (J' sermon, r is a), 1629

personal experience, r is matter of, 1539

personal experience vs. social obligations, 1642

personal experience which grows ratio to quest, 1095

personal, must be distinguished from other high thought, 2075

RELIGION, A PERSONAL PHILOSOPHY OF, 1113

religion, personal, solvent for most moral difficulties, 2093

personal vs. institutional, 1128

Peter founded new, 2069,-91

the philosophic pressure of r, 1115

RELIGION, PHILOSOPHY AND, 1140

RELIGION, PHILOSOPHY OF, 1129

RELIGION, THE POSITIVE NATURE OF J', 1769

religion, prayer is most potent agency of r, 997

presents two phases of manifestation, 1110

primitive, had a biologic origin, 944

primitive r democratic, savage quick to borrow or lend, 1012

primitive r was insurance, 956

private matter, no danger in r becoming, 1090

problems, r does not remove, 2093

r illuminates, transcends, 2093

product of superanimal endowments, 1003

property of human race, not child of culture, 1119

provides for survival of all good, 2096

purpose: affords intellectual constancy, philosophic security, 1116

233

religion (cont'd)

religion (cont'd)

religion, true, definitions of (cont'd)
  is to know God as Father, man as brother,1091
  living, dynamic body of personal spiritual
    experience, 966
    this is essence of t r, that you love your neighbor
      as yourself, 1950

  truth and maturity of, proportional to, 28
  the truth of personal spiritual experience, 1141
  turning of other cheek, act that may typify, 1770
  turns universe outside in, 1135
U ultimately to be service of God and man, 1132
  unconscious activity, 1088
  unfailingly exhibited by postmoral humans, 68
  unfolds the truths of being, 1641
  unselfishness abstraction, or real, 196
  unwise course, neglect of truth, beauty, 43
  up to date, 2060
  upheld by authority or experience, 1729
  valid only when, 1572
  vs. environment, 1132
  vs. ethics--theology, 1141,1862
  vs. new order of society--Christianity, 2069
  vs. philosophy, 1080
  vs. science, 53,141
  vs. theological beliefs, 1095
  violence, r opposes as technique of social evolution,
    1086
  virtues of, weaknesses, 1006
W way of living, 1013,-89
  we need to know religious experiences of many
    mortals, 1130
RELIGION, WEAKNESS OF INSTITUTIONAL, 1087
religion, Western world had no soul-satisfying r, 2069
  what is r?, 1780
  what it does, 1093
  what it does for man, 2078
  when achieves most, 1086
  when it's an idea, it's a philosophy, 1121
  when strong r threatens to dominate man, 2083
  wholly spiritual in motive, makes life worthwhile,1727
  will ever remain evolutionary or revelatory, 1012
  without faith, a contradiction, 1141
  without God r an intellectual absurdity, 1141
  world r presages light and life, 807
  yields happiness, 1106
religion and science, both predicated on assumptions,
    1139
  difficulty in harmonizing, due to, 1136
  interpretations of r&s reconciled only by mota, 1139
  need more searching, fearless self-criticism, 1138
  scientists are religion's concern, 2076
religion, content of,
  vagaries, illusions, error, self-deception,
    distortion, perversions, not withstanding...1140
religion is not, system of philosophic (provable) belief
  (is more), 1104
religion of J (see under "Jesus", and above see "religion,
  J', future of")
religion, philosophy, science,
  assumptions, these are founded on, 1141
  faith, logic, reason: methods, of r p s, 1106
  in ideal state, r p s welded into unity, 1080
  r becoming real...p struggles...s in contest, 141
  r concerned with values, s with facts, p...reality,
    1110
  r is man's experience with values, s is study of
    physical environment, p is effort to unify,
    coordinate, 1136

religion, philosophy, science (cont'd)
  s discovers material world, r evaluates it,p "inter-
    prets" its meanings, coordinates s viewpoint with
    spiritual concept, 1139
  these lead to value, to coordinate, to reality,
    consciousness, 1122
  unity by action of wisdom, faith, experience, 1080

religionist, acts as if in presence of the Eternal,1119-20
  aware of contact sources of superhumam power, 1100
  knows and knows now, 1120
  not religion, proves spiritual realities, 2080
  superior social wisdom, 1087
  supreme value, 1100
  world's most whole-hearted, 2093
religionists, as group, concern with religion only, 1089
  emancipated, 1120
  enhanced cosmic foresight, 1087
  future r must live out their religion, 1091
  have believed much that was false, 1130
  immune, 1120,-24
  irreligious conduct of (result), 2095
  must foster technique for conserving values, 1076,-78
  no group has "The Truth", 1012
  on trial before bar of human needs, 1457
  seem to live emancipated, 1120
  stimulate spiritual growth mutually, 1094
  unified, how live, 1091,1120
  would do better to...1012
religions, all from identical spiritual leadings, 1012
  all teach worship of Deity, 67
    and some doctrine of human salvation, 67
  all would have "come" if J' r had been left as he
    taught it, 1670
  astrology, and mystery r, 1337
RELIGIONS, THE COMPOSITE, 1010
religions, conscientious self-examination (wrong), 1583
RELIGION'S CONTRIBUTION, 1092
religions, disagree on what is required of man, 1127
  earlier, small concern for individual, 1336
  eleven living, 1011
  emperor worship, 1336
  evolutionary r drive men by fear, 66
  evolve, and are revealed, 1407,1641
RELIGIONS, THE GENTILE, 1336
religions, great interracial faiths, Hebraic, Buddhist,
    Christian, Islamic, 1011
  higher, shape heart to God, 1781
    lower, shape ideas to human heart, 1781
  institutional, weakness of, 1087
  intellectual vs. true (Rodan), 1780
  lower vs. higher and their views of God, 1781
  many have had feeling of the inner presence, 1215
  modern r, error of, 1572
  most advanced of ancients (Judaism and Hinduism),
    1011
  mystery r, 1337
  new r cannot be invented, 1012
  of all human r, none surpassed...1045
  of authority, easy way out, 1729
  of authority, intellectual assent, 1729
  of despair crave extinction in slumber, 2063
  of earth have neglected the poor, 1608
  of Hebrews, Greeks, Paul, J, 2095
  of Occident, times of J, 1336
  of spirit, participation, experience, 1729
  of U, 67,1009,-11,-27
  of wishful fancy, 1782
  revelatory allure men toward God of love, 66
  seriously blundered, 1071

religions (cont'd)
  things common to all r, 1004
  time for presenting to all r gospel of J, 1041
  we need to know many, 1130
  we should be exposed to experiences of other, 1130
  what all live r do, 1092
  with Universal Deity, agreement on God, 1432-33
RELIGIONS, THE WORLD'S, 67,1442
religious, acid test for r philosophy, 1113
  arrogance, 1012
  assurance, genuine, 1119
  attitude evolved through, 1132
  authority vs. philosophy of living, 1098
  ceremony, contributes to...values, 994
  certitudes, 1119
  challenge of this age, 43
  conduct, result of having true religion, 1121
  conflict, deadly, 1730
  confusion, not decadence, 1092
  desire is hunger quest, 1121
  development, none without conscious effort, 1131
  devotion, three distinct forms,1728
  ecstacy, 1000
  epochs, most great, due to outstanding personality,
    1008
  epochs, seven (major) of post-Adamic U, 1009
  evolution, lost to Jews, 1340
  evolution, motion passed westward when...1340
religious experience, consequences, rewards, 1142
  consists of 2 phases, 2095
  danger of accepting symbols, ceremonies, in place
    of r e, 1728
  impossible to depict, 2096
  influenced by health, heredity, environment, 1095
  important to be exposed to r e of others, 1130
  is God-consciousness, 1121
  is realization...of having found God, 1121
  is the spiritual content of religion, 1140
  is truly supermathematical, 2080
  maintained while changing beliefs, 1130
  markedly influenced by health and inheritance, 1095
  never fully understood by material mind, 69
  not symbols, ceremonies, 1728
  of personal religion remains genuine and valid, 1140
  paramount feeling regarding moral values, social
    meanings, 1132
  personal, is God-consciousness, 17
  primitive, 1131
RELIGIOUS EXPERIENCE, PROGRESSIVE, 1111
religious experience, reality in r e proportion to
    spiritual content, 1142
RELIGIOUS EXPERIENCE, THE REALITY OF, 1129
religious experience, requires incessant activity, 1120
  superhuman insight only through genuine r e, 2075
  tests of, 1000
  3 great satisfactions from, 69
  unfailingly yields "fruits" in daily life, 1091
  unity of derives from identical nature of God fragment,
    1129
  valid, but discourse fallacious, 1140
  vs. beliefs, 1130

RELIGIOUS FAITH, THE CERTAINTY OF, 1124
RELIGIOUS FAITH, FOUNDATIONS OF, 1118
religious, force, 1119
  forms, J thawed frozen r f into liquid liberties, 1728
    primitive, persist today, 1729
  gathering vs. secular meeting, difference, 1133
  group activities, purposes, 1092
  group, should be separated from all other groups,1091

religious (cont'd)
  groups and sects, J' time, 1534
RELIGIOUS GROWTH, 1094
religious, growth, foolish to attempt too rapid
    acceleration, 1004
  growth, nature of r g is unconscious, 1095
  growth, soil for, 1094
RELIGIOUS GUARDIANS, THE, 1255
religious, habits contribute to spiritual growth, 1095
  idealism, preparedness, aggression, 804
  ideas, cardinal, go back to ghost fear, 1005
  impulse, origin in spirit presences, 1132
  insight and defeat, 2096
  knowledge, certainty of is superhuman, 1142
  leader, greatest, a layman, 2091
RELIGIOUS LEADERS, THE GREAT, 1008
religious, leaders, insincere, 1386
    leaders needed, 2082
      receive real rewards in another world, 804
  liberty, 1135
  liberty 100-200 A.D., 2074
  life, in open arenas of society and commerce, 1121
    should not become egocentric, selfish, unsocial,
      1130
  social or group aspect of, 1090
RELIGIOUS LIVING, ACME OF, 1101
religious, living, earmark is sublime peace, cosmic
    poise, 1101
  living, experience of, 1094
RELIGIOUS LIVING, MARKS OF, 1100
religious, longings, if only material, 1727
  maturity, measure of, 28
  peace, to exist, 1487
  person, identifies self with universe, 67
  philosophy, phases of growth, 1114
    ideal, 1141
  practices, currents of life, 2073
  progress, religion ministers to r p of all through r p
    of individual and r p of each is augmented by r p
    of all, 1094
  reality vs. beliefs, 1095
  renaissance, Orient and Levant 600 B.C., 1078
  renascence 600 B.C., 1033, -50
  slavery, grotesque system of, 2095
  sovereignty, only God's, 1487
  speculation, detrimental, 1121
  symbols, don't dispose of, but, 1098
  teacher, greatest was layman, 2091
  teachers, many greatest were unlettered, 1127
  tendencies are innate in humans, 1129
  traditions, danger in, 1727
  truths, capacity to perceive, 1129
  urge, three manifestations of, 1728

remains, of dead in Europe, why missing, 897
remanded, after failure of survival, T A more training,
    then, 1195
REMARKABLE IKHNATON, 1047
remembrance supper, "emblem of ministry of Spirit of
    Truth", 1941   ended singing 118th Psalm, 1943

(REMEMBRANCE) SUPPER, ESTABLISHING THE, 1941
remembrance supper, is symbolic rendezvous with
    Michael, 1942
  J' last mortal rendezvous with his chosen ambassa-
    dors, 1935
  J made the lambless Passover a r s, 1404
  Judas seized the seat of honor, 1937
(REMEMBRANCE) SUPPER, THE LAST, 1936

236

remembrance supper (cont'd)
  Lord's Supper, how originally celebrated, 2067
  menu, 1940
  new vs. Passover, 1942
REMEMBRANCE SUPPER, ON THE WAY TO, 1934
remembrance supper, reduced to... mathematical
      precision of set formula, 1942
  seating order, how it came about, 1937
  "this is the new Passover", 1943
  "this is our last supper", 1938
  upon all such occasions the Master is really present,
      1942
remission of sin, none without blood (Hebrews), 60
Remmonites, 1637
Remona, wife of Cain, 849
REMOTE REPERCUSSIONS OF SIN, 760
renaissance, great spiritual, hope of U, 2086
  moral, sixth century before Christ, 1049-50
  of Urantian religion, each r identified with leader,
      1009
  spiritual must await new teachers (if), 2082
"render unto Caesar", 1474, 1580, 1740, 1899, 1929, -57
rendezvous worlds, 147, 149
renew the spirit by worshipful communion, 1739
renewed, all things constantly, 55
renewing of your mind, spiritual, 1609
"renewing your strength, the Lord guide you", 1656
RENUNCIATION AND HUMILIATION, 976
renunciation, foolish ritual of r, 976
reorganization, of world, through spirit-born souls, 2083
  personnel of P undergoing r, 263
"repent, for kingdom of heaven is at hand" (John B), 1501
"repent! Get right with God!" (John B), 1498
"repent", mighty appeal of John's preaching, 1510
"repentance, Father accepts you before r", 1851
repentance, has led to reform and achievement, 998
  if r genuine, faith sincere, don't fear judgment, 1476
  John preached, 1584 (see also "repent")
  "our piety springs from r" (Rodan), 1785
  vs. "change of mind" by faith, 1545
  voluntary when men believe gospel, 1683
repented, rebellion's vast majority, 758
repercussions of all these realities (we witness), 1160
REPERCUSSIONS OF DEFAULT, 843
REPERCUSSIONS OF FINITE REALITY, 1159
repercussions of human growth, 1286
REPERCUSSIONS OF PRAYER, SOCIAL, 998
repersonalization, 1235
  100 Jerusem volunteers, 743
repetition, J found r necessary, 1831
  parables, 1853
repletion superimposed on completion, 1163
reprehensible, lack of spiritual brotherhood is r, 1866
representation, trained, survival of democracy
      requires, 802
representative government, divine ideal, can't be used
      too soon, 834
  divine ideal, evolution of, 801
REPRESENTATIVE GOVERNMENT, THE EVOLUTION
      OF, 801
representative government, ideal for non-perfect beings,
      517
representatives, planet r legislate at hdqtrs. world, 632
repression, moral worth can't be derived from mere,
      1572
reprobates, "you wicked r, souls are steeped in iniquity",
      1908
REPRODUCERS, THE HEAVENLY, 500
reproduction, creature ability for r from Universe
      Spirit, 404

reproduction (cont'd)
  human, controlled on spheres of light and life, 630
  regulated to requirements, light and life, 630
  selective, of mortals, 592-93, -95-96
reptiles, 732
  flying, 688
Reptilia, great animal family, 732
  nearly extinct, but ancestor to birds and mammals,
      732
REPTILIAN AGE, THE EARLY, 685
REPTILIAN AGE, THE LATER, 687
republic, advanced state, nearby planet, 809
repugnant to divine nature, to suffer deterioration, or
      inferior act, 137
requirements, even to approach knowing a divine
      personality, 30
  for friendship, moral affinity, spiritual harmony, 30
  mortal survivors must pass r, 531
  to have revelation of God; hungry for truth, dis-
      satisfied with self, wanting help, eyes of mind
      open, 1466
requires, "spirit unity" (to have), 1591
RESERVE CORPS OF DESTINY, THE, 1257
reserve corps of destiny (living men and women
      admitted to special service of superhuman
      administration of world affairs... ministry of
      mercy and wisdom, 1257)
  average world 70 corps, Urantia 12, 1257
  celestial forces prepare as guarantees against
      disaster, 1256
  fewer than 12 mortals conscious of distinction, 1257
  frequently contacted on quarantined worlds, 1191
  how chosen, 1257
  members chosen because of... 1257
  midwayers, contact guardians of human minds of U
      rc of d, 863
  mortals assigned soon as competent, 1257
  962 persons (1934); fewer than 12 (realize), 1257
  revelator is forbidden to reveal real function, 1258
  supernormal minded, of great decision, rc of d,
      personal seraphim assigned, 1241-42
  unperceived liaison associates of rc of d, midwayers,
      865
  Urantia's 12 includes 962 persons, 1257
  various, 1242
RESERVE CORPS, THE (Seconaphim), 310
RESERVE CORPS, THE, (Supernaphim), 289
RESERVE CORPS, THE VARIOUS, 339
reserve powers through prayer, 999
RESERVES, THE (Seraphic Hosts), 431, 433, 436
reservists, T A rehearses r in deep mind, 1257
RESIDENCE, THE DIVINE, 118
RESIDENT GOVERNOR GENERAL, THE, 1252
RESIDENTIAL AND ADMINISTRATIVE AREAS, 522
residential spaces, staggering number, Paradise, 121
resigned, five members of Sanhedrin, 1718
  Jairus, 1718
"resist not evil", meaning of, 1590
resistance, only conscious can prevent survival, 1206
respiration, space (see "space respiration")
response, intelligent r to total objectivity, 2095
  organismal environmental r, 738-39
responsibilities, "let him take up (full measure of) his r
      and follow me", 1760, -70
responsibility, advances us, 316
  cosmic, of self-conscious personalities, 1284
  of ethics, 316
  precludes idle meditation, 1393
  supreme, of existence, 914
  to civil order, 1929

responsibility (cont'd)
    tremendous r on earthly fathers, 1923
rest, and relaxation are problem solving, 1611
    and recuperate, all the way "up", 282, 505
REST, COMPLEMENTS OF, 296
rest, day of, on Eden, 831
    divine, 299
    "I will give you r", 1590
REST, INSTIGATORS OF, 299
rest, must learn value of r and relaxation, 1611
    nature of, 299
    relaxation after universe perfected, 1293
    sevenfold nature of, 299
    will have long, revivifying r of Paradise, 505
    worship is true soul r, 1616
restful, worship is r spiritual exertion, 1616
restraint, each r transcended, requires new r, 1302
restraints, self-imposed, concepts of justice and ideals
    of brotherhood, 1302
    self-imposed, most powerful and most tenuous of
        civilization's factors, 1302
restrictions, many imposed on revelators of U papers,
    1315
    subnormals can't breed, 812
RESTRICTIVE TABOOS, THE, 914
results conform to causes, 794
resurrect human J, (figuratively), 2090
resurrected, 1000 "experienced the r J",2024
    son mystery cults, 1081
    we are eternally r on Paradise, 299
RESURRECTION, THE, 2020
resurrection, awakening 7 times (mortals), 540
    bestowal sons, 3rd day, 596
    clarifying statement on the r, 2021
    countless individuals gone on to mansonia, 2024
    "doesn't change gospel", 2052
    Jacob insistent affair was a fraud, 2034
    (J) believed in advance, 2001,-13
    mornings, 533
    mortals, 321, 2024
    none from "cessation of existence", 37
    not of J' body, celestial hosts afforded it dissolution,
        2023
    of Adam, special, no. 26 of U, 853
    of the dead, 1900
    of the dead, belief of rabbis, scribes, 1534
RESURRECTION OF LAZARUS, 1842
resurrection,of Lazarus, first and only on U, 1846
    difficult, 1845
    "of the unjust" (cessation of life), 1247
    on Paradise, 297, 299
    our r more glorious form, 1846
    Paradise personalities present, 2020-21
    planetary roll calls, three, 2024
    so-called r, the dead called to record, 409
    statement of Midway Commission on r, 2021
    story to Sidon, Antioch, Damascus, 2054
    third day, all bestowal sons, 229
    three statements to clarify, 2021
    truth of, vs. fact of r, 2023
    what constitutes mortal's, 533
resurrection hall, morontia, by T A transit, 624
resurrection halls, 486
    throughout eternity will remember r h, 533
resurrections, after mansion world, no more literal r,
    539
    dispensational (3), 2024
    many special and millenial, 2024
    no more after your residence on system hdqtrs. , 539
    of U sons, many, 2024

resurrections (cont'd)
    periodic, 568
    special, at least every 1000 years, 568
retaliation, getting even, no, 1579
retarded, defective strain, not purged, 839
    in light and life, drastically eliminated, 627
reticence, John (apostle) never mastered r, 1554
retribution, swift, (Lucifer), 618
retrograde motion, 656-57
retrograde, sovereignty in Europe, 1489
retrogression (see "regression")
return, Michael's (Jesus'), promise to r, (see under
    "Jesus", "return of Michael", "second coming")
    no mortals r to this planet, 436, 1230
RETURN OF THE SEVENTY, THE, 1806
return, to high spiritual concept of J, 1866
reunion of Orvonton Master Sons on Paradise, (J
    present), 371
revealed truth, evolutionary man can't accept suddenly,
    1012

revelation

revelation, affirms: First Cause of science and
    religion's God are one, 1106
    affirms: science, religion, philosophy, are one, all
        good, 1122-23   always contaminated, 1022
    Amenemope conserved morals of r, 1046
    angels; r often through a., 1241
    awe for Deity inspired by r, 766
    Bible as, work of men, some holy, 1767
    bridges gulf between man and God, 1106
    can't reveal God to those who don't seek, 1466
    compensates for lack of truth mota in material world,
        1136
    compensatory for lack of morontia, 57, 1106
    concept of God through. . . 28
    continuous human experience, 1107
    cosmology of any r outgrown soon, 1109
    dependent on capacity to receive, 27, 50, 66, 71
    difficult to induce (men) suddenly to accept revealed
        truth, 1012
    divine beings to mortals, not because of trances, 1099
    each mortal epoch receives more, 591
    enlarged to come, when kingdom in fruition, 1914
    epochal, when through some celestial agency, group,
        personality, 1109
    essential to realize brotherhood on U, 597
    evolution doing what r failed. . . 937
    experiential r still in progress, 128
    extended by Magisterial Son, 594
    extended to central universe, post-bestowal age, 598
    extended to include super-universe, 596
    for all worlds of local creation, Master's life, 2087
    function of, 1138
    ghost fear only religion up to time of r, 955
REVELATION, THE GIFT OF, 1007
revelation, great r in times of great testing and
    threatened defeat, 2082
    harmonizes 3 contending philosophies of religion,1090
    harmonizes trinity approach, reason, faith, logic,1106
    hope of U lies in possibility of new r of J, 2086
    the hunger for truth is a, 1122
    ideal r of personality of God, J, 30
    ignorers of, woe to, 1826
    in and through J, shall not fail, 2097
    influence on dogma, 1006
    initial presentations of r simple, 591
    is compensation for frailties of evolving philosophy,
        1140
    is evolutionary, 1007

revelation (cont'd)

is validated only by human experience, 1106

J was a r of God, 1856

keeps in touch with evolution, 1007

limit on r, can't discuss Personalized Adjuster
ministries, 1202

REVELATION, THE LIMITATIONS OF, 1109

revelation, living, appropriate fruits always, 1931

lucky numbers, 3 and 7, from, 968

Magisterial or Teacher Sons yet to come, 598

man to God, and God to man, 1406, 1578, 1914, -85,
2000, -03

mankind ripening for r, 1004

man's only religion before r, 955

many events of religious r, but only 5 epochal, 1007

master universe is partial r of the Infinite, 1153

Melchizedek (like U Book) no fanfare, 1024

mission of, 1122

mission of is to censor religions of evolution, 1007

more to come (my Father will continue r), 1010, 1914

must be in touch with evolution, not go too fast, 1007

"my life giving r, the Father in the Son, and the
Son...", 1711

never can this supernal r come to end, 1181

never in this u, God such a living reality as in human
J, 2087

never renders science unnatural, religion unreason-
able, philosophy illogical, 1106

new and undreamed r of pursuits (activities), 391

new, of J' life needed to spiritually baptize modern
culture, 2084

new r of salvation of God, no one can take away, 1952

next r of progression, demands inherent in, 1915

not limited to one people or generation, 1768

of cosmology not inspired, 1109

of Deity through quality values of truth, beauty, etc.,
646

REVELATION OF THE FATHER, THE SUPREME, 88

revelation, of God, supreme purpose of Christ's
bestowal, 1331

of God to world, shall not fail, 2097

of God's love, 1826

of the goodness of God, the gospel, 1683

of identity of Trinity, this disclosure, first since
A. D., 1145

of love, personal experience, 1629

of Spirit of Truth, 1782

Old Testament, as a r of truth, 1767

only hope for atoning for conceptual deficiency, 1137

Paradise Trinity r to a few individuals, 1145

part of plan, 1110

permission to include seven prayers, 1624

reconciles science and religion, 1135-36

religious r essential to brotherhood on U, 597

required to unify God of religion, science, philosophy,
59

science, philosophy, religion, unity, 1122

seven Absolutes, described in these papers as
follows, 1155

sifting of errors of evolution from truths of r, 1110

sixteenth proscription, mandate of this r, 351

socialized religion of new r pays price of compromise, 1626

sooner or later, evolutionary religion receives
expansion of r, 1110

sought by early men, 987

speeds up evolution, 1129

substitute for morontia insight, 1106

sudden, spectacular conversion of Paul, 1099

supernal r through Adjuster never ends, 1181

revelation (cont'd)

supreme r of the... Father, J, 1417

synthesizes apparently divergent sciences and
theology, 1106

technique needed due to man's deficiency in
conceptual data, 1137

technique saves ages of time, 1110

tends to make man godlike, 1122

"through bestowal of his Son", 1796

through contact personalities (see under "personalities, contact")

through human, still divine, 1732-33

times past, in spite of mystic phenomena, 1099

to Apostles, of J' divinity, 1747

to creatures of space by Paradise Sons, 233

to a world is determined by world's capacity, 591

too much stifles imagination, 330

transiently clarifies knowledge by, 1109

two kinds, auto r and epochal r, 1109

unconscious levels' memories mistaken for r, 1099

Unity of philosophy, First Cause of science, God of
religion, all one, 59

usual to worlds, ever-expanding, 1007

vs. evolution in religion, 66, 1122

we may engage in r some day, 247

"when I have finished this r, I will continue...", 1807

why, 1136

why "hard things" are first in U Book, 215

will continue throughout ages, 1599

"woe upon those who despise the r", 1826

world will be slow to recognize r of Father's love,
1533

your r of truth, enhanced by, 1917

Revelation, Book of

greatly abridged and distorted, 1555 (see also under
"Bible")

John wrote while in exile on Patmos, 1555

revelation, this (see also "Urantia Book)

at time of this r, climate is secular, 2081

authorized by Nebadon (our universe) commission
(1935), 1319

by Corps of Superuniverse Personalities, 17

by a technique authorized by superiors (1934), 648

carries more than 1000 highest human concepts, 17

city of this visitation, 1243

contact personalities (see under "personalities,
contact")

contactual subject of this r, 1243

cosmology not inspired, 1109

date of U Book (1934-35), 354, 648, 707, 710, 716, 828,
1313

departed "here" more widely from substance of
Master's teachings... 1487

difficult due to circumscribed language, 1

Divine Counselor speaks with authority, 32

Divine Presence aids man grasp this r, 17

during time of this r, first hearing Gabriel vs.
Lucifer, 616

for enhanced... planetary knowledge, 17

for next 1000 years, 330

forbidden to include... undiscovered facts, 1109

Foreword by Commission sent to U, 1

greetings to U not approved, 717

human sources exhausted before superhuman used,
1343

human subject of this, 1243

is an epochal r, 1008

mandate for the U Book (1934), 354

mandate of superuniverse rulers, 16

many Christian groups, time of this r, 2075

revelation, this (cont'd)
  midwayers part in, 865
  most recent of r of truth to races of U, 1008
  must stay close to thought and reactions of own age, 1007
  narrative of J' life, how gathered, 1332
  narrative of Universal Father, 72
  not permitted discuss ministries of P T A, 1202
  notes from commission, 1323, 1486-87
  of Universal Father, by Divine Counselor, 53
  personal guardian of human used in this r, 1243
  priority given to human concepts, 16
  pure r only when no...previous expression, 16
  put into English through fortuitous cosmic adjustments, 1258
  seraphim in disagreement on U Book r, 1486
  seven prayers for this record, 1624
  sponsored by numerous personalities, 1319
  these papers differ from all previous r, 1008
  twelve midwayers portrayed this narrative, 1343
  unique, composite r by many beings, 1008
  we present this narrative as a sequence, however... 1158
  what a transcendent service if through this r S of M recovered from tomb, 2090
  will stand on record, but revision will be needed, 1109
revelational evolution, techniques of progress, 2094
revelations, age of these r many maintain J' ideas are unsound, 1720
  commissions sent to enlarge r, 260
  essential, two truths in J' teachings, 1593
  extended to superuniverse, 596
  first on a planet, prince and staff, 591
  five epochal on U, 1007
  flash upon the earth in lives, 1467
  J' spiritual only, 1839
  new r of truth, post-Adamic ages, 594
  not necessarily inspired, 1109
  "of truth, sealed by ignorance", 1768
  promised by J for future, 1863
  to Elizabeth, 1345
revelators of truth, 260
revelatory, concepts limited by, 1163
  religion, defined, 1007

revenge, crystallization of Judas' r, 1567
  for civil governments, and God, 1580
  harbored by Judas, 2056
  "he who plans vengeance...in danger...1576
  "is mask of cowardice", 1632
  J rebuked Zebedees for words of vengeance, 1788
  J sought to minimize elements of retaliation, vengeance, 1764
  J warned against retaliation, no allowance for r, or getting even, 1579
  Judas bent on getting even with Peter, James, John, 1925
reverence, (J taught), free from fear and superstition, 1673
reverse, modern society is in r, 780
REVERSION DIRECTORS, THE, 416, 547
reversion, evolutionary, caused many distressful diseases, 736
  plants to prechlorophyll levels (bacteria), 736
revile, "when men r you", 1570
revival, during greatest r of spiritual thinking since Adam, J came, 1332
  must come of the actual teachings of J, 1866
  of spiritual consciousness, 6th century B.C., 1009, 1033, -50, -78
REVIVAL, THE SAMARITAN, 1615

revolt, secular ok, but not r against God, 2081
  when present superstition r is over...J' gospel will persist gloriously, 2082
  radical r is nearly fatal to civilization, 767
revolutionary movements, our (rotations, etc.), 168
revolutions, axial, electronic, beyond imagination, 477
  electron, 1 million million 1 second, 462
reward, every act shall receive its r (Buddhism), 1447
  follows effort as result of causes, 579
  great r of personal satisfaction, being just, 315
  on earth, for entering kingdom, 1537
rewards, for J' children, spiritual joy, divine communion, eternal life, 1593
  for noble living are spiritual prizes, 2056
  for withstanding evil, 619
  in this world, hereafter, 1804
  material, cannot equal satisfaction of achievement, 435
  material, transcended by, 435
  of faith, 1766
REWARDS OF ISOLATION, THE, 578
rewards, of religion, this life, 1593
  of spiritual content of experience, 1142
  of temporal life flow in...channels, 1779
  set off (differential) individuals from the average, 579
rhinoceros, 695
rhythm, less exhausting, 504
  recorders (poets), the, 504
rhythms, beauty sponsors r of all human experience, 647

ri

rib, creation of woman, dates from "operation" 450,000 years before Adam, 837
  myth, given origin by, 742
rich, man and beggar, allegory, 1854
  man, counselled by J, 1462
  only, thought heavenbound, 776
  toward God, man was not, 1821
RICH YOUNG MAN AND OTHERS, THE, 1801
riches, and the love of wealth, 1801
  J used no influences of, 1520
  "the love of r often obscures...vision", 1822
  possession of r vs. love of r, 1803
  when a curse, 1464, 2093
riddle, atomic, explained by mesotron, 479
  contests, 916
ridicule, Judas could not stand r, 1887
  poison darts of, 1897
  Sadducees hoped to r J, 1900
Rig-Veda, 1216
  attempt to combat the "Salem teachers", 1028
right, divine, of personality survival, 761
  doing, wrong doing, consequences for all, 619
  hand not know what left hand does...1583
  human, every h r is associated with a social duty, 906
  of ascent, risk is better than to deprive being of r of ascent, 1233
  thing, easier to do--day by day, 1740
  to enter kingdom, 1583
right and wrong, concept, before revelation, 956
  recognition of r&w exhibits wisdom, 1141
  wisdom chooses between r&w shows spirit leading, 1142
righteous, be r by faith, then DO, 1584
  being r must precede doing righteousness, 1584
  life, because saved, 1683
  living, no material reward for, 435
righteousness, acquire by faith (excess r by works), 1861
  "be valiant in defense of r", 1931
  believers, belief in triumph of r, 1739
  faith in triumph of, 1739

righteousness (cont'd)
    four steps of inner r, 1862
    helps creative spirit, 1965
    is the divine thought, love the... attitude 41
    is fruit of spirit born life of sonship, 1683
    is natural fruit of... 1683
    is volitional, not automatic, 238
RIGHTEOUSNESS, JUSTICE AND, 36
righteousness, must hunger and thirst for, 1774
    not automatic with free will beings, 238
    not by "slavish works" like Pharisees, 1861
    Spirit must quicken formulas of, 380
    virtue, 193
        consists in r, 1576; result of, 1862
    you cannot earn r, 1683
rights, asserted by society now, 793
    equal, to all, no, 794
    few in Middle Ages, 794
RIGHTS, HUMAN, 793
rights, must not encroach, 614
    natural, only a life and world, 793
    natural r, none, 793-94
    none to deprive others... 614
    not even Supreme Rulers violate, 614
    not even to live if, 793
    of society (10), 793
    social, not natural, 794
Rimmon, Ramman, 1637
riot, Pilate was afraid of a tumult or r, 1996
riots, and bloodshed due to Pilate's ruling, 1988
    at Mt. Gerizin, temple vessels, 1989
riptides, sociologic, of cyclonic transitions of a
    scientific era (20th century), 1090
risk, better than deprive mortal of ascendant privilege,
    1233
    everything, proof of God-knowing, 1733
    everything you are and have on survival, 1733
ritual(s), "childlike and meaningless r" (J), 1404
    don't destroy it, reform it, 1076
    hampered society, cursed civilization, 1000s of
        years, 992
    of poverty, unfortunate, 976   outworn, 1012
    pageantry, origin, 2070
RITUALS, PRIESTS AND, 992
ritual(s), priests use foreign words to awe common
    people, 992
    tends to become substitute for religion, 992
ritualistic purification, meaningless ceremony, 976
rivalry, keen and laudatory r developed, 575
river bed is not the river, 1098
river cult, 947   river of life, 404
river of truth, running down the centuries, 2082
rivers of energy and life... from Deities, 468
rivers, supernatural infants adrift on r, 947

ro

"road of robbers" to Bethany, 1874
roads, between major centers, J' time best ever, 1332
    paved, 12,000 miles, Garden, 824
robe of J, seamless vestment, unusual garment, 2007
robust J, 1415
rock, of spiritual reality, 1747, 1897
    on this is sonship (divine), 1747
    "upon this foundation will I build", 1747
rocks, "spiritual foundations of the eternal", 1897
Rocky Mountains, 690, 696
RODAN OF ALEXANDRIA, 1772, -87, 2044, -68 (Greek
    philosopher, 1772; one of the greatest of his race,
    1782; a disciple of J, 1772; made 10 addresses to
    group at Magadan, 1772)

Rodan of Alexandria (cont'd)
    death, persecutions, in Greece, 1787
    debate with Nathaniel, Thomas, 1783
RODAN (OF ALEXANDRIA), FURTHER DISCUSSIONS
    WITH, 1783
Rodan, intellectual vs. true religions, 1780
    mighty man in kingdom, killed in Greece, 1787
    morontia appearance, J (R and 80 believers), 2044
    one of the greatest of his race, 1782
    taught Greeks (the enquiring), 1924
    taught to win, instead of fighting, 1778
    won to belief in personality of Father, 1784
RODAN'S GREEK PHILOSOPHY, 1772
roll call of justice, roll call of mercy, 1247
roll call, second judgment, 830
Roman, captain, 1974-75, -77
    Christian, Greek, dovetailing, 2073
    education bred great loyalty, 2072
    Empire, apart from Jews, receptive to Christian
        teachings, 2069
        believers from all over, 1657
        one of early 2, 1487
        turned upside down, 2077
ROMAN EMPIRE, UNDER THE, 2073
Roman, Empire, why failed, 2074
    feast days, reduced to 135 a year, 961
    guards seized with fear, 2023
ROMAN INFLUENCE, THE (after Pentecost), 2072
Roman, state, 801
    door open always for talent, ability, to rise, 1335
    half population slaves, 1st century A.D., 1335
    yoke, Jews hated reminder of, 1794
romance, imagination and fantastic r make divorces, 929
    man's ascent from seaweed, 731
romancing, man's universe r, very much is truth, 2096
Romans, 945, 960-61, 964
    accepted Paul's Christianity, 2072
    could govern Occident because governed selves, 2072
    early, honest, 2072
    good religion couldn't save empire from: 2074
    no word for "unselfishness", 2073
    sublimely consecrated, 2072
    these R were a great people, 2072
    took over Greek culture, 2072
    tribute to, 2072
Rome, 1522
    adopted Christ as its moral philosophy, 2072
    art or religion, R cared little for, 2072
    brought new tolerances, 2072
    church leaders not tradition bound, 1456
    collapse, too rapid expansion plus internal degenera-
        tion, 801
    failed due to 10 things, 2074
    government feeding the people, 1461
    great blunder (Pilate), 1989
    J at R prepared way for reception of his followers'
        message, 1455
    J contacted 500, 1461
    J prepared way for Christianity in R, 1455
ROME, THE MELCHIZEDEK TEACHINGS IN, 1080
Rome, moral decline, J' time, 2074
    no middle class, 1333
ROME, ON THE WAY TO, 1427
Rome, one of 3 greatest factors, spread of Christian-
    ity, 1456
    persecutions due to word "kingdom", 2072
    policy of intrigue to curb other powers, 1334
    purpose of J' trip to R, 1423
    racial deterioration, J' time, 2074
    rapid spread, Christianity through R and Empire, 1456

Rome (cont'd)
   religious leaders taught, 1455
   sex promiscuity at baths, 1461
ROME, THE SOJOURN AT (see under "Jesus")
Rome, 2,000,000 population, J 6 months, talked with
    32 religious leaders, 1455
   what if J' gospel, instead of Greek Christianity?,2074
   why failed, even with religion, 2074
room for expansion, 156,163
roots, feed grafted branch, which is Godless moral man,
   1126
round trip to Divinington, seconds, 1511
routes, optional, to Havona, 538,552
royal roads, none to Paradise, 551

ru

ruffians hired to harass J, 1684,-86
Rufus and Alexander, sons of Simon of Cyrene became
   gospel teachers in Africa, 2006
rule, golden (see "Golden Rule")
   of life, basic, 1650
RULE OF LIVING, 1650,1805 (see under "Jesus", also
   "Golden Rule" under "G")
rule of Most Highs, greatest good to greatest number,
   1488
Ruler of u of u, is power, energy, etc., is personal, 53
rulers, planetary, appear on their worlds, 1025
   Melchizedek may return here, 1025
   (religious) of Jerusalem conspire with Herod, 1705
    (see also "Sanhedrin")
   remarkable (2), 1037
   "the sin of these r is", 1906
   universe, know all instantaneously as all occurs, 105
   why r wanted to kill J, 1791
rules of conduct, no, principles yes, 1584
rules of living, Pharisees had 613 vs. J' one commandment, 1805
ruminants, N.A. soon overrun by r, 696
run on bank, moral, of the ages, 2076
runaway boy and J, 1475
rush of life, believers should step aside from, 1739
"Russia", 871, 891, 893, 946
   spiritual nonprogression cannot long persist, 2095
Ruth (daughter of Matthew), 1679
Ruth (sister of J) (born A.D. 9), 1389,1720-21,2007,1724
   alone, unwavering loyalty, 1538,1721
   and Jude, went with Mary to J at end, 1997
   "baby sister", never doubted J, 1628
   chief comfort to J, 1628
   fifteen years old, long talks, 1483
   loyal to the end, 1721
   married to D. Zebedee, 2031
   refused to help dissuade J from work, 1721
   sunshine of house, 1402
   taken in hand by Miriam, Martha, 1396
RUTH, VISIT WITH, 1628
ruthless with sin, I am (J), 1766
Ryonin, teacher, 1040

S

SABBATH AT BETHANY (see under "Jesus")
SABBATH DAY, THE EVENTS OF, 1532
Sabbath, day, origin, 832,837
   family observance, J modified, 1402
   how used originally, 832-33
   reason for keeping S changed in Scriptures, 1549
SABBATH SERVICE, THE, 1655
Sabbath, "was made for man", (J), 1655
sacrament, J established only one s, 1942

sacrament (cont'd)
   (marriage, no), 927,929
   Melchizedek substituted bread and wine for
    sacrifice, 1018
   of most primitive of viands, 1004
SACRAMENTS AND SACRIFICES, 983
sacred, all s in lives of spirit led, 1732
SACRED AND PROFANE HISTORY, 1070
sacred book, fetishes, 969
   Paul had no idea his letters would be made, 1084
sacred literature, best authors of world's literature
   recognized eternal God, 1433
"sacred scriptures", include spurious document, 838
   (see also "Word of God, Bible all inspired?")
SACRED SPHERES OF PARADISE, THE, 143
SACRED WORLDS OF THE ETERNAL SON, 149
sacredness, don't attach to non-sacred things, 1727
sacrifice, beginnings of human s, 722
   child should learn to, 1575
   crucifixion not a s, but a joy!, 1944
   death of J no connection with Jewish system of s, 2002
   detracts from efficacy of true prayer, 996
SACRIFICE, EVOLUTION OF HUMAN, 980
sacrifice, firstborn sons common, Moses taught how to
    avoid, 1352
   human, ended cannibalism, 980
   insurance against ill luck, 974
   Jephthah's daughter (civilized people), 981
   J demands loyalty, not s, 1945
   J, not a s, 1936,-45,2016
   J portrayed conquest by s of pride, selfishness, 1590
   kinds of, 977
   material things, receive manifold more (with per-
    secutions), 1804
SACRIFICE, MODIFICATIONS OF HUMAN, 981
sacrifice, not for forgiveness, 1545
   of droves of animals, 1378
   of Sons not to "coax God", 39
   old man insisted self be sacrificed, 980
SACRIFICE, ORIGINS OF, 716,974,977
sacrifice, penance, primitive and puerile religion, 60
   prophets: to obey is better than to sacrifice, 2049
   rituals of s, exorcism, coercion, all merge, 974
   -self, no, self-forgetfulness, yes, 1951
   Semites returned to s, gospel of faith too advanced,
    1021
SACRIFICE, SIN, ATONEMENT, 974
sacrifice, slaves, to show disdain of wealth, 777
   sons, two buried alive in foundations, 983
   substitutes material in place of consecrated wills, 996
   system grew up around savage ideas, 974
   temple s for mother's purification after babe born,
    1352
   vs. faith, 1017,-21
   vs. loyalty, 1945
SACRIFICES AND CANNIBALISM, 978
SACRIFICES AND SACRAMENTS, 983
sacrifices, early s not gifts to gods, but bargaining, 983
   no, faith yes, 1545
   not expressions of true worship, 983
   of Egyptian ruler, 978
   religious, origin of, 716
   to God, bribes to men, 978
sacrificial animal profits, 1888
Sadducean, Annas, onetime high priest, 1420 (see
   "Annas")
Sadducees (priesthood and certain wealthy Jews--a
    religious party), 1534
   and Pharisees delighted by each others' failures, 1902
SADDUCEES AND THE RESURRECTION, 1900

salvation (cont'd)
     was and is the new and living way, 1113
     "whosoever will may come", 1567
     "you cannot buy", 1683
Salvington, capital of Nebadon, 174, 197
     "Christ's" accustomed place, 1315, 2057
     cluster of 490 architectural spheres around S, 387
     hdqtrs. of Nebadon, local Universe, 358
     to acquire residence on S, train on 490 worlds, 387
SALVINGTON WORLDS OF THE FINALITERS, 401
Samaria, 2013
<u>SAMARIA, GOING THROUGH,</u> 1607
Samaria, J and James did not avoid, 1399
     Nazarenes avoided, 1374
     "we go into S", 1611
Samaritan, the good, 1809
     leper vs. Jews, 1827
SAMARITAN REVIVAL, THE, 1615
SAMARITAN, STORY OF THE GOOD, 1809
Samaritan Temple to Yahweh, 1612
Samaritans, 1788
     among lepers, Simon wanted them passed by, 1827
     Jews and, 1610, -12, 1788
     Pilate deposed due to slaughter of S, 1988
     prejudice against, 1607
     revival, 1615
     with whom "the Jews had no dealings", 1535
SAMUEL--FIRST OF THE HEBREW PROPHETS, 1062
Samuel (prophet), he did act (chopped king), 1062
     "The Lord enriches and impoverishes", 1063
     Scripture changed in S, 1599
     "Yahweh, changeless", 1063
SANCTITY OF SERVICES, 316
sanctuary, first places of s were market places, 775
     J wrote words in the s, 1793
SANGIK, THE SIX RACES OF URANTIA, 722
Sangiks, ancestors of all 6 colored races, 722, 735
     normal animal passion, little imagination, 914
     presence of Andites created outmating desire, 919
     primary, secondary, 904
     primary, secondary mating, small scale, not bad, 920
     were all cannibalistic. 979

Sanhedrin

Sanhedrin (rulers of Jews, high priests, supreme court;
     enormous temple profits, 1888-89; condemned J
     in advance of trial, 1847, -72, 1910; falsified
     charges, 1990; bribed tomb guards to lie, 2043, -45;
     fearful due to own divided views, 1789), 1602-03,
     1797, 1809, -11, -27, -35, 1905, 2000, -24
     about to arrest J, 1720
     Abraham of S, member, believed in J, 1665
     accepted Judas' services, 1926
     adulteress, agents of S used a. in attempt to ensnare
          J, 1793
     against J, why, 1791
     appointed spies, 1654
     assassination of J proposed, 1911
     authority, usurpation of, 1718
     bade spies return, 1667
     banquet for J, all Bethany and Bethpage, in defiance
          of S, 1878
     believers, full score out of S, 1903
     believers in J among Sanhedrists, were Pharisees,
          1978
     believers in J in S were 14, 1810
          resigned in a body, 1847
     blasphemy, must charge J with, 1713
     breathed easily after J taken, no uprising, 2000
     bribed guards to lie about stone at J' tomb, 2023, -45
     broadcast, "J condemned to die", 1871

Sanhedrin (cont'd)
     challenge, J' open c to S, 1813
     charged the poor week's pay for pair doves, 1889
     charges against J formulated, 1850
     charges to go to Pilate, 1985
     (chief priests and leaders) secret meetings, 1654
     clerk of S court, "man (J)...is worthy to die", 1989
     closed all Palestine synagogues to J, 1718
     closed Capernaum synagogue to J, 1717
     condemned J in advance of a trial, 1847, -72, 1910
     conference with Herod, 1717
     confusion bordering on panic, 2033
     confusion, S disbanded in, 1792, 1814
<u>SANHEDRIN COURT, BEFORE THE,</u> 1978
SANHEDRIN COURT, SECOND MEETING OF, 1985
Sanhedrin, court went to Pilate with J, 1987
     courts of temple profaned, 1889
     dared not arrest J, 1796, 1815
     death of J unjustly and irregularly decreed, 1986
     death sentence for 7 reasons, 1911
     death to J without trial, 1910
     decided Lazarus too, must die, 1880
     decision to destroy J without trial, 1847
     determined to "try" J, 1654
     doubted J under Roman protection, 1791
     Eber, officer of S sent to arrest J, 1791-92
     enlisted Jewish leaders, 1899
     false judges, 1989
     false witnesses, score of, 1982
     false written charges to Pilate, 1990
     fateful meeting, death at all costs, 1909
     53 Pharisees and Sadducees, ordered to Capernaum,
          1707
     frantic, due conversion of young Abraham, and 3 spies
          baptized, 1672
     greedy priests, 1889 (see also "priests (rabbis)
          money", under "P")
     grim determination to destroy J, 1932
     healing blind man, challenge to S, 1813
     Hebron synagogue resisted S, was burned, 1718
     Herod plotted with, 1719
     high priest demanded J' death, 1995
     hired men to make trouble, 1686-87
     hostility of (leaders), 1672
     Jerusalem religious rulers antagonistic, 1617
     J and 24 fled from officers of S, 1723
     J' death decreed many times, 1909
     J explained S would conspire to destroy him and
          apostles, 1705
     J must be speedily destroyed, 1891
     J once more offered Israel and S salvation, 1810, 1906
     J work through "power of prince of devils" said S, 1847
     Joseph and Nicodemus, quit S, 2013
     Josiah (healed from blindness) before the S, 1813
     Lazarus death decreed, 1849, -80
     Lazarus resurrection, meeting on, 1847
     leader of S sought Roman soldiers, 1973
     leaders bribed guards and Roman soldiers to lie,
          2023, -45
     led mob in "crucify him", 1994
     loved J, many members of S, 1810
     many members S secretly believed or..., 1789
     Matadormus, member of S, 1802
SANHEDRIN MEETING, THE FATEFUL, 1909
Sanhedrin, meeting in violation of rule, 1813
SANHEDRIN, MEETING OF THE, 1847
Sanhedrin, meeting, special on resurrection, 2033
     meetings amid profanation, 1889
     member (Pharisee) at J' Philadelphia breakfast, 1833
     member questions J, 1711

Sanhedrin (cont'd)
  members, 5, resigned, 1718
  members of S joined kingdom, 1118, 1789, 1910, 2013
  members (some) believed in J, 1606, 1789, 1810, -13,
    1847, -78, -82-83, 1903, -10, -78, 2013
  "mischief-maker, evildoer, wicked man" (said of J),
    1992
  mob overthrew bazaars at temple, 1889
  murderous intrigues of wicked S, 1849
  murderous S, J revealed his nature to, 2011
  new problems, in J' resurrection, 2034
  Nicodemus, elderly, visited J, 1601
  nineteen members of S ejected J, 1847
  observers, new from S, 1698
  overcharged people exorbitantly, 1889
    charged week's labor for pair of doves, 1889
    30%, 80% commission for changing money, 1889
    temple treasury and rulers profited tremendously,
      1889
  own Jewish laws, rules, ignored, 1813, 1982, -84-85
  panic, due to desertion of 3 spies, 1672
  perjured witnesses, 1982, -99
  Philadelphia, S never controlled, 1831
  planned for J' destruction, 1673
  profits, enormous (animals), 1888
  religion of authority (sterile), 1729
  requested tomb be made secure, 2014
  resentment was general against S, 1741
  resurrection, new problems, 2034
  resurrection: trouble with J just begun, 2033
  Sadducees became majority, 1892
  sat in judgment on (J) innocent life, 1986
  Simon, member, publicly espoused J, 1606
  sin of the rulers, 1906
  sitting in judgment on Sabbath violation of own rule,
    1813
  6 spies asserted discipleship, joined J' family of
    followers, 1654
  spying Pharisees confessed faith, 1667
  Stephen's preaching, conflict with S, 2068
  "stop Galilean or world will go after him", 1882
  supreme court, S was, 1909
  synagogues, closed all s to J, 1718
  ten million dollars in treasury--common people poor
    and overcharged, 1889
  "these maddened and blinded rulers of the Jews", 1927
  30 prejudiced judges in judgment of J, 1984
  throw out any who mentioned...2033
  trial court, 23 constituted, 1978
  trial of J proceeded along unfair unjust lines, 1815
  trial of J, so-called, 1982
  tribunal, highest on earth, 1987
  tribunal, supreme, of all Israel, 1815
  trouble, real, had just begun, 2033
  try J on flouting...1719
  Tues., April 4, A.D. 30, unanimously "voted death",
    1909
  23 members constituted trial court, 1978
  unlawful to execute, got Pilate to do it, 1989
  upset by conversion of young Abraham, 1665-66, -72
  vengefulness of the, 1880
  visitors resented profiteering, desecration, of
    temple, 1889
  warfare, open, on J, 1708
  was fearful due to its own divided views, 1789
  "we can't kill him, you do it", 1989
  why S wanted to kill J, 1790-91
  "will deliver me to be put to death", 2052
  with 19 men "out" could try J with solidarity, 1847
SANHEDRISTS, BEFORE THE COURT OF, 1982
Sanhedrist tribunal, the written charges of, 1990

sanitary advance, disease-destroying properties of sunlight, 748
sanitation, J' camp at Bethsaida a model of s, 1657
  hygiene, methods lost for 500,000 years, 747
sanity, health, happiness, integrations of, 43
sanobim, 550, 1243
SANOBIM, CHERUBIM AND, 422
SANOBIM, EVOLUTION OF CHERUBIM AND, 423
Sansa, Adam's mortal daughter, 847
Sarah, (wife of Abraham), 1019
  cause of Abraham's cowardice, 1023
sarcasm, cynicism, 1765
Sargan, Sansa married, 847
Sargon, King of Assyria, carried 25,000 Jews into
  captivity, 1612
Sargon, priest of Kish, 876
Sartaba, Mt., J and apostles, 1610
Sasta, Buddha's name to followers, 1036
Satan, approved Jews' plans to kill J, 1971
  a brilliant creature of light, 754
  "falling as lightning from heaven", 490, 609, 1807
  first lieutenant of fallen Lucifer, System Sovereign,
    600
  "get thee behind me", 609, 1760
  hearts of all Edentia closed against S, 490
  "how can Satan cast out S?", 1714
  in Peter's interpretation of parable, 1690
  interned rebels with S on prison worlds, 611
  a Lanonadek Son, 602, 754
  mandate S confined to prison world, 616
  never had power to touch faith Sons of God, 610
  not appropriate to his part in Job, 1663
  not "devil" (who is Caligastia), 602
  pleased by Judas' defection, 1938
  present with J, 1493
  provoked David to number Israel, 1599
  shortly after inspection by S, rebellion!, 755
  visited U until time of this Book, 611, 616
  why S permitted to continue in rebellion, 620
  worked mischief to time of J, 615-16
Satania (our local system, 1 of 100 that comprise con-
    stellation; composed of over 7000 astronomical
    groups, 456-57)
  astronomic center is dark island, 457
  composed of over 7000 physical systems, 457
  oldest inhabited world in S, is Anova, 559
  only 61 life-modification planets in, 486, 559, 664
  over 2000 brilliant suns in S, 458
  neighboring systems are named...457
SATANIA PHYSICAL CONTROLLERS, 456
Satania, probation nursery of, 516
  619 inhabited worlds in over 500 physical systems, 359
  sparse in inhabited worlds, 359
  two thousand brilliant suns in S, 458
  worlds, some in S peopled since L R, 609
satellite worlds (see also "mansion worlds")
  Lanonandek cluster, administrative spheres, 394
  Life Carriers' 7 spheres, 42 s w, 397
  of Evening Stars, 7 with 42 s w, 408
  of Spirit-fused Mortals, 42 around 7 spheres, 411
  700 around 70 spheres around Edentia, 485
  7 s w of Jerusem, have 49 subsatellites, 509
    each of 7 almost 10x size of U, 509
    subsatellites (49) about size of U, 509
  7 spheres, 42 s w, acme of ascenders' education, 391
  70 worlds, 420 tributaries, "Melchizedek University",
    387
  six s w of "Melchizedek" for special study, 388-89
satisfaction (consciousness of achievement) transcends
  any conceivable material reward, 435
SATISFACTION OF SERVICE, THE, 312

satisfaction (cont'd)
  personality, only in unity of cosmic constancy,
    consistency, 1120
satisfactions, from religion 3, 69
  of living, one is skill, 1779
  spiritual vs. material, 1000 to 1...501
  supreme s of the loving service of man, 1863
  supreme subjective s, 1094
Sato, led progenitors of Greeks (descendant of Adamson),
  895
SATURDAY EVENING, THE (J), 1715
Saturn and Jupiter, 656
Saul (citizen of Tarsus), (see also "Paul" under "P"),
  1411
Saul (King), and witch of Endor, 1646
  army "upped" from 3000 to 330,000 by exiled priests,
    1072
  and David, 1072
  Hebrew history begins with...1072
  priests faked S's prophecied kingship to create
    "divine line of descent", 1072
savagery, U languished in s 35,000 years ago, 868
savage(s), and civilized men alike, 951
  not obscene or prurient, 968
  not what killed him, but who, 794
  primitive, didn't like work, 773
  talked all night when one died (wake), 958
  the s was a slave to usage, ritual, 767
"save his life selfishly (whoever would) shall lose it",
  1760
"save men, don't judge them", 1571
saved, countless mortals already, 2024
  God would have all men s, 39
  how many will be?, 1828-29
  Jewish theology s by intervention of Babylonian
    teachers, 1339
  "justified" (synonym) by faith, 2094
  not because live righteous life, but vice versa, 1683
  "others, himself he cannot save", 1578
  what must I do to be s, 1682, 1802, -09
  who then can be s, 1803
"saving truth of the gospel", 2052
savings are a form of survival insurance, 775
savior, J correctly called s, 2017-18
Savior Sovereign, (Michael) system of Palonia, 1311

sc

scaffolding, conceptual frames of...are serviceable s
    before enlarging comprehension, 1260
  for the God concept, 990
  personality and relations, are never s, 1235
  stages of developments, 1488
  transient s, bridges over to promised land, 364
  war an indispensable s in building civilization, 786
scalping, head hunting, 955
Scandinavia, cremation, therefore no remains found in
  Europe, 897
scar of resentment (Judas), 1927
scene, distant, made visible, 327
scheme, of creation, is, 1261
    potentialities into actualities, 1261
  society is co-op s to gain freedoms, liberty, 906
school, and work combined, 751
  the entire universe is one vast s, 412, 417, 558-59
SCHOOL OF THE PROPHETS, A NEW, 1657
school, plan, learning and doing, 1658
  play (social), home (passing the cultural torch), 909
schools, Capernaum, none better, 1548
  Dalamatia, curriculum, 751
  early, of planet, perverted, 576
SCHOOLS, THE MELCHIZEDEK, 517

schools (cont'd)
  of Adam and Eve, 586
  of ethics, administration, social adjustment, 551
  of evangelists, 1657
  of Paradise attainment, 339
  of philosophy, divinity, spirituality, 551
  of the prophets, new, 1657
  of religion, 1486
  of thinking, feeling, doing, 551
  of universe administration and spiritual wisdom, 388
  on neighboring planet
    feeble-minded, 812
    for self-support, 812
    military, naval, 817
    parental schools, 812
    philosophy, 817
    precollege 5 to 18, 812
    professional, 817
    statesmanship, 816, 818
    technical, 817
  on worlds of Planetary Prince, 586, 743
  parental s of child culture compulsory, 811
SCHOOLS, PLANETARY HEADQUARTERS AND, 575
schools, planetary hdqtrs. s wrecked swiftly,
    completely, 576
  preparatory, 339

science

science (after "science", see "science and religion",
    "s, religion, philosophy", and "s.vs. religion")
  adds greatly to mortality of false gods, 1124
  agelong contest between truth, error, 141
  ancient magic was cocoon of modern s, 973
  and credulity, 1125   and magic, 970-72
  and physical can't explain...738
  and professions emerged from parasitical priest-
    hoods, 1006
  assumptions of, 191, 1139
  becomes thought domain of...1139
  birth of the first Primates, 706
  birth of s due to search for truth, 901, 972-73
  contribution of, 907-09
  deals with phenomena, 2077
  destroy not faith, but superstition, 2078
  destroyed childlike illusions, 2076
SCIENCE, DISCOURSE ON (J), 1476, 1727
science, effort to solve riddles, material, 2096
  emancipated women, 937
  energy, weight, antigravity, 175
  experiment, religion experience, 2076
  facts, 150,000 incompatible with chance cosmic
    origin, 665   facts of s are unproved, 1127
  the false s of materialism, 42
  fights for deliverance from bondage, 141
  first Cause and God of religion are one, 59, 1106
  from magic, 972-73
  grounded in reason, imagination, conjecture,
    helpful, 1137
  idea precedes realization, 1122
  is the domain of knowledge, philosophy the realm of
    wisdom, religion the sphere of faith experience,
    1110
  is sobering man, 1093   is sustained by reason, 1137
  knowledge of s not essential, 141
  left J' religion untouched, 2076
  mental attitudes of s prevent fanaticism, 1089
  method of, 1106
  morality, religion constitutive factors of man, 196
    survive civilizations, 196
  more you know, less sure you can be, 1119
  must progress, not be thwarted, 988

science (cont'd)
   must purify religion, 1088
   must refine, ennoble religion, 906, 1006
   needs wisdom's guidance, 909
   never can attain satisfactory comprehension of soul,
     1215
   never hurt faith if, 1727
   no quarrel with true religion, 2078
   not more real or certain than spiritual enlighten-
     ment, 2077
   not real until facts become meaning in thought
     streams of mind, 1120
   of mathematics could not know, 141
   "of mind over matter?" man can modify physical
     reality, 1222
   on Uversa certain energies known as triata, 471
   or religion, no, 1135
   philosophy, couldn't predict H_2O, 141
   physical, but scientist super-material, 2077
   planetary council on art and s, 748
   predicated on 3 assumptions: matter, motion, life,
     1139
   providing new basis for knowing philosophy, 1306
   providing new basis for knowing values of spiritual,
     1306
   pursuit of knowledge constitutes s, 1122
   quantitative experience, a, 2077
   religion, and controversy, 2076
   sanitation, 1657
   seeks to identify, analyze, classify, 1122
   slowly destroying superstitions, 1306
   (so-called) no base for universe philosophy, 480
   sorts men, religion loves men, 1122
   stabilizes philosophy, purifies religion by destruction
     of superstition, 907
   suggests existence of Absolute, 1106
   vainly strives to create brotherhood of culture, 1122
   what s should do for man, 2078
   "where s leaves off, we begin", (J), 1641
   without idealism, 2086
   yields knowledge, 1106
SCIENCE AND RELIGION, 1137 (see also "science vs.
   religion")
science and religion
   both based on assumptions, 1110, -39
   both essential to understanding of universal truths,
     1135-36
   difficulty in harmonizing, 1136
   fiery furnace of s refines r, 1006
   grounded in reason and faith, 1137
   in complex scientific age, 1139
   materialistic panic, but spiritual bank of the ages
     (permanently solvent), 2076
   mind can create energy relationships and living
     relationships to dominate... in universe, 1222
   mota reconciles both... 1139
   need more searching, self-criticism, 1138
   play parts in 15 factors on which civilization is
     predicated, 906-11
science, religion, philosophy, 141, 1110, -36, -39
   ideal welded into unity by experience, faith, wisdom,
     1080
   lead to fact, value, and coordinate consciousness, 1122
   proofs: reason, faith, logic, 1106
   what each is founded on, 1141
   what God is to each of these, 1125
science vs. religion
   certainties and certitudes, 1119
   entire p, maximum of being, 1122
   first contest, 774

science vs. religion (cont'd)
   method of experiment vs. of experience, 2076
   quantitative vs. qualitative experience, 2077
   respective appeals of, 1119
   s sorts men, r loves men, 1122
   to God a possibility, to r a certainty, 1125
   two extremes of u perception, harmonized through
     mota, 1139
   what each leads to, 1122
scientific discoveries, revelators not at liberty to
   anticipate, 1109
scientific discovery, every s d demonstrates freedom
   and uniformity, 2078
SCIENTIFIC KNOWLEDGE, 907
scientific knowledge
   and action, only antidote for "accidental" ills, 957
   as factor in U civilization, 907
scientific materialism, offspring is tyrannical state, 2081
scientific method, faces forward, 970
   an intellectual yardstick, 2078
   useless in evaluation of spiritual... 2078
scientific minds, highest, 2076
   materialistic tendencies, 2075
scientist, can never produce life, 403, 468, 737
   can't discern dynamics of living protoplasm, 737
   higher any s progresses in his science... 1125
   not science, perceives, 2080
   Thomas (Apostle), mind of true scientist, 1563
   Universe like s, not like science, 2080
   vs. idealist, 1457
   vs. mystic, 1125, 1434
scientists, and Supreme Mind, 1125
   can never tell what are gravitation, light, electricity,
     1476; personality, 1225
   confusion of s due to, 1439
   materialistic and extreme idealists at loggerheads,
     1457
   no right to assert "materialism", 1457
   on trial before bar of human needs, 1457
   philosophers, prophets, 1110
   powerless to create matter, or energy, 468
     to add life to matter, 468
   secrets of life, s never will find, 737
   started run on moral bank, 2076

scourging of J, (Pilate), illegally, 1995, 2004
scribe of Damascus (J), 1423, -56, -59, -68, -92
Scripture, (J quoted S throughout his work for kingdom)
   J rejected negative half of a S, 1770
   never believe records that God directed slaying, 1768
     (see also "word of God, Bible all inspired?")
Scriptures, "altogether human in origin, but..."(J), 1767
   "are sacred because..." (J), 1768
   "best collection of religious wisdom" (J), 1767
   cream of S used by J, 1769
   doctrine of perfection of S confuses, disheartens
     seekers of truth, 1768
   "even the S have said: 'out of him...' ", 1795
   excerpts by J and Ganid from S, 1444
   "gathered together in recent times" (J), 1767
   "the Gods created the heavens and the earth"
     (Trinity), 1598
   Greek, neighbors listened to boy J read, 1389
   Greek, only 2 copies in Nazareth, 1359
   Hebrew, misapplied to J, 1347-48
   invalidity of the S, 1670
   J' discussion of, 1767
   J presented Greek translation of, 1355
   J used positive half of a S, 1770
   J' words seemed to detract from S, 1767

Scriptures (cont'd)
>   "Lord moved David" became "Satan provoked David",
>   1599
>   much misrepresentative of F in heaven, 1767-68
>   not the word of God, 1768
>   Psalms read in temple, 1795
>   sad feature of belief S are sacred, 1767
SCRIPTURES, THE TALK WITH NATHANIEL ON THE,
>   1767
Scriptures, used wrongly as guide, 1769
>   "what is the truth about the S?", 1767
>   wisdom, best collection of religious w, 1767
sculptors, Dalamatia, 748
sculpture, Amenhotep III, 1500 B.C., 1215
Scythopolis, Greek city, once Beth-Shean (Hebrew),
>   1370,-74, 1788

se

sea of glass, circular crystal 30 miles deep, on Edentia,
>   487
>   Jerusem feature we see first on m w 2, 534
>   Jerusem, Sovereign holds conclave on s of g every
>   10 days, 511
>   Lucifer mainfesto issued, Satania conclave on s of g,
>   604
>   Lucifer's successor landed on s of g with staff, 608
>   receiving stations, transports arrive, pearly
>   observatory, 521
>   saw a s of g mingled with fire, 539
sea serpents, threatened destruction entire fish family,
>   686, 688
sea squirt uses vanadium for oxygenation, 737
sea trade, Mediterranean s t full swing 4500 years ago,
>   898
search for God, is search for everything, 1289
>   new amazing discoveries of new greater love, 1289
seas, cleared of pirates, trade advancing, J' time, 1333
>   foraminifers in s marked Cretaceous period, 688
>   high s of unexplored truth, 1729
seasons, why?, 657
seaweed, romance of man's ascent from s, 731
SECONAPHIM, THE, 307
seconaphim, are retentive or record personalities, 201
>   lone, accompanied Michael to bestowal 3, 1312
SECONAPHIM, MINISTRY OF THE, 317
seconaphim, offspring of Reflective Spirits, 201
SECONAPHIM, THE PRIMARY, 307
SECONAPHIM, THE SECONDARY, 310
SECONAPHIM, THE TERTIARY, 313
second century A.D., travel universal, thought
>   untrammeled, 2074
second coming (see also "return of Michael" under
>   "Jesus")
>   apocalyptic account in Gospel of Matthew, 1915
>   apostles believed near, 2067
>   J intimated would be seen by eye of spiritual faith,
>   1919
>   J promised some day to come back, 1863, 1918
SECOND COMING, THE MASTER'S, 1914
SECOND GARDEN, THE, 847
second mile, 2084
"second milers", few genuine, 2084
second, one-millionth of s electron in orbit, 462
SECOND OR SYSTEM STAGE, THE, 632
Second Source and Center, 5, 1151, 1262 (see also
>   "absolute actuals")
SECONDARY CAUSATION, PRIMARY AND, 1298
SECONDARY DISSOCIATORS, 325, 328
Secondary Lanonandek, authored papers 50 and 51 in the
>   U Book

secondary (cont'd)
SECONDARY MIDWAYERS, THE, 862
SECONDARY MODIFIED ORDERS OF ASCENSION, THE,
>   570
SECONDARY NEBULAR STAGE, THE, 653
secondary races, some respects biologically superior,
>   920
SECONDARY SUPREME FINITE INTEGRATION, 1164
secoraphic hosts, mothers of the, 308
secoraphic personalities are staff for Reflective Spirits,
>   201
secoraphic Voices of the Creator Sons, 452
secrecy, fraud and superstition, 992
secret, do good deeds in s, 1560,-64
>   love is s of beneficial association between personali-
>   ties, 141
>   of atomic constitution, 478
>   of a better civilization, 2064
>   of energy, 1777
SECRET OF GREATNESS AND THE SOUL OF
>   GOODNESS, THE, 317
secret, of Paradise ascension, 84
>   of purposeful growth of society, 433
>   of Sonarington (incarnation), 1317
>   of survival, imitation of God, 1221
>   "sins, purge me from", 1640
>   societies, 790
>   spheres, seven of the Universal Father, 143
>   writings, were beginning of Jewish, Christian Bibles,
>   1074
secrets, energy s of physical universe lead to man's
>   manipulation of energy, 1222
>   no arbitrary s in Universe, 221
>   of cause and effect, man slow about 990
>   of life, scientists will never find, 737
Secrets of Supremacy, 149
SECRETS OF SUPREMACY, TRINITIZED, 207
secrets, storehouse of s natural realm, being unlocked,
>   1306
sect, believers in J were s within Judaism, 2060
>   of Jewish faith (believers), no longer within Judaism,
>   2068
sectarian rivalry, no place for, 2085
sectarianism, dogmatism, disease, 1092
SECTOR GOVERNMENTS, THE, 181
secular, alliances for religion, bad, 1089
>   and spiritual, gigantic, struggle, 2075
>   church must not be s, 1089,-92
>   history is not sacred, 1071
>   optimism, social, political, is an illusion, 1282
>   superstition, revolt, when over, J' gospel!, 2082
SECULAR TOTALITARIANISM, 2081
secularism, betrays man into tyranny, 2081
>   blights souls, 2081
>   broke bonds of church control, now threatens new
>   mastery, 2081
>   can never bring peace to mankind, 2081
>   a disease of institutional religion, 1092
>   frees man from church, enslaves him to state, 2081
>   from two influences, 2081
>   ignores God, 2081
>   inception was protest against church, 2081
>   leads to disaster, 2082
>   mistake of s was, 2081
>   philosophic, brought tyrannical state, 2081
>   progress from, 2081
>   tends to affirm man does not need God, 2081
>   threatens new type of mastery, 2081
>   vs. materialism, 2081
>   weakness of s discards ethics and religion for politics
>   and power, 2082

secularism (cont'd)
  whence?, 2081
  without God (nothing) leads to peace, 2082
secularistic revolt, brought amazing creativity of
    industry, 2081
secularists, majority of Christians are actual s, 2081
secularization, complete s of science, etc., leads to
    disaster, 2082
securities, temporal, are vulnerable, 1096
security, against dangers and racial perils, through
      guild of civilization, 906
  age, the, 576
  guild of civilization exacts costly admission fees,
      imposes discipline, exacts penalties, 906
  safeguarding of J, 1718
  sense of s in (one who) grasps Supreme, 1101
  society's prime gift to men, 792
  with uncertainty, 1223
see yourself as others see you (help to), 553
seed, his s and her s, 844
  "new kingdom is like a..." (J), 1536
  of Christianity, harvest of moral character, spiritual
      achievement, 1335
  of purposeful growth of society, 433
  of soul, 1459
  of theoretical truth is dead unless, 380
  -plant period, the, 683
  time and harvest, interval between, 616
seeds, of potential existence, 91
  of wisdom, proved by...1302
seek, and you shall find--law of universe, 1838
  "first the kingdom of heaven", 2088
  "the greater thing", 1823
  or can't get revelation,1466
  "you shall s, but not find me", 1872
seeking for one not lost (J), 1525
segregata, pure energy, 126
selection, natural, must be superseded by intelligence,
    734
  uncontrolled, chance survival, 734
SELECTIVE ASSORTERS, 544
selective reproduction on advanced worlds, 630
Seleucid Syria, 1334

self

SELF, THE, 1227
self, Adjuster-expression (of real and better s), 2078
  admiration leads to...614
  cognition of sonship, 448
  don't take s seriously, 555
  has rights, as well as neighbors, 1134
  in morontia state, has become a more enduring
      reality, 1238
  integration of s with the u is...2097
SELF, THE MORONTIA, 1235
self, pity, of recently liberated women, 936
  religious person seeks identify s with universe, 67
  transcend the, 1222-23
self-acting Adjusters (see "Self-Acting Adjuster" under
    "Thought Adjuster"), exploits, numerous, within
    and without mortal subjects, 1196
self-assertion
  and liberty--Lucifer, Satan, 602, 604
  delusions of, 604, 607
self-assertiveness
  leads to wars, 2065
self-centered
  in prayer, guard against, 1639
self-completion
  finding God, 2094
self-concepts
  displace spirit-nucleus, 142

self- (cont'd)
self-confidence
  presumptuous (Peter), 1962
  reasonable, ok, 1223
self-conscious
  human, divine, 1228, 1479, 1528
self-consciousness
  can't be explained, 1228
  connotes, consists in, 194
  endowment of super-material world, 1228
  human, 4 universe-reality realizations inherent in, 196
  in essence is a communal consciousness, 196
  not explained materialistically, 196, 1228
  secret of s-c of man's spiritual nature, 1229
self-control
  achievements in, rungs of ascending ladder, 975
  acme of all human virtues, rugged s-c, 927
  ancient, primitive customs taught savages s-c, 976
  at last makes representative government unnecessary,
      599
  better than self-denial, 977
  ethical prayer seeks wisdom to enhance s-c, 998
  ever increasing demand of advancing mankind, 914
  the Father's children are always masters of self, 1610
  food hoarding developed s-c, 775
  form of government unimportant, vital is s-c, 806
  greatest warrior is he who subdues self, 1447
  greatness on U evidenced by s-c, 317
  ideal state, few laws, enhanced s-c, 803
  individual s-c eliminates representative government,
      599
  J was perfected specimen of, 1609
  leads to altruistic service, 614
  making laws unnecessary on advanced worlds, 630
  new message of, 1609
  only with emotional maturity, 598
  poverty, penance, taught savage s-c, 976
  prayer mighty force for promotion of s-c, 999
  quarantine of women helped toward s-c, 936
  self-liberty, balance needed, 1302
self-criticism, 1459
self-deceived
  easy to become, 1609
self-deception
  maidens and consorts in sex service, 982
self-denial, 1605, -10
  bondage of, 1609
  (John) vs. self-control (J), 1609
self-destruction, cosmic
  possibility of s-d can't be avoided, if free will, 1301
self-determination
  fallacy, 1401, -90
self-discipline
  all-encompassing motivation imposes, 1100
SELF-DISTRIBUTION OF THE FIRST SOURCE AND
    CENTER, 108
self-examination
  spiritual, no, 1583, 1609
  vs. self-forgetfulness, 1609
self-expression
  and Adjuster-expression, 2078
  gratification of human hunger for supernal s-e, 508
  potential for s-e is unlimited in Godlikeness, 507
  sublime in Havona worship, 304
  worship: gain this satisfaction of s-e, 304
self-forgetfulness, 2088
self-glorification
  becomes ridiculous, 549
self-government
  height of ideals of s-g, Havona, 155

self-government (cont'd)
  of Melchizedeks, 385
  true...on Havona, 155
  under true s-g fewer and fewer restrictive laws, 597
self-gratification
  a basic urge that led to capital accumulation, 776
SELF-GRATIFICATION, DANGERS OF, 942
self-gratification
  excessive s-g destroys society, 764, 766
  family provides certain...forms of s-g, 937
  institutions of, one of 3 groups of human i, 772
  mating, varying degrees of s-g, 931
  modern threat, 770, 942
  moral discipline needed, place of s-g, 2086
self-maintenance
  vs. self-gratification, 764, 766, 772
  vs. self-realization, 764
self-realization
  duty of society to provide opportunity for s-r, 794, 803
  enhanced in...and comprehension, 1951
  goal of s-r should be spiritual, not material, 1096
  leisure devoted to increased s-r, 814
  normal mortals, innate drives toward s-r, 1095
  religious growth presupposes s-r, 1094
  through worship and service, 1572
  true cosmic s-r results from...1039
  vs. self-perpetuation, s-maintenance, s-gratification,
    764-766
self-relationship
  of I AM, 1157
self-respect
  debase s-r by using religions of authority, 1729
  do not lessen or destroy men's s-r, 1765
  idleness is destructive of s-r, 1764
  is not self-admiration, 1740
  J aimed at superb s-r in his life, 1582
  loss of, paralysis of will, 1765
  measure of (love of fellows), 1740
  moral society aims to preserve s-r, 803
  spiritual living mightily increases true s-r, 1740
self-restraint
  gives personality freedom, 1460
  lack of s-r balanced in early man by...1302
  little to start with, 1302
self-sacrifice
  old religion, 1951
  vs. self-forgetfulness, 1951
self-surrender
  intellect vs. emotion, 2065
self-will
  response to primordial s-w of self-existent self-will,
    1160
self-worth
  consciousness of s-w augmented by...1100
selfhood, 1232
  in study of s, helpful to remember...1227
  iniquity reveals transient reality of all God unident-
    ified, 1301
  is material, subject to vicissitudes, 1238
  of personality dignity...is the bestowal of Father, 104
  totality of, 1096
  volitional, T A never violates, 1204
selfish, creature can't receive unselfish glories of P,
    1638
  gain, sin to use divine talents for s g, 1519
  men and women, 2083
  mire of own production, 1309
  political sagacity suicidal, 598
  qualities of love, 1096
  thoroughly s soul cannot pray, 1639

selfishness, defined, 613
  folly of unmitigated s, 597
  prejudice is inseparably linked to s, 1774
  unmitigated s, the acme of ungodliness, 613
"sell, go and s all that you have" (J), 1802
seller, chew wood to soften his heart, 971
Selta, author of apocalyptic about Messiah (copied into
    Gospel of Matthew), 1915
selves emerge from 3rd Source and Center, 1285
semispiritual work on U, 864
semistates, reversions or nucleuses of future states, 801
Semites, after Abraham and Melchizedek, religious
    beliefs caused certain tribes to be called...
    Hebrews, Jews, 1055
  Bedouin, 1042
SEMITES, DEITY CONCEPTS AMONG THE, 1052
Semites, Egypt, forlorn, ignorant, dejected, 1055
  Egypt, spectacular night flight, 1056
  henotheistic, 1054, -78
  northern absorbed Sumerians, 876
  racially blended, almost all 9 races, 1054
  thought soul resided in bodily fat, 955
SEMITIC PEOPLES, THE, 1054
Semitic, tribesmen went back to sacrifices and atone-
    ment, 1021
SENDING THE APOSTLES OUT TWO AND TWO, 1681
sense, new, of spiritual joy, security, confidence, 2059
  of guilt, badge of transcendent distinction for man-
    kind, 984
  of proportion, concerned in exercise of virtue, 193
  of spiritual dominance essential to personality unity,
    1480
senses, approach universe through s, turns universe
    inside out, 1135
  higher spiritual orders have 70 to 210 s, 154
  Nalda brought to her s, 1613
SENSITIZERS, ETHICAL, 433
sensual urges, not suppressed by religious rebuke or
    legal prohibitions, 1582
sentiment, false, that perpetuates defective strains, 592
  the supreme, 1546
SENTINELS, ASSIGNED, 268, 413
separation, church and state, great peace move, 784
Sepharvites, installed in place of Jews, 1612
Sepphoris, 1350, 1992
  boy J heard unjust decision of Herod at S, 1393
  heartbroken Rebecca induced father, move to S, 1403
  J advised associates avoid S and Tiberias, 1531
  J worked as smith at S, 1410
  Joseph (J' father) killed at S, derrick fell, 1388
  low morals, 1684
  one of many Galilean cities rebuilt by Antipas, 1334
  3 miles from Nazareth, 1368
sepulchers, whited, 1826, 1908
sequence, complex content to simple, (U Book), why, 215
  epochal U revelations, 1007
    Caligastia, Planetary Prince, 500,000 years ago,
      701
    Adam and Eve, 38,000 years ago, 735, 741, 828
    Melchizedek, 4000 years ago, 1015
    Jesus, 2000 years ago, 1351
    Urantia Book (dated 1934), 707
    (see also "date of Urantia Book")
Serapatatia, 840, 849
  lieutenant of Adam, led to Eve's downfall, 840, 842, 849
  played into hands of Caligastia, Daligastia, 841
seraphic and other space velocities, 260 (see also
    "seraphim")
SERAPHIC COMMANDER, A LOYAL, 606
seraphic, departures from U, 327, 348

250

seraphic (cont'd)
SERAPHIC DESTINY, 440
SERAPHIC DOMAINS OF ACTION, 1245
seraphic estates, beauty and vastness, 420
SERAPHIC EVANGELS, 552
seraphic guardians, increasing numbers as mortals
   attain circles, 626
SERAPHIC GUARDIANS OF DESTINY, 1241
seraphic, guardians of J, 1357
   guidance helped assemble 100 scattered mortals, 742
   helpers make selves visible, 574
SERAPHIC HOSTS, THE, 426
SERAPHIC MINISTRY TO MORTALS, 1245
SERAPHIC ORGANIZATION, 421
SERAPHIC PLANETARY GOVERNMENT, 1250
seraphic reunions, each millenium, 420
SERAPHIC SPIRITS OF BROTHERHOOD, 437
seraphic supervision on U, 1254, -57
SERAPHIC TRAINING, 420
seraphic, transport techniques, 430
   vision, reinforced, 439
SERAPHIC WORLDS, THE, 420
seraphim (see also "angels" and "guardian angels")
   (Planetary government rules chiefly through seraphim,
      1250; of origin in local u, 440; 500 million pair on
      U, 1250. Individuals (human) have their guardian
      angels, 136; who influence you every way con-
      sistent with dignity of your personality, 1245)
SERAPHIM, ADMINISTRATOR, 434
SERAPHIM, ADOPTED, 348
SERAPHIM AND THE ASCENDANT CAREER, 1248
seraphim, and supernaphim, recording, 302
   are personal agency of Infinite Spirit, 1245
   are the traditional angels of heaven, 1241
   attain Paradise in 100s of ways, 440
   attending humans, exclusive s privilege, 422
   become guardians of destiny, 1242
   cherubim, sanophim, become s, 551
   Chief of Seraphim, authored the following papers in
      the U Book, 82-84, 113-114
   closely associated with material creatures, 421
   constantly manipulating environment, 1245
   defenders of mortals, why, 428
   disagreement between s of churches and s of progress,
      1486
   do not invade sanctity of mind, 1245
   essential part of mortal progression, 1245
SERAPHIM, EVOLUTIONARY, 443
seraphim, fall into seven orders, groups, 422, 426
   formal statement in extenuation, 1223
   function on spiritual and literal levels, 419
   guardian s drawn from all ranks of experienced...440
   high orders can't necessarily perform what lower
      can, 426
SERAPHIM, THE HOME, 1256
seraphim, how assigned to mortals, 1241
   is teacher of man's evolving nature, 1245
   known as (J') "mighty angels", 422
   live in pairs, negative and positive, 420
   lone, accompanied Michael on 6th bestowal, 1315
   manipulate environment, 1244-45
SERAPHIM, MASTER, OF PLANETARY SUPERVISION,
   1254
seraphim, mathematical prodigies, 419
   may range all Nebadon, even Orvonton, 421
   mind-stimulators, toward circle-making decisions,
      1245
   ministers, are, 418
   most nearly standard of spirit beings, 418
   no "supreme s" lost in rebellion, 608
   not male, female, but "aggressive", "retiring", 938

seraphim (cont'd)
   number on U "at noon" 501, 234, 619 pairs, 1250
SERAPHIM OF THE FUTURE, 440
seraphim, of planetary supervision, 12 corps on U as:
      1255
   of U, sang over J' manger, birthday, 1352
   on mansion worlds, will be conscious of, 1245
   on U now; teach--exchange your mind for J' m, 553
SERAPHIM, ORIGIN OF, 418
seraphim, report of s on her mortal subject, 1223
SERAPHIM RESERVES, THE, 431, 433, 436, 439
seraphim, seek to promote circle-making decisions, 1245
   still being created, 418
SERAPHIM, SUPERIOR, 429
SERAPHIM, SUPERVISOR, 432
SERAPHIM, SUPREME, 427
seraphim, told Ardnon, J was coming, 1317
   the traditional angels of heaven, 1241
   trifle ahead of mortal races, 419
   12 legion (plus other beings) at J' service, 1516
   usually serve in pairs, 1243
   with cherubim and sanophim, angelic corps of local u,
      418
   work through social, ethic, moral environment, 1245
Seraphington, 443   "bosom of Son and Spirit", 146
   destiny sphere for angels, 441
   mystery, spirit servers closely related to us, 147
SERMON ON FORGIVENESS, THE, 1762 (see also
   "sermons" under "Jesus")
SERMON ON THE KINGDOM (see "sermon" under
   "Jesus")
SERMON ON THE LIGHT OF THE WORLD, 1794
"SERMON ON THE MOUNT", 1570, -72, -75
Sermon on the Mount, is not the gospel, little
   instruction, 1572
sermon, Peter's Pentecost, 2060
serpent, has been revered, 968
serpents, 946   Hebrews worshipped, 946
   "wise as", 1580, -84, 1801, 1930
servant, apostles reluctant to be s of the others, 1937
SERVANT, THE CENTURION'S, 1647
servants, transition, Jerusem, 523
   usually served meals, none at last supper, 1936
serve, in humiliation, 1965
   "men as I have served you" (J), 2041, -44
served people, J, 1461
server of all, "he who would be greatest" (J), 316
service, all s is sacred and exhilarating, 273
   and joy, highest in establishment of homes, 1839
   essential, sacred, 273, 316
   finaliters serve in own s u last, 345
   for courageous, 1608
   goal of time, 316
   highest concept of brotherhood, 2017
   highest honors, 1839
   is the KEY, 316
   loving, great privilege, 1600
   measure of capacity for self-respect, 1740
   motive, must augment "gain" motive, 787, 805
   news-gathering of all creation in constant operation,
      201
SERVICE, THE SANCTITY OF, 316
SERVICE, SATISFACTION OF, 312
service insensitivity, 786
service ministry, filled with mercy, motivated by love,
   1175
service of self, is distorting (non-religious human
   activities), 67
servile, Caligastia and Daligastia now s, 610
SERVITALS, THE HAVONA, 273

Servitals (cont'd)
  138 billion on Uversa's 490 satellites, 274
  vanish, Graduate Guides appear, 271
servitude, involuntary
  mental defectives, social delinquents, compelled to
    labor, 585
  normal in early times, 585
Set, god of darkness and evil, 1048
  lost eye restored by spit, 1044
Seth, oldest surviving son Adam & Eve, 2nd garden, 849
Sethard, one of 7 outstanding human teachers, 1339
Sethite priesthood, ancestors of present Brahmans, 882
  by 2000 B.C. Mesopotamia had about lost teachings
    of S p, 1042
  dominated one of 7 major religious epochs (post-
    Adam), 1009
  lineal cultural descendants of priests of second
    garden, but, 882
  made marriage a religious ritual, 929
  many to India, influenced leaning to religions, 881
  modified Levantine religious evolution, 1007
  16,000 B.C. nearly converted 1/2 of India, 881
  tithing in ancient times, 1016
  true educators, 850
  zeal of S equaled by followers of J, 1084
Sethites, 873,876,898
SETTING OF THE STAGE, THE, 1707
seven Absolutes, infinite reality is existential as s A,
    named, listed, 4-5   (see also "Absolutes")
SEVEN ABSOLUTES OF INFINITY, 1154-55
seven aspects of salvation, 1112
"seven circles of the universe", 947
seven, colors in the natural spectrum, 480
  commandments, the (Salem), 1017
  coordinate Absolutes, total infinite reality
    existential as s c A, 4
  developmental epochs, civilization, 577,589
  higher spiritual influences, the, 2062
  periods of s, basic elements in order of atomic
    weights, 480
  significance of the number 7, 479-80
  vs. ten, where each prevails, 479
  why the scheme of 7, 184   (see also "sevenfold")
Seven Circuit Spirits, 1272
SEVEN CRUCIAL YEARS, THE (J), 756
SEVEN MANSION WORLDS, THE (see "mansion
  worlds")
SEVEN MASTER SPIRITS, THE, 184 (see also "Master
  Spirits")
Seven Master Spirits, 150,271,273,287
  and Infinite Spirit, 186
  and Morontia, 189
  are coordinating directors of grand universe, 197
  bestowals and, 1318
  Conjoint Actor's primary personalities, 206
  direction of the grand universe, 150
  distributors of Infinite Spirit to universes, 106
  in Zoroastrianism, 1050
  origin of 7-fold, 184
  portrayal of sevenfold Deity, 185
  tradition lingered in Ur, 1049
SEVEN MASTER SPIRITS, VOICE OF THE, 308
seven prayers from other worlds, 1621
SEVEN PSYCHIC CIRCLES, THE, 1209
SEVEN SACRED WORLDS OF THE FATHER, 144
SEVEN SPIRITS OF THE CIRCUITS, THE, 202
"seven spirits of God", 378
seven stages (of settled existence) on a planet, 627
SEVEN SUPERUNIVERSES, 164
SEVEN SUPERUNIVERSES, PURPOSES OF THE, 181

seven (cont'd)
SEVEN SUPREME EXECUTIVES, 198,268-69
SEVEN SUPREME POWER DIRECTORS, 271,273
SEVEN SUPREME SPIRIT GROUPS, THE, 197
SEVEN TRIUNITIES, 1147
sevenfold, appeal of... spirit influences, 2062
Sevenfold Deity, 184-45,1291
sevenfold electronic organization of prematter, 479
Sevenfold God, the, (see "God, the Sevenfold")
sevenfold, persistence of creative constitution, 480
  salvation, 1112
  scheme, atomic world, a birthmark indicative of...
    479
    because only 7 Master Spirits possible, 184
    electronic organization of matter, 479
    of superuniverse organization and government, 164
    reality of s diversity of creations, 480
    seven is basic to central universe and... 479
    seven possible associations of triune Deity, 186
    suggested 7 day week, 751
    Trinity, 7 different singular and plural capacities,
      110
seventh day for worship, incidental in Eden, 837
seventh heaven, 174
SEVENTH OR SUPERUNIVERSE STAGE, THE, 636
Seventy, The (teachers, trained, experienced in pro-
    claiming the gospel, selected from some 250
    evangelists and disciples ordained by J, 1800)
  coincident, the number in, 1806
  consisted of Abner and... 1800
SEVENTY, FAREWELL TO THE, 1804
seventy, the, instructions to, 1800,-04
  Jew and gentile, sent to... 1800
  most drawn from over 100 evangelists, 1658
SEVENTY, ORDINATION OF THE, AT MAGADAN, 1800
seventy, the, Peter's ordination sermon, 1805
  preached for 6 weeks, 1801
SEVENTY, THE RETURN OF THE, 1806
seventy times and seven, origin of phrase, Tubal
  Cain, 1764
"seventy times seven", after 490 opportunities,
  ascenders fail, 449
seventy times seven, opportunities for fusion, 449
seventy, the, training, 1800,-04
sewage disposal, Garden of Eden, 825
sex, and birth, connection not seen by primitives, 931
  and nonsex liaison, midwayers origin, 862
  attitudes, 1574
  attraction causes serious problems, 914
  Babylonians and others clung to disguised forms of s
    worship, 1042
  charms well used, 935
  Christianity imposed s obligations upon man, 937
  civilizer of the savage, 922
  compels thinking, leads to love, 922
  compensations on mansion worlds for sex-deficiency
    here, 516
  control, early peoples, 791
  each s will remain supreme in own domain, 938
  fatal price for s if marriage collapses as institution,
    943
  festivities of May Day, imitative magic, 972
  free love never approved above scale of rank
    savagery, 915
  gratification, 939,982
  home building should be essence of all educational
    effort, 931
  hunger of soul can't be satisfied with physical
    pleasures, 942
  insures men, women, coming together, 913

sex (cont'd)

laxity, 982

maiden to be sacrificed could instead enter temple s service, 982

male, female, but not s, 939

man's first form of trading was woman exchange, 776

marriage not founded on s, 931

Mesopotamian women submitted s to strangers, 1042-43

no consideration to T A, in considering indwelling, 1186

no reproduction of mortal kind after death, 516

one of 8 basic urges that led to capital, 776

primitive indulged s freely, no family responsibilities, 931

promiscuity, Roman baths, 1461

propensity must be regulated, 906

"pure in heart" referred to more than s attitudes, 1574

rewards improved hunting skill, 722

Salem teachers never overcame Ishtar's popularity (spirit of sex fertility), 1042

self-gratification incidental, non-essential, 765

(The Spirit and the Flesh), 382

temple sex service, subtle species of self-deception, 982

unrecognized, unsuspected civilizer of savage, 922

urge, lures man to become better than animal, 922

urge, unbridled, 914

used by intelligent women, 935

woman could redeem life from head-hunters by sexual surrender, 982

women earned dowries in temple sex service, 982

sex code, of evolutionary races, red man had highest, 913

sex control, a right of society, 793

sex-emotion creatures, we, not above us, 419

sexes, complete understanding between the s, no, 938

cooperation, but personally antagonistic, 939

equal, 564

sh

Shabattum, the seventh day, 1042

shackles of animalism, 231

shadow, can't reveal actuality, 29

"shall follow the substance", 1823

shadows of creation

brighter T A shines in man, greater the shadow cast by mind upon...141

God is light whose interruptions are creation shadows of all space, 1124

matter is...shadow of Paradise...shining of Deities, 648

personality, image-shadow cast by Creator p, 29

shadows of truth, material, 1641

Shalmaneser III, decided to control Mediterranean coast, 1074

shaman, often would gain all wealth of tribe, 988

SHAMANIC THEORY OF DISEASE AND DEATH, THE, 989

SHAMANISM--MEDICINE MEN AND PRIESTS, 986

SHAMANISTIC PRACTICES, 987

shamans, female, became snake venom addicts, 946

SHAMANS, THE FIRST, MEDICINE MEN, 986

SHAMANS, MEDICINE UNDER THE, 990

shamans, terribly expensive, but worth all they cost, 1006

"shame on false teachers" (J), 1731

sharing, master design for all who attempt perfection, 614

sharks, 679-80

shattered, plan for Jews as light-bearers, 1910

Shawnee Teuskwatowa, prophet, 988

sheep, go to lost s of Israel, 1681

God and Son search for, 1851

"in the midst of wolves" (J), 1584

lost, parable, 1762, -70

"not of this flock" (J), 1577

"not of this fold" (J), 1818-19

"search for the s gone astray" (J), 1851

shear, one man, ten men, 1476

sheep's clothing, 1571

shekel, fish with a s in his mouth, 1744

Shekinah, doctrine of, 1510

Shema, Jewish creed of faith, 1685

Sheol, phantom replica of man down to S, 953

SHEPHERD, THE LIFE OF A, 1497

SHEPHERD, SERMON ON THE GOOD, 1818 (see "Sermon" under "Jesus")

shepherds, the true and the false, 1818

wise men, homage at J' birth, no, 1352

shield against meteors, 660

shields, energy, for interplanetary transport, 438

Shin sect, Japan, progressive, 1041

Shinto (religion), 1011, 1451

Shintoism, proto-Taoism, 1033, -38

ship, is your mind, T A is pilot, will is captain, 1217

social, has steamed out of sheltered bays, 1086

shock, affects minds, 1976

shooting stars, 658, 967

short circuited, Solitary Messengers can be, 257

shortcomings of all who labor on U, 1189

shortcuts, J scorned using, 1520

never will you gain by impatient s, 846

to mansion worlds through advanced standing, 1232

SHREWD STEWARD, PARABLE OF THE, 1853 (see also "parables")

shrines, 25 on 1 planet, consuming bodies, 622

shudder of indignation swept over vast Universe, 1984, 1995, 2011

shut off, when spiritual appeals to men are shut off, hard to change attitudes, 1672

si

Siberia, huts like Cro-Magnon, 891-92

Sicily--and bridge to Africa, 826, 891

sick, "and afflicted, words of good cheer", 1649

material and spiritual methods, "kingdom's first hospital", 1658

shamefully neglected for long ages, 991

sickness, afflictions, 4 reasons for, 1649

"all s shall be taken away from you", 1629

"not to the death" (J), 1836, -42, -44, -48

should be banished (intimated by J), 1632

Siddim, battle of Abraham, 1020, -24

Sidon, J and associates 2-1/2 weeks in, 1734

siege, time of s you will be driven to eat (your dead), 1709

Sierras, 689-90, 696, 698

sifting, great, through which gospel believers...passed, 1741

of believers, the kingdom, 1715

sign, give us a s of your authority, 1714, -45

SIGNIFICANCE OF ORIGINS, THE, 314

SIGNIFICANCE OF PENTECOST, THE, 2060

SIGNIFICANCE OF THE SUPREME TO UNIVERSE CREATURES, 1281

significant, occurrences in all inhabited creation, recorded, 281

"signs of the times", 1745

Sikh, India divided among S, Hindu, Mohammedan, and Jain, 1011

Sikhism, adaptable, 1012
  budded and blossomed out of... 1012
  one of most advanced religions of Asia, 1010
  synthesized from Islam, Hinduism, Buddhism, 1010

Silas and Timothy joined Paul at Corinth, 1472

silent, cosmic contemplation, 622
  receptivity after prayer, 1641

Siloam, 1794
  taught use of material healing, 1813
  tower of S fell, killed 18 men, 1830

Silurian seas and inundation, 676, 678

silver, thirty pieces of, 1998 (see also "Judas" under "Apostles")

"silver, woman and 10 pieces of" (J), 1851

silvery trumpets, solemn blasts of the, 1794

Simeon and Anna at temple, 1353

Simeon, tomb of, "high place of Baal", 1387

Simian tribes, origin of the, 705

simians, ancestors survived by hiding from battle, 706
  due to retrograde, 700, 706
  from retarded twins, 706

similitude of the 3 Gods embraced in 1, energy, 468

Simon, a boat named S, built by J, 1628

Simon (brother of J) born A. D. 2, 1364, -96, 1410-12, -84
  to Passover with J, 1441

Simon from Cyrene, bore J' cross, 1438, 2006

Simon, member of Sanhedrin, 1606

Simon of Bethany, camp of J on plot of, 1895
  J said goodbye to the aged S, 1897

Simon Peter (Apostle), 1548 (see "Peter" under "Apostles")

Simon, the Pharisee, J read the mind of, 1651-52

SIMON THE PHARISEE, VISITING, 1651

SIMON THE ZEALOT (Simon Zelotes), 1564 (see under "Apostles")

simultaneous awareness with happening
  universe rulers, how, 105

simultaneous events, presented as sequential transactions, 6

sin, and forgiveness, 1861
  and suffering permitted, why?, 615, 1861
  "bondservant of s not likely to abide forever in master's house", 1796

SIN, THE CONCEPT OF, 975

sin, conscious choosing to oppose spiritual progress, 754
  conscious, deliberate rebellion, 2016
  conscious disloyalty to Deity, 984
  depicts failure to perceive obligations and duties of ... 1301
  depicts immaturity dazzled by freedom of will, 1301
  desire to s, not with sonship, 1683
  disloyalty to Deity, degrees of, 984
  effects never merely local, 761
  error, evil, iniquity, suggest, 613, 754-55

SIN, EVIL, AND INIQUITY, 1659

sin, experience of creature consciousness, 1898
  father of s turned face away from the horror, 1972

SIN, FORGIVENESS OF, 984

sin, full opportunity for s-expression is cure for plague of evil and s, 618
  God's foreknowledge of (?), 49
  good, and evil, 842
  harvest of naked facts, faced, 1998
  if God chooses to foreknow s, doesn't stop it, 49
  (is according to one's light) "now you have no excuse", 1947
  is act of conscious, deliberate rebellion, 2016
  is deliberate transgression, unwillingness to be led, 1660

sin (cont'd)
  is final result of, 37
  is measure of resistance to divine leading, 1660
  is rebellion brought by rebels, 1660
  knowingly resisting cosmic reality, 754
  new concept, 975
  no remission of s without blood (Hebrews), 60
  not due to defective nature, 1861
  not hereditary, 2016
  not part of God's consciousness, 1898
  not self-existent in finite world, 1222
  not transmitted parent to child, 2016
  nothing to do with bestowal plan, 2003
  offspring of a knowing mind, dominated by unsubmissive will, 1861
  origin, 1222
  original, mankind has no racial guilt, 2003
  original, origin of, 952, 974
  original, Paul's theory of, 1339
  the penalties of s inevitable, 1661
  personal, despite repercussions, 761
  pleasant adjustment to, 1566
  proves temporal liberty, even license, of finite will, 1301
  prevail, no?, 2063
  realization of true nature of s, 1998

SIN, REMOTE REPERCUSSIONS OF, 760

sin, result--annihilation, 37, 41
  retards, doesn't deprive of salvation, 761

SIN, SACRIFICE, AND ATONEMENT, 974

sin, sinner, and love, 41
  suggests, 755
  this man or his parents?, 1811
  "to convert wealth to treasures", 1821
  true nature, Judas, 1998
  vs. evil, 754, 842, 1660
  "wages of s is death", 529, 612
  "within every s is... seed of its own destruction", 612

Sinai, 1054, -56, -76
  clans, Yahweh, 1598

sincerity, has become sublime by arrival at Havona, 290
  J placed great value upon, 1582
  needs discretion, 1961
  of prayer assures hearing, 1639
  a pure heart, 1582

sin-darkened sphere of U, 1984

sinful, human nature not, 1739
  man, "depart from me Master, for I am a s m", 1629
  pleasures of time vs. righteous realities of eternity, 1745

singers, the, 501

Singlangton, 724, 885, 1032-33
  teacher of the "One Truth", 887

single-eyed can't comprehend reality, 1454

SINGLE-ORIGIN BEINGS, 332

Sinkiang, dominated by Andites, 872-74, 885
  Eastern Turkestan, 878

sinners (Lucifer rebellion), why not adjudicated, destroyed quickly, 619

"sins forgiven if you confess", 1736

sins, of rulers of the Jews, 1906

sinus (?), gas chambers close to Adam, Eve, brains, 834

situation, alarming, fewer and fewer people with Self-Acting T A, 1207
  tough, crisis at Capernaum, 1711

situations, 3 recurring s throughout his ministry (J), 1523

Siva, 1031

six races, purpose of the, 726

Sixth Century B. C.
  awakening, new, to monotheism, 1078
  great religionists, 1009

Sixth Century B.C. (cont'd)
    Salem gospel restated, 1033
    unique century of spiritual progress, 1033
    Zoroaster, great man, 1050
SIXTH DECISION, THE, 1523
sizes of spheres of constellation, 485

skeletal structures, 3, 905
SKEPTIC, THE, 1336
skill, is acquired, ability is inherited, 1779
    necessity for, 1779
skip, the mansion worlds, highly cultured beings, 288,
    537 (see "mansion worlds, at once after death")
    none of seven Havona circuits (billion worlds), 288

sl

slate or shale (organic carbon), 671, 674
slaughter of animals, why?, 1375
slave, Borneans kill s to make ghost journey with
    master, 960
    savage was a s to usage, 767
    wife buried alive at master's death, 860
slavery, and race decadence, Rome, 2074
SLAVERY AS A FACTOR IN CIVILIZATION, 778
slavery, came with agriculture, 902
    compelled backward and lazy people to work, 779
    compelled invention of social regulations, 779
    early church tolerant of s because, 1335
    gave origin to beginnings of government, 779
    gravest of all destructive social maladies, 779
    grotesque systems of religious s (without God), 2095
    in Roman state, time of J, 1335
    indispensable link in civilization, 779
    led to social advancement, 779
    like polygamy, is passing, doesn't pay, 779
    Lucifer claimed ascendant plan for mortals enslaved
      celestials, 604
    no grave economic results, abolition, 813
    of church, then of state, without God, 2081
    of custom, races never liberated from, 749
    one of civilization's first four great advancements, 901
    origin, 774, 778, 934
    origin of s, early ages on planets, 585
    polygamy recognized slave wives, 926
    sex, polluted superior peoples, 776, 892, 895-96
    slaves built alive into walls, 981
    tasks making low grade demands are s for higher
      types, 771
    threat of industrial s, 786
    to tradition, 749
    usually ends after Adamic arrival, 585
    was advancement over massacre, cannibalism, 779
    weapons ended s to food, 768
    woman's liberation from domestic, 937
slaves, Claudius freed 117 after J' talk, 1461
    early church largely lower classes and s (Rome's
      conquests), 1335
    erode civilization, 895
    half the Roman state, 1335
    inferior deported, better were made citizens, 813
    inferior, numerous, Romans, 1468
    inferior s adulterated religion in Greece, 1077
    many (freed) slaves rose to high positions, 1335
    master fear concepts into God-love, 1013
    Mediterranean society, 1st century A.D., 1335
    progeny of s deteriorated blue man, 892; Greeks,
      895-96
    "shall your disciples own slaves?", 1603
    sudden liberation disastrous, 779

slavish creatures
    convert energies into physical state not known on U,
      328
    order of life beyond our comprehension, 328
    primary associators are the most, 328
sleep, five years or 5000, same reaction, 341
    J did not s that night, 1532
    there shall be no more, 299
    transit, 296-97, 318
    watchdogs made s possible for clan, 778
slothful deserter, who refuses to survive, 1199
slow thinkers, billions on worlds of space, 1557
slumbering spiritual forces, lures to man's, 1777
slumbers, J' concept of kingdom now, 1866
smiths, early, were magicians, 774
    first nonreligious with privileges, 774
smoke signal, primitive message, 775
smugness, social, vs. stoical resignation, 1268

snake, female shamans became s venom addicts, 946
    (serpent) revered in Palestine, 946, 968
snakes, barren wives become, 928
    60 million years ago, true s, 691
sneezing, soul's attempt to escape, 954
snow, crystals, hexagonal, no two alike, 1220
    deep in Nazareth, 1361
    20,000 feet deep, 699

so

soar, no bird can soar except by outstretched wings
    (prayer), 1002
social action church
    displaced spiritual concept of kingdom, 1864
social
    activities, all must become spiritually motivated, 794
    advancement, J no rules for, 2093
    and civil realms, J ignored, 1580
    and recreational life neglected, 1388
social architects, 432
SOCIAL ASPECTS OF RELIGION, 1090
social attainment, ideal of s a., how, 2093
social
    attitude (apostles), 1580
    brotherhood and spiritual b, 1865
SOCIAL CHANGES, 911
social
    changes as factor in U civilization, 911
    changes, imperative to avoid disaster, 1086
SOCIAL CLASSES, 792
social
    classes, flexible, indispensable, 793
    consciousness, from moral nature, 1131
      is alienable, 196
      is dependent on...196
    cooperation requires leadership, 911
    customs uplifted vs. exchanged, 749
    deprivations, victims of s d by smug...1268
    development, most advanced, white, yellow, 763
      next age of, 910
    disgust, for idleness and unearned wealth, 814
    evils, indiscriminate kindness blamed for s e, (J),
      1580
    evolution, accelerate only by applying spiritual
      pressure, 598
      based on marriage, 913
      basic facts of, 801
      only technique for accelerating, spiritual
        pressure, 598
      rebellion cannot accelerate, 830

social (cont'd)
    fraternity on U, 597
social gospel,(reform), vs. proclaiming truth, is
    failure, 1043
    religion aids progress of all through fostering
        progress of each individual, 1094
social group, how gets all knowledge, 1776
    in working harmony, force greater than sum of
        parts, 1477
    most effective, 1775
    responsiveness to sufferings of s g through religion
        only, 1086
    three persons are a minimum, 110
social
    groups, right to use force, 1929
social growth, cannot be secured by legislation, 1097
social harmonization, 504
social
    harmony, not at cost of free personality and spiritual
        originality (J), 1591
SOCIAL HOUR, THE LAST (J), 1927
social ills, evils, 1580
social improvement, slow but effectual method, (the
    100), 749
social improvements, and J, 1576
social
    improvements, natural fruits of kingdom, 1865
    inheritance, man stands on shoulders, 909 *
    laboratories of Edentia, 433   *(see non-religionist)
    "lever, fruits of the spirit", 1930
social maturity, true badge of...pursuit of spiritual
    realities, 1773
    vs. immaturity, 1772-73
social mechanism, insurance plan to protect against
    antisocial, 906
    a single, from 3 practices, 772
Social Ministry, (see also under "Jesus")
social ministry, religion's s m highest when no secular
    connections, 1086
social
    misunderstanding, avoid sin through tact and
        tolerance, 1740
    morality, not determined by evolutionary religion,
        1005
    optimism (secular), illusion without God, 2082
social order, change it very slowly, 782
    change, make certain it's for better, 782
    new, introduced, (on high), 536
    not business of kingdom, 1565,-76,1605-10
    serene, not for a millenium, 1086
    to be reconstructed, 1087
    value to s o in J' teaching, is ministry of genuine
        personal religious experience, 1585
social
    parasites, professional alms-seekers, 1580
    problem, 3 or more persons grouped for service, 433
    problems, moral power, spiritual energy...for
        difficult s p, 1739
SOCIAL PROBLEMS OF RELIGION, THE, 1086
social
    progress, comes from 907
        only if leisure used for more valuable tasks, 909
SOCIAL PROGRESSION, FACTORS IN, 764
social
    reaction to J, replacing spiritual, is tragedy, 1864
    readjustment, U on brink of amazing, enthralling
        s r, 2082
    reconstruction, extensive s r continuing in 20th
        century, 1086
SOCIAL RECONSTRUCTION, RELIGION AND, 1086

social (cont'd)
    reconstruction (cont'd)
        world-wide, impending, 1087
    relations new, require religion, 1087
SOCIAL REPERCUSSIONS OF PRAYER, 998
social service, comes from "brotherly" affection, 1603
    derives from, 1133,1770
    fruits of personal religion, 1862
    is a certain effect of...true religion, 1770
    J didn't teach essence of his r consisted in s s, but,
        1770
    manifestation of religion, 1862
    no substitute for gospel, 1931
    not business of kingdom, but of kingdom believers,
        1565,1603,-24,1770
    not essence of J' religion, but effect of it, 1770
    people ever progressing to goal of, 806
social ship, on high seas of evolutionary destiny, 1086
social situations, (J), patience, tolerance, forgiveness,
    1580
social smugness in the fortunate, 1268
social
    spiritual, relationships of home, 1922
    stability purchased at cost of lessened personal
        initiative, 793
    standing, independent of money, 1392,1402
    strata, exceptions, 792
social structure, civilization of mortal maturity, 1777
    great, glorified s s from effective small units of
        human association, 1777
social system, J recommended no, 1580
    without morality, doomed (like solar system without
        gravity), 2075
social
    systems, industrial policies, faulty, 2086
    "tolerance, patience, forgiveness", 1580
social uplift, by improving a race's own mores, 749
social
    usage, not good to follow, 1457-58
        rapid changes in s u make character-forming hard,
        1772
SOCIAL VALUE OF WAR, THE, 785
social vs. religious gatherings--communion, 1133
socialists, 1091
socialization, of personality, seven things to learn,
        constellation training worlds, 494
    of religion, a real purpose in, 1092
    yes, of gospel, no, 1565,1624,2082
    protective, 763
    real, supernal cultural acquirement, 494
    70 spheres of advanced s, 1248
socialize, we learn to s egoistic ambitions, 508
SOCIALIZING INFLUENCE OF GHOST FEAR, 766
socializing value of friendship, 1775
socially, downtrodden, joy to, 1541
    indifferent, low standards, 1457
    unfit, not needed, ample other opportunities for
        exercise of noble traits, 592
society, beneficent club, no, 906
    better than ancestors, 782
    breaks down without superhuman help, 766
    can improve--neighboring planet, 811,815
    character trend of s set by preceding generation, 909
    complex, requires augmented spirit energies, 1777
    concerned with 3 things, 764
    controlled by a law (population, land arts, standard
        of living), 769
    a cooperative scheme for securing...906
SOCIETY, CULTURAL, 905
society, cultural s a recent phenomenon, 764

society (cont'd)
duty of s, 3-fold, 794
evolves cyclically through "fear" and reluctant cooperation, 763
founded on needs, basic urges, 766
good, impossible with weak and wicked lying in wait, 804
greatest factor (probably) in evolution of, 766
has limits without superhuman help, 766
human, plunging forward, 912
ideals this generation, carve destiny of next, 909
immature if, 1772
in reverse, 780
is as the families, 939
is guild of earth-workers, 906
is not a divine institution, 911
made best by J' religion, 2093
measure of advance of a, 797, 802-03, 1462
measure of its institutions, 1388
Mediterranean, 5 well-defined strata, 1335
modern, and marriage, great inconsistency of, 929
modern, in dangerous phase, 765
must continue to evolve, 804
must evolve if it is to remain, 804
must have superhuman help, 766
must prevent, 798
must provide for self-realization, 794, 803
new order of, 1862
none has endured loss of mores, except for better, 767
now, thanks to ancient taboos, 975
organized s has right to use force in execution of its mandate (J), 1470, -75
organized, use force against unjust minorities, 1891
phenomenon of progressive evolution, 911
plunging forward, 912
primitive, 4 divisions, 777
savagery to barbarism, 10 groups, reasons for, 792
staggers under guilt of... 2086
strain of dangerous phase now, 765
this s slowly disintegrating, 2082
through fire, slavery, animals, property, 777
two goals, self-control, social service, 806
two problems, 1773
ultimate achievement can't surpass, 2093
will fail to grow up to maturity if... 1772
sociological pronouncements, no (J), 1580
sociologist, J was not a s, 1580
materialistic, of today, 2077
sociologists, skilled, on m w, 553
sociology, displaced for first time by theology, 1075
sociophilosophical system of J' followers, 1866
Socrates, what he taught, 1079
Socratic, ideals of western world, 1077
sodium, atom, capable of light and energy locomotion, 462
Sodom, and Gomorrah, natural destruction legend fabricated, 1021-22
Lot went to S to go into business, 1019
soft answer turns away wrath... 1555, 1687
soil, architectural worlds, 527
for religious growth, 1094
work with s, not a curse but a blessing, 752
sojourn, we mortals will s on a billion worlds, 270
Sojourns of Jesus (see under "Jesus")
Sol Invictus (sun-god), 1082
solar, emanations, 170
energy for life maintenance, 1276
SOLAR-ENERGY REACTIONS, 464
SOLAR ENERGY, SOURCES OF, 463

solar (cont'd)
extrusion, Angona, 657
SOLAR RADIATION, 460
solar, spectra, why s s show iron so importantly, 462
supergases, density like iron, 460-61
solar system, all planets and satellites of s s growing, 658
evolved from gases, 656
few have had similar origin, 655
fifth planet of s s fragmentized by Jupiter, 658
functioning as today for 3 billion years, 658
location of our, 168
name, Monmatia, 655
not plunging headlong... cosmic path is well charted, 165
of atom, energy units faintly similar to our s s, 477
origin, 651
double, 656
from Angona solar extrusion, 657
gravity-explosion, 170-71
ours is diminutive, 652
ours named, registered 3 billion years ago, 658
planets, twelve, 656
Saturn, Jupiter middle planets, 656
Saturn, Jupiter still largely gaseous, 656
SOLAR SYSTEM STAGE, THE -- the planet-forming era, 657
solar system, stage set for unique origin of our s s, 655
sunspot cycles, 11-1/2 years, 655
three planets suitable to harbor life, 173
SOLAR SYSTEM, THE URANTIA, ORIGIN, 655
solar system, without gravity, 2075
soldiers and J' garments, 2007
SOLEMNITY OF TRUST, 315
SOLITARINGTON, 146
Solitarington, "bosom of Father and Spirit", 146
solitary, existence enjoyed, only one group, 257
meditation not necessary to receive spirit, 2064
SOLITARY MESSENGERS, THE, 256, 413
Solitary Messengers, all equal, 256
SOLITARY MESSENGERS, ASSIGNMENTS OF, 257
Solitary Messengers, go and come, Urantia, 841
billions mps, 261
SOLITARY MESSENGERS, NATURE AND ORIGIN OF, 256
Solitary Messengers, not lonesome spirits, 256
personality coordinators, 262, 1190
questions about, 262
sense nearness of T A, 257
seven divisions of service, 258
SOLITARY MESSENGERS, SPECIAL MINISTRY OF, 262
SOLITARY MESSENGERS, TIME AND SPACE SERVICES OF, 260
Solitary Messengers, unique, 256, 261, 329, 413
withstand temperatures and terrible conditions, 329
solitary wanderings, year of J' s w, Palestine, Syria, 1492
Solomon (son of David and Bathsheba), 951, 1073
and taxation, 1072
bankrupted the nation, 1073
continued all the tyranny and taxation of David, 1073
"even S in all his glory" (J), 1823
harem almost 1000, 1073
purged father's political machine of all northern influences, 1073
"so are... men snared in an evil time", 951
vast Hebrew navy, Syrian sailors, 1073
Solomon, Wisdom of, evidences penetration by Stoicism and Platonic philosophy, 1338
SOLOMON'S PORCH, TEACHING IN, 1790, -96, 1815

Son of Man (cont'd)
Nazareth, a divided sentiment regarding, 1398
SON OF MAN ON URANTIA, THE, 609
Son of Man, "Psalmist, erroneous ideas about S of M",
1725
represented last chance of Jews to attain world
dominion, 1522
stood in John (B's) immediate presence (for baptism),
1504
term "S of M", idea from Book of Enoch, 1390
"will not lead armies in battle... for power... or
glory, 1536
"you shall know... as Prince of Peace", 1536
"your leaders plan the murder of the", 1826

SONARINGTON, "BOSOM OF THE SON" SPHERE, 145,
1327

sons, and daughters of God, in kingdom all are equally
s and d of G, 1679
(children) of the Supreme God of experience, 1240
SONS, CREATURE-TRINITIZED, THE, 251, 296
sons, divine s of the P F of all personalities, 1240
in reserve for next age, 1280
liberated faith s, 1942
"of Annas", 1889
of destiny, trinitized, 251, 262
"of faith and truth", 2034
of the kingdom, liberated, 1589, 1930
of the kingdom, three obligations, 1930
of space, what a glorious destiny for (mortal), 354
of thunder, 1955
trinitized s of unrevealed destiny, 262

sons of God, ascending s achieve status by evolution, 223
because, 448
by faith alone, 2003
children of the Highest, 448
drawn to one another, 1949
faith-enlightened, spirit-liberated, 1930
freedom from fear, 1655
God loves you, his s, 2052
grow in grace by faith... 1656
how to become truly the s of G, 1797
"I have revealed you as the s of G on earth", 2052
men are the s of G, through faith realize this
ennobling truth, 2052
"men who through faith and love have become s of G",
1991
no matter mens' status, to J were all God's children,
2093
perfected, 295
praise Infinite for what he is, not does, 1675
"proclaimed joy", 87
robust, liberated, 1861
salvaged, 1851
Trinity-embraced, of dual or single origin, 243
Urantia mortals, why, 448
you... are all indeed the, 2053

Sons, all Paradise Sons are as the SON of God, 232
"and Daughters of God" J spoke on, 1686
are perfect personalities, 28
SONS, ASCENDER-TRINITIZED, 251
Sons, caused suffering, 1632
Creature-trinitized, 198, 251
SONS, CREATURE-TRINITIZED, 296
Sons, divine, determine successive planetary ages, 589
divine Sons are "Word of God", 111
divine, unexpected visitations of d S may or may not
occur, 514
divine, why?, 58

Sons (cont'd)
SONS, GLORIFIED MATERIAL, 349
SONS, THE LANONANDEK, 392
SONS, THE MAGISTERIAL, 224
Sons, Magisterial, personalized by Son and Spirit, 88
Magisterial, Teacher will come to U, 598
SONS, MASTER, RELATION TO THE UNIVERSE, 240
(see under "M")
SONS, MATERIAL, 415, 514
SONS, MATERIAL, GLORIFIED, 349
SONS, THE MELCHIZEDEK, 385
Sons, of Attainment, Trinitized, 243-44
SONS OF DESTINY, TRINITIZED, 251
Sons, of Perfection, Trinitized, 243-44
of Selection, Trinitized, 243-44
of the Trinity, Stationary, 144
SONS OF THE TRINITY, STATIONARY, 218
Sons, Origin and Nature of Creator, 234
original Michael, 234
Paradise, attribute of bestowal inherent in P S, 1308
SONS, THE PARADISE CREATOR, 234
Sons, Paradise-Havona trinitized, 251
SONS, PARADISE, OF GOD, 87
Sons, Stationary, of the Trinity, 218
SONS, THE TRINITY EMBRACED, 243
SONS, THE TRINITY TEACHER, 214, 230
SONS, UNITED MINISTRY OF THE PARADISE, 232
SONS, THE VOICE OF THE CREATOR, 308
SONS, THE VORONDADEK, 389
SONS, THE WORLD OF THE, 510

Sons, Creator
how created, 88
over 700,000, 235
rule of C S is for spiritualization, 37
SONS, CREATOR, VOICE OF THE, 308
Sons, Creator, well nigh 1,000,000 C S of Paradise, 1299

Sons of God
SONS OF GOD, THE, 335
SONS OF GOD, THE ASCENDING, 443
SONS OF GOD, BESTOWAL OF THE PARADISE, 227
SONS OF GOD, CIRCLES OF THE, 523-24
Sons of God, clearly discernible by... created intelli-
gences, 44
SONS OF GOD, THE DESCENDING, 223
Sons of God, devoted to helping us gain goal, 232
SONS OF GOD, THE FAITH, 447
Sons of God, Lanonandek, 741
Lanonandek, tendency to fall into error, 395
SONS OF GOD, THE LOCAL UNIVERSE, 384
Sons of God, made the universes, 21, 24
SONS OF GOD, MATERIAL, ORIGIN AND NATURE OF,
349, 415, 514, 580, 828
SONS OF GOD, PARADISE, 223
SONS OF GOD, PARADISE, BESTOWALS OF, 227
SONS OF GOD, PARADISE CREATOR, 234, 307
Sons of God, Paradise, of threefold origin, 224
SONS OF GOD, PARADISE, UNITED MINISTRY OF, 232
Sons of God, THE PLANETARY ADAMS, 580
THE PLANETARY PRINCES, 572
3 groups, descending, ascending, Trinitized, 243
SONS OF GOD, TRINITIZED, 243
SONS OF GOD, UVERSA REGISTER, 334-35

sonship, accepted, not enough, 1916
and brotherhood existed throughout eternity, 2002
SONSHIP AND CITIZENSHIP, DISCOURSE ON (J), 1929
(see also "Jesus, on")
sonship, by grace, through faith, 1621
divine s by faith, 1725

sonship (cont'd)
    experience of faith, 2097
    four orders of s have visited U, 584
    human stones (make) living temple of s, 1747
    incompatible with sin, 1683
    is the supreme relationship, 454
    local universe, 4 orders, 384
    mighty stimulator, 1931
    ministry, normal success of 4 orders of, 584
    no capacity for, mind not normal, 1441
    only experience that makes fatherhood certain, 1126
    stimulus to powers of personality, 1931
    with God, actuality of, 2097

Sontad, wife of S, his oldest sister, 713
sophistries, twin s, self-determination and sovereignty,
    1489
sordid performances called "spiritualism", 865
sordid scenes, man dominated by own baser passions, 57
sorrow, capacity to withstand brooding in deep s, 1740
    for vast universe, (crucifixion), 2011
    J man of s, NO, 1766, 1954
    the most terrible, wounded in house of trusted friend,
      1677
    much s, ambitions disappointed, pride wounded, 1674
    none in face of divine duty...performed, 274
    upon death replaced by joy, 623
SOUL, THE ADJUSTER AND THE, 1215 (see "Thought
    Adjuster")
soul, affirmations of He (vs. intellectual It), 2093
    all races have word for s, 1216
    ancients believed s could leave body, 954
    and Adjuster, 1215
    and Adjuster's memory pattern, 1230
    ascending, judgment of s based on service, 274
    attitude of vs. behavior, 1584
    believers, step aside from life, refresh the s, 1739
    birth of s, first moral decision (T A), 1478
    birth of s gradual, joint offspring...1218
    -bound powers of divinity, how release?, 1777
    can evolve without mental culture, but not without
      capacity and desire, 739
    characteristics of, 1478
    child of...1288-89
    -conflict, all forms of, lack of harmony between
      moral and intellectual self-consciousness (J), 1478
    consciousness, the ideal of God, 69
    creation of s, three factors, not two, 1218
SOUL, DISCOURSE ON (J), 1477 (see also "Jesus, on")
soul, divine invasion of s, with moral choice, 2095
    each, develop in its own way, 1582
    earmark of great, 1740
    elemental needs of, 1771
    emancipation of mind and s, not without...1773
    every...mortal knows of his s as a real experience,
      1479
    evolution of s possible because mind is personal, in
      contact with superanimal realities, 1218
    evolved by Adjuster upon mind in accord with
      choosing of personality bestowed by parental act
      of F, 333
    evolved from mind by T A with cooperation of
      personality, 1216
    evolves, supreme undertaking where mind and spirit
      dualize s, 195
    evolves within the mortal mind, 404
SOUL, THE EVOLVING, 1218
soul, evolving, difficult to describe, 1478
    evolving, indwelt by T A and I S, 1178
    evolving vehicle for selfhood continuity, 1218

soul (cont'd)
    expansion, faith helps, 1619
    an experiential acquirement, 8
    flowering of an immortal s, 1282
    from inception is real, has survival qualities, 195
    God-knowing s dares to say: "I know", 1125
    growth comes on morontia worlds, 744
    healer and spirit liberator, J, 1345
    "her s is in progressive motion" (J), 165
    hope-door of man's s, 2083
    human s, the reborn child of the indwelling spirit,
      1670
    -hunger, can't satisfy with physical pleasure, 942
    -hunger, spiritual disquiet, religion is cure, 1078
    -hunger, T A arouses unfailingly, 1119
    if change in s ceased, soul would cease, 1226
    "if wealth does not invade precincts of the s", 1804
    immortal s, is spiritualized mind, 1286
    insight of s, approach through (4 things), 2076
    is, 1288
    is embryonic in mortal, 744
    is matter of eternal import, 276
    is mustered into the Corps of the Finality, 1286
    is real, 195
    J could see into heart of God and at same time into
      depths of man's s, 1603
    J on the s, 1477-78, 1653 (see also under "Jesus, on")
    J portrayed needs of s with new insight, 1771
    "jointly created, living growth", 1738
    joy of outpoured S of T unfailing energy for s, 2065
    known through cosmic insight, spiritual discovery,
      1215
    learn to feed, 1440
    made divine by striving, 557
    man's fear-ridden, 1710
    material and spiritual brings into existence, 71, 1159
    morally conscious mortal knows his s exists, 1479
    mortal, become the reborn child...1676
    must refresh (how), 1739
    mystery of evolution, 147
    naked before Universal censors, 313
    nature of the, 1217
    new reality (spirit is father of, material mind is
      mother of), 8
    newly appearing entity, s, survives, 1234
    not life, has identity, survives, 404
    of expression is absent unless truth, beauty, goodness
      unified, 507
    of mortal man is created out of, 1287
SOUL OF PHILOSOPHY, THE, 311
soul, of third circler passes at death to mansion worlds,
    1232
    only aggressive, progressive, s on earth is truth-
      learning believer, 2063
    perplexing mystery, building of s in human mind, 147
    personality identity survives by soul survival, 195
    portrays harvest of temporal decisions, 1216
    powers, degree yielded to T A, measured by love...
      1642
    preparation of s for ascending career occupies T A,
      1192
    primitive doctrine of survival from...953
    product of union of divinity and humanity, 1196
    progress of s retarded by mental and physical
      poisons, 1204
    reconstruction, testing process of self-destruction
      and self-r, 1782
    requires mental capacity, desire, to evolve, 739-40
    requires moral thinking, spiritual activity, 1478
    requires spiritual exercise well as nourishment, 1000

soul (cont'd)

resolves divinity tension, 1276

second generation of s is, 1459

seed of s is immortal spirit, 1459

severe strain on the s to serve good and evil, 1480

"shall have become reborn child of this indwelling spirit", 1676

sleepers awakened gradually so s get back in body, 954

son of man and son of God, 1196

spirit growth of s, 66

spiritual capacity of, 1621

a stagnant s is a dying soul (J), 1478

Stoics thought divine s imprisoned in evil physical body, 1336

surviving identity, of material personality, spirit prepersonality, 71

"there was but one...s among multitude", 2065-66

to unbeliever: "how do you know that I do not know", 1125

unique, new, original universe value, 1218

vs. divine spirit, 1478

what helps it?, 1388

will faithfully portray harvest of...decisions, 1216

worship is tuning in s, 1621

worth and attitude of, 1584, 1739

worth of, how judge, 1739

souls, "cannot lead unwilling", 1466

cowardly, 1766

divinely watered s independent of environment, 381

"ease-drifting", 1931

"Father and I live in s of each of you", 1949

"God looks into your s", 1838

God's refreshment of our souls, 1777

high climbing, 1778

human "no previous existence", (J),1811

hungry s famish in presence of bread...1766

impoverished majority rich, refuse believe it, 556

J spoke to consciences and s, 1632

SOULS OF PEACE, THE, 437

souls, prayer digs deeper channels to s for...2066

timid, aid of illusions, 1779

SOULS, THE UNION OF, 311

souls, world is filled with lost s (directional sense),1098

sound, designers, the, 506

distant, made audible, 327

reflections of glorious spirit-souls, 506

spiritual, 499

sour grapes, 1630

SOURCE, FIRST S AND CENTER (see under "First Source and Center")

SOURCE OF EVOLUTIONARY GROWTH, THE, 1280

sources, of all reality expression, triunities, 1148

SOURCES OF SOLAR ENERGY, 463

SOURCES OF SUPREME REALITY, 1263

South America, 727, 905

–Africa connections disappear, 683

drifted westward with North America, 663

"Japanese" (Andites) in boats reached S A, 873

race of superior potential, highlands of, 728

SOUTHERN JUDEA, IN, 1605

souvenirs of material days on peripheral P, 120

Sovereign Jesus, we appear before, 1238

sovereign of his self-made u, Michael, 1323

SOVEREIGN OF NEBADON, THE, 367, 2057

sovereignty, concept of equality never brings peace except...1487

SOVEREIGNTY, DIVINE AND HUMAN (J on), 1486

sovereignty, free will beings require a supersovereignty to avoid conflict, 1487

sovereignty (cont'd)

global, will prevent g wars, nothing else will, 1490

illusive notions of unlimited national s, 1487

in Europe, retrograde, 1489

is power, grows by organization, 1488

SOVEREIGNTY, LAW, LIBERTY, AND, 1490

sovereignty, Life Carriers planned beings for social sovereignty, 856

SOVEREIGNTY, LOCAL UNIVERSE, 237

sovereignty, moment you lose sight of spiritual s, 1487

national s is a disease, 1491

of God is unlimited, 52

of the mortal free will, absolute, 71

of Nebadon, 1493, 1512-13

of universe earned by 7 bestowals, 1318

SOVEREIGNTY OF URANTIA, THE, 1250

sovereignty, only 2 levels of, on world, 1488

Paradise and creature viewpoints, 1324

SOVEREIGNTY, POLITICAL, 1487

sovereignty, political, critical stage of evolution on U, 1487

political, is innately the peoples', 1489

spiritual s of God, above all, 1487

super s over men is required for peace, 1487

two levels of relative s on a world, 1487-88

sow a mortal body, reap a morontia form, 431

sows, whatsoever a man s, 37

sp

space, acts as an equilibrant on gravity, 125

all s filled by Paradise Deities, 91

alternately contracts, expands, 123 (see "space respiration")

SPACE AND MOTION, 133

space, and pattern, 1297

SPACE AND TIME, 134

space, and time, where they originate, 120

as 12 oranges in U, 458

(assembly of chemicals (miracle)), 1530

bodies, disruption of, 658

blanket, 462, 475

SPACE BODIES, THE ORIGIN OF, 170

space, body, disruption occurs when...658

charge of universal force, 476

cloud, dense, long obscured both sun and moon, 837

communication, 539

conditions and motions, 7 between Paradise and Super U, 152

confusion, due to...461

currents, 494

cushions explosive action, 125, 128

SPACE, DISCOURSE ON TIME AND (J), 1438 (see also "Jesus, on")

space, does the pattern of an idea occupy s?, 1297

drift, universal, 476

"emptiest", about 1 electron cubic inch, 473

–energies (antidotal), 826

–energies, source of, 123

–energy unknown on U, 667

fleeting shadow of Paradise...2021

for all on Paradise, 121

force, 468, 470-71, 479

SPACE FUNCTIONS OF PARADISE, 124

space, in atomic system, pervaded by energy influence, 478

in outer s 70,000 more superuniverses to form?, 354

intrusion, unique, 153-54

is not infinite, 135

is pervaded, especially by...461

is real, moves, 133

space (cont'd)
    is a system of associated points, 1297
    is womb of...forms of matter...123
SPACE LEVELS OF THE MASTER UNIVERSE, 128
space, man perceives s by synthesis, 1297
    measurable vibrations in s from ultimatons, 474
SPACE, THE MESSENGER HOSTS OF, 273
space, mother force of s, 122
    motions, 4 kinds, 133
    not empty, confused scientists fail to recognize
       reality of s, 1439
    not empty, gravity-responding energy currents,
       power circuits, etc., 473
    not empty, various forms of energy and matter
       circulate...461
    not empty, vast ocean of out-spread force-energy,
       476
    permeation by calcium because, 462
    personalities throng the universes of s, 417
    pervaded and unpervaded, 123-24
    pervaded by presence of Divine Minister, 455
SPACE POTENCY, 469
space, presence of Divine Minister pervades Nebadon,
    455
    processions, opposite directions, 125, 134, 153
    rays, life fully resistant to amazing flood of, 667
    reports, 288, 439, 522
    reports of archangels, 2001
    "reports of glory", 270
    reservoirs, 123-24 (vertical space)

space, seven different conceptions of, 1439
    shadow of eternity upon moving panoply of s, 1117
    time, neither is absolute or infinite, 31
    travel (see also "enseraphim", "Solitary Messengers",
       "travel", "velocities")
    travel distortions, 134
    travel or passage, individuals, 561-62, 570, 1248
    unorganized outer, 2015
    vertical cross-section...like Maltese cross, 124
    vibrations in content of s (ultimaton), 474
    within an atom is not empty, 476-78
    zones, non-pervaded, periphery of Paradise, 121
    zones, width of, 130

space energy conditions, do not modify inheritance
    factors, 667
space potency, called "ABSOLUTA" on Uversa, 469
    difficult term to define, 126
    energy reality, from s p to monota, 1149
    free space presence of the Uqa, a prereality, 469
    homogeneous organization of s p, unique to Isle of
       Paradise, 120
    is a prereality, 469
    mind potency, spirit potency, potentials transmuted
       into actuals, 1261
SPACE RESPIRATION, 123
space respiration, the motion of space itself, 133
    totality of s r destroys local value as time source, 135
    two billion year cycles of s r, 123-24, 134, 149
space traversers (see "transport", "transporters")
spark, spirit s of the God who is spirit, 1434
spark of divinity, immortal, functions to perpetuate
    personality, 1459
spark of infinity indwells finite man, 1221 (see
    "indwelling spirit", "Mystery Monitor", "spirit
    indwells mind of man", "Thought Adjuster")
spark of life (life activation spark), 404
    creative force alone can supply, 404
    Life Carriers impart, 399
    Spirit of God contributes the vital, 404

sparrow, "one of them shall not fall", 48
sparrows, 1682, 1820
spatial environment, 666
"speak peace, but mischief in hearts", 1677
speak, "spirit will s through you", (J), 1584
spear invented, 725
SPECIAL COLLEGES, THE, 816
SPECIAL WORK OF THE MELCHIZEDEKS, 388
SPECIALISTS, COORDINATION OF, 910
specialization, ever increasing, expanding, next age, 910
SPECIALIZATION OF LABOR, 773
species improvement, hybridization makes for s i
    because of...920
species, living, over 99, 500 reduced to less than 500,
    682
spectacle, awful, of human limitations, 59
    healing s, 683 persons made whole in moment, 1633
    inspiring, contemplate Father through starry realms,
       1840
    Son of God, about to die, 1996
spectra, iron registry varies--temperature, 462
spectroscopic estimations, 134
spectrum, races appear in order of s colors, 589
speech, careless and offending s, and prayer, 1640
    inspired, Josiah before court, 1815
speed(s), 260 (see also "velocities")
    Solitary Messenger, 841 trillion mps, 261
sphere to sphere, after mansion worlds, conscious for
    travel, 544 (see also "space travel")
    as we progress, we are advance-tuned, 544
    grow less material, more intellectual, 535
    you may depend on going, 63
SPHERES, THE ARCHITECTURAL, 174 (see "archi-
    tectural spheres, worlds")
spheres, architectural, by fiat of Deity, 172, 174
    dark energy-charged, 457
    demortalizing s, (7 mansion worlds), 539
    five major divisions of, 172
    for mortals, from collisional debris, 171
    glorified, present plenty of real and potential evil, 625
    of advanced socialization (70), 1248
SPHERES OF LIGHT AND LIFE, THE, 621
spheres, of Nebadon diverse nebular ancestry, 455
SPHERES OF SPACE, THE, 172
spheres, origin of vast majority, 170-71
    seven immense s of Infinite Spirit, 143
    seven luminous s of Eternal Son, 143
    seven secret s of Universal Father, 143
    sizes of s in constellation, 485
    units in superuniverses, etc. (table), 167
spies, appointed to follow J (6), 1654
    became divided in attitude toward J, 1665
    confessed faith in J, were baptized (3), 1667
    desertion of Sanhedrin s for J, 1672
    found J again, 1655
    front row at healing, 1666
    new from Sanhedrin, 1698
    of Sanhedrin defected to J, 1667
    questioned J, 1713
spikenard, cruse of, Mary (sister of Lazarus), 1879

spirit

spirit, advancement, sudden when, 740, 1317
    all is circuited in Eternal Son, 71
    and thought, 1213
    appeals to s are essential to brotherhood, 1672
    appeals to s when shut off by men, 1672
spirit artisans, no caste in the ranks of s a., 508
spirit, "baptism of the s", 2061
    basic personality reality of the universes, 141

spirit (cont'd)
  becomes dominant, 484, 1276

spirit beings, all always engaged in self-improvement,
    422
  are real, 25
  closely related to us, unrevealed, 147
  the few without forms, 483
  inhabit material spheres, 154

spirit, bestowal, (divine) secret of man's self
    consciousness, 1229
  bestowal of s is domain of spiritual gravity, 139

spirit-born, individuals, 1096
  life of sonship, 1683
  man, fellowship with God, 1931
  never thirst, 381

spirit, born of (see "born of the spirit")

spirit-born sons, characterized by spontaneous,
  generous, and sincere friendliness, 1951

spirit, capacity, measure of, 1740
c career follows morontia training, 537
  career, Super-U, 342
  circuits between man, Maker, 1638
  cohesiveness, 82
  comes from Paradise through Havona, 1164
  communion, channel of, 2062
  communion, not promoted by ornateness, 1840
  conjuring, comparable to ("mass?"), 987
  conquest of energy matter through mediation of mind,
    1281
  -consciousness, borderland of, 2097
    realization of spirit reality of God, 69
  content of any value, imperishable, 2097
  cooperation, never abrupt transitions of, 739
SPIRIT COORDINATORS, 430
spirit, cult, under s c life a gamble, 963
d designs and types, controlled by Trinity, or... 236
  determines form, 1236
  destiny conditioned by, depends on, 1739
  destiny, difficulties help attain, 1719
  divine, fruits are, 2054
  the divine s that indwells mind, the T A, 8
  divine, within heart of man (J), 1457, 1661
SPIRIT DOMINANCE, 1275
spirit, dominance of mind, conditioned upon, 1216
  down-grasp, how it occurs, 1099
  ebb and flow, 150
  ecstasy, calmness, 1000
  endowment, symmetry of, 380
    3-fold, 1108, 2061
    (3-fold), of evolutionary realms, 639
    uniform, 63
  energy, and mind, unification in reflectivity, universe
    rulers simultaneous information, 105
    laws of, 505
    strength for weakness, 1777
    undiminished in transmission, 82
  experience in any environment, 2064
f finding the s, effect on apostles, 2065
  forces, (are like gravity--return), 380
    conspire to help man (17), 379
    universe, 5
  forms (our) as we ascend, personal and unique, 483
  four tasks, 2061
  fringe of conflict, flesh, 1766

spirit (cont'd)
  fruits of the, 381, 1602, 2054, -62
    God's will discernible increasingly in, 138
    guidance "into all truth", 383
    not borne by "the flesh" naturally, 382
  goal of existence, all personalities, 140
  goals, cosmic allurements of... 141

spirit gravity (see also "gravity, spirit")

SPIRIT-GRAVITY CIRCUIT, THE, 81 (see also "gravity,
    spirit-, circuit")
spirit, -gravity pull and response between individuals
    and groups of i, 82
  gravity, requires constant, instant readjustment, 82
  growth depends on, 1095-96
  guidance like gravity, 1276
  "guide, give your s g little trouble", 1673
  has body, not vice versa, 483
  help descends, returns, 380
  "helper, I will send you a s h", 1947
  highest personal reality, 140
  hovers, to help, 304, 379, 2062
  hunger, prevented, 381
i identification, matter of, 1217
SPIRIT IN MAN, THE, 380
spirit, indwelling, give opportunity to speak to soul, 1641
  indwelling, 3 evidences of, 1711, 2094

spirit indwells minds of men (see also "Mystery
    Monitor", and "Thought Adjuster")
  all who yield to "teaching of Father's indwelling
    spirit", 1711
  "already does s of F indwell you", 1602
  "and my spirit shall dwell with you", 2049
  "appeal to spirit which lives within mind", 1705
  "association of mind... with indwelling spirit of...
    eternal God", 1931
  "comprehend that God dwells within you", 1664
  "Father sends s to indwell minds of men", 1536
  Father "spirit sent to live within you", 1609
  "God has become what you are that he may make
    you what he is", 1664
  "his spirit actually dwells within you", 1609
  "I will... return as a spirit indweller of each of
    you", 1953
  indwelling of God's s of love and... grace, 1545
  "J has taught us God lives in man" (Rodan), 1777
  J' spirit alongside F's that indwells m of m, 1700
  "make appeals to divine spirit that dwells within"
    ... 1765
  man is "dwelling place of gift of the Gods" (Rodan),
    1779
  "only uniform thing about men is the indwelling
    spirit", 1676
  "soul... become reborn child of this indwelling
    spirit", 1676
  spectacle of God... sending his spirit to dwell
    within (man), 2065
  "spirit of God dwells in you", 381
  "spirit of living God who dwells...", 1742
  "there is spiritual part of... F in every f son", 1661

spirit, influence in hearts, 1700
  influences (see also "spiritual influences", "Thought
    Adjusters", "Adjutant Mind Spirits", "Spirit
    of Truth", "Holy Spirit")
  all as one, 95-96, 1244
  impersonal, 1244
  in human mind, 1105

spirit (cont'd)
    influences (cont'd)
        in man, many, 2094
        many, but can't be segregated, 95-96
        on man, 7 ams, later 7 higher, 2062
    instant transformation to s, no, 541
    is always intelligent, minded in some way, 102
    is architect, mind is builder...484
    is basic personal reality in universes, 141
    is divine purpose, 102
    is fundamental reality of personality experience, 140
    is goal, flesh is fact, 1778
    is unchanging, transcendent, 140
    is value, energy is thing, mind is meaning, 102
    is willing but the flesh is weak (J), 196
    joy of outpoured s is tonic for health, 2065
    kingdom, enter for deliverance, 382
    law of s decrees, 1689
    laws as reliable as physical laws, 505
    laws of s, mind, matter, 1638
    leading, shown by choices between right, wrong, 1142
    -led, all sacred in lives of s-led, 1732
    -led mortals, "goodly heritage", 1674
    liaison, dual, hovers over worlds, seeking to...379
    lines trace back to s, physical energy to P, mind to
        T S C, 105
    "load-pulling", 911
    luminosity, 143, 1246
m man's, known by 3 phenomena, 1108
SPIRIT, MATTER, MIND, AND, 139
spirit, "may have something to impart others have
    refused to hear", 1731
SPIRIT MIND, THE, 78
spirit, mind and energy, 102
    mind is divine purpose in action, 102
    -mind, neither material nor creature, 482

spirit ministries to man, adjutants leading men to...
        spiritual ideals, 379
    all coordinate as one mind and soul, 96, 100-01
    are many spiritual influences and they are all as
        one, 95
    combined Action of U F and Eternal Son, 95
    combined denote symmetry of spiritual endowment,
        380
    Conjoint Creator is the universal mercy minister,
        95
    coordinate functioning of three divine ministra-
        tions, 1003   coordinated, 1244
    Divine Minister (spirit) works as one with S of T,
        379
    Divinity (is) plural in manifestation, but singular
        in human experience, 380
    evolutionary r arose through 3 ministries, 1003
    liaison of all spiritual ministry (5-fold), 96
    ministry of Holy Spirit makes possible T A, 379
    more coordinate as "mind control" achieved, 380
    numerous impersonal spirit influences indwell,
        surround, impinge upon... (man), 1244
    of Creator Father-Son and Creative Mother-
        Spirit, 379
    personality credits established by combined
        ministries, 556
    seven adjutants, the spirits of promise, 379
    seven higher spirit influences hover over and
        dwell in man, 2062
    Sons of God reveal F, angels from I S guide us,
        94-95
    Spirit of Truth automatically prepares man for
        T A, 379
    that surround you and impinge upon you, 64

spirit (cont'd)
    ministries to man (cont'd)
        T A's work coincides with influences of I S and
            local u Mother Spirit, 95-96
        vast ministries of I S, made more personal, 1244
        within you a conspiracy of spiritual forces, 381
    ministry (endowment) to men, 2061-62
    ministry, vs. healing sick, 1634
    must dominate human experience, 381
    "my s shall dwell within you", 2049
n never compromised by compulsion, 381
    never drives, only leads, 381
    nucleus in mind of man, 2094
SPIRIT OF BESTOWAL, THE, 86
spirit, of divinity, humbly obedient to will creatures, 150

spirit of God (see "Mystery Monitor" and "Thought
        Adjuster"; also above see "spirit indwells minds
        of men")
    dwells in the minds of man, 1742
    Infinite Spirit is referred to as "s of G", 96
    liaison of all spirit ministry, 96

spirit, "of idealistic beauty", 1732
    of infirmity, persons relieved from, 1836
    of the Master's injunction, 1950
    of wisdom, first function on U, 709
    only uniform thing about men, 1672

spirit patterns, exist in relation to space, don't occupy
    or displace it, 1297

spirit personality, J attained full realization of s p in
        human experience, 30
    may have human complement for cosmic achieve-
        ment, 1196

spirit, polarity, 2024
possession, no more, 1807

spirit...poured out (see "Spirit of Truth, poured out"
    below)

spirit, "pray for tranquility of s", 2048

spirit presence (Son), mind presence (spirit), 1288
spirit presences, activate to unselfishness, 1132
    three always with man, 380

spirit, progression, J' teaching requires, 1782
    quickens, 380
    realities, love is the greatest of all s r, 1608
SPIRIT-RECEPTION SERIES (of mortals), 566
spirit, renew by worshipful communion, 1739
    rich vs. poor in s, 1573-74

spirit servers, unrevealed, closely related to us, could
s   almost comprehend, 147

spirit, shut off appeal to s, little can be done, 1672
    strives for mastery through mind, 140
    substance, more real than the material, 141

spirit, symmetry, 380
    takes origin only from spirit ancestors, 403-04
    teaches what to say, 1912
    things and spiritual things are real, 118
    those born of the, 381
    Thought Adjuster, prepersonal, 8 (see "Thought
        Adjuster")
    unity despite individual original endowments, 1592

spirit (cont'd)
spirit value in mind flashes on high, 84

spirit, value sorter, the Adjuster, 2095
    when men shut off appeal their s, 1672
    will return to divine source, 26, 1676
    "will speak through you", 1584

spirit world, is a reality to spirits, 498
    only one way to have communion with, 1681
    will not coerce, 381, 1802

spirit worlds, can't conceive now of glories and beauties
    of (future) worlds, 507

spirit, yours, the potential of achievement, 1438
    SPIRIT DEIFIED
SPIRIT AND THE FLESH, 382
Spirit, children of S are the "Act of God", 111
    contributes the vital spark, 404
    divine S descends in long series of steps, 380, 445

Spirit, domination of S never tainted with coercion, 381
    exerts direct influence on created beings, 96
    -fused ascenders, 1197
SPIRIT-FUSED MORTALS, 416, 450
Spirit, -fused mortals, no former consciousness, 451
    -fused mortals, worlds of the, 411
    fusion, descendants, Andon & Fonta, 717
    gives life, 380
    the Holy, 2062 (see also "Holy Spirit")
    Holy, in all, 1003
    Holy, is local, 95   paves way for T A, 379, 1003
    Holy vs. Infinite, 95
SPIRIT, IN MAN, THE, 380   perfect and changeless, 98

SPIRIT, INFINITE, 90
    INFINITE SPIRIT, God, Deity of Paradise, 4, 13;
    Third Person of Trinity, God of Action, 90; omni-
    present, 95; Conjoint Creator of all things, beings,
    universes, 96; possessing amazing anti-gravity
    power, manipulator of energy, acts personally for
    the Father and Son, 101; Third Source and Center,
    107; is mind God, 638; is to mind as Son is to Spirit,
    140; known in local system as "Divine Minister", 375)
    (see also "INFINITE SPIRIT")

Spirit, Infinite
    draws near to every being, 95
    family of I S falls into 3 great groups, 107
    is "eyes of the Lord. . . and the divine ears", 95
    is love applied, and ministry, 94
    is ministry, 94
    is to mind, as Son is to spirit, as Paradise to
      physical, 140
    "not in word only, but in power and in the Holy Spirit,
      380
    on Paradise, Holy Spirit is local, 95
    possesses amazing power, antigravity, 101
    "the S gives life", 380
    your power and achievement is "according to his
      mercy, through the renewing of the Spirit", 380

Spirit, labor of S effected through 7 adjutants, 379
    ministry, limited by reception capacity, 379
SPIRIT, MINISTRY OF THE, 379
SPIRIT, MOTHER, THE LOCAL UNIVERSE (see
    "Mother Spirit", same as "Divine Minister", 375)
Spirit, never drives, leads, 381
SPIRIT OF DIVINE MINISTRY, THE, 94

Spirit (cont'd)
    of God, (the Bible) confuses Paradise Spirit and
      Creative Spirit of Local Universe, 95 (Holy Spirit
      is circuit of later)
    of the Lord, where there is S of the L is liberty",
      2063, -65

Spirit of Truth, 17, 33, 42, 241, 383, 639, 647, 864, 1105,
    1782, 1917-18, -31, -47, -61, 2041, -44, -53, -66
SPIRIT OF TRUTH, THE, 1949
Spirit of Truth, and Divine Minister, dual spirit, hovers
      over worlds, 379
    apostles more spiritual progress in month, 2061
    baptised with, 2043
    believers, to lead all into truth, 2061
SPIRIT OF TRUTH, BESTOWAL OF, 2059
Spirit of Truth, brings enhanced fellowship with Michael,
      2061
    "come into the fellowship of the", 2032
    consciousness of true meanings, 1949
    creates consciousness of Michael, not self, 2061
    directs the loving contact of human. . . 1951
    dwells in men's hearts, 2061-62
    eliminates mental conflict, 1957
    "endow you with power from on high", 2055
    energy, unfailing, for soul, 2065
    foundation for human race to achieve, 820
    the four missions of, 2060-61
    fruits in man, forgiveness, sweetness, etc., 2064
    health, a tonic for, 2065
    in each believer a well of water, 2035
    intellectually conscious of, no, 2061
    is also the spirit of idealistic beauty, 1732
    is of Universe Son, 380
    is spirit of both Father and Son, 2061
    is spirit of the Son, 379
    is a world influence which is universal, 2065
    joint spirit of bestowal Avonal and Creator Michael, 596
    last of the spirit endowment to aid men, 2062
    lead you. . . into all Truth, 1948
    leads to proper life purpose, 2065
    leads upward, urges onward, 2063
    "let the S of T do his own work", 1932
    limited by man's reception of bestowal Son, 379
    loneliness for men without the S of T, 2061
    (male) "when he has come", 1948, -51, -61, 2053
    the mighty, 1930
    mind, a stimulus for, 2065; missions of, 2060, -62
    new teacher comes into your heart, 1958-59
    new teacher, forever unfolding. . . 2064
    the new teacher to abide in your hearts, 1954
    Pentecost, S of T came to mankind on, 2062
    poured out (upon all flesh), (see also "poured out"
      under "Jesus, Quotes"), 241, 365, 381, 596, 1594,
      1601, -42, 1795, 1930, -48-49, -54, 2035, -59-61
    poured out upon all normal mortals, to be, 1328
    power multiplying fulcrum, 1930
    prepares mind automatically to receive T A, 379
    proof of fellowship is fellowship with Michael, 2061
    provides for ever expanding religion, 2064
    purifies the human heart, 2065
    a religion neither radical nor conservative, 2063
    reveals Creator Son, 2062
    saying ever: "this is the way", 1287
    "shall endow you with power", 2055
    Son's spirit is, 2061
    spirit (in a sense) of both Father and Son, 2061
    spiritual bestowal of selflessness, 2065
    "then shall I live in you", 1948
    this (cup) emblem of. . . divine S of T", 1941

Spirit (cont'd)
Spirit of Truth (cont'd)
  "this is the way", 1287
  this must be the coming of the, 2059
  to all sincere believers, 2063
  to capacity to grasp spiritual realities, 2063
  to lead all believers into all truth, 2061
  tonic for health, stimulus for mind, 2065
  transformations wrought by, 1931
  unfailing energy for the soul, 2065
  "a well of living water springing up", 1954
  world influence, mighty, 2063
  a world influence which is universal, 2065

SPIRIT, THE OMNIPRESENT, 100
Spirit, Original and Infinite, by series of "stepdowns"
    draws near, 445
  provides spark of life and endowment of mind, 404
SPIRIT, THE WORLD OF THE, 510
SPIRITINGTON, "bosom of the spirit", 145
spiritists don't drift, they use oars, 2080
spirits, accredited, after mortals finish morontia
    career, 342
  alcohol known as s, why, 945
  all work on physical spheres, 139
  (angels) seen by humans, seraphim sometimes, 438
  bad s in world only, rebellion period to Pentecost, 962
  belief in unclean s, 1659
  do not return to earth, 1646,-80
  doctrine of good and evil, hurts idea of cosmic unity,
    961
  dual liaison of s hovers over world, 379
  few lost s entered minds before Pentecost, 1807
  have forms, 483; homes, 501
  kindred, 82
  many mighty among midwayers, 866
  ministering spirits of Paradise, 285
  minor, 1807
  of Creator Father-Son and Creative Mother Spirit
    not individually segregated to man, 379
  of the Divine Presence, assist man to God-
    consciousness, 17
  of evolutionary origin vs. revelation, 948
  of the Gods indwell you, 304
  react uniformly to all spirit appeals, 1672
  return to earth? never, 1230, 1646,-80
SPIRITS, SEVEN ADJUTANT MIND (see "adjutant mind
  spirits")
spirits, seven, of advancing worlds hover over man, 2062
  variable under God, 137
  "we will send our s into minds of men" (J), 1805

spirits, unclean (evil), (see also "evil spirits")
  Elman tried teach about evil (unclean) s, 1658
  J, lesson for apostles on u s, 1541,-91
  Kheresa lunatic thought self possessed by u s, 1696
  mother believed daughter possessed by u s, 1734
  powerless after spirit poured out on all flesh, 1646
  universally believed u s caused sickness, 1659
  young man, epilepsy, not u s, 1631
  youth possessed of unruly s, 1713

SPIRITS, THE DISCERNER OF, 313
SPIRITS, FUNCTIONS OF THE SUPREME, 205
SPIRITS, INSPIRED TRINITY, 219
SPIRITS, LOCAL UNIVERSE CREATIVE, 203
SPIRITS, MINISTERING, OF THE CENTRAL UNIVERSE,
  285
SPIRITS, MINISTERING, OF THE SUPERUNIVERSES,
  306

Spirits (cont'd)
  of the Circuits, 287
SPIRITS OF TRUST, THE, 437
SPIRITS, THE REFLECTIVE (see "Reflective Spirits")
SPIRITS, THE SEVEN MASTER (see "Master Spirits")
spiritual, achievement through facilities, 1845
  assurance, formula for, 1641
  age, initiated when time is ripe, 231
  age, millenium of cosmic enlightenment, 231
  and intellectual training, 181
  and moral, changes can be sudden, 911
  approach to unify mankind, 2065
  aristocracy, 222
  "assault, take kingdom by s a", 1726, 1829
  assets of human race (ample), 2076
  assurance equal to, 1641
  attainment, by gradual growth or specific crisis, 1096
  bastion, 1096
  beings, eclipsing emotion of s b is joy of high duty,
    274
  "births" sudden or gradual, 1130
  bi-unification, guardian angels, 1249
  bondage, created out of J' life (wrong), 2084
  brotherhood before social, 597
  causes, don't assign s c to common physical events,
    1812
  civilization, how advanced, 1258
  cohesiveness among spiritized personalities, 82
SPIRITUAL COMMUNION, 1133
spiritual, confusion, 1766
  content of experience, rewards of, 1142
  content transcends all else, 1142
  currents of the universe, ascending (use), 1002
  darkness, time of deepening s d, 389
  death, intellectual crystallization, 1120
  decadence? not necessarily, (confusion before growth),
    1092
  decline, alarming picture, 1207
  depth vs. miracles, 1808
  development
    civilization at a standstill in, 909
    depends on, 1095
    self-mastery is measure of, 1609
  difficulties, gospel solvent for, 2060
  disloyalty (Jewish leaders), 1932
  dominant over material, in personality relationships,
    274
  doubts, mortals grow weary, entertain, 361
  drive, used for material achievement, 1405
  economy, 855, 1196
  ecstasy, 1773
  endowment, 3-fold, 2061
  energies, in mortal life, 1090
  energization, 84
  energy, acts according to laws to drive mechanisms
      of material achievement, 1405, 1739
    economic problems, 1739
    manipulators, 505
    sustains supernaphim, 286
    techniques for intake, improved, 505
    unfailing, new, 2065-66
  enlightenment, enthralling epoch of s e ahead, 2082
    Urantia on brink of enthralling e, 2082
  ennoblement, J contributed to, 1461
  evolution is an experience, 1460
  experience, in s e real is good, good is real, 1123
    no special environment required, 2064
    remains valid, 1140
  experiences described, not to convince unbelievers,
    but for satisfaction of believers, 30

spiritual (cont'd)
  exquisitely s types (mortals) harbored on older
    worlds, 569
  faith, revealed by, 1108
  fellowship, intimate, with J, 1593
  fixation, danger of, 1094
  food, attractive, 1474
  food for eternal life, 1710
  force, use of, 1829
  forces, conspiracy of s f, 381
    lures to call forth man's slumbering s f, 1777
    unerringly seek own original levels, 380
  forward urge, most powerful driving force, 2063
SPIRITUAL FREEDOM, DISCOURSE ON (J) (see under
  "Jesus, on")
spiritual, "graduates", end of the circle of Havona
  worlds, 292
  gravity, centers in Eternal Son, 86
    circuit leads directly back to Eternal Son, 81
    functional vs. postulated, 132
    is absolute, 82
    of Eternal Son, 139, 155
    reactions are predictable, 82
    realm of Eternal Son, 139
  greatness consists in, 1758
SPIRITUAL GROWTH, 1095
spiritual, growth, apex of, 1425
    laws of, 1931
    transforming embrace of, 1002
  guidance, at every crossroad, 383
    to child, family, 1922
  healings, not physical, 1649
  heritage, value of, 2082
  hunger (see "soul hunger")
  idealism, is energy that advances civilization, 910
  illumination, floodtides of s i swept over J, 1376
  "incarnation in souls", 1953
  indolence, 1918
  infallibility, no place for, 2085
  influences, discover through T A, 64
    surround you, 64 (see also "spirit influences" and
      "spirit ministries to man")
  insight (defined), 2095
    accrues due to T A, 1105
    approached through..., 1105, -20, 2076
    brotherhood predicated on fatherhood, 598
    on U, 598
    through s i we find God, 2076
  invincibility, 2088
  jeopardy, none for J' universe in his absence, 1326
    of man, 1090
  joy, new sense of, 2059
    not under microscope, 2095
  laws, reliable as laws in material realms, 505
  leaders and patriotic issues, 1397
  level of maximum status, much beyond finite remains
    unproved, 1139
  liberty, gospel endows man with s liberty 7 ways,
    1859
  life, J' only concern, 1580
  living and self-respect, 1740
  longings, 2069
  lowlands of mortal existence, 441
  luminosity of Father, 25
  meditation, healthful attitude in worship and prayer
    of thanksgiving, 1100
  midway creatures help between material and s, 523
  nature, man grafts humanistic branches on s n,
    but... 1126
  never thirst, 381

spiritual (cont'd)
  nobility of that day, 1816
  nonprogression can't long persist, 2095
  originality, preserve, 1591
  personalities continue to ascend life to life, 361
  -physical coordination, 2136
  polarity of planet, place of (resurrection call), 2024
  possibility is potential reality, 2096
  potentiality of religion is dominant over duty actuality
    of... evolution, 1124
  power, in Deity loyalty, 1776
    J, no limitations, 1700
    required for s work, 1758, -65
  powers involved in U life beginnings, 667
  preparedness, sermon (J), 1820
  presence determined by, 150
  progress, faith's part in, 1619
    not a daydream, 2078
    nothing can take place of, 2077
    predicated on, 1095
  progression, 1736
  realities, can't always be known by apparent facts,
    2023
    essential to society as gravity to solar system,
      2075
    of the kingdom, 1821
    separate from social, other problems, 1605
  reason is soul intelligence, 1108
  receptivity, imagination, dependent on glands, 566
    Rodan on, 1777
  records assembled by reflectivity and preserved... 201
  reflex, conditioned, 1095
  regeneration of men, 2082
  rhythm of the soul, religious, 2080
  sifting, 1705
  socialization, 1985
  sound, 499
  sovereignty is God's alone, 1487
  "springtime", 1915
  stability, immunity to disappointment, 1101
  stagnation, dark ages, 1090, 2075
  "strangers, you are s s", 1829
  "strength, I will give", 1590
  strength, new consciousness of (S of T), 2059
  striving, age of real s s threshold to utopian, 820
  summons, transcendent, 2083
  sureties are impregnable, 1096
  symmetry comes from H S, S of T, T A, 380
  teacher vs. Messiah, 1351
  teaching more important, 1634
  tide, Paradise sometimes engulfed in, 304
  times good when J came, 1332
  transformations, in... superconsciousness, 1199
    sudden when, 740
  treasure, greatest, 2083
  types, mortals, supervisors favor measures to
    foster, 1207
SPIRITUAL UNIFICATION, 639
SPIRITUAL UNITY, 1591
spiritual, unity, faith union with J, 2085
    J on, 1591
  urge not a psychic illusion, 2096
  value, everything of s v is registered in duplicate, 201
  values, and forces are real, 82
    augment mind's s v by pooling ideas, 1776
    come first, 1581
    to validate, how, 1116
  vision, effort required, 1097
  will prevail, 2076
  work, can't do in absence of s power, 1758

spiritualism, sordid performances called s, 865
  (trance prophet), 1230, 1666
spirituality, angels aid us through circles, 1242
  "now", but grace can grow, 1120
spiritually, blind individual, 1458
  blinded mortals, 1999
  decadent centuries, China, 1035
  indolent, low standards, 1457
    souls, 2085
  insolvent is already dead, 1229
  minded persons, attractive kinship, 82
  stagnant, Jews, 1727
  we must grow, 1840

spironga, 416, 485, 523
spit, high compliment to be s upon, 968 (see also
  "saliva")
  upon J, 1984, -95
spitting could drive out devils, 968
spittle, as healing agent, Egypt, Arabia, Mesopotamia,
  1044
  mixed with clay, blind man, 1812
Splandon, major sector--we pass through 10, our
    super U, 211
  surrounded by 70 spheres, intellectual training, 174
sponges, 677
  survive, part of gradual transition, 731
spontaneity from cosmic mind, 2078
spontaneous friendliness, 1951
spores vs. seeds, 737
spornagia, 532, 539
  animals, seem to be perfect, 416
  beautiful, 485
  care for, maintain 57 hdqtrs. architectural worlds, 509
  described, 528
  directed by celestial artisans, 526
SPORNAGIA, THE, RECTANGLES, 527
spring, a social center of Nazareth, 1364
square circles, God cannot create, 1299
SQUARES, THE EXECUTIVE-ADMINISTRATIVE, 527

st

stability, cosmic, upon completion of the 7 super-
    universes, 1274
  dependent on personality choice, 1217
  insured at expense of progress, 1301
  is product of... 135
  no real s in cosmos until... 1274
  of atom depends on, 477
  of mechanical statics vs. divinity of spiritual
    dynamics, 1303
  of personality only through God, 1774
  wholly, always, proportional to divinity, 135
STABILIZATION, CRUSTAL, 660
stabilization, of physical gravity, 125
  of social maturity, from family life, 1777
stable, caravan
  J born in former grain storage room, 1351
  Joseph and Mary 1 night, in inn 3 weeks, 1351
staff of Caligastia
  brought 50,000 midwayers into being, 745
  100 from 100 different planets, 742
  superhuman potentially sexual procreators, 744
  ten groups, functional, 745
stage, 3 vital factors setting s for Christianity, 1456
  world, for Christianity, 2069
stages, (four) of J' human life, 1749
  of existence, 7 settled, 627
  of morontia progression, 2041
stagnation, civilization evidences striving, not s, 764

stagnation (cont'd)
  spiritual, 1090
"stand at door", 1765
standard of life and living, Father's will man should
    better his estate on earth, 1661
standard of living, becomes suicidal if too complicated,
    luxurious, 770
  inversely to population, 769-70
  on high, 1001 things of supreme value, 501
  return to more simplified s of living after Magisterial
    Son, 595
  tied directly to land arts, 769
standardization, none at camp, 1658
standards, alternatives, 1457
  non-material are transient, 1457
star, cultists, 947
  double, one type of, 458
  largest, Antares, 458
  "of Bethlemen, the", (legend), 1352
STAR STUDENTS, THE, 338
STARRY ASSOCIATES, OUR, 458
starry hosts, endless but orderly procession of, 47
stars, best discerned from depths, 556
STARS, THE BRILLIANT EVENING, 407
Stars, Brilliant Evening, superangels, ascendant, 407
stars, "he calls them all by... names", 49
  shooting, 658
STARS, WORLDS OF THE EVENING, 408
start afresh, "set men free so can s a as children" (J),
  1583
startling words, 1604
stasis of infinity, 1155
state (see also "nation")
  best which governs least, 803
  can't transcend moral values of citizenry, 803
STATE, DEVELOPMENT OF THE, 800
state, doomed when 50% idle, defective, etc., 818
STATE, THE EMBRYONIC, 800
state, the enduring, 797, 806, 1462
  exalted, compels work, 803
  goal of, 806
  how prevent becoming parasitical?, 805
  ideal is organic, 818
  J' teachings applied not to s, 1580
  moral myth, man obligated to live and die for s, 800
  most enduring, single nation, common language,
    mores, institutions, 800
  regulates only, 805, 818
  should coordinate, 803
  status of s determined by, 797, 803, 1462
  strongest most enduring s is, 800
  three mighty drives in ideal, 803
  tyrannical, offspring of materialism, 2081
  weakness of Roman s, 801
statecraft, technique for adjusting competition, 800
STATEHOOD, THE CHARACTER OF, 806
statehood, earmarks of ideal, 807
  evolution of, through 12 levels of progress, 806
  great problem in, 805
STATEHOOD, THE IDEALS OF, 803
statehood, ideals of s only through evolution, 803
  a people's characteristics are reflected in, 806
statement, frank vs. strategy, 1397
states, advanced, highest honors for civil, social
    servants, 804
static concepts, deficient in wisdom, devoid of truth, 1436
static, dead concepts, potentially evil, 1436
stationary, absolutely nothing is s except I of P, 133
STATIONARY SONS OF THE TRINITY, 114, 219
"stations to which you... ascend", 1947

statisticians, atoms, and people, 478
stature, mortal, tends to decrease, red race to indigo, 584
status, advanced, on neighboring planet, 808
STATUS OF INDIVIDUAL JEWS, 1909 (see also "Jews")
status, on secret worlds, 148
  prerequisite to s, achievement, 1260
STEADFAST, VAN THE, 759
steam, Urantia in blanket of s 1000's of years, 659
steam-power, 500,000 years ago, 748
steering paddle of ship, J helped repair, 1429
stellar body, vast, collapsed in 40 minutes, 464
stellar gas clouds, energy potential unbelievably
  enormous, 170
step, every s willingly, cooperative, 381,383
Stephen, and Barnabas converted by Greeks, 2068
  brought conflict with Jews, 2068
  four hour discussion with J, 1411
  Hellenist, converted by pupils of Rodan, 2068
  martyr, first Christian, 1411,2068
  one of 3 greatest factors (Paul), 1456
  organization of church, cause of, 2068
  stoned to death by Jews, 1411,2068
steps of inner righteousness, 1862
stereoscopic effect of mota, 554
stereovision of world, 1434; of U, 554
stewards and king, parable, 1763
stewardship and wealth, 1822
stifles imagination, overrevelation, 330
stigma, none attaches to animal origin beings, 361
stimulus, of external aggression's danger lacking, 887
Stoicism, ascended to a sublime morality, never since
    transcended, 1336
  Fourth Book of Maccabees, 1338
  remained a philosophy, never became a religion,1336
  witnessed in Wisdom of Solomon, 1338
Stoics, 1083,1336
  better prepared Rome to receive Christ, 2073
  "the wise man is king", 1991
stone, at tomb, rolled by midwayers, 2023
  "book" of world record, 671-72
  formations resembling animals, 944
  is basic building matter, 462
  not one upon another, 1912
Stone of Scone, 967
stone, rejected, became cornerstone, 1894
  tomb door, 2013,-23
  worship, 944,967
  worship, widespread over world, 945
stoned, to death on spot (Stephen), 2068
Stonehenge, 898
STONES AND HILLS, WORSHIP OF, 944
stones, in sea, 751
  "lest these s by the roadside cry out", 1882
  precious, Garden of Eden, 823
stop-moments in reel of picturization, 57
stopping places, mortal, 1475
storehouse, man beginning to unlock s of secrets of...
  1306
storm on the lake, 1694
STORY OF THE GOOD SAMARITAN, 1809
story tellers, stop during hunting, 787
straight, and narrow is the way, 1828
  and narrow way, new version,1829
strain, of existence, religion to reduce, 1727
  relax by restful worship, 1616
strains, most valuable, some lost, 714
Strait of Gibraltar closed, 697
strange form, morontia J, 2032
STRANGE PREACHER, THE, 1764
strange spirit occurrences, 1196

strangeness between Judas and others, 1751
stranger, "no man is s to one who knows God", 1431
strangers, customary to kill all s, 787
  women submitted to s, fertility sacrifice, 1042-43
strategy, public, J resorted to, 1397
stream of cosmic events, Father may place hand in,1305
stream of, divine ministry, 1638
  eternity, currents within, 1285
  human history, mistake to believe in supernatural
    sedimentation in, 1071
strength, action achieves, 556
  for social culture, from cooked food, 778
  for weakness through worship, 1777
  greater than sum of units, 763
  in living for others, 1776
  Lord guide you continually... renewing your s, 1656
  of weary (of no might) increased, 1392,1662
  "shall renew", 381,1069,1774
  spiritual, never hesitate to ask God for s s, 999
  "spiritual s I will give", 1590
  technique of gathering s and wisdom, 1774
strengthened, by hope, 1400
  with power, 381
strife, fratricidal, sinfulness of, 597
strive, all s in achievement, all participate in the
    destiny, 1276
  "do not s with men", 1593,1932
  "my messengers must not s with men", 1577
  "s not with souls you would win", 1956
strives, Supreme Mind s for mastery of energy-matter,
  1276
structures, unevolved artificial s doomed, 870
struggle, Adjuster cannot alter your career s, 1223
  advances worst traits of man, 770
  all mortal races must s, 578
  at every crossroad in the forward s, 383
  basic s of man always, for land, 769
  Christianity faces ominous s, 2075
  eternal purpose of this...uphill... 1223
  for life, painful, 951
STRUGGLE FOR TRUTH IN CHINA, 1032
struggle, gigantic, between militarism and industrialism
    on U, 786
  gigantic, between secular and spiritual, religion of J
    will... triumph, 2075 great, this u age, 1284
  land yield reduced, s inevitable, 770
  long bloody, of primitive man, why, 590
  one only for those of kingdom, 1766
  religion's s between 3 philosophies, 1090
  theory of s between higher, lower natures, 1131
struggles, of mortal living, 68
  three: for existence, standard of living, quality of
    thinking, 910
stubborn associates, more tolerant with?, 1740
STUDENT VISITORS, THE, 339
student visitors, 1254
  allowed on all inhabited planets, 546
  Uversa, over one billion, 340
students, crafty, hypocritical, question J, 1899
STUDENTS, MANSION WORLD, 341
students, 100,000 foreign at Melchizedek schools, our
    universe, 388
  what learned in A M, they taught in P M, 1658
study, apostles, night after night at J' feet, 1534
  apostles, 3 hours every evening, 1533
  ascent should be supreme s of man, 449
  becomes voluntary, M W #5, 537
  first s on mansion worlds, 2 languages, 546
  in library at Alexandria, J-Ganid, 1432
  intense, 5 nights a week, J, 1420
  "lower to higher", 4 errors likely, 215

study (cont'd)
worlds, billion of perfect central creation, 288
490 surrounding Uversa, spiritual preparation, 317
seventy around Umajor the fifth, intellectual
training, 181
stumble, "at my words", 1715
"in fear", 1823
into error, do not, 1951
"not", 2042
stumbles, mankind, in darkness, 2084
stumbling block of J' disciples, 1510
stunned multitude (J would not be king), 1702
stupid, to mechanize idea of God, 53

su

subadministrative centers, 626
subbreathers, live on subatmospheric planets, 561
subconscious, emanations of vs. revelations of superconscious, 1207
subconscious vs. superconscious
contrast between subc emanations and superc revelations, 1207
hypothesize subc? then postulate a superc, 1099
mind may respond either to subc or superc, 1000
mystical state gravitates consciousness toward subc
rather than superc, 1100
religious growth is in superc, not subc, 1095
subjecting total personality to...contacting...divinity,
1774
subjects taught, garden schools of Adam and Eve, 587
schools of Planetary Prince, 587
sublime religious experience, time man had, 1091
submission, J (not patient s) energy and enthusiasm in s,
1770
negative s, J didn't teach, 1770
to outworn system of religious forms unnecessary,
1731
vs. divine privileges,
subnormal, are increasing enormously, 771
subnormal man, breeding should be controlled, 770
only few needed, 771
subnormal mind, no capacity for sonship, 1441
subordinate intelligences, can be variable, changeable,
unlike God, 137
subordinates, errors, misdeeds, of Sons (administrative)
cause suffering, 1632
subpersonal living things, mind energy-matter, activated
two ways, 1301
"substance of", J' religion, 1769
substance, of soul is morontial, 8
substitute, ceremony no s for compassion, 1951
substitutes, peaceful s (for war) must be provided, 786
substituting innocent for guilty, (atonement) childish
scheme, 2017
substitution, Christian church for kingdom in hearts of
men, 1865
success, charm, tact, tolerance, 1774
circle attainment augments potential for s, 1211
despite failure, 1780
factors of material, 1739, -79
failure, and ego, 555
in eternity, failure here, 1780
in modifying reality through, 1222
in quest of Infinite proportional to Fatherlikeness, 1174
material, essentials of, 1739, -79
material (making a living) religion required for ideal
solution, 1778
normal planetary s of 4 orders of sonship, 584
successful living is, 1773
suckled, no infanticide after babe, 770

sudden appearance, new group of human feelings, 708
sudden "appearances" (see "mutations")
sudden, mental, spiritual transformations, 740
Sudna, servital, becomes Graduate Guide, 271
Suduanism, now Jainism, 1450
suffer, does the Paradise Father s?, 53
"suffer...for sake of gospel", 1947
suffering, faith and confidence inspired in the s, 1659
four causes for, 1649, -64
J on, 1662, -64
SUFFERING, THE MISUNDERSTANDING OF--
DISCOURSE ON JOB, 1662
suffering, not God's judgment, 1664
sin and s permitted, why, 615, 1861
why, 1605, -32, -61
SUFFRAGE, THE PLAN OF UNIVERSAL, 817
suffrage, universal, 802
universal, weakness in u s, corrected on neighboring
planet, 817
suggestion, negative and positive, 987
suicidal, evil, error, sin, iniquity, 37
pleasures, 943
too high standard of living, 770
suicide, as ancient social vogue, 790
common over trifles, among primitive, 795
cosmic, 1283
custom, widow commits s on grave, 960
intellectual and moral, 2079
Judas, 1567
Pilate, 1989
retaliation, Serapatatia, 843
soul, cosmic self-destruction, 1301
testifies to...1773
sum is more than additives, 141
Sumeria, 881
by 5000 B.C., purest Adamites in S, 896
Sumerian, 886
clay tablets tell of earthly paradise, 860
kings, longevity of earlier vs. later, 857
language, like Aryan, 860
Sumerians, became Semites, 876
descendants of Nodites, 857
Egyptian civil administrators were, 1044
elaborate records left by S, 860
SUMERIANS--LAST OF THE ANDITES, THE, 875
Sumerians, medicines, castor oil and opium, 992
Melchizedek resembled Nodites and S, 1015
Nodite ancestry blended with Adamites, 860
origins 200,000 years ago, 860
records dug up, kings for several thousand years, 857
summary of new gospel after Pentecost, 2066

summation

summation (for further listings on these subjects, look
under their own letters of alphabet)
acceptance of kingdom teaching, enriches man 7 ways
(J), 1859   adjutant mind spirits (7), 401
angels, 12 functional groupings, U, 1255
atonement, 2017
brotherhood, 5 "steps" to achieve, 597
capital, urges that led to, 776
central u ministering to 7 orders of u intelligence, 160
challenge, the great c to modern man, 2097
character transformation, process of (J), 1705
Christian religion arose through, 1084
Christianity and dark ages, 2074
Christianity, factors of paramount value, setting stage
for spread of C, 1456
Christianity's compromise, 2069
Christianity's history in paragraph, 2075

summation (cont'd)

Christianity's problem, 2082, -86
Christianity's triumph over cults due to, 2070-71
church, unholy alliances, commerce, politics, 2085
circles, attaining c and guardians, 1242
circuits, super and local u, 177
civilization, first 4 great advances, 901
   4 great steps march of c, 768
   progressive program of c embraces, 804
   U, predicated on 15 factors, 906
civilizations, high c born of, 911
classes, reasons for social, 792
classless society, evolutionary through...793
communism, counter to 4 proclivities, 780
cross, symbolism of, 2019
death, three kinds, 1229
democracy, dangers of...801
developmental epochs (seven) races pass through
   under Planetary Prince (normally), 576
divine nature of J, 1785
energies, Paradise forces and, 467
energy manifestations (10) wavelike, 475
energy systems, non-spiritual, 469, 480
escape, modes of terrestrial, 568
Eternal Son, nature of, 74
events, 3 groups of e may occur in life, 1830
evil, three ways of contending with (J), 1770
f fables, allegories vs. parables (J), 1692
faith-insight, triple gift and bestowal, 1108
faith, spiritual, revealed in, 1108
fall of man, 845-46
   original sin, 1339, 2003
false charges of Sanhedrist tribunal, 1990
family is founded on 7 facts (J), 1604
fathers, seven, we experience, 587
feast of tabernacles, ceremony, 1795
F S and C, functions of, outside Havona, 111
freedom, to prevent loss of, 798
freewill, self-conscious, of personality is evolved in,
   194
God concept of Hebrews, evolution of, 1053
God, the nature of, 33
gospel message, changed to proclamation of risen
   Christ, 2066
gravity, universal, 131
habits make character, 1777
handicap, great, confronting U, 626
happiness, factors constitutive of, 794
Havona worlds, seven basic forms of living things,
   beings, 156
high spiritual orders, only 3 divine injunctions for,
   1179
history of Christianity, 2075
human life, 2094
human rights, presently, 793
i inalienables of human nature, 192
indictment of J, Sanhedrist court, 1985
indictment of scribes, Pharisees (J), 1907
industry, perils of i on U, 786
Infinite Spirit, nature of, 92
institutions, human, 3 general classes, 772
intellectually, mankind 3 classes, 1241
intelligence, central u, how satisfies 7 orders of u
   intelligence, 160,
issues of eternal life transferred from individual to
   church, 1865
j Jerusem, local system capital, description, 519
Jesus: apostles' failure at healing, 1758
J, events extraordinary in his life on U, 2091
J, the faith of, 2087

summation (cont'd)

Jesus' farewell admonitions to apostles, 1955
J' farewell talk to the 70, 1804
J: feelings that prompted his tears at Lazarus' tomb?,
   1844
J: 5 cardinal features of gospel, 1863
J' healing miracles, due to, 1669
J' human life, four stages of, 1749
J' ideal concept failed, but Paul "built" progressive
   society, 1865
J' instruction, teachers and believers, 1765
J' kingdom concept, tendencies that changed it, 1864
J: kingdom of heaven, 1693
J, levels of meaning, Golden Rule, 1650
J, the man, 2090
J' morontia visits with apostles, two and two, 2047
J, prayer, thanksgiving, worship, 1638
J, the religion of, 2091
J, salvation, growth in grace through faith, 1682
J' 6 great decisions on Mt. Hermon, 1516, -26
J, 60 days in retirement, why, 1617
J' s to brothers of Emmaus, 2034-35
J' teaching methods, Stoics, Cynics, cult leaders,
   Rome, 1455
J' teachings about God, only 2, 1857
J', 2 essential revelations are business of gospel
   teachers, 1593
Jews, status of individual Js, 1909
Judas met defeat because, 2056
kingdom, distortion of J' concepts of k, 1864
   double viewpoint of, double nature of, 1860
   J noted 5 phases, 1862
   steps of inner righteousness, 1862
   teachings of, four groups of ideas, 1859
   three essentials k consists in, 1585
l laws of living, 2 fundamental (J), 1603
learning goals, m w through constellation, 494
levels of reality, three, 192
life: essentials of temporal, 1778
life, modern national, essentials to, 800
   two major problems of, 1778
light and life, seven stages of settled existence
   advanced worlds, 627
living, art of, factors of higher levels of, 1775
Lucifer rebellion, delayed adjudication, why, 617
magic, superstition (J), 1680
mankind, approximately 3 racial classes, 905
man's spirit endowment, 3-fold, 2061-62
mansion worlds, 530
material development, acme of, 629
matter, 10 grand divisions of, 471
midwayers' explanation of resurrection, 2015
mind, dominant on planet, reaches out towards:, 483
mistakes, great, made in early Christianity, 1670
moral values of u, become man's through 3 choices,
   2094
mortal stages of being, three, 1177
Mother Spirit, 6 phases of career, 203
motions, opinions on, 133
Nathaniel's s of two parables, 1876
mysticism, etc., test of, 1000
of life: man, educated by fact, ennobled by wisdom,
   saved by faith, 2094
organization, physical, of s u s, 166
p Paradise, between P and s u s 7 space conditions,
   motions, 152
Paradise, sacred spheres of, 143
   3 domains of activity, 119
Pentecost, significance of, 2060
personality, dimensions of, 1226

summation (cont'd)
  personality (cont'd)
    14 things known about, 1225
    phases p performs in, 1226
  Pharisees' objections to J' teachings, 1850
  Pharisees's strictness, 1827
  philosophy's three beginning assumptions, 1111
  physical types, planetary, 560
  positive demonstrations you (J) know God, 1733
  prayer: answers to, 1848
    conditions of effective, 1002
    effective, must be: (J), 1620
    kinds of, 1001
    vs. worship (J), 1616
  purpose, the eternal and divine, 364
r races, evolutionary r of color, 723
  realities, 3 basic mind r of cosmos, 195
  reality, concepts presented limited by, 1163
    cosmic mind responds on 3 levels of u r, 192
    forms and phases of, 1162
    functioning levels of finite, 140
    repercussions of finite, 1159
    three elements in universal r, 2094
    transcendental levels of, 1160
  realizations, 4 reality-r are latent and inherent, 196
  reassembly of personality involves, 1235
  reflectivity, universe, 105
  religion, cures and benefits of, 1117
    dangers of formalized, 1092
    distinguished from men's other high forms of
      thought, 2075
    early influences on man, 1003
    evolution fear to love, 1675
    five epochal revelations, 1007
    four kinds of on U, 1129
    quality of a, 1013
    seven great religious epochs, 1009
    true (Rodan), 1782
    20th century Urantian, 1011
  religious growth, habits which favor, 1095
  religious philosophy, 4 phases in evolution of, 1114
  religious urge, 3 manifestations of (J), 1728
  representative government, essentials to, 802
  reserve corps of destiny, basis for choosing, 1257
  resurrection, clarification of, 2021
  revolutionary (revolving) movements in U, multiple,
    168
  Roman Empire failed as results of, 2074
  Rome, successful state, based on, 801
  Rome's failure, 2074
  rulers of the superuniverses, 178
S Sadducees reasons for wanting to do away with J, 1911
  salvation, J' way 7 provisions, 1112
    real, based on 2 realities, 2017
  Scriptures: J' use of, 1767, -69
    the work of men, 1767
  secular totalitarianism, 2081
  selfhood, in study of s, 4 things to remember, 1227
  skeletal types, originally 5 on U, 904
  social manifestations to be outgrowth of experience of
    individual believers, 1865
  sovereignty over local universe, 7 step technique for
    obtaining, 238
  space bodies, 10 kinds of origins, 170
  space levels encircling central Isle, 129
  space levels of master universe, 128
  spheres of space, 5 major divisions, 172
  spirit, in man, the, 380
  spirit indwelling of mind, 3
    evidences of, 2094

summation (cont'd)
  spirit influences, higher, 7, to help men, 2062
  Spirit of Truth, 4 tasks, 2060-61
  spiritual development depends on, is predicated on,
    1095
  state, ideal, functions under 3 mighty drives, 803
  statehood, evolution 12 levels, 806
  strata of people, J' time, 1335
  substitution of earthly church for kingdom in hearts,
    1865
  success, essentials of material (J), 1739
  suffering, man s from (J), 1664
    reasons for (J), 1649
  superuniverses, constitutive organization of, 166
t Thought Adjusters, 7 classifications, 1178
    harmony, ways to augment, 1206
  three great satisfactions from religion, 69
  time cognizance, levels of, 135
  Trinity, functions of the, 113
  two ways mortals may live together, 1775
  Urantia advisory council of, 24, 513
  Urantia, reasons for uniqueness, 1250
  virtues to cherish, 1805
  war, 5 values to past civilizations, 785
    7 early causes of, 784
  wealth, attitudes toward, 1463
    10 ways of amassing, 1462
  why world didn't embrace gospel, 1670
  wisdom, the ascending levels of, 806
  words: God, Deity, Father, Elohim, Yahweh, 1856
  worship, benefits of practice of w, 1774

"summertime of new visitation" (J), 1915
summons, transcendent spiritual, 2083
sun, age of, associates of, etc., 458-59, <u>465</u>, 666
  Antares 450 times our sun's diameter, 458
  chief element in, 462
  death-dealing rays, 666
SUN DENSITY, 459
sun, density at core 3 tons per cubic inch, 458
  density, near-by s, 1 ton cubic inch, 460
  density 1/1000 of Urantia atmosphere, 460
  diameter 1 million miles (minus), 458
  dispersion, spectacular period of s d begins, 654
  electron from center to surface, 500,000 years, 460
  electrons of, energized by x-ray, 462
  formation, almost 100 different modes of, 172
  gaseous but dense, 459
  gaseous stone surface, 6000 miles thick, 462
  heat of our s could boil all oceans in 1 second, 464
  in interior almost no whole atoms exist, 463
  is generator, 460
  its number is 1,013,572...655
  light, 1 two-billionths, reaches U, 665
  much matter recaptured by solar g, 656
  ordinary--trillions of years old, 172
  ours in 6 billionth year, 465
  radiates 100 billion tons of matter annually, 465
  shine on as now 25 billion years, 465
  size of U, 60,000x density of our s, 460
SUN STABILITY, 465
sun, temperature ,
  higher than believed, 463
  internal 35 million degrees, 463
  surface 6000 degrees, 462
Sunday morning with the apostles, 1886
SUNDOWN, THE HEALING AT (see under "Jesus", also
  see "healing")
sunlight, economical at $1,000,000 a pound, 460
  health-giving, disease-destroying, 748

suns, all are originally truly gaseous, 458
   Anova exposed to light of 3 s, 559
   are the stars of our... system, 172
   burned out, 171
   cold or dead, collapsed matter, 472
   dead, majority will be revivified, 464
   dead, tremendous gravity, 173
   diameter, average, about million miles, 458
   disappearing s yield energy of rarest form, 464
   local accelerators of energy circulation, 172
   many as glasses of water in oceans, 172
   mother wheels of, 169
   nonsolid reach density equal to iron, 460
   Orvonton illuminated, warmed, by over 10 trillion
     blazing s, 172
   planets, spheres, 10 groups, 170
   power control stations (dynamos), 172
   ray, transformed into heat, liberation of other
     energies, 461
   serve as universe lighthouses, 459
   some can shine on forever, 464
   the stars of space, 1 class of spheres, 172
   turn matter into energy, dark suns energy into
     matter, 473   years, trillions upon trillions, 173
sunspots, 666
   cycles, 11.5 years, 459, 655
   function as enormous magnets, 666
Suntites, in Garden after default, 826
SUPERANGEL WORLD, THE, 510
superb self-respect, J' aim, 1582
superbreathers, live on superatmospheric worlds, 561
supercitizens of Paradise, one thousand groups
   (transcendentalers), 350
superconductors, living, for over 15 energies, 327
superconscious, spiritual truths resident in, 1209
   vs. subconscious (see "subconscious vs. super
     conscious" above)
superconsciousness, spiritual transformation in s
     through T A, 1199
   spiritual truths resident in s, 1209
   sublime experiences... in s, 1203
superco-ordinators of grand universe, 351
superfinite levels, seeking to find God on, 163
supergases, solar, 459
supergovernment, basic unit of s is the system, 166
supergovernments, deliberative assemblies, 317
   differential of energy segregates transactions, 429
supergravity presence constitutes force-charge of
   pervaded space, 139
superhuman, agencies (miracle), 1530
   J deprived self of s, 1516
   knowledge of reality of religious experience is s, 1142
SUPERHUMAN MINISTRY, THE ANGELS OF, 1256
superhuman values, mind and spirit, potential for
   creation of, 757
superior races, primary, 919
supermind bestowal, initial, Holy Spirit, 1003
supermortal, body is of s design, therefore cannot be
   controlled by man alone, 1303
   material beings, 407
supernal activities, our future s-a, no words to describe, 391
supernal experience, finding God, 1731
supernaphim, angelic hosts, children of I S, 285
   in Havona, piloted by s whose natures, like ours,
     derived from MS of O, 290
SUPERNAPHIM, THE MIGHTY, 286
supernaphim, ministering spirits of Paradise and
   central universe, 285
supernaphim, primary
   command seraphic hosts on isolated worlds, 298

supernaphim, primary (cont'd)
SUPERNAPHIM, PRIMARY, MINISTRY OF THE, 298
supernaphim, primary
   serve ascendant pilgrims and Paradise Citizens, 287
supernaphim, recording
   7 grand orders, each 1 million subdivisions, 302
supernaphim, seconaphim, seraphim, cherubim,
   sanobim (where they serve), 418
SUPERNAPHIM, THE SECONDARY, 289
supernaphim, secondary, 287
   directors of affairs of ascending beings, Havona, 287
   seven classifications, 289
supernaphim, shares transit after death, 1244
   solitary s accompanied Michael, 4th bestowal, 1313
SUPERNAPHIM, THE TERTIARY, 288
supernaphim, tertiary, 285, 287
   create superaphic ministers, 287
   record story of u of u, 281
supernatural, causes explained all for early men, 901
   experience, messenger appears to J (age 12), 1376,
     1408; second s e episode at baptism, 1408
   occurrence, only 1, about birth, 1347
   power, only after baptism, 1408
superphysical adjustment, animals adapting to air,
   water, land, 737
superpower mother systems of creations called triata,
   126
supersovereignty over equals, necessary for religious
   peace, 1487
superstition (see also "fetishes")
   charms, relics, gross s, 1681
   chew hard wood to soften seller's heart, 971
   devils could be driven out by spitting on person, 968
   exalted family of sword makers, 774
   fetish of eye falling by chance on vital book passage,
     969
   first s of prenatal marking of babies, 962
   ghosts near, dogs howl, cocks crow, 964
   God's approval, disfavor, shown in "personal
     condition", 1830
   hardly complimentary to U races, 590
   man increasingly liberated from slavery of s, 767
   not compatible with material achievements, 590
   of civilized man was ignorance of savage, 951
   phallus thought capable of overpowering evil eye, 962
   pool at Bethesda, 1649
   revolt when over, J' gospel will illuminate way, 2082
   science slowly destroying s, 1306
   spittle believed to be healing agent, 1044
   stars twinkling, souls of worthy dead, 1044
   statement of J on s, 1680
   that God afflicts man, 1664
   touching garment, not faith, healed woman, 1698
   was early moral and social police force, 797
superstitions, 1012
superstitious ceremonies, religion's, 1729
superstitious, prevent machinations of ignorant agitators,
   798
   relic worship, 2008
   savages feared run of good luck, 950
superuniverse, billion local systems in each s u, 157
   confederation (local universes), requisites for
     admission to, 177
   development, 6 purposes not pertaining to mortal
     ascent to Paradise, 1163
   each constituted of 10 major sectors, 166
   each unique, 182
   executive groups of, 178
SUPERUNIVERSE OF ORVONTON, THE, 167
superuniverse, organization of, 166-67
   ours, Orvonton, 182

survival (cont'd)
  dependent on (cont'd)
    decisions determine s potential, 69
    decisions make for sojourn for eternal ages, 435
    desire to do F' will, 52
    evolvement of soul within mind, 404
    gain the final goal of faith, 1225
    gift of the Gods being desired, 1204
    identity transfer; material body to morontia soul,
      1229
    intentions and desires of survival value, 1233
    kind of death, 1229-30
    mind that craves s, 403
    mind with spirit insight, 403
    mind without immortal spirit can't survive, 565
    not comprehension, but what mind desires to c,
      1217
    personality divinely stable, who has become
      eternally existent, 1303
    spiritual level, s decisions have been made, 1238
    submission to spirit direction, 484
    supreme desire to be Godlike, 1206
  eternal, is matter of faith in word of truth, 1641
    of all true believers, 1642
  existence, reality, and grandeur of, 417
  failure, 1243, -47
    guardians of those who experience f, 1243
    if mortal f guardian makes complete report, 1247
    in some phase of Deity adventure, 284
    result of wholehearted sin, annihilation, 37
  faint flicker of faith only for s, 447
  heritage of the ages is yours, 1240
  how attained, 26
  ignorance alone can never prevent s, 1206
  inferior, unfit ancestors may virtually disqualify
    offspring for s, 1198
  jeopardized only by one's self, 761
  J' death illustrated mortal s, 2017
  may be rejected any time, 1218
  must be desired, 1204, -17
  national s demands preparedness, 805
  necessary credit to assure s of all, 314
  no antagonism to Adjuster, 565
  no one's sin deprives another of s, 761
  not dependent on knowledge, wisdom, 740
SURVIVAL OF ADAM AND EVE, 853
SURVIVAL OF ANDON AND FONTA, THE, 717
survival, of the fittest, 589, 704-05
  of the fittest, not on Jerusem, 521
SURVIVAL OF THE HUMAN SELF, 1232
survival, of religion due to... 1132
  one must do as well as be, 1260
  only conscious resistance can prevent, 1206
  or extinction, goal of destiny, 764
  orders of s and ascension, 568-70
SURVIVAL, PERSONALITY, 1225
survival, possibilities increase through cooperation, 764
  price of, 290 (see also "kingdom, price of entrance
    to")
  real life... to which present life is but vestibule, 1225
  rejected, man moves counter to universe, 1285
    may be prior to mortal death, 1218
    results sometimes in Personalized Adjusters, 1179
    secrets of Supremacy lie dormant, 1284
    Supreme to that extent is delayed, 1283
  requires decisions (J), 1458
  scheme, vast, for mortals, 1241
  secret of, 1206, -21
  (seed of the soul) eternal, 1459
  technique of, 26

survival (cont'd)
  two basic reasons for believing in, 1106
  value, morality without God, has no s v, 1126
    nothing of s v is ever lost in all the universe,
      1197, 1200
      whatever has s v held for master architects, 1201
  we'll know each other on mansion worlds, 1235
  who all survives?, 447
  you shall serve throughout the universes, 1240
survive, if man does not choose to, 2097
survives, how man, 1458
  all worth saving, 1200
  what s and how, 1230
surviving mortals, countless on Paradise, 127
survivors, ascendant beings candidates for seeing S and
  F, 187
  of rebellion: "not a single Jerusem citizen was lost",
    608
SURVIVORS, SLEEPING, 341
Susa, Ur, 875, 1481
Susanna, women evangelists chose S as chief, 1679
SUSATIA, THE, 414
susatia, permanent citizenship local u, 414, 416, 452
suspense, of being a transient reality in u, 1116
  profound, pervaded Nebadon, 1409
suspicion, bred by ignorance, incompatible with love, 597
  inherent reaction of the primitive, 437
sustain you, tranquility, patience, faith... 2048

SW

swamp, pagan, Christianity drains many a, 2083
swear by temple, vs. gold (Jews), 1907
sweat of face, not a punishment, 751, 848
sweep net cast into the sea, 1694
sweet, man can be s in midst of gravest injustice, 2064
sweetness, of goal attainment, 1294
  of uncertainty, 438
swine, 315, 975, 1765
  pearls before, 1571, -85, 1696, 1999; (related idea,
    subnormal "mind", 1440; "dogs", 1571)
swing around circuit of s u s countless times, 63
swing of the great ellipse, 125
Swiss, 945
Switzerland, J visited, 1466
swords, J, no comment on, 1880
  the Simons ordered 100, 1871

Sychar, J' morontia appearance at, 2053
  near Jacob's well, 1611, -15
SYCHAR, THE WOMAN OF, 1612
symbolism, (Bible) for backward age's childlike thought,
  1493
  difficulty is "hangup" between scientific attitude
    and... 966
  distinguish from idolatry, 946
  J' religion needs new appropriate s, 966
  J' s reduced to precise formula, 1942
  must find adequate s for new ideas, loyalties, 966
  new appropriate, needed, 965
  simple spiritual supper sacrament, 1942
symbols, and ceremonies in place of religious exper-
    ience, 1728
  in religion, good and bad, 946
  last supper, why, 1942
  men can communicate with, 1775
  why J used, 1942
symmetry of J' personality, unique, 1101
symmetry of spiritual endowment and ministry due to, 380
sympathize not with... who will merely s with you, 1766

sympathy, compassion, J taught, 1580
 false, avoid, 1766
 unsalvable not to be given s, 592
SYNAGOGUE, AFTERNOON AT THE, 1629
synagogue, at Philadelphia became Christian church,
 1831
 Capernaum, open warfare, 1707-08
 Capernaum s closed to J, 1717
 cast out of s into nobility (Josiah), 1816
 fire destroyed s after leaders defied Sanhedrin, 1718
 head of s at Philadelphia deposed, 1836
 J conducted services in new s more than half the
 time, 1420
 J' epochal sermon, 1709
 J had often spoken in Nazareth s, 1684
 J "preached" in, 1391, 1532, -34, 1629, -65, 1707, -09
 largest in world, Alexandria, 1433
SYNAGOGUE, LAST WORDS IN THE (J), 1713
synagogue, leader deposed for criticizing J, 1836
 man cast out of s becomes associated with Creator,
 1816
 Roman "proselyte" gave s to Capernaum Jews, 1420
 service, details of, 1684
 tolerated gentiles, 1333
synagogues, all s Palestine closed to J, 1718
 scattered everywhere, 1333
synchrony of automatic forgiveness, 1638
synthesis, a growing experiential s on an ever-increasing
 complexity of relationships, 482
 Paradise attitudes and creature viewpoint, 240
Syria, legatus of S (Pilate), 1987
Syrian, confederation, Serapatatia, 841
 David laid tribute on Syrians, 1073
 later appearing Assyrians, 859
SYRIAN WOMAN, THE, 1734
Syrians, 1048, -54, 1669
system, about 1000 inhabited worlds, 166
 basic unit of supergovernment, 166
 capital, attain Jerusem citizenship, 494
 group and coordination discipline, 494
 Jerusem, almost 100x size of U, 509
SYSTEM CO-ORDINATORS, 543
system, each has architectural hdqtrs., 166
 entire s under quarantine, 529
SYSTEM GOVERNMENT, THE, 512
SYSTEM HEADQUARTERS, THE LOCAL, 519
system, in bad s something is missing or displaced, 1227
 in a good s all factors are in cosmic position, 1227
 in human s, personality unifies all, 1227
 of Satania in isolation, 578
SYSTEM (POWER) CENTERS, 322
SYSTEM SOVEREIGN, THE, 511
systems, near us, names of, 457
 vs. aggregations, relationships, 1227

T

Tabamantia, an agondonter, 579
 veteran finaliter, 565, 822
Tabamantia's, inspection of this planet, 821
 tribute to Chief of T A, 1189
tabernacle, of flesh and blood, 483, 532, 1193
 physical, for mortal, evolved by, 483
TABERNACLES, AT THE FEAST OF THE, 1788
tabernacles, earthly (mortals), 1196
 feast of, 1379
 of the flesh, 103
 T As rarely leave their mortal t, 1197
TABOO, THE, 974
taboo, on man-eating, gradual, 980

taboo (cont'd)
 one not afflicted unless t violated, 990
 restrictions against in-marriage, not biologic, matter
 of t, 919
taboos, and mores, marriage, 928
TABOOS, THE RESTRICTIVE, 914, 1042
tabulation, physical organization of the universes, 167
tact, and tolerance, 1740, -78
 and tolerance, you must have, 1774
 charm and wisdom, 1740
 J' tactful explanation of "Jonah story", 1428
 John's t enabled him to live, 1555
 Nathaniel's t (humor) relieved tension, 1559
 required of Judas to manage J' financial affairs, 1566
tactful, are you becoming more, 1740
tadpole, to become frog, best way, 1094
"take heed that no man deceive you" (J), 1912
taken away (that he has not), 1689, -92
talent, ability, should not be for aggrandizement...1519
 always is an ancestral foundation for t, 507
 help from system hdqtrs. for the gifted, 507
 the one universal t entrusted to all, 315
 spirit artisans may aid those with, 508
talents, not arbitrary gifts, 507
 parable of the 5 (see "parables")
TALK ABOUT ANGELS (J), 1840
TALK ABOUT THE KINGDOM, THE, 1746
TALK WITH NATHANIEL, THE, 1767
Tannach, where Deborah and Barak defeated Sisera, 1387
TAOISM, 1032, -38, 1451
Taoist and Confucian teachings, China follows, 1011
TARENTUM, EMBARKING AT (J), 1470
Tarichea, 1542, -87, 1655
tarry in valley of decision?, 1820
TARRYING AND TEACHING BY THE SEASIDE, 1688
TARRYING TIME IN GALILEE, 1524
task, Adam (and beautiful mate) almost hopeless t, 846
 J' single, 1520
tasks, angels perform with ease, difficult, 419
taste, "and see that the Lord is good", 41
 designers, the, 506
tatooing, 983
taunted, Abel t Cain on fact Adam wasn't his father, 848;
 on relative value of offerings, 848
tax, collector and harp, 1402
 collector, the temple, 1743
 "does not your Master pay the temple t?", 1743
 no progressive income t on advanced world, 625
TAXATION, 815
taxation, census for, 1350
 handicapping industry, how prevent?, 805
TAXATION (NEIGHBORING PLANET), 815
taxation, overmuch, Rome, 2074
taxes, citizens must control levying of t, 807
 disguised, easier to collect, 792
 Egyptian ruler sorely taxed toiling subjects, 978
 golden ages, light and life, 10%, 625
 graduated inheritance tax, 1 to 50%, 816
 heavy, payer gets extra votes, 817
 inheritance, king would exact, 781
 J circumvented, 1393
 J registered as skilled craftsman for t, 1420
 on neighboring planet, 815
 properties used for home purposes, free from t, 811
 spheres of light and life, 10% to public treasury, 624
 state assigned property to people, had right to tax, 782
 tithing, 625, 792

teach, apostles resented those who had not sat at J' feet, would t in his name, 1765
"teach us how to pray", 1618
teacher, advanced, very great t, Amenemope, 1046
   Amenomope, Egypt, advanced ideals, 1046
   exalted instead of truth, 1413
   intolerant, contentious, or interfering, prompt, summary dismissal, 1486
Teacher, Jesus the great (Andrew), 1524
teacher, J was counselled to function...as t, 1328
teacher-leaders, some of the great t-l of earth
   (*means, "see multiple page references in proper alphabetical location")

Adam and Eve*	Jesus*
Amadon, 757	Lao-Tse*
Amenomope*	Mansant, 726
Angamon, 1456	Mardus, 1457
Apostles (see)*	Mek, 748
Asoka, 1037	Melchizedek, Machiventa*
Buddha*	Moses*
Caligastia*	Nabon, 1459
Confucius*	Onagar*
Cymboyton*	Onamonalonton*
Fad, 746	Orlandof, 725
Fantad, 724	Orvonon, 725
Gautama Siddhartha*	Paul*
Hap, 747	Philo*
Hebrew prophets	Porshunta, 724
Amos and Hosea*	Rodan*
Elijah and Elisha*	Sethard, 1339
Isaiah, first*	Singlangton*
Isaiah, second*	**Tenskwatawa, 988
Jeremiah*	Todan, 1637
Samuel, 1066	Van*
Ikhnaton*	Zoroaster*

teacher, "master t of all, experience", 1961
   new, spirit of Truth, 1954, -58-59, -64, -66, 2064
     so can judge wisely, 1951
   not a preacher (J), 1594
   of Alexandria (J), 1492
   -pupils (see "pupil-teachers")
   religious, greatest was layman, 2091
Teacher Sons, 88
   "parents" are the Trinity, 230
   prevent segmentalized conceptions, 215
   serve individual planets, 214
   Trinity, personalized by Trinity, 88
   (21 billion) in service, 214
teacher, -students gain what they skipped, 624
   tendency to exalt t instead of teachings, 1413
   the true, remains learner, 1433
   true t maintains intellectual integrity, 1453
   vs. truth he teaches, 1413
TEACHERS AND BELIEVERS, INSTRUCTION FOR, 1765
teachers, ascending career, advanced are required to teach, 498
TEACHERS, ASSISTANT, 430
teachers, attitudes should be, 1670
   billions upon billions in Satania, 550   camp, 1868
   Chinese t taught Salem religion at See Fuch
     (1500 B.C.), 1032   false, 1571
   future, augment brotherhood, not the opposite, 1010
   instruction for, 1765
TEACHERS, MANSION WORLD, 550
teachers, many true t have appeared, 988 (see "teacher-leaders" above)
   Melchizedek t reached all peoples on Asian continent, 1032

     **Teuskwatawa

teachers (cont'd)
   new, for social, moral, economic, political reorganization of the world, 2082-83
   of Bible traditionalism, know truth, are cowards, 1769
   of gospel, only business, 1593
   of Israel, greatest feat, 1076
   of J' religion should...1670
   of new religion about J, 2068
   of religious truth, more to come, 1010
   of rest, 505
   of science and religion, 1138
   older Jewish t tolerated (with Essenes) idea of (reincarnation), 1811
   pupils are t all way to Havona, 279
   pupils become assistant t after 3 years, 812
   (religious) know truth, withhold it, 1769
   seven outstanding human, 1339
   superb...Eternals of Days, 156
   true, challenge priests, 988
TEACHING ABOUT ACCIDENTS (J), 1830
TEACHING ABOUT THE FATHER (J), 1590
TEACHING ABOUT THE KINGDOM (J), 1593, 1862
teaching, about marriage (J), 1838
   at camp, not dogmatized, 1658
   brief, vs. lifetime beliefs, 1831
   by staff from on high, 745
   conference, questions, answers, 1579
TEACHING COUNSELLORS, THE, 428
teaching, difficulty t about God if not wanted, 1466
   elemental needs of soul, 1771
   graph technique of Havona, 289, 303
TEACHING IN SIDON (J), 1735
TEACHING IN SOLOMON'S PORCH (J), 1815
TEACHING IN THE TEMPLE (J), 1596 (see under "Jesus")
teaching, incomprehensible techniques, 303
   J' parables and discourses, 1546 (see also "parables" and "Jesus, on")
   J' questions and answers, 1546
   J' supernal, 1457

teaching
   methods of Jesus
     admonish brethren to keep busy, 1765
     allowed each soul to develop in its own way, 1582
     appeal to feelings is transitory and disappointing, 1705
     appeal to intellect (exclusively) is empty and barren, 1705
     appeal to spirit, accomplish marvelous transformations, 1705
     aroused and quickened mind is gateway to the soul, 1705
     arrest and focus intellectual attention through emotions, 1705
     avoided distracting details, poetic image, 1771
     compassion boundless, but sympathy was practical, 1874
     condemn wrongs but accord recognition for praiseworthy, 1765
     demanded vigorous, active, courageous expression of...personality, 1770
     demonstrate (2 ways) fact you are God-knowing, 1733
     denunciations largely against pride, cruelty, oppression, hypocrisy, 1582
     didn't attack older teachings, taught something additional, 1582
     do not indulge in sarcasm at expense of simple-minded, 1765
     do not lessen or destroy self-respect, 1765

teaching (cont'd)
  methods of Jesus (cont'd)
    do not strive... always be patient, 1593
    do something positive to save the wrongdoer, 1770
    do something to challenge the unrighteous, 1770
    don't try to prove you have found God, 1733
    effectively used antithesis, comparing minute to
      the infinite, etc., 1771
    emotionally, men react individually, 1672
    encouraged slow-thinking mortals to ask questions,
      for help, 1557
    essence of religion is not social service, but s s
      is certain effect of true religion, 1770
    exalted love--truth, beauty, and goodness, 1583
    exemplified in life what he taught, 1749
    failing to reach minds in illustration, would use
      another, 1590
    faith must dominate attitudes of body, mind,
      spirit, 1733
    first, fact of F's love, truth of his mercy, then
      news man is faith-son, 1460
    frequently set out to help by asking for help, 1875
    graciousness is aroma of friendliness from love-
      saturated soul, 1874
    growth of spiritual nature by technique of living
      progress, 1749
    he was a charming listener, 1874
    he went about doing good, 1770
    indwelling spirit is only uniform thing about men,
      1672
    "it is not your kingdom, you are only
      ambassadors", 1593
    learned, from others, then made their lives
      richer, 1460
    let light shine, but with wisdom and discretion,
      1692
    make direct appeals to indwelling divine spirit,
      1765
    Master did not grow weary in his teachings, 1590
    men astonished at originality and authoritativeness
      of his t, 1672
    mind is not seat of spiritual nature, it is gateway
      to s n, 1733
    ministry banished fear and destroyed anxiety, 1658
    never attacked errors or flaws in teachings of
      others, 1456
    no dogmatic formulation of theologic doctrines, 1658
    no immunity to accidents, but fearlessness when
      they occur, 1767
    no solutions for nonreligious problems, 1583
    no spiritual self-examination, no religious intro-
      spection, 1583
    parable promotes sympathy without antagonizing,
      1692
    parables, how he used and why, 1692
    parables used, advised against use of fables,
      allegories, 1692
    patience in dealing with backward and troublesome
      inquirers, 1672
    positive action instead of negative compliance, 1769
    positive teacher of true virtue, 1582
    present good news of God as Father, then of son-
      ship, 1592
    proceed from known to discernment of unknown,
      1692
    proclaim: God is your F and you are his sons, 1593
    progression of J as teacher, teacher-healer, Son
      of Man, Son of God, 1749
    put lamp on a stand, 1692
    put spirit of positive action into passive doctrines,
      1769

teaching (cont'd)
  methods of Jesus (cont'd)
    react positively, aggressively, to every life
      situation, 1770
    resist not evil injury to your feelings of personal
      dignity, 1590
    respect the personality of man, promote no
      righteous cause by force, 1765
    selected truths of other teachers and embellished
      it to crowd out error, 1456
    sensual urges not suppressed by religious rebuke
      or legal prohibitions, 1582
    showed his faith in people, 1875
    soft answer turns away wrath, 1687
    spirits react uniformly to spiritual appeals (within
      experiential limits), 1672
    spiritual victories can be won only by spiritual
      power, 1765
    spread good cheer everywhere he went, 1874
    story can teach to varying people, 1692
    strength of teaching was in naturalness, 1771
    suit teaching to minds and hearts before you, 1692
    take nothing out of hearts, put something in, 1592
    taught character growth, not character building,
      1583
    taught not so much from law as from life, 1672
    taught spirit easy victor over both intellect and
      instinct, 1749
    theme for teachers, common motive for life
      service, (F's will), common goal (to find F),
      1592
    think not alone of "how they hear" (but also) "how
      you hear", 1692
    "this good news if you believe is your eternal
      salvation", 1593
    three ways of contending with, and resisting evil,
      1770
    to those he taught most, he said the least, 1460
    use neither physical nor psychic force, 1765
    used only parts of Scriptures not misrepresenta-
      tive of God, 1767
    used 3 stories at same time, 1853
    usually asked questions, ended by receiving
      questions, 1460
    utilized just one feature from a parable, 1672
    warned against creeds, traditions for guiding
      believers, 1592
    was supremely interested in men, 1557
    won 30 of 32 religious teachers in Rome, 1456
    your religion testifies that God has found you...
      ennobled you... 1733

teaching, mind vs. heart, 2052
  most misunderstood t of J, 1918
  "new, don't attach to old", 1914
  new--on old, not good, 1576,-79
  one hour is 10,000 years, 303
  one hour not change beliefs of lifetime, 1831
  platforms (at Temple), 1888
  required, 279,498
  to darkened minds one age, not this, 1600
  "vacillating and indefinite", 1725
  words distorted, 1915,-46, 2050

TEACHINGS ABOUT PRAYER AND WORSHIP, 1616
teachings, beautiful, 1769
  circulating, of the Trinity Teacher Sons, 286
  eternally true, divinely beautiful, 1769
TEACHINGS IN ARABIA, THE SALEM, 1050
TEACHINGS IN THE LEVANT, THE MELCHIZEDEK, 1042

teachings (cont'd)
TEACHINGS IN THE OCCIDENT, THE MELCHIZEDEK, 1077
TEACHINGS IN THE ORIENT, THE MELCHIZEDEK, 1027
TEACHINGS IN ROME, THE MELCHIZEDEK, 1080
TEACHINGS IN VEDIC INDIA, THE SALEM, 1027
teachings, J' about prayer, worship, other worlds grasped, 1616
    J' apostles departed from, 1825
    J' t grossly perverted, 1582
    J', 3 days with Peter, James, John, reorganized for this record, 1593
    J' will prevail, 1616
    material problems of equity, justice, 1605
TEACHINGS, MELCHIZEDEK'S, 1016
TEACHINGS OF AMENEMOPE, 1046
TEACHINGS OF MOSES, THE, 1057
teachings, philosophic, lost in battle against temple harlotry, 1043
    poisoned by Caligastia, 576
    6th century B.C., 1033,-50
    spirit, not apropos of sordid affairs, poverty, economics, etc., 1605

teamwork, dependent on leadership, 911
    one of most important lessons, 312
tears of agony, Peter, 1981
TECHNICAL ADVISERS, 279, 414
Technical Advisers, law counselors to Life Carriers, 280
    61 trillion in Orvonton, 279-80
technical analysis does not reveal what person or thing can do, 141
TECHNICIANS (SERAPHIM), 554
technique, for cure of plague of evil and sin, 617-18
    of conjoint revelational evolution, effects all progress, 2094
    of gathering strength and wisdom, 1774
    of germ plasm metamorphosis, 857
    of progress, revelational evolution, 2094
    of science, no spiritual good, 2095
    of self-revelation, through recognition of reality of... 192
    of social contact, J' usual, 1460
    there is a divine t in approach to Divinity, 301
TECHNIQUES (LAND)--MAINTENANCE ARTS, 768
techniques, new needed, 984
TECHNIQUES OF LIFE, EVOLUTIONARY, 737
techniques, of memory, reconstruction, 450-51
    of terrestrial escape, 568
technology develops faster than worship-wisdom, 1302
teeth, man's (first 36, then 32, now toward 28), 737
Teherma the Persian, 1592
telepathy (?), Adam and Eve, communication over 50 miles, 834
telephone number, doesn't identify personality, 141
telescopes, increasingly powerful, 130
    more powerful will err in velocities, 134
    reveal millions of universes forming, 130
telescopic technique will improve, 459
"TV" (space reports), all Nebadon looked on... amazed at boy J, 1373
    before visiting U saw and heard ideation of some great minds of U, 503
    curtailment of reflective associates, "living mirrors of space and presence projectors of time", 318
    fullest u publicity of all that transpired (J on U), 1316
    interplanetary "millions of... worlds... trillions of creatures... one more look at J on the cross", 2018
    Perfectors of Wisdom, hear and see high or low beings' original expressions of wisdom, 310

"TV" (space reports) (cont'd)
    recorded human emotions and divine thoughts of J, 1844
    render distant scene visible, distant sound "audible", 327
    transmitters... all forms of communicable perception, 327
"tell no man" (see under "Jesus, Quotes"), 1545
temperature in energy-matter evolution, 473
TEMPERATURE TYPES, THE, 562
temperatures, exceedingly low t of open space, 473
    in layers of atmosphere, 666
temple, beauty of illuminated t, "these buildings to be destroyed?", 1912
    boy J sickened by terrible sight, t rites, 1378-79
    ceremonies, puerile and insignificant, 1399
TEMPLE, CLEANSING THE, 1888
temple, "destroy this t", 1895, 1982,-85
    discourse, last t, 1905
    disillusionment of J, in inner, 1377
TEMPLE, FIRST AND SECOND DAYS IN THE, 1381
TEMPLE, THE FOURTH DAY IN THE, 1383
temple, "gate beautiful", 1379
    harlotry, 965, 982, 1043,-65
TEMPLE, JESUS VIEWS THE, 1378
temple, memorial to Michael as a Melchizedek, bestowal 1, 1310
TEMPLE, THE MORONTIA, 622
temple, morontia, average seats about 300,000, 622
    of Artemis of the Ephesians, 1477
    of the Father, devastated at Dalamatia, first capital of world, 759; at Eden, first garden, 826
    of God, 381
Temple of New Life, 533
temple, of records on system capital, 436
    of religion, Cymboyton, 1485
    of religious philosophy, 1486
    of religious philosophy burned down, 1492
TEMPLE, THE PRESENTATION IN THE, 1352
temple, profanation of, 1889
    profits, 1888-89, 1978-79
    sex service, 982
    sight of, enthralled J, 1375-77
    slaughter of droves of animals, 1378
TEMPLE-TAX COLLECTOR, THE, 1743
temple, teaching conferences, 1380
TEMPLE, THE THIRD DAY IN THE, 1382
temple, treasury, 1888,-91
    treasury, held $10,000,000 while poor languished, 1889
      profited tremendously from commercial, 1889
      received percentage from money-changers, 1889
      wealthy while poor paid levies, 1889
    200,000 worshippers at one time, 1377
    (ways to gouge) profits, animal inspectors, 1888
      enormous, 1888-89
temples, of God (men), 1609
"temples of God", physical bodies of mortals, 26
temples, of sun, circular, roofless, 898
temporal, concerns, "perish", 1431
    issues, to decide t i man needs, 1093
    life, the essentials of, 1778
    matters are concerns of men, 1605
    welfare, not concern of T A, 1204
temporary T A indwelling, 410
tempt not angels of your supervision, 1931
temptation, 1222
    and human nature, 1739
    beat t through love for better conduct, 1739
    in t endowed with power of perfect will of God, 1609
    intelligently redirect energies to beat t, 1738
    lead us not into t, "why?", 1738

temptation (cont'd)
TEMPTATION OF EVE, THE, 841
temptation, the real (2 years), 1386
    save us in t (prayer), 1620
    tests for spiritual capacity, 1740
    through own selfishness, 1738
    to gain power and authority in absence of super-
        sovereignty, 1487
    will (power) alone can't combat, 1739
temptations, J', confused and puerile symbolism, 1514
    one of J' greatest, 1412
    transform into uplifting mortal ministry, 1739
tempted during 40 days, no, 1514-15
ten commandments, the earlier, 1599
Ten Commandments in Greek, in charcoal, 1392
Ten Commandments, precursors of, 751
TEN LEPERS, THE, 1827
ten trillion suns, universe of Orvonton, 172
ten vs. seven, numeration, 479
tenderness, not t to give sympathy to degenerate,
    inferior, 592
tension, divinity t resolved by evolution of soul, 1276
    personality t, relax by worship, 1616
    profound cosmic t, resolved only in synthesis, 1277
    spirit communion relieves, 1774
tensions, among J' followers, 1610, -17
    make possible all universe growth, 1262
    talking no cure for t, 1610
    to relieve t, 739, 774
    vs. worship, 1579, -81, 1616
    wars come from t, 2065
Tenskwatawa (Teukswatowa), Shawnee prophet, 988
tentmaker of Antioch (J), 1456
tents, new, for Salem school, 1021
Terah, father of Abraham, 1018
    migrated from Mesopotamia to Palestine, 1019
TERRESTRIAL ESCAPE, 568
terrestrial escape, seraphim indispensable to, 568
TERTIAPHIM, THE, 306
tertiaphim, lone, accompanied Michael to second
    bestowal, 1311
TERTIARY AND QUARTAN STAGES, 654
TERTIARY LANONANDEKS, 392
tertiary maximums, are things, meanings, values, 1158
TERTIARY SECONAPHIM, 313
TERTIARY SUPERNAPHIM, THE, 288
test, filth t for fidelity of man's wife, 795
    final and supreme t, achievement, 291
    for entering kingdom, 1569
    great t of idealism, 804
    Havona t for disappointed pilgrims, 295
    J passing through great t of civilized man, 1521
    J' t for every institution, every use of religion, 1388
    life on U is short intense t, 158
    of civilization, men have power, don't use it wrongly,
        1521
    of degree to which spirit controls, 1642
    of examiners for spiritualization, 544
    of faith, mortals and Planetary Prince, 575; of Sons
        with Father not present, 573
    of religious experience, 1000
    of time almost over, (attainment third circle of
        Havona), 295
    of yielding to T A, 1642
    subject yourself to t at will, proceed when passed, 544
tested, J' t in all things, 1407
TESTING, FIVE MONTHS OF, 1546
testing, J provided t opportunities for chosen
    messengers, 1708
    of Apostles, 1546
    ours relatively short and intense on U, 1237

testing (cont'd)
    season of intense t, 1959
    "time of t soul is revealed", 1824
tests, crucial t of will creature, 315
    even on Havona, 291, 294, 295
    for Life Carriers, 396
    material t for spiritual problems, J refused, 1523
    required to pass t, Havona circles, 291

th

thank you, "I am not like other men", 1838
    to seconaphim for journey to Havona, 343
"thanks, I will give t", 1640
thanks, with all your prayers, give t, 1443
"thanksgiving", Nathaniel's confusion, 1638
thawing out frozen forms of religion (J), 1728
Thebes, Egyptian capitol, 1048
THEFT OF LIBERTY, THE, 614
theme oft used by J, no dogmatism, creeds, for con-
    trolling believers, 1592
theologians, define instead of worship, 993
    usually have held people back, prophets opposite, 1128
theologic, difficulties, due not to First Cause, but
    subordinate and secondary causes, 1298
    difficulties, many caused by man's dislocation of
        Deity, 1298
    doctrines, apostles taught no standardized, 1658
theological, arrogance, 1012
    beliefs vs. reality of r, 1095
theology, an advancing t to world through gentiles, 1340
    and revelation, tell content of religious experience,
        1107
    attempt to define God, 993
    can be false, but religion OK, 1140-41
    can kill religion, 1141
    can never depict real religious experience, 2096
    does not produce religion, r produces theologic
        philosophy, 1130
    error, substituting facts for message, 2059
    for first time theology displaced sociology, 1075
    from man's study of self and u from inside, 1135
    imperfection of lover's insight does not invalidate
        reality or sincerity of his love, 1140
    is the psychology of religion, 69
    is the study of actions and reactions of human spirit,
        1135
    is study of your r, study of another's is psychology,
        1135
    not standard at Bethsaida camp, 1658
    of mind vs. true religion of spirit, 1731
    to do with intellectual content of religion, metaphysics
        (revelation) with philosophic aspects, 1140
    when t masters religion, r dies, 1141
THEORY OF DISEASE AND DEATH, THE SHAMANIC, 989
theory of God, no substitute for realizing presence, 1733
thief, convinced J was Son of God, 2009
THIEF ON THE CROSS, THE, 2008
thieves, delayed crucifixion, 2001
things, all t work together for good of God-knowing, 1306
things, meanings, values (see also "meanings",
    "meanings and values", and "values")
    constitutive mind endowments of mortals, innate
        recognition of tmv, 1139
    cosmic intuitions (3) give validity, reality to...tmv,
        192
    energy is t, mind is m, spirit is v, 102
    first 3 of 7 ascending levels of mortal wisdom, 806
    in physical life, senses tell of t, mind discovers m,
        spiritual experience reveals true v, 1098
    mind for unification, be aware of material things,
        intellectual meanings, spiritual values, 1120

things, meanings, values (cont'd)
  only in harmony of functional triunity (tmv) is there
    unity, 1120
  outline of meanings to be attached to...concepts of
    tmv, 1
  soul and energy of philosophic dynamics is...
    spiritual insight (unity of tmv), 1120
  tertiary maximums, result of relationships between
    primary and secondary m, 1158
  3 elements only in universal reality, fact, idea,
    relation...(designated) t,m,v, 2094
think as men, pray as children, 555
"think before you speak", 1962
thinkers are few, 192,1213
thinking, essential to progress, 901
  leads to wisdom, wisdom leads to worship, 1228
  leisure for t essential for civilization, 902
  man, afraid to be held by a religion, 2083
  -mentation, 503
  spiritual serviceableness of all mere t, discounted,
    1121
  sublime t is prayer, 1616
  wisdom, worship, 1228
"third day", Jewish expression meaning "presently",
  1872
Third Person of Deity, 4,13,102 (see also "Third
  Source and Center", "Infinite Spirit","Spirit,
  Infinite")
  is bestower of mind, source of mind, Conjoint
    (Creator) Actor, 103
THIRD OR CONSTELLATION STAGE, THE (light and
  life), 633
THIRD SOURCE AND CENTER, ATTRIBUTES OF THE,
  5,98,1151,1262 (see "Infinite Spirit" and "absolute
  actuals")
Third Source and Center, 136,186
  executive, exclusive, of Father and Son, 91
  functional family of the, 106
  is universal unifier for U F, 98
  nucleus of functional family of, 205
  one of "absolute actuals", 1151,1262
thirst, "for divine perfection", 1683
  "for righteousness--for God", 2054
  "never t, for spiritual water is a well", 381
thirty pieces of silver, the, 1998
"this is the way", 383,1286
"this is the way, walk therein", 1664
THOMAS AND JUDAS, THE CALL OF, 1542
THOMAS DIDYMUS, (APOSTLE), 1561 (see under
  "Apostles")   Thor, 893,948
THOSE HIGH IN AUTHORITY, 243,246,316
THOSE WITHOUT NAME AND NUMBER, 243,246
Thoth, wise god restored Horus' eye, 1044
"thou shalt not", 975

Thought Adjuster

Thought Adjuster (see also "Adjusters", and following
  this listing "Thought Adjuster, Personalized (Jesus)"
  etc. See also "indwelling spirit", and "Mystery
  Monitors"). The Thought Adjuster is an actual fragment of the living God, 62; arriving in each mortal
  mind, simultaneously with that mind's first moral
  activity, 1478. The Thought Adjuster and material
  mind collaborate to create the soul of man, 1286; it
  arouses hunger for perfection, 1119; is bestowed on
  all mortals (U) since Pentecost, 1187; and fused with
  mortal (after spiritual attainment) is eternity partner
  of mortal ascender, 1179.

  absolute volition, but prepersonal, 1183
  actual fragment of living God, 62

Thought Adjuster (cont'd)   T
  aided J to organize intellect, 1398
  "all those who yield to T A will...come to me",1711
  "already does the spirit of the Father indwell", 1602
  altruistic urge of Monitor, 1133
  and material mind create soul of man, 1286
  and personality are basis for transcendental
    personality, 1111
  and personality are changeless, 1226
ADJUSTER AND THE SOUL, THE, 1215
  and volition, 1183
  antagonism toward T A, no, 565
  appeal to mortal partner, 1213
  arouses unfailingly, hunger for perfection, 1119
  arrival of J', 1357
  arrival of T A, also guardians, 446
  arrival of T A constitutes identity, 569
  arrival signified by emergence of...1131
  arrives in humans on U, just prior to 6th year, 1187
  arrives upon emergence of moral impulses, 1131
  arrives with first moral activity of mind, 1478
  arrives with plan for an ideal life, 1204
  aside from personality domains and T A bestowal,
    Father is least active of P Deities, 362
  at communion, J' spirit fraternizes with T A, 1942
  at-onement authorization, 1237
  attaches reality to cosmic insight, 1122
  attunement of man to T A advances the Supreme, 1278
  augments personality, 194
  autorevelation is from T A, 1109
b becomes father of new reality, morontial, 8
  before T A, evil midwayers could influence inferior
    minds, 863
  bestowal edict of T A, 596
  bestowal of Son's spirit prepared way for T A, 2061
  bestowal spirit of Father, 63
  bestowed on all U mortals (moral) since Pentecost,
    1187
  better approach to T A is through...1099
  birth of soul, 1478
  bodies are temples of God's indwelling, 26
  Brahmanism came near to idea of T A, 1030-31
  brought up shadowy memories in J' mind, 1424
  Buddhism, clear presentation of T A in B, 1039
  business of T A, prepare you for survival, 1192
  by faith recognize the T A of God...1682
c came to J, Feb. 11, 2 B.C., 1357
  can know mind of God because of T A, 1123
  can you realize true significance of?, 1181
  can't alter your career struggle, 1223
  can't be compared with marriage, 929
  career of a mortal indwelt by T A, 340
  certain way to discover God's presence, 64
  chief mission of...Son, to effect coming of T A, 567
  children too young for T A repersonalized on parent
    arrival, 570
  children who die before choosing Paradise career, 569
  children with T A follow parent of highest spiritual
    status, 569
  circumstances under which T A is released, 1229
  coexists in human mind in midst of unrighteousness,
    1193
  comes to man as the divine will, 86
  communion with T A involves...65
  completed assigned service (J) on Mt. Hermon, 1493
  comprehend T A only by ministry of mind, 638
  conception of the soul, 551
  concern not so much with temporal affairs, 1195
  consciousness of T A based on, 1139
  contact especially in sublime experiences of worship,
    1203

Thought Adjuster (cont'd)

contact with human, exclusive Creator prerogative, 1203

contact with T A, don't confuse mystical with, 1100

contact with T A facilitated by loving service, prayer, 1000

ADJUSTER, COOPERATION WITH THE, 1205

cooperation with T A not a conscious process, 1206

cooperation with T A, price of survival, 290

creates hunger and thirst for...1107

creates within man unquenchable yearning...1176

creates within you a hunger for...1105, -19

d death due to non-Adjuster fusion, 365

deepest and realest thing in soul, 1105

depend on leading of T A, 365

depends, for personality, on mortal, 1233

destiny of is as mortals', Corps of Finality, 1238

detailed during sleep (Paul's) projection to 3rd m w (II Cor. 12:2), 553

develop high type of religious insight, 1129

divine lover (T A) lives in man, 2094

divine spirit nucleus, 142

divine spirit that indwells man, 8

do not confuse with...conscience, 1207

due to T A, no mystery to know mind of God, 1123

dwells within human mind, fragment of God, 17 (see "indwelling spirits" under "Thought Adjusters") this listing, and in "I")

efficient when mortal is enseraphimed, 431

enables close contact God with creatures, 35

energies of the universes, in touch with T A, 1207

enlightened prayer must recognize, 997

equips man to search for God, 2096

essence of infinite being imprisoned in mind of finite creature, 1176

eternal custodian of your identity, 1234

eternal destiny assured by fusion with T A, 64

evolution of T A progress enlarges Supreme, 1284

evolves the spirit soul upon material mind, 333

experience of man and T A must find...1287

expression, real, better, self, 2078

extrahuman service of T A, 1196

exudes a personal flavor of divinity, 1130

f facilitates communion, 31

factors of pure energy are also present, 1182

failure, never, 444

faith can be elevated only by experience with T A, 1137

faith from assurance of presence of T A, 1766

Father actually present in T A, 363

Father close to man through T A, 445

Father entrusting himself to man, 437

"Father sends his spirit to indwell minds", 1530, -36

Father's indwelling presence, your spirit, 1642

"Father's spirit, T A, does live within man", 1711

Father's way of direct communication with creatures, 1184

feeling of reality, due to insight from T A, 1122

finaliters find Father through T A, 643

first arrive on world, guardians also arrive, 568

first extraordinary event of J' bestowal, 2091

focal point for human personality, 1479

a fragment of God, ever seeks for divine unification, 43

fragmentized spirit of God, 24-25

ADJUSTER FUSION, 1237

fusion after irrevocable choice, 1237

fusion assures eternal destiny, 64

fusion in flesh instead of death, 598-99

fusion usually in mortal's local system, 1237

fusion with T A may transcend death, 1237

Thought Adjuster (cont'd)

fusion with T A perfected 6th mansion world, 538

futile efforts but for indwelling T A, 33

"the gift of eternal life, Father's spirit", 1642

gift of the great God himself, 34, 1610

God adjusts with mind of imperfection through, 47

God-concept, enlargement possible because of T A, 33

God-consciousness is resident in T A, 2095

God may suffer through T A, 53

God most easily discovered through T A, 64

God rules, but Father sends T A, 1857

goodness is growing toward recognition of T A, 1458

great challenge, better communication with...2097

great days in a T A career are...1212

great intellectual and spiritual leaders chiefly due to T A, 1198

greatest adventure, contact with T A, 2097

greatest manifestation of divine love, 40

ADJUSTER GUIDANCE, ERRONEOUS CONCEPTS OF, 1207

h harmony with T A how to augment, 1206

has eternal identity, 71

has eternal plans, 1458

has no mechanism to gain self-expression, 1104

"he will guide you into all truth", 382

helped curb rebel midwayers, 863-64

here God acts uniquely, directly, exclusively, 45

hereafter, remember past through T A, 498

heroism of J' indwelling T A, 2092

holds secrets of your faith...1111

how affect your life, 1191

how and when Cain received a T A, 849

how we thwart T A, 1199

human inheritance, factor in assignment, selection of T A, 1185

i if then the spirit T A dwells within, 1609

if withdrawn, world would return to primitive, 1198

an impersonal (pre-personal) entity, 31, 62, 1130

in depths of the mortal mind, 363

in intellect of every normal...mortal, 62

in man a fragment of infinity, 50

in Paradise Corps of Finality after fusion, 1179

individualizes love of God to each soul, 40

"indwelling heavenly Father", 1712 (see "indwelling spirit")

ADJUSTER INDWELLING, MATERIAL HANDICAPS TO, 1199

indwelling of God's...love and...grace, 1545

indwells the mortal intellect, 24

indwells you and will speak through you, 1584

indwelt by T A, no power can prevent ascent, 63

influence of T A, mostly a superconscious experience, 1208

initiates morontia life on earth, 551

insensitivity of T A to time, 1516

insight born of activity of T A, 2087

interested in 3 qualifications of human candidate, 1186

interpreter, evaluator, part of Universal Unity, 2094

is bestowed spirit of the Universal Father, 2062

is cosmic window, faith-glimpse the U F, 1129

is the essence of man's evolving nature, 1245

is identity of mortal, angel is trustee, 1247

is in keeping of man, with fraction of Supreme, 1285

is indestructible despite mortal's choice, 1283

is nucleus of human personality, 70

is prepersonal, 28-30, 62

is pilot, mind is ship, will is captain, 1217

is preceded by Holy Spirit, 379

is presence of Universal Father, 363

is spirit Monitor, 24

Thought Adjusters (cont'd)
associates of T As, many unrevealed, 1177
augment 3 divine ministrations, 1003
avail selves of reflectivity system, 201
Caligastia...servile before Paradise T As, 610
Caligastia's 100 staff, as yet unfused with T As, 744
Caligastia's 100 staff detached from T As, 758
call, distant echo of T As, 1223
came in great numbers, days of Onagar, 717
ADJUSTERS, CLASSIFICATION OF, 1177
classifications: many ways these mysterious God
fragments can be classified, 1179
College of Personalized T A, Divinington, 186
communication throughout Universe, 1176,-81,-91,
1196
continue to come on advanced worlds, 630
custodians of sublime values of creature character,
1203
deserted T As return to Divinington, 444
ADJUSTERS, DESTINY OF PERSONALIZED, 1201
detached from 100 of Prince's staff, 744,758
ADJUSTERS, DEVELOPMENT OF, 1195
difficult task on U because, 1207
difficult to experience consciousness of, 65
difficulties due to races, 1225
direct connection with Universal Father, 100
direct voice heard when, 1213
divine love, T As greatest show of, 40
ADJUSTERS, DIVININGTON HOME OF, 1179
Divinington is Paradise rendezvous of, 144
do not diminish God, 50
do not indwell on some worlds, 410
due to God's paternal affection, 39
dwelt only in some, before J, 1642
effect on Solitary Messengers, 220,257
enable F to draw personalities...1271
enjoy equivalent of human thinking, 78
epoch, majority of world mortals indwelt, 595
essence of God, 1112
essential to fostering immortal soul, 1188
evolutionary will creatures alone get T As, 1184
experiential classifications (3) functional class (1),
1196
experiential or transient with the primitive, 445-46
Father fragments, natives of Divinington, 143
flawless technique, 1192
form, appear to be without, 483
fragmented entities, 25
fragments of the ancestor of gravity, 1183
full touch with universes, intelligence, energies,1207
function many ways with reserve corps, 1258
fused, are finaliters, 1179
fused, eternity partners of ascenders, 1179
fusion types, 445-47
gain experience on planets of loan order, 1212
gifts of God, 139,445,1108
goal of destiny for all T A is...1239
impersonal Mystery Monitors, 34,46
increasingly bestowed upon post-Adamic men, 593
increasingly fuse with subjects on earth, 599
individualizations of...reality of U F, 380
indwell numerous types, 70
indwell thinking centers of mind, 379
indwelling spirits (mortals indwelt by) (see also
"indwelling spirit" under "I") 24, 25, 28, 30, 33, 35,
39, 62-65, 70, 139, -95, 363, -80, 443, -45, 572, 1181,
1487, 1536
information, receive stream of cosmic i, 1207
known to Solitary Messengers as divine gifts, 1184
liaison of 2 T A transfers vital data, 1258

Thought Adjusters (cont'd)
liaison vs. fusion, 1197
"light man by the true light", 590
light & life planets, midwayers and T A, 627
loaned for lifetime on series two worlds, 1197
"make mortals accessible to ministry of T A"
(Immanuel), 1328
manipulate but never dominate, 1217
masculine, are, 8
Melchizedek observers to U when T As came to
Andon, Fonta, 736
ministries to man prior to T A, 379
ADJUSTER'S MISSION, THE, 1191
ADJUSTERS, MISSION AND MINISTRY OF, 1185
more progress with 3-brained than 1, 2-brained, 1197
mortals, some without T A before J, 1642
mortals with transiently indwelling T A, 410
Mystery Monitors, are,35, 64 (see under "M)
mystery of mysteries, 26
name hardly appropriate, 1192
ADJUSTERS, NATURE AND PRESENCE, 1180
nature of inter-communication? "we do not know",
1181
never fail, 1205
never fail, never default, 1191
no limit to number God can send, 50
no relaxation from this bestowal to human death, 1183
non-fusion (virgin or experienced), 445-46
not the only fragmentations of Father, 333
not organic part of mortal, divine superimpositions,
1197,1203
not possessed by Material Son uplifters, 581
nucleus of human personality, 70
numbers and records of T As are on Uversa, 1199
of naturally gifted individuals, 507
of Planetary Prince assistants, not fused, 574,744
of unusual distinction, subjects (may still) reject
survival, 1179
on nursery (mansion) world, 532
on other worlds, 1188
on worlds where loaned, survivors fuse through
spirit, 1197
ADJUSTERS, ORGANIZATION AND ADMINISTRATION,
1188
THOUGHT ADJUSTERS, ORIGIN AND NATURE OF, 1176
THOUGHT ADJUSTERS, ORIGIN OF, 1177
Paradise rendezvous of T As, 144
patiently indwell, 364
potent on earth, 1198
prepersonal presence of (T A) Mystery Monitors, 572
ADJUSTER'S PROBLEM, THE, 1223
react uniformly to spiritual appeals, 1672
realities of purest order known in u, 1183
register adoration of Father, 65
rejoice when can flash messages to human partner,
1193
ADJUSTERS, RELATION OF, TO MORTAL TYPES,1197
ADJUSTERS, RELATION TO OTHER SPIRIT
INFLUENCES, 1244
ADJUSTERS, RELATION TO OTHER SPIRITUAL
INFLUENCES, 1190
ADJUSTERS, SELECTION AND ASSIGNMENT, 1185
share life vicissitude experiences of humans, 1185
Spirit of Truth prepares minds for, 379
spornagia are not T A indwelt, 528
superacting As are those who...1197
Supreme, 1178,-96
experienced, can leave human body at will, 1197
they are God, 1177
to all normal minded after Spirit of Truth, 596

Thought Adjusters (cont'd
to mortal creatures as Circuit Spirits to...203
torment to T A, selfish, sordid thoughts, 1193
tormented by our wrongdoing, 45
total classifications, 7 orders, 1178
traitors (of rebellion) servile on U before T As, 610
traverse mind-gravity circuits, 333
uniform through 7 super-universes, 1188
unify creatures with God in Paradise, 1259
universal reflectivity system available to, 201
unlimited ability to communicate with each other, 1181
but, 1196
Urantia, As advanced or supreme type, 1198
utilize material gravity circuits, not subject thereto,
1183
valor and wisdom exhibited by...1180
very rarely, even temporarily, leave their mortal
tabernacles, 1197
volunteer to indwell, 1191
where Spirit of Truth not present, how T As are
bestowed, 1187
will recall, rehearse, essential memories, 1235
with many unrevealed associates, undiluted divinity,
1177
ADJUSTER'S WORK IN THE MIND, THE, 1207
you are indwelt by Mystery Monitors, 25

Thought Adjusters, Personalized
are before, are, and are after, personality, 1201
are nontime beings, 1516
are omnipersonal, 1201
certify model careers for mortals, 1204
executives of Architects of Master Universe, 1201
extraordinary human divinities, 1202
highest order of ascending Sons of God, 445
ADJUSTERS, PERSONALIZED, 444
sovereign stabilizers of the universes, 1201
two groups: a) served with incarnated Paradise Sons,
b) distinguished As whose subjects rejected
survival, 1179

Thought Adjusters, Self-Acting
act as though fusion already achieved, 1196
alarming, few persons who can function with, 1207
can communicate with those in other realms, 1196
do intercommunicate on levels of mutual work, 1196
have functioned in interplanetary matters in crises,
1197
scarcity, planetary supervisors advocate remedy,
1207

thought, and spirit, 1121, 1213
can be bad, 1937
cosmologic levels of
curiosity, aesthetic appreciation, ethic sensitivity,
646
attainment of, 646
creator t always precedes creator action, 42
five forms of, 2075
THOUGHT, GREEK PHILOSOPHIC, 1078
thought, preservers, 503
THOUGHT RECORDERS, THE, 503
thought, recorders, preserve noble ideas in tongue of U,
503
revelation is meeting ground for scientific and
religious t, and philosophy of scientific stability
and religious certainty, 1139
untrammeled, 100-200 A.D., 2074
thoughtless pagan, the, 1466
thoughtless, (the) t are dead, 1447

thoughts, and emotions of J recorded, 1844
certain abrupt t sometimes from T A, but...1207
your t, not feelings, lead you Godward, 1105
Thracians, immortality, 1010
threat, greatest to the home, 942
threats to freedom (12 things), 798
three, basic judgments of human mind, 2094
basic mind realities of cosmos, 195
drives of life, the, 1772
THREE PERSONS OF DEITY, THE, 110
three, priests from Ur, the, 1352
threes, joints, legs of stool, for tents, etc., 1143
thrill, building new, transformed society, 2084
men, new call to J' adventure, 2084
THURSDAY AFTERNOON ON THE LAKE, 1579

ti

Tiberias, conference, Herod and Jews, 1717
TIBERIAS CONFERENCE, THE SECOND, 1719
Tiberias, J at, 1419
J "avoid T", 1531
J avoided, 1587
TIBERIAS, SABBATH AT, 1680
Tiberius Caesar (Roman ruler)
and Augustus, overlapped, 1512
compliment to J, 1455
died while Pilate enroute, 1989
Tibet, Andites to China by way of T, 873
Chinese reinforced by superior peoples from...T, 885
Christianity in, 1038
TIBET, RELIGION IN, 1038
Tibet, some parts, 1/2 of males are non-producers, 988
today, traces of Andites blood among Tibetans, 879
tidal, convulsions may be started by dark island of
space, 170
friction, brake on planetary axial revolution, 657
sympathy (opposite sides), 170, 656
upheavals, 170
wave, engulfed Dalamatia, noble culture obliterated,
759
tide of public enthusiasm, why rejected?, 1708
tides flushed city's streets, sewers (Caesarea), 1429
tiger, facing cave-man, your ancestor, 1098
Tiglath, lad named T, accompanied J, 1492, 1752
Tigris and Euphrates
ancient civilization fell, superior people emigrated,
inferior immigrated, 877
grain growers harassed by barbarians, 875
group at mouth, Nodite ancestry of Sumerians, 860
Nodites journeyed toward pleasant regions between,
847
superior Andites refused to leave T&E home, 874
tiles (roof) loosened for paralytic, 1667
time, abridged, 2024
abrogated only, "miracle", 1530
absolute is eternity, 135
accelerated, body of J to dust, 2024
all must wait upon (J), 1436
allusions, impossible, 73
and eternity, 1293, 1426
TIME AND ETERNITY, 1295
time
and space, 1294
insulate man from absolute, limit actions, 1303
so finite can exist with Infinite, 1303
why Gravity Messengers are independent of, 260
TIME AND SPACE, 134
TIME AND SPACE, DISCOURSE ON AT CARTHAGE, 1438
TIME AND SPACE, EVOLUTION IN, 739
TIME AND SPACE, MORTALS OF, 445

time (cont'd)
time and space (cont'd)
TIME AND SPACE, THE SON AND SPIRIT IN, 376
TIME AND SPACE, SUPREME AND ULTIMATE, 1294
time, "avoid loss of t (and) overmuch trivialities" (J),
     1805
  becomes shadow of eternity, 1117
  circular simultaneity replaces linear t, 1439
  cognizance, three levels of, 135
  coming into existence of t itself (through incon-
     ceivable transactions), 1158
  consciousness in intellect, relationship to maturity,
     1295
  cushions escape from barriers to too free action,
     1302
  day, 1000 years, inner circuit, 153
  dimensions, seven, 1439
  direct relationship between t and maturity in intellect,
     1295
  failure to improve, retards ascent, 315
  fragments of eternal continuum are called t, 1296
  from t to eternity, J showed way, 1426
  germane to Havona circuits, 153
  -governor, Lucifer sought to disrupt, 1302
     of progressive human evolution, Caligastia by-
        passed, 1302
  here and there, 174
  hereafter clarifies U memories, 1235
  how used by humans of Prince's schools, 575
TIME, IMPORT OF, 315, 372
time, is criterion intellect uses to evaluate facts of
     existence, 1295
  is relative (illustration, crime, punishment), 618
  is stream of events, 1439
  is a succession of instants, 1297
TIME LAG, THE MERCY, 615
TIME LAG OF JUSTICE, THE, 615
time, man perceives t by analysis, 1297
  moment is day, 271
  moving image of eternity, 2021
  not on Paradise, 153, 739
  "of testing, soul is revealed", 1824
TIME OF WAITING, THE, 1494
time, open break, t for, has now come, 1805
  our t and the circle of eternal purpose, 364
  passage on mission, 259
  -penalized, every mortal born since Caligastia, 761
  relativity of (Lucifer rebellion), 618
  required, change basic ideas, 1705
  required for God, 1733
  ripening of t, J on, 1436
  segments--our Universe, 372
  shorten only when, 1758
  -space descension, ascension, 4
  -space image-shadow, human personality is, 29
  -space, neither absolute or infinite, 31
  -space perceptibility, only man has, 1297
TIME-SPACE RELATIONSHIPS, 1297
time, -space shadow, 29, 648
  a technique of dodging situations, 551
  to lengthen t unit in experience (wisdom, judgment),
     1295
  too little t given to eternal realities, 1733
  too little t spent by men to know God, 1733
  25,000 years of system t equals 20,000 years U, 619
  ultimately events come to be a related cycle, 1439
  unit of maturity, immaturity, 1295-96
  unlimited for progress through circuits, 288
  use, advanced races, 1000 things unknown here, 599
  vs. circle of eternity, 364

time (cont'd)
  vs. space, miracles, 1516, -30
  without space exists in Paradise level mind, 135
  years vary in...on circuits, 153
times, of great testing are t of great revelation, 2083
TIMES OF MICHAEL'S BESTOWAL, 1332
times of transition, now, dangerous, 1086

timid, vacillating individuals seek escape...through
  religion, 1121
tithe, Abraham, spoils of battle tithed, 1020
  mint, anise, cummin, 1908
tithers, over 100,000 on rolls of Melchizedek brotherhood, 1021
tithes, for taxes, light and life worlds, 625
tithing, derived from times of Sethites, 1016
  10% on spheres of light and life for public treasury,
     625
titles of Deity, various, defined, 1053
TITUS THE NOBLEMAN, 1644
Titus of Capernaum, son, 1644

to

"to him who has...from him who has not", 1692
Toda, tribe of India, 994
Todan, gospel to Mesopotamia, 1637
today, culture budding, social progress beginning, have
  time to think, 901
today's condition, material comfort era merging into
  quest for knowledge, wisdom?, 577
toil, liberation from t will continue, 902
tolerance, born of confidence in J and F, 1958
  earmark of great, 1098, 1740
  Ganid mightily moved by J' t, 1467
  grows into friendship, ripens into love, 1098
  J to John: "give up your intolerance", 2047
  Nathaniel revered J for his t, 1559
tom-toms, to influence spirits, 991
TOMB, DISCOVERY OF THE EMPTY, 2025
tomb, J' body rested 1-1/2 days in, 2014-15
  of Joseph, 2012
     burial of J, 2013
     discovery of the empty t, 2025
     empty, not because body resurrected, 2023
     "is empty, J has risen"...2030
     Jews bribed guards to lie, 2023
     Jews sought guard for, 2014
     message from Michael, to J in t, 2016
     Peter and John at, 2027
     stone rolled, guards seized with terror, 2023
TOMB OF LAZARUS, AT THE, 1843
TOMB, SAFEGUARDING THE, 2014
tomb, ten Jewish guards, ten Roman soldiers, 2014
TOMB, THE TIME OF THE, 2012
tombstones, 945, 964
tones, "recognize four instead of one", 1465
tonic for health, joy of outpoured spirit, 2065
tongue is a member few men can tame, 1640
tool, Serapatatia used as t of Caligastia, 841
TOOLS OF CIVILIZATION, 901
torchbearers, as factor in U civilization, 909
torment to Adjusters, sordid, selfish thoughts, 1193
torn in heart, J, by opposing courses, 1515
total depravity, doctrine destroyed much, 1091
total reality is infinity, 1146
totalitarianism, ecclesiastical, hold gains of secular
  revolt from, 2081
TOTALITARIANISM, SECULAR, 2081
totality of selfhood, 1096
TOTEMISM, 970

transition (cont'd)
times of t dangerous, 1086
TRANSITION YEARS, THE, 1483
TRANSITIONAL CULTURE WORLDS, 509
transitions, cyclonic t of a scientific era, 1090
of mortal, 1st: death; 2nd: ideal sleep; 3rd: relaxation
of the ages, 297
translate human values to spiritual, 1118
TRANSLATED MIDWAYERS, 444
translated, sphere to sphere you will be, 63
TRANSLATION, DEATH AND, 623
translation, from living on advanced worlds, 631
from living on U, 624
not death, 623, 1208
shrine, 623
temple, blazing glory of consumer fire, 622
to Morontia, Van, 833
translators, 1, 503
TRANSLATORS AND INTERPRETERS, 546
transmigration, 946, 953 (see also "reincarnation")
Buddha, valiant fight against t of souls idea, 1035
replaced early Vedic faith in spirit progress, 1029
souls of men into bodies of animals, no, 1431
stultifying belief, 1029
transmissions of character, spiritual, (seven is basic
to), 479
transmit messages, 100 light years by messenger, 261
TRANSMITTERS, ENERGY, 327
emergency communications outside the circuits, 327
living superconductors, 327
transmutation of...mortal mind...into mortal soul, 26
TRANSMUTATIONS, ENERGY AND MATTER, 472
transplant of life plasm, early, 742, 744
TRANSPLANTATION, LIFE, 399
transplanted, if t to normal world, would seem heaven
to us, 598
transplants of life plasm (rib myth), 742
transport, 222, 324-25, 430, 433, 436, 509, 535, 543, 582,
828-29, 833, 844, 1250
advisors, 505
departure of a seraphic t, 438
dispatcher, summons living energy, 439
Most Highs sent shrub of Edentia to U (tree of life),
745
on Jerusem 2 to 500 mph, 521
TRANSPORT PERSONALITIES, 289, 310
transport, techniques, seraphic, 430-31
TRANSPORTERS, THE, 430, 433, 436
transporters, all groups of ministering spirits have
transport corps, 430
celestial beings, 438
transports, seraphic, from Jerusem, 844
seraphic, landed with A&E in Garden, 828
travel, ascending mortals freely t mansion worlds, 534
desire for t will be fully gratified, 340
good to know life as lived on earth, 1674
great influence for civilization, culture, 909
interplanetary, ascending mortals, 534
interplanetary (mansion worlds), 538
J desired to, 1381
J thought about, 1411
mansion world sojourners, once a year to finaliter
sphere, 509
morontia worlds, Jerusem, Edentia, and on and on,
1248
mortals who fuse in mortal life traverse space freely,
570
one superuniverse hdqtrs. to another, direct, only
Solitary Messengers, 259
seraphim in large numbers, 434

travel (cont'd)
timeless technique of Gravity Messengers, 347
Uversa to Urantia, 109 days, 222
was universal, time of J, 1333
traveler, British (J met), 1475
travesty, on character of God (atonement), 60
to worship nature, 57
treason, first capital offense, 796
treasure, greatest spiritual, 2083
"where your t is", 1822-23
treasures, "in heaven, failed to lay up", 1821
"lay up t in heaven", 1577
make certain of t laid up in heaven, 1853
treaties, diplomacy, foreign policy, cannot maintain
peace, 1491
of peace, first were "blood bonds", 788
treaty, first tribal t was for salt, 775
tree, cults, divining rods, relic of ancient t c, 946
"first make the t good", 1582
of forbidden fruit, figurative, 975
"of knowledge, good and evil", 825
TREE OF LIFE, THE, 825
tree of life, become as "gods if...partook of t of life",
826
in rebellion, loyalists had possession of priceless t
of life, 756
Melchizedek had not t of life, 1015
shrub of Edentia sent to U, 745
trees, and flowering plants, 688
leafless, 670-80
TREES, WORSHIP OF PLANTS AND, 945
trend of the circle, 125
trephining skull, among first operations, 991
triad gods, many countries, 1143
triads, man generally tends to think in t, 1143
trial, balance, 314
TRIAL BEFORE PILATE, THE, 1987
trial, "discloses what is in the heart", 1824
Josiah's testimony spontaneous, 1815
marriage, primitive tribes, 917
on t before bar of human needs, scientists and
religionists, 1457
TRIANGLES, THE JERUSEM, 528
Triassic period, 685, 687
triata, 126, 156
TRIBAL COORDINATION AND RACIAL COOPERATION,
THE SUPREME COURT OF, 749
tribal government of Onagar, not equalled for many
1000s of years, 716
TRIBAL RELATIONS, THE GOVERNORS OF ADVANCED,
748
tribal struggles, kept great Indian civilization from
coming, 723
TRIBES, THE BADONON, 720
TRIBES, CLANS AND, 788
tribes, twelve, there never were 12, 1071
TRIBULATION, THE AGE OF BIOLOGIC, 682
tribulation, "coming up through great t" makes...
mortals kind, 538
error of each man augments t of all, 138
only through much t will many enter kingdom, 1533
tribulations, suffering for sins of others, transient t,
619
tribunal of nine, equals Ancients of Days, 217
tribunals, aims of constitutional, 798
TRIBUNALS, THE SUPREME, 180
tribute to Caesar, lawful for us to give?, 1899
trifles, of living, crosscurrent conflicts of, 1778
vs. high, holy obligations, 1987
trillions upon trillions of celestial beings spring from
I S, 119

289

TRILOBITE AGE, THE, 673
trilobites, in tens of 1000s of patterns, 676
   nearing extinction, 681
   some had 25 to 4000 tiny eyelets, 676
Trimurti, Hindu trinity, Brahma, Siva, Vishnu, 1031
trinitarian postulates vs. triads, 1143-44
trinities, two post-Havona t, experiential, Ultimate
   and Absolute, 16
TRINITIES, THE, 15
TRINITIES AND TRIUNITIES, 1146
Trinities, experiential, 645
TRINITIES, THE LEVEL OF THREE, 1171
Trinities, the Trinity of, 645
trinitization, supreme creative performance, 249
TRINITIZATION, TECHNIQUE OF, 249
TRINITIZED AMBASSADORS, 243, 248
Trinitized Ambassadors, classes of 7000, 248
TRINITIZED CUSTODIANS, 243, 247
TRINITIZED SECRETS OF SUPREMACY, THE, 207
Trinitized sons of destiny, 251, 262
TRINITIZED SONS OF GOD, THE, 243
Trinity, 105, 200, 291, 1271
   (absolute unity, 41; original Deity, 1263,-76;
   absolute center-source of perfect and infinite
   stability, 1265; three individualized but eternally
   associated persons, God the Father, God the Son,
   and God the Spirit, 90; existent from eternity, 90;
   each knows all that transpires in all universes, 77;
   incomprehensible to mortal man, 112, 1269; functioning in nonpersonal capacity but not in contravention
   of personality, 112)
Trinity Absolute, the, 1167
Trinity, an absolute inevitability, 185
   absolute unity, 41
   all three existent from eternity, 90
TRINITY AMBASSADORS, THE, 370
Trinity, and triune associations, 1146
   and unity, 31
   appearance of post-Havona universes dependent on
      others than T, 136-37
   benediction of the T, 53
TRINITY BEYOND THE FINITE, THE, 116
Trinity, concept, expression, life realization, inherent
   in T, 405
   concept, helps in grasp of others, 1146
      long dormant in Jewish theology, 1339
      revealed by Adam, never lost by Sethites, 1009
   concepts, Adam and Eve, 1143
      Agni, Vedic 3-headed God, India, 1143
      Caligastia staff, 500,000 years ago, 1143
      Melchizedek, 1143
TRINITY CONCEPTS, URANTIAN, 1143
Trinity, concerned only with the total, 115
   creation of central universe is threefold (T), 154
   crudely illustrated by corporate entity, 112
   Deity is unity, existential in T, 1282
   Deity, undivided, indivisible, 1147
   diverse associations of the, 1318,-24
   each person of T has gravity circuit, 176-77
   each person of T knows all that transpires in all
      universes, 77
   emblem of T government, three azure concentric
      circles on white, 606, 1015-16,-42
TRINITY-EMBRACED SONS, 243
Trinity, embraces groups of 700,000, 70,000 and 7,000,
   245, 247-48
   embraces High Son Assistants who personify original
      ideas, 253
   eternally associated persons, 90
   existentially overcare of m w probably attributed to
      T, 136

Trinity (cont'd)
   experiential, 1166,-70
   factual identity disclosed in this book, 1143,-45
   Faithful of Days is representative of P T in Edentia,
      489
TRINITY, FUNCTIONS OF THE, 113
Trinity, functions of each person, 99
   functions on all levels of cosmos, 112
   futile to attempt to elucidate T mystery, 112
   God the Supreme is T to creatures, 1292, 1304
   growth of concept, 1143
TRINITY GUIDES, THE, 292
Trinity, in a service of creation and control... are one,
   97
   incomprehensible to mortal man, 112, 1269
   an (inescapable) inevitability, 15, 108
   inevitabilities, Seven Master Spirits, 1266
Trinity Infinite, 113
Trinity, infinity, eternity, universality (3 circles), 1016
   is eternal, actual, and undivided Deity, 1264
   is functional rather than organic, 1147
   is God the Supreme, 1292
   is one, 640
   is original Deity, 1263
   "is primal source of all reality", (Lao-tse), 1033
   is to God the Supreme as Adjuster to man, 1282
   is undivided and indivisible Deity, 1147
   J used Hebrew word for plural God (the T) and not
      Yahweh, 1856
   man's relation to God, Son, Spirit, 66
   masculine, all 3 members (Infinite Spirit, "He"), 112
   members of T as personalities, 8, 90
   Messengers of the P T, "can't reveal much about", 258
   more than simple sum of... 1145
   mystery, futile to try to elucidate, 112
   nearness to man of persons of T, 572
   non-Father capacities, relationships (12), 1146
   nonpersonal corporate entity, father, son, grandson,
      (crude T), 112
   nonpersonal function, not in contravention of
      personality, 112
   oath to, from Son, 1308
   of Paradise, Original Deity, 1276
TRINITY OF TRINITIES, THE, 1170
Trinity of Trinities, 3-level concept, 1170
Trinity, on Paradise 3 personalizations of Deity, but in
   T they are one, 640
   order of origin of Deities, 90
TRINITY ORIGIN BEINGS, THE COORDINATE, 214
Trinity, origin beings vs. trinitized beings, 148
   origin sovereigns (Master Spirits) midway between P
      and us, see and know both ways, 1272
   our relation to T personalities, 66
TRINITY, THE PARADISE, 108
Trinity, Paradise T is existent, 91
   P T is first triunity, 112
TRINITY PERSONALITIES, THE SUPREME, 207
Trinity, Philo helped Paul "restore", 1339
   presence circuits of, 176
   the principals of T, and personality, 8
   qualities, functions of T, more than simple sum, 1145
   regime extends from... 181
TRINITY, RELATION OF THE SUPREME TO THE
   PARADISE T, 1264
Trinity, revelation of 500,000 years ago, Caligastia, 1143
   service (mortal's) of P T is about to begin, 305
   Sethites converted 1/2 of India 16,000 B.C. to P T, 881
   shows interrelationship of law and love, 1145
   Sons, embrace 10 types, personalities, 114
      forever on duty in Nebadon, 1317

Trinity (cont'd)
  source of the Supreme is in the P T, 1264
  Spirit is attained first, 94
  spirit, mind, energy, proceeding from T of P, 1090
  spirit personality of Supreme is derived from P T, 1265
TRINITY SPIRITS, INSPIRED, 219
Trinity, spiritual design is controlled by T, or by... 236
TRINITY, STATIONARY SONS OF THE, 114
Trinity, "stumbled" Mohammedans, 1011
  the Supreme... experiential spirit personalization of the P T, 1270
  Supreme T Personalities are the justice and executive judgment of P T, 207
TRINITY TEACHER SONS, THE, 214, 230
Trinity Teacher Sons, 88, 179, 598
Trinity Teacher Sons--the Daynals, 223
Trinity, three beings, one Deity, undivided, indivisible, 640, 1147
Trinity Ultimate, 1166, 1291; Michael, Creator Son, also member of corps of T U, 1318
Trinity, unification as comprehended by finite beings is the Supreme, as comprehended by absonite beings is the Ultimate, 12
  unification of infinity is existential in P T, 1173
TRINITY UNION OF DEITY, THE, 112
TRINITY UNITY AND DEITY PLURALITY, 1145
Trinity, unity of, 97, 101
  unity of Deity, 640
  U F, E S, I S, is eternal Deity union, the Paradise T, 15
  U Book, first revelation of T since J, 1143, -45
  vs. Adjuster, 1282
  vs. triunity, which is functional, 1146
  we are children of the 3 Paradise Deities functioning as T, 114
  why, 185, 1145-46

TRIODITIES, 1151
triodities, (non-Father triunities), 1261
  are associate or coordinate triunities, 1151
  fifteen triunities and associated t, 1170
  non-Father triune relationships, 1151
  operative t on finite level impinge on Supreme, 1266
TRIODITIES, RELATION OF THE SUPREME TO THE, 1265
triodities, two, actual and potential, 1264
triodity, growth of the Supreme is matter of t relationship, 1265
  of actuality, Son, P Isle, Conjoint Actor, 1151
  of potentiality; Deity, Universal, and Unqualified Absolutes, 1151
tri-partite functions, early council of elders, 789
tri-partite government, evolution of statehood, first creation of 3-fold g, 806; sacred feature of human g, 806
tri-partite legislative body, constellation, 487
TRIP TO BETHLEHEM, THE, 1350
trip, when trial t in flesh is finished, 26
  wise, learned, tried to t J, but he did not stumble, 1674
TRIPS ABOUT ROME, 1466
trips to planets, 1252
triumph, certain t of righteousness, 1739
  of Christianity in the Occident, reasons for, 2070
TRIUMPH OF LOVE, 618
triumph, of technique, love of creatures gives full satisfaction to infinite love of Father, 305
  religion of J will, 2075
triumphant masters of self, children of faith, 1610

TRIUNE DEITY, RELATION TO (Seven Master Spirits), 185
triune, existence of spirit, mind, energy, attain unification within Deity of Supreme, 1090
  manifestation of personality, 1144
TRIUNE-ORIGIN BEINGS, 330
TRIUNITIES AND TRINITIES, 1146
triunities, 1261
  fifteen t and associated triodities, 1170
  help avoid misunderstanding of Trinity, 113
TRIUNITIES, THE SEVEN, 1147
triunities, seven, nature and meaning of, 1148
  never homologous with a trinity, 1146
  only in t of functional reality is unity, 1120
  P T is first t, 112
  partners rather than corporative, 1147
  total reality functions through, 1147, -57
TRIUNITY, UNITY, DUALITY AND, 1157
trivial, present is t seen alone, 1776
trouble, Jude, often, clashes with authority, 1416
  much due to 3 things, 1740
  part of divine plan, 258
  real only after self-concepts displace... 142
  why, in this world, 258
"troubled, be not" (J), 1912
troubles, are creations of fear, 1611
  can't talk men out of t when... 1610
  each age must evolve remedies for own t, 1581
  from fear and apprehension, 1611
  origin in fear soil of own heart, 1674
  religion dissolves, absorbs, illuminates, transcends t, 2093
TRUE AND FALSE LIBERTY, 613
true believer, does not grow weary, 1740
  object of t b is always to act but never to coerce, 1034
true, causes, seek for t c, 1812
  church (the J' brotherhood), unity, not uniformity, 2085
  healing, 1758
  "light which lights every man", 447
TRUE MONOGAMY--PAIR MARRIAGE, 927
TRUE RELIGION, 1104
TRUE RELIGION, THE DISCOURSE (J), 1728
true, religion, must act, 1121
TRUE VALUES, 1456
TRUE VALUES, THE PERSISTENCE OF, 1200
TRUE WORSHIP, 65
trumpet, alms, 1651
  blasts of middle ages, great mistake today, 2077
trust, "and confide in one another", 2055
  betrayal of t distorts personality, 754
  the crucial test of will creatures, 315
  God in order to know him, 1119
  "in riches", no salvation, 1803
  is the crucial test of will creatures, 315
  most sacred, "loyalty to one's own flesh and blood", 1403   no overloading as trusts augmented, 316
  seconaphim weigh t in living scale of unerring character appraisal, 316
  secures heavenly ascent, 1118
TRUST, THE SOLEMNITY OF, 315
TRUST, THE SPIRITS OF, 437
trustful, the Gods are very, 437
trustworthiness, true measure of self-mastery, character, 315
trustworthy estimate of ancestral factors and... status of any (man) on any world, 314

truth, accompanies faith, 1141
  advanced t, man can't suddenly accept, 1012

truth (cont'd)

the all-powerful, 1470
all t takes origin in God, 1125
analyzed too much, 2075
TRUTH AND BEAUTY, DIVINE, 42
truth, and fact, 554, 1297
TRUTH AND FAITH, 1459
truth, and faith, discourse on (J), 1459
   artistic triumphs of t are...555
   attracts only those who...1815
   authority of truth is...1768
   basis of science and philosophy, 647
   bearers, persecuted by church, 2085

TRUTH, BEAUTY, GOODNESS, 646
truth, beauty, goodness, 40, 157, 507, 647, 2078, 2096
   absonite levels beyond concept levels, 1263
   Adjuster reveals Father source of all, 2096
   appreciation of, inherent in perfection, 52
   approach insight of the soul through, 2076
   base life on highest consciousness of, 1206
   believes, admires, reverences, doesn't worship, 1114
   cannot perish in human experience, 2097
   concept generates superanimal effort to find, 2096
   correlated in Spirit, Paradise Son, and Supreme, 1279
   Deity must provide original, 1299
   Deity provides the pattern, 1299
   do phenomena enhance love for?, 1000-01
   embrace full revelation of divinity reality, 648
   Father life is predicated on, 1175
   God not a hypothesis to unify, 2095
   God the Sevenfold in loving ministry of, 1164
   God the Supreme is, 1279
   highest concepts of tbg, modern religion, 2083
   in choosing, mind enters premorontia career, 1237
   long settled in light and life planets, example of, 1306
   man must through tbg evolve, progress, 641
   Paradise Deities are presented as, 233
   Paradise values of eternity and infinity, 2078
   prayer answered by increased revelation of, 1002
   pursuit of tbg leads to God, 2078
   quality values embrace revelation of Deity, 646
   some can't revere tbg without ritual, 999
   tithe, 9/10 devoted to, sphere of light and life, 625
   true spirit values, 1950
   true spiritual concept of supreme reality, 1089
   understandings of tbg, etc. only relatively true, 1260
   values of that which is real, 43
   when universes have achieved...destiny, 1293

truth, beauty, holiness, 1841
  can be acted out, can be lived, 42
  can know God is changeless, perfect, his universe evolving and imperfect, 31
  can know, live, but not imprison t, 1949
  cannot compel men to love t, 1713
  communal vision of supreme t, 1782
  comprehension, high liberty, 2060
  confusing when dismembered, 2075
  the "conviction of" in the heart, 1949
  conviction of t, living, growing, 1949
  crystallized into a creed, Jews, 1727
  dead, only d t can be held as a theory, 1949
  deals with reality values, 1459
  defined by living (J), 1459
  desire for t can come two ways, 1466
  divine, dies under human formulation, 1949

truth (cont'd)

discern t that comes through non-traditional oracles, 1731
discerning t by intellect, 40
discovered, delight of the soul, 1459
distorted by fact, 1615
divine, adaptable to every human requirement, 1950
   apparent human origin, 1733
   best known by spiritual flavor, 42
   defined, 1949
   is best known by its spiritual flavor, 42
   is a living reality, 1949
   is spirit-discerned, 1949
domain of, 1435
drives out error, 1592
ennobling, men experience, 2052
eternal, and obsolete ideas, 1119
   hold fast, 2082
   is discernment of divine goodness, 43
exists only on high spiritual levels, 1949
faith, men can't possess t without f, 1459
fall in love with, 1745
flexibility and adaptability of divine t to requirement and adaptability of every son of God, 1950
flexible, everlasting, vs. rigid fact, 549
God the Supreme is the t of cosmic mind meanings, 1304
great t your faith may grasp--sonship, 445
Greeks and Jews loved t, 2071
guide for those who teach, 1765
half world grasping eagerly for light of t, 973
human formulation of divine t kills it, 1949
hunger, 1861
hungry, must be h for t, 1466
"I am the t", 1428, 1947
imprison t, you cannot, in dogmas, 1949
TRUTH IN CHINA, THE STRUGGLE FOR, 1032
truth, in heart with living roots, 1927
inconcussible, 1297
institutional religion tends to fossilize t, 1092
is...647, 1615
is both replete and symmetrical, 42
is everlasting, 1947
is experienced, 1435
is a flexible factor, 42
is living, 1459, 1917
is relative, 888
is spiritual reality value...1949
Jesus, loyal to all t, 1101
J taught t for an entire age, 1594
J was the t, 1428
know t, experience compassion, choose goodness, 1583
knowledge, and wisdom, 1435, -59
like goodness, is relative (J), 1457
living, teaches t-seeker when, 2075
living t can enjoy only experiential existence, 1949
living t is flexible, 888, 1138
-loving soul, admitted by faith, 1865
momentous discovery of, 961
more t you know, the more t you are, 1297
new, from seeker and giver, 1428
not through the traditional oracles, 1731
one may be right in fact, wrong as to t, 555
the "One Truth" proclaimed 100,000 years ago, 724
only an experiential existence in...mind, 1949
only dead t can be held as a theory, 1949
originates in religious living, 1459
people would not believe the, 1645
perceived (spiritual) t when experienced, 557
personal discovery of t, applied to life, 1222
possessed only through faith, 1459

truth (cont'd)
    presents intellectual foundation of religion, 647
    progressive, purposive evolution is a t, 1125
    promulgation of t, be mighty in, 1931
    remains unchanged, associated teachings change,1119
    resents not criticism, 1641
    revealed t threatened with extinction, 1014
    right and duty, new philosophy, 963
    seed of theoretical t is dead, 380
    seeker, t giver, enlightenment!, 1428
    seekers rewarded now, 1574
    "shall make you free", 1796
    should dominate thinking, 1140
    sovereignty of, 1089
Truth, Spirit of (see "Spirit of Truth")
truth, spirit reality and eternal values, 2023
    spirits... assist man in (taking) t contributory to
        G-consciousness, 17
    "stand in vigorous defense of t when unbeliever
        attacks you", 1932
    static t is dead, 1949
TRUTH TEACHER, ONAGAR--THE FIRST, 715
truth, to know the way of t, 1118
    triune existence of spirit, mind, energy, 1090
    understanding of cosmic relationships, etc., 1138
    (U Book) assigned to enlarge t, 247
    U Book most recent presentation of t, 1008
    vs. knowledge, 1435,-59
    vs. the teacher, 1413
    "what is the t about the Scriptures?", 1767
    "what is t--who knows?" (Pilate), 1991
    wise man is occupied with search for t, 1453
    you cannot imprison t, 1949
    "you shall know the t", 1594
truths, central in universe, 2018
    concealed in Christianity, 2061
    great, almost lost, 2070
    greatest man can ever hear, 2086
    new of the kingdom, 1595
    spiritual, resident in superconscious, 1209
    two of first import in teaching "kingdom", 1593

tu

Tubal-Cain, "I shall now be avenged...", 1764
tuned, advance-t (re-keyed) to keep in synchrony with
      morontia life, 544
    our bodies (morontia) modified, t, for food require-
        ments, etc., 544
tuning in the soul... is worship, 1621
tuning in to spiritual broadcasts, 1621
Turanians, ancestors of, upstepped, 873
turban, J wore t, sandals, girdle, cloak, 2007
turbulence that led to Jewish destruction, 1913
Turkestan, 879
    Adamites many generations all through T, 891
    and Iranian barbarians harassed Sumerians, 875
TURKESTAN, THE ANDITES OF, 878
Turkestan, aridity drove Andonites back into T, 898
    bronze culture 9000 B.C., 903
    Chinese pushed Andonites into Siberia and T, 884
    cradle of civilization for 35,000 years after Adam,
      included T, 900
    highlanders, virile, vigorous people, 870
    Nodites entered T, blended with superior... 872
    people were first to build wood houses, 902
    present Russia and T occupied in south by... 871
    stock in conquerors of Mesopotamia, 876
    vestiges of once Adamsonite headquarters, 862
turmoil, cosmic poise, absence of doubt and t, 1101
    results, gift of J rejected, 1682

turtle, 20 feet across, 691
Tut, 757
Tutankhamen, nephew of Ikhnaton, 1048

TWELVE APOSTLES, THE (see "Apostles")
TWELVE, FIRST WORK OF THE, 1545
twelve "illustrations" of religious faith, 1107
TWELVE, ORDINATION OF THE, 1568
TWELVE, ORGANIZATION OF THE, 1547
twentieth century, transition from old religious
    loyalties to emerging new meanings and values, 1089
twenty-nine, before 30, J well-nigh perfection of man,
    1426
Twenty-third Psalm, original of, 552
twins, 706-08,770,948
TWINS, THE CALL OF THE,1541
twins, first Primates, first simians, 706
TWINS, FLIGHT OF THE, 712
twins, no two exactly alike, 1220
TWO CRUCIAL YEARS, THE, 1386
two mistakes of early Christianity, 1670
"two or three of you", 1763
two original manifestations, the constitutively perfect,
    the evolutionally perfected, 1158

Tyrannus, school of T at Ephesus, Paul taught, 1478
tyranny, of political and economic slavery, secularism,
    2081
    of usage, savage and ancient men, 767
Tyre and Sidon, judgment, 1807
TYRE AND SIDON, THE SOJOURN AT, 1734
TYRE, AT, 1737
TYRE, JESUS' TEACHING AT, 1737
Tyre, manufacturers spread gospel, 1737
Tyrian purple, 1737

U

U major the fifth, hdqtrs. of Splandon, 174
U minor the third, hdqtrs. of Ensa, 174
Ukraine, 898
ultimacy of Deity, 1298,1304
ultimata, 126
Ultimate-Absolute, 1201
ULTIMATE ADVENTURE, 352
Ultimate and Absolute, two post-Havona Trinities, 16
ULTIMATE DEITY, 1166
Ultimate Deity, omnipotent, omniscient, omnipresent, 2
ultimate goals and work, 1239
ULTIMATE, GOD THE, 12
Ultimate, is,12
    is transcendental unifier, 1305
ULTIMATE QUARTAN INTEGRATION, 1166
ULTIMATE, THE TRINITY, 1166,1292
ultimates, 1162
ultimaton, first measurable form of energy, 467
    has Paradise as its nucleus, 467
    long before physicists discover the u, 474
    100 to electron, proton 1800x weight of electron, 477
ultimatonic, activities throughout organized space, 473
    activity, acceleration of, 463
    activity, in collapsed matter, 472
    condensation, 459-60,464; stores of energy, 460
    cooling to critical explosion point of u condensation,
      459
    matter, one of 10 grand divisions of matter, 471-72
    rays from minute ultimaton spheres, 474
    suns that have lost u stores of energy, 460

ultimatons, 464-65, 472, 479
    aggregate into electrons, condensation stores energy, 475
    are minute spheres, 474
    are within electrons, don't orbit, 474
    are without linear-gravity response, 476
    as begin to assume form, infraultimatonic rays, 474
    basic units of materialized energy, 473
    can't be converted back into puissant energy, 473
    cosmic ancestry of u (ultimatonic units), 169
ULTIMATONS, ELECTRONS, AND ATOMS, 476
ultimatons, electrons, etc., force and energy...in space, 473
    "emptiest" space, about 100 u per cubic inch, 473
    energy in its primitive state, 473
    function by mutual attraction, 476
    have 3 varieties of motion, 476
    humbly obedient to temperature extremes, 473
    1/860 in diameter of wavelike ripples, 474
    100 held together to form electron, 476
    100 interassociated u in intraelectronic positions, 476
    100 mutually interassociated in electron, 476
    respond only to circular Paradise gravity pull, 476
    suns can "degrade", break up, all but u, 463
    throughout space, organized into electrons, 473
    turned into circuits and revolutions of the electron, 473
    unassociated, no gravity pull on, 476
    unknown on U, 476
    veer toward electronic organization...475
    velocity to point of partial antigravity behavior, 476
ultraindividualistic, Caligastia, it might have been noted, 752
ultra-violet dangerous (ozone), 665
umbilical cord, first necklace, first toy, 968

un

UNATTACHED MINISTERS, 429
unattainable, essential to cult, 966
unbelief, "help thou my", 1757
"unbeliever, if superior civil servant, question your truth", 1931
unbelievers, caviling, 1712
    "ennobled to love", 2042
unbelieving materialist, his hopes, 1118
uncertainty, children of time have learned to feast on u, 291
    days of u ending with attainment of U F, 295
    during transition to kingdom, 1766
    is secret of contented continuity, 438
    look beyond mists of, 1194
    sublime u, matchless adventure, opportunity for, 1194
    sweetness of u, charm of the unknown, 438
    with security is essence of P adventure, 1223
UNCHANGING CHARACTER, GOD'S, 57
UNCLASSIFIED AND UNREVEALED ORDERS, 333
UNCLASSIFIED (POWER) CENTERS, 322
"Uncle Joshua, tell us a story" (J), 1416
Uncle Simon (Zealot) estranged from J, 1397
unclean spirits (see also "evil spirits")
    J gave apostles first lesson on u s, 1541
    none on U after Pentecost, 1646
    often called "evil spirits", 1591
    youth epileptic and demon-possessed, 1755
unconscious, healing by J, beneficiaries of, 1669
    type of religious activity, great weakness of, 1088
unconsciousness, none during Edentia training, 494
    transition ends after seventh mansion world, 540, 544
underdeveloped people, democracy not for, 517
understand, J apparently strange doings if you discern his purpose, 1425

understand (cont'd)
    man praiseworthy because you u him, 1098
    much in universe a Divine Counselor doesn't u, 55
    tolerate, be friendly, then love, 1098
    you will u "strange doings" as you advance, 590, 1306
understanding, comes from wisdom, 620
    connotes...impressions integrated into network of principles, 1220
    finite knowledge and creature u are relative, 42
    God has full u of need of every intelligent creature... 362
    is only relatively true, 1260
    is relative, 42
    mercy follows as climax to adjuncts to group u, 315
UNDERSTANDING, THE SPIRIT OF, 402
undesirable--prolonged isolation of personality, 1099
undiscovered energy (see "energy, undiscovered on this planet")
unemployed, build military defenses on neighboring planet, 819
    help them get work, 1765
unemployment, danger of, 910
    early, due to oxen, 909
unequal, celestial beings, Lucifer in best 100 of 700,000, 601 (see also "equality")
unfair, unholy advantage taken by weak or wicked, 804
unfit, degenerate, delinquent; handling of (see also "defectives", "eugenics")
    church has universally helped perpetuation of racially degenerate stocks, 1088
    degenerates, etc., those who have lost moral heritage and destroyed spiritual birthright, 592
    high civilization demands, first, ideal type of citizen, 1088
    post-bestowal period disease and delinquency problems virtually solved, 596
    race improvement should be attacked early in evolution, 592
    U handicap, problems of disease, degeneracy, war, multicolored races, multilingualism, 626
    why so many defective degenerates on U, 592
unfolding in man, truth folded in J, 2064
unfortunate, and needy enough, degenerates unneeded, 592
    persons, frightened by every new discovery, 1731
ungodlike, omnipotence gives no power to do the u, 49
unholy alliances, churches in politics, commerce, 2085
unholy secular alliances, (religion's), 1089
unification, never can religions of authority come to u, 1732
    of energy, idea, and spirit systems for efficient living, 43
UNIFICATION OF EVOLUTIONARY DEITY, 641
unification, of whole constellation of settled systems attended by, 633
    only hope for u of Christianity is the living J, 2085
UNIFICATION, PERSONALITY, 639
UNIFICATION, SPIRITUAL, 639
unified, all Deity and Paradise derivatives, 1157
    divine law and divine love u in philosophy to appreciate F S C, 1222
    mankind can be u only by spiritual approach, 2065
unified personality, Deity reality is spirit-mind u p, 140
    endowments of supermaterial world, 1228
    growth in spirit, mind, energy leads to u p, 102
    imparts the qualities of identity and creativity, 1227
    is purpose of cosmic evolution, 1229
    possibility of u p is inherent in (7 things), 1229
    predictions of decisions impossible after u p, 136
    true worship realized on 4 levels, 66
    Universal Father is a divinely u p, 639

UNIFIER, THE SUPREME, 643
unifier, Ultimate is the transcendental u of all things, 1305
uniform, only u thing about men is the indwelling spirit, 1672
  physical facts are fairly u but truth is... flexible, 42
uniformity, A of Ds (impose) administrative u on creative diversity, 209
  of laws, world, universe, 1736
unify, divine law and love in philosophy, 1222
  with goals not deeds, 1091
unifying influence, most powerful world has known, 2065
Union of Days, 617, 1311
  advice and counsel of, 237
union, of God and man, 1176
  of human nature with divine foundation truth of kingdom, 1748
  of love, mercy and ministry, 1148
  of material and spiritual energies, 542
UNION OF SOULS, THE, 311
union, of 2 natures, J, stumbling block, 1510
  with divinity enables man to be Godlike, 1774
  with God, not like drop in ocean, 31
UNIONS OF DAYS, THE, 179, 212
Unions of Days, one represents Trinity to each local creation, 212
  700,000, but not all commissioned, 212
unique, space, wave movements, 153-54
  Urantia's colored races after will creatures, 723
  worlds, billion diverse individual w, each is u, 159
UNIQUENESS OF PARADISE, THE, 126
uniqueness of personality, 138, 369, 1284
UNITED ADMINISTRATION, 587
United Brotherhood of Urantia Midwayers (see also "midway creatures" and "midwayers")
  authorized to record... life... of J of Nazareth, 1332
UNITED MIDWAYERS, THE, 864
United Midwayers, acknowledgment to sources of record and concept, 1343
UNITED MINISTRY OF THE PARADISE SONS, 232
"united nations", 1487-88
  leagues, J on, 1489
  peace groups enlarged to nations, encouraging, 788
United States, example of federation, 1489
  government analogous to Super U but not separate judicial personnel, 180
units in organization of universes, 167
unity, all physical force, matter, and energy are one, 123
  among men only through appeal to spirit within, 1672
  based on goals, not creeds, 1091
  characterizes true church, 2085
  concept of u in association with indivisibility implies transcendence, 31
UNITY, DEITY, 640
UNITY, DUALITY, AND TRIUNITY, 1157
unity, human, only through religion of spirit, 1732
  in an evolving selfhood (J), 1479
  in face of diversity, apostles, 1591
  in human experience through philosophy, 1120
  in infinity is the I AM, 1261
  in the nature of Deity, 41
  in self from a consciousness sorter, 1480
  in time and space, never to be found by physical yardstick, 1306
  in universe, 1477
UNITY, INTELLECTUAL, 638
unity, is derived from "indweller", 1591
  not uniformity, in religions
    group can experience spiritual u, can't attain philosophical uniformity, 1129

unity (cont'd)
  not uniformity, in religions (cont'd)
    J prayed for unity, not uniformity among followers, 1965
    kingdom in hearts will create r unity (not... uniformity), 1487
    r of spirit requires only unity of experience... making allowance for diversity of belief, 1732
    r... requires uniformity of insight, not of viewpoint and outlook, 1733
    r requires unity of spirit feeling, not uniformity of intellectual views, 1732
    security of r group depends on spiritual unity, not theological uniformity, 1135
    "spiritual unity... in face of utmost diversity of thinking, feeling, conduct", 1591
    spiritual u is fruit of faith, uniformity is earmark of physical world, 2085
    true church... characterized by unity, not... uniformity, 2085
  of experience, of destiny, otherwise diversity, 1732
  of God, Conjoint Actor is revelation of, 98
  of ideals and purposes rather than of... opinions and beliefs, 1091
  of ideals, correct basis for religionists cooperation, 1091
  of men only by... 1672
  of personal ministry, 4 coordinates, 1245
  of selfhood is supermaterial endowment, 1228
  of spiritual ministry to mortal personality, 1244-45
  of truth, beauty, goodness, 2096
  of universe is in common causation, 1477
  only in harmony of the triunity, 1120
  organic, in universe, 56
  political, cultural, religious thought (Rome), 2073
  required, Christianity now subdivided, secularized, 2084
UNITY, SPIRITUAL, 1591
unity, spiritual, implies 2 things, 1592
UNITY VS. DIVERSITY, 1262
Universal Absolute, 14, 133-34, 1298, 1303
  eternalized Father-initiated divinity-tension, 7
  is resolution of... divinity-tension, 7
  unfathomability of cosmic relationships of, 116
UNIVERSAL ABSOLUTE UNITY, 644
Universal Censor, authored the following papers in the U Book: 10, 15, 16, 29
  where U C is present, there is the judgment of Deity, 218
UNIVERSAL CENSORS, THE, 217, 280
Universal Censors, unerring and divine totallers, 218
UNIVERSAL CONCILIATORS, 275, 414
Universal Controller, 45
Universal Creator, simultaneously all-powerful, all-merciful, 1598
UNIVERSAL EVOLUTIONARY REPERCUSSIONS, 642
UNIVERSAL FATHER, THE, 21
Universal Father (see also "Father" and "God, the Father")
  actually lives in every rational mortal, 1126 (see "Thought Adjusters")
  after attaining U F, more circuits to traverse, 294
  always U F before universal sonship and brotherhood, 1299
  exploring infinity of, 163
  gives of self to be part of personality of (man), 1178
  is the personal cause of the Absolutes, 1148
  known by various names, 22-23
  of all, 1326
UNIVERSAL FATHER, PERSONALITY OF THE, 27

Universal Father (cont'd)
  primal member of each triunity, 1147
  recognized J as sovereign ruler of Nebadon, after U,
    1317
Universal First Cause, It, He, and Father, 2093-94
UNIVERSAL GRAVITY, 131
UNIVERSAL KNOWLEDGE, GOD'S, 48
UNIVERSAL MANIPULATOR, THE, 101
universal, mechanism moves on majestically, 364
Universal Mother, Supreme Being is the, 1288
universal, mystery, secret of incarnation of divine Sons,
    (see under "mystery")
UNIVERSAL NONSPIRITUAL ENERGY SYSTEMS
    (MATERIAL MIND SYSTEMS), 480
UNIVERSAL OVERCONTROL, 135
universal, peace rarely attained until, 594
  phenomena, to contemplate properly, 136
  reality, 3 elements in, 2094
  regime, in u r must teach, 279
UNIVERSAL SPIRIT, GOD IS A, 25
UNIVERSAL SUFFRAGE, THE PLAN OF, 817
universal, truth, finaliters bringing u t into being, 249
UNIVERSAL UNITY, 637
Universal Unity, interpreter in mind, 2094
universal, upholder, 98
universe, administrators, Master Son, Union of Days,
    Morning Star, 633
  affairs, J in touch with directors of u a, 1659
  age, during present u a finaliters return to service
    in universes of time, 345
  age, each is antechamber, 1294
UNIVERSE AIDS, 406
UNIVERSE AIDS, CIRCLES OF THE, 523, 525
universe, and God not identical, one is cause, one
    effect, 1126
  apparent "accidents" in u, a part of finite drama...56
  apparently self-maintaining, 482
  ascension scheme of u, A&E became subject to, 826
  assemblies (have programs), 411
UNIVERSE ATTITUDE OF THE FATHER, 54
universe, business at a standstill (crucifixion), 2001
  by universe, guided to Paradise personality of the
    U F, 39
  cannot be explained, 1260
  career of Adjuster-indwelt mortal, 340
  causes are higher than U effects, 53
Universe Center (name for God), 22
UNIVERSE, CENTRAL, THE PURPOSE OF, 160 (see
    also "Central Universe")
universe, central
    architecture, lighting, heating, biologic and artis-
      tic embellishment beyond (any) stretch of
      imagination, 156
    instantly eternalized in stupendous eruption, 91
    nowhere else such enormous spheres for habitation,
      156
    u of 3-fold creation (Trinity), 154
Universe Circuit Supervisor, Andovontia, 413
UNIVERSE CIRCUIT SUPERVISORS, 265
universe, circuits, local, 177
  circular, 468
  classes, those who do and don't know God, 1468
  comprehension, 1951
  conscious citizens, 1258
  creation of mind, a mechanism of law, 481
UNIVERSE CREATIVE SPIRITS, THE LOCAL, 203
Universe Daughter is of Infinite Spirit, 380
universe, diametrically opposite ways to approach, 1135
Universe Divine Minister, 162
universe, educational system, 4-fold training, 394

universe (cont'd)
  equilibrium established before Creator Son leaves his
    capital planet, 1274
  every impulse of every electron, thought, spirit, is
    ...unit in whole universe, 647
  every u planned and fashioned by, 93
  evolution will transcend past, 263
  evolving u of relative imperfections, 31
  finite, 468
  foundation of u is material, 467
  friendly, assurance of citizenship in, 1950
  friendly, "entire u is f to me", 1470
  friendly, "real u is f to every child...", 1477
  friendly, "u...on your side", 1437
  fundamental cause of, 1477
  glorious u, personal and progressive, 846
UNIVERSE, GOD'S RELATION TO, 54
universe, grand (see "grand universe")
  great day in the life of a u, 1632
  a growing u is an unsettled u, 1274
  has outer limits, 468
  highly predictable only in...sense, 136
  history, inconceivable transactions mark beginning
    of u h, 1158
  how bound into integrated administrative unit, 456
  "I assume jurisdiction of your u for the time of your
    incarnation" (Immanuel to Michael), 1325
  illuminated by 3 kinds of light, 9
  "in my Father's u...are many abodes", 1934
  in my Father's u, many tarrying places, 1947
  in which righteousness triumphs, this is, 2063
  in which truth prevails, this is, 2062
  inside out, when studied through physical senses, 1135
  intelligence circuits, at space junctions transporters
    can change destination, speed, 433
  intelligences, ascending men not exclusive occupation
    of u i, 54
  is dependent, 1126
  is Fatherly, 1573
  is friendly to the individual, 1470, -77, 1574, 2094
  is non-static, 135; only God is changeless, 222
  is school, 412, 558
  is seven dimensional, 1439
  is the nature and reactions of, 1477
  is a whole, 647
  J' creation, 1984, -99
  J' life was lived to instruct entire, 1999
  J running his from U, "Father's business", 1659
  lawful and dependable, 1735
  lawful and friendly, 1574
UNIVERSE LEVELS OF REALITY, 1162
universe, levels, three, 1160
  like scientist, not like laws scientist discovers, 2080
  local, another in Nebadon, is Henselon, 393
    embraces 1/100,000 part of superuniverse energy,
      169
    400 billion years ago, 1309
    making, unmaking, remaking, 176
    master, definitely delimited and bounded, 130
    master u, 1
    mechanism, mind of u m is creative spirit mind, 482
UNIVERSE MECHANISMS, 481, 1303
universe, mechanisms are nonvolitional patterns of
    Infinite's plan, 1303
  Michael's supreme sovereignty of u established by
    bestowals, 1318
Universe Mother Spirit, 162, 368, 551; cosovereignty,
    equality with Son, 204
universe, moving over vast elongated circle around F's
    central dwelling place, 365

universe (cont'd)
new, firstborn of parents of a n u unique, supernal personality, 369
non-stable, 222
not like artist's art, but like artist, 2080
not like science, but scientist, 2080
not self-existent, 52
of energy, at center of every minute u e is a stable nucleus, 477
of law and order, 952
of mass-energy, mind, spirit, 1477
UNIVERSE OF UNIVERSES, THE, 128
universe, of universes
is mind planned, made, administered, 481
is vast mechanism controlled by one infinite mind, 637
Paradise is actual source of u of u, 7
only sin is isolated and evil gravity resisting on mental, spiritual, levels, 647
organization, 167, 1254
UNIVERSE ORGANIZATION, 358
universe, organized, chief business of, 558
UNIVERSE ORIENTATORS, 428
universe, ours, doesn't belong to settled order, 177
ours, near outer border, 129
ours, organization began 400 billion years ago, 1309
perfect central, 16
UNIVERSE, PERSONALITY IN THE, 29
universe, physical aspects of local, 455
UNIVERSE POWER, 470
UNIVERSE POWER DIRECTORS, THE, 319, 336
universe, presence, I S is, is a cosmic power, a holy influence, a universal mind, also a true and divine personality, 96
real, friendly to God's children, 1477
UNIVERSE REALITY, 6
universe, reality realizations, four, 196
records, mortal is dead when mind circuits of will-action are destroyed, 1230
UNIVERSE REFLECTIVITY, 105
universe, reflectivity
all levels of u actuality coordinated, 105
sees, hears, senses, knows, all things, 105
UNIVERSE, RELATION OF THE ETERNAL SON TO THE, 81
UNIVERSE, RELATION OF THE INFINITE SPIRIT TO, 98
UNIVERSE, RELATION OF MASTER SONS TO THE, 240
universe, romancing, not all fact, but much is truth, 2096
ruler who subsequently became J of Nazareth, 1325
rulers know remote conditions instantly (as occur), 105
seven-dimensional, 1439
UNIVERSE SON AND SPIRIT, THE, 368
Universe Son, good spirit of U S poured out upon all flesh, 365
is of Eternal Son, 380
Universe Sovereign, experience an eternal possession of, 1405
not U S until, 1309
universe, spirit influence, 7-fold, 1962
stood at attention, 2000
supreme engagement of, 1329
"TV" (see also "TV" under "T")
unseen hosts of a u stood, gazed at Creator dying on cross, 2008
throughout u every unit part of whole, 52
to feel at home in, 1117
two-fold gravity embraced, 91
unfailing in techniques to equalize opportunity, 624

universe (cont'd)
unorganized realms of, 2015
unsettled because growing, 1274
value, creature achieves, 1238
was not inevitable, not an accident, 52
well-ordered, 373
without significance apart from I AM, 2080

universes, adornment of eternal God, 125
are eternally stable, 55
common spiritual experiences, 1085
conducted in law and order, 560
constituted, how, 166, 182
controlled by one infinite mind, 637
do not run down, 176
enormous training schools, 417
entirely different, plans of Creator Sons, 523
future, in force--charge of space, 139
gigantic creation to be "run" by (us), 1239
glorious purpose in march of u through space, 364
made by Sons of God, 21
names of u nearest Nebadon: Avalon, Henselon, Sanselon, Portalon, etc., 360, 393
UNIVERSES--NEBULAE, THE ANCESTORS OF, 169
universes, new system of u organizing... 354
of outer space, 130, 351, 1318
organization of (see "Urantia, in cosmic organization")
outer--in preliminary assembly, 634
outer rings of u encircle inhabited creation, 131
permeated by energy lanes, 1276
UNIVERSES, PHYSICAL EMERGENCE OF, 357
universes, physical u, symbolic of perceivable reality of Almighty Supreme, 1276
throughout, names by which God is known, 22
the time u are not perfect; that is their destiny, 1274
untold numbers now forming, 125, 130-31
vast integrated mechanism, 637

university, high, of spiritual training, 269
University, Melchizedek, 387
UNIVITATIA, THE, 493
univitatia, ... administer constellation morontia worlds, 633
experience of living with u, 433
permanent residents of local u constellations, 222, 414-16
unlike us except intellectually, 494
unknown energy, space-force reaction of the U Absolute? 479 (see also "energy undiscovered")
unlearned, most can dispel darkness, 1118
unlucky, Friday 13, 968
unmarried persons, breakdown of mores, 928
UNNAMED TYPES, THE, 563
unpervaded space, confluence of u s and pervaded s under nether P, 123
means... 123
unpredictable decisions, free will personality, 136
unpredictables, unknown, unfathomable, what is explanation of?, 136
Unqualified Absolute, 4, 5
and Deity Absolute become one in Universal Absolute, 13
UNQUALIFIED ABSOLUTE, THE DOMAINS OF THE, 130
Unqualified Absolute, pervades all space, 137
regions beyond superuniverses, domain of U A, 130
Unqualified Supervisors of the Supreme, 636, 1291
unreality can't exist forever, 41
UNREVEALED ANGELS, 420
unrevealed, associates (many) of T As, 1177

unrevealed (cont'd)
  beings, hosts of b unrevealed to us, 145
    origin by acts of Father and Son, 145
    spirit servers "closely related" (to us) we can
      almost comprehend, 147
  orders from E S and I S, 1189
unseen, hosts of a u stood in silence, gazed upon J on
    cross, 2008
  "messenger will run by your side", 1967
  spirit helpers unrevealed to us, too closely related,
    147
unselfish, drive from T A, 1134
  good, do u g as you go about daily duties, 1875
  interest, origin, 1129
  love of man, is kingdom, 1860
unselfishness, 317, 1572
  desirable?, 51-52
  due to religion, or it is abstraction, 196
  not natural, 196
unstable, civilizations are, because not cosmic, 196
untrammeled executives, System Sovereigns, 511
unvarying, physical authority, presence, function, 150
unwilling souls can't be led, 1466
unwise acts of thoughtless offspring, father restrains,
  1608
unwritten law, crimes of honor, pretense under u law,
  917
  murders under pretense of the u law, 795

Upanishads and Brahmanas, later scriptures of Hindu
  faith, 1029
upbreeding, 585
UPHEAVAL, THE GARDEN'S FIRST, 832
uplift, spiritual, through group prayer, effective social
  repercussions, 998
uplifted, what mortal not u by extraordinary f J has in
  him?, 2093
UPPER PARADISE, 120
upper, room 1933
  strata of society, deaf ear to helpless in past, 1087
uprising against profiteers, 1890
upward and downward evolution, mortals, T As, 1196
Ur, Abraham and brother left, 1598
  Chaldeans near Ur, among advanced Semites, 1054
  idea of a real God best preserved near Ur, 1060
  Salem doctrines proclaimed in Ur, 1019
  Zoroaster learned of r traditions at Ur, 1049

URANTIA

Urantia (name of this planet we live on), 1, 182
  aborigines of U, Andonic people, 904
URANTIA ADVENTURE, THE, 734
Urantia, advisory council (names of 24), 513
  after U life, more material than spiritual, 521
  age, more than billion years old at surface, 659
  all eyes in universe focused on U, 33 years, 1317
  all planetary schools perverted, 576
  all U is waiting for... ennobling message, 1041
  always has a resident governor general, 1251
  amazing, enthralling epoch ahead, 2082
  among the least in all creation until J, 466
  ancestors' blunders and rulers' mistakes plunged U
    into hopeless state, 853
  and superuniverse, 164
  announced 4000 years ago as selection for M's
    bestowal, 486; selection of U, 853, 1324, -44, -63
  archangel headquarters on U, 408; why, 1259
    circuit on U, 1250, -53-54
      opened with planetary resurrection, 2024

Urantia (cont'd)
URANTIA ATMOSPHERE, THE, 665
Urantia, awaiting unencumbered Jesusonian message,
  1041
  backward, 177, 624
  barbarism, long in, 591
  belongs to one of relatively recent universes, 165
  bestowal Son at close of Adamic period, not usual, 595
  billion years old on its surface, 659-60
  broadcast from Salvington that J was born on U, 1316
  celestial eyes focused on Palestine, 1409
  celestial workers on U difficulties due to quarantine,
    318
  certain, one thing is, Michael's promise to return,
    226, 598 (see under "Jesus--return of Michael")
  certainty of Magisterial and Teacher Sons to come,
    1025
  chief (sentimentally), of 10 million inhabited worlds,
    1319
  chosen for bestowal because so hopeless, 853
  communication experts (12), 505
  concepts in U Book limited by, 1163
  confusion and turmoil, 258, 578
  confusion, because all supernatural ascribed to God,
    583
    due to ignorance of multiple Sons of God, 87
    sacred books don't distinguish personalities, 60
  conspicuous for 35,000 years, 1316
  created by the pre-infinite, 1268
  Creators could make U a paradise, but... 258
  crises 33 on U, M Hs intervene, 1253-57
  curse of lowest strata of deteriorated, antisocial,
    feeble-minded, outcast, 920
  the dead of a U dispensation rise, 2124
  decimal (experimental) planet, 398, 565 (see also
    "experimental planet")
  departs far from average course, 591
  deprived of help from above and beyond, 1008
  deprived of interplanetary communication, 580
  despite bad natural history will achieve light and life,
    600
  destructive wars, one victor with enhanced reputation,
    J, 2064
  discussed, identified, 182
  disordered and disturbed planet, 1325
  distraught, 631
  divisional hdqtrs. for universe archangels, 409
  double tragedy, rebellious P P, and defaulting Mat S,
    578
  dual origin planet, 170-71, 465, 656
  dual origin planet, less violent... career, 466
URANTIA DURING THE EARLY LAND-LIFE ERA, 685
Urantia, eighth race to appear on U, 857
  emergency regency, 1201
  end of most beautiful natural creation, Eden, 827
  energy misbehavior on, 458
  energy (space) unknown on, 667
  epochal revelations, chronology (1007) dates
    Caligastia, Planetary Prince, 500,000 years ago,
      701
    Adam and Eve, Material S & D, 38,000 years ago,
      735, 741, 828
    Melchizedek (highest local u Son), 4000 years ago,
      1015
    Jesus (Creator Son), 2000 years ago, 1351
    Urantia Book (dated 1934), 707 (see also under
      "date of U Book")
  ethics of might and right, only recent concerned, 908
  evil dominated, sin-stricken, 629
  evolutionary path, not average, 591
  executive of U new every 100 years, 1252

U BOOK

value (cont'd)
  supreme, may or may not be a cosmic reality, 1100
  supreme spiritual v flashes to Absolute Spirit
    Personality, 84
  that which is v vs. that which has v, 1096
  thing, meaning, v (see "things, meanings, values")
  unique element in reality, 1261
values, always both actual and potential, 1097
  are experiences of individual, 1477
  are "felt", meanings known, 1219
  can never be static, 1097
  crystallize thoughts about v of infinite nature and
    eternal import, 365
  discover v in associates by discovering motivation,
    1098
  experiential realization of, 1097
  four levels of realization, religion in all, 68
  human, more adjustment of 1 generation than in
    2000 years, 1013
  mind does not create, 2094
  none in naturalism, 2077
  of eternal survival, 1431
  of the real, truth, beauty, goodness, 43
  of sacred and secular, even Bushmen distinguish,
    1132
  quest for personality v, a latent, inherent reality
    realization, 196
  relative vs. supreme, 2075
VALUES, TRUE, 1456
values, true, discourse on (J), 1456-57
Van, A&E awakened on U in presence of V, 829
  A&E proclaimed rulers of U by V, 830
  and Amadon, proposed sites for Garden, 847
    sustained on U over 150,000 years, 759
    translation to morontia, 833
  assembled loyal midwayers and others, 756
  believed to have been taken up alive, 860
  council of V was court of appeals, 749
  devoted to loyalists 7 years, 756
  early associates settled on shores of Lake V, 860
  headed 1 of 10 commissions, Prince's staff, 749
  joined by descendants of rebellious Dalamatians, 822
  message sustaining V "lost" in transmission, 760
  N.W. of India, culture of days of V, 870
  one of 100 new sojourners on U, 743-49
  preaching for 100 years, advent of Son of God, 822
  protested desire to worship A&E, 832
  7-hour address indicting rebels, 755
VAN--THE STEADFAST, 756,759
Van, steadfastness due to 9 things, 756
  titular head of loyal corps until Adam, 856
vanishing personality control, 755
Vanites, the, 860
vanity group of emotions, 765
variety is restful, 555
VARIOUS RESERVE CORPS, 339
varying, will creature's recognition of spiritual
  presence, 150
vast, gulf between experience of truth of God and
  ignorance of fact of God...1125
  time involved in attainment of God, 63
  universal family circle and fraternal circuit of
    eternal God, 71

ve

Vedas, ancient rituals of the, 1031
Vedic, -Aryans, 1027
  faith corrupted, 1029
VEDIC INDIA, THE SALEM TEACHINGS IN, 1027
Vedic, priesthood, 1029
  rejected gospel, terrible price, 1029

Vedism, priests refused "one God, one simple faith",
  1028
vegetable, to animal, gradual transition, 731
  to animal life, transition 450 million years ago, 669
  type of organisms, disease causing, Urantians would
    have been immune to, 736
vegetarians, Adam and Eve, 850
  corporeal staff, nonflesh diet, 744
  great forward step when flesh added to wheat, rice,
    vegetables, 901
  herbivorous, carnivorous, omnivorous, 593-94
  morontia vegetation eaten, all energy, no residue, 492
  no carnivorous creatures on architectural worlds, 492
  practice dates from Caligastia 100, superhumans,
    3-fold beings, 744
vegetation of energy growth, no "residual", 492
vegetative, incarnation, energy source for mortals, 286
VEGETATIVE LAND-LIFE PERIOD, THE, 678
velocities, Adjusters, transit time practically none, 1186
  axial revolutions, orbital v beyond imagination,
    dangerous, how braked, 125
  enseraphimed ambassadors average only 550,000 mps,
    260
  Gravity Messengers transcend time and space, 347
  instantaneous v of gravity traversers, 261
  midwayers attain double v, 372,560 mps, 260
  most nonenseraphimed beings, limit 186,280 mps, 260
  of culture, 909
  orbital v of calcium atom, quadrillionth of second, 462
  physical controllers travel at v approaching S M, 324
  radium particles, rate of 10,000 mps (positive),
    186,000 mps (negative), 477
  reach any point in s u from hdqtrs. in less than year,
    222
  seraphim and others, triple v, 558,840 mps, 260
  Solitary Messengers, almost unbelievable v, 222
  spirits this u use gravity, go anywhere--instanter--
    but they're not persons, 260
  transporters superimpose v of energy upon v of
    power, to 550,000 mps, 433
  triple, traveling courts of the worlds, 276
  Uversa to Urantia 109 days, 222
velocity, J' T A to Divinington and back in seconds, 1511
  Solitary Messenger 841 billion mps, 261
Veluntia, large sun, density 1/1000 of U atmosphere, 460
vengeance, days of gentile, 1913
  rebuke for words of, 1788
  a wrong is not righted by v, 1580
ventriloquism, first used by shrewd priests, 987
venture, "eternal, I am on my way with you" (Rodan),
  1781
Venus, superbreathers, if any inhabitants, 561
verdict rendering by highest and most noble types, 247
Veronica of Caeserea-Philippi, cured of scourging
  hemorrhage by f, 1698-99
versatile J ("anything you can't do?"), 1481
versatility, multiplied by dual associations (as male,
  female), 938
  of ultimate performances through rewards following
    causes, 579
vertebrates, fish, 678-79
vertical fault, 4 mile, California, 696
"the very hairs of your head are numbered", 1820
vestal virgins, duty of watching sacred fires, 947
veto scepter, God unerringly wields, 52
Vevona, with Adam on U, still on U, 437

vi

vibrations, in content of space, from ultimatons, 474
  of material and morontia activities (at tomb), 2021

vividness gives power to an idea, 961,1005

VO

vocation builders, the, 502
vocation can reflect light of your life, 1572
voice, humans seldom hear Adjuster's v, 1213
  "in the Garden" rebuked, remonstrated, 583,842
VOICE OF THE ANGELIC HOSTS, 309
VOICE OF THE CONJOINT ACTOR, 308
VOICE OF THE CREATOR SONS, 308
VOICE OF MERCY, 430
VOICE OF THE SEVEN MASTER SPIRITS, THE, 308
VOICE OF WISDOM, THE, 310
voice, still, small v speaks within heart, 1664
VOICES OF THE GARDEN, 437
"Voices" (Seconaphim), 308-10
volcanic age, the, 659
volcano, one of greatest eruptions in history, Kentucky,
  675
Volga and Don, 892
volition, and T As, 1183
  choice to be like God is superfinite, 1300
  exhibits inheritance factors from unique First
    Causes, 1299
  God's foreknowledge is not abrogation of v, 1300
  is relative, 1299-1300
  only in creature v, deviation, 139
  personality v not predictable, 155
  range of will is finite-limited except in...1300
  temporal v and spiritual v, 1300
  T A absolute v, but prepersonal, 1183
voluntary, J taught "v conformity to God's will", 1582
  military conscription, do not influence world peace,
    1491
volunteers, all T As are v, opinion of Solitary
    Messengers, 1185-86
  T A v on basis of data on candidate, 1185-86
Volvox, 732
voodoo doctors, 972
Vorondadek Son, authored paper 36 in the U Book
  still resident on U, 1253
VORONDADEK SONS, 389
Vorondadek Sons, historians of the local u, 390
  1 million in our u, Orvonton, 389
  1 of 4 groups of local u sonship in U Book, 384
votes, more in recognition of achievement, 518,817
voting compulsory on neighboring planet, 818
vows, foolish, 981
voyage of discovery, unending for First Source and
  Center, 1174
VULNERABILITY OF MATERIALISM, THE, 2078
vulnerable, temporal securities are v, but...1096

W

"wages of sin is death" (eternal obliteration), 529,613
  (see also "annihilation", "cessation of existence",
  and "extinction")
wait on m w for others to "catch up", 539
WAITING (J) THE TIME OF, 1494
"wakes", ancient methods still in vogue as w, 964
  candles for the dead, 959,964
  savages sat up all night with dead, 958
"walk humbly with God", 1676
walk, on water, J did not, 1520
  uprightly, no good thing will God withhold from those
    who w u, 1445
wall, defense, 2nd Garden, 847
  40 feet high, Urantia's Dalamatia, 743-44
  protection from beasts, 746

walls, of crystal gems, 524
  of prejudice, self-righteousness, 1879
THE WANDERER OF SPACE, CALCIUM--, 461
wanton and irreligious, rich were usually, 2093
war (see also "wars")
  ambition, invention, better ferment than w, 786
  ancient decimated inferior people, 786
  animalistic reaction to misunderstandings, irrita-
    tions, 783
  another world w will teach...1490
  chiefs, not fond of peace, 789
  destroys society sometimes, kills patient, 785
  early causes of (7), 784
WAR, THE GENESIS OF, 783
war, has always been a kingmaker, 789
  has fallen into disrepute, 614
  heritage of early evolutionary man, 614
  "in heaven", after 2 years, Lucifer's successor
    installed, 608
    fought in terms of life eternal, 606
    spread to every planet in system, 756
    very terrible, 606
  is a symptom, not a disease, 1491
  is violence, law of nature, carried on collectively,
    783
  like slavery, must sometime be abandoned, 785
  madness, Christianity lowered its ideals before w m,
    2083
  modern w disrupts civilized culture, 786
  modern w no longer selects great leadership, 786
  natural state, 783-85
  none on advanced worlds, 630
  peace, sovereignty, 1491
  prevention of (J on), 1489
  result of self-preservation reactions, 786
  should be honored as school of experience, 786
  sinfulness of fratricidal strife, 597
WAR, SOCIAL VALUE OF, 785
war, strong medicine, costly, dangerous, 785
  urge, sex appetite used to combat w u, 788
  will continue unless substitutes are found, 786
  without religion preparedness leads to w, 805
ward, U is personal ward of Christ Michael, subject to
  his plans, 227
WARDS, SUPERUNIVERSE, 342
warfare, ancient w decimated worst, now the best, 786
  efforts to humanize 500,000 B.C., 749
  rules of "civilized", 785
  Sanhedrin against J, 1708
  threatened early race with extinction, 714
warn, unjust hatred of Jews unjustified, 1909
warned against mischief in hearts, 1676
warning, all olden teaching not be replaced, 1656
  miscegenation, 586
warnings, divine, useless, when, 1567
WARNINGS, FINAL ADMONITIONS AND, 1953
warp of morontia is spiritual, woof physical, 9
warrior king rides horse, peace king on ass, 1881
wars, all participants defeated on U, 2064
  and peace, religious, 1487
  become more suicidal, 1490
  eliminate whole peoples, 591
  explanation of, 1220
  genesis of, 783
  global w will go on until government of mankind is
    created, 1490
  harvest of world w, why?, 2081
  Indian, the more intelligent perished, 723
  made by self-assertiveness, 2065
  major, why, 1488

wars (cont'd)
  no end on U until, 1487, -90
  now destroys best human stocks, 786
  only one victor in all w, J, 2064
  tribal, 714
  victors defeated, 2064
  world, due to secularistic revolt, too far, 2081
  world wide disaster unless, 2081
  worse, prophesied (1934) why, 2081-82
waste, avoid w of time, 1805
  better than abrogation of liberties, 805
  in funeral rituals and death ceremonies, 960
  words, why? "no spiritual capacity", 1440
watch-care, 136
watchtower for the guards, 1893
watchword of Universe is "progress", 54
water, ability of animals to adapt to air, w, land is
      superphysical adjustment, 737
  as drop of w returns to the sea, 1284
  circulation, subsoil system, 520
  divine Spirit, w of life, prevents consuming thirst,
      381
  divining, 946
  formula for w should have prevented materialistic
      philosophy, 141
  the garden of your heart, 554
  "give me a drink" (J), 1612
  heat from our sun boils all oceans 1 second, 464
  holy, and floor sweepings, drink for fidelity test, 795
  holy w protection against ghosts (priests washed feet
      in), 964
  in 3 forms, made J think, 1367
  J never walked on, 1519
  J poured into foot basin, washed apostles' feet,
      1938-39
  J walking on w (Peter's dream), 1703
  "living", 1613, 1954
  "of life", 1795, 1820
    "I did not teach you my blood is the", 1712
  of the (living) Spirit, 1613, 1954
  one drop, energy of 100 hp for 2 years, 463
  one drop, 1 billion trillion atoms, 463
  Pilate made Jews pay for aqueduct for millions of
      Jewish visitors, 1988
  supply from upturned rock outcrops, 690
  turned to wine, 1328-30
  union with God not as w finds u with ocean, 31
  well of spiritual w, 381
  "why come down into w to greet me?" (JB), 1505
watered in soul by spirit, 1712
waters, living, of combined spiritual communion and
      social service, 1931
Waters of Merom, 1745, -59
watersheds, many ancient w drain into so-called
      Christianity, 2083
WAVE-ENERGY MANIFESTATIONS, 474
wave, tidal w engulfed noble Dalamatia culture, 759
wavelike energy manifestations, 10 groups, 474
waves (see also "rays")
  light, these due to "force blanket" of space and... 476
  of cultural evolution vs. line of biologic e, 906
  of energy, no, direct lines, 461
  wavelike behavior, 474-75
way, on the w to Jerusalem, 1867
  "this is the w" Spirit of Truth, 383, 1287
  "this is the w; walk therein" (Father), 1664
  "the w, the truth, and the life", 242
  we work, 435
ways, mortals may live together, two, 1775
  "my w are higher than your w", 1068

we, achieve universe value, 1238
  appear before J, 1238, -48
  are devoid of courageous decisions, 1207
  are part of immense plan, 364
  are surrounded by spiritual influences, 64
  forever recognize associates of former existence, 498
  get 570 bodies, 542
  go to billion Havona worlds, 209
  have developmental stages, three, 1177
  have training on 490 worlds, 387
  how w advance, 316
  live and move in him, 139, 1155
  minister to God in others, 1475
  not in recognized spiritual family, 177
  pass through 10 divisions of s u, 211
  reach Paradise eventually, 417
  remember people, 498
weak, and inferior, always contend for equal rights, 794
  and wicked prevent ideal society, 804
  elements in civilization, brutality, 577
  exploitation of, 1803
weaker, always make disproportionate social gains, 937
weaklings, gradually subjugated by advancing civiliza-
      tion, 577
weakness, in w made powerful, 1327
  James' spells of unaccountable silence were a w, 1553
WEAKNESS OF INSTITUTIONAL RELIGION, 1087
wealth, and the kingdom, 1803
  channels of, 1779
  deliver from love of w, not w, 1802, -21
  disciples did not part with w, 1802
  from labor, knowledge, organization, 773
  handling, 1462
  "if one's w does not invade precincts of the soul",
      1804
  "is unenduring", 1822
  J, injustice of wealth, 1581
  J never taught w was wrong, 1803
  J on, 1462, 1821-23
  Matadormus, 1801
  no sin in, 1821, -23
  not a gift, w comes from, 773, 1779
  not sign of God's favor, 1662
  of wisdom and truth, your T A, 1207
  on earth, treasure in heaven, 1821
  Pharisees much given to acquirement of riches, 1854
  power, worship of, 786
  (Rodan), 1778-79
  support of kingdom's work, 1822
  10 ways of amassing (J), 1462
  3 questions all who gain w must answer, 1822
  undeserved w may be greatest of human afflictions,
      1305
  uneven distribution, 1581
  vs. what it causes, 1581
  without work, 2086
weaned, Eve's children at 1 year, 834
  intellect protests against being w from, 1097
weaning, early women, w at 4 or 5 years old, 934
weapon tools, relief from food slavery, 768
weathervane cock, origin, 964
WEDDING AT CANA, THE, 1528
WEDDING CEREMONY, THE, 924
wedding, ceremony, grew out of, 924-25
  double, James and Esta, 1418
    Simon and Jude, 1420, -84
  presents, origin, 916
weddings, red man first to develop elaborate, 924
Wednesday, day off, usually, J and apostles, 1920

week, 5-day, 811
WEEK OF COUNSEL, A, 1717
WEEK OF INTENSIVE TRAINING, THE, 1542
WEEK OF REST, A, 1718
week, 7-day, Dalamatia, 751
 10 days on Jerusem, 511
weep, had seen Master grieve, but none had seen him w,
 1587
weeping, replaced by joy, 623
weight, light has w, 173; sunlight economical at $1
  million per pound, 460
 nearby sun, 1 ton pci, 460
 ocean beds, plus water, approximate w of higher,
  lighter continents, 668-69
 ocean floor water pressure, ca 5000 lbs. psi, 669
 (of energy) is relative depending on velocity, mass,
  antigravity, 175
 of 1 cubic inch of old star, 6000 pounds, 459
welfare, fail in holy obligations, be meticulous in what
  is unimportant in human w, 1987
 of part vs. whole, considered in God's doings, 47-48
 temporal, Adjuster deeply interested in, 1204
well of spiritual water, 381
wept, because of family (J), 1587
 bitterly, Peter, 1981
 over people and Jerusalem, 1375, -81, 1882
west, got advancing theology when Jews defaulted, 1340
Western Hemisphere, no contact with rest of world
  until 1000 A.D., 884
western, man's ancestors, 893
 thinking progressively secularized for 300 years, 2081
 world ready for one God, 2073
 world, spiritual longings, 2069

wh

whales, dolphins, etc., origin, 696
what did J commend to the F's hands?, 2014-15
"what is truth?", 1991
WHAT MUST I DO TO BE SAVED?, 1682
what prayer meant to J, 2088-89
what religion is; living, dynamic experience, 66
"what shall I do to be saved?", 1682
"what shall we do with J?", 1719
"what will they do with J?", 1910
wheat, spies condemned eating of, 1654
wheel, staff of 100 taught use of w on U, 746
 used ages before 5000 B.C., 904
wheels, bulk of mass of s u originates in nebular w, 170
 dark islands of space, vast balance w, 173
 mother w, comets wild offspring of, 173
  of direct-origin suns, 169
  throwing off vast suns, 169
 of energizing forces, tremendous, 130
"when brought up before governors and rulers", 1912
when man gives all that he has, God makes that man
  more than he is, 1285
whence energy? "look to your Master", 1777
"whence, why, and whither?", philosopher failed to
  explain, 1641
"where 2 or 3, there am I", 1763
"wherefore did you doubt?", 1703
whip of cords, J used, 1890
whirled stars, 170
white, invaders exterminated inferiors, 892-93
 invaders of Europe, eliminated blue man quickly, 893
 light, the whole visible light of the suns, 475
 man, in N. America first about 934 A.D., 729
 normally, amalgamated races are w, 593
 people, no classifying, 899
 races, Christianity well adapted to secular mores of,
  1084

white (cont'd)
 races (cont'd)
  considerable Andonite and Nodite stock in w r, 889
  500 years in Europe, ancestor veneration, 887
  origin, 725
   from Andite-blue union, 894
   northern, 4 most desirable stocks, 897
WHITE RACES, THE THREE, 897
white races, why no early remains found in Europe, 897
whited sepulchres (dead men's bones), 1826, 1908
"whither shall I flee from your presence?", 44
"who do men say that I am?", 1745
"who is this man?" (J), 1883
WHOLE, THE PART AND THE, 137
"whosoever will may come", 1567
why, anxieties, sorrows, anguish, permitted?, 258
 the apostles failed to heal, 1758
 bestowal Sons live and die as mortals, 229
 confusion and turmoil, 258
 diseases?, 736
WHY DO THE HEATHEN RAGE?, 1725
why, do men ("explore outer space"), climb high
  mountains?, 483
 "do the rulers seek to kill you?", 1790
 "do you call me good?", 2088
 (Father) permit...so many afflictions?", 1661
 is Father not always merciful?, 1605
 Jews presumed to dictate to Pilate, 1989
 Pilate was threatened by Jews as treasonable, 1989
 Pilate yielded to bloodthirsty Jews, 1989-90
 rebellion?, 393
 religious fanatics (Jews) could gain death of man
  Pilate proclaimed innocent, 1989
 scheme of seven, 184
 sin?, 1861

wi

wicked, only the w who say: "universe has neither truth
  nor a ruler", 1449
wicked, weak, take unholy and unfair advantage, 804
wickedness, "spiritual hosts of w in heavenly places"
  (Paul), 611
WIDESPREAD FAME OF JESUS, THE, 1668
widow, poor w, 2 mites into the trumpet, 1883
 rich, wanted healing, no gospel, 1670
widowhood, to be feared, early times, suicides, 916
WIDOW'S MITE, THE, 1883
wife, accused by husband, fidelity test, 795
 beater and J, 1470
 if A&E first couple, whence Cain's Nodite wife?, 1660
 "in the resurrection, whose w shall she be?", 1900
 lending, still obtains among...917
 man loves w but can't explain, 1140
 of Peter, 1552; of Philip, 1557
 purchase, advance over killing girl babies, 770
 second, of Adamson, 895
 white man's like cat, costs nothing (African), 923
wild oats, 791

will, activated to be unselfish by spirit presences, 1132
 "be done, thy w", 1860
 birth and death of, recorded by Salsatia, 413
 creature, equipped to discern fact, law, and love of
  God, 195
  registered upon first act of w, 267
WILL CREATURES, EVOLUTIONARY, 564
will, creatures, only after 7 adjutant mind-spirits
  achieve, 709
 dangerous 1218
 defined by J, 1431

will (cont'd)
  determining factor in man's experience, 1863
  divine, shines brighter as life is enlarged, 138
WILL, THE FATHER'S, 1971 (see "will of the Father"
  and under "God, Father's will")
will, free w supreme in moral affairs, 753
  gradually changing man's w, 1863
  human, constitutes, 730
  in mind of primitive man, 741
  indwelling spirit and w, 757
  is captain, mind is ship, T A is pilot, 1217
  is deliberate choice... based on intelligent reflection,
    1431
  is determiner of spiritual presence, 150
  is relatively free, 81
  "it is my w that your w be done", 1221, 1303
    "not my w, but yours be done", 1200, 1514
    "your w be done", 1574, 1774
  man with dignity of w since 991, 509 B.C., 710
  mind (on loan to man) is about all of u reality subject
    to his w, 1216
  moral, (the personality), 1458
  mortal w, God has decreed sovereignty of, 71
  no interference of w by angels, 1246
  not enough vs. temptation, 1739
  not negation of, but affirmation of, 1221
  not a surrender of, an expansion of, 1221, -85
  of Deity, adjust to, 1001

will of the Father, 1515, -18, -65, -91, 1615, 1706, -60
  abiding by w of F is limit of gifts, 1831
  choosing goodness, will to be in harmony with,
    1583
WILL OF THE FATHER, DOING THE, 1579
will of the F, "enter k, he who does the", 1569
  freedom, initiative, proportional to actuality of
    doing, 2078
  "further reveal the", 2022
  "gospel and kingdom, supreme desire to do", 1931
  heart of J' religion, development of compassionate
    character and doing w of F, 1582
  "I always have been...will be...subject to the
    w of F", 1417
  "I am in this world to do", 1947-48
  "I must do the", 1528
  "I wait upon the", 1529-30
  "I will be subject to", 1523
  "ideal of my life, the doing of", 1953
  "if petition is not inconsistent with", 1763
  invincibility of man dedicated to doing, 1970
  J convinced w of F he submit to course of human
    events, 1999
  J deferred slightest wish to the, 1555
  J drink...cup of mortal experience, 1972
  J exhibited unquestioning loyalty to, 2088
  J focused in mind, w of F as holy, just, great,
    true, beautiful, good, 2087
  J interpreted r wholly in terms of, 2088
  J' life devoted to one great purpose, 2090
  J sacrificed all hindrances to doing, 2093
  J sought to know, 1755
  J subjected himself in all things to, 1531
  J won world in potential by submission to, 1522
  J would die as a man--doing, 2008
  kind of character man can perfect...when chooses,
    2000
  leave untangling of complicated situation to...1532
  "my meat is to do the", 1615
  never fail in life of progress in divine kingdom if
    you do, 1601

will (cont'd)
will of the Father (cont'd)
  Nicodemus didn't know how submit his w to, 1602
  nothing in the cross required by, 2019
  "pay price of dedication to doing", 1869
  pray for a fuller revelation of, 1758
  "rebellion against the", 1766
  r of J demands seek knowledge of, 2083
  seek for a larger knowledge of, 1758
  shocking, inhuman experiences of J' final hours,
    not the, 1972
  "tarry with me, thus learn to do", 1533
  that Son pass through creature experience of
    death, 1969
  "thus shall we fulfill", 1877
  "tolerance born of...perfect submission to", 1958
  unswerving determination to do, 2063
  when w of F becomes truly your w, then you are
    in kingdom, 1589
  "when the w of F is your law, you are hardly in
    kingdom", 1589

will of God (see also under "God, the will of"), 1609
  "ask for grace and courage to do that w", 1723
  "attempt to discover the w of G", 1733
  "can be done in any earthly occupation", 1732
  endowed with power of, 1609
  "erroneous ideas, Psalmist", 1725
  "exchange w of G for mind of self" (Rodan), 1777
  faith in effectiveness of supreme human desire to
    do the w of G, 1586
  fellowship of kingdom fulfillment of, 2088
  is...1278
  is the way of G, 1431
  it is not surrender, doing w of G, 1221
  J showed "w of G" to other sheep also, 1577
  pattern of doing, 1577
  power of performance of the perfect, 1609
  preeminence of, in man's experience, 1863
  prevails, 1262
  sharing inner life with G is doing w of G, 1221
  to extent we do w of G we help actualize the
    Supreme, 1278

will, "of man is the way of man" (choice), 1431
  of man, of God (J on), 1431
  operates within limits set by Master Architects, 1300
  the power of choosing to worship and ascend, 710
  preeminence of w in man's experience, 1863
  proof of its liberty, 1301
  proof of man's moral, 1458
  results of subjecting creature w to F's w, 1221
  seraphim do not manipulate w, 1245
  sovereignty of human, 71, 1232, -99, 1300, -03
  spirit-illuminated w of a God-knowing human, 1217
  spirit liberates, mechanism limits, function of w, 1301
  submit w as a little child, 1602
  though range is limited is true will, 1300, -03
  to believe vs. w that believes, 1122
  unsubmissive, 1861
  U only planet in Satania, w appeared in pre-colored
    race, 736
  usually arrival of w, then P P arrives, 741
  whole souled choice of w no defeat for, 740
  you fail
    the God of time
    the Supreme personality
    the great brother?, 1285
willful, rejection of truth is error, 613
  unbeliever, stand against, 1932

willing learner, if you are a, 381
willingness to believe, key to Havona, 290
WILLINGNESS TO COOPERATE, 810
wills, human, occupied with temporal doomed to
     perish, 1431
   ours determine spiritual presence, 150
wind, behold manifestations, cannot discern spirit, 1602
   "in leaves, you hear, don't see", 1602
window, cosmic, T A is, 1129
winds, "angels... shall gather... his elect from the
     four w", 569
wine, at Cana wedding, 1529
   J refused narcotized w on cross, 2007
   "new, into old w skins", 1655
   sour, commonly called vinegar, 2010
winebibber, J called, 1627
wings, air currents ascending, outstretched w to soar
     (prayer), 1002
   angels' explained, 438
   "as a mother hen her chicks under her", 1872, 1908
Wisconsin fossils, 670

wisdom, all treasures of w and knowledge hidden in J,
     1417
   allow faith to do what knowledge and reason cannot,
     1119
   all w in J and knowledge, 1417
   and worship, 1228
   as used on Uversa, 310
   ascending levels of, 806
   authoritative, 453
   can serve in lieu of transcended barrier of
     restraint, 1302
   capacity for w from experience with religious, 1101
   comprises... 1949
   cosmic, essential to cosmic understanding, 620
   culture, and knowledge, 1780
   dark ages of interrugnum of w, 1302
   disheartening miscarriage of w, 846
   divine and safe only when cosmic in scope, spiritual
     in motivation, 614
   divine, functions through Perfectors of W, 215
   dominates knowledge, glorifies culture, 1780
   "embraces discretion, and courage", 1958
   embraces ideas formulated from... 1111
   exhausts material potential, can taste absonite
     grandeur, 631
   exhibits spirit leading when... 1142
   expanding, to balance transcended restraints, 1302
   experience, judgment, concomitants (human
     experience), 1295
   experiential w, balances restraints, internal,
     external, 1302
   experiential w, society needs swift augmentation of,
     1302
   facts are building blocks... of w, 1222
   fails, balance lost between self-liberty and self-
     control, 1302
   failure is cultural experiment in acquirement of w,
     1780
   from facts adjusted to ideals, 1779
   from failures, 1779
   "give these men", 1569
   imperfections of w of extra-Paradise creatures mars,
     errs, etc., 56-57
   indispensable to true culture, 908, 911
   interpretation of the universe, 2094
   interpretation of w and spiritual insight prevent pur-
     suit of knowledge leading to despair, 2076
   introduces man to a world of truth, 1141

wisdom (cont'd)
   is super-knowledge, 1776
   J on, 1481
WISDOM, KNOWLEDGE, AND INSIGHT, 1121
wisdom, knowledge... experiential reason, divine
     revelation, 1004
   light and life make feasible techniques disruptive
     earlier, 1302
   love, worship; 3 separate evidences of indwelling of
     human mind, 2094
   makes impossible to doubt realest, deepest thing,
     1105
   Master displayed great w in all dealings, 1589
   material comfort era merging into quest of knowledge,
     w?, 577
   more w, love, required in home life, 1922
   most valuable human w, knowledge of J, 2090
   must evolve, spiritual insight is a gift, 1109
   never hesitate to ask God for w, 999
   no limit to attainment of, 631
   no limit to intellectual evolution, 631
   of Creators, imperfect creation, climb to perfection,
     361
WISDOM OF DELAY, THE, 617
wisdom, of Union of Days is time reflection of w of T,
     617
   outrun by material development, 1302
WISDOM, THE PERFECTORS OF, 215
wisdom, premium put upon, always, 989
   pursued to gain insight 5 things, 806
   reason, faith, 2094; man's highest human attain-
     ments, 1141
   religion provided discipline and self-control that
     made w possible, 1006
   restraints in accord with moral w, 1302
   secured only through experience, 908
   seven ascending levels of mortal w, 806
   seventy functional divisions of, 303
   social group in union of w, shares all knowledge, 1776
   source of all w, sublime partnership with G, 1119
WISDOM, SPIRIT OF, 402
wisdom, subordinate physical-life machine to w of
     experience, 1301
   test of, 770
   transcendental (atom), 480
   twofold in origin, 216
WISDOM, THE VOICE OF, 310
wisdom, world wide vogue, pursuit of w (12th level of
     statehood), 807
   worship-w outrun by material, seeds of retrogression,
     1302

WISE LEADERSHIP, EFFECTIVE AND, 911
wise man, friendly in the midst of his enemies, 1447
   "is king", Stoics, 1991
   is occupied with search for truth, 1453
wise men (3) knew of J' impending birth, 1317, -52
wise, saying, child of insight looks for S of T in every
     w s, 1949
   to withhold certain details, 410
witchcraft and the devil, 987
wives (see also "wife")
   believed to become snakes, 928
   choicest went to hunters, 720
   compared to cats (Africans), 923
   leave w of others alone, taught, 791
wizards, 979

woe (see under "Jesus, quotes")
wolves, send you as lambs among w, 1800
"wolves, sheep in the midst of", 1584
wolves, sheeps' clothing, ravening w, 1571
woman, accused by husband, test for fidelity, 795
    "behold your son!"..."I desire that you depart", 2009
    bent, straightened by faith, 1836
    childbearing made w dangerous, unclean, 935
    degradation of w, Rome, 2074
    food provider, beast of burden, abused companion, 765
    healed of hemorrhage, 1698
    hopeless under Mohammedanism, 937
    loose labor methods improved when men took over, 935
    man has usually chosen easier path, 934
    moral standard bearer, 938
    no longer can man monopolize ministry, 2065
    now undergoing the crucial test of her long existence, 937
    of Sychar, 1612
WOMAN, THE PARTNERSHIP OF MAN AND, 938
woman, Peter's wife very able w, 1552
    ruled the Hebrews, Deborah, 784
    shrewd manager of men, 935
    social paradox, slave and master, 935
    spirit of infirmity, 1835
    stand great abuse without violent resentment, 765
WOMAN TAKEN IN ADULTERY, THE, 1792
WOMAN UNDER THE DEVELOPING MORES, 936
woman, vs. man, 934
    was first slave, 778
    weakness of, 840
    where w was, always regarded as home, 765
    who used perfume on J, 1652
    why indispensable, 764
WOMAN WITH THE SPIRIT OF INFIRMITY, THE, 1835
woman's, affliction, mental, bowed back healed, 1836
    liberties, precipitous augmentation of w liberties caused problems, 930
    status, declined during pastoral age, 768, 778
WOMAN'S STATUS IN EARLY SOCIETY, 935
womb, how enter into his mother's?, 1602
    of space, children of the, 304
women, after crucifixion, 2013, -25
    all true, not one denied or betrayed J, 1680
    and children, fattened to eat, 979
    animal husbandry reduced w to...slavery, 768
    believed report of resurrection, 2030
    believers helped change gospel, 2051
    children, fattened for slaughter, 979
    courageous w of Jerusalem wept for J, 2005
    decent man couldn't address woman in public, 1612
    deciding factor in struggle Christianity vs. Mithraism, 1083
    dependence, lower status, due to, 934
    devoted mother love of human female, 765
    emancipation proclamation, 1679
    employed early as spies, commerce a sideline, 774
    equality after Pentecost, 2065
    forbidden to eat human flesh, 980
    have souls, 1614
    held first markets, 775
    hiding near, saw J placed in tomb, 2013
    how J overcame difficulty of counseling w, 1679
    in early industry, 774
    Jerusalem Jews divorced wives for trifling reasons, 1838-39
    J accorded equality to, 1546
    J' recognition of equality of w, 1671

women (cont'd)
    Master taught w to be accorded equality with men, 1839
    men and w, highest service and joy in...homes, 1839
    men and w need each other, 939
    men and w partners with God to create beings, 1471
    mission to anoint J' body, 2025
    outgeneral men at home, 934
    "parents...copartners with Makers of heaven and earth, 1839
    primitive w aged early, 926
    public, 1472
    rabbinic teaching against, 1671
    recognition, Eden, 831
    rejoiced to be included, 1682
    rights are not men's, to be lost?, 938
    rights of w by no means men's, 938
    sent to home of Elijah Mark after J' death, 2011
    society of Jewish w offered drugged wine to lessen suffering of the crucified, 2007
    synagogues confined w to gallery, 1679
    teachers and ministers called deaconesses in early church, 1679
    today's liberated w pity themselves, 936
    12 at Peter's house, upset, but none deserted, 1715
    uniform consideration J gave to all sorts of men, w, children, 1546
    were first traders, 774-75
    why priests?, 777
    why tactful, 934
    young men and w should be taught realities of...930
WOMEN'S EVANGELISTIC CORPS, THE, 1678
women's evangelistic corps
    and Abner's associates working in n Perea, 1825
    astounding for that time, 1679, 1762
    evil resorts, preached in, 1680
    financed themselves, 1679
    furnished own funds, 1679
    instructed: return for a while to Bethsaida, 1783
    J counseled Abner let w go to Jer Passover, 1870
    J emancipated w for all time in "charge" to, 1679
    J' parting advice given to w c, 1897
    joined joyous procession from Bethany to Jer, 1882
    none deserted, 1715
    not one denied or betrayed J, 1680
    nursed sick, 1817
    Peter's wife member of, 1552
    Susanna elected chief, Joanna treasurer, 1679
    ten w selected for wec, names, 1679
    trained corps of 50, 1808
women's rights, may lose chivalry, 938
women's secret clubs, 791
"wonder, no w our hearts burned", 2036
wonders of world, 7 (Pharos), 1432
"Word is made flesh", 227
word "love", painful to use due to mortal use, 40
word, none for "God-consciousness", 1130

"word of God", Bible all inspired? (see also "Bible")
    (Scriptures "contain best of higher thoughts of Jewish people...but also contain much not representative of character and teachings of Father in heaven...These writings are the work of men, some of them holy men, others not so holy...Scriptures are faulty and altogether human in origin, but...constitute the best collection of religious wisdom and spiritual truth..." (J), 1767; Hebrews 500 B.C. did not consider "these writings" to be divine revelations, 838; "when you read the Scriptures look for those eternally true and beautiful teachings" (J), 1769)

word of God (cont'd)
    can be discerned by, 1732
    those born of spirit shall discern it, 1732
    vs. living God, 1782
words, descriptive w don't equal seeing, 2083
    Father will provide, 1582, 1912
    represent performances of mind within scope...
        directed by...limited by, 2080
    valueless in prayer, 85, 1002
    vs. alphabet, 2080
work, able-bodied, should be compelled to w, 780
    all-important, eliminating defectives, degenerates
        from human strains, 839
    all upright w is sacred, 1732, 2049
    alternate with play, 1616
    and play--even in ascendant life, 547
    and schooling combined, 751
    and wealth, 773
    "as for God", 2049
    awaiting us on first mansion world, 1248
    can do important w if...555
    elevate drudgery of w: how, 1475
    faithfulness, will not assure one of wealth, 1779
    in the mines (J), 1643
    less important than way you w, 435
    menial, no such thing as m w in spiritual world, 273
    no w, no eat, 773
    nothing takes precedence over, 555
    of the kingdom, last phase in spiritual depth, 1808
    of the realm is sacred, 2049
    of U A&E prematurely launched, Voice remonstrated,
        583, 842
    "out your own salvation", Buddha, 1036
    power-energy w vs. space w, 134
    primitives did none, willingly, cheerfully, 773
    progress, play (service, study, relaxation), 526
    resting matter can perform w, 474
    savages didn't like, 773
    should be compelled, 780
    (vocation) "reflector", 1572
workday, short, safe for ethical, intelligent mortals,
    595
    two and one-half hours, post- magisterial age, 594
worker made slave to idler, the suicidal weakness of
    communism, 780
workers, elevate toil, 1475
working in Jericho, 1595
works, good, not enough for salvation, 1802
    (healing) not to tempt man, 1834
    of faith come not at bidding of...unbelief, 1757
workshop, Havona is the w of finaliters, 163
world, administration, normal planets, 588
    advanced, recently visited, no progressive tax, 625
        returns to more simplified forms of living, 595
        stage of civilization, Anova, 559
    age of, 659
WORLD, THE ANGELIC, 510
world, another type, beings don't fuse with T A, 410
    beset by evil, 1395
    "birth sphere of spirits", 1675
    brain series: one-two-three, 446, 565, 1197
    brotherhood, helped by travel, commerce,
        competitive play, 597
        needs common language, multilinguists, national
            interchanges of...597
    citizens, better through service and worship, 1930
    confused status of, pre-Eden, 824
    conquer with forgiveness, good will, love, 2064
    court, advisory, moral, high level of statehood, 807
    creation in 6 days, origin of tradition, 836-37

world (cont'd)
    crisis, J intimated unexpected event, part of a w c,
        1863
    distraught by sin, 1395
    dominated by selfishness, sin (J), 1473
    dominion, last chance of Jews for, 1522
    driving force, most powerful in w, 2063
    enlarged revelation--when, 1914
    eternally changing, settled goals impossible, except
        God, 1774-75
    "even before this w was", 1819
WORLD, THE FINALITER, 509
WORLD, THE FINALITERS', 530
world, finite w made by an infinite Creator, must be
    good, 1222
WORLD, THE FIRST MANSION, 532
world, friendly (see also "universe, friendly"),   1737
    "gain the w and lose your soul", 1822
    glimpse of this and next required, 1776
    glory of God being shed abroad in the w, 598
    "go into all the", 2042-44, -53-55, -57
    good, 1222
    government, Adam made heroic effort to establish
        w g, 833
        in creating global g nations creating a lasting
            sovereignty, 1491
        need for w g increases as great powers grow
            fewer, 1489
        supreme planetary tribunal, 807
        U better prepared (than others) for...planetary g,
            820
        U celestial g on plane of equality with most, 1259
        U no peace until mankind g, 1489
    history, changed for 2000 years by 4 imperfect
        gospel records, 1342
    "I will go with you into all the", 2053
    influence, Spirit of Truth, which is universal, 2065
    inhabited; is required that a bestowal Son live life on,
        228
    intercommunication, by angels, 1841
    is filled with lost (directional) souls, 1098
    J living life of inspiration for every person...of u,
        1585
    J a man of great experience in things of this w, 1582
    judgment at end of an age, 1915
    largely ruled by organized, superior minorities, 908
    law must come (J), 1491
    leadership, test of, 770
    light system, 520
    Magisterial Sons usually materialize, are visible on
        w missions, 226
    may have many magisterial visitations, before and
        after bestowal Son, 226, 595
    membership in super universe, 177
WORLD, THE MORONTIA, 510
world, most needs J now, 2084
    most powerful driving force in w, 2063
    most powerful unifying influence in w, 2065
    need of w today, 380
    needs more firsthand religion, 2083
    never sincerely tried ideas of J, 1863
    never tried J' teachings, 1720
    new teachers, leadership and inspiration for social,
        moral, economic, political reorganization of the
        w, 2082-83
    next, we have knowledge of this, 1481
    not an enemy, 1579
    not fundamentally evil, 2093
    not...a new w, but makes old...new, 1945
    ocean and the first continent, the, 660

worlds (cont'd)
   other, and J' life (cont'd)
      vast concourse hovered over momentous scene on
         earth, 1911
      vast...host astir in unified action (12 seconds)
         Lazarus sat up, 1846
   other, isolated, 1252
   potential, 175
   rebellion-isolated, 37 in system, 1252
WORLDS, THE SERAPHIC, 420
WORLDS, THE SEVEN MANSION, 530
      FIRST, 532
      SECOND, 534
      THIRD, 535
      FOURTH, 536
      FIFTH, 537
      SIXTH, 537
      SEVENTH, 538
worlds, seventy training, Edentia age, 181, 494
   sinless advanced w, description of, 629
world's, social center headquarters, 750
worlds, spawning ground of mortal races, 559
   study w of central creation, billion, 156, 388, 417, 489
   teem with angels, men, and...260
   36 other rebellion-isolated w, 1252
   this and other, beautiful relations, man and Maker
      from eternity, 2002
   to come, no marriage, 1900
   training schools, 181, 387, 494
WORLDS, TRANSITIONAL CULTURE, 509
worlds, 200 (ca) more w our system ready for life next
      few million years, 559
   U in an infinite family of w, 183
   use quarantine to protect selves, 46
WORLDS, THE VORONDADEK, 391
worlds, we visit, 209
   we will sojourn on billion w, 221, 489
   where Paradise Son has lived in bestowal, 23
   without protective friction atmosphere, 563, 658-59
   worry, 1823
      anxiety, 1579
      discouragement, indolence--moral immaturity,
         1773
worship, 1781
   alternate with service, 1616
   and prayer, explained, compared, 1616
      the great difference between, 65
WORSHIP AND PRAYER, TEACHINGS ABOUT, 1616
worship, and prayer
      w God; pray to, commune with Son; work details
         out with I S, 66
WORSHIP AND WISDOM, THE ADJUTANTS OF, 948
worship, animals were objects of w (Andonites), 716
   builders, the, 502
   by w man aspires to be better, thereby eventually
      attains the best, 2095
   can't estimate quality of w, 2095
   causation, duty, 192
   communion with source of reality, 2095
WORSHIP, CONDUCTORS OF, 303
worship, connotes mobilization of all powers of
      personality, 66
   contemplation of the spiritual, 1616
   creates energy (Rodan), 1777
   defined, 195, 303
   divine heart of the Gods completely satisfied by w,
      304-05
   -experience consists in...66
   experience realized on 4 cosmic levels, 66
   foretaste of divinity, 2094

worship (cont'd)
   God, three-step progression, 196
   "God where you are", 2053
   illuminates destiny, 1123
   in tabernacles of nature best, 1840
   interchange of strength for weakness, courage for
      fear, God's will for self-will, constitutes w, 1777
   is divinely creative, 1616
   is encircuited to person of the Creator, 65
   is for its own sake, 65
   is a growing passion, 304
   is highest joy of Paradise existence, 304
   is personal communion with Father, 1616
   is (series), 1616
   is superthinking, 1616
   is time striking step with eternity, 1616
   is transforming experience, 1641
   is tuning in the soul, 1621
   is a yardstick, 1616
   J' w, understanding communion with Father, 1620
   lost by black peoples, 725
   love, wisdom
      3 separate evidences of indwelling of human mind,
         2094
   makes one like being worshipped, 1641
   man aspires by w to be better, 2095
   man has worshipped everything on earth, 944
   man through w attains the best, 2095
   mind's assenting to spiritualizing self, 66
   mobilizes personality powers, 66
   more essential than prayer, 1123
   most exquisite pleasure, 303
   not self-deception, 2095
WORSHIP OF ANIMALS, THE, 946
WORSHIP OF THE ELEMENTS, 946
worship, of God, what is not, 68
WORSHIP OF THE HEAVENLY BODIES, 947
worship, of images, 1478
WORSHIP OF MAN, 948
WORSHIP OF PLANTS AND TREES, 945
WORSHIP OF STONES AND HILLS, 944
worship, of wealth power, 786
   on Paradise, necessary to direct its expression, 304
WORSHIP, ORIGINS OF, 944
worship, outgrown systems defended, 2085
   outgrown systems of, 2085
   prayerful w shuns evil and forbids sin, 1443
   prelude to true w, 1133
   privilege, is, highest, 303
   public and family, Eden, 836
   reflects back onto life, 1616
   relaxation sets capacity for spiritual receptivity, 1777
   releasing touch of, 1779
   rest or w, clearer head, steadier hand, 1611
   salvation for mortals, 1621
   a satisfaction of self-expression, 304
   satisfaction to Father's love, 305
   self-interest diverts w to prayer, 65
   sequence to, 1675
WORSHIP, THE SPIRIT OF, 402
worship, spirits of the Gods inspire you to...304
   spontaneous reaction, 65
   strain of living needs balance of w relaxation, 1616
   techniques, otherwise 100s years required to express
      appreciation, gratitude, 304
   to sacrifice, one step, 977
   to w is duty of created intelligences, 303
WORSHIP, TRUE, 65
worship, true, homage to the Father, 1599
   on 4 cosmic levels, 66

worship (cont'd)
  true (cont'd)
    religious w, 2095
    sincere, great privilege, 1600
  tuning in the soul, 1621
  voluntary only to w, love, recognize God, 22
  what constitutes reality of true w, 22
  when we w Father, we w Son and Spirit, 74
  when w evolves into real religion, 948
  where you are, 2053
worshipful, communion, refresh soul, 1739
  form of the cosmic discrimination (1 of 3), 192
  habits, strength-giving, repetition makes mature p, 1777
worst is over, 2076
wound healing, chemical action and reaction, 735
"wounded in house of friend", most terrible sorrow, 1676

wr

wrath, Cain in w turned upon, slew, Abel, 848
  flee human w, live for God, 1934
WRATH, GOD'S, 1597
wrath, "of God", J would not accept as true, 1378
  placate unbelievers, 1958
wrestled in spirit, 1493
writing, ideographic w system placed limit on learned classes (China), 887
  J left none, why, 1330, 1768
  J' w, every vestige destroyed, 1527
  slates of white boards, 1387
  system, 500,000 B.C., 746
  system, from Dilman, 860
wrong, "don't only condemn w", 1765
  ideas about God, 59
  ideas from making allegories out of J' parables, 1672
wrongdoing, glamor, fascination, intoxication of w had vanished, 1998
  torments our T A, 45

X

Xenophanes, 1079
X-ray, stimulated electron, 1/2 million years center of sun to surface, 460
X-rays, modify germ plasm, like life circuit, 857

Y

Yahweh, 1859
  Alexander, permission to Samaritans to build temple for Y worship, 1612
YAHWEH AND BAAL, 1064
Yahweh, became Elohim, chiefly under Elijah, 1065
  brought to low point in eyes of Canaanites, 1072
YAHWEH--GOD OF THE HEBREWS, 1052
Yahweh, had become God of all nations, 1068
  Hebrews henotheistic but believed other gods subordinate to Y, 1054
  in man's image, wrathful, so Moses' followers could comprehend, 1057
  J explained to apostles growth of idea of Y, 1598
  J to Jacob, concept of Father's nature changes, 1597
  J used Y text, first pretentious effort of public career, 1536 (Exodus 19:16)
  Joash, boy king, crusaded for Y, 1074
  Moses proclaimed Y Lord God of Israel, 1057
  one of hundreds, and thousands of Semitic peoples' nature gods, 1053
YAHWEH--THE PROCLAMATION OF, 1056

Yahweh (cont'd)
  prophets taught you Y. "I proclaim a greater truth", 1629
  savage demon to loving and merciful Father, 1076
  vs. Hebrew word signifying Trinity, 1856; vs. Elohim, 1856
  the volcano spirit, 1051
  word for progressive conception of tribal God of Jews, 1856
yang and yin, soul and spirit (Chinese), 1215
yardstick, "physical" not adequate for "time and space", 1306
yawn, might permit malignant ghost into body, 960

ye

year, constellation y equals 5 U, 390, 488
  Egyptian, 365 days, 858
  Orvonton--3000 days, 174
  super universe, 8-1/5 U years, 174
  ten months on neighboring planet, 812
years, for 10s of 1000s years, looked forward to 7th bestowal, 1316
  "a 1000 y are but a watch in the night", 36
  1000 y a day with God, "but a watch in the night", 153
YELLOW MAN, THE, 724
YELLOW MAN AND RED MAN, 883
yellow man, apt pupil in art of warfare, 883
  Buddhism to China first 1000 years after J, 1038
  China, once head of human society, fell behind, 1035
  Chinese 15,000 B.C., fewer than 12 million, 885
  first to learn strength of union, unity, 883
yellow race, after Adam, 869
  ancient, superior because, 885
  children docile, 941
  first large (12 million) scale civilization, 885
  first out of barbaric bondage, 1033
  superiority due to 4 things, 885
  survived because peaceful, 724
  would have dominated world but for mountain barriers, 886

yo

Yoga, Gautama, 6 years of futile practice of, 1035
yoke, "gospel y is easy", 1590, 1766
  Master's y is indeed easy, but never imposed, 1590
  of the gentiles, 2035
  of iron, alien, 1709
  of the kingdom of heaven, 1685
  "take my y upon you", 1808
you, are all God's planetary children, 72
  are human parent, T A the divine parent, of soul, 1193
  are known fully on high, 313-14
YOU ARE THE SALT OF THE EARTH, 1572
you, be uplifted by J' faith in y, 2093
  cannot earn righteousness, 1683
  evolve inward, upward, T A evolves outward, downward, 1196
  (reader) are becoming more and more adorable, 538
  "shall adore God because...", 1675
  "shall be to me a kingdom of priests", 1536
  shall face God, 64
  "should love your neighbor as yourself", 1769 (see also "love your neighbor..." under "Jesus, Quotes")
  should not fail to accept (God), 51
  to draw truth seekers, 1726
  torment T A, 45
THE YOUNG MAN WHO WAS AFRAID, 1437
young, "man with God in hills", 1921
  master universe will always be y, 1170
  people, J one night a week with, 1420

your, frame is dust, 1240
    mind and will and T A's mind and will, 1205
    spiritually valuable ideas, no power can prevent
        reaching God, 84
youth, civilization in jeopardy when y...1220
    failure to educate for marriage, 929
    immaturity dazzled by freedom, failing to see
        duties...1301   J met with young weekly, 1420
    would respond to J' gospel, 2085
youths, mated, likely one a fool, 916
    spoiled, poor marriage hopes, 928
    teaching, 2086

Z

Zaccheus, 1875
    visit to, 1873
Zacharias (father of John the Baptist), 1354,-75,-83
    belonged to Jewish priesthood, 1345
    Joseph invited to Jerusalem to talk to Z, 1351
    Simeon and Anna, intimates of priest Z, 1353
    skeptical of vision (Gabriel), 1345
    visited Nazareth family with boy John, 1359
Zadoc (adopted ancestor of Joseph), David line, 1347

zeal, loveless, 1089, 1773
Zealots, any and all methods ok against Romans, 1535
    J with Simon, a Z, 1397
    Jude, J' brother, propaganda work for Z, 1415
    sought J again as leader of tax rebellion, 1522
    sought J support, J "no", influence negative, 1397
Zebedee (boatbuilder of Capernaum, father of James
        and John, apostles)
    alone, knew of J' trip around Roman world, 1423,-83
    daughters of, 1421
    David (son of Z) (see under "D")
    family, almost worshipped J, 1420
    for Z, J created new style of boat, new methods, 1419
    James (son of Z) (see under "Apostles")
    J became partner of Z, in boatbuilding, 1419
    J worked with Z little more than year, 1419
    John (son of Z) (see under "Apostles")
    Joseph (father of J) deal in Capernaum with Z, 1405
    moderately well-to-do, 1420
    sons of, 1421
Zebulun, 1741
    teachings at, 1642, 1742
    the visit at, 1642
Zechariah (prophet), 1884
    J decided Z correct, spiritual Messiah, 1881
    J quoted Z to apostles, 1638
    slain, 1908
Zeus, 1078

ZO

Zone of Infinity, on nether P, 122
zones, energy, 4 in atoms, 478
Zoroaster, featured in one of greatest centuries of r
        awakening, 1009
    followers militant against Mithraic cult, 1082
    heroically died for "truth of the Lord of light", 1050
    one of world's 7 greatest ethical, religious teachers,
        1339
    revived embers of Salem gospel, 1049
Zoroastrian Rimmonites, 1637
ZOROASTRIANISM, 1449
Zoroastrianism, only creed, perpetuates Dalamatian
        and Edenic teachings, 7 Master Spirits, 1050
    a Urantian religion as U Book revealed, 1011

Zoroastrians, had a religion of morals, 67
Zulus, 1010

Z

PERSONAL REFERENCES AND NOTES

PERSONAL REFERENCES AND NOTES